PRINCIPLES

OF

INTERNATIONAL

LAW

Second Edition

By
Sean D. Murphy

Patricia Roberts Harris Research Professor of Law
George Washington University
Member, United Nations International Law Commission

CONCISE HORNBOOK SERIES®

WEST®

A Thomson Reuters business

© West, a Thomson business, 2006
© 2012 Thomson Reuters
  610 Opperman Drive
  St. Paul, MN 55123
  1–800–313–9378
Printed in the United States of America

ISBN: 978–0–314–26268–4

For Julie

Preface

International law is continually transforming the world in which we live. So many of the daily transactions in which we or our society are engaged occur in an environment of transnational rules—such as when we make a transatlantic telephone call, fly to Mexico, export computers to Brazil, watch an Australian-made movie, eat Belgian chocolate confident that it is unadulterated, send troops to Afghanistan or Iraq, call for prosecution of war criminals in The Hague, pursue extradition of a suspected murderer who has fled abroad, condemn genocide in Sudan, organize global reductions in ozone-depleting gases, or extract natural gas for our homes from an undersea continental shelf.

This book is about such transnational rules. It explores the basic foundations of international law: its nature, history, and theoretical underpinnings, and the players that make it all happen (states, international organizations, others). The manner in which international law is created, interpreted, and enforced is addressed, as well as mechanisms for dispute resolution. Several chapters are devoted to discrete subject matter areas, such as human rights, environment, international crimes, and the laws of war. Further, the inter-relationship of international law with national law is explored, with particular focus on U.S. foreign relations law.

The objective of this book is not to provide a comprehensive account of these areas, for doing so would require several volumes and even then would be incomplete. Rather, this book seeks to illuminate the central principles that animate the field and to convey basic information of use to students and practitioners alike, with appropriate citations for those interested in further study. So as to "bring the material alive," relevant and contemporary incidents involving international law are provided throughout. While traditional international law is central to the book, new developments in transnational cooperation are also addressed, such as the tremendous influence of non-governmental organizations.

I wish to express my profound appreciation to Judge Thomas Buergenthal, since our prior collaborations helped inspire this volume. My thanks to Allison Hellreich, Jered Matthysse, José E. Arvelo–Vélez, and Joseph Clark for outstanding research assistance on this project, for comments received from other professors and

v

practitioners in the field, and for the support of Dean Paul Berman, and my other colleagues, at George Washington University Law School.

SEAN D. MURPHY
WASHINGTON, D.C.

January 2012

Summary of Contents

Table of Contents

List of Graphics

1. Source: United Nations (http://www.un.org/en/aboutun/structure/org_chart.shtml).

2. Source: International Court of Justice (http://www.icj-cij.org).

3. Source: World Public Opinion.org, *World Public Opinion on International Law and the World Court* (Nov. 2009)(http://www.worldpublicopinion.org).

4. Source: U.S. Constitution.

5. Source: United Nations (http://www2.ohchr.org/english/structure.htm).

6. Source: Canadian Government (http://www.charts.gc.ca/about-apropos/fs-fd/008–eng.asp).

7. U.S. Extended Continental Shelf Project (http://continentalshelf.gov).

8. Source: Intergovernmental Panel on Climate Change Fourth Assessment Report (2007), Figure 1–1 (http://www.ipcc.ch/graphics/syr/fig1–1.jpg).

9. Source: United Nations (http://www.un.org/Depts/Cartographic/map/dpko/PKO_BN.pdf).

List of Abbreviations

AFR. J. INT'L & COMP. L.	African Journal of International and Comparative Law
AM. J. INT'L L.	American Journal of International Law
AM. U. J. INT'L L. & POL'Y	American University Journal of International Law and Policy
ARIZ. J. INT'L & COMP. L.	Arizona Journal of International and Comparative Law
BRIT. & FOREIGN STATE PAPERS	British and Foreign State Papers
BRIT. Y.B. INT'L L.	British Yearbook of International Law
B.H.R.C.	Butterworth's Human Rights Cases
C.F.R.	Code of Federal Regulations
Cal. 2d	California Reports (Second Series)
CARDOZO L. REV.	Cardozo Law Review
CHI. J. INT'L L.	Chicago Journal of International Law
Cl. Ct.	United States Claims Court Reporter 1983–92
Ct. Cl.	Court of Claims Reports 1863–1982
COE Doc	Council of Europe Document
COLUM. L. REV.	Columbia Law Review
Common Mkt. Rep.	Common Market Reporter
Cong.	United States Congress
CONG. REC.	Congressional Record
Consol. T.S.	Consolidated Treaty Series
Const. Comment.	Constitutional Commentary
Daily Comp. Pres. Doc.	Daily Compilation of Presidential Documents
Dall.	Dallas Series 1790–1800
DEP'T ST. BULL.	United States Department of State Bulletin
ECOSOC Res.	United Nations Economic and Social Council Resolution
E.H.R.R.	European Human Rights Reports
Eur. Ct. H.R.	European Court of Human Rights
Eur. H.R. Rep.	European Human Rights Reports
EUR. J. INT'L L.	European Journal of International Law
EUR. PARL. DOC.	European Parliament Document
Europ. T.S.	European Treaty Series
Exec. Order.	Executive Order

F.2d	Federal Reporter 1932–1992 (Second Series)
F.3d	Federal Reporter 1993–present (Third Series)
F. Supp.	Federal Supplement 1932–1960
F. Supp. 2d	Federal Supplement 1960–present (Second Series)
Fed. Appx.	Federal Appendix
Fed. Reg.	Federal Register
FOREIGN INVESTMENT L.J.	Foreign Investment Law Journal
G.A. Res.	United Nations General Assembly Resolution
G.W. INT'L L. REV.	George Washington International Law Review
GEO. L.J.	Georgetown Law Journal
GEO. J. INT'L L.	Georgetown Journal of International Law
H.R.	House of Representatives Resolution
H.R. Con. Res.	House of Representatives Concurrent Resolution
H.R. REP.	House of Representatives Report
HARV. INT'L L.J.	Harvard International Law Journal
HARV. L. REV.	Harvard Law Review
HUM. RTS. L.J.	Human Rights Law Journal
ICAO Ass. Res.	International Civil Aviation Organization Assembly Resolution
ICAO Doc.	International Civil Aviation Organization Document
ICC Doc.	International Criminal Court Document
I.C.J.	International Court of Justice, Report of Judgments, Advisory Opinions and Orders
ICSID REV.–FOREIGN INVESTMENT L.J	International Centre for Settlement of Investment Disputes Review–Foreign Investment Law Journal
I.L.M.	International Legal Materials
I.L.R.	International Law Reports
Inter.-Am. C.H.R.	Inter–American Commission on Human Rights
Inter.-Am. Ct. H.R.	Inter–American Court of Human Rights
INT'L & COMP. L.Q.	International Law and Comparative Law Quarterly
Int'l Arb. Awd.	International Arbitration Awards
INT'L ARB. REP.	International Arbitration Reporter
Int'l Crim. Trib. former Yugo.	International Criminal Tribunal for the former Yugoslavia

Int'l Crim. Trib. Rwanda	International Criminal Tribunal for Rwanda
Int'l Hum. Rts. Rep.	International Human Rights Reports
Int'l J. Mar. & Coastal L.	International Journal of Marine and Coastal Law
Int'l Law.	International Lawyer
Int'l Org.	International Organization
Int'l Trib. L. of the Sea	International Tribunal for the Law of the Sea
Iran–U.S. Cl. Trib. Rep.	Iran–United States Claims Tribunal Reports
J. Leg. Stud.	Journal of Legal Studies
L.N.T.S.	League of Nations Treaty Series
Max Planck Y.B. U.N. L.	Max Planck Yearbook of United Nations Law
Mich. L. Rev.	Michigan Law Review
N.Y. Times	New York Times
NAFTA Ch. 11 Arb. Trib.	North American Free Trade Agreement Chapter 11 Arbitration Tribunal
Nat'l Rev. Online	National Review Online
Nav. War College Rev.	Naval War College Review
Neb. L. Rev.	Nebraska Law Review
Neth. Q. Hum. Rts.	Netherlands Quarterly of Human Rights
Neth Y.B. Int'l L.	Netherlands Yearbook of International Law
Nuclear L. Bull.	Nuclear Law Bulletin
OAS Doc.	Organization of American States Document
OAS G.A. Res.	Organization of American States General Assembly Resolution
OAS Res.	Organization of American States Resolution
OECD Doc.	Organisation for Economic Co-operation and Development Document
O.J.	Official Journal of the European Union
P.2d	Pacific Reporter (Second Series)
P.C.I.J.	Permanent Court of International Justice Report
Pub. L.	Public Law
R.C.A.D.I	Recueil des Cours de l'Académie de Droit International
R.I.A.A.	United Nations Reports of International Arbitral Awards
Rev. Belge de Droit Int'l	Revue Belge de Droit International

S. Con. Res.	Senate Concurrent Resolution
S. Ct.	Supreme Court Reporter
S. Exec. Rep.	Senate Executive Report
S. Rep.	Senate Report
S. Res.	Senate Resolution
S. Treaty Doc.	Senate Treaty Document
S.C. Res.	United Nations Security Council Resolution
S.C.R.	Supreme Court Reports (Canada)
So. 2d	Southern Reporter (Second Series)
S.W.3d	Southwestern Reporter (Third Series)
Stat.	United States Statutes at Large
T.C. Res.	United Nations Trusteeship Council Resolution
T.I.A.S.	Treaties and Other International Agreements Series
Temp. State Dep't No.	Temporary State Department Treaty Number
Tex. Int'l L.J.	Texas International Law Journal
Tex. L. Rev.	Texas Law Review
U. Chi. L. Rev.	University of Chicago Law Review
U. Pa. L. Rev.	University of Pennsylvania Law Review
UCLA L. Rev.	University of California, Los Angeles, Law Review
U.N. Doc.	United Nations Document
U.N.T.S.	United Nations Treaty Series
U.S.	United States Supreme Court Reports
U.S. Const.	United States Constitution
U.S.C.	United States Code
U.S.C. App.	United States Code Appendix
U.S.C.A.	United States Code Annotated
U.S.C.S.	United States Code Service
U.S.T.	United States Treaties and Other International Agreements
Va. J. Int'l L.	Virginia Journal of International Law
Vand. L. Rev.	Vanderbilt Law Review
Wash. Post	Washington Post
Weekly Comp. Pres. Doc.	Weekly Compilation of Presidential Documents
WTO Doc.	World Trade Organization Document
Yale J. Int'l L.	Yale Journal of International Law

PRINCIPLES

OF

INTERNATIONAL

LAW

Second Edition

PART I

SYSTEMIC ELEMENTS OF INTERNATIONAL LAW

Chapter 1

FOUNDATIONS OF
INTERNATIONAL LAW

The field of international law is principally concerned with legal norms that operate among nations (often referred to as "states"), but it is also concerned with certain legal norms that operate between a nation and persons within its jurisdiction, and with certain legal norms that regulate the transboundary relationships of persons. Unlike national law, international law is largely decentralized; there is no single legislature, judiciary, or executive responsible for the creation, interpretation, and enforcement of international law, but instead a variety of ways international law seeks to perform those functions. As such, the origin and nature of international law are both unusual and exciting; the field allows a lawyer to "think outside the box" as to what law is and how it shapes human behavior. At the same time, fully understanding the field of international law may take years of study, for it encompasses an enormous range of topics, from the grander norms that seek to prevent war to the less dramatic norms that regulate trans-Atlantic telephone calls.

The purpose of this chapter is to introduce the reader to the basic structure of international law, to some of the theories that exist in explaining the nature of international law, and to the basic history of the field from its origins to the present. By understanding these foundations of international law, and the "actors" of international law discussed in Chapter 2, it will be possible to discuss in detail the manner in which international law is created (Chapter 3), interpreted (Chapter 4), and enforced (Chapter 5).

A. Structures of International Law

Basic Horizontal Structure: Interaction of States

In the first instance, international law arises from a horizontal structure that consists of 193 nation states.[1] Each of these nation states is fully sovereign; none of them regards itself as subordinate

---

1. As of 2011, there are 193 member states of the United Nations. There is a further state, the Vatican State, which is not a member of the United Nations. Other entities, such as Kosovo and Pal-estine, are recognized by some states as being a "state," but have not been admitted to the United Nations. For a discussion of what constitutes a "state," see Chapter 2(A).

to any other state nor, as a general matter, subordinate to a supranational organization. This horizontal structure is very decentralized and means that states can only be exposed to restrictions that they have affirmatively accepted, which occurs when they regard the restrictions as advancing their national interests.

Imagine that you are a member of a group of 193 persons stranded on an island. No one in the group is willing to cede power to any single person or small group of persons for the purpose of making rules that would bind the group as a whole. At the same time, two persons on the island might develop rules as between themselves, such as "whenever you give me two coconuts, I will light a fire for you." Entering into such a bilateral agreement serves the interests of the two persons; they both gain more by cooperating than by not cooperating. This bilateral agreement does not bind other persons; it only binds the two persons who have entered into the agreement. Whether the agreement is "legally" binding in some technical sense is of less interest to the two persons than whether the agreement leads to compliance.

If one of the persons fails to abide by the rule, then the other person likely would reciprocate by no longer cooperating in the arrangement. This dynamic of reciprocity helps keep such bilateral agreements operating, for the two persons entered into the agreement because it was in their interests to do so and, unless those interests change, there is no reason to deviate from the rule. Moreover, a failure to abide by the rule may have reputational consequences; if it is known that you received two coconuts but then refused to light the fire in exchange, you will be seen as an untrustworthy partner by others on the island. Before long, you will not be able to enter into any agreements with other persons, such that your short-term gain (obtaining two coconuts for free) is at the expense of your long-term survival. Even if you could survive, most persons do not like being outcasts; they instead strive to be regarded by others as community members in good standing. All told, the more rational choice for each person is to abide by her agreements.

Such dynamics are quite common in international law. For example, in the field of trade law, states have agreed under the General Agreement on Tariffs and Trade (GATT)[2] to the entry of goods and services from each other without restriction, or pursuant to negotiated tariff levels or quotas. A failure to abide by the

---

2. General Agreement on Tariffs and Trade, Oct. 30, 1947, T.I.A.S. 1700, 55 U.N.T.S. 187. The agreement was revised as part of the Uruguay Round, so as to create a "GATT 1994." *See* Marrakesh Agreement Establishing the World Trade Organization, Annex 1A, THE LEGAL TEXTS: THE RESULTS OF THE URUGUAY ROUND OF MULTILATERAL TRADE NEGOTIATIONS 17 (1999), 33 I.L.M. 81 (1994).

agreement can lead to retaliation by your trading partner and can have reputational consequences in dealing with other trade partners. In most instances, the rational choice for a state is to abide by its trade agreements.

Agreement to a rule need not be solely bilateral. Every person on the island may realize that it is in his or her interest for certain general rules to exist, such as a rule that physical attacks by a person against another person are prohibited. Consequently, the members of the group might all agree to a rule prohibiting physical attacks. If so, a rule of non-aggression is created even without a legislature, for the community of persons is small enough that, through consensus of the persons directly affected, a new rule can emerge. Such a rule is similar to Article 2(4) of the United Nations Charter, which prohibits the use of force by one state against the territorial integrity and political independence of another state.[3]

Issues may arise regarding the enforcement and interpretation of the non-aggression rule. Consequently, everyone on the island (or a sub-group) might further agree that if a person is seen physically attacking someone else, then all the other persons on the island (or the members of the sub-group) will band together to stop the attacker. If so, a means for enforcing the rule through collective security has emerged; so long as the community of persons is truly willing to gang up on an attacker, it is likely that the rule will have "teeth"—violations of the rule either will not occur because they have been deterred or, if they do occur, will be dealt with quickly and effectively. Such a rule is similar to Article 5 of the Charter of the North Atlantic Treaty Organization (NATO), by which member states agree that an armed attack against one NATO member in Europe or North America shall be considered an attack against all NATO members.[4] Many observers believe that this rule helped prevent armed conflict in Europe throughout the Cold War.

There may, of course, be grey areas in applying the non-aggression rule. What if you think someone on the island is about to attack you; may you preemptively attack them? The island has no judicial court to consider such a matter, so instead you may have to rely upon the manner in which the community as a whole responds to such a preemptive act (either accepting an instance of preemptive self-defense or not accepting it). Indeed, over time the practice of the community may serve to interpret and reinterpret the meaning of the rule. In 2002, the United States issued a national security strategy that claimed, among other things, an evolving right under international law for the United States to use military force preemptively against the threat posed by "rogue

---

3. U.N. Charter art. 2(4), 59 Stat. 1031, T.S. No. 993.

4. North Atlantic Treaty, art. 5, Apr. 4, 1949, 63 Stat. 2241, 34 U.N.T.S. 243.

states" possessing weapons of mass destruction (WMD).[5] The reaction of the international community was largely unfavorable, suggesting that such a right may not exist in international law.

Looking at this simple horizontal structure, jurisprudence scholars have expressed differing views as to the nature of "international law." On one end of the spectrum, the British scholar John Austin in 1832 denied that international law was really "law," since law is best understood as a command issued by a sovereign that was backed by a sanction. Since international society lacked such an overarching sovereign, Austin felt that the field referred to as "international law" was best understood as simply a collection of moral rules.[6] At the other end of the spectrum, the Austrian scholar Hans Kelsen, writing in 1960, saw international law as primitive in nature, but nevertheless as sitting at the top of a global legal order of which national laws are a subsidiary part.[7] Somewhere in the middle of the spectrum fell H.L.A. Hart, a British scholar who in 1961 regarded international law as a series of "primary rules" (*e.g.*, a rule to trade coconuts for fire), but as lacking the important "secondary rules" (*e.g.*, rules about how the primary rules can change over time and how they are to be interpreted) which are needed to create a true legal system.[8] These starkly differing views continue to attract adherents today, but are made vastly more complicated when one introduces the other, more "vertical" aspects of contemporary international law.

Vertical Structure: International Organizations

International law is not limited to a simple horizontal structure. Over time, states have come together to establish some supranational organizations capable of creating laws that have a binding effect on their member states. For example, within the European Union (EU), the 27 member states have delegated to the EU sweeping powers to regulate broad sectors of their economies, including the movement of goods, services, labor, and transportation. On matters such as completion of the internal market, the environment or consumer protection, EU legislation is adopted jointly by the European Council and European Parliament under a "co-decision procedure." Certain provisions of the EU treaties and various EU legislative measures apply directly within the member states, superseding national law in case of conflict. To that extent, EU law has a status within the member states comparable to

---

5. *See* WHITE HOUSE, THE NATIONAL SECURITY STRATEGY OF THE UNITED STATES OF AMERICA 13–17 (Sept. 17, 2002).

6. *See* JOHN AUSTIN, THE PROVINCE OF JURISPRUDENCE DETERMINED 142, 200–201 (H.L.A. Hart ed., 1954) (1832).

7. *See* HANS KELSEN, PURE THEORY OF LAW (Max Knight trans., 1967) (1960).

8. *See* H.L.A. HART, THE CONCEPT OF LAW (1961) (especially Chapter X).

federal law in the United States. Other international organizations typically have less sweeping powers than those found in the European Union. Nevertheless, as discussed in Chapter 3(E), there are other international organizations and autonomous treaty bodies capable of creating new rules that bind their member states without the further consent of those states.

Likewise, in some instances, states have created and submitted themselves to the compulsory jurisdiction of international courts or tribunals. For example, 66 states have submitted themselves to the compulsory jurisdiction of the International Court of Justice (the judicial wing of the United Nations) if they are sued by another state that has also accepted the Court's compulsory jurisdiction. Hundreds of treaties concluded by states also provide for the Court's jurisdiction when a dispute arises with respect to one of those treaties. The International Court is also available if states mutually agree to bring a particular dispute before the Court, even if jurisdiction on a compulsory basis does not exist. Each year, the International Court decides cases on matters such as territorial and maritime disputes, diplomatic immunities, or disputes over the use of military force. While the International Court is one of the oldest and most venerated fora for pacific settlement of disputes, there are a wide array of such fora in existence, as discussed in Chapter 4.

Some international organizations are capable of helping enforce international rules. As discussed in Chapter 5, the Security Council stands at the center of such entities, with extensive power to impose sanctions and to authorize the use of military force to address threats to peace and security. However, there are numerous other ways that international organizations help to enforce international law, such as the process for authorizing retaliatory trade sanctions by the World Trade Organization, or the indictment and prosecution by the International Criminal Court of persons for violating the laws of war.

Vertical Structure: Interface with National Law

A different aspect of the vertical structure of international law concerns the interface of international law with national law (also referred to as "domestic law"). National legal systems typically contain rules about whether international law is automatically received into the national legal system. Some countries view international law and national law as part of the same system of law (the "monist" approach), and thus international law is automatically a part of the national legal system. Thus, in most civil law countries, treaties are regarded as being a part of the internal law as soon as they are ratified. Indeed, in some countries, such as the Netherlands, treaties have the same rank as constitutional law, and thus are paramount even with respect to subsequent national legislation.[9] Other countries, such as the common law and Scandinavian countries, tend to view international law and national law as separate, distinguishable bodies of law (the "dualist" approach). However, national legal systems usually are much more complicated than these broad approaches suggest, and one must look at the constitutional rules and judicial practice to fully understand how any given national legal system relates to international law.

As discussed in Chapter 7, Article VI of the U.S. Constitution provides that treaties concluded by the United States are part of the "supreme law of the land," which has been interpreted to mean that, in some instances, a treaty properly concluded by the United States is immediately capable of creating a rule that binds *within* U.S. national law. Thus, a private individual may be able to sue in U.S. court using a provision of the treaty as a rule of decision in the case. By contrast, in the United Kingdom, treaties never have an immediate effect within U.K. law; there must always be U.K. legislation enacted that implements the treaty.

Alternatively, a national statute may exist that calls for use of international law in application of the statute. In the United States, the Alien Tort Statute, 28 U.S.C. § 1350 (2006) provides that federal "district courts shall have original jurisdiction of any civil action by an alien for a tort only, committed in violation of the law of nations or a treaty of the United States." Thus, non-U.S. nationals may sue persons in U.S. courts for commission of a tort in violation of the law of nations, such as the torture of a prisoner by a government official, which is prohibited under both the 1984 U.N. Convention Against Torture[10] and under customary international law.[11]

Many areas of international law have become extremely complex, such that the reception into national law leads to detailed national statutes and regulations. For example, after the sinking of the *Titanic* in 1912, states joined together to conclude a multilateral treaty designed to promote the safety of merchant ships at sea. The agreement was repeatedly revised with increasing detail over the course of the twentieth century, culminating in the 1974 adoption of the International Convention for the Safety of Life at

9. *See* GRONDWET [CONSTITUTION OF THE KINGDOM OF THE NETHERLANDS], art. 94 (1983) ("Statutory regulations in force within the Kingdom shall not be applicable if such application is in conflict with provisions of treaties that are binding on all persons or of resolutions by international institutions.").

10. Convention Against Torture and Other Cruel, Inhuman or Degrading Treatment or Punishment, Dec. 10, 1984, S. TREATY DOC. No. 100–20 (1988), 1465 U.N.T.S. 85 [hereinafter Convention Against Torture]. The convention entered into force for the United States in 1994.

11. *See, e.g.,* Filartiga v. Pena–Irala, 630 F.2d 876 (2d Cir. 1980).

Sea (SOLAS), to which the United States is a party.[12] SOLAS has been amended and supplemented many times, and now contains numerous regulations setting minimum standards for the construction, equipment and operation of ships. One of those regulations requires certain types of ships to be fitted with an identification system that automatically informs shore stations (and other ships) of the ship's identity, type, position, course, speed, navigational status, and other safety-related information.[13] Rather than simply regard SOLAS as binding law within the United States, or simply making reference to SOLAS in a brief statute, the United States implements this obligation, in the first instance, through relatively detailed statutory provisions[14] and, in the second instance, through detailed federal regulations.[15] Although these statutes and regulations make explicit reference to SOLAS, in many instances it may not even be apparent to the reader that the U.S. laws are implementing detailed obligations arising under international law.

National law also can play an important role in the interpretation and enforcement of international law. To the extent that a national court is called upon to decide a case based on a rule of international law, the national court provides a forum for interpreting that law. In 2004, the U.S. Supreme Court considered whether an individual had been arbitrarily arrested in violation of either treaties (such as the International Covenant on Civil and Political Rights[16]) or customary international law. The Court found that there was no relevant treaty obligation enforceable in U.S. courts.[17] Further, the Court found that "a single illegal detention of less than a day, followed by the transfer of custody to lawful authorities and a prompt arraignment, violates no norm of customary international law so well defined as to support the creation of a federal remedy."[18] While the Court's decision was carefully tied into the U.S. standard for bringing a claim under the Alien Tort Statute, the decision nevertheless provides guidance for the U.S. government and foreign governments when interpreting more generally what constitutes an unlawful arbitrary arrest under international law. Further, had the Court found that the arrest was a tort in violation of international law, the plaintiff likely would have succeeded in pursuit of a civil judgment against the defendant, thus allowing national law to assist in the enforcement of international law.

---

12. Nov. 1, 1974, 32 U.S.T. 47, 1184 U.N.T.S. 276 (entered into force May 25, 1980).

13. *Id.*, ch. V, reg. 19.

14. *See* 46 U.S.C. §§ 70114, 70117 (2006).

15. *See* 33 C.F.R.§ 164.46 (2010).

16. Dec. 19, 1966, 999 U.N.T.S. 171, 6 I.L.M. 368.

17. *See* Sosa v. Alvarez–Machain, 542 U.S. 692, 734–35 (2004).

18. *Id.* at 738.

Vertical/Horizontal Structure: Interaction of Persons

Another dimension in the structure of international law concerns the presence and importance of legal and natural persons operating across borders. Traditional studies of international law focus on states and international organizations as the principal means by which international law is created, interpreted, and enforced. However, over the past century, the field of international law has seen other "actors" emerge as important participants, including mid-level government bureaucrats, non-governmental organizations, corporations, and private citizens. As discussed in Chapter 2(D) and (E), states and international organizations remain the dominant features on the international law landscape, but these other actors play key roles in the lobbying of governments and international organizations, the creation of specialized norms at an expert-level, the development of codes of conduct for private entities that inculcate international legal norms, the monitoring of compliance, and the pursuit of international and national litigation to enforce international law. Looking at international law as simply a matter of monolithic states interacting with one another misses this important dimension, for behind the facade of the "state" are real people operating both within and outside government, capable of promoting in various ways international law creation, interpretation, and enforcement. The structure of this interaction is vertical in the sense of the hierarchy between a state and the persons within it, but also horizontal in the sense of persons operating as among themselves across boundaries.

B. Theories of International Law

Among the foundations of international law are theories about the nature of such law; in what sense is it "law" and how does that law "bind" states and other relevant actors? As is the case with national law, there are various and sometimes conflicting theoretical strands that seek to explain the nature and functioning of international law.

International Natural Law

For a natural law theorist, international law consists in part of fundamental principles of right and wrong. These principles are fixed and universal; they do not change depending upon political inclinations or cultural predispositions of states. Moreover, these principles are not identified by studying enactments by states; rather, they are determined through a process of "right reason," which to a large degree focuses on whether a particular principle is inherent in the notion of a society of states and in the essential characteristics of humanity.

In the initial stages of the development of international law (discussed *infra* Section C), international law theorists such as Francisco de Vitoria, Francisco Suarez, Hugo Grotius, and Samuel Pufendorf relied heavily on natural law theory to construct what they believed to be the "law of nations."[19] For them, many of the rules that comprised international law could be explained by reference to moral philosophy, ethics, and theology, particularly the teachings of the Christian tradition. More recently, overt reliance on such metaphysical sources to construct legal rules has fallen into disrepute, replaced instead by positivism (discussed below). Yet in many respects, natural law continues to lurk beneath the surface of international law.

Thus, in seeking to explain the most rudimentary norms of contemporary international law, theorists invariably are still led to a form of natural law reasoning. For example, a *grundnorm* of contemporary treaty law is that every treaty in force is binding upon the parties to it and must be performed by them in good faith, a concept referred to as *pacta sunt servanda* (an agreement must be kept). But why are states bound to this rule? It is certainly true that they initially consented to be bound by the treaty, but why can they not, at some later point in time, simply decide that they no longer wish to be bound? There must be some rule outside the scope of the treaty itself that binds the state to the treaty. It is possible that states have agreed to a rule of *pacta sunt servanda* by adhering to a "treaty on treaties" that contains the rule.[20] Yet, even then, by what theory is a state bound to abide by that "treaty on treaties"?

In the end, it seems that there must be some first principles of international law separate from those consented to by states, ones that are rooted in pre-existing understandings. These metaphysical norms undergird the norms that arise from the express consent of states. Other such norms might include principles on the independence and legal equality of states, the duty of non-intervention, and the right of self-defense.[21]

Further, while it appears that most of contemporary international law consists of norms that arise from the express consent of states, the intellectual heritage of those norms can often be traced to earlier natural law reasoning, such that the reasoning remains of relevance to us. Thus, norms constraining the conduct of warfare so as to protect civilians, while embedded today in treaties such as the

19. *See* ARTHUR NUSSBAUM, A CONCISE HISTORY OF THE LAW OF NATIONS ch. 4 (rev. ed. 1954).

20. *See* Vienna Convention on the Law of Treaties art. 26, May 23, 1969, 1155 U.N.T.S. 331 [hereinafter VCLT].

21. *See* ALLEN BUCHANAN, JUSTICE, LEGITIMACY AND SELF-DETERMINATION: MORAL FOUNDATIONS FOR INTERNATIONAL LAW (2004).

1949 Geneva Conventions and the 1907 Hague Regulations,[22] derive from norms that date back at least as far as the Book of Deuteronomy. Similarly, the prohibition on the use of force by one state against another (unless undertaken in self-defense) is today expressed in a treaty consented to by states, but the norm is one that has a rich heritage in the "just war" doctrines that emerged during the theological debates of the Middle Ages. Indeed, certain norms appear to reflect fundamental beliefs of governments and persons worldwide (e.g., the abhorrence of genocide), such that the norm is best viewed as not solely anchored in the existence of a treaty commitment or some other form of state consent. International law even recognizes the possibly of norms from which states may not deviate under any circumstances, regardless of their treaty practice, a concept known as *jus cogens* (peremptory norms).[23] While most scholars would view those norms as being very limited in number, the belief that they exist reflects the enduring influence of the natural law tradition.

Finally, while most contemporary international law is reflected in treaties or the practice of states, there remain gaps in those positive acts of state consent, which invariably must be filled by decision-makers through resort to other concepts. Likewise, there are times when the law needs to change to accommodate new developments. Policy-makers, practitioners, judges, and scholars confronted with such gaps, or a need for change, will often turn to basic notions of equity, justice, or "fairness,"[24] which in turn seem rooted in natural law thinking. Thus, the international military tribunal at Nuremberg convicted certain German defendants for committing "crimes against peace" because they embarked on an aggressive war, and for committing "crimes against humanity" because they inflicted atrocities against their own citizens. The tribunal did this even in the absence of a treaty or clear customary practice that created such crimes. While the tribunal's judgment sought to make references to various treaties and state practice in existence prior to the commission of the criminal acts, many observers see the judgment as resting most securely on more fundamental notions of what natural law requires.

International Legal Positivism

The central problem with the natural law tradition is in identifying what norms are compelled by natural law reasoning. One can posit the existence of universal norms of international law, but how do we know what they are? States may well disagree on

---

22. *See* Chapter 14(B).

23. *See* VCLT, *supra* note 20, art. 53; *see also* Chapter 3(B).

24. *See* Thomas Franck, Fairness in International Law and Institutions (1995).

the existence and content of such norms, leading to uncertainty and instability in inter-state relations. Consequently, states are much more attracted to the idea of establishing international norms through the affirmative (or "positive") practice of states, typically captured either expressly in written treaty instruments or tacitly in the customs that develop among states over time that they regard as part of their legal obligations.

This approach emphasizes the importance of state consent; a state is bound to a legal norm because it has affirmatively consented to the norm. While the natural law theorist may dwell on what the law "ought" to be as a matter of equity, justice, and fairness, the positivist theorist is more focused on what the law "is" through a systematic study of ratified treaties and state practice. The Permanent Court of International Justice (the judicial wing of the League of Nations) stated in the *Lotus* case:

> International law governs relations between independent States. The rules of law binding upon States therefore emanate from their own free will as expressed in conventions or by usages generally accepted as expressing principles of law and established in order to regulate the relations between these co-existing independent communities or with a view to the achievement of common aims. Restrictions upon the independence of States cannot therefore be presumed.[25]

International lawyers for the most part continue to see international law in this way; a judge of the International Court of Justice recently wrote that "[i]nternational law rests on the principle of the sovereignty of states and thus originates from their consent."[26]

For example, rather than ask whether state-sponsored torture violates fundamental rights held by humans regardless of the practice of states (a natural law approach), the positivist wants to know whether: (1) states have enacted a treaty containing a provision that prohibits such torture;[27] (2) the state that committed the torture is a party to the treaty; and (3) if so, when ratifying the treaty the state filed a reservation of some kind by which it prevented application to it of the relevant provision. If a treaty provision does not bind the state, the positivist wants to know if there is evidence of uniform practice by states accepting a customary rule prohibiting state-sponsored torture, such that the state's consent to the norm can be found even in the absence of a treaty obligation. If no such consent can be found, then the state cannot be said to be in violation of international law.

---

25. S.S. "Lotus" (Fr. v. Turk.), 1927 P.C.I.J. (ser. A) No. 10, at 18 (Sept. 7).

26. Advisory Opinion on Legality of the Threat or Use of Nuclear Weapons, 1996 I.C.J. 226, at 291, para. 10 (July 8) (separate opinion of Judge Guillaume).

27. *See, e.g.,* Convention Against Torture, *supra* note 10.

Exactly how states adhere to treaties and develop customary rules of international law will be considered further in Chapter 3. For now, it is sufficient to note that most international lawyers (and most national lawyers, for that matter) tend to think like positivists; they are more comfortable analyzing rules arising from affirmative acceptance by states than they are speculating about rules derived from "right reason."

International Legal Realism

Classic positivist theory regards international law as something akin to a hard science; rules that have been established by states can be determined through careful, rational analysis and, where necessary, empirical observation. For every controversy over a particular rule of international law, there is a "right answer," which can be discerned neutrally or objectively. For the realist, however, focusing on rules that are "out there," waiting to be discovered, is misguided, for it ignores important aspects of process that permeate the international legal system. The realist is impatient with the idea that black-letter rules govern international society, that judges and decision-makers are mechanically applying such rules free of their own biases, and that international law is devoid of significant gaps, ambiguities, and uncertainties. Consequently, realism has led to two different but important approaches to how we think about international law.

First, international legal realism has led to the development of an approach known as "international legal process." This approach accepts that decision-makers are strongly influenced by their own policy preferences and seeks to understand (and to a certain extent constrain) the use of such preferences in the development and application of international law. To do so, the international legal process approach carefully studies the allocation of decision-making powers in inter-state relations and exactly how those powers, formal and informal, are exercised and restrained.[28] Recent scholarship of this type has stressed the manner in which international rules are internalized by states and the variety of entities other than states that now participate in the international legal system. The "vertical dimensions" of international law referred to in the first section of this chapter capture some elements of this approach.

The second strand of international realism also accepts that decision-makers are strongly influenced by their personal policy-preferences, but warmly embraces the use of those preferences in

---

28. *See* ABRAM CHAYES, THOMAS EHRLICH & ANDREAS F. LOWENFELD, INTERNATIONAL LEGAL PROCESS: MATERIALS FOR AN INTRODUCTORY COURSE (1968); Harold Hongju Koh, *Transnational Legal Process*, 75 NEB. L. REV. 181 (1996); Jacob Katz Cogan, *The Regulatory Turn In International Law*, 52 HARV. INT'L L.J. 322 (2011).

the development and application of international law, so long as the preferences promote desirable social and economic objectives. The leading version of this approach is the "policy-oriented jurisprudence" developed largely by Harold Lasswell and Myres McDougal.[29] For them, law is not "out there" waiting to be found by, in essence, looking backwards; it is instead the very decisions that are made by persons who are authorized by the community to make them, where those persons have the effective power to secure compliance with their decisions. For the policy-oriented approach, the important step lies in establishing the best criteria and procedures that such decision-makers should follow when making decisions about where society wants to go in the future. To do so, the policy-oriented approach borrows tools and techniques from a variety of social-science disciplines, including economics, psychology, and sociology, thus engaging in a much wider empirical inquiry than is the case for the positivist. Policy-oriented scholars have identified certain analytic tools—referred to as "phase analysis," "value analysis," and "analysis of decision functions"—as a means of examining the context in which decisions are made and past trends in decision-making. Among other things, they have developed a set of values that they believe society desires (such as enlightenment, wealth, and well-being), and urge policy-makers to approach decision-making so as to advance those values.

Critics of the policy-oriented approach assert that the use of values to determine the legality of a course of action is a recipe for undesirable indeterminacy in the law, and charge that it provides major powers (such as the United States) with far too much discretion in claiming what the law requires or allows. Law cannot be a check on the exercise of power, the critics claim, if it becomes subsumed as part of the political preferences of decision-makers. For the policy-oriented approach, however, law is inescapably intertwined with the values of authoritative decision-makers, and it is far better to recognize the role of such values, to identify what those values should be, and to judge the conduct of decision-makers based on fidelity to those values.

New Stream

Building upon the insights of the international legal realism approach, the "new stream" approach agrees that the positivists are wrong in approaching international law as though it consists simply of neutral rules waiting to be discovered. Yet, with a heavy reliance on linguistic theory and philosophy, the new stream approach seeks to understand the hidden ideologies, attitudes, and structures of international law, so as to expose contradictions or

---

29. *See* HAROLD D. LASSWELL & MYRES McDOUGAL, JURISPRUDENCE FOR A FREE SOCI- ETY: STUDIES IN LAW, SCIENCE, AND POLICY (1992) (two volumes).

antinomies.[30] A core contradiction lies in the idea of a legal system created by the consent of sovereign states, which then is supposed to bind and constrain those very same states. For the new stream school, many of the rules of international law attempt to mediate back and forth between concepts of sovereign independence and sovereign constraint, a dynamic that can be achieved by, for instance, having common rules competing with exceptions to those rules, by having general rules competing with more specialized rules, or by having rules oriented toward sovereignty competing with rules oriented toward community. In short, these binary oppositions are embedded within international legal rules, such that international law can be manipulated to reach contradictory results. Thus, while a state is said to be bound by a treaty that it has ratified or a customary rule to which it has not objected, a state might also be bound to a conflicting peremptory norm of *jus cogens* that is not based on the state's consent (discussed above). Given such core contradictions, two international lawyers are capable of making completely respectable, formal arguments that reach the exact opposite conclusion by assigning greater significance to one or the other norm.

The new stream approach does not seek to reconcile such conflicts; for them, doing so is pointless. The new stream approach also does not follow the policy-oriented approach in seeking to define optimal values; rather, new stream scholars see themselves as engaging in a value-free methodology, an effort simply to understand the true structure of international legal rules.

Critics of the new stream approach charge that it cynically deconstructs international law as being an arbitrary and empty system, without providing any means for reconstructing the field. Most new stream scholars, however, accept that international law continues to function in practice; that international lawyers believe in and pursue formal, doctrinal arguments. For the new stream scholar, the value in their theory is in pointing out that international law is not determinate and neutral in nature, but instead a vehicle for ideology. Such theorizing has helped open the door for a variety of new voices in the debate over international law theory, including those advancing feminist theory and "Third World" theory. Thus, feminist theorists argue that the international legal system—a product of governments and international organizations almost exclusively dominated by men—is crafted in a manner that covertly perpetuates the unequal position of women. For them,

---

30. MARTII KOSKENNIEMI, FROM APOLOGY TO UTOPIA: THE STRUCTURE OF INTERNATIONAL LEGAL ARGUMENT (2005) (reissue of 1989 edition with new epilogue); Philip Trimble, *International Law, World Order, and Critical Legal Studies*, 42 STAN. L. REV. 811 (1990); David Kennedy, *A New Stream of International Law Scholarship*, 7 WIS. J. INT'L L. 1 (1988).

international legal rules should be transformed so as to be less litigious, less confrontational, and less patriarchal.[31] Third World theorists focus on how international law developed so as to support the interests of powerful, mostly European, colonizing states, whose interests lay largely in promoting the "values" of the developed world. For these theorists, international law should incorporate the doctrine and principles of non-European states, and should be redirected toward addressing distributive justice, poverty, and development, and upholding the principles of sovereignty and non-intervention.[32] One means of doing so is to regard General Assembly resolutions as having a binding legal effect, since the majority of states within it are developing states.

International Law/International Relations

Running parallel with theories by international lawyers about international law are theories by international relations scholars about the role of "norms" and "regimes" in inter-state relations. To a large extent, international lawyers and international relations specialists have operated in different spheres, but in recent years they have done better at taking account of each other's work, which in many respects is mutually reinforcing. While the work of international relations specialists is varied and not easily reduced to a brief summary, it may generally be described as following one of four approaches.[33]

International relations "idealists" believe that international society has reached a stage where resort to warfare is no longer tenable; states collectively share strong interests in peaceful co-existence. Those interests can be furthered by states pursuing cooperative strategies through treaties, international organizations, and mechanisms for the pacific settlement of disputes. Idealism in the United States was at its zenith in the early 1900's, when many influential American leaders believed that the political and legal institutions successfully crafted within the United States could be recreated at the international level, thus bringing worldwide peace and prosperity. Such idealists pushed for the creation of international organizations like the League of Nations and international agreements, such as the 1928 Kellogg–Briand Pact,[34] in which states codified in law the idea that resort to the use of force to achieve foreign policy objectives was no longer permissible. While

---

31. HILARY CHARLESWORTH & CHRISTINE CHINKIN, THE BOUNDARIES OF INTERNATIONAL LAW: A FEMINIST ANALYSIS (2000).

32. THE THIRD WORLD AND INTERNATIONAL ORDER: LAW, POLITICS AND GLOBALIZATION (Antony Anghie et al. eds., 2003).

33. See INTERNATIONAL LAW AND INTERNATIONAL RELATIONS (Beth A. Simmons &

Richard H. Steinberg eds., 2007); FOUNDATIONS OF INTERNATIONAL LAW AND POLITICS (Oona A. Hathaway & Harold Hongju Koh eds., 2005).

34. General Treaty for the Renunciation of War, Aug. 27, 1928, 46 Stat. 2343, 94 L.N.T.S. 57.

such thinking (also referred to disparagingly as "utopianism") remained prevalent in the United States during the 1920's and 1930's, it lost favor when such efforts failed to avert the outbreak of World War II. Idealism still holds a place in American foreign relations; some glimpse it in George W. Bush's call in his second inaugural address for a United States committed to the vigorous promotion of democracy worldwide.[35] European foreign policy has strong elements of idealism, perhaps because the creation of a supra-national institution (the European Union) has succeeded in ending the conflict among European states that sparked two world wars.

International relations "realists," who became ascendant in the United States after World War II, generally posit that there is no essential harmony of interests between states, but rather a web of conflicting national objectives in an anarchical world.[36] For classical realists, power or state capabilities, rather than common interests, shape relations among nations, and only through a balance of power can harmony be effectively achieved. Cooperation among states might occur when their interests coincide, but such cooperation is not the product of moral or ethical principles shared universally by states. Rather, it is the product of certain a priori assumptions about human nature; that persons leading states seek wealth and power, and will use international law and institutions only when doing so serves that purpose. Thus, cooperation among states is part of a fluid process of changing politics, not part of a stable legal framework to which states must adhere. "Neo-realism" departs from classical realism in trying to provide a more systemic or structural account of international relations, as opposed to describing the ethics of statecraft. For example, international economic regimes (such as the World Bank) are reflections of structural power in the international system, allowing certain powerful states to serve their interests by controlling and bringing stability to the global economy.

"Liberal international relations" theorists accept some of the core tenets of realism, but see realism as falling short in fully capturing how nations behave.[37] Liberal theorists assert that, as states modernize and move away from habitual warfare, promotion of economic and social welfare becomes more important than preserving the state's security, and hence cooperation among states through treaties and international organizations becomes more likely than conflict. For liberal international relations theory, states are not uniform in nature; those with democratic traditions and a

---

35. *Inaugural Address*, 41 WEEKLY COMP. PRES. DOC. 74 (Jan. 24, 2005).

36. *See, e.g.*, KENNETH WALTZ, REALISM AND INTERNATIONAL POLITICS (2008).

37. *See, e.g.*, HEDLEY BULL, THE ANARCHICAL SOCIETY: A STUDY OF ORDER IN WORLD POLITICS (1977).

commitment to the rule of law approach international relations differently than states that lack such features. By and large, democratic states do not go to war with one another, and they find sophisticated ways of cooperating across borders. Moreover, liberal theorists believe that realists fail to account for individuals and non-governmental organizations in international relations. These key actors have added a new (and less state-centric) dimension to how one should think about international politics.

"Constructivism" does not espouse a substantive international relations theory of its own, but rather criticizes other theorists for failing to take account of the full content and sources of state interests. For constructivists, the international system is an ideational construct of state actors, in which there are widely shared inter-subjective beliefs (ideas, conceptions, assumptions). States "construct" one another in their relations; a concept such as "sovereignty" is not objectively true, but is the product of states constantly defining and redefining it through social interactions. To fully understand the "interests" of states, one must seek to understand human consciousness and its role in international society, for it helps explain why certain norms—such as a norm favoring the use of force to protect human rights—can emerge within the society of states.[38]

All of these theories on international relations make important points about the way states and persons act in international relations. To understand fully why states create treaties and international organizations, or other norms and regimes, it is useful to understand the basics of these theories, as well as those who criticize them.

C. History of International Law

Ancient Times

The oldest known treaty appears to date back to 3100 B.C. Written on a stone monument in Sumerian language, the treaty ended a war and helped mark a boundary between two city-states in Mesopotamia—Lagash and Umma. Among other things, the treaty records an oath taken by both sides to powerful Sumerian gods, who they worshiped in common, and in this sense these gods became the guarantors of the treaty. There are, of course many other examples of such treaties in ancient times, such as among the Hittites of Asia Minor, Babylon, Assur, and Egypt. While many were treaties of peace, others were collective defense treaties, some had extradition provisions, and still others set up autonomous

---

38. *See, e.g.,* ALEXANDER WENDT, SO- (1999); MARTHA FINNEMORE, NATIONAL IN-
CIAL THEORY OF INTERNATIONAL POLITICS TERESTS IN INTERNATIONAL SOCIETY (1996).

regions for ethnic groups, such as the Greek cities in the delta of the Nile.[39]

Early religious texts also codified rules that, if not themselves a form of "international law," presaged by some centuries the emergence of such law. Thus, as noted above, the book of Deuteronomy contains probably the oldest written canons on warfare, prohibiting the killing of women and children and expressing a duty to uphold sworn promises to an enemy, even when difficult to do so. Similarly, in ancient India and China may be found warrior codes that called for humanity in warfare, as well as emergent rules on how rulers should treat envoys, the predecessors of today's diplomats.

As in many things, laws developed by Greece in the fourth century B.C. would have important influences on later Roman law and the development of the European legal system. Among the Greek city-states there developed an elaborate treaty system, one probably not again seen until the 1800's. These Greek treaties covered the typical topics of peace and alliances, but also addressed trade issues, coinage, the granting of personal liberties, protection of property, intermarriage, and rights to attend public games. An important Greek contribution came in the development of arbitration as a method of inter-state dispute settlement, on matters such as delimitation of boundaries or the use of streams and springs. Among other things, the arbitrators had to take an oath to the Greek gods to act impartially and sometimes were from a third state. Yet perhaps Greece's greatest contribution to contemporary law, including contemporary international law, lies in the development of the idea of "natural law" (discussed above), whereby universally applicable rules are derived not from man-made law but from "right reason."[40]

Law is regarded as one of ancient Rome's paramount cultural achievements. Some important substantive doctrines in Rome's relations with its enemies would later prove important for international law. Thus, it is in early Roman history that the concept of the just war emerged, consisting of elaborate proceedings in which a special group of priests would decide whether a foreign nation had violated its duties to the Romans (if so, the Romans felt that the gods would side with them in war). Roman treaties, however, were not particularly sophisticated, perhaps due to Rome's success in simply conquering foreign dominions. Rather, Rome's greatest significance for modern international law appears to lie in the general development of Roman private law. For when European scholars and statesmen in the sixteenth and seventeenth centuries (dis-

---

39. *See* Nussbaum, *supra* note 19, Ch. 1.

40. *See* Coleman Phillipson, The International Law and Custom of Ancient Greece and Rome (1911) (2 vols.).

cussed below) were casting about for a foundation on which to build international law, it was natural to look to Roman law which was held in high authority throughout Europe. Roman law contained important principles that seemed, by analogy, appropriate to use in inter-state relations. Thus, Roman rules on private ownership of property were found useful in developing rules on territorial sovereignty (for example, a rule that sovereignty over a newly discovered land requires actual possession of that land), Roman rules on private contracts were seen as appropriate for the development of treaty law, and Roman rules on powers accorded by superiors to inferiors were seen as relevant in developing rules on diplomatic agents.

The Roman body of rules known as the *jus gentium* had nothing to do with relations among empires let alone among "states" as we know them today. Rather, such law concerned the rules applied to non-Romans living or present within the Roman empire, which were more liberal than the older Roman civil law. Ultimately, these liberal rules came to be applied even among Romans, and became the core of what we now consider classical Roman law.[41]

Middle Ages in Europe

After the fall of the Roman empire, Europe entered an extended period of decline and stagnation known as the Middle Ages. During this time, there were various barriers to the growth of international law in the form of alternative systems of rules. First, there was imperial law, by which the Holy Roman Emperor was the supreme and universal authority. Given the existence of imperial law, there was little need to develop a system of law that would mediate among the princes of Europe. Some rules regarding relations with those outside the Empire did form, mostly relating to peace treaties and arbitration. Second, feudal law emerged due to a need for organizing the hierarchy of power at the local level. Third, ecclesiastical law provided an extensive system of rules compelling obedience over all the Christian world. While this law was principally concerned with spiritual and moral matters, it strayed into secular matters. For example, the doctrine of the just war was significantly defined and developed by both Saint Augustine and Saint Thomas Aquinas, thus influencing the later development of international law on war and peace.[42]

Important systems of rules began to emerge in the private sphere that later would be recognized as a part of international law,

---

41. *See generally* DAVID BEDERMAN, IN-
TERNATIONAL LAW IN ANTIQUITY (2001).

42. *See, e.g.,* FREDERICK H. RUSSELL,
THE JUST WAR IN THE MIDDLE AGES (1975);

STEPHEN C. NEFF, WAR AND THE LAW OF
NATIONS: A GENERAL HISTORY ch. 2 (2008).

at least as broadly defined. Thus, a rich body of customs concerning the treatment of vessels and seamen plying trade across the oceans coalesced into early maritime law. Likewise, the *lex mercatoria* (or mercantile law) emerged about nine centuries ago, when Europe experienced a commercial renaissance associated in part with the opening of trade with markets in Asia. This law—virtually an autonomous legal order—formed from the practice of merchants across Europe, and governed a special class of people (merchants) in special places (fairs, markets, and seaports). The *lex mercatoria* was truly transnational in nature, based upon an amalgam of Europe-wide customs, and even administered by speedy, informal, and equity-oriented mercantile courts, rather than by regular judges. By developing over time useful standardized contract terms, shipping terms, and letter of credit terms, this *lex mercatoria* remains very much alive today and is kept vibrant through trade associations.[43]

The end of the Middle Ages saw the collapse of feudalism and of imperial power. The grip of the Catholic Church in Europe declined with the Reformation, which in turn sparked the Counter–Reformation. Such developments led to vicious religious warfare between Catholics and Protestants in Europe, and the rise of nation-states as a means of creating stability.

The Rise of Nation–States

The Peace of Westphalia in 1648 largely brought an end to European religious wars (and specifically ended the "Thirty Years War"). In essence, Westphalia checkmated the Counter–Reformation by solidifying territorial state structures whereby the authority of a government over a certain territory containing certain people was acknowledged regardless of that government's religious affiliation. Typically, therefore, 1648 is selected as the year when international law "began," although in reality it had antecedents in prior times (as discussed above) and emerged only over a protracted period with the rise of nation states, especially Spain, England, France, and The Netherlands.

With the rise of nation-states, an obvious question emerged: what law governed their relations, if any? Various scholars of international law across Europe sought to define the content of, and defend the existence of, such law. Thus, a school of "Spanish scholastics" emerged who sought to advise the Spanish emperor on international law, including Francisco de Vitoria (1486?–1546) and Francisco Suárez (1548–1617). These scholars were highly versed in civil and ecclesiastical law, but they also relied heavily on Catholic

---

43. *See, e.g.,* Lex Mercatoria and Arbitration (Thomas E. Carbonneau ed., rev. ed., 1998).

theology in their writings, which invariably failed to win over Protestant communities. The Italian Alberico Gentili (1552–1608), who became a renowned professor of civil law at Oxford, wrote a widely-read treatise entitled *De Jure Belli* [Law of War] (1589) and another on the rights of ambassadors, entitled *De Legationibus* (1585). Gentili was the first international law scholar to move away from theology and to focus instead on Roman law as a source for international rules. Such a move was shrewd, in that Roman law was respected throughout Europe, in both Catholic and Protestant communities. Many scholars regard Gentili as the founder of a systematic law of nations.[44]

Yet it is typically the Dutchman Hugo Grotius (1583–1645) who is regarded as the "father of international law."[45] An amazing child prodigy who was already crafting Latin poems at age seven, Grotius ultimately wrote numerous non-international law treatises that were widely read and relied upon, even up until the twentieth century. His signature achievement, however, was his 1625 treatise *De Jure Belli ac Pacis* [Law of War and Peace], which presented for the first time a system of international law that proved widely acceptable among states and heavily influenced later scholars. Living in a time of religious warfare, Grotius essentially tried to mobilize the forces of jurisprudence, philosophy, history, and theology as a means of restoring peace in Europe. Published widely in many languages (including fifty editions in Latin!), the treatise was an incredibly thorough inquiry into international law and its subdivisions, sources, and foundations. Grotius sought to draw on many of the natural law insights of the Spanish scholastics, but followed Gentili in decoupling those insights from Catholic theology. One might say that his treatise was inspired by Christian ideals, but was secular in nature; the Pope and the Catholic Church have no legal position in Grotius's international law. Grotius also wrote an important pamphlet entitled *Mare Liberum* [Freedom of the Seas] (1609), which sought to advance Dutch seafaring interests and counterbalanced Englishman John Selden's treatise, *Mare Clausum sive De Dominio Maris* [The Closed Seas, or the Dominion of the Seas] (1635). Although it took time, Grotius' doctrine favoring freedom of the seas for navigation and fishing became commonly accepted.

Because he was writing at an early stage in the formation of international law, Grotius recognized but was not fixated upon the positive practice of nation states, for there was little to be found other than certain customary practices. Rather, Grotius' theorizing about international law is typically placed more in the natural law

---

44. *See, e.g.,* J.G. STARKE, INTRODUCTION TO INTERNATIONAL LAW (9th ed. 1984).

45. *See* HUGO GROTIUS AND INTERNATIONAL RELATIONS (Hedley Bull et al. eds., 1992).

tradition. Many of the scholars who initially followed him remained within this tradition, such as the German Samuel Pufendorf (1632–1694). Author of three works on international law, including *On the Law of Nature and of Nations* (1672), Pufendorf insisted on the natural equality of states, an idea readily traced to Thomas Hobbes. With the Englishman Richard Zouche (1590–1661) and Swiss diplomat Emmerich de Vattel (1714–1767), however, may be seen a clear movement away from natural law thinking to a more positivist inquiry into the actual practice of states, including their treaty practice. Among other things, Vattel's great work on *The Law of Nations* (1758) divided positive law into three classes: (1) voluntary law arising from the presumed consent of states; (2) conventional law arising from the express consent of states; and (3) customary law arising from the practice of states.[46]

The Rise of Positivism

As international law matured, states and scholars began looking less to natural law sources as a means of determining the content of international law, and more toward the positive acts by sovereigns through treaty or custom. With this development came an increasing emphasis after 1700 on the sovereign consent by states to a norm before they can be said to be bound by that norm. Treaties were an important first place to look for such consent, for conclusion of a treaty was clear evidence of the existence of a binding norm and usually was clear about the content of the norm. Yet in the absence of an applicable treaty, the customary practice of states over time, if universal enough and consistent enough, could establish the existence of a customary norm, at least if the practice showed that states regarded adherence to the norm as a legal obligation. As a practical matter, customary international law served a critical role during the first centuries of international law, when treaty practice was sparse or uneven. By the twentieth century, as treaties became commonplace and addressed the wide array of concerns in the field of international law, custom became less dominant, but still featured as an important means of filling in gaps.

During the nineteenth and early twentieth centuries, international law experienced both a widening and a deepening. It widened in the sense that international law spread from Europe and North America to South America and the Far East, with the emergence of those region's own nation states, and the opening of China and Japan to the West. It deepened in the sense that an enormous number of treaties were crafted going well beyond traditional

46. *See generally* Francis Ruddy, In- (1975).
ternational Law in the Enlightenment

matters, such as war and commerce, to cover consular affairs, extradition, monetary matters, postal, telegraph, railway, fishing, copyrights, patents, and many other subjects. Some have estimated that between the Congress of Vienna Final Act in 1815 and World War I, about sixteen thousand treaties were concluded.

At the same time, the world saw the emergence of international organizations and non-government, transnational organizations as important actors in international law.[47] The industrial revolutions in Europe and then North America fomented concerns by like-minded groups in different states (*e.g.*, labor groups), while at the same time creating the transportation and communication links for those groups to organize on a transnational scale. Consequently, from 1815 to World War II, it is estimated that more than four hundred non-governmental, transnational organizations emerged, concerned with commerce, labor rights, humanitarian law, and other matters. Concomitantly, about forty international (or inter-governmental) organizations appeared, in part as a governmental response to the organization of non-governmental, transnational organizations.

Post-World War II Trends

In the aftermath of World War II, international law truly flourished. The increasing interaction of states and non-state actors across boundaries spurred by economic growth and technological progress necessitated the development of increasingly complex and sophisticated treaty regimes. Many of the specialized regimes discussed in Part III of this treatise principally grew to maturity during this period.

Further, international law became truly global in the sense of beginning to accommodate the views and interests of developing states; while in 1945 there were only 45 states in existence, today—after decolonization and fragmentation of states such as the Soviet Union—there are at least 193 states, the vast majority of which represent the developing world or economies in transition. This development has begun to have an enormous impact on the agenda for developing international law and international organizations, with many multilateral negotiations reflecting a struggle between the interests of developed and developing states.

International organizations have continued to proliferate and, in the case of the European Union, to become supra-national in nature. Likewise, non-governmental organizations have continued

47. Bob Reinalda, Routledge History of International Organizations: From 1815 to the Present Day (2009); Anna-   Karin Lindblom, Non-Governmental Organisations in International Law (2005).

their rise as important actors in both the creation and monitoring of international law.

International Law in American History

Since its inception, the United States has played a special role in the development of international law.[48] Colonial America emerged at roughly the same time as the systematic study of international law. Alberico Gentili—the renowned Italian scholar discussed above—died in 1608, one year after the founding of Jamestown. Hugo Grotius, probably the most famous of the early writers on international law, published his systematic treatise in 1625, just five years after the Mayflower landed at Plymouth. By the time of the Treaty of Westphalia in 1648, English colonists were present all along the Eastern seaboard, Spanish colonists occupied Florida, Dutch colonists had settled in present-day New York, and the French had developed trading posts in present-day Canada. Thus, the development of international law coincided with the emergence of early American law.

Colonial lawyers became quite interested in the application of certain aspects of international law, such as international maritime law, including law on the seizure of vessels as prize, piracy, and awards and allowances for the salvaging or saving of vessels damaged or in distress. Moreover, on the eve of the American Revolution, the central intellectual problem confronting the American colonists was how to recognize the English Parliament as sovereign, yet deny to it a power generally recognized as necessary for any supreme legislative authority—the power to tax.[49] In determining the appropriate level of political representation and revenue authority at the central and local levels, the colonists referred to, and drew upon, European international law theorists, such as Grotius, Pufendorf, and Vattel. Indeed, in describing the political pamphlets published in the colonies just prior to the Revolution, Barnard Bailyn has stated that "[i]n pamphlet after pamphlet the American writers cited ... Grotius, Pufendorf, Burlamaqui, and Vattel on the laws of nature and of nations, and on the principles of civil government."[50] Jack Rakove, in his treatise *Original Meanings,* states that "There can be no question that the framers and many of their contemporaries were familiar not only with the great works of such luminaries as Locke, Hobbes, Montesquieu, Hume, and Blackstone, but also with ... the disquisitions on public law of such

---

48. Mark W. Janis, America and the Law of Nations 1776–1939 (2010).

49. *See* Bernard Bailyn, The Ideological Origins of the American Revolution 202 (1967).

50. *Id.* at 27; Pamphlets of the American Revolution 24 (Bernard Bailyn ed., 1965); *see also* Benjamin Fletcher Wright, Jr., American Interpretations of Natural Law: A Study in the History of Political Thought 7 (1962).

respected European authorities as Grotius, Pufendorf, and De-lolme."[51]

Colonial interest in the law of nations had a cascading effect on U.S. attitudes in the early American republic. One can readily chart the influence of the law of nations upon John Marshall as he, within a relatively brief period of eight years, argued before the Supreme Court as debtors' counsel in the test case against pre-Revolutionary British creditors, represented the United States in an important diplomatic mission to France, served in the House of Representatives, and then directed U.S. foreign policy as secretary of state.[52] All of this occurred before he penned the opinions as Supreme Court Chief Justice for which he is well known. It is no surprise that in the first great treatise on U.S. law, Chancellor James Kent in 1826 wrote that the "faithful observance" of the law of nations "is essential to national character, and to the happiness of mankind."[53] Kent's *Commentaries on American Law*, in turn, were edited in their 12th edition in 1873 by a young Oliver Wendell Holmes,[54] who later as Supreme Court justice would author decisions such as *Missouri v. Holland*, strongly endorsing international treaty obligations as constituting a part of U.S. law.[55]

The first U.S. treatise dedicated exclusively to international law was written by Henry Wheaton. Wheaton had served as a Chief Justice of the U.S. Marine Court in Washington, D.C. and, based on that experience, had written *A Digest of the Law of Maritime Captures and Prizes* (1815). In 1836, his *Elements of International Law* addressed the field of international law generally, and was of such high quality that it ultimately went through several editions and translations, reaching a worldwide audience.[56]

During the American Civil War, important international legal issues arose for both the Union and the Confederacy concerning the status of belligerents and neutrals, possible foreign recognition of the Confederacy, and the laws of war. Indeed, a code of conduct developed for the Union armies by Dr. Francis Lieber (known as the "Lieber Code") served as a template for the later development of the Hague Conventions of 1899 and 1907. President Abraham Lincoln's efforts to adhere to international law, admittedly in an imperfect way, in matters relating to the laws of blockade, the

---

51. JACK N. RAKOVE, ORIGINAL MEANINGS: POLITICS AND IDEAS IN THE MAKING OF THE CONSTITUTION 18 (1996).

52. *See* FRANCES HOWELL RUDKO, JOHN MARSHALL AND INTERNATIONAL LAW: STATESMAN AND CHIEF JUSTICE (1991).

53. JAMES KENT, COMMENTARIES ON AMERICAN LAW, pt. 1, lect. 1, at 1 (1826–30) (four vols.).

54. *See* KENT'S COMMENTARIES ON AMERICAN LAW (Oliver Wendell Holmes, Jr. ed., 1873).

55. Missouri v. Holland, 252 U.S. 416 (1920).

56. On Wheaton's life, see ELIZABETH FEASTER BAKER, HENRY WHEATON, 1785–1848 (1937).

treatment of blockade-runners as prisoners of war, and the treatment of hostages, presents another fascinating aspect of Civil War history.[57]

U.S. interest in international arbitration also dates from early in its history, although for more than one hundred years that interest was principally focused on disputes with its "mother country," the United Kingdom. The 1794 "Jay Treaty"[58] established three boards of arbitration to resolve disputes between the United Kingdom and its former colony. After the American Civil War, the 1871 Treaty of Washington[59] established four arbitrations for addressing Britain's conduct during that war, including Britain's responsibility for allowing construction in the United Kingdom of the Confederate raider *Alabama*.[60] Other U.S./U.K. arbitrations addressed fur seals and the boundary between Canada and Alaska. In the years leading up to World War I, the United States entered into a few treaties providing for international arbitration, principally with Latin American states, but broader efforts foundered in the U.S. Senate.

After the First World War, the U.S. Senate never consented to U.S. ratification of the Covenant of the League of Nations, nor of the separate protocol embodying the Statute of the Permanent Court of International Justice. There were supporters of U.S. adherence to such institutions. Perhaps the best known of these was Eleanor Roosevelt, a visionary in her efforts in the 1930's for the United States to join the Permanent Court of Justice, a woman with an unwavering desire to mitigate the plight of refugees, and a social activist taking courageous and mostly unpopular stands in favor of what we now call human rights, particularly in the area of race relations.[61] Yet strong voices of realism and exceptionalism, particularly in the U.S. Senate, argued that submission to such institutions would harm U.S. national interests, and would diminish or jeopardize U.S. sovereignty. Dispute resolution on a more limited scale was possible. Thus, the United States concluded a convention with Mexico in September 1923 (which took effect in March 1924) creating a General Claims Commission. The purpose of the commission was to settle claims arising after July 4, 1868, against one government by the nationals of the other, for losses or damages suffered by such nationals or their properties, "originating from acts of officials or others acting for either government and

---

57. *See* Mark E. Neely, Jr., The Fate of Liberty: Abraham Lincoln and Civil Liberties 139–59 (1991); Stephen C. Neff, Justice in Blue and Gray, A Legal History of the Civil War (2010).

58. The Treaty of Amity, Commerce and Navigation, U.S.-U.K., Nov. 19, 1794, 8 Stat. 116.

59. U.S.-U.K., May 8, 1871, 17 Stat. 863.

60. *See* Tom Bingham, *The* Alabama *Claims Arbitration*, 54 Int'l & Comp. L.Q. 1 (2005).

61. *See generally* Blanche Wiesen Cook, 2 Eleanor Roosevelt (1999).

resulting in injustice.''[62] Composed of three members (from the U.S., from Mexico, and from a third country), the commission met from 1924 to 1937 in Washington, D.C. and Mexico City. Final settlement was reached in 1941.

The cataclysm of World War II led the United States to host meetings that would lead to the creation of the United Nations and to become a member of both that institution and the Statute of the International Court of Justice. Moreover, the United States was instrumental in the creation of numerous other multilateral organizations in the immediate aftermath of the war, such as the World Bank and the International Monetary Fund.[63]

With its rise as the preeminent superpower, the United States has evinced conflicting attitudes toward international law and institutions. While the United States historically has articulated a desire for cooperation with other states as co-equal sovereigns—and, indeed, has been a leader in many respects for the promotion and development of international law and institutions built around the concept of sovereign equality—the United States has innate historical and cultural characteristics that push it toward an attitude of "exceptionalism" in its foreign policy, meaning a belief that the United States formally and informally is entitled to be treated differently from other states. This conflict reflects certain factors quite unique to the United States, including its present role as a military and economic powerhouse and a country in many respects uniquely insulated from the vicissitudes of international relations.

Further, the United States is often conflicted over whether international law should be "embedded" in U.S. law. On the one hand, the United States at its founding saw adherence to international obligations as an important means of establishing the international legitimacy and security of a nascent republic, and so adopted constitutional and judicial principles that made international law a part of U.S. law and superior to the law of the several states. On the other hand, the United States has certain constitutional and democratic traditions that make it difficult to adhere to and implement international law at the national level. As discussed in Chapter 7, U.S. constitutional law has created certain hurdles to U.S. adherence to international law and institutions by dividing power between the president and the legislature, and by maintaining a federal system that accords extensive rights to the several states. With respect to its democratic tradition, the United States places a central emphasis on self-governance, and resists adherence to rules that have not been generated by the people through their

---

62. Convention for Reciprocal Settlement of Claims, U.S.-Mex., art. I, Sept. 8, 1923, 43 Stat. 1730.

63. *See* David Armstrong et al., From Versailles to Maastricht: International Organisation in the Twentieth Century (1996).

elected representatives. As such, there is a general skepticism if not hostility to being bound by rules that were generated collectively by nation-states, where the United States has a significant but not controlling influence. Moreover, the United States has always accepted the importance and significance of a judiciary for the resolution of disputes, but has also viewed unelected judges as potential agents for usurping popular governance, a concern that is aggravated when the judges or other decision-makers in question are non-American and issuing their decisions from afar.

Further Reading:

Antony Anghie, *Imperialism, Sovereignty and the Making of International Law* (2005).

Robert J. Beck et al., *International Rules: Approaches from International Law and International Relations* (1996).

Samantha Besson & John Tasioulas, *The Philosophy of International Law* (2010).

Jutta Brunnée & Stephen J. Toope, *Legitimacy and Legality in International Law: An Interactional Account* (2010).

Doris Buss & Ambreena Manji, *International Law: Modern Feminist Approaches* (2005).

James L. Brierly, *The Basis of Obligation in International Law and Other Papers* (Hersh Lauterpacht ed., 1958).

Jack L. Goldsmith & Eric A. Posner, *The Limits of International Law* (2005).

Andrew T. Guzmán, *How International Law Works: A Rational Choice Theory* (2008).

Andreas Hasenclever et al., *Theories of International Regimes* (1997).

Jan Klabbers et al., *The Constitutionalization of International Law* (2009).

Martti Koskenniemi, *The Politics of International Law* (2011).

Charlotte Ku & Paul F. Diehl, eds., *International Law: Classic and Contemporary Readings* (2009).

Mary Ellen O'Connell, *The Power and Purpose of International Law* (2008).

Sundhya Pahuja, *Decolonising International Law* (2011).

D.S. Pradhan, *Third World Attitude Towards International Law* (2010).

Steven R. Ratner & Anne–Marie Slaughter, eds., *The Methods of International Law* (2004).

Gregory C. Shaffer & Tom Ginsburg, *The Empirical Turn in International Legal Scholarship* 106 *Am. J. Int'l L.* 1 (2012).

Joel P. Trachtman, *The Economic Structure of International Law* (2008).

Chapter 2

ACTORS OF INTERNATIONAL LAW

This chapter considers the principal "actors" (sometimes referred to as "subjects") of international law: states; international organizations created by states; non-governmental organizations; persons and groups of persons; and transnational corporations. These actors are capable of possessing international rights and duties, and have the capacity to take certain kinds of action in the international sphere. States and international organizations remain the dominant international actors in making, interpreting, and enforcing or complying with international law. Yet, increasingly, the other actors are also playing roles in the field of international law. For example, while corporations are formed under the national law of a state and often conduct their activities solely within the confines of national law, it is possible for a corporation to obtain certain rights under a bilateral treaty addressing foreign investment, including a right to sue a state before an international tribunal.[1]

A. States

States remain the central actors in the field of international law; most international law is created, interpreted, complied with, or enforced by the governments of states. Yet what exactly is a "state" and what entity is permitted to be the "government" of a state? Why are entities as vastly different in geographic size and population as China and Liechtenstein both considered states? Why are Antarctica and Quebec not considered states? How does the international community handle a situation where two different entities—say in China, Haiti, or Libya—both claim to be the government of the same state?

Though decisions on whether a state exists, and on what entity is the government of a state, are imbued with political considerations, certain basic rules of international law have emerged as a guide. When an extraordinary political event occurs—the emergence of a new state or the rise to power of a new government by other than routine processes—other states in the world community indicate their willingness to accept both the fact of change and the

---

1. *See* Jordan J. Paust, *Nonstate Actor Participation in International Law* *and the Pretense of Exclusion*, 51 Va. J. Int'l L. 977 (2011).

legal consequences arising from that fact by either explicitly or implicitly "recognizing" the new state or government.

Recognition of States

The question of whether a particular entity should be recognized as a state can arise from various scenarios. An existing state might fragment into several new states, such as occurred when the Socialist Federal Republic of Yugoslavia broke apart after 1990 to form Bosnia–Herzegovina, Croatia, Kosovo, Macedonia, Montenegro, Serbia, and Slovenia. Alternatively, a portion of an existing state might secede to form a new state, as occurred when Eritrea seceded from Ethiopia in 1994, or when South Sudan seceded from Sudan in 2011. It is possible for two states to merge together to form a new state, such as occurred in 1958 when Egypt and Syria merged to form the United Arab Republic (they chose to return to being independent states in 1961). During the twentieth century an enormous number of states were formed out of colonies of the major European powers, particularly in Africa. At the same time, many entities have aspired to statehood without success, such as the Basque region in Spain, Biafra in Nigeria, Katanga in the Congo, Turkish-dominated northern Cyprus, Chechnya in Russia, Tibet in China, Nagorno–Karabakh in Azerbaijan, and the Kurdish peoples of Iran, Iraq, and Turkey.

There are considerable advantages in being recognized as a state. Doing so allows the new state to consolidate sovereign control over its territory in the eyes of the world; it brings the new state into a normative system that protects it from foreign interference and intervention. The new state can conclude with other states treaties that advance its interests, such as on trade and investment, and can directly seek foreign aid. The new state can pursue admission to international organizations where, again, it can pursue policies that secure its interests. The new state can also obtain access abroad to assets associated with its territory and can sue in international or national fora to vindicate its rights.

Under traditional international legal theory, an entity aspiring to be recognized as a new state must first meet certain factual conditions. The aspiring entity must have: (1) a defined territory; (2) a permanent population; (3) an effective government; and (4) the capacity to enter into relations with other states.[2] For example, the Anglican Church is not a state in part because it does not have a defined territory. Antarctica is not a state because it has neither a permanent population nor a government. The state of California is not a state under international law because, while it has a defined

---

2. *See* Inter–American Convention on the Rights and Duties of States, Dec. 26, 1933, 49 Stat. 3097, 165 L.N.T.S. 19 (Montevideo Convention).

territory, a permanent population (relatively speaking), and an effective state government (again, relatively speaking), it does not have the capacity to enter into formal relations with foreign nations; that power is reserved to the federal U.S. government. Note that no aspect of these conditions speaks to magnitude; even a small geographic area with a small population (such as Liechtenstein, Monaco, or the Vatican City) can qualify as a state. International law has not sought to achieve uniformity of states in terms of size or population; while doing so might allow for greater democracy in the decision-making of international organizations, historical and cultural influences have been inescapable forces in the creation of states of all sizes.

For the most part, these four conditions continue to be taught today as the fundamental elements of statehood. With respect to the third condition, the emphasis has been on the control that the government exercises over the relevant territory, to the exclusion of other entities. The degree of control necessary may be a function of the manner in which the government came to power. If the prior sovereign in the territory consented to the creation of a new state, then a relatively lower degree of control by the new government may be tolerable in finding statehood. Thus, when Belgium granted independence to the Congo in 1960, it was quickly recognized as a state even though its government was engulfed in a civil war and did not control large portions of its territory. With respect to the fourth condition, it is possible for a state to assign some of its foreign relations capacity to another state (such as Liechtenstein has assigned to Switzerland) or to an international organization (such as has occurred in the European Union) without losing its status as a state.

While the conditions for statehood are broadly accepted in traditional international legal theory, who gets to decide whether these conditions are met is less clear. Some theorists contend that an entity is *ipso facto* a state once these conditions are met, regardless of what other states do or say (the "declaratory theory of recognition" since other states are only declaring something that already exists). For example, the Charter of the Organization of American States provides that the "political existence of the State is independent of recognition."[3] Other theorists, however, contend that only when other states decide that such conditions have been met, and acknowledge the legal capacity of the new government, is a new state actually constituted (the "constitutive theory of recognition"). While the declaratory theory is probably more widely subscribed to, in reality a new entity can only achieve many of the

3. Apr. 30, 1948, 2 U.S.T. 2394, 119 U.N.T.S. 3, as amended by protocols of 1967, 1985, 1992, and 1993 [hereinafter OAS Charter].

benefits of statehood (*e.g.*, access to international organizations) when other states agree to accord it such benefits.

Modern Trends in Recognition of States

The dissolution of the Union of Soviet Socialist Republics (USSR) after 1989 is both an example of recognition practice and an illustration of modern trends in this area. In December 1989, the Congress of the USSR People's Deputies found that the July 1939 Molotov–Ribbentrop Accords, by which the USSR first occupied and then annexed the Baltic states (Estonia, Latvia, and Lithuania), were contrary to international law. On this basis, the Baltic states held referenda in early 1991 on whether to seek independence. The overwhelming response was positive, and the Baltic states then waged a successful campaign for full independence. The State Council of the Soviet Union released the Baltic states and recognized their independence on September 6, 1991. The Baltic states were then admitted to the United Nations on September 17, 1991.

Thereafter, several of the other republics of the Soviet Union held referenda on whether to secede. Most proclaimed their independence in 1991, while Russia proclaimed itself as the successor state to the former Soviet Union. Virtually all other states recognized the republics of the former Soviet Union as new states and they were admitted as members of the United Nations, with Russia simply succeeding to the Soviet Union's membership. A notable aspect of this recognition was the approach taken by the European Community, which in December 1991 issued a Declaration on the "Guidelines on the Recognition of New States in Eastern Europe and in the Soviet Union."[4] In that declaration, the European Community and its member states affirmed

> their readiness to recognise, subject to the normal standards of international practice and the political realities in each case, those new states which, following the historic changes in the region, have constituted themselves on a democratic basis, have accepted the appropriate international obligations and have committed themselves in good faith to a peaceful process and to negotiations.

The declaration then set down general conditions requiring the new state to: (1) respect the U.N. Charter, the Helsinki Final Act, and the Charter of Paris, "especially with regard to the rule of law, democracy and human rights"; (2) guarantee rights for ethnic and national groups and minorities; (3) respect existing borders; (4) accept relevant arms control commitments; and (5) commit to settle by agreement all questions regarding state succession and regional

---

4.   31 I.L.M. 1486 (1992).

disputes. The European Community and United States recognized the statehood of the republics of the former Soviet Union based on these principles.[5]

Thus, while the traditional Montevideo Convention criteria still reflect the minimum requirements for the formation of a new state, in some situations the willingness of other states to recognize a new state may turn on additional requirements relating to more modern notions of human rights and democracy.

Further, while international law does not expressly account for the existence of "quasi-states," in fact various entities are regarded as having certain levels of sovereign autonomy, even though not fully accorded the status of "state." Taiwan is not generally regarded as (and has not sought recognition as) a state, despite fitting the four traditional criteria, but has concluded certain trade agreements and has been accorded rights to participate in certain international fishing agreements.[6] Palestine has not been admitted to the United Nations, despite fitting the four traditional criteria, yet has been accorded unique rights as an observer at the United Nations.[7] Kosovo also has not been admitted to the United Nations, but even before it declared independence the Security Counsel endorsed "substantial autonomy and self-government in Kosovo" within the state of Serbia and Montenegro.[8] Such anomalies reflect an effort by the international community to cope with a situation where certain sovereignty or autonomy is warranted, but where full recognition of a new state would severely aggravate political relations and could possibly lead to armed conflict.

Recognition of Governments

Under traditional international legal theory, the establishment of a new government through normal, constitutional processes within a state raises no questions regarding the recognition of the government. In such situations, the new government is entitled to all the rights and obligations accorded under international law. By contrast, an entity that comes to power through non-constitutional means is not automatically accorded such rights and obligations. Rather, its status as the government of the state may be in doubt until such time as it is widely recognized by other states. The central (and often determinative) issue for a state when deciding whether to recognize a newly formed government has been whether the new government is in "effective control" of its state (sometimes

5. For a similar declaration relating to the dissolution of Yugoslavia, see 31 I.L.M. 1485 (1992).

6. *See, e.g.,* Convention on the Conservation and Management of Highly Migratory Stocks in the Western and Central Pacific Ocean, art. 9(2) & annex 1, Sept. 4, 2000, 40 I.L.M. 278.

7. *See* G.A. Res. 3237 (Nov. 22, 1974); G.A. Res. 52/250 (July 7, 1998).

8. *See* S.C. Res. 1244, para. 11 (June 10, 1999).

referred to as the "de facto control test"). "Effective control" has largely been measured by the degree to which the government commands the obedience of the people within the state. Although in a given case there may be extremely complicated facts concerning what factions control what portions of a territory, the "effective control" test is a relatively simple one, and allows states to proceed pragmatically in their relations with the new government.

The decision to recognize a new government, however, has not always been dictated simply by whether its passes the effective control test. For instance, capital exporting states, such as the United States, at one time found relevant whether the new government had declared its willingness to honor the international obligations of its predecessor, including debt obligations. Further, states have also found relevant the political nature of the new government, including the degree to which it is democratic.

For example, from the time the Beijing-based communist government in China gained control of the Chinese mainland in 1949 until the 1970's, that government was not generally recognized by the global community (other than the communist bloc) as the government of China. Instead, the government based in Taiwan was accorded that status and allowed to represent China at the United Nations. In 1971, the political winds had shifted sufficiently that officials of the Beijing-based government were allowed to represent China at the U.N. General Assembly,[9] and throughout the 1970's individual states began recognizing the Beijing-based government as the government of China, including the United States in 1979.[10]

The notion of states "recognizing" a new government of a state, however, is anathema to those states that see it as an interference in national affairs. The 1930 Estrada Doctrine, named for Mexican Foreign Secretary Genaro Estrada, stands for the proposition that the manner in which a new government comes to power is wholly a matter of national concern.[11] As such, states should not seek to influence the outcome of an internal power struggle by granting or withholding recognition. The Estrada Doctrine is attractive because many states find it politically difficult to announce publicly whether they "recognize" a new government, and would prefer simply to open diplomatic channels or otherwise develop relations without issuing a pronouncement that could be construed as approval of the new government. In such instances, determination of the legal effects of the new relationship is often

9. *See* G.A. Res. 2578 (Oct. 25, 1971).

10. *See* U.S. *Normalizes Relations with the People's Republic of China*, 79 Dep't St. Bull. 25, 26 (Jan. 1979) ("[T]he United States of America recog-

nizes the People's Republic of China as the sole legal government of China.").

11. *See* Philip Jessup, *The Estrada Doctrine*, 25 Am. J. Int'l L. 719 (1931).

left to national courts, which must pass upon the legal rights and obligations of the new government in the absence of a clear statement of recognition.

Establishing diplomatic relations with a new government is not required as a part of the recognition process, although they usually go hand in hand. Breaking diplomatic relations merely signifies that one state declines to deal with another's government; it does not vitiate the recognition of that government.

Modern Trends in Recognition of Governments

As is the case with the recognition of states, contemporary attitudes in favor of democracy and human rights have influenced some incidents of recognition. For example, Haitian President Jean–Bertrande Aristide was democratically elected in 1990 but then deposed in a 1991 coup by Haitian military and police authorities. Aristide fled the country, which fell under the complete control of the junta. Nevertheless, the international community rallied around Aristide, refusing to recognize the new Haitian authorities and instead imposing comprehensive economic sanctions through resolutions of both the Organization of American States and the U.N. Security Council. When the Security Council in 1994 authorized military intervention to depose the junta,[12] the military and police authorities fled Haiti, paving the way for Aristide's return to power.

The reaction of the international community to such military coups, however, has not been uniform. For example, in July 1999, the democratically-elected Prime Minister of Pakistan, Nawaz Sharif, was ousted in a coup by military authorities, led by General Pervez Musharraf. While various states lamented the coup and urged a return to democratic rule, no U.N. sanctions were imposed on Pakistan and no military effort was undertaken to restore Sharif to power. Most states continued to engage in diplomatic relations with the new Pakistani government headed by Musharraf, who pledged a return as soon as possible to democratic rule.

Modern trends in favor of human rights may also be influencing recognition practice with respect to an existing government that engages in abusive treatment of its people. For example, in early 2011, peaceful protests in Libya in favor of greater democracy met with a crack-down by the government of Muammar Gaddafi, in which considerable violence was inflicted upon Libyan civilians. Rather than quell the protests, the crack-down spurred the emergence of a full-blown rebellion, in which the rebels seized control of about half of the country and banded together to form a "National Transitional Council" (NTC). Moreover, the U.N. Security Council

---

12. *See* S.C. Res. 940, para. 4 (July 31, 1994).

passed two resolutions that: imposed an arms embargo on Libya; froze the assets of Gaddafi and ten members of his inner circle and restricted their travel; characterized their conduct as possibly constituting crimes against humanity; referred the situation to the International Criminal Court; demanded a ceasefire; banned most flights within Libya; and authorized Member States "acting nationally or through regional organizations or arrangements, and acting in cooperation with the Secretary–General, to take all necessary measures . . . to protect civilians and civilian populated areas under threat of attack in [Libya]. . . ."[13] Thereafter, a multi-state coalition commenced military operations against Libya to implement the resolution.

For several months, the status of the two competing factions in Libya was unclear. The previously recognized Gaddafi government presumably remained the recognized government, though defections of officials (such as the Libyan Ambassador to the United Nations) clouded the situation. A handful of governments began making statements that the NTC represented the "people of Libya", but outright recognition of the NTC as Libya's government— which would have allowed it access to Libyan assets abroad and to other forms of assistance—was not initially forthcoming. On July 15, however, a group of 32 countries known as the "Contact Group on Libya" (including the United States) met in Istanbul, Turkey, to consider their next steps in dealing with the civil war in Libya, including their relationship with the NTC. Among other things, the Contact Group issued a statement in which they declared that:

> The Contact Group reaffirmed that the Qaddafi regime no longer has any legitimate authority in Libya and that Qaddafi and certain members of his family must go. Henceforth and until an interim authority is in place, participants agreed to deal with the National Transitional Council (NTC) as the legitimate governing authority in Libya.[14]

From that point forward, the NTC was able to act as the interim government of Libya in its relations with those 32 states. After the NTC seized complete control of the country, the collapse of the Qaddafi government, and the disappearance (and later death) of Qaddafi, the NTC became generally recognized as the interim government in Libya. The Security Council terminated its mandate for the use of force in Libya and stated that it *"[l]ooks forward* to the establishment of an inclusive, representative transitional Government of Libya, and *emphasises* the need for the transitional

13. *See* S.C. Res. 1973, U.N. Doc. 1973 (Mar. 17, 2011); S.C. Res. 1970 (Feb. 26, 2011).

14. Fourth Meeting of the Libya Contact Group–Chair's Statement, para. 4 (July 15, 2011).

period to be underpinned by a commitment to democracy, good governance, rule of law and respect for human rights."[15]

Recognition in U.S. Practice

In the United States, the power to recognize foreign governments is inferred from the express grant to the president of the power to "receive Ambassadors and other public Ministers."[16] The Supreme Court has consistently stated that whether a government should be recognized is a political question whose determination is within the exclusive prerogative of the executive branch.

The rights of governments recognized by the U.S. government include the right: (1) to bring a law suit in U.S. court; (2) to claim sovereign immunity in U.S. courts and to receive diplomatic protection to the same extent as other recognized governments; and (3) to have access to the bank deposits and other property of the state located in the United States. Courts will not deny a recognized government the rights that it would normally have under United States law solely because diplomatic relations with it have been broken.[17] Recent examples of U.S. recognition practice may be seen with respect to Afghanistan, Iraq, Macedonia, and Libya.

Afghanistan. After the Soviet withdrawal from Afghanistan in 1989, a group known as the Taliban seized control of Afghanistan and became its de facto government. The United States, however, declined to recognize the Taliban as the government of Afghanistan. In the fall of 2001, the United States invaded Afghanistan as a response to the terrorist attacks of September 11, 2001, and joined Afghan opposition groups in successfully deposing the Taliban. Shortly thereafter, major leaders from the Afghan opposition groups and diaspora met in Bonn, Germany, and agreed on a plan for the formation of a new government. That plan led to the inauguration on December 22 of Hamid Karzai as Chairman of the Afghan Interim Authority (AIA). In anticipation of Karzai's inauguration, the U.S. Department of State in essence recognized the new government by announcing that the United States would deal with the AIA when it assumed power.[18]

In June 2002, the AIA held a nationwide Loya Jirga (Grand Assembly), and Karzai was elected president by the Transitional Islamic State of Afghanistan (TISA). In late 2003, the TISA convened another Loya Jirga for the drafting and approval of a new constitution, which was signed in 2004. In October 2004, the TISA

15. S.C. Res. 2009, para. 2 (Sept. 16, 2011).

16. U.S. Const. art. II, § 3; *see* Louis Henkin, Foreign Affairs and the United States Constitution 38 (2d ed. 1996).

17. *See* Banco Nacional de Cuba v. Sabbatino, 376 U.S. 398, 410 (1964).

18. *See* U.S. Dep't of State Press Release on Afghanistan: Reopening of U.S. Mission (Taken Question) (Dec. 14, 2001).

held nationwide elections, in which millions of Afghans voted to select representatives of a new government under the new Constitution through secret ballot. In November, the Joint Electoral Management Board in Kabul officially announced the final results of the election, including Karzai's selection as Afghanistan's first democratically elected national leader.

Iraq. In March 2003, the United States invaded Iraq, asserting that Iraq had failed to abide by its obligations under Security Council resolutions to cooperate in the elimination of weapons of mass destruction. After ousting the government of President Saddam Hussein, the United States and United Kingdom, operating as "occupying powers under a unified command,"[19] governed Iraq through an entity known as the Coalition Provisional Authority (CPA). The CPA, in conjunction with the United Nations, undertook a lengthy process culminating in the establishment of an interim Iraqi government, which would govern Iraq until a permanent government could be established.

In June 2004, the U.S. government announced: "On June 28, 2004, full sovereignty was transferred to a new Iraqi interim government. The Coalition Provisional Authority, led by Ambassador Paul Bremer, ceased to exist. The Iraqi Government is now running the day-to-day operations of its country."[20] As such, the United States recognized the new Iraqi government and opened a U.S. embassy in Baghdad for the conduct of diplomatic relations.

Macedonia. Following the breakup of the former Socialist Federal Republic of Yugoslavia in 1991, several of its constituent republics became independent states, including the republic of Macedonia. Macedonia established a parliamentary democracy with multiethnic party representation and a popularly elected president. While the new state proclaimed itself the "Republic of Macedonia," the government of Greece protested the use of such a name, stating that it implied territorial designs on the northern Greek province of "Macedonia." Greece stated that it would seek to block the new state from joining the United Nations, NATO or the European Union unless the dispute over the name was resolved. In April 1993, the General Assembly decided to admit the new state as a member of the United Nations, with the state being "provisionally" referred to as "The former Yugoslav Republic of Macedonia," pending settlement of the disagreement that had arisen over its name.[21]

19. S.C. Res. 1483, pmbl. & paras. 4–5 (May 22, 2003).

20. *See* U.S. Dep't of State Fact Sheet on Iraq's Transition to Self–Government (June 28, 2004).

21. *See* G.A. Res. 47/225 (Apr. 8, 1993).

On November 4, 2004, the U.S. Department of State spokesman announced that "[w]e have now decided to refer to Macedonia officially as the Republic of Macedonia.... We have taken our decision on Macedonia's name without prejudice to the negotiations under UN auspices that have been ongoing since 1993 on differences between Macedonia and Greece over the name. We hope those talks will reach a speedy and mutually agreeable conclusion."[22] Some observers asserted that the U.S. action was a reward to the Republic of Macedonia for supporting the 2003 U.S. intervention in Iraq, and a reprimand to Greece for not providing such support. In any event, the announcement reflected a recognition of the name of the new government and a belief that it was entitled to entry in international organizations under such a name.

Kosovo. Once the constraints of the Cold War began dissipating in 1990, both the Soviet Union and the Socialist Federal Republic of Yugoslavia (SFRY) collapsed, spinning off almost twenty new countries. Kosovo—an autonomous province within the SFRY Republic of Serbia rather than itself a SFRY "republic"—was not viewed by the international community in the early 1990's as entitled to a sovereign status, and hence remained within Serbia (which resided within the new Federal Republic of Yugoslavia (FRY), later renamed Serbia & Montenegro, and then just Serbia). Yet it was Serbia's actions against Kosovo in 1989–90, stripping Kosovo of many of its rights under the SFRY Constitution, that led the other SFRY republics to fear an unacceptable imbalance in the SFRY federal system, prompting Slovenia, Croatia, and Bosnia–Herzegovina to pursue and win sovereign status. The cost of doing so, however, was to unleash the brutal Balkans conflict of the early 1990's, brought to a close only with the 1995 Dayton Accords.

After Dayton, Kosovar Albanians (the dominant ethnic group in Kosovo) continued to seek greater rights, and the Kosovo Liberation Army began engaging in violent tactics against Serbian authorities. Those tactics prompted in 1998 a major crack-down by Serbian authorities in Kosovo,[23] which by 1999 became so threatening that NATO countries launched an air campaign against the FRY/Serbia to secure the withdrawal of all FRY/Serbian authorities from Kosovo. Belgrade ultimately relented, withdrawing its forces, and consenting to the deployment of both NATO forces and civilian authorities operating under U.N. auspices.[24] From mid–1999 onward, these international military and civilian authorities governed

22. Richard Boucher, Spokesman, U.S. Dep't of State Daily Press Briefing (Nov. 4, 2004).

23. *See Prosecutor v. Milan Milutinović, Nikola ainović, Dragoljub Ojdanić, Nebroja Pavković, Vladimir Lazarev-* *ić, Sreten Lukić,* Case No. IT–05–87–T, *Judgment,* vol. 2, para. 1178 (Feb. 26, 2009).

24. *See* S.C. Res. 1244 (June 10, 1999).

in Kosovo, transforming it into an "internationalized" territory, and in the process building up local Kosovar governing authorities.[25] The end-game in Kosovo, however, was never clear, with possible final status solutions ranging from Kosovo as a autonomous province within Serbia with extensive, entrenched rights, Kosovo as a federal unit within the FRY on par with Serbia and Montenegro, Kosovo as an independent country, or other options in between.

Final status talks led by the United Nations, and supported by the major powers (in the form of a "Contact Group"), failed to secure agreement between Belgrade and Pristina, with the former seeking a provincial status and the latter a sovereign status. Ultimately, the relevant U.N. envoy concluded that further talks were pointless, but also that the existing interim status was not sustainable given the volatile political and ethnic tensions within Kosovo. With the Security Council unable to take any further steps (due to disagreement between the major powers over how to resolve Kosovo's status), Kosovar authorities proceeded on their own to declare independence on February 17, 2008.[26]

On February 18, President George Bush sent a letter to the President of Kosovo stating: "On behalf of the American people, I hereby recognize Kosovo as an independent and sovereign state." Among other things, the letter noted "Kosovo's desire to attain the highest standards of democracy and freedom," and its "embrace of multi-ethnicity as a principle of good governance and ... commitment to developing accountable institutions in which all citizens are equal under the law."[27] By 2011, Kosovo had been admitted to membership in some international organizations, such as the International Monetary Fund and World Bank, and recognized by some 70 states, but was not yet a member of the United Nations.

South Sudan. In the 1980's, Sudan's government sought aggressively to expand Islamic law from the Arabic-speaking and dominantly-Muslim northern part of Sudan to the African-influenced, non-Muslim southern part of Sudan, an area consisting of the three historic provinces of Bahr el Ghazal, Equatoria, and Upper Nile. Among other things, the government sought to incorporate traditional Islamic punishments drawn from Islamic law into the penal code operating in southern Sudan. Further, the Government sought to exploit valuable natural resources located in south-

---

25. For a discussion of this phenomenon in Kosovo and elsewhere, *see* GREGORY H. FOX, HUMANITARIAN OCCUPATION (2008).

26. *See* Kosovo Declaration of Independence, 47 I.L.M. 461 (2008); *see generally* MARC WELLER, CONTESTED STATEHOOD: KOSOVO'S STRUGGLE FOR INDEPENDENCE (2009).

27. Letter to President Fatmir Sejdiu of Kosovo Recognizing Kosovo as an Independent and Sovereign State, 44 WEEKLY COMP. PRES. DOC. 236 (2008).

ern Sudan, principally oil resources, so as to provide much-needed revenue for the central government. Steps of this kind first led to serious tension between the government and political leaders in southern Sudan, and then led to unrest, violence, and ultimately civil war. Following this first Sudanese civil war, a Southern Sudan autonomous region was formed in 1972, which operated until tensions again flared up in 1983. A second Sudanese civil war ended in 2005 with a Comprehensive Peace Agreement, which called for a referendum in January 2009 by the people living in southern Sudan on whether southern Sudan should remain as a part of Sudan or should become an independent country.[28]

The referendum overwhelmingly supported independence and South Sudan declared itself to be an independent state on July 9, 2011. That day, President Obama issued a statement saying "I am proud to declare that the United States formally recognizes the Republic of South Sudan as a sovereign and independent state upon this day, July 9, 2011."[29] Within two weeks, South Sudan then became the 193rd U.N. member state and the 54th member of the African Union.

Rules on State Succession

Whenever an existing state breaks apart to form two or more states, or a portion of an existing state secedes, or two existing states merge to form a new state, issues arise regarding whether the newly formed state "succeeds" to the rights and obligations of the prior state. For example, when a state such as the Soviet Union or Yugoslavia breaks apart, what are the rights of the newly formed states to assets of their predecessor state that exist abroad in bank accounts or in the form of properties, such as embassy buildings? Do they have any obligations arising from treaties entered into by their predecessor state? Do persons residing in the new states automatically lose their old nationality and gain a new one, or do they have a choice in the matter?

Various efforts have been made to codify the rules on state succession, but to date such efforts have not received widespread acceptance. For example, the 1978 Vienna Convention on Succession of States in Respect of Treaties[30] sought to establish rules for whether states are bound by the treaty commitments of their predecessor state. Generally speaking, the convention provides that a state emerging from the break-up of an existing state is bound to the predecessor's treaties (the principle of continuity), whereas a

---

28. *See* Ted Dagne, Cong. Research Serv. R41900, The Republic of South Sudan: Opportunities and Challenges for Africa's Newest Country (2011).

29. Statement Recognizing South Sudan as an Independent and Sovereign State, 2009 Daily Comp. Pres. Doc. 201100497 (July 9).

30. Aug. 23, 1978, 1946 U.N.T.S. 4.

state emerging from colonialism is not (it has a "clean slate"), unless it so consents or unless the treaty relates to territorial boundaries. The convention creates various special rules, such as the idea that where the predecessor state owes a national public debt, and part of the state secedes, the debt should pass to the new state in an equitable proportion. Although the convention entered into force in 1996, only a handful of states have ratified it, casting doubt that its rules have passed into customary international law. Similarly, the Vienna Convention on Succession of States in Respect of State Property, Archives, and Debt[31] has failed to attract significant adherence and has not even entered into force. Only recently has the Council of Europe adopted a convention on the avoidance of statelessness for persons when state secession occurs.[32] Consequently, while there may be certain international legal presumptions that operate in a situation of state succession, many issues are sorted out *ad hoc* as situations arise.[33] For example, in 1991 several of the successor states to the Soviet Union signed a treaty dividing proportionally among the new republics (and the Baltic states) Soviet debts and assets,[34] while the former Yugoslav republics completed such a treaty in 2001.[35]

Rules on Delimitation of Land Boundaries

In the course of states being formed, uncertainties may exist as to the exact location of the land boundary between them. Those uncertainties may remain unresolved for years, even centuries, if they are in remote regions that involve few natural resources. Yet such uncertainties can blossom into major disputes, even wars, so states will often attempt to resolve them through bilateral negotiations or dispute settlement.

For example, in July 2005 the International Court of Justice issued a decision determining the boundary between Benin and Niger. Both states were a part of French West Africa during the period of European colonization and gained independence in 1960. After decades of disputes about their boundary, the states jointly requested the Court to indicate the course of the boundary and to

31. Apr. 18, 1983, 22 I.L.M. 3066 (1983).

32. Convention on the Avoidance of Statelessness in Relation to State Succession, May 19, 2006, Europ. T.S. No. 200.

33. *See generally* TAI-HENG CHENG, STATE SUCCESSION AND COMMERCIAL OBLIGATIONS (2006); KONRAD G. BÜHLER, STATE SUCCESSION AND MEMBERSHIP IN INTERNATIONAL ORGANIZATIONS (2001); P.K. MENON, THE SUCCESSION OF STATES IN RESPECT TO TREATIES, STATE PROPERTY, ARCHIVES, AND

DEBTS (1991); OKON UDOKANG, SUCCESSION OF NEW STATES TO INTERNATIONAL TREATIES (1972); DANIEL P. O'CONNELL, THE LAW OF STATE SUCCESSION (1956).

34. Treaty on Succession with Respect to the State Foreign Debts and Assets of the Soviet Union, Dec. 4, 1991; *see* Paul Williams & Jennifer Harris, *State Succession to Debts and Assets: The Modern Law and Policy*, 42 HARV. INT'L L.J. 355 (2001).

35. Agreement on Succession Issues, June 29, 2001, 2262 U.N.T.S. 251.

determine which state owns islands located in the Niger river, particularly Lété Island. The joint agreement called upon the Court to apply international law, including the principle that states emerging from colonization succeed to the existing administrative boundaries (referred to as *uti possidetis*). Neither party convinced the Court that it had title over the Niger river based on administrative acts during the colonial period, so the Court decided the case based on evidence of more contemporary effective exercise of authority. That evidence established "that the boundary between Benin and Niger follows the main navigable channel of the River Niger as it existed at the dates of independence," with the precise location to be based largely on a 1970 scientific study.[36] Further, the Court found that sovereignty over most of the islands follows the line of the main navigable channel; as such, the island of Lété fell under Niger sovereignty. In another border area, the Court found that the boundary followed the River Mekrou according to the principle of *uti possidetis*.

The *uti possidetis* principle also featured in the Court's 2007 decision concerning the border between Nicaragua and Honduras. In that case, the Court considered whether the colonial power (Spain) had allocated the disputed territory to one of its colonial provinces. Finding that it had not, the Court assessed whether there was evidence of colonial *effectivités*, meaning conduct of the administrative authorities during the colonial period that demonstrated an allocation of the territory to one of the provinces. Finding that no such evidence existed, the Court then sought to identify any post-colonial *effectivités*, and concluded that Honduras over time had exercised a "modest but real display of authority" in the disputed territory, such as by enforcing its criminal and civil law, and by regulating immigration and fisheries activities.[37] Consequently, the Court concluded that the disputed territory was Honduran.

B. International Organizations

Formation

Rather than conduct inter-state relations solely through direct contact among governments, states have also formed hundreds of international organizations (sometimes referred to as "inter-governmental organizations") as more permanent fora for addressing various issues. An international organization (such as the United Nations) can be very large in membership and permanent staff, and

---

36. Frontier Dispute (Benin/Niger), 2005 I.C.J. 90, 133, para. 103 (July 12).

37. Territorial and Maritime Dispute in the Caribbean Sea (Nicar. v. Honduras), 2007 I.C.J. 659, 721–22, para. 208 (Oct. 8).

can be responsible for addressing a wide array of issues. Alternatively, an international organization (such as the International Whaling Commission) can be quite small and focused on a discrete topic. Membership can be global, regional, or bilateral, and need not be based on geography. For example, the Organization for Economic Co-operation and Development (OECD) has select members from the Americas, Europe, and Asia. Some international organizations have only states as members, while other international organizations have both states and other international organizations as members. The International Labor Organization (ILO) has states as members, but is unusual in that each member sends to the ILO Governing Body two government delegates, one delegate representing employers, and one delegate representing employees.

Whatever its mandate and membership, an international organization is typically created by a treaty, which is often (but not necessarily) labeled a "charter" or a "constitution." Such a treaty is governed by the law of treaties[38] in the same way as any other treaty. At the same time, the treaty is also regarded as having a special status as the constituent instrument of an international organization. An international organization is expected to evolve over time, and its constituent instrument is regarded as needing to evolve with it, rather than remain static. Consequently, such an instrument is often interpreted not just by focusing on the ordinary meaning of the treaty language, but also by considering the organization's basic purpose and goals, and how those goals may be achieved in a changing world. This purposive—or "teleological"—approach to interpretation of the constituent instrument attempts to give greater vitality to the international organization than might otherwise exist under standard treaty interpretation.

Unlike regular treaties, the constituent instrument of an international organization is often interpreted in light of the practice of the organs of the organization,[39] rather than just the practice of its member states. Further, the organs may play a role in various matters concerning the functioning of the treaty, such as the ability of a state to join the treaty, the compatibility of a state's reservation to the treaty,[40] or whether the treaty should be revised.

---

38. *See* Chapter 3(A).

39. *See, e.g.*, Advisory Opinion on Legal Consequences for States of the Continued Presence of South Africa in Namibia (South West Africa) Notwithstanding Security Council Resolution 276 (1970), 1971 I.C.J. 16, 22 (June 21) (using such practice to interpret the voting requirements of U.N. Charter article 27(3)); Advisory Opinion on Competence of the General Assembly for the Admission of a State to the United Nations, 1950 I.C.J. 4, 9 (Mar. 3) (looking to the practice of the Security Council and General Assembly when interpreting U.N. Charter provisions on admission of states to the United Nations).

40. *See* Vienna Convention on the Law of Treaties art. 20(3), May 23, 1969, 1155 U.N.T.S. 331.

The treaty provides the basic framework for the work of the international organization. It normally: (1) sets forth the purposes of the organization; (2) specifies which kinds of states may join the organization, how they can join, and—once they join—how they may participate in the work of the organization; (3) indicates the structure of the organization, such as the creation of one or more organs and their associated powers; (4) creates a secretariat as a permanent staff of the organization and identifies where the organization will be located; (5) indicates how disputes concerning the treaty will be resolved; and (6) addresses the privileges and immunities that the organization and its staff shall have.

Not all international organizations are created by treaty. The U.N. General Assembly has created several international organizations—such as the U.N. Children's Fund (UNICEF)—simply by adopting a resolution. In such instances, the resolution serves as the constituent instrument of the international organization.

Legal Personality

Once an international organization is created, questions may arise as to whether the international organization has certain attributes. Does the international organization itself have the power to conclude international agreements, to bring claims on behalf of the organization, or to be sued by others? One place to look when answering such questions is the constituent instrument of the organization. If the member states have expressly provided for such attributes, then the questions are more easily answered. If not expressly provided, these attributes might be implied based on the overall purpose of the international organization. Further, some tribunals and scholars assert that certain attributes are inherent in any international organization. That is, such attributes arise as a matter of international law given the "international personality" of the international organization as an entity separate from that of its member states.

In the *Reparation for Injuries* advisory opinion,[41] the International Court considered whether the United Nations was capable of bringing a diplomatic claim against Israel for the death of a U.N. representative. In that case a Swedish national, Count Bernadotte, was acting as a U.N. mediator in the Middle East in 1948. While performing his duties in Palestine, Bernadotte was assassinated, and the evidence suggested that Israeli agents were responsible. Under traditional international law, the state of the person's nationality would bring an international claim for damages against Israel (thus, in this case, Sweden would bring the claim). Yet, as a

---

41. *See* Advisory Opinion on Reparation for Injuries Suffered in the Service of the United Nations, 1949 I.C.J. 174 (Apr. 11).

policy matter, the assassination was clearly an affront to the United Nations and its entire membership, not just to Sweden. Moreover, to the extent that U.N. representatives of differing nationalities are often at risk in dangerous parts of the world, it would be rather inefficient to rely on individual states for pursuing such claims.

The General Assembly asked the International Court to advise on whether, as a legal matter, the United Nations could bring a claim against Israel. Nothing in the U.N. Charter expressly accorded the United Nations such a power, nor had any international organization previously exercised such a power. The Court first determined that "to achieve [U.N.] ends the attribution of international personality is indispensable."[42] Among other things, the Court noted that the U.N. Charter defines the relationship between the United Nations and its members, requiring them to give the United Nations every assistance and to obey Security Council decisions. Further, the Charter provides privileges and immunities to the United Nations in each member state, and allows for the conclusion of agreements between the United Nations and its members. Having found the existence of an international personality, the Court unanimously concluded that the power to pursue claims for direct injury to the United Nations necessarily followed. According to the Court, "it is impossible to see how [the United Nations] can obtain reparation unless it possesses capacity to bring an international claim. It cannot be supposed that in such an event all the Members of the Organization, save the defendant State, must combine to bring a claim against the defendant for the damage suffered by the Organization."[43] On similar reasoning, but with some judges dissenting, the Court found that the United Nations could also seek reparations for personal injury to the U.N. agent (as opposed to the injury to the United Nations as a whole). Further, the Court found that such claims could be pursued even against a state who was not itself a member of the United Nations (which Israel was not at that time).

In an effort to help protect U.N. personnel from attack, a Convention on the Safety of United Nations Associated Personnel was adopted in 1994.[44] Among other things, the convention prohibits any attack against U.N. personnel and premises and obliges state parties to take appropriate measures to ensure their safety and security. An optional protocol entered into force in 2010 expanding the scope of the convention to U.N. and associated personnel engaged in operations delivering humanitarian, political

---

42. *Id.* at 178.

43. *Id.* at 180–81.

44. *See* G.A. Res. 49/59 (Dec. 9, 1994), *reprinted in* 34 I.L.M. 482 (1995).

or development assistance in peace-building or delivering emergency humanitarian assistance.[45]

Legal Responsibility

The creation of an international organization also raises issues as to when it is responsible for wrongful acts. As is the case for state responsibility (see Chapter 6), it would appear that an international organization is responsible for the consequences of wrongful conduct that can be attributed to the organization. Yet the rules on the responsibility of international organizations are somewhat less settled than their counterparts that deal with the responsibility of states. While the International Law Commission (ILC) in 2011 completed a series of draft articles on the responsibility of international organizations,[46] which largely track the ILC's 2001 articles relating to state responsibility, the ILC's general commentary to the articles noted:

> The fact that several of the present draft articles are based on limited practice moves the border between codification and progressive development in the direction of the latter. It may occur that a provision in the articles on State responsibility could be regarded as representing codification, while the corresponding provision on the responsibility of international organizations is more in the nature of progressive development. In other words, the provisions of the present draft articles do not necessarily yet have the same authority as the corresponding provisions on State responsibility.[47]

Even so, some core rules appear widely accepted. Every internationally wrongful act of an international organization entails the international responsibility of that organization.[48] An internationally wrongful act can arise from conduct that is either an action or omission, when it is both attributable to the organization and constitutes a breach of an international obligation of that organization.[49] Conduct will be attributed to an international organization when it is committed by one of the organization's organs or officials, or by a person entrusted with one of the functions of the organization. Even if the organ, official, or person is acting *ultra vires* (outside the scope of their powers), attribution may occur if there is a close enough connection to the official work of the organization.

---

45. U.N. Doc. No. A/C.6/60/L.11 (2005), *reprinted in* 49 I.L.M. 1659 (2010).

46. Draft Articles on Responsibility of International Organizations, in Report of the ILC on the Work of its Sixty-third Session, U.N. Doc. A/66/10, at 54–68 (2011).

47. *Id.* at 70.

48. *Id.* at 54 (art. 3).

49. *Id.* at 55 (art. 4).

Because of the unique character of international organizations, a thorny question that sometimes arises is whether the organization itself is responsible for a wrongful act or its member states either directly or on a subsidiary basis (*i.e.*, when the international organization cannot bear the responsibility). There is a general presumption that member states have not created an agency relationship with an international organization simply by ratifying the constituent treaty and participating in the work of the organization, and therefore that member states are not responsible. That presumption is even stated explicitly in the constituent instruments of some international organizations.

An often-discussed case is that of the International Tin Council (ITC), an international organization created by thirty-two states that bought and sold tin on the world market in times of oversupply and scarcity for the purpose of keeping tin prices stable. By the mid–1980's, the ITC had incurred enormous debt which it could not repay. Its creditors proceeded to sue the ITC in courts of the United Kingdom, where the ITC was headquartered, and to seek appointment of a receiver who would pursue proceedings *against the ITC's member states*. Ultimately, the House of Lords determined that, as a matter of U.K. law, the ITC had a legal personality separate from its member states, such that contracts concluded by the ITC did not create liability for its member states. At the same time, the House of Lords stated that any liability of the member states under international law could not be enforced in U.K. courts without appropriate U.K. implementing legislation.[50]

Another well-known case concerns the creation by four Arab states of the Arab Organization for Industrialization (AOI) to develop their arms industries. The AOI entered into a joint venture agreement with a company, Westland Helicopters. The agreement provided that disputes would be resolved by international arbitration. AOI then went bankrupt and Westland Helicopters invoked the arbitration clause to bring a claim against AOI *and against the four Arab states*. In 1984, an arbitral body established under the auspices of the International Chamber of Commerce found in *Westland Helicopters*[51] that it was possible to "pierce through" the AOI. The arbitrators found that, under international law, member states are liable for injury by their international organization to third parties, at least where the constituent instrument fails to exclude such liability. This arbitral decision, however, was later annulled during enforcement proceedings before Swiss courts on

---

50. *See* Romana Sadurska & Christine M. Chinkin, *The Collapse of the International Tin Council: A Case of State Responsibility?*, 30 VA. J. INT'L L. 845 (1990); *see also* Dan Sarooshi, *Conferrals by States of Powers on International Organizations: The Case of Agency*, 74 BRIT. YRBK. INT'L L. 291, 321–24 (2003).

51. *See* 80 I.L.R. 652 (1988).

grounds that the arbitral panel had not been granted jurisdiction over the member states. The outcome suggests that the difficulty lies not just in establishing a legal right to pierce through an international organization, but also in the ability to secure jurisdiction over (and execute against the assets of) sovereign states.

More recently, issues have arisen regarding whether conduct by military personnel deployed in association with an authorization from the United Nations is to be attributed to the United Nations or to the state that has supplied the personnel. In the *Behrami & Saramati* case,[52] the European Court of Human Rights decided that actions of French troops undertaken in Kosovo as part of an "international security presence" authorized by the U.N. Security Council,[53] known as KFOR, were not the responsibility of France, but of the United Nations. As such, a claim could not be brought against France for allegedly wrongful acts by those personnel. By contrast, in the *Al-Jedda* case, the U.K. House of Lords found that actions of U.K. troops with respect to detainees undertaken in Iraq *were* the responsibility of the United Kingdom, even though the Security Council had authorized those troops to intern persons when necessary for security reasons.[54] According to three of the Lords, the occupation of Iraq by the United Kingdom (and the United States) after the intervention in March 2003 was only authorized or regularized by the Security Council retrospectively; U.K forces did not intervene in Iraq on behalf of the United Nations (unlike KFOR in Kosovo).[55] As such, a claim for wrongful conduct of those troops could be brought against the United Kingdom, a finding later upheld by the European Court of Human Rights, which determined that "the United Nations Security Council had neither effective control nor ultimate authority and control over the acts and omissions of troops within the Multi–National Force and that the applicant's detention was not, therefore, attributable to the United Nations."[56]

The level of responsibility of the international organization itself may differ depending on whether national law or international law is being applied. Under the former (such as with respect to the U.K. law in the ITC litigation noted above), the national law may largely consist of local rules on agency, contract, and corporations. Under international law, many of the rules of state responsi-

---

52. Behrami & Behrami v. France/Saramati v. France, Germany & Norway, App. Nos. 71412/01 & 78166/01, Eur. Ct. H.R., Grand Chamber, Decision on Admissibility (May 2007), *reprinted in* 46 I.L.M. 743 (2007).

53. *See* S.C. Res. 1244 (June 10, 1999).

54. *See* S.C. Res. 1546 (June 8, 2004).

55. Al-Jeddah v. United Kingdom, 2007 U.K.H.L. 58, *reprinted in* 47 I.L.M. 607 (2008).

56. Al-Jeddah v. United Kingdom, Judgment, Eur. Ct. H.R., para. 84 (July 7, 2011).

bility applicable to states that are discussed in Chapter 6 would appear to apply. In either event, as noted above, difficult issues may arise as to whether the injury resulted from an action taken within the scope of the official powers of the organization (*intra vires*) or from an action outside the scope of such powers (*ultra vires*). Further issues may arise as to whether the injury resulted from the action of an organization official who was acting outside the scope of his official duties, or from the action of a person hired temporarily by the organization (such as a chauffeur), in which case the organization may not be responsible.

Structure and Powers

An international organization normally has "organs" created pursuant to its constituent treaty, which also sets forth the powers of those organs. There is no single blueprint for how many organs an international organization should have, nor for the size or powers of those organs. Having said that, it is common to have one plenary organ in which all member states are represented and which meets annually or biennially to provide overall guidance for the work of the organization, while a second organ—consisting of a smaller sub-group of the member states—meets more often to decide on the details for implementing that guidance. Further, there is typically a permanent staff of the organization—a "secretariat"—that pursues the work of the organization on a day-to-day basis. The exact powers of these organs are indicated in the first instance by the constituent treaty, but are also supplemented by rules established by the organs themselves, by the practice of the organs over time, and often by the opinions of the Legal Office of the organization. An example of such a structure and division of powers may be seen with respect to the principal organs of the United Nations.

General Assembly. The organ of the United Nations at which all members are represented and which has a wide-ranging agenda is the General Assembly.[57] Every member state is represented with one vote; since there are presently 193 member states of the United Nations, there are 193 seats in the General Assembly. The General Assembly may discuss any matters within the scope of the U.N. Charter, which in practice means anything that has a transnational component. Most resolutions adopted by the General Assembly do not directly bind states; they are merely recommendations. Nevertheless, such resolutions may have an effect on the development of international law as discussed in Chapter 3, for they may be evidence of emerging legal norms. Each regular session of the General Assembly begins in September and runs through May of

57. *See* U.N. Charter ch. IV.

the following year. The General Assembly has also occasionally convened an emergency special session, such as on the topic of "Occupied East Jerusalem and the rest of the Occupied Palestinian Territory."

During the course of each regular session, there are several committees which prepare reports for review and decision of the General Assembly. In addition to the General Committee, which considers the session's organization and agenda, and the Credentials Committee, which reviews the credentials of each member's delegation, there are six key committees: Disarmament and International Security (First Committee); Economic and Social (Second); Social, Humanitarian, and Cultural (Third); Special Political and Decolonization (Fourth); Administrative and Budgetary (Fifth); and Legal (Sixth). In recent years, the Legal Committee has considered various issues, such as: the annual report of the International Law Commission; criminal accountability for peacekeeping operations; and whether to recommend observer status for various entities, such as the Parliamentary Assembly of Turkic-speaking countries.

After a matter is reported out of a committee, it is discussed on the floor of the General Assembly. Often the General Assembly will adopt a resolution to address the matter, in which case a simple (or sometimes a two-thirds) majority vote is sufficient. Each year the General Assembly adopts about 300 resolutions.

While the General Assembly has a wide-ranging agenda, the U.N. Charter provides that while "the Security Council is exercising in respect of any dispute or situation the functions assigned to it in the present Charter, the General Assembly shall not make any recommendations with regard to that dispute or situation unless the Security Council so requests."[58] Thus, while the General Assembly has a broader range of issues that it can address than does the Security Council, in the area of peace and security the General Assembly is expected to defer to the Council.

Security Council. The Security Council is a smaller organ than the General Assembly, consisting of just fifteen member states.[59] Of those fifteen, five members are permanently on the Security Council: China, France, Russia, United Kingdom, and United States. The remaining ten non-permanent members are elected by the General Assembly to serve two-year terms. The Security Council meets throughout the course of the year and focuses exclusively on matters of peace and security. In recent years the Security Council has considered numerous matters, such as: whether to authorize military action by a coalition of states to protect Libyan civilians from their government; whether to authorize a U.N. peacekeeping

---

58.   U.N. Charter, art. 12(1).   **59.**   *See* U.N. Charter ch. V.

deployment to help deter violence in South Sudan; and whether to authorize an international coalition to maintain a military presence in Afghanistan.

Security Council resolutions require nine votes for adoption. If the matter is substantive (not procedural) in nature, then all five permanent members must vote in favor of the resolution or abstain. Each year, the Security Council adopts approximately sixty resolutions. When a resolution is adopted pursuant to the Council's powers under Chapter VII of the Charter, the resolution is binding upon all member states,[60] and has the effect of superceding any existing contrary treaty obligations.[61] Thus, if the Security Council decides to impose economic sanctions on a state under Chapter VII (as it has done in recent years to Côte d'Ivoire, Libya, and Sudan), all states are obligated to abide by those sanctions. Moreover, as part of addressing the threat of terrorism, the Security Council has imposed sanctions on certain individuals and organizations.[62]

Various proposals have been made for altering the structure of the Security Council. Some observers favor expanding the Council to include major economic powers, such as Germany or Japan, while others favor an increase in the overall size (perhaps to twenty-one or twenty five) to reflect the larger overall membership of the United Nations. Other observers worry that adding permanent members and increasing the size might make it more difficult to reach agreement on taking action. Removal of any of the existing permanent members does not at present appear to be politically feasible. In any event, such alterations would likely entail an amendment to the U.N. Charter, which is difficult and would require the consent of the existing permanent members.

Economic and Social Council. Operating under the authority of the General Assembly, the Economic and Social Council (ECOSOC) focuses solely on economic, labor, development, human rights, and other social progress issues.[63] ECOSOC is not a plenary organ; the General Assembly elects fifty-four member states to serve on ECOSOC. Though there is no permanent membership, the permanent members of the Security Council are always elected. The remaining states typically are from a variety of economic and social backgrounds.

ECOSOC can initiate studies relating to topics within its ambit and make recommendations either to states or to the General Assembly. ECOSOC can also draft conventions for submission to

---

60. *See* U.N. Charter art. 25.

61. *See* U.N. Charter art. 103; *see also* Rain Liivoja, *The Scope of the Supremacy Clause of the United Nations Charter*, 57 INT'L & COMP. L.Q. 583 (2008).

62. *See* Chapter 5(B) & (C).

63. *See* U.N. Charter ch. IX.

the General Assembly, which then adopts them and opens them for signature. ECOSOC can also convene conferences of states for the purpose of drafting a convention, on a global or regional level. In an effort to coordinate the work of the U.N. system, ECOSOC receives and reviews reports from a wide array of U.N. specialized agencies, such as the International Labor Organization (ILO), the Food and Agriculture Organization (FAO), the World Health Organization (WHO), the World Bank, the International Monetary Fund (IMF), and the International Civil Aviation Organization (ICAO). In conducting its work, ECOSOC is assisted by various commissions and committees. Some commissions address particular subject matter areas, such as the Commission on the Status of Women,[64] while others are regional in nature, such as the Economic Commission for Europe, which has drafted various conventions for European and North American states.

Trusteeship Council. The Trusteeship Council was set up in the aftermath of World War II to monitor eleven territories that—until they were ready for independence or to join a neighboring state— were placed under the administrative authority of another state. Such territories were left over from a similar, earlier system under the League of Nations (the "mandate" system), were colonies detached from the Axis Powers, or were territories voluntarily placed in the trusteeship system by states.

The Trusteeship Council is made up of the five permanent members of the Security Council. For fifty years, various states such as Cameroon, Nauru, Togo, and Western Samoa emerged as new states from trusteeship arrangements, while others were merged with adjacent territory, such as Italian Somaliland (which now forms part of Somalia). In November 1994, the Trusteeship Council suspended its operations upon the independence of Palau, the last remaining U.N. trust territory.[65]

International Court of Justice. As discussed in Chapter 4(D), the International Court of Justice is the judicial organ of the United Nations, which sits in the Peace Palace in the Hague and hears cases between states when accorded the jurisdiction to do so.[66] The Court consists of fifteen judges elected by the General Assembly and the Security Council, and issues two kinds of decisions: judgments in contentious cases and advisory opinions when asked a legal question by a competent organ (*e.g.*, the General Assembly) or international organization.

64. *See* ECOSOC Res. 1996/6 (July 22, 1996).

65. *See* T.C. Res. 2199 (May 25, 1994).

66. *See* U.N. Charter ch. XIV.

Secretariat. The U.N. Secretariat is the permanent officers and staff of the United Nations.[67] At present, the Secretariat consists of about 44,000 staff members from some 160 states. While the Secretariat's headquarters are in New York, it has offices worldwide. In general, the Secretariat carries out all the day-to-day work of the United Nations, both servicing the work of the other principal organs and administering the myriad programs and policies established by them. The secretary-general heads the Secretariat and is appointed by the General Assembly, upon recommendation of the Security Council, for a five-year renewable term. The current secretary-general, Ban Ki-moon, is the eighth in the United Nations' history.

International Law Commission. Although not one of the principal organs of the United Nations, the International Law Commission (ILC) is an important actor in the field of international law. The ILC was created by the U.N. General Assembly in 1947, and consists of thirty-four persons experienced in the field of international law, who are nominated by member states and elected by the U.N. General Assembly to serve five-year terms. These persons are expected to act in their personal capacities (not as representatives of governments), yet they maintain close contact with governments in developing the ILC's work. As a former member from the United States has written:

> Individuals with the experience and character required for election to the Commission by the General Assembly generally do not extend undue deference to the views of their own or any other country. Nevertheless, most Commission members do not labor in a vacuum or for abstract ends. Most are sensitive to the fact that the utility of their work requires acceptance by a broad community of states, large, small, and in between. States do not give orders, but they are the clients without whom the Commission's work comes to little.[68]

The ILC meets in Geneva each summer (with working groups and rapporteurs continuing their work throughout the year) to study particular topics of international law, often for the purpose of developing a draft convention for the consideration of states. Thus, the ILC is responsible for the initial drafts of important conventions on the law of treaties[69] or on the law of diplomatic and consular immunities,[70] and for codification of rules in a non-binding instrument, such as the ILC Rules on State Responsibility.[71]

67. *See* U.N. Charter ch. XV.

68. Robert Rosenstock, *The ILC and State Responsibility*, 96 Am. J. Int'l L. 792, 793–94 (2002).

69. *See* Chapter 3(A).

70. *See* Chapter 9(A).

71. *See* Chapter 6.

The above describes the basic structure and powers of the principal organs of the United Nations. Yet the entire U.N. system is far more complicated, involving dozens of subsidiary bodies, programs, funds, functional and regional commissions, specialized agencies, and organizations with relationships to the United Nations. A sense of the complexity of the U.N. system is apparent from the chart on the "United Nations System" which appears below.

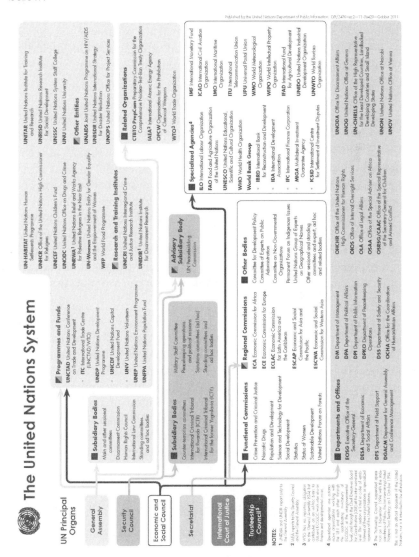

Privileges and Immunities

It is generally thought that international organizations and their officials must have certain privileges and immunities in order to undertake their work without interference by the states in which they are operating. The law in this field, however, is uneven. There is no global convention on the privileges and immunities of all international organizations and their staffs. In 1958, the ILC embarked on a study of such privileges and immunities, but abandoned the effort in 1992. Consequently, the relevant laws on such privileges and immunities largely arise from whatever agreement has been negotiated relating to a particular organization, including any agreement between the organization and its "host state," as well as the national laws of that state.

Persons that represent states before international organizations also are normally accorded certain privileges and immunities. In 1975, the U.N. General Assembly adopted a global convention to address the privileges and immunities of such persons,[72] but that convention has still not entered into force. While several states supported the convention, many states who are hosts to international organizations abstained on the vote that adopted the convention, believing that the convention does not protect their interests. While the convention may reflect customary international law since it is based upon the widely-adhered to convention on privileges and immunities of diplomatic personnel,[73] the unwillingness of states to ratify the convention suggests that its norms are not uniformly accepted.

Here as well, the United Nations serves as a useful example of the types of privileges and immunities that exist for international organizations. First, the U.N. Charter provides that the United Nations shall enjoy in its member states "such privileges and immunities as are necessary for the fulfillment of its purposes."[74] It also provides that representatives of members of the United Nations (meaning persons sent to the United Nations to represent a member state) and U.N. officials shall similarly enjoy such privileges and immunities.[75] The Charter, however, does not spell out these privileges and immunities in any further detail.

Second, in 1946 the United Nations adopted a General Convention on the Privileges and Immunities of the United Nations.[76] This

---

72. *See* Vienna Convention on the Representation of States in Their Relations with International Organizations of a Universal Character, Mar. 14, 1975, U.N. Doc. A/CONF.67/16 (1975).

73. *See* Chapter 9(A).

74. U.N. Charter art. 105(1).

75. *Id.*, art. 105(2).

76. Feb. 13, 1946, 21 U.S.T. 1418, 1 U.N.T.S. 16. The United States became a party in 1970.

convention applies to the United Nations itself, while a similar 1947 convention applies to the specialized agencies of the United Nations. These conventions have served as models for many other international organizations in crafting similar agreements for ratification by their member states. The 1946 General Convention provides that the United Nations, its property and its assets are immune from process, that U.N. premises, archives and documents are inviolable, and that the United Nations is exempt from taxes and customs duties. With respect to representatives to the United Nations from member states, the convention provides that they are immune from personal arrest, exempt from immigration restrictions, are accorded freedom of speech, and as a general matter enjoy the same privileges and immunities as diplomats. With respect to officials of the United Nations, the convention provides immunity from suits for acts performed in their official capacity, exemptions from taxes on their salaries, and other privileges and immunities. High-level U.N. officials (such as the secretary-general) are accorded the same privileges and immunities accorded to diplomats. The convention also accords miscellaneous protections for U.N. "experts on mission," a category of persons that has spawned two advisory opinions of the International Court of Justice.[77] Such immunities can always be waived by the United Nations and often are in situations where there is credible evidence that a U.N. employee has engaged in serious criminal behavior. For example, in 2007 the U.S. government determined that a U.N. translator was involved in a conspiracy to sell U.S. visas to Uzbek nationals seeking to enter the United States. The United Nations waived the individual's immunity, allowing his trial to go forward in U.S. courts.[78]

Third, the United Nations and the United States in 1947 concluded a bilateral Headquarters Agreement[79] which further clarified the privileges and immunities to be accorded the United Nations. The agreement provides that U.S. law continues to apply within the "headquarters district" of the United Nations, yet accords various protections to the United Nations. For instance, U.S. authorities may not enter the headquarters district without the consent of the U.N. secretary-general and may not restrict the travel of persons to and from the district on official U.N. business.

---

77. *See* Advisory Opinion on Applicability of Article VI, Section 22, of the Convention on the Privileges and Immunities of the United Nations, 1989 I.C.J. 177 (Dec. 15); Advisory Opinion on Difference Relating to Immunity from Legal Process of a Special Rapporteur of the Commission on Human Rights, 1999 I.C.J. 62 (Apr. 29).

78. *See* Colum Lynch, *U.N. Worker Jailed in Visa–Sale Scheme*, Wash. Post, Aug. 7, 2007, at A2.

79. June 26, 1947, 61 Stat. 3416, 11 U.N.T.S. 11.

Fourth, there exist national laws implementing privileges and immunities of the United Nations and other international organizations. For example, in the United States the International Organizations Immunities Act (IOIA),[80] enacted in 1945, permits the president to designate an entity as an "international organization" by executive order. Once so designated, the international organization is accorded various rights, such as the right to contract and acquire property under U.S. law. Further, the statute states that the international organization (and its property and assets) enjoy the same immunity from suit as enjoyed by foreign governments, making relevant the rules established by the Foreign Sovereign Immunities Act.[81] The IOIA also contains provisions directed at the personnel of (or representatives to) the international organization, such as concerning entry to the United States and immunity from suit for official acts. The U.S. Diplomatic Relations Act[82] is principally directed at the privileges and immunities of diplomats, but the language and legislative history appears broad enough to cover representatives to international organizations and, if so, accords them the privileges and immunities accorded to diplomats under the Vienna Convention on Diplomatic Relations.[83] Finally, certain specialized statutes provide protections for U.N.-related personnel. For example, the Act for Prevention of Crimes Against Internationally Protected Persons[84] criminalizes acts of violence against "a foreign official, official guest, or internationally protected persons" in certain situations.

Examples of International Organizations

The Organization of American States. In 1948, twenty-one Western Hemisphere states signed a Charter creating an Organization of American States (OAS).[85] At present, all thirty-five states of the hemisphere have ratified the OAS Charter; Cuba is a member, but its government has been excluded from participation in the OAS since 1962. The OAS has its headquarters in Washington, D.C. The purpose of the OAS is to promote cooperation among the states of the Western Hemisphere, advance their common interests, and provide a forum for undertaking action.

The General Assembly—the supreme organ of the OAS—has a wide range of powers to decide on actions associated with the OAS mission. It consists of representatives from all member states, who each have one vote. The General Assembly convenes annually for a period determined by the Assembly's rules of procedure and at a place selected in accordance with a principle of rotation.

80. 22 U.S.C. § 288(a) (2006).

81. *See* Chapter 9(C).

82. 22 U.S.C. §§ 254(a)–254(e) (2006).

83. *See* Chapter 9(A).

84. 18 U.S.C. § 112 (2006).

85. OAS Charter, *supra* note 3.

A separate organ, the "Meeting of Consultation of Ministers of Foreign Affairs," exists to consider problems of an urgent nature. Any member state may request that a Meeting of Consultation be called. A third organ, the Permanent Council, is charged with monitoring the maintenance of friendly relations among the member states, and reports directly to the General Assembly. Consisting of one representative of each member state, the Permanent Council carries out the decisions of the General Assembly or of the Meeting of Consultation if implementation of those decisions have not been assigned to another body.

The European Union. The European Union (EU) is a confederation of states often referred to as the only "supra-national" organization, meaning an international organization that has extensive powers to bind its member states (but not so extensive that it is regarded as a state). The legal and political system of the European Union has been continually evolving since its inception sixty years ago. As of 2011, there are twenty-seven member states of the European Union, all located in Europe.

The EU is founded on a series of treaties, beginning with those signed in Paris (adopted in 1951) and Rome (1957) and continuing through to more recent treaties of Maastricht (1992), Amsterdam (1997), Nice (2001), and Lisbon (2009). Originally, there were three European communities: the European Coal and Steel Community (ECSC); the European Atomic Energy Community (Euratom); and the European Economic Community (initially referred to as the EEC, and then as the European Community or EC). The ECSC ceased functioning in 2002. Euratom also ceased functioning as an independent entity; its functions were absorbed into the EC. The Maastricht Treaty established the EU, but it had a fragmented legal structure, operating under three "pillars," one of which concerned economic integration through the EC. The Lisbon Treaty changed the legal structure of the EU by merging the three "pillars" into a single legal entity with a single legal personality, known as the EU.

Originally, the EU was designed to create a single economic market among its member states by allowing for the free movement of goods, services, and capital, and by establishing a common system of customs or tariffs with respect to goods, services, and capital from other countries. Over time, this economic union has deepened with extensive regulation of many sectors, such as agriculture and fisheries, and the pursuit of regional development within the member states of the EU. Moreover, the EU has evolved so as to encompass common controls in a wider array of areas, such as the provision of aid to developing countries, environmental policy, foreign affairs, and security. The 1985 Schengen agreement abolished passport controls among EU states and many non-EU states in Europe. In 1999, a common currency—the euro—was introduced, which has been accepted for use in seventeen EU member states. The EU engages as an institution in diplomatic relations worldwide, including at the United Nations, the World Trade Organization, and at major multilateral meetings of the "G–8" or "G–20." To coordinate such relations, the Lisbon Treaty created a High Representative of the Union for Foreign Affairs and Security Policy (who also serves as Vice–President of the European Commission).

The EU, however, is not a state. EU member states retain their sovereignty; they have just pooled certain sovereign attributes for specific common purposes. Thus, understanding the EU requires understanding the division of competencies between the EU and its member states. The EU has been given *exclusive competence* with respect to rules on the customs union, on competition (or antitrust) where necessary for the functioning of the EU market, on monetary policy for those states in the European monetary zone ("euro-zone"), on the EU's common commercial policy, and on the conservation of marine biological resources. The EU and its member states have *shared competence* in certain other areas. In some of these areas, such as the environment, consumer protection, and transport, the member states can establish rules so long as the EU has not already done so. Conversely, in other of these areas, such as research, technological development, and humanitarian aid, the EU can act only act if doing so does not intrude upon decisions reached by individual member states. Many other areas are left to competence of the member states, such as culture, tourism, education, or disaster prevention, with the EU simply exercising a *supporting competence* by helping to coordinate or supplement the member states.[86]

The mechanisms for creating EU rules are sophisticated. In the first instance, the various treaties and amendments to those treaties establish the different EU institutions and their powers. Further, there is—in addition to the "primary legislation" of the constituent treaties—a large body of "secondary legislation" created by EU institutions, known as regulations, directives, decisions, and recommendations or opinions. "Regulations" are directly binding on all member states without the need for any national implementing legislation. "Directives" bind member states to objectives that must be achieved within a certain time-limit, but leave to national authorities the means for achieving those objectives. Directives have to be implemented in national legislation, but only in accordance with the procedures of the individual member states. "Decisions" are binding upon those to whom they are addressed,

---

86. *See generally* THE CONSTITUTIONAL INTEGRITY OF THE EUROPEAN UNION (Fabian Amtenbrink & Peter A. J. van den Berg eds., 2010).

whether a state, company, or person; thus, decisions do not require national implementing legislation. "Recommendations" and "opinions" are not binding.

Such laws are the product of decision-making by three main EU institutions: the European Parliament (EP) (which represents the people of Europe); the Council of the European Union (which represents the member states); and the European Commission (intended as a politically independent body that pursues the collective European interest).

The parliament consists of 736 members who are directly elected every five years. Rather than sitting in national groups, EP members sit in one of seven political groups, with each group reflecting one of the political ideologies that spans across the member states. The parliament resides in Strasbourg and is charged with examining and adopting EU legislation under a "co-decision procedure" whereby it, in effect, has a legislative veto over matters in most policy areas under consideration by the council. The parliament also approves the EU budget, monitors the work of the commission and council (and can even bring suit against them before the European Court of Justice), and must assent to important international agreements, including decisions to allow the accession of new EU member states.

Despite the role of the European Parliament, the Council of the European Union (formerly known as the Council of Ministers) is the focal point for initiating and finalizing EU legislation and decision-making. It is composed of the representatives of the member state governments, who meet regularly in Brussels and Luxembourg at the level of ministers, ambassadors, or working groups. There are presently twenty-seven representatives on the council, with the presidency rotating among the member states every six months. A member state's representative changes depending on the topic under discussion, so that there are essentially multiple councils addressing foreign affairs, agriculture, finance, and other matters. Council decisions are taken by vote. Votes are weighted so that the larger a state's population, the more votes it controls. The number of votes required to adopt a measure depends on the subject matter, with some votes requiring unanimity but most requiring a qualified majority.

The European Commission is in many respects the driving force of the EU. Located in Brussels, the commission is basically the E.C. executive body, responsible for conducting the day-to-day work of the EU. The commission drafts proposals for new laws, which are presented to the parliament and the council. Once the laws are adopted, the commission monitors whether they are properly implemented by member states. The commission also supervises the expenditure of EU funds, such as agricultural subsidies, and represents the EU internationally, such as through the negotiation of agreements between the EU and non-EU states.

The Commissioners of the European Commission are twenty-seven persons nominated by member governments and approved by the European Parliament for a five-year term (they may also be dismissed by the Parliament). The president of the commission is appointed by the council and the parliament. The commission is assisted in its work by about 38,000 civil servants. While the commission consists of persons from EU member states, it acts independently of the member state governments.

In addition to the three law-making institutions, there are certain other important EU institutions. The European Council is comprised of the heads of state or government of the EU member states, plus the president of the commission, and holds meetings approximately four times per year. The European Council is headed by a president, who serves for a thirty–month term that can be renewed once. The European Council has no formal legislative power, but was charged by the Treaty of Lisbon with deciding upon the general political direction and priorities of the EU. As such, the European Council serves as a key body for deciding on the strategic direction of the EU and on how the EU should react in crisis situations.

The European Court of Auditors audits the accounts and the implementation of the EU budget. In doing so, it seeks both to improve financial management and to promote transparency by reporting to the citizens of Europe on the use of public funds by EU authorities.

The European Court of Justice (ECJ) settles disputes over the interpretation of EU treaties and legislation. Further, when national courts are uncertain about how to apply EU legislation, they may ask the ECJ for guidance. The ECJ, located in Luxembourg, consists of one judge from each member state.[87]

The European Central Bank independently manages monetary policy for those member states that have adopted the euro as their common currency. Like the Federal Reserve Bank in the United States, the European Central Bank determines the level of interest rates within the European monetary zone for the purpose of maintaining price stability. Based in Frankfurt, the bank is empowered to conduct foreign exchange operations and has the exclusive right to issue euro banknotes. At present, the European monetary zone—in which the euro is the only currency—includes seventeen EU member states.

87. *See* Chapter 4(F).

The African Union. In 1963, African states created the Organization of African Unity (OAU). The principal objectives of the OAU were to eliminate all vestiges of colonization and apartheid, promote unity and solidarity among African states, promote cooperation for development, and safeguard the sovereignty and territorial integrity of the member states. By the late 1990's, the OAU sought to extend such cooperation so as to pursue deeper economic and political integration. To that end, the African Union was officially launched in July 2002, to replace the OAU. The African Union, which is based in Addis Ababa, Ethiopia, and consists of fifty-four African states, is loosely structured along the lines of the European Union, yet is at a much more nascent stage. The African Union's objectives include increasing the political and socio-economic integration of the continent, promoting and defending common positions of the member states on issues of interest to the African continent and its peoples, securing peace and security in Africa, and advancing democratic institutions, good governance and human rights in Africa.[88] Time will tell whether the African Union can achieve the success of the European Union.

The principal organ of the African Union is the Assembly, which is composed of the heads of governments or their representatives. The Assembly meets at least once a year to determine, among other things, the common policies of the Union. Decisions are taken by consensus or, failing that, a two-thirds majority (procedural matters require a simple majority). There is also an Executive Council composed of foreign ministers which meets at least twice a year to prepare decisions for the Assembly. A third organ, the Permanent Representatives Committee, is charged with preparing the work of the Executive Council. The Commission, consisting of a chairperson, the deputy chairperson, eight commissioners, and staff members, serves as the Secretariat of the Union. A Pan–African Parliament consisting of 235 members has consultative and advisory powers; in time, the intention is to accord it legislative powers. An Economic, Social and Cultural Council, composed of different social and professional groups of the member states, provides advice to the principal organs. A Court of Justice decides disputes over interpretation of African Union instruments.

To date, efforts at economic integration in Africa have had limited success. Most economies are relatively weak and highly dependent on agriculture, while intra-regional trade is a lower percentage of total foreign trade than in other regions of the world. Nevertheless, some successes exist through the operation of sub-

---

88. Constitutive Act of the African Union, art. 3, July 11, 2000, OAU Doc. CAB/LEG/23.15 (2000); *see generally* Zeray Yihdego, *The African Union:* *Founding Principles, Frameworks and Prospects*, 17 Eur. L.J. 568 (2011); Diedre Badejo, The African Union (Peggy Kahn ed., 2008).

regional organizations, such as the Economic Community of West African States (ECOWAS), the Economic Community of Central African States (ECCAS), and the Common Market for East and Southern Africa (COMESA). The African Union has played a limited role in conflict management. It regularly condemns military coups that occur in African states, such as in the Central African Republic (2003), Guinea–Bissau (2003), São Tomé and Príncipe (2003), Togo (2005), Mauritania (2005 and 2008), Guinea (2008), Madagascar (2009), and Niger (2010). Yet it has minimal tools for preventing such unconstitutional changes in government and even less tools for military intervention, including for the protection of human rights. The African Union has engaged in some peacekeeping operations deployed with the consent of a host government. In 2003, the African Union deployed a peacekeeping force of soldiers from Ethiopia, Mozambique, and South Africa to Burundi (AMIB) to monitor implementation of certain peace agreements. In 2004, African Union peacekeeping forces (AMIS) deployed to Darfur, Sudan, but AMIS was unable to contain the violence there, and was replaced at the end of 2007 by a UN peacekeeping force. The African Union also sponsored in 2007 the deployment of peacekeeping forces to Somalia (AMISOM) to support the transitional government, train its security forces, and create a secure environment for the delivery of humanitarian aid.

ASEAN. The Association of Southeast Asian Nations (ASEAN) was founded in 1967 with the signing of the ASEAN Declaration (Bangkok Declaration).[89] The objective in forming the association was to promote economic growth and regional stability. For some forty years, the association operated without a constituent instrument, but in 2007 the ASEAN states created a formal legal personality for the association by adopting the ASEAN Charter, which entered into force in late 2008.[90] The Charter sets forth certain fundamental principles agreed upon by the member states, including: respect for the independence, sovereignty, equality, and territorial integrity; a shared commitment and collective responsibility in enhancing regional peace, security and prosperity; renunciation of aggression; reliance on peaceful settlement of disputes; and commitment to non-interference in each other's internal affairs.[91] Moreover, like the treaties of the European Union, the ASEAN Charter pursues a single and integrated regional economy by creating a free market as among the ten ASEAN states (Brunei Darussalam,

---

89. Association of South East Asian Nations Declaration, Aug. 8, 1967, 6 I.L.M. 1233 (1967).

90. Charter of the Association of Southeast Asian Nations (Nov. 20,

2007), *at* <http://www.aseansec.org/publications/ASEAN–Charter.pdf>.

91. *Id.*, art. 2.

Cambodia, Indonesia, Laos, Malaysia, Myanmar, Philippines, Singapore, Thailand, and Vietnam).

The Charter also established or formalized certain institutional structures. ASEAN's supreme policy-making body is the ASEAN Summit, a meeting of the heads of state or heads of government of member states, which occurs twice per year.[92] Further, the Charter establishes an ASEAN Coordinating Council, consisting of the foreign ministers of member states, who meet at least twice annually to coordinate the ASEAN Summit and other operations.[93] Three ASEAN Community Councils address matters of political security, economic issues, and socio-cultural issues respectively, so as to implement decisions of the ASEAN Summit[94] through Sectoral Ministerial Bodies.[95] An ASEAN Secretariat funded by the member states was established, based in Indonesia and headed by a secretary–general and four deputy secretaries–general.[96]

The ASEAN Charter provides that ASEAN states shall respect, promote, and protect fundamental freedoms and human rights,[97] and further called for the creation of a human rights body.[98] In July 2009, terms of reference were adopted for the establishment of an ASEAN Intergovernmental Commission on Human Rights, consisting of representatives of the member states, which is charged with developing strategies for pursuing such freedoms and rights.[99]

C. Non–Governmental Organizations

In addition to states and international organizations, there is a further type of organization relevant to international law known as private or non-governmental organizations (NGOs). NGOs are generally regarded as groups of persons or societies, voluntarily created, that act independent of governments on a non-profit basis. Obviously, NGOs of interest to international law are those that are concerned with matters that transcend national boundaries.

NGOs, however, come in many different shapes and sizes. Some NGOs are principally the creature of a single national legal system, but with transnational scope to its activities (such as the International Committee of the Red Cross, which was created under Swiss law and whose members are all Swiss nationals). Other NGOs have a headquarters office created under a single national legal system, but are then affiliated with numerous offices worldwide that have legal status under other national legal systems (such as Greenpeace International, which is headquartered in the Nether-

---

92. *Id.*, art. 7.
93. *Id.*, art. 8.
94. *Id.*, art. 9.
95. *Id.*, art. 10.
96. *Id.*, art. 11.

97. *Id.*, art. 2.
98. *Id.*, art. 14.
99. *See* 48 I.L.M. 1161 (2009).

lands, but is affiliated with twenty-seven national and regional offices operating in forty-one states who are licensed to use the name "Greenpeace"). While many NGOs firmly retain independence from states by not accepting government donations (*e.g..*, Greenpeace), other NGOs embrace government involvement. Perhaps the most unusual is the IUCN/World Conservation Union, which has a membership of more than 900 NGOs, but also 87 states and 117 government agencies.

NGOs are creations of national law. While there have been some efforts to accord NGOs a formal status under international law, for the most part those efforts have been unsuccessful. In 1986, the Council of Europe adopted a Convention on the Legal Recognition of Personality of International Non–Governmental Organizations, which requires parties to recognize the legal personality and capacity accorded to an NGO by any other party.[100] Nevertheless, even this convention has only eleven parties as of 2011.

Some NGOs are focused specifically on the study and development of international law, often with academics as members. The Institut de Droit International, established in France in 1873, consists of 132 persons elected by the Institut based on their achievements in the field of international law. The Institut adopts resolutions setting forth what it considers to be the rules of international law on particular topics, which in turn are often cited by states, tribunals, and scholars. Similarly, the International Law Association is an organization of specialists in the field of international law, consisting of both a global organization and "branches" in many states. Resolutions adopted at its biennial conferences, as well as the reports and studies of its committees, have influenced the development of international law.

Other NGOs (such as the ICRC or Greenpeace) are more activist in nature, seeking to raise public awareness of transnational problems.[101] NGOs have found that they can directly affect transnational private behavior by shining a spotlight on corporations engaging in poor labor or environmental practices, and organizing boycotts of such corporations. They also often engage in transnational lobbying campaigns to influence how governments and international organizations address transnational problems. The U.N. Charter itself calls upon the Economic and Social Council to consult with NGOs that are concerned with matters within ECOSOC's competence. To that end, ECOSOC developed procedures for receiving advice from hundreds of NGOs operating in either a general or special consultative status, which allows the NGOs to attend and participate in U.N. meetings and confer-

---

100. Apr. 24, 1986, E.T.S. No. 124.

101. *See* MARGARET E. KECK & KATHRYN SIKKINK, ACTIVISTS BEYOND BORDERS: ADVOCACY NETWORKS IN INTERNATIONAL POLITICS (1998).

ences.[102] Such consultation practice has now spread throughout the U.N. system, providing NGOs with opportunities to speak before the U.N. General Assembly and, sometimes, before the U.N. Security Council.[103]

Further, NGOs have found that they can be important players in the creation, interpretation, and enforcement of international law on matters of interest to NGOs. NGOs increasingly participate as observers in multilateral treaty negotiations, commenting on draft treaty text and otherwise seeking to influence the views of states. NGOs also actively participate in conferences of the parties to multilateral treaty regimes, where important decisions are made on how the treaty should be interpreted and implemented. NGOs have submitted amicus briefs directly (or through states) to various international tribunals, such as World Trade Organization and North American Free Trade Agreement (NAFTA) dispute resolution panels, the International Criminal Tribunal for the former Yugoslavia, and the International Court of Justice. NGOs are very active in programs that assist states (especially developing states) in implementing their obligations under international law, such as through training programs and technology transfer. NGOs are active in monitoring the conduct of states, such as on matters of implementation of human rights regimes, as a means of shaming states into compliance. Thus, while NGOs are created under and governed by national (rather than international) law, they play important roles in the promotion of international law and in its observance.[104]

Critics of NGOs highlight their overall lack of accountability. NGOs are not democratic in any normal meaning of the term; while they may represent their members in a general sense, their members typically have not elected or appointed the NGO's leadership. Certainly NGOs cannot be said to represent all persons who may have concerns about labor, environmental, human rights, or other matters. Indeed, NGOs that are focused on a particular sector, such as the international environment, are often in conflict with one another over the desired course of action. Further, the best-known and best-equipped NGOs are often funded by persons from developed states, and thus tend to be more interested in issues of concern to those persons (*e.g.*, radiation from ozone depletion) than issues of greatest concern to the developing world (*e.g.*, clean drinking water).

102. *See* U.N. Charter art. 71; ECO-SOC Res. 1996/31 (July 23, 1996).

103. *See generally* "THE CONSCIENCE OF THE WORLD": THE INFLUENCE OF NON-GOVERNMENTAL ORGANISATIONS IN THE UN SYSTEM (Peter Willetts ed., 1996); CONSTRUCTING WORLD CULTURE: INTERNATIONAL NONGOVERNMENTAL ORGANIZATIONS SINCE 1875 (John Boli & George M. Thomas eds., 1999).

104. *See* Peter Spiro, *New Global Potentates: Nongovernmental Organizations and the "Unregulated" Marketplace*, 18 CARDOZO L. REV. 957 (1996); NON-STATE ACTORS AND HUMAN RIGHTS (Philip Alston ed., 2005).

D. Natural Persons and Groups

While states are the dominant actors in the field of international law, they are governed by (and govern) natural and legal persons. Even in the early history of international law, rules developed to protect natural persons, such as diplomatic envoys. Over time, protections for persons have grown enormously, especially with the dramatic rise of human rights and international humanitarian law in the latter half of the twentieth century.[105] Various economic treaties, such as on trade and investment, are designed to create rights for individuals or corporations (see below) to sue states before international or national fora to vindicate rights. In limited situations, natural persons can even sue their own states before international tribunals to vindicate rights, such as before the European Court of Human Rights. Conversely, natural persons may now be criminally prosecuted for violations of international law, including before international tribunals.[106]

A person's nationality is an important aspect of the rights and protections accorded the person under international law. Each state has the right to determine how a person may acquire its nationality. However, to be entitled to recognition on the international plane, that nationality must be based on a genuine link between the state and the person or entity.[107] As a general proposition, nationality may be acquired as the result of birth, either by being born within a state's territory (*jus soli*) or through the nationality of one's parents (*jus sanguinis*). Further, "naturalization" can occur by voluntary application and acceptance in a formal process or as the result of marriage, adoption, or the reacquisition of an original nationality by operation of law. An individual may also become a national of a state that acquires the territory on which he or she lives, although the consent of an individual is normally required before a state can impose its nationality upon that person. Individuals may also have more than one nationality; that is, they may be dual nationals. For example, a person may have the nationality of state X by operation of the *jus soli* principle and of state Y under the *jus sanguinis* principle.

Groups of persons may also have certain rights or obligations under international law. Groups such as the Bosnian Serbs or the Kurdish peoples of Iran, Iraq, and Turkey have not be able to establish their own state, but they have been permitted to participate in certain international negotiations concerning their future. Such groups are often referred to as "minorities" or "peoples,"

---

105. *See* Chapters 10 & 14(B).
106. *See* Chapter 13.

107. *See* Nottebohm Case (Liech. v. Guat.), 1955 I.C.J. 4 (Apr. 6).

meaning a group that sees itself as having a unique bond based on cultural, ethnic, historical, linguistic, racial, or religious identity. Indeed, the rights of indigenous peoples are increasingly being recognized in international treaties.[108] For example, the Convention on Biological Diversity states that parties shall, as far as possible and subject to their national law,

> respect, preserve and maintain knowledge, innovations and practices of indigenous and local communities embodying traditional lifestyles relevant for the conservation and sustainable use of biological diversity and promote their wider application with the approval and involvement of the holders of such knowledge, innovations and practices and encourage the equitable sharing of the benefits arising [therefrom].[109]

Generally speaking, however, groups of persons have not been accorded positions of strength in international law. Their participation in the system and the rights accorded to them are bestowed and thus controlled by states or, in some instances, international organizations. Groups of persons do not have ready access to international law making, interpreting, or enforcement, but over time international law may transition to a system in which greater account is taken of groups of persons organized at a sub-state level.

E. Legal Persons (Corporations)

Multi-national corporations (MNCs)—by which is meant corporations with affiliated business operations in more than one country—have become extremely important actors in the transnational arena.[110] While a corporation is deemed to have the nationality of the state where it is incorporated,[111] the activities of MNCs can be global in scope, and provide significant benefits by creating wealth in states where they operate. Through their investments and trade, MNCs create jobs, produce goods and services, introduce technologies, and develop markets. While much of the increased MNC activity since the 1990's has been among states of the developed world, a portion of that activity includes the movement of MNC operations to the developing world to take advantage of a cheaper supply of labor and other resources.

There are various ways that MNCs become involved in the creation of, interpretation of, and compliance with international

---

108. *See* S. JAMES ANAYA, INDIGENOUS PEOPLES IN INTERNATIONAL LAW (2d ed. 2004); ANNA MEIJKNECHT, TOWARDS INTERNATIONAL PERSONALITY: THE POSITION OF MINORITIES AND INDIGENOUS PEOPLES IN INTERNATIONAL LAW (2001).

109. Convention on Biological Diversity, art. 8(j), June 5, 1992, 1760 U.N.T.S. 79, 31 I.L.M. 818.

110. For a brief discussion of what constitutes an MNC, see PETER MUCHLINSKI, MULTINATIONAL ENTERPRISES AND THE LAW 12–15 (1995).

111. *See* Barcelona Traction, Light & Power Co. (Belg. v. Spain), 1970 I.C.J. 3, 168 (Feb. 5).

law. In some situations, MNCs are directly involved in the creation of international agreements, such as the role employer representatives play in the tripartite (government/employer/labor) representation established for the International Labor Organization (ILO) Assembly. In other instances, MNCs have developed or availed themselves of international legal norms in their relations with states in which they do business. Thus, MNCs have often "internationalized" their investment contracts with such states, meaning that the contract becomes governed by international law and, when disputes arise, is adjudicated by international arbitration between the investor and the host state ("investor-state arbitration"), rather than the local courts of the host state.

Indeed, during the 1960's to 1980's many developing countries sought to nationalize or expropriate foreign investment as a means of stemming post-colonial economic "neo-colonization." Such actions prompted MNCs to pursue greater protections in their contracts with developing states, including the ability to take disputes to investor-state arbitration. Simultaneously, many inter-state negotiations between developed and developing states became enmeshed in fierce arguments about the protections to be accorded foreign investors under international law, such as whether an expropriation should lead to the payment of "full compensation" or some lesser amount. These arguments have lessened somewhat since most developing states now see great benefits in attracting foreign investment and technology through appropriate investor protections. In any event, many international rules protecting foreign investors have emerged from both international agreements and arbitral decisions.[112]

MNCs have also been important players in the field of private international law as it relates to economic matters. MNCs engage extensively in the international sale of goods, the licensing of intellectual property across borders, and other forms of international business transactions. A variety of treaties and codes have developed in the field of private international law to address these transactions.[113]

Finally, MNCs are also the source (and target) of efforts to develop certain forms of non-legally binding norms (sometimes referred to as "soft law"), which often draw on international laws relating to labor, human rights, and the environment. Chapter 3(F) discusses such "soft law" in the form of transnational corporate codes of conduct that have emerged in recent years as a means of constraining the behavior of MNCs.

---

112. *See, e.g.,* Zachary Douglas, *The Hybrid Foundations of Investment Treaty Arbitration*, 74 BRIT. YRBK. INT'L L. 151 (2003).

113. *See, e.g.,* RALPH H. FOLSOM ET AL., PRINCIPLES OF INTERNATIONAL BUSINESS TRANSACTIONS (2d ed. 2010).

Further Reading:

Chittharanjan F. Amerasinghe, *Principles of the Institutional Law of International Organizations* (2d ed. 2005).

Jean d'Aspremont, ed., *Participants in the International Legal System: Multiple Perspectives on Non–State Actors in International Law* (2011).

James Crawford, *The Creation of States in International Law* (2d ed. 2006).

Leland Goodrich, Edvard Hambro & Anne Simons, *Charter of the United Nations: Commentary and Documents* (3d rev. ed. 1969).

Thomas D. Grant, *The Recognition of States* (1999).

Trevor Hartley, *The Foundations of European Union Law* (7th ed. 2010).

Anna–Karin Lindblom, *Non-Governmental Organisations in International Law* (2005).

Lisa Martin & Beth Simmons, eds., *International Institutions: An International Organization Reader* (2001).

Janne Elisabeth Nijman, *The Concept of International Legal Personality: An Inquiry Into the History and Theory of International Law* (2004).

M.J. Peterson, *Recognition of Governments: Legal Doctrine and State Practice, 1815–1995* (1997).

Philippe Sands & Pierre Klein, *Bowett's Law of International Institutions* (5th ed. 2001).

Dan Sarooshi, *International Organizations and Their Exercise of Sovereign Powers* (2007).

Bruno Simma, ed., *The Charter of the United Nations; A Commentary* (2d ed. 2002) (2 vols.).

Stefan Talmon, *Recognition of Governments in International Law* (2000).

U.N. Dep't Public Information, *The United Nations Today* (2008).

Cynthia Day Wallace, *The Multinational Enterprise and Legal Control: Host State Sovereignty in an Era of Economic Globalization* (2002).

Nigel D. White, *The Law of International Organisations* (2d ed. 2005).

Ralph Wilde et al., *United Nations Reform Through Practice: Report of the International Law Association Study Group on United Nations Reform* (Dec. 11, 2011).

Chapter 3

INTERNATIONAL LAW CREATION

International law is not created by a global legislature, for no such institution exists. Rather, the "sources" of international law are to be found elsewhere. In seeking to identify the appropriate sources of international law to be applied by the Permanent Court of International Justice (PCIJ), the drafters of the 1920 PCIJ Statute identified the following sources: (1) treaties; (2) international custom; (3) general principles of law; and (4) judicial decisions and the teachings of scholars.

These same sources—now identified in Article 38(1) of the 1945 Statute of the International Court of Justice (ICJ)[1]—remain the classic starting point for discussing international law creation. However, contemporary international law has evolved such that there are at least two other methods of international law creation that merit study. First, in certain circumstances, international organizations have been accorded the power to generate rules that bind their member states. While they are not global legislatures with plenary power to legislate, these organizations operate somewhat like legislatures in the narrow areas of their authority. Second, non-binding instruments have also had important effects on the behavior of states and non-state actors, and over time have helped crystalize international law on a particular topic. Both the classic sources of international law and these more contemporary sources are discussed in this chapter.

A. Treaties

Introduction

When two persons wish to enter into a legal relationship, they typically do so by concluding a contract, which provides in writing the rights and obligations of the two parties. Such contracts can be on a wide variety of substantive issues, can be short or lengthy, can be of limited or unlimited duration, and often contain important provisions regarding performance, dispute settlement, and suspension or termination of the contract. The contract itself does not define the entire legal relationship between the two parties, for there has to be a "background" set of procedural and substantive

1. Art. 38, June 26, 1945, 59 Stat. 1055 [hereinafter ICJ Statute].

rules that, among other things, explain when it is that a contract is formed. Background rules may be found in national laws on contract, such as the contract codes of each of the fifty states of the United States.

In the international arena, "contracts" between two or more countries are commonly referred to as "treaties" or "conventions."[2] Like contracts between persons, treaties can be on a wide variety of substantive issues, can be short or lengthy, can be of limited or unlimited duration, and often contain important provisions regarding performance, dispute settlement, and suspension or termination of the treaty. Background rules for treaties, however, are not found in national laws; rather, they exist in international law itself. These background rules emerged over the centuries in the practice of states. In May 1969, a U.N. conference adopted the Vienna Convention on the Law of Treaties (VCLT)[3]—sometimes referred to as the "treaty on treaties"—as a means of codifying the background rules states were following in their treaty practice. As of 2011, 111 states are parties to the VCLT.

The VCLT directly applies to treaty relations between two VCLT parties, but only for treaties concluded after the date the VCLT entered into force for those parties.[4] For treaties concluded prior to that date, and for treaties concluded by states that have not yet ratified the VCLT (including the United States[5]), the VCLT does not directly apply. Even so, many states and international tribunals regard the VCLT as largely reflecting the customary practice of states, and thus accept the VCLT as relevant when considering how states should behave in their treaty relations.

For example, in a case between Hungary and Slovakia, the ICJ was confronted with an international agreement that predated the entry into force of the VCLT. Nevertheless, the Court applied the provisions of the VCLT on termination and suspension of treaties as customary law, even though those provisions were somewhat controversial when they were originally adopted in the convention.[6]

The VCLT sets forth a wide variety of rules relating to treaties, which may be loosely grouped into five categories: (1) defining what constitutes a treaty; (2) making treaties; (3) filing reservations to

---

2. *Id.*, art. 38(1)(a).

3. May 23, 1969, 1155 U.N.T.S. 331 [hereinafter VCLT].

4. *Id.*, art. 4.

5. The Nixon Administration submitted the VCLT to the U.S. Senate for advice and consent, but the Senate as a whole has never voted on the treaty. Subsequent administrations have tried to obtain such consent without success.

The U.S. acceptance of the VCLT as largely reflecting customary international law appears to have taken away any urgency in joining the convention, such that other treaties have received greater attention and priority.

6. *See* Gabčikovo–Nagymaros Project (Hung. v. Slovk.), 1997 I.C.J. 7, paras. 42–46 & 99 (Sept. 25).

treaties; (4) the operation of treaties; and (5) terminating or suspending treaties. Each category is discussed in turn.

What is a Treaty?

The VCLT defines a treaty in Article 2 as

> an international agreement concluded between States in written form and governed by international law, whether embodied in a single instrument or in two or more related instruments and whatever its particular designation.

Thus, the VCLT only speaks to *written* treaties concluded *between states*. Nevertheless, general international law accepts that there can be binding oral treaties between states, although they rarely occur. International law also accepts that there can be binding treaties between a state and an international organization, or between two or more international organizations.[7] The VCLT's definition recognizes that a treaty may consist of not just a single written instrument but of multiple instruments, such as an exchange of diplomatic notes between two states.

The definition also recognizes that a treaty must be governed by international law. If two states conclude a written instrument, such as a military sales contract or the lease of property for an embassy, which calls for the application of a state's national law to the instrument, then it is not a treaty. Rather, it is a contract between two states that will be interpreted and enforced in accordance with national law. A treaty need not expressly state that it is governed by international law; its intention to be so governed can be determined from the language and context of the instrument. At the same time, if two states conclude a written instrument containing language that is non-legally binding in nature, then it will not be regarded as governed by either international law or national law. For a non-legally binding agreement, the U.S. government regards it as appropriate to avoid the use of various types of terms, such as "treaty," "agreement," "parties" (instead use "participants"), "shall" (instead use "should"), "agree to" (instead use "intend to" or "expect to"), "undertake," "enter into force" (instead use "is to come into operation" or "activities are to commence"), "done at," "concluded at," and "equal authenticity" when referring to multiple language versions of the agreement.[8]

---

7. *See* Vienna Convention on the Law of Treaties Between States and International Organizations or Between International Organizations, Mar. 21, 1986, 25 I.L.M. 543. This convention has not yet entered into force, but its provisions (which parallel those of the VCLT) are generally regarded as expressing customary international law.

8. *See* U.S. Dep't of State, *Guidance on Non–Binding Documents* (n.d.), *at* <http://www.state.gov/s/l/treaty/guidance>.

Finally, the definition recognizes that the instrument's exact label is not significant; it can be called a "treaty" or "convention" or "agreement" or "charter" or some other name. Some labels, such as "memorandum of understanding," may be viewed as potentially significant if they signal an intention to create a non-legally binding instrument. Nevertheless, if the language of the instrument demonstrates an intent to create a legally-binding instrument, then it will be a treaty no matter its label.

Making Treaties

Representation. Every state has the capacity to make treaties.[9] Further, many contemporary multilateral treaties also provide for certain international organizations to become parties, such as the European Union. Those entities, of course, act through persons. When a state or international organization authorizes a person to represent it in the negotiation or adoption of a treaty, it provides to the person a document referred to as "full powers."[10] Alternatively, if the treaty is being negotiated as part of a multilateral conference, the person's credentials to the conference may serve a similar function.

Negotiation. For a bilateral treaty, the process of negotiation is fairly straightforward. The two states meet for one or more sessions to hammer out the details of the treaty and then normally initial the final text once the negotiation is completed. For a multilateral treaty, the process can be somewhat more complicated. Usually a government or an international organization invites states to participate in the negotiation of the new treaty and hosts the negotiating sessions, which may last several years if there are many states involved and the subject is politically or technically difficult. To indicate that a multilateral negotiation has ended, states *adopt* the treaty, typically by consensus or at least a two-thirds majority vote.[11] Simultaneously, the states may issue a "Final Act" providing a summary of the negotiations, including which states attended, how often they met, and who presided over them. Adoption of a treaty does not mean that the treaty becomes binding upon the states; it simply establishes that the negotiations are over. At the same time as (or just after) adoption, the treaty is often *authenticated*, meaning that the definitive text, including all translations, is certified by such procedure as agreed upon by the states involved.[12]

For example, in 1994, the U.N. General Assembly launched the negotiation of a treaty to establish a permanent International Criminal Court (ICC). Those negotiations lasted four years and entailed several negotiating sessions in New York and Rome. On

---

9. *See* VCLT, *supra* note 3, art. 6.

10. *Id.*, art. 7.

11. *Id.*, art. 9.

12. *Id.*, art. 10.

July 17, 1998, a U.N. diplomatic conference attended by 160 states adopted the "Rome Statute," by a vote of 120 in favor, 7 opposed (including the United States), and 21 abstentions. The Rome Statute was then authenticated by the U.N. Secretariat and sent to all states who participated in the negotiations.[13]

Signature. Once a treaty has been adopted, the manner in which a state consents to be bound to it is usually indicated in the treaty itself. A treaty might provide that a state's *signature* establishes the state's consent to be bound to the treaty.[14] If there is no indication in the treaty that any further steps are anticipated after signature, then signature alone will be regarded as establishing a state's consent to be bound.

A multilateral treaty is normally *opened for signature* for a discrete period of time, such as one year from the date of adoption. At any time during that year, an authorized representative of a state may sign the treaty. Once the period for signing has closed, a state may no longer sign the treaty. Most treaties, however, allow states to *accede* to the treaty after the end of the signature period by filing an instrument of *accession*.[15] For example, the Rome Statute provided that it would be open for signature from July 17, 1998 to December 31, 2000. During that time period, 135 states signed the Rome Statute, including the United States.

Ratification. Often a treaty is written so that a further step by the state is anticipated after its signature, such as *ratification* (also referred to as *acceptance* or *approval*) of the treaty, in which case signature alone does not establish the state's consent to be bound.[16] The principal reason for this second step is that many states have internal constitutional requirements mandating legislative or parliamentary approval of a signed treaty before it becomes binding on the state. For example, in the United States, the president or his representative signs the treaty and it is then sent to the U.S. Senate for advice and consent.[17] Only after receiving such consent, which may require the passage of implementing legislation, may the president proceed to the next step of ratifying the treaty.

When this two-step process exists, a state's signature simply reflects a commitment by the state to pursue whatever measures are necessary to ratify the treaty. Signing does not obligate the state to ratify a treaty; if internal approval is not secured, the VCLT accepts the state's inability to ratify. Having said that, VCLT

---

13. *See* Rome Statute of the International Criminal Court, July 17, 1998, 2187 U.N.T.S. 3 [hereinafter Rome Statute]; *see also* Philippe Kirsch & John T. Holmes, *The Rome Conference on an International Criminal Court: The Negotiating Process*, 93 Am. J. Int'l L. 2 (1999).

14. *See* VCLT, *supra* note 3, art. 12.

15. *Id.*, art. 15.

16. *Id.*, art. 14.

17. *See* Chapter 7(C).

Article 18 provides that, in the period between signature and ratification, a state "is obliged to refrain from acts which would defeat the object and purpose" of the treaty. The exact contours of this obligation are unclear, but it apparently means that a state may not undertake any act that would impede its ability to comply fully with the treaty if the state eventually becomes a party. Thus, State A would probably violate Article 18 if it signed a treaty with State B providing for the free flow of river water from A to B but then, prior to ratification, proceeded to dam several of its rivers that flowed into B.

If a bilateral treaty anticipates ratification, then the instruments of ratification are simply exchanged by the two parties once both have completed their internal processes. If a multilateral treaty anticipates ratification, then the state submits its instrument of ratification to an entity designated as the *depositary* of the treaty, which could be a state or an international organization.[18] For example, the Rome Statute designated the U.N. secretary-general to serve as the depositary.[19] It may take many years for a state to file its instrument of ratification, acceptance, or approval; indeed, the United States took forty years to ratify the 1948 Convention Against Genocide.[20] Further, it is possible for a state to notify the depositary that it has no further intention of seeking ratification (sometimes referred to by non-lawyers as "unsigning" a treaty). Just prior to entry into force of the Rome Statute, the United States decided that it had no intention of pursuing ratification. Therefore, on May 6, 2002, the Department of State notified the secretary-general that "the United States does not intend to become a party to the treaty."[21]

Entry Into Force. A treaty enters into force as agreed upon in the treaty.[22] Bilateral treaties normally provide for entry into force upon or shortly after both sides consent (by signature or exchange of instruments) to be bound. Multilateral treaties normally provide for entry into force within a set period of time after a specified number of states have ratified the treaty. Only once a treaty enters into force does it bind those states who have ratified it. Thus, a state can file its instrument of ratification, yet not become bound until some later point in time when a sufficient number of ratifications have been deposited. After a treaty enters into force, states

---

18.   *Id.*, art. 16.

19.   *See* Rome Statute, *supra* note 13, art. 125.

20.   Convention on the Prevention and Punishment of the Crime of Genocide, Dec. 9, 1948, 78 U.N.T.S. 277 [hereinafter Convention Against Genocide].

21.   Press Statement, Richard Boucher, U.S. Dep't of State, International Criminal Court: Letter to U.N. Secretary General Kofi Annan (May 6, 2002).

22.   *See* VCLT, *supra* note 3, art. 24(1).

who then file instruments of ratification or accession become bound immediately or after the passage of a specified period of time.

For example, the Rome Statute was written so that it would enter into force sixty days after ratification by the sixtieth country.[23] Consequently, the Rome Statute entered into force on July 1, 2002, sixty days after ten states simultaneously filed their instruments of ratification, which made for a total of sixty ratifications.

Reserving to Treaties

When a state consents to be bound to a multilateral treaty, it is sometimes possible for it to file a reservation to the treaty. VCLT Article 2(1)(d) defines a reservation as

> a unilateral statement, however phrased or named, made by a State, when signing, ratifying, accepting, approving or acceding to a treaty, whereby it purports to exclude or to modify the legal effect of certain provisions of the treaty in their application to that State.

Normally, reservations are not made to bilateral treaties, since the two states can simply change the treaty in the course of the negotiations to suit their desires. However, the negotiation of a multilateral treaty often involves so many states that it cannot be drafted to the complete satisfaction of all, so the issue of whether to permit reservations to the treaty presents itself during the course of negotiations. Ideally, even a multilateral treaty containing detailed rights and obligations could be crafted so as to attract widespread adherence without any reservations, for this exposes all state parties to the same detailed rights and obligations. The Rome Statute, for example, is a very detailed treaty that has attracted some 115 parties even though it permits no reservations.[24] Yet states are so diverse worldwide in their political needs and interests, that it is often difficult to achieve consensus on detailed provisions in a treaty. Consequently, the negotiators of a multilateral treaty often are confronted with one of two possible scenarios: (1) adopt a treaty that allows no reservations (and thus preserves uniformity of obligations), but that must be very superficial or that attracts very few parties; or (2) adopt a very substantive treaty that allows reservations (and thus sacrifices uniformity), thereby permitting many states to join because they can make necessary adjustments.

VCLT Article 19 provides that a state may file a reservation unless: (1) the treaty prohibits reservations; (2) the treaty provides for only some reservations, which do not include the reservation in question; or (3) the reservation is incompatible with the object and

---

23. *See* Rome Statute, *supra* note 13, art. 126(1).

24. *Id.*, art. 120.

purpose of the treaty. While it is relatively easy to determine whether (1) or (2) applies, it may be more difficult to determine whether (3) applies. If a state filed a reservation to the Convention Against Genocide saying that it wished to exclude from the definition of "genocide" the mass killing of a particular indigenous group, then such a reservation clearly would be incompatible with the object and purpose of the treaty. In contrast, a reservation by a state to the Convention Against Genocide saying that it did not accept that disputes arising under the convention could be adjudicated by the ICJ would not be regarded as contrary to the object and purpose of the convention, since the object and purpose of the convention is not to ensure the Court's jurisdiction.[25]

Yet determining the exact "object and purpose" of a convention can be difficult, especially for complex treaties, and there may well be no authoritative place to go for an interpretation of the issue.[26] One controversial effort to provide such an interpretation involves the U.N. Human Rights Committee, which was established by the 1966 International Covenant on Civil and Political Rights.[27] The Human Rights Committee consists of eighteen highly respected persons in the field of human rights, operating independent of governments, who are charged with certain tasks, such as reviewing and commenting on periodic reports made by the parties to the Covenant. The Committee has not been empowered, at least expressly, to issue decisions that are binding upon the parties. Nevertheless, in General Comment No. 24 issued in 1994, the Committee stated that it was empowered to opine on the status and legal effect of a party's reservation to the Covenant.[28] Many states have criticized the Committee for adopting such an important role.

In 2001, the International Law Commission (ILC) adopted a *Guide to Practice on Reservations to Treaties*,[29] which in paragraph 3.2 states that treaty monitoring bodies "may assess, within their respective competences, the permissibility of reservations to a treaty formulated by a State" and in paragraph 3.2.2 states that when "providing bodies with the competence to monitor the application of treaties, States or international organizations should specify, where appropriate, the nature and the limits of the competence of such bodies to assess the permissibility of reservations." The *Guide* avoids indicating whether a treaty body such as the U.N. Human Rights Committee has been accorded such competence.

---

25. *See* Advisory Opinion on Reservations to the Convention on Genocide, 1951 I.C.J. 15, 24–26 (May 28).

26. For the European Court of Human Rights' assumption of such a role, see Belilos v. Switzerland, 132 Eur. Ct. H.R. (ser. A) 4 (1988).

27. *See* Chapter 10(C) & (D).

28. *See* Human Rights Committee, General Comment No. 24, U.N. Doc. CCPR/C/21/Rev.1/Add.6 (1994), *reprinted in* 34 I.L.M. 839 (1995) [hereinafter General Comment 24].

29. U.N. Doc. A/66/10, para. 75 (2011).

Assuming that a reservation is deemed by some authoritative body as incompatible with the object and purpose of the treaty, a further question rises as to the effect of that incompatibility. The VCLT does not make clear whether the state is to be regarded as a non-party or as a party who has ratified without making an effective reservation.

In General Comment 24, the U.N. Human Rights Committee took the position that reservations violative of the treaty's object and purpose may be severed from the instrument of ratification, such that the treaty remains "operative for the reserving party without the benefit of the reservation."[30] The ILC's *Guide*, however, in paragraph 4.5.3 sets forth the following rules:

1. The status of the author of an invalid reservation in relation to a treaty depends on the intention expressed by the reserving State or international organization on whether it intends to be bound by the treaty without the benefit of the reservation or whether it considers that it is not bound by the treaty.

2. Unless the author of the invalid reservation has expressed a contrary intention or such an intention is otherwise established, it is considered a contracting State or a contracting organization without the benefit of the reservation.

3. Notwithstanding paragraphs 1 and 2, the author of the invalid reservation may express at any time its intention not to be bound by the treaty without the benefit of the reservation.

4. If a treaty monitoring body expresses the view that a reservation is invalid and the reserving State or international organization intends not to be bound by the treaty without the benefit of the reservation, it should express its intention to that effect within a period of twelve months from the date at which the treaty monitoring body made its assessment.

In most instances, there is no authoritative body available to review the compatibility of a proposed reservation to a multilateral treaty and consequently it is solely reviewed by the non-reserving parties to the treaty. If a non-reserving party regards a reservation as incompatible with the object and purpose of the treaty, then that party should object to the reservation. Yet even if the non-reserving party does not regard the reservation as incompatible with the treaty, it may still wish to object on policy grounds, if it simply does not like the reservation. In either event, a difficult question arises:

30. General Comment 24, *supra* note 28, para. 18.

what happens if some non-reserving states object to the reservation but others do not?

At one time, international law called for *all* other parties to indicate their acceptance of the reservation before the reserving state could become a party to the treaty. This "rule of unanimity," however, was generally abandoned after a 1951 advisory opinion of the International Court found it too cumbersome for contemporary treaty practice.[31] As now expressed in VCLT Articles 20–21, several scenarios are possible for a state that seeks to file a reservation to a multilateral treaty:

1. If a state files a reservation to a multilateral treaty and the treaty expressly authorizes such a reservation, then no acceptance by the other parties is necessary (unless the treaty so provides). The reserving state becomes a party to the treaty with the reservation in force.

2. If the treaty is of a type where it appears that the rule of unanimity should apply because the consent of all parties to the entirety of the treaty is essential, then all the parties must consent to the reservation before the reserving state may become a party. An example would be a multilateral treaty involving just a few states, where a failure of any state to abide by all the terms of the treaty would dramatically change the effectiveness of the regime.[32]

3. If (1) and (2) are not applicable, the reserving state can become a party to the multilateral treaty so long as at least one other state expressly or tacitly accepts the reservation. In such an instance, the treaty enters into force as between the reserving state and the accepting state (and any others who accept the reservation), as modified by the reservation. The reservation does not solely benefit the reserving state; the accepting state has its rights and obligations under the treaty vis-á-vis the reserving state modified to the same extent as that of the reserving state. *Tacit* acceptance occurs when a party is silent for twelve months after being notified that a state has sought to join a treaty subject to a reservation. In practice, this scenario is the one most commonly seen if a treaty permits reservations.

4. A third state might object to the reservation, but unless that state says otherwise, the treaty will enter into force as between it and the reserving state, except that the provi-

---

31. Advisory Opinion on Reservations to the Convention on Genocide, *supra* note 25.

32. Further, when a treaty is the constituent instrument of an interna-

tional organization, a reservation requires the acceptance of the competent organ of the organization, unless the constituent instrument provides otherwise.

sion(s) to which the reservation relates "do not apply to the extent of the reservation."[33] In practice, most objecting states allow the treaty to enter into force as between them and the reserving state.

5. A fourth state may object to the reservation and assert that, as a consequence, the treaty does not enter into force as between it and the reserving state. This scenario is possible, but rarely seen in practice.

One area of uncertainty has been whether there is any difference in the resulting treaty relationship when a state accepts a reservation (scenario 3 above) and when a state objects to a reservation but allows the treaty to enter into force (scenario 4). In situations where the reservation seeks to exclude a provision of a treaty (an "excluding reservation"), there would appear to be no difference in the outcome; a state that accepts a reservation agrees to exclude the provision from the treaty, while a state that objects but allows the treaty to enter into force has in essence decided to allow a treaty relationship but without any "meeting of the minds" on the provision, which results in the provision dropping out of the treaty. Hence, the outcome is the same.

Yet in situations where the reservation seeks to modify a provision of a treaty (a "modifying reservation"), the outcome from the two scenarios is less certain. Some commentators have asserted that this situation is the same as that of an "excluding reservation"; a state that accepts the modification creates a treaty relationship with the modified provision, while a state that objects but allows the treaty to enter into force creates a treaty relationship in which the provision operates except "to the extent of the reservation," which means operates with the modified provision. Other commentators, however, have argued that it makes little sense for the two scenarios to lead to the same result; if a state is objecting to the modification, then the modification should not apply in the treaty relationship. Instead, since there is no meeting of the minds with respect to the content of the provision, the result should be that the treaty enters into force but without that provision at all. The ILC's *Guide* appears to take the latter position, asserting in subparagraphs (3) and (4) of paragraph 4.3.6:

3. To the extent that a valid reservation purports to modify the legal effect of certain provisions of the treaty, when a contracting State or a contracting organization has raised an objection to it but has not opposed the entry into force of the treaty between itself and the author of the reservation, the objecting State or organization and the author of the reservation are not bound, in their treaty relations, by

33. VCLT, *supra* note 3, art. 21(3).

the provisions of the treaty as intended to be modified by the reservation.

4. All the provisions of the treaty other than those to which the reservation relates shall remain applicable as between the reserving State or organization and the objecting State or organization.

For example, suppose there is a multilateral treaty that provides in Article I for free trade in wheat and in Article II for free trade in corn. State A seeks to join the treaty, but files a reservation that once imports of wheat exceed one million tons in a calendar year, Article I no longer applies for that year. If State B accepts this reservation, the treaty is in force as between States A and B, except that if either state exceeds one million tons of wheat imports in a calendar year, that state is no longer obligated to accept such imports from the other state. If State C objects to the reservation but does not reject entry into force of the treaty, then the treaty enters into force between States A and C, and Article I falls out of the treaty. Consequently, the only obligation as between States A and C relates to free trade in corn under Article II. If State D objects to the reservation and declares that it does not regard the treaty as having entered into force, then there is no treaty relationship as between States A and D.

These provisions introduce much greater complexity into the treaty relations of states within a multilateral regime than was the case under the rule of unanimity. Multiple states can file multiple reservations which other states can accept and still other states reject. The consequence can be a treaty regime where there are numerous variations in rights and obligations as between any two parties to the treaty, such that the regime looks more like a network of bilateral treaty relationships than a unified multilateral treaty.

Separate from the filing of reservations, it is also possible in treaty practice for a state to file an "understanding" or "declaration" (reservations, understandings, and declarations are sometimes referred to as "RUDs"). Whereas a "reservation" changes a treaty obligation and requires the acceptance of the other party(ies), an "understanding" is an interpretive statement that clarifies or elaborates upon a treaty provision without altering it. A "declaration" is a statement expressing the state's position or opinion on matters relating the treaty, such as whether to accept an optional form of binding dispute resolution. In the United States, it is also common for the U.S. Senate to include a "proviso" in its consent to the treaty, which relates to an issue of U.S. law or procedure, and is not included in the instrument of ratification deposited or exchanged with other states. "Understandings" can be important when interpreting the meaning of a treaty since, if other states do not object, or offer alternative ones, the understandings might be viewed as evidence of the parties' interpretation of the treaty. When a state files an understanding or declaration that seeks to modify the legal effect of a provision of the treaty, other states may declare that the filing is actually a reservation and may object to the submission in accordance with the procedures discussed above.[34]

Operation of Treaties

Once a treaty has entered into force, the principle of *pacta sunt servanda* provides that each party to the treaty must perform its obligations in good faith. A party cannot invoke the provisions of its national law as grounds for not performing those obligations.[35] Thus, if there is a conflict with national law, the party should seek to alter its law prior to joining the treaty. Normally, a party's obligations under a treaty are not retroactive; they are only prospective in application.[36] When a new treaty conflicts with an earlier treaty, the new treaty will govern with respect to relations between states who are parties to both treaties. If, however, a third state has not joined the new treaty, then that state's treaty relationship with all parties to the earlier treaty remain intact.[37]

Invariably, there is a need to interpret the meaning of treaty provisions. The approach to treaty interpretation advocated by VCLT Articles 31–32 and widely used by states and international tribunals is as follows. First, a "treaty shall be interpreted in good faith in accordance with the ordinary meaning to be given to the terms of the treaty in their context and in the light of its object and purpose." Second, the "context" of the terms of a treaty includes not just the entire text (including its preamble and annexes), but also any agreement relating to the treaty that was made by all the parties in connection with its conclusion (or made by one party and accepted by the others). Third, account should also be taken of any subsequent agreement reached by the parties regarding interpretation of the treaty, any subsequent practice of the parties regarding its interpretation, and any relevant rules of international law applicable to the relations between the parties.

Once an interpretation has been reached following the above steps, it is appropriate to examine the preparatory work (or "legislative history") of a treaty—often referred to as the *travaux préparatoires*—in order to confirm the interpretation. Preparatory work is generally understood to include successive drafts of a treaty and

---

34. *See* Cong. Research Serv., S. PRT. 106–71, Treaties and Other International Agreements: The Role of the United States Senate 11 (2001).

35. VCLT, *supra* note 3, arts. 26–27.

36. *Id.*, art. 28.

37. *Id.*, art. 30.

other records from the negotiations. Resort to preparatory work is also appropriate if the initial interpretation leaves the meaning of the relevant terms ambiguous or obscure, or leads to an absurd or unreasonable result.[38]

In addition to these basic rules, there are interpretive techniques that international lawyers often use, many of which are familiar to national lawyers. For instance, if a particular right or obligation exists only in one part of a treaty (or in one treaty but not in a similar treaty) then, by the *a contrario* principle, the right or obligation does not exist where it is not mentioned.[39] If there are two possible rules that would apply to the same issue, then by the *lex posterior derogat legi priori* principle, the later in time rule should prevail, while by the principle of *lex specialis derogat legi generali*, the specific rule should prevail over the general rule. Such interpretive techniques are rarely dispositive in a dispute; indeed, legal realists will point out that for many such principles there are opposite principles that may be equally employed. Nevertheless, such interpretive techniques are commonly used.

Withdrawal, Termination or Suspension

Treaties often have a provision that provides for their automatic termination after a certain period of time (*e.g.*, ten years after entry into force), or for their automatic renewal after such a period of time unless one of the parties provides advance notice that it wishes the treaty to lapse. Alternatively, many treaties simply provide that they remain in force indefinitely unless a party provides notice of termination, which would then take effect after a certain period of time (*e.g.*, six months).

Prior to the automatic termination of a treaty, a party may withdraw from, terminate or suspend a treaty under certain circumstances. The treaty itself may allow for such action, in which case it occurs in accordance with the terms of the treaty. Further, all the parties to a treaty can agree at any time that a treaty should be terminated or suspended.[40] It is even possible for a few members of a multilateral treaty to suspend the treaty as among themselves, so long as such suspension is not prohibited by the treaty and does not inhibit the rights of those states who have not suspended the treaty.[41]

38. *See* Richard K. Gardiner, Treaty Interpretation (2008).

39. *See, e.g.*, Avena and Other Mexican Nationals (Mex. v. U.S.), 2004 I.C.J. 128, para. 151 (Mar. 31) (stating that the *a contrario* principle should not be applied to the Court's interpretation of the Vienna Convention on Consular Relations).

40. *See* VCLT, *supra* note 3, arts. 54 & 57.

41. *Id.*, art. 58.

Where a treaty contains no provision allowing for withdrawal or termination, the VCLT states that withdrawal or termination is not allowed unless the possibility of withdrawal or termination can be shown from the intent of the parties or can be implied by the nature of the treaty. If such a possibility can be shown, a state must provide at least twelve months advance notice.[42] For many treaties (*e.g.*, boundary treaties, peace treaties, and perhaps human rights treaties), the ability of a state to terminate or withdraw is disfavored.

Termination or suspension of a treaty by a party also may occur when another party has committed a "material breach."[43] A material breach is either a repudiation of a treaty that is not permitted by the treaty or a violation of a provision essential to the object and purpose of a treaty. Termination or suspension of a multilateral treaty on this basis is complicated; a state may only suspend a treaty if it is especially affected by the material breach or the breach radically affects every party to the treaty. Otherwise, all parties to the multilateral treaty (other than the defaulting state) must agree on the steps to be taken in response to the breach.

Further, termination of or withdrawal from a treaty is permitted if performance has become impossible.[44] Impossibility of performance arises when a object which is indispensable for the execution of the treaty permanently disappears or is destroyed. For example, it would be impossible to perform a treaty that imposed rights or obligations with respect to an island which later sank below the seas. The standard for impossibility of performance appears to be a high one; the financial difficulties of a state, for example, are not grounds for claiming impossibility of performance.[45]

Finally, termination of or withdrawal from a treaty is permitted if there has been a fundamental change of circumstances.[46] Changed circumstances (also referred to as *rebus sic stantibus*) occurs when a fundamental change, unforeseen by the parties at the time of the treaty's conclusion, arises with respect to circumstances that were an essential basis of the consent of the parties to the treaty, thus radically transforming the obligations to be performed under the treaty. States have sometimes invoked this doctrine, but international tribunals have resisted applying it, since doing so frequently would undermine the foundation of binding treaty relations. For example, in the *Gabčikovo* case, the International Court rejected the argument that a treaty concluded during the Cold War between two communist governments (Hungary and

---

42. *Id.*, art. 56.

43. *Id.*, art. 60.

44. *Id.*, art. 61.

45. *See* Gabčikovo–Nagymaros Project, *supra* note 6, para. 102.

46. *See* VCLT, *supra* note 3, art. 62.

Czechoslovakia) for the building of hydroelectric projects along the Danube River had been radically transformed by the fall of communism in Eastern Europe, the rise of environmentalism, and the diminishing economic viability of venture.[47]

Under the VCLT, a party seeking to withdraw from a treaty, or to terminate or suspend a treaty, must notify the other parties to the treaty in writing. If there is no objection within three months, the party may proceed. If there is an objection, the VCLT calls for states to resolve the matter through appropriate methods of dispute settlement, including mediation, conciliation or arbitration.[48] An annex to the VCLT outlines a process for conciliation through use of the U.N. secretary-general. For disputes concerning *jus cogens*, either party may take the matter to the ICJ for resolution.

B. Customary International Law

Introduction

As treaties have grown in number and depth, treaty law has become the dominant source of international law. Nevertheless, there are many general topics of international law for which treaties have not been developed, such as on the rules of state responsibility[49] or on head-of-state immunity.[50] Moreover, even if there exists a treaty addressing a particular topic, certain states might not be a party to the treaty and therefore not bound by it. Even if states are bound, treaties typically have gaps or ambiguities that require reference to rules outside the treaty for its application and interpretation.

Consequently, there is a second main source of international law known as customary international law.[51] For a lawyer trained in a common law system (like the United States), it may be helpful to think of customary international law as akin to common law. In other words, there may be a statute (treaty) addressing a particular issue but, if not, then a lawyer may resort to the common law (customary international law) to find the applicable norm.

Unfortunately, there is no single place to look for the rules on formation of customary international law; there is no "Vienna Convention on Customary International Law."[52] Rather, states through their practice, and international lawyers through writings

47. *See* Gabčikovo–Nagymaros Project, *supra* note 6, para. 104.

48. *See* VCLT, *supra* note 3, arts. 65–67.

49. *See* Chapter 6.

50. *See* Chapter 9(B).

51. *See* ICJ Statute, *supra* note 1, art. 38(1)(b).

52. There are, however, useful studies, such as Int'l L. Assoc., *Statement of Principles Applicable to the Formation of General Customary International Law*, Report of the Sixty–Ninth Conference, London (2000). As of 2011, the International Law Commission is set to embark on a study of this source of law.

and judicial decisions, have agreed that customary international law exists whenever two key requirements are met: (1) a relatively uniform and consistent state practice regarding a particular matter; and (2) a belief among states that such practice is legally compelled. Each of these requirements is discussed below, along with the concepts of the "persistent objector" and of *jus cogens*, the relationship of treaties and custom, and certain criticisms of customary international law.

Uniform and Consistent State Practice

The first requirement of customary international law is that there be a relatively uniform and consistent state practice regarding a particular matter. Such state practice can take many forms: acts taken by states in their diplomatic relations with one another; acts taken internally by states through their legislatures or courts; acts taken by states before international organizations; and even inaction by states when they are confronted with a particular matter. Whether the practice of international organizations (*e.g.*, resolutions of the U.N. General Assembly or the work of the International Law Commission) should be included as evidence is more complicated and sometimes controversial. In any event, state practice must be relatively uniform and consistent, but it need not be perfect. Ideally, it should be evident over some extended period of time, rather than a very short period of time. Overturning an existing rule may require a higher level of evidence of state practice than creation of a new rule where none existed before.

For example, in the famous *Paquete Habana* case before the U.S. Supreme Court,[53] the issue was whether coastal fishing vessels of an enemy state could be seized by the United States as prizes of war. There was no treaty on the matter that bound the United States, yet since the Court regarded customary international law as part of U.S. law, it embarked on an analysis of state practice from the 1400's through the 1800's. The Court reached the following conclusion: "By an ancient usage among civilized nations, beginning centuries ago, and gradually ripening into a rule of international law, coastal fishing vessels, pursuing their vocation of catching and bringing in fresh fish, have been recognized as exempt, with their cargoes and crews, from capture as prize of war."[54] Consequently, the Court found that the United States should not have seized the coastal fishing vessel *Paquete Habana* as a prize of war.

The determination that sufficient state practice exists is both a science and an art. In the *Anglo-Norwegian Fisheries* case, the International Court stated that there must be "constant and suffi-

53. *See* Chapter 7(C).   **54.** The Paquete Habana, 175 U.S. 677, 686 (1900).

ciently long practice," but also that "too much importance need not be attached to the few uncertainties or contradictions, real or apparent" that may exist in the practice.[55] Similarly, in *Military and Paramilitary Activities in and against Nicaragua*, the Court stated that "absolutely rigorous conformity with the rule" was not required; rather, "instances of state conduct inconsistent with a given rule should generally [be] treated as breaches of that rule, not as indications of the recognition of a new rule."[56]

In theory, the practice of all states contributes to the creation of customary international law, but on certain topics the practice of some states might be deemed of greater relevance than the practice of others. For example, if the matter concerns the treatment of representatives to international organizations, the practice of states who host major international organizations may be of particular relevance. Further, the practice of larger and more powerful states is often given greater weight than the practice of smaller states, in part because the former are leaders of blocs of states and in part because they are better at publicizing their practice through written digests or other materials.

Scholars have debated whether practice in the form of words is sufficient, or whether there must also be action. For example, some scholars contend that it is a form of state practice when a state affirms before the U.N. General Assembly that it opposes state-sponsored torture, while others contend that what really counts is whether the state is actually engaging in torture at home. On the one hand, a refusal to take account of the state's verbal positions seems to ignore an important and fertile area for assessing state practice; on the other hand, empty rhetoric seems to be a tenuous reed upon which to build legal norms.

Rules of customary international law are often global in nature, but they can also be regional. For instance, in the *Asylum* case,[57] the International Court accepted that there could exist a customary rule of international law special to the states of Latin America regarding the right of a state to issue a unilateral and definitive grant of political asylum. In that case, however, the Court found that Colombia had failed to prove the existence of such a regional customary rule.

Opinio Juris

The second requirement of customary international law is that states engage in their practice out of a belief that they are com-

---

55. Fisheries Case (U.K. v. Nor.), 1951 I.C.J. 116, 138–39 (Dec. 18).

56. Military and Paramilitary Activities in and against Nicaragua (Nicar. v.

U.S.), 1986 I.C.J. 14, 98, para. 186 (June 27).

57. Asylum (Colom. v. Peru), 1950 I.C.J. 266 (Nov. 20).

pelled or permitted by international law. This requirement is referred to as *opinio juris sive necessitatis* (or *opinio juris* for short). The first requirement is referred to as the "objective" element of customary international law, while the requirement of *opinio juris* is referred to as the "subjective" element.

There is, of course, a certain tautology to this second requirement ("state practice cannot become law unless states regard it as law"). Indeed, it is hard to see how customary international law can possibly evolve over time if states must deviate from an existing rule while at the same time regard the deviation as lawful. The principal idea in the *opinio juris* requirement, however, is to distinguish customary international law from everyday customs of states followed out of courtesy or habit. For example, during the visit of a foreign head of state, the host country typically flies the head-of-state's flag alongside the host country's flag at major public events. Such a practice is relatively uniform and consistent worldwide. Yet, no state regards itself as legally obligated to undertake this practice; it is simply a matter of courtesy. If a state failed to fly a foreign head-of-state's flag, it would be regarded as a gaffe and perhaps an insult, but not as a violation of customary international law.

One difficulty in establishing *opinio juris* is that states often engage in a practice without publicly stating whether they believe the practice to be legally compelled. Indeed, to the extent that the relevant practice consists of inaction, there may be no obvious opportunity to articulate such a belief. Consequently, whether *opinio juris* exists is often surmised from the context in which the practice took place.

Persistent Objector Rule

Even if both requirements are met so as to establish a norm of customary international law, a state is not bound if the state persistently objected to the norm as it emerged. This "persistent objector" rule[58] is a nod to the centrality of state consent in international law; if a state refuses to consent to the new norm of customary international law, then the state will not be bound by it. Obviously, if there are a large number of persistent objectors, a customary international law norm cannot emerge at all, for the state practice would not be uniform or consistent. Yet if most states agree on the emergence of a norm, a few "hold out" states will not prevent the norm from coming into existence, but the objector states will not be bound by the norm.

---

58. *See* Jonathan Charney, *The Persistent Objector Rule and the Development of Customary International Law*, 56 Brit. Y.B. Int'l L. 1 (1985).

An example of the persistent objector rule arose in the *Anglo-Norwegian Fisheries* case. In that case, the United Kingdom sought to argue that there existed a customary rule of international law that a state may only draw a "baseline" along its coast[59] in a manner that closes off a bay only if the bay has an opening of ten miles or less. The International Court found that such a rule of customary international law had not yet crystalized, but further found that "[i]n any event, the ten-mile rule would appear to be inapplicable as against Norway, inasmuch as she has always opposed any attempt to apply it to the Norwegian coast."[60] Likewise, in the *Asylum* case, the Court found that even if a Latin American customary rule had emerged regarding the grant of asylum for a political offense, it could not be invoked against Peru, which had rejected the rule by declining to ratify certain treaties. According to the Court, even "if it could be supposed that such a custom existed between certain Latin–American States only, it could not be invoked against Peru, which, far from having by its attitude adhered to it, has on the contrary repudiated it."[61]

Concept of Jus Cogens

In Chapter 1(B), reference was made to the concept of *jus cogens* (peremptory norms), which the VCLT defines as a norm "accepted and recognised by the international community of States as a whole as a norm from which no derogation is permitted and which can be modified only by a subsequent norm of general international law having the same character."[62] One way to think about *jus cogens* is as "super" customary international law—law so fundamental to the inter-relationship of states that a state cannot, through its treaty practice or otherwise, deviate from the law. At the same time, *jus cogens* appears not to arise from the normal processes of customary international law; the emphasis is less on consensual state practice and more on notions of universal morality or justice. Perhaps for that reason, there is often disagreement on which norms are *jus cogens*. There are only a handful of decisions by international tribunals that help clarify the matter. Thus, the ICJ has referred to the prohibition on the use of force by one state against another as "a conspicuous example" of *jus cogens*, the Inter–American Court of Human Rights has advised that the prohi-

---

59. *See* Chapter 11(B).

60. Fisheries Case, *supra* note 55, at 131.

61. *Asylum*, *supra* note 57, at 277–78.

62. VCLT, *supra* note 3, art. 53; *see* Draft Articles on Responsibility of States for Internationally Wrongful Acts, art.

40, cmt., paras. 2–3, *in* Report of the ILC on the Work of its Fifty-third Session, U.N. GAOR, 56th Sess., U.N. Doc. A/56/10 (2001). A classic article is Alfred von Verdross, *Forbidden Treaties in International Law*, 31 AM. J. INT'L L. 571 (1937); *but see* Georg Schwarzenberger, *International Jus Cogens?*, 43 TEX. L. REV. 455, 467 (1964–65) (doubting the existence of *jus cogens*).

bition against racial discrimination is *jus cogens*, and the International Criminal Tribunal for the former Yugoslavia declared that the prohibition against state-sponsored torture "has evolved into a peremptory norm or *jus cogens*, that is, a norm that enjoys a higher rank in the international hierarchy than treaty law and even 'ordinary' customary rules."[63] It seems that prohibitions on genocide, slavery, and forced disappearances might also qualify.

As an abstract notion, *jus cogens* reflects a belief that certain important norms of international law have a superior claim to authority and therefore trump other norms; it is a concept that seeks to bind states together in a fragmented world. Yet, the practical application of *jus cogens* may not be particularly significant (*e.g.*, two states typically do not enter into a treaty for the purpose of enslaving their citizens or persistently object to the existence of a customary rule against slavery) unless the range of *jus cogens* norms expands. Further, the significance of declaring a norm as *jus cogens* is not always clear. In the *Al-Adsani* case, the European Court of Human Rights declared that the prohibition against state-sponsored torture is a peremptory norm of international law, but then proceeded to find that the norm did not override state immunity, at least in the context of a civil claim brought before a national court.[64]

One future area of relevance for *jus cogens* may be with respect to international organizations. The U.N. Security Council in recent years has issued binding orders that some argue deny states their inherent right of self-defense (*e.g.*, the arms embargo on Bosnia–Herzegovina in the early 1990's) or deny individuals certain fundamental human rights (*e.g.*, ordering Libya to extradite two individuals; freezing the assets of suspected terrorists without prior notice or ability to be heard). While the powers accorded to the Security

63. Military and Paramilitary Activities in and against Nicaragua, *supra* note 56, at 100, para. 190; Advisory Opinion on Juridical Condition and Rights of Undocumented Migrants, 18 Inter–Am. Ct. Hum. Rts. (ser. A) No. 18, paras. 98–101 (Sept. 17, 2003); Prosecutor v. Furundzija, Judgment, Case No. IT–95–17/1–T, para. 153 (Int'l Crim. Trib. former Yugo. Dec. 10, 1998). Various decisions of the Inter–American Commission on Human Rights have also declared norms as *jus cogens*. *See, e.g.*, Domingues, Case 12.285, Inter–Am. C.H.R., Report No. 62/02, paras. 45–46, 64 (2002) (regarding death penalty for juvenile offenders).

In 1995, several states urged the ICJ to determine that certain principles of international humanitarian law, such as the prohibition on causing unnecessary suffering to combatants, be regarded as *jus cogens*, but the Court—although noting that such norms "constitute intransgressible principles of international customary law"—declined to explicitly reach the *jus cogens* issue. *See* Advisory Opinion on Legality of the Threat or Use of Nuclear Weapons, 1996 I.C.J. 226, 258, paras. 79 & 83 (July 8).

64. Al–Adsani v. United Kingdom, 24 Eur. H.R. Rep. 11 (2002). U.S. courts on several occasions have declined to set aside immunity in the face of an alleged *jus cogens* norm. *See, e.g.*, Ye v. Zemin, 383 F.3d 620 (7th Cir. 2004); Hwang Geum Joo v. Japan, 332 F.3d 679 (D.C. Cir. 2003); Siderman v. Argentina, 965 F.2d 699 (9th Cir. 1992).

Council under the U.N. Charter are wide-ranging, governments, courts and scholars might resort to notions of *jus cogens* in challenging the legality of such actions.[65]

Relationship of Treaties and Custom

Treaty law and customary international law can and do exist side-by-side. An important dynamic within international law is the manner in which treaties shape and develop customary international law.

For example, in *Military and Paramilitary Activities in and against Nicaragua*, the International Court found that customary international law on the right of a state to use force against another state exists separately from such rules as contained in the U.N. Charter, even where the two categories of law are largely identical. Moreover, while the rules set forth in the U.N. Charter may have initially diverged from customary international law at the time the Charter was adopted in 1945, "the Charter gave expression in this field to principles already present in customary international law, and that law has in the subsequent four decades developed under the influence of the Charter, to such an extent that a number of rules contained in the Charter have acquired a [customary] status independent of it."[66] In other words, new rules on the use of force established in a treaty (the U.N. Charter) had influenced state practice and thereby passed into customary international law.

A more recent example concerns a series of disputes between Ethiopia and Eritrea. A claims commission had to decide whether the 1949 Geneva Conventions could be invoked by the two states with respect to their 1998–2000 armed conflict. Eritrea had only acceded to the conventions in August 2000 and thus was not—as a matter of treaty law—bound to them for most of the armed conflict. However, the claims commission found that customary international law was "exemplified by the relevant parts of the four Geneva Conventions of 1949."[67] The commission noted: (1) the widespread acceptance by states of the conventions over the course of their fifty-year existence; (2) that law of war treaties "build upon the

---

65. *See* ANTONIOS TZANAKOPOULAS, DISOBEYING THE SECURITY COUNCIL: COUNTERMEASURES AGAINST WRONGFUL SANCTIONS (2011).

66. Military and Paramilitary Activities in and against Nicaragua, *supra* note 56, at 92, paras. 172–82. The Court had to reach such a finding because the U.S. acceptance of the Court's jurisdiction prevented the Court from deciding a matter arising under a multilateral treaty unless all the parties to the treaty were before the Court. Since all the parties to the U.N. Charter were not before the Court, the Court could not pass directly upon the rules embedded in the U.N. Charter, but could pass upon the rules of customary international law.

67. Partial Award on Prisoners of War, Ethiopia's Claim No. 4, para. 32 (July 1, 2003), *reprinted in* 42 I.L.M. 1056, 1062 (2003).

foundation laid by earlier treaties and by customary international law"; and (3) that "rules that commend themselves to the international community in general . . . can more quickly become part of customary international law than other types of rules found in treaties."[68] Consequently, the commission found that Ethiopia and Eritrea were bound throughout their conflict to rules of customary international law as reflected in the 1949 Geneva Conventions.

Virtually all states of the world are parties to both the U.N. Charter and the 1949 Geneva Conventions, so it is not difficult to see how those treaties may be regarded as reflecting customary international law. Treaties that have secured lower levels of ratification may or may not support the existence of a customary rule. On the one hand, a treaty such as the Convention Against Genocide—to which 142 out of 193 states are party—may well reflect customary international law, especially since Article I of the treaty is written not to "create" a new crime, but to "confirm" that genocide is a crime under international law. On the other hand, there is an obvious tension in finding that states who have declined to join a treaty are nevertheless bound to the same obligations as a matter of customary international law, for doing so renders largely meaningless the significance of joining the treaty. Indeed, absent evidence to the contrary, there is a respectable argument that a new treaty is not codifying existing customary international law since, if it were, there would be no need for the treaty. Further, the treaty might not reflect new customary international law since several states have declined to join (hence, there is insufficient uniformity to establish a customary rule). Finally, even if a treaty supports the existence of a new customary rule, it might be argued that states' refusal to join is, in effect, a persistent objection to the application of the new norm to them.

Some provisions of a treaty may be regarded as reflecting customary international law, while other provisions may not. For example, many states (including the United States) regard the VCLT provisions on treaty interpretation[69] as codifying customary international law. However, other provisions of that convention are not regarded as codifying customary international law, nor as having altered state practice over time so as to crystalize a new rule of customary international law. For example, as noted in at the end of Section A above, VCLT Article 66 provides for settlement of certain treaty disputes by the ICJ. Yet only a state's express acceptance by treaty of an international tribunal's jurisdiction (*e.g.*, by ratifying the VCLT) would be viewed as a basis for such jurisdiction.

---

68. *Id.*, paras. 30–31.

69. *See* VCLT, *supra* note 3, arts. 31–32.

Since there is no hierarchy between the different sources of international law, in theory customary international law can evolve and overtake treaty law. For example, the 1958 Convention on the High Seas proclaimed that areas outside a state's territorial seas were high seas, and thus open to all for fishing. Nevertheless, in the *Fisheries Jurisdiction* cases, the International Court found that international custom had evolved by 1974 to allow a coastal state to establish exclusive rights to a fishing zone extending up to twelve nautical miles from its coast, even though beyond its territorial sea.[70] Thus, international custom overtook a pre-existing treaty norm. Moreover, if the new customary norm is *jus cogens* in nature, then "any existing treaty which is in conflict with that norm becomes void and terminates."[71] Nevertheless, it is generally thought that the existence of a treaty between two states establishes a legal relationship with respect to the treaty's subject matter, with customary rules simply filling in the gaps.

Criticisms of Customary International Law

In addition to the apparent tautology in *opinio juris* noted above, customary international law has been criticized on many grounds.[72] First, some scholars observe that it is an imprecise source of international law. Unlike a treaty, where the relevant rule is expressed in writing, a customary rule of international law is divined from the practice of states, which may vary over time. There are no clear rules on what level of consistency or uniformity must exist in the practice, on how long the practice must exist, or on what types of practice count. Nuances, gradations, or exceptions in that practice, therefore, may be missed or misinterpreted.

Second, even if precise rules on the formation of customary international law existed, critics note how difficult it is to analyze the practice of all 193 states worldwide and even more difficult to determine whether such practice operates in conjunction with *opinio juris*. Finding such practice at best is enormously time-consuming and at worst impossible.

Third, critics note that given the difficulty of ascertaining such practice, customary international law analyses sometimes rely on the practice of just a handful of states, especially the developed countries that have resources to publish digests and other public

---

70. *See* Fisheries Jurisdiction (U.K. v. Ice.), 1974 I.C.J. 3 (July 25); Fisheries Jurisdiction (F.R.G. v. Ice.), 1974 I.C.J. 175 (July 25).

71. VCLT, *supra* note 3, art. 64.

72. *See generally* ANTHONY D'AMATO, THE CONCEPT OF CUSTOM IN INTERNATIONAL LAW (1971); Jack L. Goldsmith & Eric A. Posner, *A Theory of Customary International Law*, 66 U. CHI. L. REV. 1113 (1999); J. Patrick Kelly, *The Twilight of Customary International Law*, 40 VA. J. INT'L L. 449 (2000).

information.[73] As such, purportedly neutral assessments may mask the privileging of the practice of just some states over that of others. Alternatively, critics charge that such analyses often give up trying to scrutinize the actual day-to-day practice of states and instead rely on very abstract, general, and non-binding "declarations" or "resolutions" issued by states at politically-charged meetings, which may not be consistent with actual practice nor reflect the considered legal views of states.

Fourth, critics maintain that the imprecision in this source of law accords far too much latitude to decision-makers of powerful states or of tribunals for "finding" whatever customary rule suits their objectives. Indeed, some critics question whether customary international law really exerts any independent normative force; arguably, states agree to and follow customary international law only when it is in their national self-interest, and argue that it has "changed" when it is not.

C.   General Principles of Law

A third source of international law consists of "general principles of law."[74] Like customary international law, there is no treaty or other instrument that clearly spells out what is meant by "general principles of law." The late Professor Oscar Schachter identified several different ways that this category has been used.[75]

First, this source can mean principles that *exist in the national laws* of states worldwide. For example, the principle that "no one shall be a judge in his own cause" exists in national laws worldwide. As such, it may be transposed to an international legal setting, perhaps to preclude a state from voting on a matter before an international body which is adjudicating the wrongfulness of the state's action. Another example would be the principle that "any breach of an engagement involves an obligation to make reparation."[76] These "general principles of law" appear to have been what the drafters had in mind when they crafted the original provision of the Statute of the Permanent Court of International Justice, but the language used—"the general principles of law recognized by civilized nations"—does not actually refer to national law.

Second, this source can mean general principles of law derived from the *specific nature of the international community*. Such principles might include *pacta sunt servanda*,[77] the principle of non-intervention by one state in the affairs of another, and the principle

---

73. *See* Chapter 15(C).

74. ICJ Statute, *supra* note 1, art. 38(1)(c).

75. OSCAR SCHACHTER, INTERNATIONAL LAW IN THEORY AND PRACTICE 50–55 (1991).

76. Factory at Chorzów (Ger. v. Pol.), 1928 P.C.I.J. (ser. A) No. 17, at 29 (Sept. 13).

77. *See* Chapters 1(B) & 3(A).

of the legal equality of states. These principles are often referred to by states, tribunals, and scholars, but are not derived from legal principles operating in national laws. Rather, they arise from the rudimentary character of the society of sovereign states.

Third, this source can mean principles *intrinsic to the idea of law*. For example, the principles of *res judicata* (a final judgment on the merits is conclusive as between the parties) or of *lex posterior derogat priori* (the later supercedes the earlier law, if both have the same source) are principles that seem basic to the very idea of law. Of course, principles of this type also exist in national legal systems, such that principles falling in the first type discussed above might fit within this type as well. The emphasis here, however, is less on empirically showing the existence of a principle in national legal systems worldwide, and more on simply identifying whether the principle is basic to the very notion of "law."

Fourth, there are general principles of law that appear to arise from notions of justice or fairness. Principles barring discrimination on the basis of race or gender, or favoring equity and reciprocity, appear to fall into this category. Many of these principles are now captured in treaties and other instruments in the field of human rights, but might also operate as sources of law independent of those instruments.

For example, in the *River Meuse* case, Judge Hudson asserted in his individual opinion that the Permanent Court of International Justice was authorized to consider principles of "equity" as part of its application of "general principles of law." In that context, Judge Hudson argued that "where two parties have assumed an identical or a reciprocal obligation, one party which is engaged in a continuing non-performance of that obligation should not be permitted to take advantage of a similar non-performance of that obligation by the other party."[78] In that case, the Netherlands claimed that Belgium was constructing certain canals that would divert water from the Meuse in violation of an 1863 agreement, but the Netherlands itself previously had constructed a lock affecting the river's water level and flow rate.

In the *Corfu Channel* case, the International Court stated that Albania was obligated to notify the shipping community of the existence of a minefield in Albanian territorial waters due to "certain general and well-recognized principles, namely: elementary considerations of humanity, even more exacting in peace than in war; the principle of the freedom of maritime communications; and

---

78. Diversion of Water from the Meuse (Neth. v. Belg.), 1937 P.C.I.J. (ser. A/B) No. 70, at 77 (June 28) (individual opinion by Judge Hudson); *see also* Application of the Convention on the Prevention and Punishment of the Crime of Genocide (Bosn. & Herz. v. Serb. & Montenegro), 2007 I.C.J. 43, paras. 114–20, 124–28 (Feb. 26).

every State's obligation not to allow knowingly its territory to be used for acts contrary to the rights of other States."[79]

D. Subsidiary Sources: Courts and Scholars

The ICJ Statute describes as a source of international law "judicial decisions and the teachings of the most highly qualified publicists of the various nations, as a subsidiary means for the determination of rules of law."[80] Thus, reference may be made to the decisions of courts and the writings of scholars when identifying the content of international law. The assertion that these are "a subsidiary means" of determining the law is an acknowledgment that courts and scholars do not themselves create international law. Rather, they engage in a review of the other sources (treaty, custom, general principles of law) and then reach conclusions as to what the law is. These subsidiary sources are extremely important in clarifying the existence of norms, such as whether a customary rule of international law has emerged. The better reasoned the judicial decision or opinion of the scholar, and the more prestigious the court or scholar, the more persuasive it will be as a source.

With respect to courts, the principle of *stare decisis* does not operate for the International Court,[81] nor other international courts or arbitral tribunals. Consequently, their decisions do not directly bind states or matters outside the confines of the particular case. Having said that, judicial or arbitral decisions (especially of the International Court) serve as extremely persuasive authority in subsequent cases. Typically, the prior court or tribunal reached a particular finding by reviewing all other relevant sources. Rather than repeat the same analysis, one can simply cite to the prior decision in support of an analogous finding. Such an approach is well-known to lawyers trained in the common law, where judicial precedent is regularly used in support of a legal position. International courts and tribunals are especially likely to refer to and rely upon prior judicial decisions, since doing so promotes their own authority and legitimacy, and increases respect for and adherence to their decisions by states. It should be noted that reference to "judicial decisions" in the ICJ statute need not be limited to international decisions. The decisions of national courts as to the content of international law are also often referred to and relied upon as evidence of that law.

With respect to scholars, there are a variety of highly regarded treatises on international law generally and in various specialized

---

79. Corfu Channel (U.K. v. Alb.), 1949 I.C.J. 4, 22 (Apr. 9).

80. ICJ Statute, *supra* note 1, art. 38(1)(d).

81. *Id.*, art. 59 ("The decision of the Court has no binding force except between the parties and in respect of that particular case.").

fields, many of which are identified throughout this volume. There are also high quality, peer-reviewed international law journals, such as the *American Journal of International Law*, the *International and Comparative Law Quarterly*, and the *European Journal of International Law*, whose articles are given close attention, at least when they purport to identify existing international law (as opposed to proposals for improving international law). Moreover, there are groups of esteemed scholars whose work can be influential in establishing the content of international law. For example, the U.N. International Law Commission,[82] consisting of thirty-four highly regarded individuals in the field of international law, issues reports on various topics of international law that are often relied upon by states and international courts. In the *Gabčikovo-Nagymaros* case, the International Court referred to the work of the ILC on the rules of state responsibility even before that work had been completed.[83] Additionally, a prestigious group of U.S. scholars of international and foreign relations law were tasked by the American Law Institute to develop the 1987 *Restatement (Third) of the Foreign Relations Law of the United States*.[84] Because of the reputation of those individuals, and the scholarly quality of the *Restatement*, both U.S. and international courts often refer to the *Restatement* as evidence of the content of international law.

E. Law–Making by International Organizations

Introduction

In addition to the "traditional" sources referred to in Article 38 of the ICJ Statute, there are other ways that international law is created. A particularly important additional source is law created by international organizations. International organizations, of course, can launch or host negotiations of treaties, but in that event the ultimate source of the law is the treaty itself. The source at issue in this sub-section is law actually generated by an organ of an international organization that is regarded as binding upon the member states of that organization.

Such law arises from many types of international organizations and the manner in which it becomes binding on states can differ considerably. To demonstrate such law, this sub-section discusses in detail the law-making by two particular organs of international organizations: the U.N. Security Council and the Council of the International Civil Aviation Organization.

---

82. *See* Chapter 2(B).

83. *See* Gabčikovo–Nagymaros Project, *supra* note 6, at 55, para. 83.

84. Restatement (Third) of the Foreign Relations Law of the United States (1987) (2 vols.).

An Emergent World Legislature? The U.N. Security Council

Under Chapter VII of the U.N. Charter, the Security Council has the authority to determine the existence of any "threat to the peace, breach of the peace, or act of aggression," and to authorize either non-forcible or forcible measures to restore peace and security.[85] All member states are bound by such decisions.[86]

When the Security Council adopts a measure under Chapter VII, it creates a legal norm that previously did not exist and that binds all U.N. member states. Thus, when the Security Council imposes economic sanctions on a state (as it has done in recent years with respect to Haiti, Libya, the former Yugoslavia, and others), a legal norm is created that not only prohibits those states from importing goods or services but also prohibits all other states from engaging in such trade with that state. In this sense, the Security Council has "legislated;" it has created a norm that binds all states without any further requirement of consent by those states. The Security Council has also legislated by creating new sub-organs, such as: the *ad hoc* war crimes tribunals for the former Yugoslavia and Rwanda, set up to investigate and prosecute war criminals;[87] the U.N. Compensation Commission, created to quantify and pay damages caused by Iraq's 1990 invasion of Kuwait; or the Iraq–Kuwait Boundary Commission, established to demarcate the Iraq–Kuwait boundary.[88] Creation of these institutions, particularly the *ad hoc* war crimes tribunals, was criticized by some scholars and even some states as outside the scope of the Security Council's powers. Those doubts explain, in part, the decision to create a permanent International Criminal Court by use of a multilateral treaty rather than through Security Council legislation.

Such Security Council actions, however, were exercised only in fairly discrete situations that targeted particular states. In recent years, the Security Council has begun using its legislative authority in a manner that is more general and abstract in imposing legal obligations on all states. Security Council Resolution 1373—adopted in the aftermath of the terrorist attacks of September 11, 2001—provided that "all States shall ... [f]reeze without delay funds and other financial assets or economic resources of persons who commit, or attempt to commit, terrorist acts or participate in or facilitate the commission of terrorist acts."[89] Further, the resolution required all states to criminalize the perpetration of terrorist acts.[90] The resolution also established a committee of the Security Council

85. U.N. Charter arts. 39, 41 & 42; *see* Chapter 14.

86. *See* U.N. Charter art. 25.

87. *See* Chapter 13(D).

88. *See* S.C. Res. 687 (Apr. 3, 1991).

89. S.C. Res. 1373 (Sept. 28, 2001).

90. *Id.*, para. 2(e).

(which comprises all Council members and meets in closed session) to receive and review reports from states on the steps they have undertaken to criminalize terrorist financing and to adopt regulatory regimes intended to detect, deter, and freeze terrorist funds (the "Counter–Terrorism Committee"). In essence, this committee is charged with determining whether states have appropriate legislative and executive measures in place (or contemplated) that give effect to Resolution 1373 and associated resolutions.

Resolution 1373 is more generic in character than prior Security Council resolutions under Chapter VII. Rather than create a new legal norm or norms with respect to a particular state, terrorist organization, or person, the resolution requires all states to adhere to new norms that affect organizations and persons worldwide. The obligations contained in the resolution are similar to those that might exist within a treaty; indeed, several of the obligations do exist in the International Convention for the Suppression of the Financing of Terrorism,[91] a convention not in force at the time Resolution 1373 was adopted.

Similarly, in 2004, the Security Council adopted Resolution 1540, which imposed various general obligations on all states to prevent non-state actors from acquiring weapons of mass destruction.[92] Among other things, the Security Council ordered states to develop effective measures to account for and secure the production and storage of such weapons and related materials, to maintain appropriate border controls to detect illicit trafficking, and to develop national export and trans-shipment controls over such items. Again, the resolution created a committee charged with monitoring states' implementation of the resolution (the "1540 Committee").

Whether the Security Council will to continue to embark on "legislation" of general norms is unclear, but such actions certainly reflect a new form of international law creation that was previously the provenance of multilateral treaties. To the extent that the Security Council continues with such actions, it will fuel interest in whether there are limits to the power of the Security Council when acting under Chapter VII and whether the Security Council is a legitimate forum for such legislating.[93]

Transnational Public Regulation: The ICAO

Introduction. Law-making by the U.N. Security Council may seem quite unique; no other organ of an international organization is provided such robust authority in creating legal rights and

---

91. Dec. 9, 1999, 39 I.L.M. 270.

92. *See* S.C. Res. 1540 (Apr. 28, 2004).

93. *See* Stefan Talmon, *The Security Council as World Legislature*, 99 Am. J. Int'l L. 175 (2005).

obligations for states. Nevertheless, there are several less-noticed areas of transnational cooperation where states have relinquished significant sovereign rights in order to establish regimes of transnational public regulation—regimes that serve key public benefits in creating an infrastructure for the transnational movement of persons, goods, and services. These regimes exist in areas such as civil aviation, telecommunications, postal services, health, environmental protection, maritime transport, banking and other forms of financial regulation, law enforcement, intellectual property, and labor standards.

The emergence of these regimes has prompted new avenues of study about the nature of such "global governance" and whether it should be understood as a form of "global administrative law." Two scholars reflecting upon such developments have asserted that

> much of global governance can be understood as regulation and administration and that we are witnessing the emergence of a "global administrative space": a space in which the strict dichotomy between domestic and international has largely broken down, in which administrative functions are performed in often complex interplays between officials and institutions on different levels, and in which regulation may be highly effective despite its predominantly non-binding forms. In practice, the increasing exercise of public power in these structures has given rise to serious concerns about legitimacy and accountability, prompting patterns of responses to those concerns in many areas of global governance. Accountability problems are addressed through greater transparency, through notice-and-comment procedures in rule-making, and through new avenues of judicial and administrative review, in a vast array of disparate areas, such as global banking regulation.[94]

The only way to truly understand these regimes is to study them very closely, for they are complex both on the international level and on the level of their reception into national law, and there are significant differences among them. Having said that, there are certain salient features that these regimes have in common. Rules are promulgated at a global level in order to be effective and efficient. These rules need to change over time in response to technical advances; one-shot codification in a static treaty is inadequate. The area being regulated requires highly detailed rules in order for the system to work; broad treaty language is insufficient. The subject matter at issue is important, but is usually not politically sensitive nor characterized by significant policy differences

94. Nico Krisch & Benedict Kingsbury, *Introduction: Global Governance and Global Administrative Law in the* *International Legal Order*, 17 Eur. J. Int'l L. 1 (2006).

among states (whether developed or developing). As such, states are willing to cede control over rule-making to an international body. Finally, crafting of the rules typically is driven by a consensus achieved among technical experts of those states with the greatest expertise in the area. As such, one phenomenon of these regimes is the transfer of power from diplomats in highly public arenas to intergovernmental networks of experts often operating behind closed doors.[95]

Moreover, these regimes are characterized by methods of rule promulgation that allow for enactment of new rules or amendment of existing rules in a fairly expeditious fashion, resulting in rules that bind the membership as a whole absent individual states "opting" out in an *ad hoc* fashion. Thereafter, while adherence to these rules is by no means uniform, states largely comply by conforming their national laws and through the decisions of national courts. Explanations for such compliance may be found in the nature of the rules (non-political, uncontroversial, technical) and because states accrue benefits from the well-functioning of these regimes.

Regulation of Civil Aviation. One of the best examples of such transnational public regulation is the regime governing international civil aviation. Each year, some two billion passengers are transported worldwide on scheduled civil aviation flights, with several hundred million traveling transnationally. Further, civil aviation transports some thirty million tons of freight worldwide, of which about nineteen million tons occurs transnationally.[96] This extraordinary movement of persons, goods and services across boundaries cannot be regulated through bilateral or regional cooperation; to do so would likely result in a patchwork of potentially-conflicting regulatory systems that would impede the ability of civilian aircraft to transit the globe.

Consequently, in 1944 states adopted the Chicago Convention on International Civil Aviation,[97] which created the International Civil Aviation Organization (ICAO). At present, ICAO is a specialized agency of the United Nations, in which 190 of 193 states participate. The Chicago Convention established within the convention itself certain important substantive rights and obligations— such as the exclusive sovereignty of a state over the airspace above its territory.[98] At the same time, the convention set up a process for

---

95. *See generally* ANNE–MARIE SLAUGHTER, A NEW WORLD ORDER (2004). For a discussion in the context of international criminal law, see Jenia Iantcheva Turner, *Transnational Networks and International Criminal Justice*, 105 MICH. L. REV. 985 (2007).

96. *See* WATS: WORLD AIR TRANSPORT STATISTICS (55th ed. 2011).

97. Dec. 7, 1944, 61 Stat. 1180, 15 U.N.T.S. 295 [hereinafter Chicago Convention].

98. *Id.*, art. 1.

the adoption and amendment of "annexes" to the convention containing detailed, technical rules that regulate the safety of international air navigation and the facilitation of air transport.[99]

The central player in the adoption of the annexes to the convention is an ICAO organ that is a subset of the entire membership. The Chicago Convention created the ICAO Assembly, an organ consisting of representatives of all states that meets approximately every three years to undertake broad ICAO tasks, such as setting overall policy and approving ICAO's triennial budget. However, the Chicago Convention also created the ICAO Council, an organ consisting of representatives from just thirty-six states elected by the Assembly.[100] Among other things, the ICAO Council is charged with adopting international "standards" and "recommended practices" (referred to as "SARPs") and with designating them as "annexes" to the convention.[101] The SARPS deal with a wide range of issues concerning international civil aviation, including communications systems and air navigation aids, characteristics of airports and landing areas, and rules of the air and air traffic control practices. The fundamental provisions of the SARPs appear in the main body of the annexes, while more detailed, technical specifications may be placed either in appendices to the annexes or in manuals.

The process for developing the SARPs begins when a proposal is advanced by any ICAO member state, by ICAO itself, or by a different intergovernmental or non-governmental organization. The proposal is then placed before one of the ICAO subsidiary bodies of technical experts—the Air Navigation Commission (ANC), the Air Transport Committee, or the Committee on Unlawful Interference with Aircraft.

Most standards fall within the domain of the ANC, which consists of fifteen aviation experts nominated by member states and appointed by the ICAO Council. While these experts are typically government employees, they are expected to function independently of their states. The ANC considers a proposal through a variety of methods: by holding meetings of the ANC; by setting up conferences, technical panels, study groups, or sub-committees of experts who report back to the ANC; or by exchanging correspondence among ANC members. In effect, these methods allow all ICAO states the opportunity to voice their views regarding the proposal.

The ANC is assisted in its work by the ICAO Secretariat and in particular by the secretariat's Air Navigation Bureau. The ICAO Secretariat helps analyze the comments received from states and international organizations, and prepares a working paper on the

---

99. *Id.*, art. 12.   **101.** *Id.*, art. 54(*l*).
100. *Id.*

comments and the Secretariat's proposals for action. The ANC then establishes the final text of the proposed SARP and presents it to the Council.

The Council must then adopt the annex (or proposed amendment to an annex) by a two-thirds vote, whereupon all ICAO member states are so notified. The annex then "shall become effective within three months" (or after a longer period if so decided by the Council), unless a majority of ICAO member states "register their disapproval with the Council."[102] Since the inception of ICAO, there has never been a majority vote registering such disapproval. In practice, the ICAO Council provides that an annex (or amendment) shall become "effective" within four months from the date of adoption, so as to allow time for preparation and transmittal of the annex/amendment to states. Once the annex becomes "effective," ICAO practice normally allows for a further period of at least four months before it becomes "applicable," thereby allowing time for states to bring their national laws and regulations into conformance. All told, it takes an average of two years from the time a new SARP is proposed before it becomes applicable.

Thus, annexes to the Chicago Convention may be adopted by an ICAO organ of limited membership (the ICAO Council) that then become applicable as against the entire membership. When the Chicago Convention entered into force in April 1947 (after ratification by twenty-six states), the convention had twelve technical annexes. As of 2011, there are eighteen annexes, containing numerous SARPs, on matters such as age requirements for pilot certification, the types of information contained on an airworthiness certificate, or the duties of airplane operators handling dangerous goods.

Whether states must automatically comply with the SARPs can be analyzed through three layers of obligation. In the first layer, one must distinguish between a SARP that is a "standard" and a SARP that is a "recommendation." SARPs enacted as "standards" generally require conformance unless the state takes some action to opt out of the rule, whereas "recommendations" merely require a state to seek conformance.

In the second layer of obligation, the Chicago Convention allows states to opt out of, or escape from, conformance to "standards" where it is impracticable to comply and where such impracticality is notified to ICAO. If a member state takes no action, it is deemed to have tacitly consented to the new rule, and thereby "undertakes to keep its own regulations" with respect to the "rules of the air" for aircraft flying over its territory "uniform, *to the*

---

102. *Id.*, art. 90(a).

greatest possible extent, with those established" under the Chicago Convention.[103] Further, each member state "undertakes to collaborate in securing the highest *practicable* degree of uniformity in regulations, standards, procedures, and organization in relation to aircraft, personnel, airways and auxiliary services in all matters in which such uniformity will facilitate and improve air navigation."[104] By contrast, if a member affirmatively opts out of the new obligation on grounds of impracticality, it must notify ICAO, in which case it assumes no commitment. Thus, standards become binding on states not through the normal process of ratification that is found for norms embedded in international treaties, but rather through a "tacit consent/opt-out" procedure.

In the third layer of obligation, there are certain kinds of SARPs that appear to bind member states without any ability to opt out. For example, each state is required to adopt measures to ensure that aircraft of its nationality flying over the high seas— seas outside the territory or territorial waters of a state—conform with ICAO regulations on the "rules of the air" (*i.e.*, rules relating to flight and maneuver of aircraft).[105] Similarly, Article 33 provides that member states must "recognize as valid" certificates of airworthiness and licenses to pilots that are issued or validated by another member state, so long as the certificate or license meet the minimum standards set by ICAO.[106] States have no ability to opt out of such rules.

F. Non–Legally Binding Norms ("Soft Law")

The traditional sources of international law do not take account of non-legally binding norms, even though such "soft law" may have important effects on the ordering of relations among international actors and, over time, on the formation of international law. States (and non-state actors) see certain advantages in developing such norms. States are often less cautious about negotiating and concluding non-legally binding norms; thus, negotiation and conclusion of the norm can occur more quickly and with less procedural or bureaucratic obstacles at both the international and national level. Compromises may be more easily achieved and there may be greater flexibility for involving non-state actors. International relations theorists would explain that "contracting costs" and "sovereignty costs" are lower, making agreement more likely. Despite being non-legally binding, such norms are taken seriously by state and non-state actors (they are usually regarded as at least "politically-binding"), and once agreed upon may have the effect of

103. *Id.*, art. 12 (emphasis added).
104. *Id.*, art. 37 (emphasis added).
105. *Id.*, art. 12.

106. For the reception of ICAO rules into United States law, see Chapter 7(C).

narrowing the options that would otherwise be legally-available. These norms may also begin a process of delegitimizing an existing rule of international law and may even serve as a basis for invoking a rule of international law, such as the principles of good faith or estoppel.[107]

Non-legally binding norms may be found in various places, including: (1) treaty provisions that call only for general cooperation among states or that bind states only to reach agreement on a matter in the future; (2) non-treaty declarations or political pacts issued by states that set forth certain aspirations; (3) resolutions of international organizations that are recommendatory in nature; and (4) codes of behavior that states or non-state actors operating transnationally are invited to adopt. Examples of each are discussed in turn.

Vague or General Treaty Provisions

One form of "soft law" may be found in treaty provisions that are too abstract to be implemented automatically, that call only for general cooperation among states, or that bind states only to reach agreement on a certain matter sometime in the future. As ICJ Judge Richard Baxter once wrote:

> [T]here are norms of various degrees of cogency, persuasiveness, and consensus which are incorporated in agreements between States but do not create enforceable rights and duties. They may be described as "soft" law, as distinguished from the "hard" law consisting of treaty rules which States expect will be carried out and complied with.[108]

For example, Article 105 of the U.N. Charter provides that the United Nations "shall enjoy in the territory of each of its Members such privileges and immunities as are necessary for the fulfillment of its purposes." This provision is so vague with respect to the norm being expressed that it requires further elaboration before it can have a serious legal effect.[109]

Some treaty provisions simply call for generalized cooperation among states when possible and appropriate. Article 5 of the Convention on Biological Diversity states: "Each Contracting Party shall, as far as possible and as appropriate, cooperate with other Contracting Parties, directly or, where appropriate, through competent international organizations, in respect of areas beyond national jurisdiction and on other matters of mutual interest, for the

---

107. *See generally* COMMITMENT AND COMPLIANCE: THE ROLE OF NON–BINDING NORMS IN THE INTERNATIONAL LEGAL SYSTEM (Dinah Shelton ed., 2000).

108. R.R. Baxter, *International Law in "Her Infinite Variety,"* 29 INT'L & COMP. L.Q. 549, 549 (1980).

109. *Id.* at 552–53.

conservation and sustainable use of biological diversity."[110] Language of this nature is so vague and susceptible to myriad interpretations that it provides little if any normative guidance.

Similarly, Article 2 of the 1985 Vienna Convention for the Protection of the Ozone Layer provides that parties shall "cooperate in the formulation of agreed measures, procedures and standards for the implementation of this Convention, with a view to the adoption of protocols and annexes."[111] This provision is essentially an "agreement to agree" about the specific measures to be taken by the parties; it is not "hard" law in the sense of compelling any concrete action other than a general obligation to cooperate.

Part of the importance of such "soft law" derives from the fact that it can lead to "hard" law over time. Thus, Article 105 of the U.N. Charter served as a basis for encouraging states to enter into subsequent, more detailed treaties: the General Convention on the Privileges and Immunities of the United Nations, and the Headquarters Agreement concluded between the United Nations and the United States.[112] The Biodiversity Convention also served as a basis for promoting more detailed cooperation among states through global and regional agreements and through the adoption of national legislation. Conventions like the Vienna Convention for the Protection of the Ozone Layer have been referred to as "framework conventions" because they represent only the first step in an effort to achieve detailed norms. In that case, the framework convention envisaged subsequent agreements on specific emissions obligations as scientific knowledge developed. In 1987, the parties adopted the Montreal Protocol on Substances that Deplete the Ozone Layer[113] which, in contrast to the framework convention, provided for the progressive reduction by specified dates of the production and consumption of ozone-depleting chemicals listed in the protocol's annexes.

Declarations or Political Pacts by States

A second form of "soft law" may be found in non-treaty declarations or political pacts issued by states that set forth certain aspirations. For example, in the field of international environmental law, there are numerous non-binding declaratory instruments or action programs made by states for the purpose of promoting the environmentally sound management of resources.[114] None of these instruments are viewed by the states that agreed to them as legally

---

110. Art. 5, June 5, 1992, 1760 U.N.T.S. 79, 31 I.L.M. 818.

111. Art. 2(2)(c), Mar. 22, 1985, T.I.A.S. 11,097, 1513 U.N.T.S. 293.

112. *See* Chapter 2(B).

113. Sept. 16, 1987, S. Treaty Doc. No. 100–10 (1987), 1522 U.N.T.S. 3.

114. *See, e.g.,* Agenda 21: Program of Action for Sustainable Development, Rio de Janeiro, U.N. Doc. A/CONF.151/26 (1992).

binding and, unlike treaties, none are subject to a process of ratification. Such non-legally binding statements are an important means by which the international community pursues a consensus on environmental values, but they are not regarded as themselves altering existing international or national law.

A good example of a political pact is the Final Act of the 1975 Helsinki Conference on Security and Co-operation in Europe (CSCE).[115] The Final Act was not concluded as a treaty; the states participating did not regard it as creating legally-binding norms, nor submit the instrument to their national legal processes for approval as a treaty. The instrument was not registered with the United Nations or anywhere else as a treaty. Nevertheless, the Final Act was an extremely important political development, as it entailed an agreement by the leaders of thirty-three East and West European states (as well as Canada and the United States) in the midst of the Cold War era. Through a series of carefully formulated provisions spanning some sixty pages on security, economics, and human rights, the Western states in essence accepted the territorial security of the communist regimes in Eastern Europe in exchange for the Eastern states making significant political commitments to human rights. While the Final Act was not itself legally binding, it made reference to numerous legal principles. Among other things, the inclusion of human rights provisions in the Final Act thereafter made it difficult for East European states to claim that human rights was a matter left to their national jurisdictions. Consequently, at follow-up conferences Western states repeatedly charged that Soviet bloc states were violating human rights norms.

Whether such criticisms hastened the demise of those communist regimes is open to question (many believe they did). Regardless, over time the continued interactions of the participating states in the CSCE has influenced the development of human rights standards on both the international and national level, and more broadly helped identify linkages between security and human rights. In 1994, the CSCE became the Organization for Security and Co-operation in Europe (OSCE) which, with a current membership of some fifty-five states, is engaged in a broad range of activities, including arms control, counter-terrorism, conflict prevention, and democratization.[116]

Recommendatory Resolutions of International Organizations

A third form of "soft law" may be found in widely-accepted resolutions of international organizations, even though those reso-

---

115. Aug. 1, 1975, *reprinted in* 14 I.L.M. 1292 (1975).

116. *See* THE CONFERENCE ON SECURITY AND CO-OPERATION IN EUROPE: ANALYSIS AND

BASIC DOCUMENTS, 1972–93 (Arie Bloed ed., 2d ed.1993).

lutions are not legally binding. If the international organization has expertise or recognized competence with respect to a particular matter, if there is near-universal participation of states in the work of the organization, if a resolution is adopted with little or no dissent, and if it is adopted in a manner that speaks to the existence of an international legal norm, then such a resolution (even if not technically legally binding) can have a very powerful influence on the development of international law.

The U.N. General Assembly has the authority to adopt some binding resolutions (*e.g.*, relating to the budget of the United Nations). Most of its resolutions, however, may only be in the form of recommendations[117] and therefore (unlike the Security Council's resolutions when acting under Chapter VII) are non-legally binding. Nevertheless, on several occasions the General Assembly has adopted resolutions that speak to legal norms and that have strongly influenced the practice of states and decisions of international and national tribunals.

For example, in 1946 the U.N. General Assembly unanimously adopted a resolution in which it "affirm[ed] that genocide is a crime under international law which the civilized world condemns, and for the commission of which principals and accomplices—whether private individuals, public officials or statesmen, and whether the crime is committed on religious, racial, political, or any other grounds—are punishable."[118] The style of the language is important, in that the states of the world did not purport to create a new crime under international law but, rather, to recognize an *existing* crime. As such, it may be regarded as reflecting the *opinio juris* of the global community, which is important when considering the status of customary international law. Such a resolution may also serve to legitimize conduct occurring elsewhere, such as the prosecution of Nazi war criminals before the Nuremberg Tribunal. Finally, the resolution may accelerate the conclusion of a legally-binding treaty that contains the norm. As discussed in Section A above, the 1948 Convention Against Genocide—adopted two years after the 1946 resolution—stated in Article I that the parties *"confirm* that genocide, whether committed in time of peace or in time of war, is a crime under international law which they undertake to prevent and to punish."[119]

Giving General Assembly resolutions such weight is more controversial when the resolution is not adopted by a large majority representing the various groups of states worldwide, and even more so when it purports to progressively develop (as opposed to simply codify) international law. A good example of this controversy con-

---

117. *See* U.N. Charter arts. 13–14.

118. G.A. Res. 96(I) (Dec. 11, 1946).

119. Convention Against Genocide, *supra* note 20, art. I (emphasis added).

cerns the interpretation of General Assembly resolutions address-ing expropriation of property. A 1962 General Assembly resolution asserted that when a state nationalizes or expropriates the property of an alien (*e.g.*, when a host government seizes a foreign oil company's extraction facilities), such expropriation must be done in accordance with international law,[120] which would entail the pay-ment of full compensation. The 1962 resolution was adopted by a vote of 87–2 (12 abstentions), with wide support from both devel-oped and developing states. By contrast, later General Assembly resolutions in 1973–74[121] provided that such expropriation may occur solely in accordance with the national law of the expropriat-ing state, and thus could entail little or no compensation. The 1973–74 resolutions, however, were passed with small but solid blocs of developed states in opposition. Further, a draft of one resolution purported to be progressively developing the law. Final-ly, the resolutions were inconsistent with the state practice at the time. Consequently, when a dispute between an oil company and Libya was taken to international arbitration, the arbitrator deter-mined that the 1962 resolution reflected "the state of customary international law existing in this field" and that the later resolu-tions did not.[122]

In its *Nuclear Weapons* advisory opinion, the International Court of Justice stated:

> The Court notes that General Assembly resolutions, even if they are not binding, may sometimes have normative value. They can, in certain circumstances, provide evidence important for establishing the existence of a rule or the emergence of an *opinio juris*. To establish whether this is true of a given General Assembly resolution, it is necessary to look at its content and the conditions of its adoption; it is also necessary to see whether an *opinio juris* exists as to its normative character. Or a series of resolutions may show the gradual evolution of the *opinio juris* required for the establishment of a new rule.[123]

Codes of Behavior for States or Non–State Actors

A final form of "soft law" may be found in codes of behavior that states are invited to adopt as part of their national law, or that

120. *See* G.A. Res. 1803 (June 14, 1962).

121. *See* G.A. Res. 3171 (Dec. 13, 1973); G.A. Res. 3201 (May 1, 1974); G.A. Res. 3281 (July 26, 1974).

122. Texaco Overseas Petroleum v. Libya, paras. 87–88 (Int'l Arb. Awd. Jan. 19, 1977), *reprinted in* 17 I.L.M. 1, 30 (1978).

123. Advisory Opinion on Legality of the Threat or Use of Nuclear Weapons, 1996 I.C.J. 226, 254–55, para. 70 (July 8).

non-state actors operating transnationally are invited to adopt as part of their internal governance.

Food Safety Codes for Adoption by States. A good example of one such code concerns the development of food safety standards. In 1962 the Food and Agriculture Organization (FAO) and the World Health Organization (WHO) jointly launched a "foods standards program," and created a new entity called the Codex Alimentarius Commission to implement the program. As of 2011, more than 180 states are members of the commission, representing more than ninety-five percent of the global population. Over the past half-century, the Codex Alimentarius has emerged as a key mechanism for harmonizing national food standards worldwide, serving both to protect the health of consumers and ensure fair practices in food trade. It does so not by creating norms that directly bind states; rather, it suggests norms that states choose to adopt because it is in their interests to do so. In this sense, the norms are different from those of the ICAO regime discussed above, yet the ultimate effect is largely the same in the coordination of global legal standards.[124]

The commission meets in plenary session every two years, alternating between the FAO's headquarters in Rome and the WHO's headquarters in Geneva. Each member state sends a delegation to the session; while typically headed by a senior governmental official, delegations often include representatives from industry, consumers groups, and academia. In between meetings of the Codex Commission, there are meetings of subsidiary bodies and committees open to all Codex members.

The process for developing Codex standards—which typically extends over a period of several years and is not governed by a set timetable—is as follows. Any state (or a committee of the commission) may submit a proposal for a new Codex standard. Either an executive committee or the commission itself must then decide whether the new standard should be developed, at which point a proposed draft standard is prepared by the permanent secretariat of the commission (based in Rome) and circulated to all member states. Comments from states are considered by one of the Codex's subsidiary bodies, after which the secretariat presents a draft standard to the commission. If the recommended standard is adopted, it is sent to all states for their acceptance. Once the commission determines that an appropriate number of acceptances has been received, the standard is added to the Codex Alimentarius. The standard can be revised over time, using the same process set forth above, as scientific knowledge develops.

124. For an overall summary of the current program, see FAO/ WHO, Un-   DERSTANDING THE CODEX ALIMENTARIUS (1999).

The entire process is characterized by the involvement of not only states, but multiple ministries within states (*e.g.*, agriculture and health), concerned international organizations, and non-state actors, such as industrial groups (*e.g.*, food processors and distributors), scientific or technical professional groups, and consumer groups. For instance, U.S. Codex activities are coordinated by representatives from the Departments of Agriculture, Commerce, Health and Human Services, and State, as well as from the Center for Disease Control and Prevention, the Environmental Protection Agency, the Food and Drug Administration, and the U.S. Trade Representative.

The Codex Alimentarius contains several hundred standards.[125] The standards adopted may be commodity specific or general standards applicable to all foods. The standards typically are formatted uniformly and are very precise and detailed. Currently, the standards are published in thirteen volumes of the Codex Alimentarius, with the initial volumes focusing on general standards and the latter volumes on commodity specific standards.

Upon adoption, the standards are not regarded as legally binding upon states. Rather, the standards reflect a code of conduct which states may accept or reject. The process for signaling such acceptance, however, is a formal one. States may accept a standard through: (1) full acceptance; (2) acceptance with specified deviations; and (3) free distribution. When a state asserts that it "fully" accepts the Codex standard, it is agreeing that it will only permit the distribution within its territory of products to which the standard conforms. When a state accepts the standard with specified deviations, it can opt out of, or escape from, conformance with certain aspects of the norm where it is impracticable to comply and where such impracticality is notified to the commission. When a state agrees to "free distribution," it is saying that it will only allow distribution within its territory of products generally conforming to the "relevant requirements" of a Codex standard. Of course, a state can simply refuse to accept the Codex standard, but it may find that the goods it produces cannot easily be exported, since other states may have accepted the standard.

In part to develop national positions before the commission, many states have established a national "Codex Committee." The U.S. National Codex Committee, for example, is composed of officials from various government agencies and is chaired by the Food Safety and Inspection Service at the Department of Agriculture.

Multinational Corporate Codes of Conduct. A second example of such codes of behavior may be found in codes of conduct that seek to constrain socially undesirable behavior of transnational non-

125. *See* <http://www.codexali mentarius.net>.

state actors. Such "public welfare" codes of conduct typically focus on multinational corporations (MNCs), which are corporations with affiliated business operations in more than one country. Many MNCs operating in developing countries have done what one would expect them to do in a free market—seek out the least expensive means of conducting operations so as to maximize profits. Yet as human rights, labor rights, and environmental rights continue to advance within the global consciousness, the practices of many MNCs in developing countries have been regarded as out of step with social expectations. This gap, in turn, has led to strident criticism of MNC activity, and sometimes to consumer backlash whereby MNCs are faced with demands for products certified as having been produced without adverse social consequences.

MNCs themselves recognize this divergence and consequently many have embraced the movement toward voluntary codes of conduct that inculcate key norms in the fields of labor, human rights, consumer protection, anticorruption, and the environment. Although these codes have taken many shapes and sizes, they generally can be characterized in the following manner. The codes are voluntary in nature; MNCs are invited to pledge themselves to the code rather than forced to do so. The codes typically consist of a series of principles, standards or guidelines, which are either broad and aspirational or more detailed and operational. The codes may draw on or refer to international law norms, may focus on MNC adherence to local laws, and/or may call for adherence to norms articulated solely in the code itself. A code might be developed *ad hoc* for a specific company (sometimes referred to as an "operational" or "internal" code). Alternatively, a code might be developed for a class of companies in a particular field (*e.g.*, the apparel or extractive industries) or for companies generally (sometimes referred to as "model" or "external" codes), which can then lead to the creation of associated operational codes. The codes are often drafted by private sector entities, usually bringing together a range of stakeholders such as labor, environmental, religious, and corporate groups. The codes might be drafted under the auspices of governments or by government representatives working through international organizations, although even then relevant stakeholders are typically a part of the drafting process.

Once a code is established, an MNC can pledge itself publicly to the code and then develop internal corporate rules or policies based on the code. MNC managers are trained to comply with those rules and policies in corporate decision-making and operations. While the codes normally call upon the MNC to make public its adherence, further transparency may not be required. Different techniques of monitoring, verification, audits, or certification might be an element of a particular code, but the codes often do not require such steps by an entity external to the MNC. Since the codes are voluntary, MNCs are not exposed to any criminal or civil penalties in the event they fail to abide by the them (MNCs remain, of course, exposed to penalties if they violate relevant national laws). Thus, the codes are legally unenforceable.

Since the codes are voluntary in nature, they are not written to impose onerous constraints. Instead, the codes are crafted to promote conduct that, although it entails some costs, brings even greater benefits to the MNC. Costs include the basic expenses involved in altering internal corporate rules and policies, training personnel regarding the new policies, pursuing any associated internal or external monitoring, verification, audits, or certification, and internalizing costs that had previously been externalized (*e.g.*, paying higher wages or avoiding environmental harms). The benefits to MNCs can take various forms. There might be internal cost savings, such as from more efficient use of resources (*e.g.*, achieved when pursuing waste reduction) or from having a healthier and more productive work force. Cost savings may also arise if adherence to the code allows the MNC to save on insurance premiums or have access to capital at lower rates, if insurers or lenders are concerned about possible adverse consequences of MNC activities. To the extent a code is adopted by an MNC's competitors, it may assist in creating a level playing field for the MNC so that its "good" corporate conduct does not put it at a competitive disadvantage. Finally, by adhering to such a code, the MNC may enjoy an enhanced public image, thus avoiding shareholder dissatisfaction, consumer boycotts of MNC goods or services, labor unrest, and undesirable regulation by its host or home government.

Over the past thirty years, with the rise of MNC activities in the developing world, these codes have proliferated.[126] In the field of human rights, the U.N. Sub–Commission on the Promotion and Protection of Human Rights (a subsidiary organ of the U.N. Commission on Human Rights, as noted in Chapter 10(D)) adopted in 2003 a code on the responsibilities of transnational corporations.[127] The code recognizes that states have the primary responsibility for the promotion and protection of human rights, but also asserts that MNCs have similar obligations. The code then sets forth six types of rights or obligations that MNCs must observe: (1) the right to equal opportunity and non-discriminatory treatment; (2) the right

---

126. For a compendium containing short descriptions of several codes, see U.S. COUNCIL FOR INTERNATIONAL BUSINESS CORPORATE RESPONSIBILITY COMMITTEE, US-CIB COMPENDIUM OF CORPORATE RESPONSIBILITY INITIATIVES (2002).

127. *See* U.N. Office of the High Commissioner for Human Rights, Sub-Commission on the Promotion and Protection of Human Rights, *Norms on the Responsibilities of Transnational Corporations and Other Business Enterprises with Regard to Human Rights*, 55th Sess., U.N. Doc. E/CN.4/Sub.2/2003 /12/ Rev.2 (2003).

to security of persons; (3) the rights of workers, such as against forced labor or child labor, remuneration that ensures an adequate standard of living, and to collective bargaining; (4) respect for national sovereignty (*e.g.*, refraining from bribery) and human rights (*e.g.*, right to food and drinking water); (5) obligations with regard to consumer protection; and (6) obligations with regard to environmental protection, such as complying with relevant national and international laws.

The sub-commission's code, however, was opposed by many corporations and governments, such that it was not adopted by the U.N. Human Rights Commission. Instead, the commission asked the U.N. secretary-general in 2005 to appoint a special representative to help clarify international standards that regulated corporations. The secretary-general appointed John Ruggie, who did not accept the idea that human rights law directly imposed duties on corporations, except with respect to the most heinous of violations (*e.g.*, forced labor or human trafficking). Instead in 2008, Ruggie submitted to the Human Rights Council (the successor to the Human Rights Commission) a report setting forth his view as to the current "framework" for business and human rights, which consisted of three broad principles: the duty of the state to protect against human rights abuses by corporations; the responsibility of corporations to respect human rights; and a need for more effective remedies to curb human rights abuses by corporations. The second principle arose not directly from international human rights law but, rather, from "societal expectations," which could be enforced both through national laws and public opinion.[128]

At the request of the Human Rights Council, Ruggie then produced, in June 2011, the *Guiding Principles on Business and Human Rights,* consisting of thirty-one more detailed principles organized into three sections, which correspond to the broad principles set forth in the 2008 framework.[129] For example, principle 15 provides:

> In order to meet their responsibility to respect human rights, business enterprises should have in place policies and processes appropriate to their size and circumstances, including:
>
> (a) A policy commitment to meet their responsibility to respect human rights;

---

128. Special Representative of the Secretary–General, *Protect, Respect and Remedy: A Framework for Business and Human Rights*, U.N. Doc. A/HRC/8/5 (2008); *see* John Gerard Ruggie, *Business and Human Rights: The Evolving International Agenda*, 101 Am. J. Int'l L. 819 (2007).

129. Special Representative of the Secretary–General, *Guiding Principles on Business and Human Rights: Implementing the United Nations "Protect, Respect and Remedy" Framework*, U.N. Doc. A/HRC/17/31, annex (2011).

(b) A human rights due-diligence process to identify, prevent, mitigate and account for how they address their impacts on human rights;

(c) Processes to enable the remediation of any adverse human rights impacts they cause or to which they contribute.

In July 2001, the Human Rights Council adopted the *Guiding Principles* by consensus.[130]

MNC codes of conduct need not be developed through the United Nations or its specialized agencies; smaller groupings of states (such as the twenty-seven member European Union[131]) and even individual states have also pursued such codes. For example, the Swiss government convened various "stakeholders" so as to develop an International Code of Conduct for Private Security Service Providers (ICoC), which sets forth a series of obligations for security contractors derived from international humanitarian and human rights law.[132] Codes drafted by smaller groups of states allow for greater specificity than global codes, since they are usually negotiated among governments with similar attitudes (*e.g.*, among a group of developed states). While they are more limited in geographic scope, they can be highly relevant if the principal concern is the conduct of MNCs based within a bloc of states.

For example, in June 1976, the Council of Ministers of the Organization of Economic Cooperation and Development (OECD) adopted a declaration on international investment and multinational enterprises, which contains a set of guidelines for multinational enterprises.[133] The guidelines establish recommended standards for good conduct for all MNCs operating in or from OECD countries, including practices relating to taxation, financing, and information disclosure. Furthermore, the guidelines contain an "employment and industrial relations" section prohibiting discrimination in the employment or promotion of personnel, establishing a general standard that MNCs should respect the right of their employees to be represented by trade unions, and containing other protections for laborers. The guidelines also include a section on environmental protection, stating that MNCs should take due account of the need to protect the environment and avoid creating environmentally-

---

130. Human Rights Council Res. 17/4, U.N. Doc. A/HRC/RES/17/4 (2011).

131. *See* Resolution on E.U. Standards for European Enterprises Operating in Developing Countries: Towards a European Code of Conduct, EUR. PARL. DOC. A4–0508/98 (1998), 1999 O.J. (C 104).

132. *See* International Code of Conduct for Private Security Providers, 50 I.L.M. 89 (2011).

133. *See* OECD, *Guidelines for Multinational Enterprises*, 15 I.L.M. 969 (1976), *as revised*, OECD, *OECD Guidelines for Multinational Enterprises: 2011 Edition* [hereinafter *OECD Guidelines*].

related health problems and setting forth various means for doing so. The most recent revision of the guidelines, adopted in 2011, augments these protections by including a new policy stating that MNCs should "[r]espect the human rights of those affected by their activities consistent with the host government's international obligations and commitments."

One difficulty in regulating MNC behavior is that an MNC may not exercise corporate control over its suppliers or distributors. The OECD guidelines address this corporate structure problem by calling upon MNCs to "encourage, where practicable, business partners, including suppliers and subcontractors, to apply principles of corporate conduct compatible with the *Guidelines.*"[134] Recommendations also address the elimination of child labor and forced labor, improving internal environmental management, and contingency planning for environmental impacts. The sections on disclosure and transparency also have been updated to encourage social and environmental accountability. Finally, the guidelines contain sections on combating corruption and consumer protection and reference international law by calling for respect for human rights.[135]

The guidelines, however, are not legally mandatory on either OECD governments or OECD-based companies. Rather, the declaration containing the guidelines represents a political commitment on the part of OECD governments to foster such corporate conduct, and reflects the values and aspirations of OECD members. Both corporate and labor groups were involved in the drafting of the guidelines, and thus it has enjoyed the general support of both communities. Each OECD member has a "national contact point" (usually part of a government agency) charged with promoting the guidelines within the member state and gathering information on adherence to them.[136] Disputes concerning the guidelines can and have been referred to the OECD's Committee on Investment and Multinational Enterprises (CIME), a political body with no means of enforcing its decisions.

---

134. *OECD Guidelines*, § II(A)(13).

135. *Id.*, §§ II–VII.

136. The national contact point for the United States is the director of the U.S. Department of State's Office of Investment Affairs.

Further Reading:

José E. Alvarez, *International Organizations as Law–Makers* (2005).

Anthony Aust, *Modern Treaty Law and Practice* (2d ed. 2007).

Chris Brummer, *Soft Law and the Global Financial System* (2012).

Michael Byers, *Custom, Power and the Power of Rules* (1999).

Vladimir Duro Degan, *Sources of International Law* (1997).

Duncan B. Hollis et al., eds., *National Treaty Law and Practice* (2005).

Jan Klabbers, *An Introduction to International Institutional Law* (2d ed. 2009).

Martti Koskenniemi, ed., *Sources of International Law* (2000).

Brian D. Lepard, *Customary International Law: A New Theory with Practical Applications* (2010).

Arnold McNair, *Law of Treaties* (2d ed. 1961).

Ulrika Morth, ed., *Soft Law in Governance and Regulation: An Interdisciplinary Analysis* (2004).

Alexander Orakhelashvili, *Peremptory Norms in International Law* (2006).

Anne Peters et al., eds., *Non-State Actors as Standard Setters* (2009).

Shabtai Rosenne, *The Law of Treaties: A Guide to the Legislative History of the Vienna Convention* (1970).

Dan Sarooshi, *International Organizations and Their Exercise of Sovereign Powers* (2005).

Dinah Shelton, ed., *Commitment and Compliance: The Role of Non–Binding Norms in the International Legal System* (2000).

Ian Sinclair, *The Vienna Convention on the Law of Treaties* (2d ed. 1984).

Anne–Marie Slaughter, *A New World Order* (2004).

Mark E. Villiger, *Commentary on the 1969 Vienna Convention on the Law of Treaties* (2009).

Mark E. Villiger, *Customary International Law and Treaties: A Manual on Theory and Practice of the Interrelation of Sources* (2d ed. 1997).

Ralf Wetzel & Dietrich Rausching, *The Vienna Convention on the Law of Treaties: Travaux Préparatoires* (1978).

Chapter 4

INTERNATIONAL LAW
INTERPRETATION
AND DISPUTE RESOLUTION

Just as there is no global legislature to create international law, there is no global court with all-embracing jurisdiction to interpret vague or ambiguous rules of international law, or to resolve disputes among international actors. Nevertheless, interpretation of international law and international dispute resolution occur all the time, in various ways and before various fora. Though these processes are not centralized, they are fairly robust and often effective. Many treaty regimes require states to follow one or more of these processes when there is a disagreement arising under the treaty. In particular, international law seeks to channel frictions between states into mechanisms for pacific resolution as a means of avoiding armed conflict. Chapter VI of the U.N. Charter provides:

> The parties to any dispute, the continuance of which is likely to endanger the maintenance of international peace and security, shall, first of all, seek a solution by negotiation, enquiry, mediation, conciliation, arbitration, judicial settlement, resort to regional agencies or arrangements, or other peaceful means of their own choice.[1]

In the first instance, states (and non-state actors) seek to resolve ambiguities in the law or avoid disputes through direct discussion, which may take the form of negotiation (where two or more states engage in a dialogue) or of consultation (where a state intends to pursue a course of action and so notifies others). If disagreement remains after those measures, states may agree to bring in a third party to assist through mediation or conciliation. If a more formal method of resolving the matter is required, resort may be made to arbitration or judicial settlement. No method is inherently superior to the others, but all are regarded as preferable to the resort to armed force in interstate relations. Each of these methods of international law interpretation or dispute resolution are discussed in this chapter.

---

1. U.N. Charter art. 33(1).

A. Negotiation, Notification, and Consultation

Negotiation

States are constantly engaged in a process of interpreting their rights and obligations under international law, whether the matter relates to trade law, extradition, protection of intellectual property, or one of the many other subjects of international law. For most governments, this task falls to members of the legal office of the foreign ministry or other ministries with transnational responsibilities. International organizations and other non-state actors also engage in the process of interpretation to determine their rights and obligations, or to educate or lobby states.

The text of treaties or the customary practice of states principally guide the interpretive process. International or national decisions that have previously addressed a matter also can provide guidance, as can scholarly writings. On certain issues there may exist extensive precedent, such that the need for interpretation is minimal. As in national law, common understandings develop over time concerning how to interpret even the most ambiguous and vague international norms—understandings that then remain settled and stable. On new issues, such as whether and how to regulate the transnational effects of the Internet, there may be little precedent to assist in the interpretive process.

Inevitably, two states may disagree about a norm of international law or about the application of that norm to a particular set of facts. When such disagreements arise, the first recourse is usually for the two states to engage in bilateral discussions. Thus, when the United States believed in the 1990's that the European Community was violating its obligations under the General Agreement on Tariffs and Trade (GATT) by failing to allow imports of U.S. beef, policy-makers and lawyers for the U.S. Department of State and U.S. Trade Representative Office contacted their counterparts in the Europe. Through such discussions, the underlying facts of the dispute were clarified and the relevant GATT provisions identified. It is always possible that one side comes away from such a discussion satisfied that it had the facts wrong, or that its legal interpretation is not sustainable or desirable in the long-term.

If the dispute remains, however, the two sides may engage in detailed negotiations in an effort to find a resolution. These negotiations typically occur face-to-face, through contacts between an embassy and its host government, or through the dispatch of a delegation from one government to the capital of the other. Despite modern technology, negotiations by telephone or Internet remain uncommon, perhaps due to the need to include persons from various governmental agencies in the negotiations. Such negotiations may take days or years, involving a few simple issues or a range of complex issues.

Negotiations may involve matters of general importance to states, such as how to interpret an arms control treaty, or may concern matters of importance only to certain persons within a state. For instance, when there is an abrupt breakdown in overall relations between two states (perhaps due to a war or a radical change in one of the state's governments), State A may expropriate the property within its territory of State B's nationals, while State B may freeze any assets of State A that are within State B's territory. At whatever point the two states normalize their relations (which might occur years later), a bilateral negotiation typically occurs whereby State B's nationals are compensated for their losses and State A's assets are returned. The agreement often will involve the payment by State A to State B of a "lump sum," which may be less than the total loss sustained by State B's nationals. State B might then run a national claims program for distribution of the sum to its affected nationals on a *pro rata* basis.[2]

The settlement reached between the United States and Iran concerning the shoot-down of Iran Air Flight 655 is a good example of a complex bilateral negotiation. On July 3, 1988, a U.S. navy cruiser operating in the Persian Gulf (the USS *Vincennes*) fired two missiles at what the captain thought was an attacking aircraft, but which turned out to be an Iranian civilian airliner. The airliner was downed, killing its 290 passengers and crew. The United States immediately expressed its regret for the incident and offered to pay compensation to the families of the victims. However, the offer was not to pay money *directly* to the government of Iran, since Iran was considered to be a state sponsor of terrorism. Further, the United States maintained that Iran was partially responsible since the *Vincennes*, at the time of the incident, was engaged in surface warfare with Iranian gunboats and Iran had allowed the airliner to take off from a joint military/civilian airfield and fly over the area of the surface engagement. Consequently, the offer was to pay compensation only for the families of the victims, not for the lost aircraft. Finally, from the U.S. perspective, the shooting of the airbus was incidental to lawful military conduct and was not internationally wrongful. Therefore, the compensation should only be paid *ex gratia* (a payment out of kindness, without accepting legal liability). Iran, in contrast, believed it was entitled under international law to compensation for both the victims and the aircraft, since it was the *Vincennes* that had initiated the surface

2. *See, e.g.*, Burns H. Weston et al., International Claims: Their Settlement by Lump Sum Agreements, 1975–1995 (1999); Richard B. Lillich & Burns H. Weston, International Claims: Their Settlement by Lump Sum Agreements (1975) (2 vols.).

warfare and either intentionally or in gross negligence shot down the airliner.

With the two states at an impasse, Iran sued the United States in 1989 at the International Court of Justice (ICJ). After filing various written pleadings, the United States and Iran commenced intensive negotiations in an effort to resolve the dispute. In August 1994, the two sides agreed in principle to the general terms of a settlement, and then proceeded to sort out the details over eighteen months of negotiations between lawyers of both governments meeting in the Hague. The terms of the final settlement suggest the complexity of the negotiations (and the need for creative lawyering).[3] The settlement was silent on whether the U.S. conduct was wrongful, simply noting the U.S. "regret" over the incident and the U.S. willingness to pay "compensation," without indicating whether doing so was legally required. To address the issue of whether payment should be made for the aircraft, the two sides agreed that the United States would pay U.S. $131.8 million in settlement of a whole range of Iranian claims against the United States (not just Iran's claim for the shoot-down, but other Iranian claims dating to the late 1970's and early 1980's). Doing so allowed the United States to maintain that none of the total payment related to the aircraft, while Iran could maintain that some of it did. To address the issue of funds going directly to the government of Iran, the payment was made to three different entities outside the control of the Iranian government. First, some funds were deposited with a Swiss bank for payments directly to the families of victims upon presentation of certain information (*e.g.*, a death certificate of the family member). Second, some funds were deposited in a security account used by the Iran–U.S. Claims Tribunal (Tribunal) to pay awards rendered against Iran and in favor of U.S. claimants.[4] Third, some funds were deposited in a bank account held in the name of Iran by the New York Federal Reserve Bank for use in paying Iran's portion of the cost of running the Tribunal. Thus, the victims' families and Iran received the benefits of the funds, without any funds being provided directly to the government of Iran.

Negotiations between governments occur all the time and are the means by which most disputes are resolved. In some instances, it may be important to record a successful negotiation through completion of an international agreement, such as with respect to a land or maritime boundary,[5] while in other instances it is politically preferable not to publicize the outcome.

---

3. The settlement documents may be found either at 32 Iran–U.S. Cl. Trib. Rep. 207 (1996) or at 11:2 Int'l Arb. Rep. annex G (1996). For background, see *Agora: The Downing of Iran Air Flight 655*, 83 Am. J. Int'l L. 318 (1989).

4. For further discussion of the Tribunal, see section C.

5. *See, e.g.*, Treaty on Delimitation of Continental Shelf, U.S.-Mex., June 9, 2000, S. Treaty Doc. No. 106–39 (2000).

Duty to Notify

States can always contact each other about a matter of concern, yet is there a duty to do so? Many scholars of international law (and some states and international tribunals) have asserted that there is an international legal duty for a state to notify other states of impending harm, or a significant risk of such harm, from an activity or event occurring within the jurisdiction of the first state. This duty to notify is said to be the natural corollary to various strands of international law, including: the general principles of *sic utere tuo ut alienum non laedas* (one must use his own so as not to injure others) and of good neighborliness; decisions of international tribunals, such as the ICJ in the *Corfu Channel* case, in which the Court noted "every State's obligation not to allow knowingly its territory to be used for acts contrary to the rights of other States;"[6] and non-binding instruments that recognize each state's "responsibility to ensure that activities within their jurisdiction or control do not cause damage to the environment of other States or of areas beyond the limits of national jurisdiction."[7]

A duty to notify may be found in various bilateral and multilateral treaties. For example, the U.N. Convention on the Law of the Sea provides that when a state has a reasonable ground for believing that its planned activity may cause substantial pollution to the marine environment, it must assess the potential effects and either publish the results or notify a competent international organization.[8]

Duty to Consult

To the extent that a duty to notify another state exists, it may imply a further duty to consider the other state's views on the matter. The value in notification is not just alerting the other state to a circumstance, but also taking into account the other state's concerns and reacting, if possible, to address those concerns. For example, in an arbitration between Spain and France, Spain was concerned that the completion of certain French waterworks would alter the flow of fresh water into Spain. The tribunal in the *Lake Lanoux* case rejected Spain's claim that France was obligated to obtain Spain's consent, but did find that France was under a duty

---

6. 1949 I.C.J. 4, 22 (Merits); *see* Trail Smelter Case, 3 R.I.A.A. 1911 (1938–41).

7. Stockholm Declaration of the United Nations Conference on the Human Environment, U.N. Doc. A/CONF.48/14, princip. 21 (1972), *reprinted in* 11 I.L.M. 1416 (1972); *see* Rio Declaration on Environment and Development, U.N. Doc. A/CONF.151/5 (1992), princip. 2, *reprinted in* 31 I.L.M. 874 (1992).

8. *See* U.N. Convention on the Law of the Sea arts. 204–06, Dec. 10, 1982, S. Treaty Doc. No. 103–39 (1994), 1833 U.N.T.S. 3 [hereinafter LOSC].

to consult with Spain with respect to projects that could affect Spain.[9]

One scholar has observed: "Despite the growth of prior consultation norms, it is unlikely that there will be any all-encompassing prior consultation duty in the foreseeable future."[10] Indeed, in the *Lake Lanoux* case itself, the tribunal recognized that it was a sensitive matter to impose such a duty and held that France had met its burden. There are, however, many multilateral and bilateral treaties that require consultation whenever disputes arise. For example, the U.N. Convention on the Law of the Sea provides that when a dispute arises between two parties, they "shall proceed expeditiously to an exchange of views regarding its settlement by negotiation or other peaceful means."[11] Likewise, the Antarctic Treaty provides that, when disputes arise, the parties "shall consult among themselves with a view to having the dispute resolved by negotiation, inquiry, mediation, conciliation, arbitration, judicial settlement or other peaceful means of their own choice."[12] Bilateral investment treaties commonly include a provision that the parties "agree to consult promptly, on the request of either, to resolve any disputes in connection with the Treaty, or to discuss any matter relating to the interpretation or application of the Treaty.... "[13]

Resort to such consultation is often a pre-condition to invoking a more formal dispute settlement process. Thus, only after the United States sought consultations with Europe regarding its inability to export beef to Europe (and those consultations failed to resolve the matter within certain time limits) could the United States request the establishment of a World Trade Organization arbitration panel.[14] Had the United States not pursued consultation, it could not insist upon arbitration.

An excellent example of institutionalized consultation is the U.S.-Canada International Joint Commission (IJC). Created in 1909,[15] the IJC has a U.S. section and a Canadian section, each headed by three commissioners and supported by a secretariat. While the governments appoint their respective commissioners and fund the work of the IJC, the IJC in practice acts independently of

---

9. *See* Lake Lanoux Arbitration (Fr. v. Spain), 24 I.L.R. 101, 127 (1957).

10. FREDERIC L. KIRGIS, JR., PRIOR CONSULTATION IN INTERNATIONAL LAW: A STUDY OF STATE PRACTICE 375 (1983).

11. LOSC, *supra* note 8, art. 283.

12. Antarctic Treaty art. XI(1), Dec. 1, 1959, 12 U.S.T. 794, 402 U.N.T.S. 71.

13. *See, e.g.*, Treaty Concerning the Encouragement and Reciprocal Protection of Investment, U.S.-Jordan, art. VIII, July 2, 1997, 36 I.L.M. 1498.

14. For background on the early stages of this dispute, see 64 Fed. Reg. 14,486 (1999).

15. *See* Treaty Relating to the Boundary Waters and Questions Arising Along the Boundary, U.S.-U.K., Jan. 11, 1909, 36 Stat. 2448, 12 Bevans 319. When Canada gained the attributes of statehood in the 1920's, it succeeded to the United Kingdom's rights and obligations under the treaty.

the governments. The IJC is charged with deciding whether certain kinds of works or activities can be built on rivers or lakes that flow along or across the U.S.-Canada boundary. Thus, proposed obstructions or diversions of water by either state cannot go forward unless they are submitted to the IJC and approved. When deciding whether to approve a submission, the IJC follows certain rules and principles set out in the underlying treaty. Further, each state has enacted national implementing laws and regulations to make the decisions of the IJC effective.[16] The IJC is therefore a very sophisticated mechanism for consultation between the United States and Canada, one that allows for the sorting out of concerns prior to the point where a dispute might arise between the two states.

B.   Mediation and Conciliation

Mediation

In the parlance of international law, "mediation" is similar to negotiation, but with the presence of a third party as an active participant in the negotiations. The mediator is not expected to issue a decision on either facts or law. Rather, the mediator helps facilitate communications between the two states and may make informal proposals to assist the parties in their negotiations.

For example, when the United States and Iran sought to resolve the 1979–81 crisis concerning Iran's seizure of U.S. diplomatic and consular personnel and the ensuing U.S. seizure of Iranian financial assets, both saw value in having Algeria serve as a mediator. The United States was anxious to resolve the crisis and secure the release of the hostages. Iran did not wish to deal directly with the United States, yet was willing to receive proposals from the United States through Algeria, and to respond in the same manner. Algerian diplomats worked tirelessly over several months to transmit proposals back and forth between the two states, and to grasp the key concerns of each side so as to communicate them to the other. Ultimately, the crisis was resolved through a series of agreements known as the "Algiers Accords," which neither party signed but were issued by the government of Algeria after receiving approval from both states.

Another example concerns the border dispute between Ecuador and Peru that led to armed conflict in 1941, 1981, and 1995. Both sides were interested in resolving the matter, but found it politically difficult to do so through direct negotiations. In 1995, both states invited Argentina, Brazil, Chile, and the United States to act as mediators. Between 1995 and 1998, diplomats from those states

---

16. For the United States, see 22   §§ 401.01–401.30 (2010).
U.S.C.   § 268   (2006);   22   C.F.R.

worked with diplomats of Ecuador and Peru to develop a comprehensive border agreement. In the end, an agreement was drafted that not only delimited the land border, but established mechanisms that guaranteed Ecuador's access to the Amazon, demilitarized a fifty-mile stretch of the border, turned the most contested areas into national parks, and opened the border to trade and development. Both states signed and ratified the agreement.[17]

Conciliation

In practice, the difference between international mediation and international conciliation is sometimes blurred, but the central idea in conciliation is that the conciliator (or conciliation body) is expected to issue a non-binding decision. Thus, conciliation usually is a more formal process, often involving both sides submitting pleadings to the conciliator in the same manner as in an arbitration. Unlike arbitration, however, a conciliator's decision is not regarded as legally-binding upon the two states. Rather, it is a proposed solution by a third-party that the states can take or leave. States may be more willing to resort to conciliation than arbitration, knowing that they can disregard the decision if they do not like it. At the same time, if the conciliator's decision is well-reasoned and impartial, it may alter the negotiating dynamic between the states, making resolution of the matter easier. Indeed, some governments may find political "cover" in a conciliator's decision that allows them to overcome domestic resistance.

Many international treaties call upon the parties to pursue, or at least consider, conciliation whenever a dispute arises. For example, the Vienna Convention for the Protection of the Ozone Layer provides that when a dispute arises

> [a] conciliation commission shall be created upon the request of one of the parties to the dispute. The commission shall be composed of an equal number of members appointed by each party concerned and a chairman chosen jointly by the members appointed by each party. The commission shall render a final and recommendatory award, which the parties shall consider in good faith.[18]

Similarly, the U.N. Law of the Sea Convention provides that a party to a dispute may invite the other party to submit the matter to conciliation in accordance with Annex V(1) of the convention.[19] In 1995, the U.N. General Assembly adopted a set of Model Rules for the Conciliation of Disputes between States, which consists of

---

17. *See* Treaty of Trade and Navigation, Ecuador–Peru, Oct. 26, 1998, 38 I.L.M. 266.

18. Art. 11(5), Mar. 22, 1985, T.I.A.S. 11,097, 1513 U.N.T.S. 293.

19. *See* LOSC, *supra* note 8, art. 284(1).

twenty-nine articles covering various aspects of conciliation.[20] The Model Rules are available for states to use whenever they wish to do so. In 1996, the Permanent Court of Arbitration adopted a set of conciliation rules for use by states, while in 1980 the U.N. Commission on International Trade Law adopted a set of conciliation rules for use by parties engaged in a commercial relationship, which can include a state and a private party.[21] However, the resort to conciliation by states has been modest; on one account, the twentieth century saw less than twenty cases of conciliation.[22]

Separate from (or in addition to) conciliation, states may agree on having an "inquiry," which entails third-party investigation and fact-finding. Like conciliation, the objective of an inquiry normally is not to impose a binding settlement but, rather, to provide an impartial report on the underlying facts to assist the parties in resolving the dispute.

C. Arbitration

Commencing an Arbitration

International arbitration is a formal process for obtaining a binding decision regarding a dispute between states, without the greater costs, time, and formalities of judicial dispute resolution. In any given case, however, international arbitration may not be less expensive or quicker than judicial settlement; much depends on how the arbitration is conducted and what judicial alternatives are available. Nevertheless, international arbitration has proven a popular means for resolving disputes between states and between states and non-state actors.

International arbitration is normally commenced through one of two processes. First, *after* a dispute has arisen, the parties can agree to take the dispute to international arbitration. This process is sometimes referred to as *ad hoc* arbitration, meaning that resort to arbitration is accepted only with respect to a specific dispute. The two parties typically conclude a written instrument (a *compromis*) in which they set forth the basic terms for how the arbitration should proceed.

Ad hoc international arbitration can be used to address a dispute that arises between two states. For example, in the 1980's a dispute arose between the United States and the United Kingdom

---

20. *See* G.A. Res. 50/33 (Dec. 6, 1955).

21. *See* Permanent Court of Arbitration, Optional Conciliation Rules (1996), *at* <http://www.pca-cpa.org>; U.N. Commission on International Trade Law, Conciliation Rules, G.A. Res. 35/52

(Dec. 4, 1980); *see also* Permanent Court of Arbitration, Optional Rules for Conciliation of Disputes Relating to Natural Resources and/or the Environment (2001).

22. *See* J.G. MERRILLS, INTERNATIONAL DISPUTE SETTLEMENT 83 (3d ed. 1998).

over charges being levied on U.S. airlines at London's Heathrow Airport. The United States contended that the charges were in violation of certain bilateral aviation agreements, but the United Kingdom disagreed. In December 1988, the two states placed the matter before an arbitral tribunal, which issued a decision in November 1992.[23]

Alternatively, *ad hoc* international arbitration can be used to address a dispute between a state and a sub-state entity. For example, in July 2008, the Government of Sudan and a liberation movement within Sudan (the Sudan People's Liberation Movement) deposited an arbitration agreement with the Permanent Court of Arbitration (PCA) in The Hague. The agreement provided for a five-member arbitral tribunal to decide whether the experts of the Abyei Boundaries Commission—which was established pursuant to a Comprehensive Peace Agreement concluded by the two parties in 2005—exceeded their mandate when demarcating certain oil-rich territory in Sudan. In a decision issued in 2009, the arbitral panel concluded that those experts did not exceed their mandate when *interpreting* their mandate, but did exceed their mandate in certain areas when *implementing* that mandate.[24]

Likewise, *ad hoc* arbitration can be used to address a dispute that arises between a state and a foreign person or company. For example, in 1970 a U.S. company purchased property in Costa Rica that it wished to develop, but the property was subsequently expropriated by the Costa Rican government. Although the U.S. company believed it was entitled to compensation, Costa Rica contended that little or no compensation should be paid. Costa Rica agreed to resolve the dispute through *ad hoc* arbitration conducted under the auspices of an arbitral center located at the World Bank, known as the International Centre for the Settlement of Investment Disputes (ICSID).[25] In February 2000, the arbitral panel issued a decision finding that the company was entitled to U.S. $16 million in compensation,[26] which Costa Rica subsequently paid.

States are not required to resort to *ad hoc* arbitration, but they may find such arbitration desirable for eliminating an irritant in their foreign relations. In the case of the ICSID arbitration noted

23. *See, e.g.*, Heathrow Airport User Charges Arbitration, 102 I.L.R. 215 (1992).

24. Government of Sudan and the Sudan People's Liberation Movement/Army Abyei Arbitration Award, 48 I.L.M. 1254 (2009); *see* Wendy J. Miles & Daisy Mallett, *The Abyei Arbitration and the Use of Arbitration to Resolve Inter-state and Intra-state Conflicts*, 1 J. Int'l Disp. Settlement 313 (2010).

25. ICSID is also involved in mediation and conciliation of investment disputes.

26. Compañía del Desarrollo de Santa Elena S.A. v. Costa Rica, ICSID (W. Bank) Case No. ARB/96/1, Final Award (Feb. 17, 2000), *reprinted in* 15 ICSID Rev.-Foreign Investment L.J. 169 (2000).

above, Costa Rica only agreed to submit the dispute (and similar disputes with other U.S. investors) to *ad hoc* arbitration after the U.S. Government threatened Costa Rica with a loss of international financing and suspension of U.S. aid, pursuant to a 1994 law called the "Helms Amendment."[27]

The second process for commencing international arbitration is for two parties, *before* a dispute has arisen, to agree that, if a dispute arises between them, either party may compel international arbitration. In other words, at the time the two parties initially enter into a legal relationship of one kind or another, they might agree that any future disputes with respect to that relationship will be resolved through international arbitration. The two parties typically would conclude an instrument (*e.g.*, a treaty or a contract) that covers the legal relationship generally, and that contains a clause (a *compromissory clause*) providing for international arbitration whenever a dispute arises.

When this type of international arbitration is envisaged between two states, the compromissory clause is usually inserted in a treaty. For example, when the United States decided in the mid–1990's that the European Community was unlawfully denying the import of U.S. beef derived from cattle treated with certain growth-promoting hormones, the United States pursued binding international arbitration because the European Community had agreed, under World Trade Organization (WTO) treaties, that trade disputes arising between them may be submitted to such arbitration.[28] This agreement to arbitrate does not only cover disputes over beef; it also covers any trade disputes arising under WTO agreements between the United States and the European Community (or other WTO members for that matter). In August 1997, a WTO dispute panel found that the ban violated the European Community's WTO obligations and therefore should be lifted.[29] Other trade agreements also provide for state-to-state arbitration, such as Chapters 19 and 20 of the North American Free Trade Agreement (NAFTA).[30]

This second process of international arbitration also can be used to address disputes that arise between a state and a foreign person or company. For example, in Chapter 11 of NAFTA, Canada,

---

27. 22 U.S.C. § 2370a (2006).

28. *See* Understanding on Rules and Procedures Governing the Settlement of Disputes, Annex 2, The Legal Texts: The Results of the Uruguay Round of Multi-lateral Trade Negotiations 354 (1999), *reprinted in* 33 I.L.M. 1125 (1994).

29. *See* Panel Report, *European Communities—Measures Concerning Meat and Meat Products (Hormones)*,

WTO Docs. WT/DS26/R/USA & WT/DS48/R/CAN, para. 9.1 (Aug. 18, 1997), *aff'd*, Appellate Body Report, *European Communities—Measures Concerning Meat and Meat Products (Hormones)* (AB–1997–4), WTO Docs. WT/DS26/AB/R & WT/DS48/AB/R (Jan. 16, 1998).

30. U.S.-Can.-Mex., Dec. 17, 1992, 32 I.L.M. 289 & 605.

Mexico, and the United States agreed that whenever one of their nationals invests in the territory of another state, the investor can submit to international arbitration a dispute arising from host government actions that interfere with the investment (unless the investor elects to resolve the dispute in local courts). Such investment arbitrations are referred to as "investor-state disputes" since they are conducted with the investor and the host government as the parties. NAFTA arbitrations are conducted either before IC-SID[31] or before an *ad hoc* panel operating under U.N. arbitration rules.[32] Similar arrangements for international arbitration are often included in bilateral investment treaties (BITs). All told, more than nine hundred bilateral investment treaties (as well as about twenty national investment laws) provide that investment disputes shall be submitted to ICSID arbitration.[33]

It should be noted that two non-state actors from different countries can agree to arbitration and select international law as their choice of law. While this form of arbitration might be regarded as "international" in nature, it is more exposed to challenges under the national law of the country where the arbitration takes place than is the case for arbitration involving states. Nevertheless, such "transnational" arbitration occurs with great regularity at or under the auspices of several institutions worldwide, such as: the International Chamber of Commerce (ICC)'s International Court of Arbitration in Paris; the Arbitration Institute of the Stockholm Chamber of Commerce; the London Court of International Arbitration; the American Arbitration Association in New York; the Inter-American Commercial Arbitration Commission (IACAC); or the Chinese International Economic and Trade Arbitration Commission (CIETAC). Each of these institutions has developed its own set of arbitration rules that parties may select when concluding a commercial contract or when resorting to arbitration *ad hoc*.

How Arbitration Works

When two parties provide for arbitration, they address in the *compromis* or the compromissory clause the manner in which arbitration will proceed. The parties can specify in detail how the arbitration will proceed, but it is more common for parties simply to incorporate in the *compromis* or compromissory clause by refer-

---

31. *See, e.g.*, Waste Mgmt., Inc. v. Mexico, Award, para. 98 (NAFTA Ch. 11 Arb. Trib. Apr. 30, 2004), *reprinted in* 43 I.L.M. 967 (2004). In addition to NAFTA, several other agreements—the Energy Charter Treaty, the Cartagena Free Trade Agreement, and the Colonia Investment Protocol of Mercosur—provide for arbitration under the auspices of IC-SID.

32. *See, e.g.*, GAMI Investments, Inc. v. Mexico, Final Award (NAFTA Ch. 11 Arb. Trib. Nov. 15, 2004).

33. *See* Kenneth J. Vandevelde, Bilateral Investment Treaties: History, Policy and Interpretation (2011); *see also* Kenneth J. Vandevelde, U.S. International Investment Agreements (2009).

ence an "off-the-shelf" set of arbitration rules, such as the rules developed by the U.N. Conference on International Trade Law (UNCITRAL)[34] or the Permanent Court of Arbitration (PCA).[35] For example, when taking their dispute to arbitration in 2008, the Government of Sudan and the Sudan People's Liberation Movement selected the PCA's Optional Rules for Arbitrating Disputes between Two Parties of Which Only One is a State. Those rules address in detail where notice should be filed to start the arbitration, how the arbitral panel will be established, whether arbitrators may be challenged or replaced, the place of arbitration, the submission of written and oral pleadings (as well as evidence), the applicable law, payment of the costs of the arbitration, and the issuance of the award. While parties may use an off-the-shelf set of rules, they may also decide to deviate from those rules or to supplement them, such as by selecting a particular location for the arbitration to be conducted or specifying the number of arbitrators to serve on the panel.

Arbitral panels normally consist of an odd number of arbitrators to avoid a tie in voting. Assuming that a panel of three arbitrators is envisaged, each party would select an arbitrator and then the two party-appointed arbitrators would select a third arbitrator to preside over the arbitration. Since a party might refuse to appoint an arbitrator, or the two party-appointed arbitrators might not agree upon the presiding arbitrator, it is common for the rules to provide for an "appointing authority" (*e.g.*, the U.N. secretary-general or the ICJ president) to make the appointment so that the arbitration can go forward.

Once the arbitral panel is established, the arbitrators decide (within the scope of the rules by which they are governed) exactly how the arbitration shall proceed, including the dates for the filing of written pleadings and the oral hearing. After receiving the views and evidence of the parties, the arbitrators deliberate and issue a binding award, which may or may not be made public depending on the terms of the arbitration. An empirical study of arbitration practice in the area of investor-state disputes under investment treaties has found that: arbitral awards in recent years have

---

34. *See, e.g.*, U.N. Conference on Int'l Trade Law, UNCITRAL Arbitration Rules (2010), *reprinted in* 49 I.L.M. 1640 (2010), *at* <http://www.uncitral.org>.

35. *See* Permanent Court of Arbitration, Optional Rules for Arbitrating Disputes between Two States (1992); Permanent Court of Arbitration, Optional Rules for Arbitrating Disputes between Two Parties of Which Only One is a State (1993); Permanent Court of Arbitration, Optional Rules for Arbitration Involving International Organizations and States (1996); Permanent Court of Arbitration, Optional Rules for Arbitrating Disputes Relating to Natural Resources and/or the Environment (2001); Permanent Court of Arbitration, Optional Rules for the Arbitration of Disputes Relating to Outer Space Activities (2011). All PCA rules are available at <http://www.pca-cpa.org>.

increased; arbitration costs can be substantial; cases rarely settle; a large number of different arbitrators are used for such cases, but very few are women; developing states are not the only respondents; investors do not win more disputes than states; and tribunals generally do not award large damages.[36]

Selected Arbitral Institutions

Arbitrations can address occasional disputes that arise between states (or between a state and a non-state actor), yet in situations where there are a series of disputes or claims that must be resolved, it is possible to establish an arbitral institution charged with handling numerous claims over the course of several years, after which the tribunal is disbanded. The following are three such tribunals created in recent years.

Iran-U.S. Claims Tribunal. The Iran–U.S. Claims Tribunal (Tribunal) was created as part of the agreement reached between Iran and the United States to resolve the crisis from the 1979–81 Iranian seizure of U.S. diplomatic and consular personnel and the ensuing U.S. freeze of Iranian assets within the jurisdiction of the United States. The Tribunal sits in The Hague and consists of nine arbitrators: three U.S. nationals appointed by the United States; three Iranian nationals appointed by Iran; and three third-country nationals agreed upon by the six U.S. and Iranian arbitrators or appointed by an appointing authority (as of 2011, the third-country arbitrators are of Finnish, Italian, and Belgian nationality). When deciding cases, the arbitrators sit as a full tribunal or in chambers of three and operate under a modified version of the UNCITRAL arbitration rules. The Tribunal has jurisdiction to decide claims of U.S. nationals against Iran, and of Iranian nationals against the United States, which arise out of debts, contracts, expropriations or other measures affecting property rights. Further, the Tribunal may hear contract claims by one government against the other relating to the sale of goods or services, as well as disputes between the governments concerning the interpretation or performance of the Algiers Declarations.[37]

By January 1982 (the deadline for filing claims before the Tribunal), some 1,000 claims were filed for amounts of U.S. $250,000 or more ("large claims") and some 2,800 claims were filed for amounts of less than U.S. $250,000 ("small claims"). Large claimants represented themselves before the Tribunal, whereas

---

36. Susan D. Franck, *Empirically Evaluating Claims About Investment Treaty Arbitration*, 86 N.C. L. Rev. 1, 6 (2007).

37. *See* George H. Aldrich, The Jurisprudence of the Iran-United States Claims Tribunal: An Analysis of the Decisions of the Tribunal (1996); Charles N. Brower & Jason D. Brueschke, The Iran-United States Claims Tribunal (1998).

small claimants were represented by their government. As of 2011, the Tribunal had issued some 600 awards; most of the claims had been settled by the parties. All told, U.S. claimants have received some U.S. $2.5 billion in awards from the Tribunal, paid from a security account established in the Netherlands in 1981 from a portion of Iran's frozen assets and thereafter replenished by Iran. The remaining claims are principally those of Iran against the U.S. government relating to pre–1979 contracts for U.S. sales of military goods and services to Iran.

U.N. Compensation Commission. The U.N. Compensation Commission (UNCC) is a subsidiary organ of the U.N. Security Council based in Geneva. The UNCC was established in 1991 to process claims and pay compensation for losses resulting from Iraq's 1990–91 invasion and occupation of Kuwait.[38] Major policy decisions of the UNCC are decided by a Governing Council consisting of representatives from Security Council member states, while the detailed work of the UNCC in deciding awards of compensation was undertaken by panels of commissioners, assisted by a secretariat. The task of the UNCC was not to assess liability; Iraq's liability for the direct loss, damage or injury from its invasion and occupation previously was determined by the Security Council. Rather, the commission's task, which was completed in June 2005, was to decide: (1) whether a claimant has submitted sufficient evidence to show that a claim falls within the scope of direct loss, damage or injury for which the Security Council determined compensation should be paid; and (2) the amount to be paid for different categories of claims. Consequently, the UNCC process was less adversarial than normal arbitration and more administrative in nature. Compensation was paid to successful claimants from a special fund that received a percentage of the proceeds from exports of Iraqi oil. As of 2011, the UNCC had paid about U.S. $33 billion in compensation.[39]

Eritrea-Ethiopia Boundary and Claims Tribunals. In May 1993, Eritrea—previously a province of Ethiopia—became an independent country. Five years later, armed conflict broke out between Ethiopia and Eritrea along their border, leading to extensive fighting and widespread collateral damage to the civilian population. Eritrea and Ethiopia agreed to a cessation of hostilities in June 2000 and signed a final peace agreement in December.[40] Among other things, the peace agreement established a five-member commission to delimit the boundary, and a five-member claims commission to decide claims for damage by either state and its nationals against the other state related to the conflict. The commissions

---

38. *See* S.C. Res. 687, paras. 16–19 (Apr. 3, 1991).

39. *See* UNCC Press Release, Doc. PR/2011/7 (Oct. 13, 2011); *see also* RICH-ARD B. LILLICH, THE UNITED NATIONS COMPENSATION COMMISSION (1995).

40. *See* Peace Agreement, Eri.-Eth., Dec. 12, 2001, 40 I.L.M. 260.

were established, received extensive written pleadings from the parties, and conducted hearings and meetings principally in The Hague. The boundary commission issued its decision delimiting the boundary in April 2002.[41] The claims commission issued a series of partial awards on liability relating to prisoners of war, enemy aliens, and the fighting along the fronts.[42] Among other things, the Commission found that Eritrea violated Article 2(4) of the U.N. Charter prohibiting the use of force by one state against another when it invaded Ethiopia in May 1998.[43] In August 2009, the Commission issued its final awards on damages, finding that Eritrea owed Ethiopia $161 million, while Ethiopia owed Eritrea $174 million. Neither side, however, has paid the awards as of 2011.

D. World Court

The judicial wing of the United Nations is the International Court of Justice (ICJ). The predecessor to the ICJ was the Permanent Court of International Justice (PCIJ), the judicial wing of the League of Nations. Together, these institutions and their jurisprudence are referred to informally as the "World Court."

Permanent Court of International Justice

Caught up in the rising tide of legalistic idealism at the turn of the twentieth century, the United States was actively engaged in the negotiations that led to the establishment of the PCIJ, due in part to a belief that reliance on international arbitration for resolution of inter-state disputes was insufficient. Though such arbitration had its place, U.S. international lawyers and policy-makers—such as Elihu Root—argued that international arbitration tended toward "an essentially political process of negotiation and compromise on the basis of expedience rather than the judicial procedure of impartial adjudication of rights and duties in strict accordance with the rules of law."[44] The latter process was an option that states should have since judicial decisions, being grounded more firmly in a rigorous application of law by persons not selected by the disputants, could serve as a means for definitively and convincingly resolving certain kinds of disputes.

41. *See*, e.g, Eritrea–Ethiopia Boundary Commission, Decision Regarding Delimitation of the Border (Apr. 13, 2002), 41 I.L.M. 1057 (2002).

42. *See*, *e.g.*, Eritrea–Ethiopia Claims Commission, Partial Awards on Prisoners of War (July 1, 2003), 42 I.L.M. 1056 & 1083 (2003); Eritrea–Ethiopia Claims Commission, Partial Awards on the Central Front (Apr. 28, 2004), 43 I.L.M. 1249 & 1275 (2004);

Eritrea–Ethiopia Claims Commission, Partial Awards on Civilian Claims (Dec. 17, 2004), 44 I.L.M. 601 & 630 (2005).

43. Eritrea–Ethiopia Claims Commission, Partial Award on the *Jus ad Bellum* (Dec. 19, 2005), 45 I.L.M. 430 (2006).

44. *See* FRANCIS ANTHONY BOYLE, FOUNDATIONS OF WORLD ORDER: THE LEGALIST APPROACH TO INTERNATIONAL RELATIONS (1898–1922) 37 (1999).

The United States had pressed without success for the creation of such a court at the 1907 Hague peace conference. Only after the carnage of World War I were other states willing to go along. In 1920, the PCIJ was created as an adjunct to the League of Nations. Principally operating from 1922 to 1939, the PCIJ issued twenty-seven advisory opinions and thirty-two judgments on a variety of matters, including disputes arising under peace treaties and boundary disputes.

The U.S. Senate, however, never consented to U.S. ratification of the Covenant of the League of Nations, nor of the separate protocol embodying the Statute of the PCIJ. While the PCIJ had its supporters in the United States, strong voices of realism and exceptionalism, particularly in the U.S. Senate, argued that submission to the jurisdiction of a world court would harm U.S. national interests and jeopardize U.S. sovereignty. When put to a vote in 1935, U.S. adherence to the protocol secured fifty-two votes in favor and thirty-six against, falling seven votes short of the necessary two-thirds majority.[45] Throughout the life of the PCIJ, the United States never participated in any litigation before the PCIJ, although a judge of U.S. nationality always served on the Court.

The substantive and procedural decisions of the PCIJ remain of interest today, since the Statute of the ICJ is essentially the same as its predecessor. Indeed, while states decided in the aftermath of World War II to create a new international court, they also decided to maintain continuity in its concept and function.

International Court of Justice

In 1945, as states of the world gathered in San Francisco to adopt the U.N. Charter, it was generally agreed that the new world order needed a global court. The U.S. delegation to the 1945 San Francisco conference reported to President Franklin D. Roosevelt that "[a]s the United States becomes a party to a Charter which places justice and international law among its foundation stones, it would naturally accept and use an international court to apply international law and to administer international justice."[46] Consequently, one of the organs of the United Nations was a new international court, the ICJ, whose Statute was an integral part of the U.N. Charter.[47] Along with many other states, the Senate in 1945 consented to U.S. ratification of the Charter, by a vote of eighty-nine to two.[48] By joining the Charter, the United States *ipso*

---

45. *See* 79 CONG. REC. 1147 (1935).

46. *The Charter of the United Nations: Hearings Before the S. Comm. on Foreign Relations*, 79th Cong. 121 (1945).

47. *See* U.N. Charter ch. XIV.

48. *See* 91 CONG. REC. 8190 (1945).

facto became a party to the ICJ Statute.[49]

The ICJ is located at the Peace Palace in The Hague. Written and oral pleadings are submitted to the Court in either English or French, after which the Court privately deliberates and issues its decision. Contentious cases (cases between two states) are often heard in phases, with separate decisions issued on: (1) requests for provisional (or interim) measures of protection;[50] (2) challenges to the Court's jurisdiction or the admissibility of the claim; (3) the merits of the claim; and (4) the award of damages if liability is found. Over the course of its existence, the ICJ has heard cases on a wide range of international legal issues, issuing approximately three major decisions per year. Many decisions of the Court are extremely important to states, such as the delimitation or regulation of land or maritime boundaries.

For example, in September 2005, Costa Rica brought a case against Nicaragua concerning navigational and related rights of Costa Rica on a particular section of the San Juan river, which runs along the border of the two countries. It was not contested that this section of the river was a part of Nicaraguan territory (the border between the states lying on the Costa Rican bank), nor that Costa Rica possessed a right of free navigation on the river under an 1958 treaty. What was contested, however, was the extent of that right of navigation. After extensive written and oral pleadings, the Court issued a decision in July 2009, with detailed findings regarding both Costa Rica's and Nicaragua's rights. Among other things, the Court found that Costa Rica's right of navigation included navigation for purposes of commerce, which in turn included the transport of passengers and tourists, with no requirement that they first obtain Nicaraguan visas or tourist cards. By contrast, Costa Rica did not have rights of navigation for vessels carrying out police functions, for exchanging personnel at police border posts along the river, or for supplying those posts with equipment, arms, and ammunition. Further, Nicaragua was found to have certain key rights, such as to require Costa Rican vessels and their passengers to stop at the first and last Nicaraguan post on their route along the San Juan River, and to carry a passport or identity document.[51]

The states who negotiated the Charter and ICJ Statute did not embrace an international court that held wide-ranging and unconstrained authority. Structural features built into the ICJ sought to mediate between the desire of states for an impartial, permanent judicial forum and the desire of states to control their exposure to

---

49. *See* Statute of the International Court of Justice, 59 Stat. 1031, 3 Bevans 1179 [hereinafter ICJ Statute].

50. *See* SHABTAI ROSENNE, PROVISIONAL MEASURES IN INTERNATIONAL LAW (2005).

51. Dispute Regarding Navigational and Related Rights (Costa Rica v. Nicar.), 2009 I.C.J. 213 (July 13).

ICJ decision-making (and, when exposed, to have their concerns be heard fairly and understood). Several of these structural features are discussed below.

States, Not Persons. At the time the ICJ was created, the idea that individuals might themselves pursue claims before an international tribunal was largely unknown. Consequently, the ICJ Statute allows only states to participate in contentious cases, thus precluding voices that are not vested in the overall system of state sovereignty. This is an important design feature that provides states with a greater comfort level regarding their exposure to the jurisdiction of the Court. Although several states have accepted international courts that allow individuals to sue their own governments—such as the European Court of Human Rights—many states (including the United States) have been unwilling to do so. Jurisdiction over cases brought by persons might greatly enhance the ICJ's role in the development of international law, yet might also exacerbate the Court's relationship with many states, for it would invariably result in the Court passing upon matters that traditionally have been handled by national legal systems.

Circumscribed Jurisdiction. The dominant structural feature controlling a state's exposure to the ICJ is that states cannot be sued before the ICJ without their consent. While there was considerable support at the 1945 San Francisco conference in favor of all-embracing compulsory jurisdiction for the Court, the United States and Soviet Union were adamantly opposed. Faced with a deal-breaker, the other nations backed down.[52] Consequently, consent to the jurisdiction of the Court does not exist merely by virtue of a state being a party to the ICJ's Statute; separate consent of one kind or another must exist. This requirement of state consent is why most of the 193 states of the world have never appeared before the Court in a contentious case even though they are parties to the ICJ's Statute, and why the Court is regarded as an important but not dominant player in the field of international dispute resolution.

While state consent is necessary for the Court to have jurisdiction, the Court's Statute is structured so as to make provision of such consent as easy as possible. First, states can accept the Court's jurisdiction on an *ad hoc* basis for the adjudication of an existing dispute.[53] For example, in 1981 the United States and Canada agreed to bring to the Court a dispute over their maritime boundary in the Gulf of Maine.[54]

---

52. *See* Ruth B. Russell, A History of the United Nations Charter: The Role of the United States, 1940–45, 884–90 (1958).

53. *See* ICJ Statute, *supra* note 49, art. 36(1).

54. *See* Delimitation of the Maritime Boundary in the Gulf of Maine Area

Second, states can accept the Court's jurisdiction by concluding a bilateral or multilateral treaty that provides for such jurisdiction over cases relating to the interpretation or application of the treaty.[55] This form of jurisdiction is inherently limited; it only covers matters within the scope of the treaty. Thus, the narrower the scope of the treaty, the narrower the scope of the Court's jurisdiction. Further, the parties may include clauses within the treaty that carve out issues as being outside the Court's jurisdiction, such as matters relating to essential security interests.

The exact language in the bilateral or multilateral treaty providing for the Court's jurisdiction is important when such a case is filed. Often the treaty will only provide jurisdiction for the Court over a "dispute" about the "interpretation" or "application" of the treaty, and even then only if the matter cannot first be resolved through bilateral diplomacy. When such language exists, the state that brings the case must demonstrate that the conditions necessary for triggering the Court's jurisdiction have been met. For example, after armed conflict broke out in the Georgian territories of South Ossetia and Abkhazia in August 2008, Georgia brought a case against Russia alleging that the latter was responsible for racial discrimination and ethnic cleansing in the two territories. According to Georgia, such action violated Russia's obligations under the Convention on the Elimination of All Forms of Racial Discrimination (CERD).[56]

CERD provides for the Court's jurisdiction over any "dispute" between two CERD parties "with respect to the interpretation or application of this Convention, which is not settled by negotiation" or by certain procedures set forth in CERD.[57] Russia objected that there was no evidence of any "dispute" between the parties concerning the interpretation or application of CERD to activities in the two territories. Though much documentation was produced by Georgia, Russia argued that each document was flawed in some way by saying nothing about CERD or about racial discrimination/ethnic cleansing, by not attributing such conduct to Russia, by not being endorsed by the government of Georgia, or by not being not communicated to Russia. The Court, however, rejected this objection, finding that statements were made by Georgia's President accusing Russia of such conduct before the case was filed at the Court.[58] Russia further objected that Georgia failed to negotiate

(Can./U.S.), 1984 I.C.J. 246 (Oct. 12) [hereinafter Gulf of Maine].

55. *See* ICJ Statute, *supra* note 49, art. 36(1). Treaties pre-dating the existence of the ICJ that provide for jurisdiction of the PCIJ are also regarded,

under the ICJ Statute, as triggering ICJ jurisdiction. *Id.*, art. 37.

56. Dec. 21, 1965, 660 U.N.T.S. 195, 5 I.L.M. 350.

57. *Id.*, art. 22.

58. Application of the International Convention on the Elimination of All

this "dispute" with Russia or to follow CERD dispute settlement procedures. The Court upheld this objection, finding that CERD's obligation to negotiate first required "a genuine attempt by one of the disputing parties to engage in discussions with the other disputing party, with a view to resolving the dispute."[59] Consequently, Georgia's case was dismissed.

When ratifying a treaty that provides for ICJ jurisdiction, a state may be able to file a reservation rejecting such jurisdiction.[60] For example, the Convention Against Genocide sets forth various obligations of states with respect to preventing and punishing genocide. In Article IX, it provides that disputes between parties arising under the convention shall be submitted to the ICJ at the request of one of the parties.[61] When the United States ratified the Convention Against Genocide in 1988, however, it included a reservation stating that, before any dispute could be submitted to the Court under Article IX, "the specific consent of the United States is required in each case."[62] Consequently, when the Federal Republic of Yugoslavia (Serbia & Montenegro) sought to sue the United States under the Convention Against Genocide for acts associated with NATO's bombing in protection of Kosovo, the ICJ found that there was no jurisdiction, and dismissed the case.[63]

States Accepting I.C.J. Compulsory Jurisdiction (including year of declaration)			
Australia (2002)	Domin. Rep. (1924)	Liberia (1952)	Poland (1996)
Austria (1971)	Egypt (1957)	Liechtenstein (1950)	Portugal (2005)
Barbados (1980)	Estonia (1991)	Luxembourg (1930)	Senegal (1985)
Belgium (1958)	Finland (1958)	Madagascar (1992)	Slovakia (2004)
Botswana (1970)	Gambia (1966)	Malawi (1966)	Somalia (1963)
Bulgaria (1992)	Georgia (1995)	Malta (1983)	Spain (1990)
Cambodia (1957)	Germany (2008)	Mauritius (1968)	Sudan (1958)
Cameroon (1994)	Greece (1994)	Mexico (1947)	Suriname (1987)
Canada (1994)	Guinea (1998)	Netherlands (1956)	Swaziland (1969)
Costa Rica (1973)	Guinea-Bissau	New Zealand (1977)	Sweden (1957)
Côte d' Ivoire	(1989)	Nicaragua (1929)	Switzerland (1948)
(2001)	Haiti (1921)	Nigeria (1998)	Togo (1979)
Cyprus (2002)	Honduras (1986)	Norway (1996)	Uganda (1963)
Dem. Rep. Congo	Hungary (1992)	Pakistan (1960)	United Kingdom
(1989)	India (1974)	Panama (1921)	(2004)
Denmark (1956)	Japan (2007)	Paraguay (1996)	Uruguay (1921)
Djibouti (2005)	Kenya (1965)	Peru (2003)	
Dominica (2006)	Lesotho (2000)	Philippines (1972)	

Third, under the "optional clause," state parties to the ICJ Statute may make a unilateral declaration that "they recognize as

---

Forms of Racial Discrimination (Geor. v. Russ.), Judgment on Preliminary Objections to Jurisdiction, para. 113 (Apr. 1, 2011).

59. *Id.*, para. 157.

60. On treaty reservations, see Chapter 3(A).

61. *See* Convention on the Prevention and Punishment of the Crime of Genocide art. IX, Dec. 9, 1948, 78 U.N.T.S. 277.

62. 28 I.L.M. 754, 782 (1989).

63. *See* Legality of Use of Force (Yugo. v. U.S.), 1999 I.C.J. 916 (June 2).

compulsory *ipso facto* and without special agreement, in relation to any other state accepting the same obligation, the jurisdiction of the Court in all legal disputes ... " involving issues of law or fact governed by rules of international law.[64] Most states have not accepted this "compulsory jurisdiction" of the Court. Of the 193 member states of the United Nations, only 66 have accepted the Court's compulsory jurisdiction (as of 2011), and many of those acceptances contain conditions and reservations that significantly limit the state's consent. Moreover, the only permanent member of the Security Council that currently accepts the Court's compulsory jurisdiction is the United Kingdom. The other permanent members—China, France, Russia, and the United States—have never done so or have withdrawn from such jurisdiction. Further, the United Kingdom's acceptance is conditioned by several significant reservations that make it difficult to sue the United Kingdom before the Court.

Advisory Opinions. In addition to the Court's jurisdiction over contentious cases between two states, the Court also has jurisdiction to issue advisory opinions on legal questions. The advisory jurisdiction of the ICJ may only be invoked by U.N. organs and by the specialized agencies of the United Nations who have been authorized to do so. Although advisory opinions are non-binding, they do have juridical authority; they can legitimate certain conduct of states and organizations, and invariably have significance for a legal system in which judicial precedents are scarce. For example, the Court's advisory opinion concerning reservations to the Convention Against Genocide helped make clear that "the principles underlying the Convention are principles which are recognized by civilized nations as binding on States, even without any conventional obligations."[65] In practice, advisory opinions are relied upon and cited as legal authority as frequently as judgments rendered in contentious cases.

A recent advisory opinion that arose in the aftermath of Kosovo's declaration of independence in February 2008 (discussed in Chapter 2(A)) demonstrates how the question asked of the Court shapes the breadth of the opinion rendered. Seeking to preclude other states from recognizing a new country of Kosovo, Serbia successfully lobbied the U.N. General Assembly in October 2008 to ask the International Court of Justice for an advisory opinion on the following question: "Is the unilateral declaration of independence by the Provisional Institutions of Self–Government of Kosovo

---

64. *See* I.C.J. Statute, *supra* note 49, art. 36(2); *see also* J.G. Merrills, *The Optional Clause Revisited*, 64 BRIT. Y.B. INT'L L. 197 (1993).

65. Advisory Opinion on Reservations to the Convention on Genocide, 1951 I.C.J. 15, 24 (May 28).

in accordance with international law?"[66] Some thirty-five countries filed written statements to the Court on the matter (as did the "authors of the unilateral declaration of independence," i.e., Kosovo), with roughly half supporting Kosovo's independence and the other half supporting Serbia's position that Kosovo's declaration was unlawful, and that final status talks must continue. In December 2009, almost thirty States appeared before the Court, including Kosovo, and in July 2009 the Court issued its opinion.[67] Limiting itself narrowly to the question placed before it, the Court concluded that Kosovo's 2008 declaration of independence was not prohibited by general international law or by the relevant U.N. Security Council resolution (Resolution 1244). The Court avoided broader questions of international law, such as whether Kosovo was now a "state," whether other states could recognize Kosovo, or whether the Kosovo people could declare independence due to a right of self-determination or "remedial secession."[68] Although in their separate opinions some of the judges of the Court discussed the right of self-determination,[69] the Court as a whole avoided the issue, and avoided being drawn into any other issues, such as advising Belgrade and Pristina that they should pursue further status talks.

State Influence on Selection of Judges. Once a state is exposed to ICJ decision-making, other structural features help assure states that their concerns will be heard and understood. In this regard, a key structural feature concerns the manner in which the fifteen judges are placed on the Court. On the one hand, the *de jure* procedure entails a concurrent election of judges by the two principal organs of the United Nations (the General Assembly and the Security Council) based on their independence, character, and expertise, and not on their nationality.[70] While judges are precluded from participating in cases in which they were previously involved (which can have the effect of preventing judges from sitting in some cases involving their own states), there is no absolute bar to a judge sitting in a case involving a state of the judge's nationality.[71] Judges serve for nine-year terms and cannot be recalled or dismissed by the government of their nationalities, thus encouraging independent decision-making.

66. G.A. Res. 63/3 (Oct. 8, 2008).

67. Accordance with International Law of the Unilateral Declaration of Independence in Respect of Kosovo, I.C.J. Advisory Opinion (July 22, 2010), *reprinted in* 49 I.L.M. 1404, *at* <http://www.icj-cij.org> [hereinafter Kosovo Advisory Opinion]; *see Agora: The ICJ's* Kosovo *Advisory Opinion*, 105 Am. J. Int'l L. 50 (2011).

68. *See* Kosovo Advisory Opinion, *supra* note 67, paras. 82–83; *see also*

Secession and Self-Determination (Stephen Macedo & Allen Buchanan eds., 2003).

69. *See generally* Kosovo Advisory Opinion, *supra* note 67, Declaration of Judge Cançado Trindade.

70. *See* ICJ Statute, *supra* note 49, arts. 2, 4(1) & 8.

71. *Id.*, arts. 17(2) & 31(1).

On the other hand, the procedure for selection of judges is not blind to nationality. No two judges may be of the same nationality and judges are to be selected so that the principal legal systems of the world are represented.[72] In contentious cases, if a party has no judge of its nationality sitting on the court, the party may appoint an *ad hoc* judge to sit in the case, who can be of the state's nationality or some other nationality.[73] Further, while the permanent members of the Security Council do not have a "veto" with respect to the election of ICJ judges (a simple majority of eight votes is required), the five permanent members are in a position to influence strongly the process, such that it is no surprise that a judge of the nationality of each permanent member is represented on the Court.[74] As an informal matter, distribution of seats on the Court are allocated such that there are a set number of judges from each of the principal regions of the world.[75]

Having a judge of the state's nationality on the ICJ, of course, does not guarantee a decision in the state's favor. The center of gravity for deciding the case remains with the other judges, who decide cases by a simple majority vote of the Court, with no "veto" power accorded to judges from particular states. Moreover, most studies indicate that ICJ judges do not automatically side with their state of nationality.[76]

The ICJ Statute provides a means for two contending states to move the Court's center of gravity closer to the value systems of the states if agreement can be reached to do so. Article 26 allows the Court to establish a chamber of judges to decide a case, which the Court typically is inclined to do if two states appearing before it request such a chamber and identify the judges they wish appointed to the chamber. Moreover, unlike the PCIJ Statute, there is no requirement to compose the chamber so as to represent "the principal legal systems of the world."[77] Thus, the chamber can

---

72. *Id.*, arts. 3(1) & 9.

73. *Id.*, art. 31(2) & (3).

74. *Id.*, art. 10. A judge from each of the permanent members has been on the Court since its inception, with the exception of a gap between 1967 and 1985 when there was no Chinese judge. The ICJ judges of U.S. nationality to date have been: Green Hackworth (1946–61); Philip Jessup (1961–70); Hardy Cross Dilliard (1970–79); Richard Baxter (1979–80); Stephen Schwebel (1981–2000); Thomas Buergenthal (2000–2010); and Joan Donoghue (2010–present).

75. *See* THE CHARTER OF THE UNITED NATIONS: A COMMENTARY 1162 (Bruno Simma ed., 2d ed. 2002). The regions are: African states (three judges); Asian states (three judges); East European states (two judges); Latin American and Caribbean states (two judges); and Western European and other states (five judges).

76. *See, e.g.*, Edith Brown Weiss, *Judicial Independence and Impartiality: A Preliminary Inquiry*, in THE INTERNATIONAL COURT OF JUSTICE AT A CROSSROADS 123 (Lori F. Damrosch ed., 1987); Thomas R. Hensley, *National Bias and the International Court of Justice*, 12 MIDWEST J. POL. SCI. 568 (1968); *but see* ERIC POSNER, THE PERILS OF LEGAL GLOBALISM 130–149 (2009).

77. ICJ Statute, *supra* note 49, art. 9.

consist of judges only from certain regions. For instance, in the *Gulf of Maine* case, Canada and the United States informed the Court that they desired a chamber consisting of five ICJ judges identified by the parties.[78] Likewise, in the *ELSI* case, Italy and the United States informed the Court that they wished a chamber to be formed consisting of five specific ICJ judges.[79] In both cases, the states were clearly interested in having greater control over the legal and political attitudes brought to the judicial table, and in both cases the Court complied. Despite this nod toward party control, chamber judgments are technically[80] (and in practice) regarded as judgments of the Court as a whole.

No Direct Enforcement of Judgments In National Law. International tribunals can differ markedly in the manner their decisions are "embedded" in the national systems of states subject to the tribunal's jurisdiction. An international tribunal can be established by an agreement that makes its decisions directly enforceable in a national legal system, without any need for governments to take *post-hoc* implementing action (*e.g.*, through statutes or executive orders). Such an approach exists for the European Court of Justice.

ICJ judgments in contentious cases are final, without further appeal, and binding on the parties.[81] Further, each U.N. member state "undertakes to comply with the decision of the International Court of Justice in any case to which it is a party."[82] Yet in crafting the U.N. Charter and the ICJ Statute, states elected not to include any provisions expressly addressing the legal effect of ICJ judgments within national legal systems, such as whether they provide a basis for private rights of action in national courts. Rather, the recourse envisaged by the U.N. Charter is for the victorious party to appeal non-compliance to the U.N. Security Council, "which may, if it deems necessary, make recommendations or decide upon measures to be taken to give effect to the judgment."[83] Of all the cases before the Court that were lost by the respondent state on the merits, in only one did an applicant, Nicaragua, request that the Security Council take action to enforce the judgment against the respondent, the United States. Exercising its prerogative as a permanent member of the Council, the United States vetoed the proposed resolution.[84] An effort by private individuals to sue the U.S. government in U.S. court based, among other things, on the ground that the U.S. actions violated the ICJ's decision, was

---

78. *See* Gulf of Maine, *supra* note 54.

79. *See* Elettronica Sicula S.p.A. (ELSI) (U.S. v. Italy), 1987 I.C.J. 3 (order of Mar. 2).

80. *See* ICJ Statute, *supra* note 49, art. 27.

81. *Id.*, arts. 59–60.

82. U.N. Charter art. 94(1).

83. *Id.*, art. 94(2).

84. *See* 25 I.L.M. 1337, 1352–65 (1986).

dismissed because there is no private right of action to enforce ICJ decisions in U.S. courts.[85]

Discursive or Political Constraints. Separate from formal or quasi-formal constraints on the Court, there are also discursive or political constraints. ICJ judges know that the Court's legitimacy and credibility as an institution rest not solely on an objective correctness of its legal reasoning, but on the acceptance of that legal reasoning by international lawyers, and more broadly by the global community. Consequently, the International Court is unlikely to issue a decision that is regarded by international lawyers as misguided or by the global community as politically unacceptable. Were the Court to do so, its standing would be severely impaired. Instead, the Court strives to issue decisions that will be well-received within the international legal community and by its primary constituents—states. By doing so, the Court encourages states to bring cases before the Court, which in turn justifies the significance and importance of the Court.

To avoid politically problematic cases, the Court has embraced various techniques, including "admissibility" doctrines. Thus, even if the Court finds that it has jurisdiction over a claim, it can further find the claim inadmissible and thereby avoid passing upon the claim's merits. For example, in certain cases the Court has relied upon a rule of customary international law known as the "local remedies rule" as a means of respecting decision-making at the national level. Under the rule, before a state may espouse a claim on behalf of its national, it must show that the national has exhausted all available legal remedies in the courts and administrative agencies of the state against which the claim is brought; failure to do so will result in the claim being deemed inadmissable until such time as the rule is satisfied. In 1959, the United States successfully invoked this rule to avoid a claim filed by Switzerland at the ICJ.[86] Conversely, the United States successfully established that the rule had been satisfied in a 1989 case brought by the United States against Italy.[87] In theory, the rule is designed to permit a state to remedy a wrong at the national level before it is transformed into a dispute on the international plane, where it might disrupt unnecessarily relations between states. In practice, it provides the Court with an opportunity to decline to pass upon a dispute that might place it in direct conflict with the tendency of some states toward strong constitutional autonomy. Similarly, the

---

85. Committee of U.S. Citizens Living in Nicar. v. Reagan, 859 F.2d 929 (D.C. Cir. 1988).

86. *See* Interhandel (Switz. v. U.S.), 1959 I.C.J. 6 (Mar. 21).

87. *See* Elettronica Sicula S.p.A. (ELSI) (U.S. v. Italy), 1989 I.C.J. 15 (July 20) [hereinafter ELSI].

Court at times has seized upon doctrines of standing[88] and mootness[89] to avoid highly-charged disputes.

Even if the Court addresses a case on the merits, it is possible to detect judicial reasoning that reflects sensitivity to the political limits of the Court's authority. In the *Nuclear Weapons* advisory opinion,[90] the Court engaged in a systematic analysis of why treaties and customary rules of international law *did not* expressly prohibit the possession or use of nuclear weapons. Several states had possessed nuclear weapons since their invention, such that a formal legal analysis pointed towards their legality under international law. Yet the vast majority of states do not possess nuclear weapons and such weapons are highly unpopular among a wide range of states, non-governmental organizations, and peace activists. Consequently, the Court was likely attracted to a judicial outcome that viewed the use of nuclear weapons as unlawful, and its legal analysis ultimately concluded that certain principles of international humanitarian law generally *did* prohibit such use.

The Court, however, declined to outright declare nuclear weapons unlawful. Several of the judges no doubt were sensitive to the fact that nuclear weapons were unlikely to be eliminated based solely on an ICJ decision, and that the most powerful states in the world rejected the idea that the possession and use of such weapons were in all circumstances unlawful. Further, the judges were likely conscious that a decision banning nuclear weapons was not firmly grounded in international law; there were certainly no treaties that expressly stated as much and the position that international humanitarian law disfavored the use of nuclear weapons was plausible but not obvious. Consequently, the Court reached a conclusion that balanced strong contending views: it found that the use of nuclear weapons as a general matter was unlawful, but that in certain extreme circumstances, involving the very survival of a state, such use might be lawful. The Court, in effect, issued a Solomonic judgment by strongly condemning the use of nuclear weapons, yet providing nuclear weapon states with a legal basis for maintaining the status quo.

E.   U.S. Relationship with the World Court

Jurisdiction Pursuant to Treaties

The United States is a party to many treaties that confer jurisdiction on the ICJ, thus enabling the United States to sue and

---

88. *See* South West Africa (Eth. v. S. Afr.; Liber. v. S. Afr.), 1966 I.C.J. 6 (July 18).

89. *See* Nuclear Tests (Austl. v. Fr.; N.Z. v. Fr.), 1974 I.C.J. 253 (Dec. 20).

90. Advisory Opinion on Legality of the Threat or Use of Nuclear Weapons, 1996 I.C.J. 226 (July 8).

be sued there. The last case brought to the Court by the United States under this form of jurisdiction was in 1987 with the filing of the *ELSI* case.[91] In that case, the United States invoked a compromissory clause contained in a 1948 bilateral Treaty of Friendship, Commerce, and Navigation that provided for ICJ jurisdiction over disputes arising under the treaty.[92] The United States alleged expropriation of and interference with property of a U.S. company's subsidiary in Sicily, but the Court ultimately concluded that no compensable harm had occurred from the alleged acts.

Since the *ELSI* case, the only other dispute pursued by the United States that might have led to the filing of an independent U.S. claim before the International Court appears to have been the "hushkits" dispute between the United States and Europe.[93] On March 14, 2000, the United States initiated a dispute resolution proceeding by filing an application and memorial before the International Civil Aviation Organization (ICAO) Council in its capacity as a judicial body.[94] The dispute concerned a 1999 E.C. regulation relating to aircraft noise, which imposed design-based restrictions on aircraft registered in, or operating in, Europe. In November 2000, the ICAO Council rejected certain preliminary objections raised by the European Community.[95] In the aftermath of the ICAO Council decision, neither the United States nor E.C. member states exercised their right to appeal the Council's decision to the ICJ (as permitted under the Chicago Convention). Rather, the E.C. filed a counter-memorial in December 2000 and the parties thereafter settled the matter. This dispute was only the fifth in ICAO's history addressed by the ICAO Council in its judicial capacity, the others being India v. Pakistan (1952), United Kingdom v. Spain (1969), Pakistan v. India (1971), and Cuba v. United States (1998). Only the 1971 Pakistan v. India dispute was appealed to the International Court.[96]

Since the 1980's, the United States has consistently declined to accept or incorporate into treaties compromissory clauses calling for

91. *See* ELSI, *supra* note 87.

92. *See* Treaty of Friendship, Commerce and Navigation, U.S.-Italy, art. XXVI, Feb. 2, 1948, 63 Stat. 2255, 79 U.N.T.S. 171.

93. The United States did file a counter-claim based on a bilateral treaty of amity in a case brought by Iran for destruction of three complexes of Iranian oil platforms in the Gulf. *See* Oil Platforms (Iran v. U.S.), 2003 I.C.J. 161, para. 9 (Nov. 6). The Court rejected that counter-claim.

94. Such a dispute is brought under Article 84 of the Convention on International Civil Aviation, Dec. 7, 1944, 61 Stat. 1180, 15 U.N.T.S. 295 [hereinafter Chicago Convention], and Article 2 of the ICAO Rules for the Settlement of Differences, ICAO Doc. 7782/2 (2d ed. 1975).

95. *See* Decision of the ICAO Council on the Preliminary Objections in the Matter "United States and 15 European States (2000)" (Nov. 16, 2000) (on file with author).

96. *See* Appeal Relating to the Jurisdiction of the ICAO Council (India v. Pak.), 1972 I.C.J. 46 (Aug. 18).

adjudication of disputes by the ICJ. Whenever the United States now adheres to multilateral treaties (such as the Convention Against Genocide) containing such a clause, it files a reservation to that clause. Whenever the United States adheres to multilateral treaties that allow parties to opt for ICJ jurisdiction, then the U.S. declines to do so. If the United States ratifies the 1982 U.N. Convention on the Law of the Sea, it has announced that it will opt for binding arbitral dispute settlement, not dispute settlement before the ICJ.[97] As discussed earlier in this chapter, U.S. bilateral investment treaties (BITs) call for investor-state arbitration before the International Centre for the Settlement of Investment Disputes (ICSID) or another forum, a striking contrast to the earlier generation of Friendship, Commerce, and Navigation (FCN) treaties, which provided for ICJ jurisdiction. Investment disputes arising under the North American Free Trade Agreement (NAFTA) are sent to investor-state arbitration before ICSID or an *ad hoc* panel operating under UNCITRAL arbitration rules. U.S. trade disputes—under agreements completed in the past twenty years—are placed before World Trade Organization (WTO) panels, panels operating under NAFTA Chapters 19 or 20, or panels operating under bilateral trade agreements; they are not placed before the International Court.

Jurisdiction Under the "Optional Clause"

In 1946, the United States accepted the Court's compulsory jurisdiction in the hope that doing so would encourage other states to follow suit.[98] At the same time, however, the United States placed in its declaration certain reservations. One reservation, referred to as the "Vandenberg reservation," provided that the Court could not pass upon disputes regarding a multilateral treaty unless all parties to the treaty affected by the decision were also parties to the case before the Court. The United States successfully invoked this reservation in a case brought by Nicaragua so as to prevent the Court from passing upon U.S. obligations under certain treaties, such as the U.N. Charter.[99] At the same time, the Court concluded that the use-of-force norms contained in those treaties "correspond, in essentials, to those found in customary international law," and therefore could be adjudicated as such.[100]

A second reservation placed in the U.S. declaration accepting the Court's compulsory jurisdiction was the "Connally reserva-

97. *See* S. Treaty Doc. No. 103–39, V at IX–X (1994) (Department of State letter submitting the convention to the president for transmittal to the Senate).

98. *See* S. Res. 196, 79th Cong. (2d Sess. 1946).

99. *See* Military and Paramilitary Activities in and against Nicaragua (Nicar. v. U.S.), 1986 I.C.J. 14, 38 (June 27).

100. *Id.* at 99.

tion," which excluded from the jurisdiction of the Court "disputes with regard to matters which are essentially within the domestic jurisdiction of the United States of America as determined by the United States of America." This reservation not only carved out from the jurisdiction of the Court a certain category of disputes, it also contained a self-judging clause—"as determined by the United States"—which was designed to ensure that the United States (and not the ICJ) would decide which disputes fell outside the Court's jurisdiction. Since a reservation of this type purports to foreclose the ability of the Court to decide whether it has jurisdiction,[101] many scholars and some ICJ judges have expressed doubts as to whether it is permissible, but to date the Court has not definitively addressed the issue.

A central problem with the Connally reservation emerged early in the life of the Court. Since the Court operates on a principle of reciprocity in the application of its compulsory jurisdiction,[102] the Connally reservation had the effect of allowing any state sued by the United States to invoke the reservation against the United States, thereby requiring the Court to dismiss the case. When the United States sued Bulgaria in 1957 for an attack on an El Al aircraft flying over Bulgarian territory (resulting, among other things, in the death of six U.S. nationals), Bulgaria responded that the matter was "essentially within" Bulgaria's "domestic jurisdiction," and thus outside the jurisdiction of the Court. The United States at first objected that such a response was in bad faith, yet ultimately concluded that allowing the Court to decide the issue would defeat the entire point of the reservation, and so withdrew its case.[103] Moreover, while the United States in theory could invoke the Connally reservation at will, it declined to invoke the reservation in the case brought by Nicaragua in 1984, because it simply was not credible to declare that U.S. attacks allegedly occurring in Nicaraguan territory were matters "essentially within the domestic jurisdiction of the United States."

After the Court rejected various jurisdictional objections raised by the United States in *Military and Paramilitary Activities in and against Nicaragua*,[104] the United States notified the Court in October 1985 of its decision to terminate U.S. acceptance of the Court's compulsory jurisdiction.[105] The termination became effective in

101. See ICJ Statute, *supra* note 49, art. 36(6).

102. *Id.*, art. 36(2).

103. See Leo Gross, *Bulgaria Invokes the Connally Amendment*, 56 Am. J. Int'l L. 357 (1962).

104. See Military and Paramilitary Activities in and against Nicaragua (Nicar. v. U.S.), 1984 I.C.J. 392 (Nov. 26).

105. See United States: Department of State Letter and Statement Concerning Termination of Acceptance of I.C.J. Compulsory Jurisdiction (Oct. 7, 1985), *reprinted in* 24 I.L.M. 1742 (1985). A year earlier, in an effort to forestall the

1986 and remains so today. The reasons stated by the United States for withdrawing from the Court's compulsory jurisdiction fell into four areas.[106] First, the United States was clearly upset at the Court for finding that jurisdiction existed over Nicaragua's case, which resulted in the Court wading into the highly-charged politics of President Reagan's Latin American policy. For the United States, the Court's decision that Nicaragua had accepted the Court's compulsory jurisdiction, that El Salvador could not intervene at the jurisdiction stage, and that Nicaragua's claims were justiciable simply could not be supported as a matter of law. Second, the United States asserted that the anticipated benefits from joining the Court's compulsory jurisdiction had not materialized. The United States originally adhered to the Court's compulsory jurisdiction in the hope that other states would follow, but most states had not filed such declarations. Further, most ICJ cases that had advanced to the merits were not based on the Court's compulsory jurisdiction, and therefore such jurisdiction had not become a principal part of the Court's overall jurisprudence. The United States itself had tried seven times to sue a state on the basis of compulsory jurisdiction, but had never been successful in doing so. Third, the United States emphasized the costs of its adherence to the Court's compulsory jurisdiction: three states had sued the United States on the basis of such jurisdiction.[107] Further, the United States noted that other states might undertake "hit-and-run" tactics by waiting until they wished to sue the United States before filing a declaration accepting the Court's compulsory jurisdiction and then, after filing the case, withdrawing that declaration to avoid themselves being sued. Finally, the United States attacked the credibility and impartiality of the judges of the Court. The United States also declined to participate in the merits phase of *Military and Paramilitary Activities in and against Nicaragua*, which led to a judgment against it on several counts.[108]

While U.S. withdrawal from the Court's compulsory jurisdiction may be unfortunate, the United States is in the company of its peers. As noted above, the only permanent member of the Security Council that accepts the Court's compulsory jurisdiction is the United Kingdom. Further, the United States arguably was termi-

---

case being brought by Nicaragua, the United States attempted to modify its declaration so as to exclude "disputes with any Central American state.... " 84 DEP'T ST. BULL. 89 (June 1984).

106. *See* Testimony of Abraham D. Sofaer, U.S. Dep't of State Legal Adviser, to the S. Foreign Relations Comm. (Dec. 4, 1985), *reprinted in* 86 DEP'T ST. BULL. 68 (Jan. 1986).

107. *See* Rights of Nationals of the United States in Morocco (Fr. v. U.S.), 1952 I.C.J. 176 (Aug. 27) [hereinafter Rights of Nationals]; Interhandel, *supra* note 86; Military and Paramilitary Activities in and against Nicaragua, *supra* note 99.

108. *See* Military and Paramilitary Activities in and against Nicaragua, *supra* note 99.

nating an adherence to the Court's compulsory jurisdiction that was, from the start, illusory, given the nature, scope, and effect of the Connally reservation.

Some Recent Cases

Iran Oil Platforms Case. In 1955, the United States and Iran concluded a Treaty of Amity which, among other things, provided for ICJ jurisdiction over disputes arising under the treaty.[109] At the same time, the treaty stated that it "shall not preclude the application of measures [of a party] . . . necessary to protect its essential security interests."[110] In 1987–88, the United States attacked three Iranian offshore oil platforms in the Persian Gulf. Four years later, Iran initiated a case at the ICJ stating that the attacks violated the Treaty of Amity. The United States challenged the jurisdiction of the Court and succeeded in knocking out two of the three treaty provisions upon which Iran based its claim.[111] Moreover, at the merits phase of the proceedings, the United States convinced the Court that the remaining provision had not been violated, since the commerce protected by that provision was not disrupted by the attacks.[112] Although the Court found that the United States had not violated the Treaty of Amity, the Court engaged in an extensive analysis of why the U.S. attacks on the oil platforms violated international law on the use of force, an analysis thereafter questioned by the U.S. Department of State legal adviser.[113]

Israeli Wall *Advisory Opinion.* On December 8, 2003, the U.N. General Assembly adopted a resolution asking the ICJ for an advisory opinion on "the legal consequences arising from the construction of the wall being built by Israel, the occupying Power, in the Occupied Palestinian Territory, including in and around East Jerusalem. . . . "[114] The resolution received ninety votes in favor, seventy-four abstentions, and eight opposed (including the United States). The United States instead favored pursuing the "Quartet's road map"—a plan that the United States, European Union, Russian Federation, and U.N. secretary-general had developed in 2003 to further the process (initiated at the 1991 Madrid Conference) for peacefully resolving the Israeli–Palestinian conflict.

In its written pleading to the Court, the United States argued that the Court should decline to answer the General Assembly's request on grounds of judicial propriety. To the United States, the

---

109. *See* Treaty of Amity, Economic Relations and Consular Rights, U.S.-Iran, art. XXI(2), Aug. 15, 1955, 8 U.S.T. 899, 284 U.N.T.S. 93.

110. *Id.*, art. XX(1)(d).

111. *See* Oil Platforms (Iran v. U.S.), 1996 I.C.J. 803 (Dec. 12).

112. *See* Oil Platforms, *supra* note 93, at paras. 98–99.

113. *See* William H. Taft, IV, *Self-Defense and the* Oil Platforms *Decision*, 29 YALE J. INT'L L. 295 (2004).

114. G.A. Res. ES–10/14 (Dec. 12, 2003).

Court was being asked to pass upon a bilateral dispute (between Israel and Palestine) in the guise of an advisory opinion, even though one of the disputants (Israel) had not consented to the Court's jurisdiction over the dispute.[115] The United States hoped to convince the Court that it would be overstepping the structural constraints on its jurisdiction by answering the question. Further, the United States reiterated its view that it was not proper for the Court to address an issue that was being handled by the major powers through political negotiations.[116]

The Court, however, determined that answering the question would not impede the Middle East peace process. That conclusion no doubt was shared by a majority of states, as was the Court's conclusion that construction of the barrier in occupied Palestinian territory was contrary to international law.[117] Among other things, the Court asserted that the construction of the barrier so as to protect the settlements of Israeli citizens in the occupied territory violated Palestinian rights of self-determination.

Death Penalty Cases. Three cases before the Court concerned the treatment of aliens on death row in the United States. The crux of the *Breard/LaGrand/Avena* line of cases was that U.S. law enforcement personnel have often failed to advise aliens upon their arrest of the right to have their consulate notified, a right contained in Article 36 of the Vienna Convention on Consular Relations (VCCR).[118] Thereafter, some aliens have been convicted of serious crimes and sentenced to death.

Paraguay, Germany, and Mexico each brought a case against the United States before the ICJ by invoking an optional protocol to the VCCR on dispute settlement.[119] All three applicant states asked the Court for provisional measures of protection so that individuals would not be executed prior to a decision by the Court on the merits. Germany and Mexico also asked the Court for decisions on the merits regarding whether the United States had violated its obligations under the VCCR and what consequences should flow from those violations.

In all three cases, the Court ordered provisionally that the United States "take all measures at its disposal to ensure" (*Breard,*

---

115. *See* Written Statement of the United States of America, paras. 3.3–3.10 (filed Jan. 30, 2004), Advisory Opinion on Legal Consequences of the Construction of a Wall in the Occupied Palestinian Territory, *at* <http://www.icj-cij.org>. The United States made no oral submissions to the Court.

116. *Id.*, para. 4.6.

117. *See* Advisory Opinion on Legal Consequences of the Construction of a Wall in the Occupied Palestinian Territory, 2004 I.C.J. 136 (July 9).

118. Art. 36, Apr. 24, 1963, 21 U.S.T. 77, 596 U.N.T.S. 261.

119. *See* Optional Protocol to the VCCR Concerning Compulsory Settlement of Disputes, Apr. 24, 1963, 21 U.S.T. 325, 596 U.N.T.S. 487.

LaGrand) or "all measures necessary to ensure" (*Avena*) that the relevant aliens not be executed pending a final decision by the Court.[120] The position of the U.S. government, however, was that such ICJ provisional orders were not binding upon the United States under the U.N. Charter, ICJ Statute, or VCCR optional protocol. After the provisional measures order was issued in *Breard*, the U.S. secretary of state sent a letter to the governor of Virginia (where Breard was on death row). The secretary requested that the governor stay Breard's execution since the "execution of Mr. Breard in the face of the Court's April 9 action could be seen as a denial by the United States of the significance of international law and the Court's processes in its international relations and thereby limit our ability to ensure that Americans are protected when living or traveling abroad."[121] In declining to intervene in the case, the U.S. Supreme Court stated that it was "clear that Breard procedurally defaulted his claim, if any, under the Vienna Convention by failing to raise that claim in the state courts."[122] Further, the Court stated:

> [W]hile we should give respectful consideration to the interpretation of an international treaty rendered by an international court with jurisdiction to interpret such, it has been recognized in international law that, absent a clear and express statement to the contrary, the procedural rules of the forum State govern the implementation of the treaty in that State.[123]

Thereafter, the governor of Virginia decided not to stay the execution, and Breard was executed.

After the provisional measures order was issued in *LaGrand*, the U.S. government transmitted the order to the governor of Arizona (where LaGrand was on death row). Again, the U.S. Supreme Court declined to intervene, and the governor of Arizona decided not to stay the execution. In the *Avena* case, at the time the provisional measures order was issued, none of the individuals were on the verge of execution.

On the merits of the case, in *LaGrand*[124] and *Avena*[125] the Court found that the United States had violated its obligations under the

---

120. Vienna Convention on Consular Relations (Para. v. U.S.), Provisional Measures, 1998 I.C.J. 11 (Apr. 9); Vienna Convention on Consular Relations (Ger. v. U.S.), Provisional Measures, 1999 I.C.J. 9 (Mar. 3); Avena and Other Mexican Nationals (Mex. v. U.S.), Provisional Measures (I.C.J. Feb. 5, 2003), *reprinted in* 42 I.L.M. 309 (2003).

121. Letter from Madeleine K. Albright, U.S. Sec'y of State, to James S. Gilmore III, Gov. of Virginia (Apr. 13,

1998), *partially reprinted in* 92 Am. J. Int'l L. 671–72 (1998).

122. Breard v. Greene, 523 U.S. 371, 375 (1998).

123. *Id.*

124. LaGrand (Ger. v. U.S.), 2001 I.C.J. 466 (June 27).

125. Avena and Other Mexican Nationals (Mex. v. U.S.), 2004 I.C.J. 12 (Mar. 31).

VCCR by not informing the aliens of their right of consular notification, not notifying their consulates of their detentions, and effectively depriving the consulates of their ability to communicate with and have access to the aliens. In both cases, the Court also found that the failure to provide judicial review of the convictions and sentences in light of the lack of notification constituted a further violation of the VCCR. As for the U.S. prospective obligation the Court stated in *LaGrand* that "should nationals of the Federal Republic of Germany nonetheless be sentenced to severe penalties" without their right to consular notification having been respected, the United States, "by means of its own choosing, shall allow the review and reconsideration of the conviction and sentence by taking account of the violation of the rights set forth" in the VCCR.[126] The Court reached a similar finding on "review and reconsideration" with respect to the fifty-one Mexican nationals in the *Avena* case.[127] As to how such "review and reconsideration" should occur, the International Court found in both cases that a local procedural default rule cannot justify precluding review of a petitioner's claim.[128] Further, the Court found that VCCR Article 36 creates "individual rights," which are arguably enforceable in U.S. courts.[129] With an eye to the U.S. approach of relying on governors and parole boards to commute death sentences as a remedy for the VCCR violations, the Court in *Avena* stated that the process must entail "a procedure which guarantees that full weight is given to the violations of the rights set forth in the Vienna Convention" and "should occur within the overall judicial proceedings relating to the individual defendant concerned."[130] The Court specifically noted that "the clemency process, as currently practised within the United States criminal justice system, does not appear to meet the requirements. . . ."[131]

On February 28, 2005, President Bush issued a memorandum to the attorney general stating that the United States "will discharge its international obligations" under the *Avena* decision "by having State courts give effect to the decision in accordance with general principles of comity in cases filed by the 51 Mexican nationals addressed in that decision."[132] Having taken this step, the

---

126. LaGrand, *supra* note 124, para. 128(7).

127. Avena and Other Mexican Nationals, *supra* note 125, para. 153(9).

128. *See* LaGrand, *supra* note 124, paras. 90–91; Avena and Other Mexican Nationals, *supra* note 125, paras. 110–13, 153.

129. The Court said "Article 36, paragraph 1, creates individual rights, which, by virtue of Article I of the Optional Protocol, may be invoked in this

Court by the national State of the detained person." LaGrand, *supra* note 124, para. 77.

130. Avena and Other Mexican Nationals, *supra* note 125, paras. 139–40.

131. *Id.*, para. 143.

132. Brief for the United States as Amicus Curiae Supporting Respondent, attachment, Medellin v. Dretke, 544 U.S. 660 (2005) (filed February 28, 2005).

United States sought to ensure that it would not again be placed in such a position. On March 7, 2005, the U.S. government informed the U.N. secretary-general that was terminating its adherence to the VCCR optional protocol, thereby foreclosing future ICJ cases against the United States based on the protocol.

Of the Mexican nationals on death row, the first set for execution was José Ernesto Medellín, held on death row in Texas. Although President Bush's memorandum was communicated to the government of Texas, Texas authorities declined to engage in any review and reconsideration. The matter was appealed to the U.S. Supreme Court, but the Court found that no treaty provided for enforcement of the International Court's judgment within the United States (though Congress could enact a statute providing for such enforcement) and that the President did not have the power on his own to require Texas courts to comply with such a judgment.[133] Having exhausted all appeals, Medellín was executed in August 2008.

On June 5, 2008, Mexico filed a request before the Court seeking an "interpretation" of the Court's 2004 judgment under Article 60 of the ICJ's Statute. Among other things, Mexico sought a finding from the Court that the United States, through all its branches of government (federal or state), must take measures to ensure that no Mexican national is executed who has not received the "review and reconsideration" called for in the 2004 judgment. The Court, however, noted that a question that was not decided in the initial judgment cannot be submitted to the Court for "interpretation," and that the question of the effects of the Court's judgment on the domestic legal order of the United States was not within the scope of the 2004 judgment. Consequently, Mexico's request was denied.[134]

Overall U.S. Track Record.

Out of a total 119 contentious cases filed before the Court (1946 to 2010), the United States was involved in twenty-two. No other state has appeared before the Court so frequently. Indeed, China has never appeared before the Court in a contentious case. In ten of the twenty-two cases, the United States was the applicant (or jointly agreed to the submission of the case to the Court). In those ten cases, the United States:

- secured a boundary decision regarded by many as favorable

133. Medellín v. Texas, 552 U.S. 491 (2008); *see* Chapter 7(B)-(C).

134. Request for Interpretation of the Judgment of 31 March 2004 in *Ave-*

na and Other Mexican Nationals (Mex. v. U.S.) (Mex. v. U.S.), 2009 I.C.J. (Jan. 19).

to the U.S. position;[135]

- won one case on the merits;[136]

- lost one case on the merits;[137]

- had to withdraw or accept removal of seven cases against Soviet bloc states due to lack of jurisdiction.[138]

In twelve cases, the United States was the respondent. In those cases:

- two were resolved prior to a decision on the merits by the Court;[139]

- three were dismissed by the Court on jurisdictional, admissibility, or other grounds;[140]

- one was won on the merits;[141]

- one was partially won and partially lost on the merits;[142]

- four were lost.[143]

Of the cases the United States lost on the merits, none were taken to a damages phase, so the existence of a monetary judgement against the United States has not arisen.

In addition to its contentious jurisdiction, the International Court of Justice has issued twenty-five advisory opinions from 1946 to 2011. The United States was involved in twenty-three of those

135. *See* Gulf of Maine, *supra* note 54.

136. *See* United States Diplomatic and Consular Staff in Tehran (U.S. v. Iran), 1980 I.C.J. 3 (May 24).

137. *See* ELSI, *supra* note 87.

138. *See* Aerial Incident of 27 July 1955 (U.S. v. Bulg.), 1960 I.C.J. 146 (May 30); Aerial Incident of 7 November 1954 (U.S. v. U.S.S.R.), 1959 I.C.J. 276 (Oct. 7); Aerial Incident of 4 September 1954 (U.S. v. U.S.S.R.), 1958 I.C.J. 158 (Dec. 9); Aerial Incident of 10 March 1953 (U.S. v. Czech.), 1956 I.C.J. 6 (Mar. 14); Aerial Incident of 7 October 1952 (U.S. v. U.S.S.R.), 1956 I.C.J. 9 (Mar. 14); Treatment in Hungary of Aircraft and Crew of the United States of America (U.S. v. Hung.), 1954 I.C.J. 99 (July 12); Treatment in Hungary of Aircraft and Crew of the United States of America (U.S. v. U.S.S.R.), 1954 I.C.J. 103 (July 12).

139. *See* Aerial Incident of 3 July 1988 (Iran v. U.S.), 1996 I.C.J. 9 (Feb. 22) (ordering discontinuance of the case following a settlement); Questions of In-

terpretation and Application of the 1971 Montreal Convention Arising from the Aerial Incident at Lockerbie (Libya v. U.S.), 2003 I.C.J. 152 (Sept. 10) (ordering discontinuance of the case).

140. *See* Legality of Use of Force, *supra* note 63; Interhandel, *supra* note 86; Monetary Gold (Italy v. U.S.), 1954 I.C.J. 19 (June 15); Request for Interpretation of the Judgment of 31 March 2004, *supra* note 134.

141. *See* Oil Platforms, *supra* note 93.

142. *See* Rights of Nationals, *supra* note 107.

143. *See* Military and Paramilitary Activities in and against Nicaragua, *supra* note 99; Vienna Convention on Consular Relations (Para. v. U.S.), *supra* note 120 (lost at the provisional measures stage and then discontinued by the applicant); LaGrand, *supra* note 124; Avena and Other Mexican Nationals, *supra* note 125. At the same time, the United States prevailed on certain arguments in these cases that narrowed the scope of the Court's findings.

advisory opinions through either written or oral pleadings. Again, no other state has participated in advisory proceedings so frequently. It is hard to find any discernible trends in this practice, although it appears that the United States was more enthusiastic about using the Court's advisory opinion jurisdiction early in the life of the Court, when the United States had greater influence in the General Assembly in requesting such opinions. In more recent years (*e.g.*, the *Nuclear Weapons* advisory opinions, the Israeli *Wall* advisory opinion, and the Kosovo declaration of independence advisory opinion), the United States has opposed the requesting of advisory opinions and, once requested, has argued that the Court should decline the request.

F. Other International Courts

Several other international courts exist as well. While they cannot be described in depth, the following provides salient information on the best known of these courts.

European Court of Justice

The European Court of Justice (ECJ) is the principal judicial institution of the European Union (EU),[144] composed of twenty-seven judges and eight advocates-general appointed by common accord of the EU states for renewable terms of six years. The ECJ can sit as a full court, in a grand chamber of thirteen judges, or in chambers of three or five judges. The advocates-general assist the ECJ prior to its deliberations by delivering impartial legal opinions in open court. Several hundred cases have been decided by the ECJ since its inception in 1953, such that its jurisprudence is rich and detailed.[145]

The ECJ has jurisdiction to hear various types of actions relating to EU treaties and rules adopted by EU institutions. It also has jurisdiction over cases brought against an EU member state for failure to fulfill its EU obligations. Such cases are normally brought by the European Commission, but can also be brought by another EU state. If the challenge is successful, the EU state is obligated to comply with the ECJ's decision without delay. Further, the ECJ has jurisdiction over cases seeking annulment of an EU law. Such cases may be brought by an EU state or by one of the EU institutions (the council, the commission, or the parliament).

Moreover, persons may seek annulment of a legal measure or challenge a failure to act when the law is of direct and individual concern to them. If the EU law is successfully challenged, the ECJ

---

144. *See* Chapter 2(B).

145. *See* ANTHONY ARNULL, THE EUROPEAN UNION AND ITS COURT OF JUSTICE (2d. ed. 2006).

declares it to be void. The same type of challenge may be brought for the failure of an EU institution to act. The ECJ has jurisdiction over actions for damages (based on non-contractual liability) caused by an EU institution or its employee(s) acting in performance of their duties.

The national courts of EU states, when confronted with a need to interpret EU law about which they are uncertain, may request a preliminary ruling from the ECJ. The jurisdiction of the ECJ to issue preliminary rulings is a useful device for maintaining a uniform interpretation of EU law. Finally, the ECJ hears appeals of decisions rendered by a Court of First Instance, which has jurisdiction to decide all actions brought by individuals and EU states, with the exception of certain actions assigned to a judicial panel or reserved for the ECJ.

European Court of Human Rights

In 1950, the Council of Europe adopted the Convention for the Protection of Human Rights and Fundamental Freedoms.[146] In addition to codifying a variety of civil/political rights and freedoms, the convention provided for the establishment of a European Court of Human Rights (ECHR). Set up in 1959 in Strasbourg, the ECHR is composed of one judge for every contracting state to the convention (forty-seven as of 2011), with no restriction on the number of judges of the same nationality. The judges are elected by the Parliamentary Assembly of the Council of Europe for terms of six years.

Any contracting state, or any individual claiming to be a victim of a violation of the convention, may lodge with the ECHR an application alleging a breach by a contracting state of one of the convention's rights. The petition must meet certain admissibility requirements, which are higher for individual petitions than for inter-state petitions. If the petition is admissible, a seven-judge chamber may invite the parties to submit evidence and written observations, including any claims for "just satisfaction" by the applicant. A hearing might then be held, after which the chamber decides the matter by a majority vote. The chamber's decision can be referred to a grand chamber of seventeen judges for review. Once final, the decision is binding on the contracting state to which it is directed.

Each year, thousands of applications are filed with the ECHR. The vast majority are declared inadmissable, but a large number are also reviewed on the merits. From 1959 to 2010, the ECHR issued 13,697 judgments on the merits, of which 11,438 judgments found at least one violation of the convention. The most common

---

146. Nov. 4, 1950, 312 U.N.T.S. 221, Europ. T.S. No. 5, as amended.

issues concerned the excessive length of court proceedings (4,469 judgments), the right to a fair trial (3,461), the right to protection of property (2,414), the right to liberty and security (1,944), and the right to an effective remedy (1,372). Countries against whom the greatest number of judgments were made were Turkey (2,573), Italy (2,121), Russia (1,079), Poland (874), France (815), Romania (791), Ukraine (717), and Greece (613).[147]

When requested by the Committee of Ministers of the Council of Europe, the ECHR may also issue advisory opinions on legal questions concerning the interpretation of the convention and its protocols. Advisory opinions are given by the grand chamber and adopted by a majority vote.

Inter-American Court of Human Rights

In 1969, the Organization of the American States (OAS) adopted the American Convention on Human Rights,[148] which entered into force in 1978. The convention created two organs to promote the observance and protection of human rights: the Inter-American Commission on Human Rights and the Inter-American Court of Human Rights. Based in Costa Rica, the court consists of seven judges who are nationals of the OAS member states and who are elected by the contracting states to the American Convention. The judges serve for terms of seven years and may be re-elected no more than once.

Only contracting states to the convention and the commission may submit cases to the court.[149] Mere ratification of the convention, however, does not expose a contracting state to the court's jurisdiction. Rather, a state must consent *ad hoc* to any case brought against it before the court. Alternatively, when a state joins the convention, it may declare that it recognizes as binding the jurisdiction of the court on matters relating to interpretation or application of the convention, in which case the court has such jurisdiction within the terms of the declaration.[150] As of mid–2011, declarations to this effect had been filed by some twenty-one states. Individuals are not permitted to bring cases before the court, but they may participate in proceedings once initiated by contracting states or the commission. The court may also issue advisory opinions regarding interpretation of the convention and other treaties concerning the protection of human rights in the Americas. Such opinions include examination of whether a state's national law is compatible with its obligations under the convention.

147. ECHR, *Statistical Information: Violation by Article and by Country, 1959–2010* (Dec. 31, 2010), *at* <http://www.echr.coe.int>.

148. Nov. 22, 1969, 1144 U.N.T.S. 123, 9 I.L.M. 673. The United States is not a party to this convention.

149. *Id.*, art. 61(1).

150. *Id.*, art. 62.

The court's numerous judgments or opinions cover a range of issues, but most are focused on arbitrary detention, widespread forced disappearance, torture or cruel, inhumane, or degrading treatment, and violations of due process in criminal proceedings.

International Criminal Courts

In 1993, the U.N. Security Council created an international criminal tribunal, based in the Hague, charged with prosecuting persons for the commission of war crimes, genocide, or crimes against humanity in the former Yugoslavia from 1991 onward.[151] A year later, the Security Council created an analogous tribunal based in Arusha, Tanzania, with respect to crimes committed in Rwanda in 1994.[152] Both of these *ad hoc* international criminal tribunals have prosecution units that investigate, indict, and prosecute alleged war criminals, and judicial units that conduct trials of the suspects, determine whether charges have been proven and, if so, decide what sentences are merited. Only the prosecutor and the accused appear as parties before the tribunals (states do not appear as parties, but have been permitted to file amicus briefs to assist in interpreting relevant law). The accused may be represented by counsel of his or her own choosing, or by counsel appointed by the tribunals. Dozens of suspects have pled guilty or been convicted, and are serving their sentences in the prisons of states that have offered to assist the tribunals. The two tribunals are expected to complete their work within a few years.

As discussed in Chapter 3(A), states meeting in Rome in July 1998 adopted a Statute for a permanent International Criminal Court (ICC).[153] The Rome Statute entered into force on July 1, 2002, and thereafter the ICC began functioning in the Hague. In February 2003, the contracting states elected eighteen judges for staggered terms, so that one-third of the terms expire every three years. In April 2003, the contracting states unanimously elected Luis Moreno–Ocampo of Argentina as the first ICC Chief Prosecutor. A registry office is responsible for all the administrative work of the ICC.

The ICC is a treaty-based court with limited jurisdiction. The court only has jurisdiction over genocide, crimes against humanity, and war crimes, although decisions have been taken that may allow the court to also exercise jurisdiction after 2016 over the crime of aggression.[154] Further, the court only has jurisdiction over crimes

---

151. *See* S.C. Res. 827 (May 25, 1993).

152. *See* S.C. Res. 955 (Nov. 8, 1994).

153. Rome Statute of the International Criminal Court, July 17, 1998, 2187 U.N.T.S. 3.

154. *Id.*, art. 5.

committed after the Rome Statute entered into force.[155] Moreover, the ICC may only investigate and prosecute acts that were: (1) committed on the territory of, or by a national of, a contracting state to the Rome Statute; (2) committed on the territory of, or by a national of, a state that has consented *ad hoc* to the jurisdiction of the ICC; or (3) referred to the ICC by the Security Council.[156]

In addition to the ICTY, ICTR, and ICC, there are a series of other tribunals established through or in conjunction with the United Nations that have more of a quasi-international/quasi-national structure. Those tribunals include: the Special Panels within the District Court of Dili, East Timor (set up in 2000); the Special Court for Sierra Leone (2002); Special Court for Cambodia (2003); and the Special Tribunal for Lebanon (2007). For further discussion of all these tribunals, see Chapter 13(E).

International Tribunal for the Law of the Sea

Under part XV of the U.N. Convention for the Law of the Sea,[157] contracting states must accept one of four options for compulsory dispute resolution.[158] Two options involve arbitration, one involves the ICJ, and the fourth is for dispute resolution before the International Tribunal for the Law of the Sea (ITLOS). Based in Hamburg, Germany, ITLOS consists of twenty-one judges elected by secret ballot of the parties. Each party may nominate up to two candidates. No two judges may be nationals of the same state, and the tribunal is supposed to reflect the principal legal systems of the world, with equitable geographical distribution. As such, there are no fewer than three members from each geographical group as established by the General Assembly of the United Nations: African states; Asian states; East European states; Latin American and Caribbean states; and Western European and other states. The judges are elected for nine year terms and may be re-elected. The terms are staggered so that one-third of the judges terms expire every three years. A registry office is responsible for all the administrative work of ITLOS, including the assessment and collection of contributions from contracting states.

ITLOS has jurisdiction over all disputes submitted to it in accordance with part XV and which concern the interpretation or application of the convention (or concern an associated agreement relating to deep sea-bed mining).[159] ITLOS also has jurisdiction over any dispute concerning the interpretation or application of related conventions that provide for ITLOS jurisdiction, such as the U.N.

---

155. *Id.*, art. 11.

156. *Id.*, arts. 12–13.

157. *See* LOSC, *supra* note 8, arts. 279–99.

158. *See* Chapter 11(D).

159. *See*, LOSC, *supra* note 8, art. 288.

Convention on Straddling and Highly Migratory Fish Stocks.[160] Further, an ITLOS sea-bed disputes chamber has jurisdiction over certain disputes with respect to activities in the deep sea-bed. Finally, ITLOS has jurisdiction over applications for the prompt release of a detained vessel or its crew where the authorities of a contracting state have detained a vessel flying the flag of another contracting state, and it is alleged that the detaining state has not complied with the convention.[161] The relevant provisions of the convention call for the prompt release of the vessel or its crew upon the posting of a reasonable bond or other financial security. Such applications may only be made by or on behalf of the vessel's flag state.

The sea-bed disputes chamber has jurisdiction to give advisory opinions at the request of the Assembly or the Council of the International Sea–Bed Authority. ITLOS may also give an advisory opinion on a legal question if an international agreement related to the convention specifically provides for such an opinion.

G. National Courts

Introduction

National courts may be authorized by their states to use international law as a source of law in their decision-making. As discussed in Chapter 7(C), the U.S. Supreme Court in the *Paquete Habana* case asserted that "[i]nternational law is part of our law, and must be ascertained and administered by the courts of justice of appropriate jurisdiction, as often as questions of right depending upon it are duly presented for their determination."[162] Such statements typically do not mean that international law is supreme over all national law; rather, international law serves as one source of law among many competing sources, with hierarchies that differ depending on the peculiarities of each nation's constitutional structure.

To the extent that national law allows local courts to use international law as a source of law, those courts can be very important in implementing, refining, and developing international law. As well-functioning juridical bodies, national courts have proven important in adjudicating the meaning of ambiguous treaty language or of customary rules.[163]

---

160. *See* Agreement for the Implementation of the Provisions of the United Nations Convention on the Law of the Sea of 10 December 1982 Relating to the Conservation and Management of Straddling Fish Stocks and Highly Migratory Fish Stocks, Aug. 4, 1995, 2167 U.N.T.S. 88, 34 I.L.M. 1542.

161. *See* LOSC, *supra* note 8, art. 292.

162. The Paquete Habana, 175 U.S. 677, 700 (1900).

163. *See* Melissa A. Waters, *Mediating Norms and Identity: The Role of Transnational Judicial Dialogue in Cre-*

Example: U.S. Supreme Court and International Law

U.S. courts regularly are called upon to interpret international law, often in the context of interpreting a treaty to which the United States is a party. For example, in December 1997, Dr. Abid Hanson and his wife, Rubina Husain, traveled on Olympic Airways from San Francisco to Athens and Cairo for a vacation. During the return flight, they discovered that their seats were located near the smoking section, even though they had informed Olympic that Dr. Hanson suffered from asthma and was sensitive to secondhand smoke. The Olympic flight attendant refused to change their seats and during the flight Dr. Hanson died from an allergic reaction to the smoke.[164]

Rubina Husain then sued Olympic Airways in U.S. court for the wrongful death of her husband, citing Article 17 of the Warsaw Convention.[165] Article 17 creates a presumption of air carrier liability so long as the plaintiff shows that the injury was caused by an "accident." Olympic Airways responded that its refusal to reseat Dr. Hanson did not constitute an "accident" within the meaning of Article 17. In considering the meaning of "accident," the U.S. Supreme Court (per Justice Thomas) noted that, while the word is not clearly defined in the Warsaw Convention, the Court had previously discerned its meaning from the convention's "text, structure, and history as well as from the subsequent conduct of the parties. . . . "[166] In *Air France v. Saks*,[167] the Court had undertaken a textual analysis of Article 17, and of Article 17 in relation to the rest of the convention, finding that a passenger's loss of hearing caused by the normal operation of an aircraft's pressurization system was not an "accident." In that case, the Court found that an "accident" under Article 17 was "an unexpected or unusual event or happening that is external to the passenger," and not "the passenger's own internal reaction to the usual, normal, and expected operation of the aircraft."[168]

By contrast, in this case—*Olympic Airways v. Husain*—the Court found that the refusal to move Dr. Hanson was a "factual event" external to him, that the event was a link in the chain of events that caused his death, and that the flight attendant's conduct was unusual or unexpected in light of both industry standards and Olympic's company policy.[169] Consequently, Dr. Hanson's death was an "accident" within the meaning of the Warsaw Convention

---

ating and Enforcing International Law, 93 GEO. L.J. 487 (2005).

164. *See* Olympic Airways v. Husain, 540 U.S. 644, 646–49 (2004).

165. *See* Convention for the Unification of Certain Rules Relating to International Transportation by Air art. 17,

Oct. 12, 1929, 49 Stat. 3000, 137 L.N.T.S. 11.

166. 540 U.S. at 649–52.

167. 470 U.S. 392 (1985).

168. *Id.* at 405.

169. 540 U.S. at 651–57.

for which Olympic was presumptively liable. In conducting this analysis, the Supreme Court (both the majority and those in dissent) looked to the decisions of foreign courts construing the same treaty, just as foreign courts have looked to the decisions of the U.S. Supreme Court for guidance. In this way, a corpus of national court decisions has emerged that implements, refines, and develops international law.

Limits on National Court Jurisdiction

There are limits, however, as to what national courts can do. First, national courts may only exercise jurisdiction granted to them under national law. If national law does not provide national courts jurisdiction to decide matters relating to international law, then such jurisdiction will not exist.

Second, regardless of what national law says, in most circumstances international law requires that there be some connection between the underlying act at issue and the state whose national courts are exercising jurisdiction. Further, the exercise of national jurisdiction must be reasonable (often national law independently will require such a connection, perhaps for reasons of fairness to the defendant). Thus, it is accepted under international law that a state can exercise jurisdiction over an act committed by one of its nationals abroad (referred to as "nationality jurisdiction"), but it is generally not accepted that a state can do so when the act is by a foreign national against another foreign national.[170] This limitation (at least if respected by national courts) constrains national courts from addressing many international legal issues with which they have no connection.

Third, states historically have recognized that their national courts should not exercise jurisdiction over foreign sovereigns.[171] Few states believe that another state's national courts will impartially decide a dispute between the two states. Conversely, states worry that if their national courts allow suits against foreign states, the foreign state will respond in kind. Thus, for a long time, states were regarded as having absolute immunity from the jurisdiction of foreign courts. This constraint severely limited the role national courts could play in interpreting international law and resolving inter-state disputes.

State immunity remains a significant bar for modern national courts. Yet international law has shifted away from absolute state immunity to qualified state immunity, thereby allowing states to be sued in national courts in certain situations (*i.e.*, when a state engages in commercial activity in the territory of the national

---

170. *See* Chapter 8.   **171.** *See* Chapter 9.

courts). Moreover, there remain many cases between *non-state actors* where an issue of international law might arise and the issue of state immunity does not present itself. Thus, in the example of *Olympic Airways v. Husain* (discussed above), the parties before the court were two non-state actors—an injured plaintiff and a defendant airline—who placed before the court arguments regarding the interpretation of an international treaty. Similarly, under the U.S. Alien Tort Statute, federal district courts have original jurisdiction over "any civil action by an alien for a tort only, committed in violation of the law of nations or a treaty of the United States."[172] Such a statute, which is invoked by one person suing another for civil redress, calls upon U.S. courts to inquire into what types of actions (*e.g.*, torture, forced labor, prolonged detention) constitute a violation of international law.

172. 28 U.S.C. § 1350 (2006); *see* Chapter 7(C).

Further Reading

Chittharanjan F. Amerasinghe, *Jurisdiction of International Tribunals* (2003).

Chester Brown, *A Common Law of International Adjudication* (2007).

John Collier & Vaughan Lowe, *The Settlement of Disputes in International Law: Institutions and Procedures* (2000).

Gráinne De Búrca & Joseph H.H. Weiler, eds., *The European Court of Justice* (2002).

Terry D. Gill, *Rosenne's The World Court: What It Is and How It Works* (6th rev. ed. 2003).

Howard M. Holtzmann & Edda Krist Jansdóttir, *International Mass Claims Processes* (2007).

Natalie Klein, *Dispute Settlement in the UN Convention on the Law of the Sea* (2005).

Ruth Mackenzie et al., *The Manual on International Courts and Tribunals* (2d ed. 2010).

J.G. Merrills, *International Dispute Settlement* (4th ed. 2005).

Jo M. Pasqualucci, *The Practice and Procedure of the Inter–American Court of Human Rights* (2003).

Georgios Petrochilos, *Procedural Law in International Arbitration* (2004).

Catherine A. Rogers & Roger P. Alford, *The Future of Investment Arbitration* (2009).

Cesare P.R. Romano, *The Sword and the Scales: The United States and International Courts and Tribunals* (2009).

Shabtai Rosenne, *The Law and Practice of the International Court, 1920–2004* (4th ed. 2005) (4 vols.).

Christoph H. Schreuer, *The ICSID Convention: A Commentary* (2d ed. 2009).

Constanze Schulte, *Compliance with Decisions of the International Court of Justice* (2005).

Yuval Shany, *Regulating Jurisdictional Relations Between National and International Courts* (2009).

Yuval Shaney, *The Competing Jurisdictions of International Courts and Tribunals* (2003).

Daniel Terris et al., *The International Judge: An Introduction to the Men and Women Who Decide the World's Cases* (2007).

Andreas Zimmermann et al., eds., *The Statute of the International Court of Justice: A Commentary* (2006).

Chapter 5

INTERNATIONAL LAW COMPLIANCE AND ENFORCEMENT

An issue often raised in any discussion about international law is whether such law is enforced. For those new to the field, the lack of a centralized system of courts and police capable of ordering and imposing sanctions is a critical flaw, one that even calls into question whether international law is really "law."

Professor Louis Henkin observed: "It is probably the case that *almost all nations observe almost all principles of international law and almost all of their obligations almost all of the time.*"[1] Several points may be made about his statement. First, for all of the writing about international law over the years, there is no definitive analytical or quantitative study about state compliance with international law. Henkin's assertion that it was "probably the case" is a tacit acceptance that the best we can do is make certain broad and generalized assertions about compliance. Second, at the level of broad generalization, international law clearly is not perfect. The converse proposition to Henkin's is that some nations do not observe some principles of international law or some of their obligations at least some of the time. Such a proposition, of course, is not fatal to the idea of international law being "law," in that persons within national legal systems violate the law all the time (murders, thefts, and so on)—often getting away with it—and yet we still refer to national law as "law." Third, the thrust of Henkin's point is that, by and large, states *do* comply with the myriad rules established under international law; widespread deviation and non-conformance simply do not exist. If they did, all the time and energy placed by states into the drafting of international agreements, the development and operation of international organizations, the creation of and litigation before international tribunals, and the interpretation and application of international law by national courts would be extraordinarily misguided. The fact that states and non-state actors place so much emphasis on international law strongly suggests that there is a "there" there.

Nevertheless, understanding *why* states comply with international law is an important undertaking, for it can help explain why

---

1. LOUIS HENKIN, HOW NATIONS BEHAVE: LAW AND FOREIGN POLICY 47 (2d ed. 1979).

some international rules appear to work and others do not. Further, for those that do not, there may be techniques and tools that can be employed to promote or enforce compliance.

A. Compliance

Effect of Initial Commitment

Perhaps the simplest explanation for why states generally comply with international law is that they have consented to it. As discussed in Chapters 1 and 3, international law is heavily oriented toward a consent-based system of law creation. Thus, prior to entering into a treaty commitment, a state seriously considers whether doing so is in its interest, weighs the long-term advantages and disadvantages of such a commitment, and then makes a choice. If the state chooses to join the treaty in 2000, there should be no reason why it would reject the treaty in 2010 or in 2020 absent some radical change in circumstances. If there is a concern about such a change, it is always possible to write a sunset provision or some other form of protection into the treaty (such as a right to withdraw upon six months notice).[2] Further, when a state joins a treaty, there is usually extensive decision-making within the government's bureaucracy, leading to some portion of the bureaucracy that strongly favors adherence to the treaty becoming responsible for the state's implementation of the treaty. That portion of the bureaucracy becomes vested in the success of the treaty and, throughout the treaty's life, promotes state adherence to it. For example, having fought initially to be the agency responsible for implementation of U.S. obligations under the World Heritage Convention,[3] the U.S. Department of Interior does not now wish to see the United States fail in implementing that convention, for failure would reflect badly on the department and diminish its role in transnational affairs.

Suppose, though, that a state's continued compliance with a treaty becomes problematic and there is no legal escape from it. Why might a state continue to comply? One reason might be that while compliance in the short-term can be painful, long-term compliance can be quite beneficial. For any bilateral or multilateral trade agreement, situations will arise where short-term compliance is problematic because imports of cheap goods force some local producers out of business. Taking a short-term approach to the matter, an importing state might be tempted to denounce the treaty. Yet the long-term benefits in promoting overall growth and

2. *See generally* RICHARD B. BILDER, MANAGING THE RISKS OF INTERNATIONAL AGREEMENT (1981).

3. Convention Concerning the Protection of World Cultural and Natural Heritage, Nov. 23, 1972, 27 U.S.T. 37, 1037 U.N.T.S. 151 (1977).

development will often trump the short-term concerns. Consequently, the state continues to comply even in situations where one might predict deviation. Similarly, for any extradition treaty, it might seem counter-intuitive that a state would accept an obligation to send one of its nationals to another state for prosecution. Yet, in the long-term, doing so allows the sending state to make claims against the receiving state for extraditions in the opposite direction. Thus, both states benefit in the long-term by enhancing their overall law enforcement capabilities.

Moreover, the long-term benefits of compliance must take account not just of benefits flowing from a single treaty or other international obligation, but from the international legal system as a whole. All states benefit from the regularity and reliability of an international legal system that works. Deviating from treaty commitments and obligations simply because a state wishes to do so risks encouraging other states to do the same, not just with respect to that treaty, but other international obligations as well. To the extent that states adopt a culture of non-compliance, the system will collapse, with adverse collateral consequences for all.

In Chapter 3(E), the process of law-making at the International Civil Aviation Organization (ICAO) was described in some detail, particularly the adoption of international "standards" and "recommended practices" (SARPs). Connecting that discussion to the present discussion of compliance, the ability of member states to opt out of SARPs at the time of their creation may be the reason that a large number of states have joined ICAO, accepted ICAO's ability to establish standards that directly regulate states, and designed their national laws to receive those standards with relative ease. Moreover, the ability to opt out likely explains why states have not sought to "water down" the standards to reach a low "common denominator" of regulation. There are differing levels of capability among states to comply with detailed regulations and the ICAO system accommodates those differences by permitting flexibility in the application of its regulations.

As for whether states actually comply with SARPs, the verdict appears to be mixed. Fairly high levels of compliance have been observed with respect to SARPs concerning aircraft equipment and construction because the major states that build aircraft operate within national legal systems that tend to comply with ICAO rules. Manufacturers of aircraft benefit from the greater certainty of multilateral cooperation; compliance with a patchwork of different national regulations would be inefficient and costly. At the same time, many other countries (principally from the developing world) are fairly lax in compliance with ICAO obligations, principally due to a lack of technical and financial capacity.

Effect of Reputational Consequences

Another factor that encourages compliance with international law concerns a state's reputation in international society. A newly emerged sovereign state typically finds great value in having other states recognize it and admit it to membership in international organizations. The leaders of the new state want to be welcomed into the "club" of states, for it helps consolidate their sovereign power and otherwise bestows upon them a degree of respectability and legitimacy.[4]

International Law

Which of these two views is closer to yours?

	Our nation should consistently follow int'l laws. It is wrong to violate int'l laws, just as it is wrong to violate laws within a country.	If our government thinks it is not in our nation's interest, it should not feel obliged to abide by int'l laws.
US	69	29
Chile	58	27
Mexico	44	53
Germany	70	26
Ukraine	67	19
Poland	62	29
France	61	35
Russia	54	34
Great Britain	54	43
Egypt	63	37
Azerbaijan	60	31
Palest. ter.	50	46
Turkey	46	46
Iraq	46	31
Kenya	65	34
Nigeria	65	34
China	74	18
Taiwan*	68	24
South Korea	56	44
Indonesia	53	34
Macau*	51	37
India	49	42
Hong Kong*	47	38
Pakistan	38	56
Average	57	35

* Excluded from average   WorldPublicOpinion.org

4. *See, e.g.,* Andrew T. Guzman, How International Law Works: A Rational Choice Theory 71–118 (2008); *but see* Rachel Brewster, *The Limits of Reputa-tion on Compliance,* 1 Int'l Theory 323 (2009); Rachel Brewster, *Unpacking the State's Reputation,* 50 Harv. Int'l L.J. 231 (2009).

This desire to be a good-standing member of the global society of states appears to be a natural human instinct that continues for successive generations of leaders, long after a new state is fully established. Most government leaders do not want to be condemned by others for failing to abide by international obligations; they no more like being called "liars" or "cheaters" than do persons operating in any community. If disagreements exist, they should exist over an interpretation of law and not over a wholesale rejection of law. Deviant behavior might go unnoticed, but other states, international organizations, and increasingly non-governmental organizations can be very effective in public campaigns that spotlight bad behavior and thereby induce compliance, a phenomenon sometimes referred to as a "mobilization of shame."

Disharmony with foreign states is unpleasant, yet it may also reflect a lack of competence or intelligence on the part of a government's leaders, which in turn might have repercussions with their national constituents.[5] While there are certainly some rogue states that prefer to operate largely outside the international legal system, their number is actually quite few.

Fear of Reciprocity

A state considering deviating from an international obligation needs to be concerned not only with its own action, but with the possible counter-actions of other states. Indeed, reciprocity is a powerful force in international relations that helps promote compliance with international norms. If a state engages in a material breach of a treaty, another party to that treaty may suspend or terminate the treaty in response.[6]

Thus, if State A decides—in violation of a trade agreement—to block the import of cheap goods from State B to protect State A's steel industry, it is entirely possible that State B will respond by blocking imports of State A's textiles, thus hurting State A's textile industry. Enforcement of world trade rules turns largely on the concept of authorized retaliation as a means of coercing compliant behavior. Knowing that such retaliation is possible, states are reluctant to deviate from trade rules.

Similarly, if State A is tempted to prosecute an ambassador of State B for alleged spying (which State A is not allowed to do under international diplomatic law), State A would need to worry that State B might respond by prosecuting State A's ambassador on a similar charge, feigned or real. As such, State A would not deviate from international diplomatic law, although it might demand that State B's ambassador be recalled home.

---

5. *See, e.g.,* Xinyuan Dai, *Why Comply? The Domestic Constituency Mechanism,* 59 INT'L ORG. 363 (2005) (using game theory to analyze the European acid rain regime).

6. *See* Chapter 3(A).

Obviously, fear of reciprocity does not exist in all situations. Some states are so powerful vis-á-vis other states that they have little concern about retaliation. Further, some regimes—such as human rights treaties—are not as susceptible to retaliation; it hardly makes sense for State B to torture someone in response to State A's violation of the Convention Against Torture.[7] Nevertheless, the principle of reciprocity runs deep in international law, and it is often the case that deviation from a norm will have collateral consequences due to the reactions of other states.

Effect of "Compliance Pull" of the Norm

So far, this discussion of compliance has centered on the attitude of a state (or more precisely, its leaders) when considering whether to comply with a particular rule of international law. Yet it is also appropriate to concentrate on the nature of the rule itself. Professor Thomas Franck developed a detailed theory on why states comply with rules of international law which focuses on various aspects of the formation and content of the rules.[8] Franck argued that the "legitimacy" of the rule exerts a "compliance pull" on states; the stronger the legitimacy, the stronger the compliance pull. A rule has a high degree of legitimacy when it has been properly validated by the international community, meaning that the rule has "come into being and operates in accordance with generally accepted principles of right process."[9] In other words, one way of looking at the elaborate system for adopting, signing, and ratifying multilateral treaties as described in Chapter 3(A) is that it generates norms that states thereafter regard as highly legitimate as a matter of process and thus deserving of compliance. One reason lower levels of compliance are seen with respect to the "soft law" discussed in Chapter 3(F) is that such "law" is not generated in accordance with accepted process.

Franck also argued that a high degree of legitimacy is associated with rules of international law that are determinate (not vague) and that are coherent (not unfair or irrational). Where rules are vague or incoherent, lesser degrees of compliance may be seen, since states do not understand what the rule requires or do not see the rule as meriting fidelity. Thus, policy-makers can promote greater compliance with international law by developing rules that are determinate and coherent.

---

7. Convention Against Torture and Other Cruel, Inhuman or Degrading Treatment or Punishment, Dec. 10, 1984, S. Treaty Doc. No. 100–20 (1988), 1465 U.N.T.S. 85 [hereinafter Convention Against Torture].

8. *See* Thomas Franck, The Power of Legitimacy Among Nations (1990).

9. *Id.* at 19.

Techniques for Identifying Non–Compliance

Encouraging state compliance appears linked with whether implementation is transparent to other states. There will be little reputational consequences for a non-compliant state, and little ability to pursue capacity-building or coercive measures (discussed below), if it is not known whether the state is in compliance. Consequently, states have developed extensive processes for the reporting of state adherence to international commitments, and in some cases processes for independent verification.

Reporting/Monitoring. Bilateral treaties sometimes include requirements for reporting by one state to another regarding its compliance with the treaty. However, it is more common for there to be regular meetings between experts and diplomats of the two states at which concerns may be raised by either side regarding compliance.

In multilateral treaties, states often include a requirement for regular reporting on implementation of the treaty. For example, the Convention Against Torture[10] entered into force for the United States on November 20, 1994. Article 19 of the convention requires the contracting states to submit every four years a report to a convention committee on their implementation of the convention (the U.N. Committee Against Torture).[11] The reports are then transmitted to the other contracting parties, who can review them and raise concerns directly with the reporting state or at a conference of the parties. In October 1999, the United States submitted its first report, which was divided into two main parts and five annexes.[12] The first part explained the federal system of the U.S. government, and the second described how the United States has implemented the various articles of the convention. The annexes addressed: (1) U.S. reservations, understandings, and declarations in relation to the convention; (2) relevant U.S. constitutional and legislative provisions; (3) U.S. views on capital punishment; (4) Immigration and Naturalization Service implementing regulations; and (5) Department of State implementing regulations. Conceding that no government has a perfect record in each of the areas and obligations covered by the convention, the U.S. government provided examples of police abuse and brutality, excessive uses of force, and death of prisoners in custody. These examples included the well-known incidents of police abuse against Rodney King and Abner Louima, as well as consent decrees and settlements between

---

10. *Supra* note 7.

11. *See* Chapter 10(D).

12. *See* U.S. Dep't of State, Initial Report of the United States of America to the UN Committee Against Torture

(1999); *see also* U.S. Dep't of State, Second Periodic Report of the United States of America to the Committee Against Torture (2005).

the federal government and state, county, and city police forces regarding patterns or practices of excessive force.

Similar reporting requirements exist for many other multilateral treaties in a wide array of areas. As might be expected, some states consistently provide their reports on time, whereas others do not. Further, reports can differ considerably in their quality and detail. In some instances, they are simply circulated to other contracting states. In other instances, the treaty sets up a committee of independent experts charged with reviewing and commenting on the reports. In this fashion, monitoring can occur not just by other contracting states, but by an impartial entity charged with such oversight.

For example, on May 15, 2000, the U.N. Committee Against Torture reacted to the first U.S. report under the Convention Against Torture.[13] The committee welcomed the extensive U.S. legal protections against torture and the efforts pursued by U.S. authorities to achieve transparency in its institutions and practices. The committee also acknowledged the broad recourse to compensation for victims of torture (whether or not such torture occurred in the United States), the introduction of federal regulations preventing "refoulement" of potential torture victims, and the U.S. contributions to the U.N. Voluntary Fund for the Victims of Torture.

The committee expressed concern, however, with the failure of the United States to establish a federal crime of torture in terms consistent with Article 1 of the convention, and called upon the United States to withdraw its reservations, interpretations, and understandings relating to the convention. The committee also expressed concern about the number of cases of police mistreatment of civilians, and of mistreatment in prisons by police and prison guards—much of which seemed to be based upon discrimination, including alleged cases of sexual assault upon female detainees and prisoners. The committee noted that the electroshock devices and restraint chairs used in U.S. law enforcement may violate Article 16 of the convention, which prohibits acts of cruel, inhuman, or degrading treatment by public officials. Finally, the committee expressed concern about the use of "chain gangs" (particularly in public), about restrictions on legal actions by prisoners seeking redress for harm incurred in prison, and about the holding of minors (juveniles) with adults in the regular prison population. Whether in the long term such observations on state practice induce greater compliance with the convention is difficult to establish empirically.

13. *See* U.N. Press Release on Committee Against Torture, 24th Sess. (May   15, 2000).

Independent Verification. When states are not satisfied with simply allowing each state to report on whether it is in compliance, they may turn to techniques for independent verification of compliance. Certain organizations, such as the International Atomic Energy Agency or the Organization for the Prohibition of Chemical Weapons, have very robust inspection powers, where experts regularly are sent—sometimes on short notice—to contracting states where they inspect facilities for compliance. Other organizations have less robust powers, but have found ways of conducting at least some level of scrutiny beyond reliance on the self-reporting of states.

For example, in Chapter 3(F) and above in this chapter, attention was given to the law-making of the International Civil Aviation Organization (ICAO). An example of independent verification of compliance may be seen in the "audits" conducted by ICAO of its member states. In 1995, ICAO adopted a safety oversight program that entailed a largely unstructured, voluntary process for monitoring state compliance with ICAO "standards" and "recommended practices" (SARPs). In 1998, the ICAO General Assembly adopted a mandatory program designed to provide systematic reporting and monitoring by ICAO of the implementation by states of safety-related SARPs.[14] From 1999 to 2001, ICAO progressively audited all member states on their compliance with the safety-related SARPs set forth in Annex 1 (personnel licensing), Annex 6 (operation of aircraft), and Annex 8 (airworthiness of aircraft). The program later expanded to cover all safety-related SARPs using a "systems approach" rather than an annex-driven approach. The main conclusions of the 1999–2001 ICAO audits were made available to all contracting states and were summarized in a progress report issued in 2001. According to that report, many developed states adhered to ICAO SARPs (and often provided higher safety standards), although most states had some laws, regulations or practices that differed and that had not been notified to ICAO.[15] In the wake of the terrorist attacks of 9/11, ICAO commenced a Universal Security Audit Program (USAP) designed to evaluate security laws and policies for consistency with ICAO Annex 17 on aviation security.

Verification programs in support of multilateral rules need not be conducted solely by international organizations. For example, an audit program was conducted by the U.S. Federal Aviation Administration (FAA) in 1992–93 of ICAO member states regarding their compliance with ICAO SARPs, known as the International Aviation

---

14. *See* ICAO Ass. Res. A32–11, 32d Sess. (1998).

15. For the report on the United States, see ICAO Universal Safety Oversight Audit Programme, Confidential Final Audit Report of the Federal Aviation Administration of the United States (n.d.) (the audit was conducted June 7–25, 1999).

Safety Assessment (IASA) program.[16] The FAA stated that if a state's civil aviation authority met its minimum safety obligations under the Chicago Convention, then carriers from that state would be permitted to operate to and from the United States. If the civilian aviation authority did not meet those standards, existing carrier operations would be suspended pending compliance, and applications by new carriers from that state would be denied. As of 1998, the IASA Program had audited eighty-seven states, and the initial findings were that some two-thirds of those states were not fully complying with ICAO SARPs. Common deficiencies included inadequate regulatory legislation and technical data, inexperienced airworthiness staff, and a shortage of adequately trained flight operations inspectors.

The forty-one states of the European Civil Aviation Conference (ECAC) also launched an audit program, known as the Safety Assessment of Foreign Aircraft (SAFA) program, which identified similar deficiencies in compliance by developing states and aircraft under their registration. Under the SAFA program, foreign aircraft in each ECAC state are subject to inspection following a common ECAC procedure and report format. If an inspection identifies significant irregularities, the matter is taken up with the operator of the aircraft and the civil aviation authority of the state of registration. Moreover, where irregularities are regarded as having an immediate impact on safety, inspectors may demand corrective action before they allow the aircraft to leave. During 2003, ECAC states performed 3,414 inspections on 623 foreign operators from 131 states, operating 172 different types of aircraft. Counter-part programs—whereby states pool their resources and expertise to engage in similar audits in coordination with ICAO—now exist in other regions, such as the Central American Agency for Aviation Safety (ACSA) and the Regional Aviation Safety Oversight System of the Caribbean (RASOS) programs.

Capacity-Building

An important insight into compliance issues is that states might be in non-compliance not due to an unwillingness to comply but, rather, because they either do not understand the obligation or lack the capacity to comply. Many international obligations are rather sophisticated, such as the SARPS discussed in the context of ICAO legislation. Other international obligations may be very expensive to implement, requiring the commitment of funds or resources that a developing state simply does not have. In such instances, the solution lies not in shaming or coercing the state into compliance, but in providing the state with the expertise and resources necessary to achieve compliance. This may be particularly

16. *See* FAA, OVERVIEW OF THE FEDER-AL AVIATION ADMINISTRATION FLIGHT STAN-DARDS SERVICE INTERNATIONAL AVIATION SAFETY ASSESSMENT (IASA) PROGRAM (n.d.).

true in cases of complex, multilateral treaty regimes, where an experienced secretariat is capable of "managing" treaty compliance.[17]

For example, the International Monetary Fund (IMF) provides extensive technical assistance to the finance ministries and central banks of member states as a means of strengthening adherence to IMF obligations and policies. Similarly, when states met to chart a course of action for the twenty-first century on global environmental issues, a central focus was on "national mechanisms and international cooperation for capacity building in developing countries."[18] Indeed, in the environmental field, the commitments of developing states are often contingent on their receipt of adequate resources to fulfill those commitments. For example, the Montreal Protocol on ozone depletion provides that "[d]eveloping the capacity [of developing states] to fulfill the obligations ... to comply with the control measures ... will depend upon the effective implementation" of "financial cooperation" and "transfer of technology."[19] In this protocol, and in other environmental agreements, it is common to provide developing states with an extended "grace" period to comply with treaty commitments, in recognition that they may need more time to reach a point where compliance is feasible.

The Montreal Protocol also provides an interesting example of a more formalized "non-compliance procedure." First envisaged in Article 8 of the Montreal Protocol, this procedure was further elaborated in subsequent changes to the protocol. Under the procedure, a contracting state that cannot meet its obligations is encouraged to self-report to a protocol implementation committee (other states may also report when they believe a state is non-compliant). The committee then works with the non-compliant state to achieve compliance, which may entail approaching wealthier states for financial or other assistance. The committee seeks to resolve the matter in a non-accusatory setting, on the assumption that the issue is one of incapacity, not unwillingness to comply. If the matter cannot be resolved amiably, however, it can be reported to a meeting of all the contracting parties, which may decide to impose sanctions on the non-compliant state.

Compliance Due to National Processes

States might absorb into their national law the international commitment, such that the international obligation merges into a

17. *See generally* ABRAM CHAYES & ANTONIA CHAYES, THE NEW SOVEREIGNTY: COMPLIANCE WITH INTERNATIONAL REGULATORY AGREEMENTS (1995).

18. AGENDA 21: PROGRAM OF ACTION FOR SUSTAINABLE DEVELOPMENT, RIO DE JANEIRO, ch. 37, U.N. Doc. A/CONF.151/26 (1992).

19. Montreal Protocol on Substances that Deplete the Ozone Layer, art. 5(5), Sept. 16, 1987, S. TREATY DOC. NO. 100–10 (1987), 1522 U.N.T.S. 3, *as amended* by the 1990 London Amendment (see Annex II to the report of the second meeting of the parties).

national obligation. When this happens, national laws, regulations, and courts become available to strengthen compliance with the international commitment. At the time a state enters into a new international commitment, existing national law may already support adherence to the commitment; indeed, the United States often seeks to steer international negotiations in a direction that requires little or no alterations in existing U.S. law. If existing national law does not support adherence, then some states have a national legal system that automatically receives the international legal norm (monist system). For states whose national legal system does not automatically receive the international law (dualist system), then implementing legislation or regulations may be necessary and, if so, are usually adopted prior to the entry into force of the international obligation. Once the international norm becomes operative in national law, national courts may become available for enforcement, including though action filed by individuals. Further, by constitution, statute or judicial doctrine, states usually interpret national laws so as to be consistent with existing international obligations. The overall effect is for the international obligation to become embedded in the national legal system, thereby allowing the use of that system (by states or non-state actors) to promote compliance.

For example, the United States adheres to the Chicago Convention's "standards" and "recommended practices" (SARPs) by incorporating them into its national law through both statute and administrative regulations. Thus, a U.S. statute provides that in "carrying out" air commerce and safety duties, the secretary of transportation and the administrator of the U.S. Federal Aviation Administration (FAA) "shall act consistently with obligations of the United States ... under an international agreement,"[20] which includes obligations under the Chicago Convention. Further, the FAA administrator is obliged when issuing regulations regarding air commerce and safety to "establish only requirements applicable to foreign air carriers that are consistent with international obligations of the United States.... "[21]

FAA regulations, in turn, provide for detailed implementation of the SARPs. Codified in Title 14 of the U.S. Code of Federal Regulations, which addresses "aeronautics and space," FAA regulations in some instances incorporate SARPs by simple reference. For example, Article 12 of the Chicago Convention requires that states adopt measures to ensure that aircraft of their nationality flying over the high seas conform with ICAO regulations on the "rules of the air." The United States implements this obligation by stating in the relevant FAA regulations that "[e]ach person operating a civil aircraft of U.S. registry outside of the United States shall ...

---

20. 49 U.S.C. § 40105(b)(1)(A) (2006). **21.** 49 U.S.C. § 45106(b)(1)(A) (2006).

[w]hen over the high seas, comply with annex 2 (Rules of the Air) to the Convention on International Civil Aviation.... "[22] Further, the regulation states that Annex 2, "to which reference is made in this part, is incorporated into this part and made a part hereof.... "[23] Similarly, in regulating the system and procedures for sampling and measurement of gaseous emissions of civil aircraft, these FAA regulations simply state that the regulations "shall be as specified in Appendices 3 and 5 to the International Civil Aviation Organization (ICAO) Annex 16.... "[24] Other examples of such direct incorporation include rules that foreign carriers within the United States conduct their operations in accordance with Annex 6 on the operation of aircraft[25] and rules affirming that the system and procedures for sampling and measuring smoke emissions "shall be as specified by" ICAO Annex 16.[26]

In other instances, FAA regulations do not directly incorporate the SARPs by cross-reference, but instead provide regulations written similarly to the relevant ICAO annexes, even repeating verbatim or near-verbatim the language of the SARPs. For example, ICAO member states must "recognize as valid" certificates of airworthiness issued by other member states, so long as the certificate meets the minimum standards set by ICAO. Those minimum standards are set forth in ICAO Annex 8.[27] In setting forth a general requirement with respect to determining whether large aircraft are safe for flight, Annex 8 requires that a standard "shall be established for all applicable combinations of aeroplane mass and centre of gravity position, within the range of loading conditions for which certification is sought."[28] The comparable FAA regulation follows this SARP in near-verbatim language, providing that "[e]ach requirement of this subpart must be met at each appropriate combination of weight and center of gravity within the range of loading conditions for which certification is requested."[29] Appropriate combinations of weight and center of gravity are then laid down in FAA operational manuals and handbooks.[30] Numerous FAA regulatory provisions follow this pattern.

---

22. 14 C.F.R. § 91.703(a)(1) (2010).

23. 14 C.F.R. § 91.703(b).

24. 14 C.F.R. § 34.64 (2010); *see* 40 C.F.R. §§ 87.64, 87.71 (2010).

25. 14 C.F.R. § 129.11(a) (2010).

26. 40 C.F.R. § 87.82 (2010).

27. *See generally* ICAO, AIRWORTHINESS OF AIRCRAFT (9th ed., 2001) [hereinafter Annex 8].

28. *Id.* at IIIA–2–1 (standard 2.1.2).

29. 14 C.F.R. § 25.21(a) (2010); *see* 14 C.F.R. § 23.1519 (2010) (directing that ranges of weight and centers of gravity be established and setting a general guideline on how to do so); 14 C.F.R. § 23.25 (2010) (setting guidelines for limiting allowable weight determinations).

30. *See, e.g.,* FAA Manual AC 120–27E, Aircraft Weight and Balance Control (June 10, 2005); FAA Procedural Handbook H–8083–1, Aircraft Weight and Balance (Aug. 23, 1999).

In still other instances, FAA regulations provide standards separate from the SARPs, but which nevertheless use the SARPs as a benchmark for the operation of U.S. regulations. For example, the airworthiness standards in FAA regulations differ structurally, and at times substantively, from the relevant ICAO SARPs. Structurally, the FAA regulates the airworthiness of several aircraft categories that differ from the ICAO SARPs. Hence, whereas ICAO Annex 8 sets standards for large airplanes and helicopters,[31] the relevant FAA regulations do so separately for transport, commuter, acrobatic and helicopter aircrafts, and other categories.[32] Substantively, these FAA regulations tend to be more specific than the analogous SARPs, yet they generally build on Annex 8 requirements. For instance, within each aircraft category, both the FAA and ICAO standards follow a similar regulatory structure, outlining requirements with regard to flight, aircraft structure, design, power plant installation, onboard equipment, and operating limitations.[33] Further, the FAA regulations expand upon the broad ICAO airworthiness requirements within each of these subject headings.

Hence, be it through direct reference, repetition or paraphrase, ICAO SARPs generally are incorporated into U.S. civil aviation law. In this manner, the issue is no longer one of just compliance with an international commitment, but also compliance with a national legal obligation. When this occurs, the various tools for promoting compliance with and enforcing national legal obligations (government regulators, prosecutors, courts, and so on) also help promote compliance with the international obligation.

There are many examples of national courts being used to challenge a government's failure to abide by its international obligations, as is clear from examples cited throughout this book. Continuing with the example of ICAO SARPs, national courts have required their governments to accept SARP-consistent certificates of airworthiness issued by other states. For instance, in May 1979, a U.S.-registered DC–10 aircraft crashed on take-off from Chicago O'Hare International Airport, killing all 271 persons onboard. The subsequent investigation by the FAA determined that the DC–10 model had certain structural faults that caused the accident. Consequently, the FAA prohibited the operation in the United States of

---

31. *See* Annex 8, *supra* note 27, IIIA–1–1, IV–1–1 (setting airworthiness standards for aeroplanes over 5,700 kilograms and helicopters within Parts III and IV respectively).

32. *See* 14 C.F.R. § 23.3 (2010) (distinguishing utility, normal, commuter and acrobatic aircraft categories); 14 C.F.R. §§ 25.1–25.1587 (2010) (regulating airworthiness for transport category aircraft); 14 C.F.R. §§ 27.1.–25.1589 (2010) (regulating airworthiness for normal category rotorcraft); 14 C.F.R. §§ 29.1–29–1589 (2010) (regulating airworthiness for transport category rotorcraft).

33. *Compare, e.g.*, 14 C.F.R. §§ 25.1–25.55 (2010) (transport plane flight standards), *with* Annex 8, *supra* note 27, IIIA–2–1 to IIIA–2–3 (large aeroplane flight standards).

all U.S.-registered DC–10 aircraft and, pursuant to a special regulation, prohibited the operation of foreign-registered DC–10 aircraft as well.[34] Foreign governments initially suspended their airworthiness certificates for DC–10 aircraft, but after they adopted comprehensive national maintenance and inspection programs, they reinstated the certificates. When the FAA still refused to rescind the order, various foreign air carriers sued the FAA in U.S. court. Drawing upon U.S. statutory authority instructing the FAA to act consistently with international agreements (such as the Chicago Convention),[35] the District of Columbia Circuit Court of Appeals found the FAA's order unlawful.[36] Among other things, the court found that the FAA never questioned whether the foreign governments' issuance of the certificates failed to meet the minimum safety standards set by the SARPs. Thereafter, the FAA rescinded its order.

B. Non–Forcible and Forcible Coercion of States

When a state fails to comply with international law, other states may or may not be a position to coerce the state into compliance. Much depends on the diplomatic, economic, and military power of the non-compliant state vis-á-vis other states. Much also depends on the political will of either side. If coercion is possible, it is often a blunt instrument, meaning that it is difficult to target the coercion on the persons responsible for non-compliance. Thus, the imposition of comprehensive economic sanctions upon a state rarely results in significant personal deprivation for the leadership of that state; rather, the population at large usually bears the burden of the sanctions. Further, states with authoritarian regimes seem far less susceptible to sanctions than regimes that are accountable to their polity. Having said that, in some instances coercion can be effective in bringing about compliance, particularly if undertaken multilaterally.

Diplomatic Sanctions

States are not obligated to engage in diplomatic relations with other states. Consequently, the downgrading or terminating of diplomatic relations with another state as a sign of displeasure with its conduct—including non-compliance with international law—is always an available option. The United States has refused to engage in diplomatic relations with Cuba for more than fifty years in reaction to the government of Fidel Castro, including its seizure of U.S. property in the early 1960's without payment of compensation

---

34. *See* Special Federal Aviation Regulation No. 40, 44 Fed. Reg. 33,396 (June 11,1979).

35. *See* 49 U.S.C. § 40105(b) (2006).

36. *See* British Caledonian Airways Ltd. v. Bond, 665 F.2d 1153 (D.C. Cir. 1981).

as required under international law. Resolution of the expropriation claims would likely be necessary prior to U.S. resumption of diplomatic relations with Cuba.

International organizations are also often in a position to impose diplomatic sanctions on a state. Under the charters of some organizations, a state that fails to comply with its obligations may be suspended from participation in the work of the organization. The U.N. Charter provides that a state can be suspended from the rights and privileges of membership if the Security Council takes enforcement action against the state,[37] a provision that has never been invoked. The Charter also provides that a member can lose voting rights in the General Assembly if it is in arrears in the payment of its dues.[38] This sanction was used against Haiti in 1963 and the Dominican Republic in 1968. The United States came close to qualifying for the loss of voting privileges in 1999, but paid its dues so as to avoid the sanction. The Organization of American States (OAS) suspended Cuba from membership in 1962 due to its alignment with the communism; that suspension was lifted in 2009.[39] The OAS also suspended Honduras from membership in 2009 in reaction to the ousting by the Honduran Congress and courts of the democratically-elected President Manuel Zelaya, but then lifted the suspension in 2011 after new elections were held and an agreement was reached allowing Zelaya to return from exile without facing the threat of prison.[40]

Some charters of organizations also envisage the possibility of expulsion from the organization. The U.N. Charter provides for expulsion of a member for persistent violations of the Charter.[41] The Articles of Agreement of the International Monetary Fund contemplate "compulsory withdrawal" if a member fails to meet its obligations.[42] Sanctions of this type, however, are rarely invoked. There seems to be a general understanding that in a crisis situation it is best to have more communication, not less, between the organization and the recalcitrant state. Hence, resort may be made to other means of diplomacy or coercion.

Economic Sanctions

Economic sanctions by states (either unilateral or collective) may take the form of "freezing" or blocking the assets of the target state, prohibiting financial transactions by persons with the target

---

37. *See* U.N. Charter art. 5.

38. *Id.*, art. 19.

39. OAS Doc. AG/RES 2438 (June 3, 2009).

40. *See* OAS Press Release, *OAS General Assembly Resolution to Lift the Suspension of Honduras* (June 1, 2011).

41. *Id.*, art. 6.

42. Art. 26(2), Dec. 27, 1945, 60 Stat. 1401, 2 U.N.T.S. 39, *as amended* 15 I.L.M. 499 (1976).

state, trade embargoes, suspension or termination of foreign assistance, and other economic restrictions. Not all sanctions are undertaken in response to a target state's violation of international law, yet in many circumstances that is the purpose of the sanctions. Such sanctions may be imposed collectively at a global or regional level, or by a state or like-minded states acting unilaterally.

For example, in 1998 the U.N. Security Council demanded that the Taliban—the *de facto* government of Afghanistan—"stop providing sanctuary and training for international terrorists.... "[43] When the Taliban failed to do so, the Security Council in October 1999 adopted a resolution stating that the Taliban's failure to comply constituted a threat to the peace, and demanded the transfer of the terrorist leader Osama bin Laden to a "country where he has been indicted, or to appropriate authorities in a country where he will be returned to such a country.... "[44] The Security Council then adopted sanctions that took effect in November 1999 requiring states to deny permission for any Taliban aircraft to take off or land in their territories, and to freeze funds and financial resources owned or controlled by the Taliban.[45] In December 2000, the Security Council adopted a resolution that imposed a comprehensive arms embargo on Afghanistan (except for nonlethal military equipment intended solely for humanitarian or protective uses), and that tightened financial, diplomatic and travel sanctions on Taliban leaders.[46]

These sanctions did not succeed in stopping the Taliban from harboring terrorists, as was vividly demonstrated by the terrorist attacks of September 2001. Yet such economic sanctions appear to have induced some cooperation by targeted states. After the Security Council imposed sanctions on Libya for failing to surrender two Libyan nationals accused of bombing Pan Am Flight 103,[47] Libya surrendered the two nationals and, as anticipated by Security Council Resolution 1192,[48] the U.N. sanctions were suspended. In January 2001, a Scottish court sitting in the Netherlands convicted one of the Libyans and sentenced him to life imprisonment; the guilt of the second Libyan was found not proven.[49]

43. S.C. Res. 1214, para. 13 (Dec. 8, 1998).

44. S.C. Res. 1267, pmbl. & para. 2 (Oct. 15, 1999).

45. *Id.*, paras. 3–4.

46. S.C. Res. 1333 (Dec. 19, 2000); see S.C. Res. 1363 (July 30, 2001) (establishing a mechanism to monitor the implementation of S.C. Res. 1333).

47. *See* S.C. Res. 731 (Jan. 21, 1992); S.C. Res. 748 (Mar. 31, 1992); S.C. Res. 883 (Nov. 11, 1993).

48. S.C. Res. 1192, para. 8 (Aug. 27, 1998).

49. *See* Her Majesty's Advocate v. Megrahi, No. 1475/99, slip. op. (High Ct. Judiciary at Camp Zeist Jan. 31, 2001), *reprinted in* 40 I.L.M. 582 (2001). The convicted Libyan was released by Scottish authorities in 2009 for reasons of health (terminal prostate cancer).

Since all states must abide by Security Council decisions when taken under Chapter VII of the U.N. Charter, economic sanctions by the Security Council are probably more effective than other types of sanctions. Nevertheless, sanctions can be imposed on a regional level as well. For example, when the democratically-elected president of Haiti, Jean–Bertrand Aristide, was overthrown in a military coup in 1991, the Organization of American States (OAS) "recommended" that its members adhere to a regional trade embargo on Haiti.[50] The embargo, among other things, cut off oil exports to Haiti from Colombia, Mexico, the United States, and Venezuela. A problem with regional sanctions, however, is that they do not affect trade from outside the region to the target state, and thus may not be effective. Further, regional organizations typically do not have the power to compel member states to adhere to the sanctions, and thus compliance within the region can be uneven. The OAS sanctions were followed in 1993 by global U.N. sanctions, which were more effective.[51]

On the national level, there are a variety of U.S. statutes that authorize the president to impose economic sanctions upon foreign states in certain circumstances. The International Emergency Economic Powers Act grants the president authority to regulate a comprehensive range of commercial and financial transactions with another country in order to deal with a threat to the national security, foreign policy, or economy of the United States if the president declares a national emergency.[52] The National Emergencies Act establishes a procedure for presidential declaration and congressional regulation of national emergencies.[53] The Trading with the Enemy Act forbids trading with enemies in times of war.[54] The International Security and Development Cooperation Act bans imports from certain foreign states, such as those supporting terrorism.[55] The United Nations Participation Act states that whenever the United States is called upon by the Security Council to apply measures adopted pursuant to Article 41 of the U.N. Charter (on non-forcible sanctions), the president may act to do so.[56] Other statutes provide related authorities.

Once the United States embarks on an economic sanctions program, the U.S. Department of the Treasury's Office of Foreign Assets Control (OFAC) administers and enforces the program. The sanctions can be either comprehensive or selective, using the block-

---

50. *See, e.g.,* OAS Doc. MRE/RES.1/91, OEA/Ser.F/V.1 (Oct. 3, 1991).

51. *See* S.C. Res. 841 (June 16, 1993).

52. 50 U.S.C. §§ 1701–1706 (2006).

53. 50 U.S.C. §§ 1601–1651 (2006).

54. 50 U.S.C. App. §§ 1–6, 7–39, 41–44 (2006).

55. 22 U.S.C. §§ 2349aa–2349aa–10 (2006).

56. 22 U.S.C. § 287c (2006).

ing of assets and trade restrictions to accomplish particular foreign policy and national security goals.

For example, under U.S. export control laws, the U.S. secretary of state has designated certain foreign states as "terrorist countries," which allows U.S. authorities to block the assets of those states located within the United States or under U.S. control.[57] As of 2011, Cuba, Iran, Sudan, and Syria were so designated. Under U.S. criminal law,[58] U.S. persons may not engage in financial transactions with the governments of those terrorist states, except as provided in regulations issued by the secretary of the treasury in consultation with the secretary of state, and overseen by OFAC.

Sometimes, sub-state entities impose economic sanctions as well. On various occasions, state or local governments in the United States, or non-governmental organizations such as universities, have decided to bar transactions with foreign governments, such as South Africa or Myanmar (Burma). Such measures can lead to conflicts with federal law.[59]

Military Enforcement

As a matter of policy, states normally do not resort to the use of military measures to coerce compliance with international law. While military power can have quicker results than less coercive measures, the human and economic costs can be quite high, and the results achieved may not be those intended. Moreover, international law generally disfavors the use of unilateral military action even when being done to vindicate a state's right under international law. The rules on state responsibility allow a state to undertake counter-measures against another state that has violated international law, but those counter-measures are to be non-forcible.[60] Resort to force is permitted only in two circumstances: when a state is acting in self-defense or when authorized by the Security Council under Chapter VII of the U.N. Charter.[61]

States have resorted to military force claiming self-defense in many instances, some of which arguably were more to enforce international norms than to self-defend. Thus, the military attacks on the Federal Republic of Yugoslavia (Serbia & Montenegro) (FRY) in 1999 by members of the North Atlantic Treaty Organization (NATO) might be seen as an act of anticipatory self-defense by European states; an effort to forestall war in the Balkans that could draw in Greece and Turkey. But even the United States, a prime

---

57. Section 40(d) of the Arms Export Control Act, 22 U.S.C. § 2780(d) (2006); Section 6(j) of the Export Administration Act of 1979, 50 U.S.C. App. § 2405 (2006); section 620A of the Foreign Assistance Act, 22 U.S.C. § 2371 (2006).

58. 18 U.S.C. § 2332d (2006).

59. *See* Chapter 7(B).

60. *See* Chapter 6(E).

61. *See* Chapter 14(A).

mover in NATO's action, asserted that the use of force was justified in part to enforce the FRY's obligations under human rights law not to harm Kosovar Albanians, as well as to enforce FRY compliance with agreements with NATO and the Organization for Security and Cooperation in Europe regarding Kosovo. Whether NATO was authorized to undertake such air strikes was and remains controversial.[62]

Since the end of the Cold War, the U.N. Security Council has been active in authorizing the use of military force to uphold international legal norms, principally but not exclusively those established by the Security Council itself. For example, in Resolution 678[63] the Security Council authorized states to assist Kuwait in reversing Iraq's August 1990 invasion of Kuwait. To that end, a coalition of states led by the United States engaged in an extensive air and ground campaign that expelled Iraq, restored the Kuwaiti government, and laid the groundwork for the creation of a secure boundary between the two states. In Resolution 940,[64] the Security Council authorized military intervention to reverse the 1991 coup in Haiti (discussed above), a prospect that intimidated the coup leaders into leaving the country peaceably. In Resolution 929,[65] the Security Council authorized France to intervene in Rwanda to prevent genocide, a step many regarded as far too little and far too late. In March 2003, the United States and several allies launched an invasion of Iraq purportedly justified under prior Security Council resolutions dating back to 1990, due to Iraq's alleged failure to comply with legal obligations to dismantle its weapons of mass destruction. That military intervention was controversial, and highlighted the possible dangers of open-ended Security Council authorizations to use military force for upholding international law. In early 2011, the Security Council characterized the conduct of the Libyan government as possibly constituting crimes against humanity and then authorized states "acting nationally or through regional organizations or arrangements, and acting in cooperation with the Secretary–General, to take all necessary measures ... to protect civilians and civilian populated areas under threat of attack in [Libya]... ."[66] Thereafter, a NATO-led coalition of states engaged in extensive bombing attacks on Libyan government forces to protect civilians from the violent tactics of their government, thereby upholding core human rights norms. Yet here, too, existed controversy, with some critics claiming that the attacks were principally designed to bolster the position of the Libyan rebel forces, who eventually seized control of the country.

---

62. *See Editorial Comments: NATO's Kosovo Intervention*, 93 Am. J. Int'l L. 824 (1999).

63. S.C. Res. 678 (Nov. 29, 1990).

64. S.C. Res. 940 (July 31, 1994).

65. S.C. Res. 929 (June 22, 1994).

66. S.C. Res. 1970 (Feb. 26, 2011); S.C. Res. 1973 (Mar. 17, 2011).

C.   Non–Forcible and Forcible Coercion of Persons

Economic Sanctions

Multilateral Economic Sanctions. In some instances, the global community has imposed economic sanctions that target persons rather than states. For example, as discussed in Chapter 3(E), the Security Council has adopted Resolution 1373 directing U.N. member states to criminalize terrorist financing and to adopt regulatory regimes intended to detect, deter, and freeze terrorist funds.[67] Resolution 1373 and subsequent resolutions not only legislate (*i.e.,* create new norms for states), they also create a mechanism for monitoring these norms.

A committee of the Security Council established by Resolution 1373 (which comprises all Council members and meets in closed session) receives and reviews reports from states on the steps they have undertaken to criminalize terrorist financing and to adopt regulatory regimes intended to detect, deter, and freeze terrorist funds.[68] In essence, this committee is charged with determining whether states have appropriate legislative and executive measures in place (or contemplated) that give effect to Resolution 1373 and associated resolutions.

Moreover, the Security Council has also adopted a regime designed to impose sanctions upon specified persons and organizations associated with Al Qaeda. This regime—first established in 1999 by Resolution 1267[69] and subsequently modified and improved through additional resolutions[70]—establishes another committee of the Security Council, commonly referred to as the "Al–Qaeda Sanctions Committee" (again consisting of all Council members). States propose to the committee a person or entity that they believe is associated with Al Qaeda for inclusion on a Consolidated List; if there is no objection by other states, then the person or entity is added to the list, along with a narrative summary of why the listing has occurred.[71] Once placed upon the list, the Council's resolutions require that all states: freeze without delay the funds and other financial assets or economic resources of designated individuals and entities; prevent the entry into or transit through their territories by designated individuals; and prevent the direct or indirect supply them of arms and related material.

Concerns that the 1267 regime provides inadequate notice to persons and entities being listed, and inadequate ability to chal-

---

67.   S.C. Res. 1373 (Sept. 28, 2001).

68.   This committee is referred to as the "Counter–Terrorism Committee".

69.   S.C. Res. 1267 (Oct. 15, 1999).

70.   *See, e.g.,* S.C. Res. 1989 (June 17, 2011).

71.   For the consolidated list, *see* http://www.un.org/sc/committees/1267/ aq_sanctions_list.shtml; for the narrative summaries, *see* <http://www.un.org/sc/committees/1267/narrative.shtml>.

lenge their listing, has led to various cases and initiatives challenging the regime. The most significant to date has been a decision by the European Court of Justice annulling an EU measure that gave effect to the regime within the EU.[72] Such challenges, in turn, have led to efforts at reform by the Security Council itself. For example, in Resolution 1904,[73] the Security Council established an Office of the Ombudsperson to assist the committee in considering de-listing requests.

National Economic Sanctions. States also under their national law impose sanctions on persons for actions that violate international law. For example, the United States has adopted sanctions that apply only to members of a particular leadership group in a state that has engaged in human rights violations—such as UNITA[74] in Angola or Bosnian Serbs in Bosnia–Herzegovina[75]—or individuals believed to be engaged in narcotics trafficking[76] or terrorism. The effect of such sanctions can involve the seizure of assets, denial of entry into the United States, deportation from the United States, or other measures.

Usually multilateral sanctions programs are implemented through national sanctions programs. With regard to tracking and seizing assets of terrorists and terrorist organizations, there are principally two U.S. sanctions programs. First, the U.S. Antiterrorism and Effective Death Penalty Act of 1996 (AEDPA) sought "to provide the Federal Government the fullest possible basis, consistent with the Constitution, to prevent persons within the United States, or subject to the jurisdiction of the United States, from providing material support or resources to foreign organizations that engage in terrorist activities."[77] To that end, the AEDPA amended the Immigration and Nationality Act so as to authorize the secretary of state to designate an organization as a "foreign terrorist organization" (FTO), meaning that it is a non-U.S. organization engaged in "terrorist activity" that threatens U.S. nationals or national security.[78] Engaging in "terrorist activity" means committing, in an individual capacity or as a member of an organization, a terrorist act or an act which the actor knows, or reasonably should know, affords material support to any individual, organization, or government in conducting a terrorist act.[79] Terrorist activi-

72. Kadi & Al Barakaat Int'l Found. v. Council & Comm'n, Case C–402/05P; C–415/05P, 2008 E.C.R. I–00000, *reprinted in* 47 I.L.M. 923 (2008); for commentary, *see* 103 A.J.I.L. 305 (2009).

73. S.C. Res. 1904 (Dec. 17, 2009).

74. *See* Exec. Order No. 12,865 (Sept. 26, 1993).

75. *See* Exec. Order No. 12,846 (Apr. 25, 1993); Exec. Order No. 12,934 (Oct. 25, 1994).

76. *See* Exec. Order No. 12,978 (Oct. 21, 1995) (concerning Colombian cartels).

77. AEDPA, § 301, 18 U.S.C. § 2339B note (2006).

78. 8 U.S.C. § 1189(a)(1) (2006).

79. 8 U.S.C. § 1182(a)(3)(B)(iv).

ty includes such acts as hijacking, kidnapping, assassination, and the use of any explosive or firearm, "with intent to endanger, directly or indirectly, the safety of one or more individuals or to cause substantial damage to property." Threats, attempts, and conspiracies to commit the above acts also come within the definition.[80] The AEDPA requires the secretary of state to notify Congress of the designations and to publish them in the *Federal Register,* without first notifying the organization. No more than thirty days following publication of the designation, an organization may challenge its designation before the District of Columbia Court of Appeals. The court's review is based solely upon the administrative record, but the government may submit, for *ex parte* and *in camera* review, classified information used in making the designation.[81] Otherwise, the statute prevents the release of any classified information used as the basis for the secretary's designation.

Once an FTO has been designated, a number of consequences follow. Designated persons who are not U.S. citizens will not be admitted to the United States. All assets of the FTO located in the United States may be frozen at the discretion of the secretary of the treasury. All persons who knowingly provide material support or resources to the FTO (other than medical or religious supplies) may be fined or imprisoned for up to fifteen years.[82] Further, a "financial institution" that becomes aware that it controls funds of an FTO (or an FTO's agent) must freeze the funds and alert the U.S. government, or face substantial fines. As of 2011, almost 50 persons or entities were designated as FTOs, including Basque Fatherland and Liberty (ETA), Hamas (Islamic Resistance Movement), and al-Qa'ida in the Arabian Peninsula (AQAP). [83]

The second U.S. sanctions program concerns "specially designated global terrorists." This program emerged in the aftermath of the September 2001 attacks, when President Bush issued Executive Order 13,224 that expanded the U.S. Department of the Treasury's power to target financial support for terrorist organizations worldwide.[84] Under this program, the department has the authority to block the assets of not just financial institutions, but all U.S. persons holding funds of a designated terrorist, and to block the assets of U.S. persons "associated with" designated terrorists.

Similarly, under the Foreign Narcotics Kingpin Designation Act,[85] the president is authorized to identify and apply sanctions on a worldwide basis to "significant foreign narcotics traffickers, their

80. 8 U.S.C. § 1182(a)(3)(B)(ii).

81. 8 U.S.C. § 1189(b).

82. 18 U.S.C. § 2339(B).

83. *See* U.S. Dep't of State, *Foreign Terrorist Organizations* (Sept. 15, 2011).

84. Exec. Order No. 13,224, 66 Fed. Reg. 49,079 (Sept. 23, 2001).

85. 21 U.S.C. §§ 1901–08 (2006); 8 U.S.C. § 1182 (2006); *see* 31 C.F.R. §§ 598.101–598.803 (2010).

organizations, and the foreign persons who provide" them, "whose activities threaten the national security, foreign policy, and economy of the United States."[86] As is the case for terrorists, a list of "drug kingpins" is issued by the president on a regular basis, and sanctions are applied to them and their assets whenever they are found. From 2000 to 2011, U.S. presidents designated 94 persons as significant foreign narcotics traffickers, while the Department of Treasury issued a further 1,031 "derivative" designations of persons or entities associated with those kingpins, as permitted under the statute.[87]

Somewhat more controversial are national economic sanctions regimes that seek to pressure *third-party* states into limiting their dealings with the targeted state, a tactic sometimes referred to as a "secondary boycott." For example, the United States precludes third-party states and their companies from having access to U.S. military equipment if they provide any lethal military equipment to states regarded by the United States as terrorist states.[88] Likewise, in addition to imposing sanctions directly on Iran and Libya in the 1980's and 1990's, the United States adopted in 1996 the Iran and Libya Sanctions Act (ILSA),[89] which among other things required the imposition of certain sanctions upon foreign companies that make major investments in the energy sectors of those countries. The statute, however, allowed the president to waive the sanctions on a case-by-case basis; ultimately, no ILSA sanctions were imposed upon a non-US company. Ironically, the United States had long opposed the practice of secondary boycotts, especially those used by Arab states that sought to discourage third states and third-state nationals from doing business with Israel.

Civil and Criminal Actions to Enforce an International Norm

Persons can also be exposed to civil and criminal sanctions that seek to enforce international law. For example, the Convention Against Torture requires states to "take effective legislative, administrative, judicial or other measures to prevent acts of torture in any territory under its jurisdiction" and to "ensure that all acts of torture are offences under its criminal law."[90]

The United States implements this requirement through laws and regulations that allow for civil and criminal actions against persons who commit torture. With respect to civil actions, various

86. 21 U.S.C. § 1902.

87. *See* U.S. Dep't of Treasury Office of Foreign Assets Control, *An Overview of the Foreign Narcotics Kingpin Designation Act* (Oct. 27, 2011).

88. Foreign Assistance Act of 1961, § 620H, 22 U.S.C. § 2378 (2006).

89. Pub. L. No. 104–172, 110 Stat. 1541 (1996).

90. Convention Against Torture, *supra* note 7, arts. 2(1), 4(1).

civil remedies are available to victims of torture, including under the Alien Tort Statute[91] (allowing noncitizens to sue individuals present in the United States who commit acts of torture against them) and the Torture Victim Protection Act of 1991[92] (providing a comparable remedy to U.S. nationals). Victims of torture may seek damages against U.S. federal officials under the Federal Tort Claims Act,[93] as well as against state officials under state tort law. With respect to criminal actions, the U.S. government enacted a statute that authorizes federal criminal prosecution of U.S. nationals who commit torture abroad, as well as of any perpetrator regardless of nationality present in the United States.[94] Further, the civil rights division of the Department of Justice investigates and prosecutes incidents involving local, state, and federal law enforcement officials. Of course, not all aspects of the convention can be fulfilled through civil and criminal actions against persons. For example, Article 3(1) of the convention obligates the parties not to "expel, return ('refouler') or extradite a person to another State where there are substantial grounds for believing that he would be in danger of being subjected to torture." The United States implements this obligation through Immigration and Naturalization Service (INS)[95] and Department of State[96] regulations.

Many states have adopted criminal laws allowing for the prosecution of individuals who violate particular norms of international law, such as the prohibition on genocide. Further, since the 1990's, international criminal tribunals have emerged that are capable of investigating and prosecuting persons for violations of the laws of war and associated crimes. Several tribunals have focused on acts that occurred within a particular state during a particular period of time (Cambodia, East Timor, Lebanon, Rwanda, Sierra Leone, or the former Yugoslavia), while the International Criminal Court has more general jurisdiction. Whether these tribunals truly deter conduct by individuals is unclear, but they are certainly capable of punishing those individuals who are apprehended.[97]

Civil Actions to Enforce a Private Transaction

International law can also assist in the enforcement of obligations undertaken by persons as part of an international business transaction. For example, the Convention on the Recognition and

---

91. 28 U.S.C. § 1350 (2006); *see* Chapter 7(C).

92. 28 U.S.C. § 1350 note (2006).

93. 28 U.S.C. §§ 1346(b), 2401(b) & 2671–80 (2006).

94. 18 U.S.C. §§ 2340, 2340A & 2340B (2006).

95. *See* 8 C.F.R. pts. 3, 103, 208, 235, 238, 240, 241, 253 & 507 (2010).

96. *See* 22 C.F.R. pt. 95 (2010).

97. *See* Chapter 13(D).

Enforcement of Foreign Arbitral Awards (New York Convention)[98] obligates 146 states to enforce a private contract to submit a dispute to arbitration, and further to enforce foreign arbitral awards once rendered. The United States ratified the New York Convention in 1970 and enacted implementing legislation (chapter 2 of the Federal Arbitration Act).[99]

For example, suppose that John Exporter from the United States contracts with Sally Importer of the United Kingdom for the sale of a good, and the contract provides that disputes shall be submitted to arbitration before the International Chamber of Commerce's Court of Arbitration in Paris, France. If a dispute arises under the contract and John seeks to sue Sally before in a U.S. court under U.S. contract law, the court will agree with Sally Importer that John Exporter must take the matter to arbitration in Paris. Moreover, if the matter is arbitrated and Sally Exporter wins an award of compensation against John Exporter, a U.S. court will enforce that arbitral award against John Exporter, unless he can establish certain circumstances as set forth in article V of the New York Convention. Those circumstances include whenever the agreement to arbitrate was invalid (*e.g.*, if John Exporter was not mentally competent to enter into a contract) or the opposing party was not given proper notice of the arbitration proceedings.

In practice, U.S. courts regularly enforce arbitral awards that fall within the scope of the New York Convention, extending deference to the decisions of foreign arbitral tribunals and rejecting spurious article V defenses. For example, in *Karaha Bodas Co.*,[100] the plaintiff was a Cayman Islands company that contracted with the defendant to build and operate an electricity-generating facility in Indonesia. The contracts provided that disputes would be arbitrated in Geneva, Switzerland. After the contract was terminated, the plaintiff initiated arbitration proceedings in Geneva. The arbitral tribunal received extensive written and oral pleadings and issued a final award in favor of the plaintiff for U.S. $261 million. The plaintiff then sued the defendant in U.S. court to enforce the award. The defendant challenged the award on various grounds under article V: that the arbitral tribunal improperly consolidated the claims into one arbitration proceeding; that the selection of the arbitrators violated the relevant rules of the arbitration; that the defendant did not have a fair opportunity to present its case; that the award was contrary to U.S. public policy because it violated the

---

98. June 10, 1958, 21 U.S.T. 2517, 330 U.N.T.S. 38. An analogous convention for just Western Hemisphere states is the Inter–American Convention on International Commercial Arbitration, Jan. 30, 1975, 1438 U.N.T.S. 245, 14 I.L.M. 336 (Panama Convention).

99. 9 U.S.C. §§ 201–208 (2006).

100. Karaha Bodas Co. v. Perusahaan Pertambangan Minyak Dan Gas Bumi Negara, 364 F.3d 274 (5th Cir. 2004).

doctrine of abuse of rights under international law; and that the award had been annulled by an Indonesian court. The Fifth Circuit Court of Appeals rejected each argument. The court noted that "the rulings of the Tribunal interpreting the parties' contract are entitled to deference. Unless the Tribunal manifestly disregarded the parties' agreement or the law, there is no basis to set aside the determination that Swiss procedural law applied,"[101] allowing consolidation of the claims. Further, the court found that the tribunal reasonably interpreted the rules for appointment of arbitrators, and that the defendant received a fair hearing and was able to present ample evidence in support of its position.[102] In rejecting the defendant's public policy argument, the court stated that the "public policy defense is to be 'construed narrowly to be applied only where enforcement would violate the forum state's most basic notions of morality and justice.' "[103] The court also noted that the abuse of rights doctrine was not established in U.S. law and, in any event, the plaintiff's conduct did not trigger application of the doctrine. Finally, the court held that Swiss, not Indonesian, law dictated whether the award should be set aside because Switzerland had primary jurisdiction in the dispute.[104]

More recently, the 2005 Hague Convention on Choice of Court Agreements[105] provides that a choice-of-court agreement made by two private parties as part of an international business transaction (or other transnational civil matter) must be accepted by all states who are party to the convention. Thus, the court selected by the private parties has exclusive jurisdiction and other courts must decline to hear any case relating to the agreement. Moreover, once a judgment is rendered in the state of exclusive jurisdiction, the Hague Convention provides for recognition and enforcement of that judgment in the courts of other parties to the convention. As of 2011, however, only one state (Mexico) had joined the convention.

101. *Id.* at 290 (footnotes omitted).

102. *Id.* at 298–305.

103. *Id.* at 306.

104. *Id.* at 288, 291–92.

105. June 30, 2005, 44 I.L.M. 1294 (2005); *see* Ved. P. Nanda, *The Land-mark 2005 Hague Convention on Choice of Court Agreements*, 42 Tex. Int'l L.J. 773 (2007).

Further Reading

Gauthier de Beco, ed., *Human Rights Monitoring Mechanisms of the Council of Europe* (2012).

Sonia Cardenas, *Conflict and Compliance: State Responses to International Human Rights Pressure* (2007).

Abram Chayes & Antonia Chayes, *The New Sovereignty: Compliance with International Regulatory Agreements* (1995).

Lori Fisler Damrosch, "Enforcing International Law Through Non–Forcible Measures," 269 *Recueil des Cours (Hague Academy of Int'l Law)* 9 (1997).

Domenico Di Pietro & Martin Platte, *Enforcement of International Arbitration Awards: The New York Convention of 1958* (2001).

Jeremy Farrall & Kim Rubenstein, eds., *Sanctions, Accountability and Governance in a Globalised World* (2009).

Laura Picchio Forlati & Linos–Alexander Sicilianos, eds., *Economic Sanctions in International Law/Les Sanctions Économiques En Droit International* (2004).

Thomas Franck, *The Power of Legitimacy Among Nations* (1990).

Vera Gowlland–Debbas, ed., *National Implementation of United Nations Sanctions: A Comparative Study* (2004).

Vera Gowlland–Debbas, ed., *United Nations Sanctions and International Law* (2001).

Robert Lutz, *A Lawyer's Handbook for Enforcing Foreign Judgments in the United States and Abroad* (2006).

Elena Katselli Proukaki, *The Problem of Enforcement in International Law* (2010).

Christian J. Tams, *Enforcing Obligations Erga Omnes in International Law* (2005).

Tulio Treves et al., eds., *Non-Compliance Procedures and Mechanisms and the Effectiveness of International Environmental Agreements* (2009).

Antonios Tzanakopoulos, *Disobeying the Security Council: Countermeasures Against Wrongful Sanctions* (2011).

Oran R. Young, ed., *The Effectiveness of International Environmental Regimes: Causal Connections and Behavioral Mechanisms* (1999).

Chapter 6

RULES ON STATE RESPONSIBILITY

At its heart, the field of state responsibility is concerned with rudimentary rules about when a state is responsible for a breach of international law and the consequences that flow from such a breach. For example, the rules establish: (1) when particular conduct may be attributed to a state; (2) when a state's wrongful conduct might be excused, such as in a situation of distress; (3) what kinds of remedies are available to a state that has been wronged, such as restitution or compensation; and (4) when a wronged state may respond through the use of countermeasures. The rules on state responsibility are background or default rules; two or more states may always choose to craft alternative rules as among themselves. Yet typically states do not address these rudimentary rules in their relationships and thus the background rules become relevant when something goes wrong.

Rules on state responsibility are not oriented toward any particular substantive field of international law, such as trade, human rights, or the environment (sometimes referred to as "primary" rules). Nor are the rules oriented toward any particular source of international law, such as treaties, custom, general principles, or otherwise. Rather, rules on state responsibility are more general in application ("secondary" rules), drawn from the practice of states, the decisions of courts and tribunals, and the writings of scholars in a wide range of areas. Having said that, historically many studies of the rules on state responsibility focused on the treatment of aliens in the territory of a state,[1] and much of the law in this area has arisen in that context.

In 1956, the International Law Commission (ILC) commenced a study of the rules on state responsibility, an effort that encountered considerable divisiveness and significant changes over the course of forty-five years. In August 2001, the ILC finally adopted a series of fifty-nine articles that purport to codify and progressively develop the rules in this area.[2] Thereafter, the U.N. General Assem-

---

1. *See* Chapter 10(B).
2. *See* Draft Articles on Responsibility of States for Internationally Wrongful Acts, *in* Report of the ILC on the Work of its Fifty-third Session, U.N. Doc. A/56/10, at 20 (2001) [hereinafter ILC Articles].

bly commended the articles to the attention of governments.[3] To date, these articles have not been transformed into a treaty; thus, they were not drafted by, let alone adopted and ratified by, states. Moreover, some aspects of the articles have been challenged by states and scholars. Nevertheless, the ILC articles and their associated commentary are an important reference point for the law in this area, and will be referred to as appropriate in this chapter.

A. The General Principle of Responsibility

The threshold principle underlying the rules on state responsibility is that an internationally wrongful act of a state entails its international responsibility.[4] Once an internationally wrongful act (or breach) occurs, it triggers a new legal regime of rights and duties, which are set forth in the remaining rules on state responsibility.

On first glance, this principle seems obvious enough, and has been stated by various international tribunals, such as the Permanent Court of International Justice (PCIJ),[5] the International Court of Justice (ICJ),[6] and highly regarded arbitral decisions.[7] Such wrongful acts may relate to just one other state or several states. The same rule likely applies to the conduct of an international organization,[8] although here the practice is less settled.

On second glance, however, the principle appears tautological and unhelpful, for it does not explain what exactly is required to establish a wrongful act of a state. When considering wrongfulness, much must be left to the specific treaty, customary rule, or other international norm at issue with respect to the conduct of a state. Indeed, the essence of an internationally wrongful act is the nonconformity of a state's conduct with conduct it was supposed to adopt in order to comply with a particular legal obligation—typically referred to as a *breach* of that international obligation.[9] The general principle does not address important broad issues, such as whether a state must be at fault in order for a breach to occur or

---

3. *See* G.A. Res. 56/83, para. 3 (Dec. 12, 2001); *see also* G.A. Res. 59/35 (Dec. 2, 2004).

4. *See* ILC Articles, *supra* note 2, art. 1.

5. *See, e.g.,* Phosphates in Morocco (Italy v. Fr.), 1938 P.C.I.J. (ser. A/B) No. 74, at 28 (June 14).

6. *See, e.g.,* Corfu Channel (U.K. v. Alb.), 1949 I.C.J. 4, 23 (Apr. 9); Military and Paramilitary Activities in and against Nicaragua (Nicar. v. U.S.), 1986 I.C.J. 14, 146, para. 292 (June 27); Gabčikovo–Nagymaros Project (Hung./

Slovk.), 1997 I.C.J. 7, 38, para. 47 (Sept. 25).

7. *See, e.g.,* Rainbow Warrior (N.Z./ Fr.), 20 R.I.A.A. 217 (1990).

8. *See* Draft Articles on Responsibility of International Organizations, *in* Report of the ILC on the Work of its Sixty-third Session, U.N. Doc. A/66/10, at 54, art. 3 (2011); *see also* Advisory Opinion on Reparation for Injuries, 1949 I.C.J. 174, 179 (Apr. 11).

9. *See* ILC Articles, *supra* note 2, art. 12.

whether there must be actual injury to another state. The law of state responsibility appears to leave such matters to the particular treaty or customary rule at issue, even though such "primary" rules rarely address these matters.

B. Attribution of Conduct to a State

The general principle discussed above requires that the internationally wrongful act be *of a state*. Yet "states" do not directly commit acts; acts are committed by governments, organizations, and people with differing levels of connection to a state. As such, to determine that an act (which can be an affirmative act or an omission) was committed by a state, there need to be rules on the attribution of conduct to a state.[10]

The ILC Articles, which in this regard are generally regarded as codifying state practice, maintain that the following conduct can be attributed to a state:

- conduct by the organs of a state, meaning legislative, executive, or judicial bodies at the national level or at a lower level of government;[11]

- conduct by persons who are not an organ of a state, but who are empowered by the state to exercise elements of governmental authority (*e.g.*, private security firms), with respect to acts undertaken in that capacity;[12]

- conduct by the organs of a state placed at the disposal of another state, such as an army;[13]

- conduct directed or controlled by a state;[14]

- conduct carried out by persons exercising elements of governmental authority in the absence of official authority, such as might occur in a failed state;[15]

- conduct of an insurrection that then becomes the new government of a state;[16] and

- conduct acknowledged and adopted by a state as its own, such as occurred when the government of Iran in 1979–80 condoned the taking of U.S. hostages by Iranian militants.[17]

Further, the ILC Articles assert that, with respect to the first and second items above, conduct can be attributed to a state even if the

10. *See id.*, art. 2.
11. *Id.*, art. 4.
12. *Id.*, art. 5.
13. *Id.*, art. 6.
14. *Id.*, art. 8.
15. *Id.*, art. 9.

16. *Id.*, art. 10.

17. *Id.*, art. 11; United States Diplomatic and Consular Staff in Tehran (U.S. v. Iran), 1980 I.C.J. 3, 32–33 (May 24).

organs or persons exceed their authority or instructions.[18]

While these standards have the benefit of brevity and provide a framework for legal analysis, their application to situations of fact can be difficult. Hence, it is not entirely clear what it means for a person to be under the "direction or control" of a state; at best, one can refer to various prior cases where attribution of conduct did or did not occur in such circumstances. For example, in 1979, a U.S. national named Kenneth Yeager sought to leave Iran in the wake of Iran's revolution. At the Tehran airport, he was stopped by "revolutionary guards" (or "Komitehs") who were searching baggage and confiscating property. When Yeager filed a claim before the Iran–U.S. Claims Tribunal for recovery of his loss, the government of Iran responded that the revolutionary guards were not part of the government of Iran. The Tribunal, however, noted that the guards were performing immigration, customs, and associated functions at the airport that normally would be governmental functions. Even if such functions were not actually authorized by the government, the guards "at least exercised elements of governmental authority in the absence of official authorities, in operations of which the new Government must have had knowledge and to which it did not specifically object."[19] Consequently, the Tribunal adopted an approach to attribution consistent with the fifth item noted above, in which attribution is found in conduct carried out by persons exercising elements of governmental authority in the absence of official authority.

By contrast, a government can have a significant general connection to a non-state actor without having the specific conduct of that non-state actor attributed to it. In the early 1980's, the U.S. government provided considerable support to Nicaraguan rebels, referred to as the *contras*, including general planning, direction, and funding. When Nicaragua brought a case against the United States for various acts committed by both the United States and the *contras*, the ICJ agreed that the United States was responsible for its general support of the *contras*, but was not responsible for every specific act committed by the *contras*, such as a political assassination. The Court found that

> despite the heavy subsidies and other support provided to them by the United States, there is no clear evidence of the United States having actually exercised such a degree of control in all fields as to justify treating the *contras* as acting on its behalf. . . . All the forms of United States participation mentioned above, and even the general control of the [United States] over a force with a high degree of dependency on it, would not in

18. *See* ILC Articles, *supra* note 2, art. 7.

19. Yeager v. Iran, 17 Iran–U.S. Cl. Trib. Rep. 92, 104, para. 43 (1987).

themselves mean, without further evidence, that the United States directed or enforced the perpetration of the acts contrary to human rights and humanitarian law alleged by [Nicaragua]. Such acts could well be committed by members of the *contras* without the control of the United States.[20]

In the *Bosnia v. Serbia Genocide* case, the Court was confronted with allegations of involvement of Serbia (previously the Federal Republic of Yugoslavia or FRY) in atrocities committed by an army formed by Bosnians of Serb ethnicity (the V.R.S.). The Court concluded the FRY's own army was not involved in the atrocities.[21] Further, the VRS was not a formal or *de jure* organ of the FRY, even though the FRY paid some salaries and benefits to VRS soldiers.[22] The VRS was also not a *de facto* organ of the FRY, because the VRS was not "completely dependent" upon the FRY; political, military, and logistical relations were strong between them, but the overall strategic decisions of the VRS were not taken by the FRY.[23] Finally, the Court concluded that the FRY did not effectively control the VRS, since there was no evidence to that effect. Moreover, the Court asserted that, when invoking this "effective control" test, a claimant must establish such control "in respect of *each operation* in which the alleged violations occurred, *not generally* in respect of the overall actions taken by the persons or groups of persons having committed the violations."[24] At the same time, the Court found that the FRY was responsible under Article 1 the Convention Against Genocide for failing to use its influence to prevent the VRS from committing atrocities at the town of Srebrenica (this wrongful conduct of the FRY *by omission* did not require any attribution of VRS conduct to the FRY).[25] The Court declined, however, to award any compensation for that violation, since it was not clear that the FRY's efforts would have made any difference to the VRS's actions.[26]

C. Concept of Breach

When a state fails to act in conformity with an international obligation, it has breached the obligation. That failure may arise from an affirmative act of the state or by an omission. Further, the failure may consist of a single act or may occur through a series of acts that in the aggregate are wrongful.[27] A state which aids or

20. Military and Paramilitary Activities in and against Nicaragua, *supra* note 6, at 64–65, para. 115.

21. Application of the Convention on the Prevention and Punishment of the Crime of Genocide (Bosnia v. Serbia), Judgment, 2007 I.C.J. 202, para. 386 (Feb. 26).

22. *Id.*, 202–03, paras. 387–88.

23. *Id.*, 205–06, paras. 394–95.

24. *Id.*, 208, para. 400 (emphasis added).

25. *Id.*, 225–26, para. 438.

26. *Id.*, 233–34, para. 462.

27. *See* ILC Articles, *supra* note 2, art. 15.

assists another state in committing a wrongful act can also be regarded as internationally responsible for the breach.[28]

There are, however, some circumstances where an act by State A that fails to conform with an international obligation will not be regarded as wrongful with respect to State B. The ILC Articles maintain that the following circumstances preclude wrongfulness:

- State B consents to State A's action, such as consent by State B to the transit through its airspace of a military aircraft registered in State A, an action that would otherwise be a violation of State B's sovereignty;[29]

- State A acts in lawful self-defense, such as an attack by State A on military bases in State B after State B has invaded State A in violation of the U.N. Charter;[30]

- State A takes "countermeasures" against State B in order to induce State B to comply with its international obligations (for a discussion of countermeasures, see section E below);[31]

- State A's action is due to *force majeure*, meaning "the occurrence of an irresistible force or of an unforeseen event, beyond the control of the State, making it materially impossible in the circumstances to perform the obligation";[32]

- State A's action is taken in a situation of distress for the purpose of saving lives, such as entering State B's airspace to land a damaged aircraft; this situation differs from the situation of *force majeure* discussed above, in that the act is taken voluntarily (an alternative action, such as downing the aircraft on the high seas, is possible);[33] and

- State A's action is necessary to safeguard an essential interest against a grave and imminent peril and does not seriously imperil an essential interest of State B, such as setting fire to an abandoned oil tanker registered by State B that is leaking oil into State A's marine environment; this situation differs from the situation of distress in that the act is not taken to save lives but, rather, to address a grave danger to State A as a whole.[34]

These reasons for nonperformance of an international obligation do not terminate the obligation; they merely provide a

---

28. *Id.*, arts. 16–19.

29. *Id.*, art. 20.

30. *Id.*, art. 21.

31. *Id.*, art. 22.

32. *Id.*, art. 23. This formulation by the ILC is more welcoming to the notion of *force majeure* than is the case with respect to treaty termination. *See* Chapter 3(A).

33. *Id.*, art. 24.

34. *Id.*, art. 25; Gabčikovo–Nagymaros Project, *supra* note 6, at 39–45.

justification for State A's failure to meet the obligation while the relevant circumstance exists.

If a state has breached an international obligation and there are no circumstances precluding wrongfulness, then two legal consequences flow from the breach. First, new obligations arise for the breaching state. Second, new rights arise for the injured state or states. The remainder of this chapter discusses these new obligations and rights. The discussion focuses on the simple situation of one state injuring another, but it is entirely possible for multiple states to be involved and, in some situations, for nonstate actors to pursue claims and receive reparation.

D. Obligations of a Breaching State

When a breach occurs, the breaching state remains bound to the underlying international obligation.[35] As such, the breaching state is obligated to stop any act contrary to that obligation. The ILC Articles further assert that a state is obligated to offer assurances and guarantees of non-repetition,[36] although state practice on that point is sparse.

Moreover, the breaching state is obligated to make reparation for its breach. In the *Chorzów Factory* case, the PCIJ confronted whether a state was obligated to make reparation for breach of a treaty, even if the treaty did not address the issue of reparation. In that case, Poland had confiscated the property of German nationals in violation of treaties associated with the end of World War I. The Court famously found:

> It is a principle of international law that the breach of an engagement involves an obligation to make reparation in an adequate form. Reparation therefore is the indispensable complement of a failure to apply a convention and there is no necessity for this to be stated in the convention itself.[37]

The Court further found, in a subsequent phase, that

> reparation must, as far as possible, wipe out all the consequences of the illegal act and reestablish the situation which would, in all probability, have existed if that act had not been committed. Restitution in kind, or, if this is not possible, payment of a sum corresponding to the value which a restitution in kind would bear; the award, if need be, of damages for loss sustained which would not be covered by restitution in kind or payment in place of it—such are the principles which

---

35. *See* ILC Articles, *supra* note 2, art. 29.

36. *Id.*, art. 30.

37. Factory at Chorzów (Ger. v. Pol.), 1927 P.C.I.J. (ser. A) No. 9, at 21 (July 26).

should serve to determine the amount of compensation due for an act contrary to international law.[38]

Reparation can be made in three principal forms—restitution, compensation, or satisfaction—which might be made singly or in combination.[39] Each is discussed in turn.

Restitution

Restitution essentially entails reestablishing the *status quo ante*, meaning the situation as it existed prior to the wrongful conduct, to the extent that is possible.[40] If property was wrongfully taken, then it should be returned. If persons were wrongly detained, then they should be released. However, restitution may not be possible or desirable. For example, goods that were wrongfully seized may have spoiled, such that their return hardly makes the injured state whole. Further, while the PCIJ in the *Chorzów Factory* case seemed to favor restitution over compensation, most international tribunals appear reluctant to order states to take acts of restitution; it is apparently considered less intrusive on sovereign functions to order the payment of compensation.

Compensation

Compensation is a second form of reparation.[41] Compensation normally entails monetary payment to the injured state for the damage it has suffered or its nationals have suffered. Thus, according to the official commentary to the ILC Articles, compensation

> encompasses both damage suffered by the State itself (to its property or personnel or in respect of expenditures reasonably incurred to remedy or mitigate damage flowing from an internationally wrongful act) as well as damage suffered by nationals, whether persons or companies, on whose behalf the State is claiming within the framework of diplomatic protection.[42]

Compensation is not punitive in nature. Rather than to teach the breaching state a lesson, the objective in compensation is to make the injured state whole.

There is extensive case law and settlement agreements that address issues of compensation. Two areas that often arise in interstate disputes concern the appropriate compensation standards for personal injury and for the taking of property. With respect to personal injury, the official commentary to the ILC Articles states:

---

38. Factory at Chorzów (Ger. v. Pol.), 1928 P.C.I.J. (ser. A) No. 17, at 47 (Sept. 13).

39. *See* ILC Articles, *supra* note 2, art. 34.

40. *Id.*, art. 35.

41. *Id.*, art. 36.

42. James Crawford, The International Law Commission's Articles on State Responsibility: Introduction, Text and Commentaries 220 (2002).

Compensable personal injury encompasses not only associated material losses, such as loss of earnings and earning capacity, medical expenses and the like, but also non-material damage suffered by the individual (sometimes, though not universally, referred to as "moral damage" in national legal systems). Non-material damage is generally understood to encompass loss of loved ones, pain and suffering as well as the affront to sensibilities associated with an intrusion on the person, home or private life.[43]

With respect to the taking of property, the official commentary provides:

Compensation reflecting the capital value of property taken or destroyed as the result of an internationally wrongful act is generally assessed on the basis of the "fair market value" of the property lost. The method used to assess "fair market value", however, depends on the nature of the asset concerned. Where the property in question or comparable property is freely traded on an open market, value is more readily determined. In such cases, the choice and application of asset-based valuation methods based on market data and the physical properties of the assets is relatively unproblematic, apart from evidentiary difficulties associated with long outstanding claims. Where the property interests in question are unique or unusual, for example, art works or other cultural property, or are not the subject of frequent or recent market transactions, the determination of value is more difficult. This may be true, for example, in respect of certain business entities in the nature of a going concern, especially if shares are not regularly traded.[44]

In situations where business that is a going concern has been expropriated, the preferred approach is to "examine the assets of the business, making allowance for goodwill and profitability as appropriate."[45] Where this is not possible, the alternative valuation method is the determination of net book value (total assets less total liabilities). If the business is not a going concern, the preferred approach is to determine the liquidation or dissolution value, meaning what might have been achieved in selling off the individual assets of the business.[46]

43. *Id.* at 223 (footnotes omitted).

44. *Id.* at 225–26 (footnotes omitted).

45. *Id.* at 226.

46. *Id.* at 226–27. On the valuation of property that is "indirectly" expropriated (*i.e.*, the state does not formally take the property but so interferes with it that property rights are rendered useless), see W. Michael Reisman & Robert D. Sloane, *Indirect Expropriation and Its Valuation in the BIT Generation*, 74 BRIT. YRBK. INT'L L. 115 (2003).

Satisfaction

A third form of reparation is satisfaction, which is a remedy sometimes employed when an injury cannot be compensated financially.[47] This remedy often arises when State A's violation of international law has been an affront to State B, such as from an insult to State B's flag, an encroachment on State B's territory without permission, or ill treatment of State B's visiting prime minister. In such circumstances, there may be no injury that can be financially assessed, but there may be a "non-material" injury that international law seeks to remedy.

Satisfaction may be given in various forms. Public acknowledgment by State A that it injured State B is a form of satisfaction. Satisfaction also may be given through a public statement of regret or apology. Disciplinary action might be taken against the persons in State A who caused the affront. A payment by State A of symbolic damages also can be a form of satisfaction.

Often recognition by an independent tribunal that one state has affronted the other is deemed to constitute satisfaction. Thus, in the *Corfu Channel* case, Albania felt affronted by an unlawful mine-sweeping operation by the British Navy in Albania's territory waters. The ICJ said that

> to ensure respect for international law, of which it is the organ, the Court must declare that the action of the British Navy constituted a violation of Albanian sovereignty. This declaration is in accordance with the request made by Albania through her Counsel, and is in itself appropriate satisfaction.[48]

Interest

The breaching state is also obligated to pay interest on the principal sum due, from the date the sum is due until the date it is paid, if interest is appropriate for ensuring full reparation. The level of interest used by states when making a payment, or awarded by international tribunals in contentious proceedings, has varied considerably. The PCIJ in the *S.S. "Wimbledon"* case awarded six percent interest,[49] while commercial claims before the Iran–U.S. Claims Tribunal were typically (but not uniformly) awarded twelve percent interest.[50] Sometimes a tribunal has awarded differing levels of interest in the same claim for different types of losses.[51] International law accords states and tribunals the latitude to award

47. *See* ILC Articles, *supra* note 2, art. 37.

48. Corfu Channel, *supra* note 6, at 35–36.

49. *See* S.S. "Wimbledon," 1923 P.C.I.J. (ser. A) No. 1, at 32 (Aug. 17).

50. *See* GEORGE H. ALDRICH, THE JURISPRUDENCE OF THE IRAN-UNITED STATES CLAIMS TRIBUNAL 475–76 (1996).

51. *See* The M/V "Saiga" (No. 2) (St. Vincent v. Guinea), 120 I.L.R. 143, 200 (Int'l Trib. L. of the Sea 1999).

a level of interest deemed appropriate for compensating the injured party.

Virtually all international courts and tribunals have awarded simple, not compound, interest. Some states, tribunals, and scholars, however, assert that compound interest is the only appropriate way of insuring full reparation to an injured state or national.[52]

E. Rights of an Injured State

When a breach occurs, new rights arise for the injured state or states. These rights principally concern the right to invoke the breaching state's responsibility and the right to pursue countermeasures.

Invocation of Breaching State's Responsibility

Introduction. An injured state may invoke the breaching state's responsibility by notifying the breaching state of a claim. The claim should specify the conduct complained of, steps the breaching state must take to correct its conduct, and what form of reparation should be made.[53]

If there are several injured states, each one may make a claim against the breaching state (or against any one of several breaching states), although no injured state may recover compensation exceeding its damages.[54] The possibility of multiple states being involved in an injury is particularly apparent in the field of international environmental law, where noxious emissions from several states may cause harm in several other states. Moreover, the ILC Articles posit that an uninjured state may invoke a breaching state's responsibility if the breach is of an obligation owed collectively to a group of states of which the invoking state is a member (*e.g.*, a regional human rights treaty) or owed to the international community as a whole.[55] Obligations owed to the international community as a whole are often referred to as *erga omnes* obligations, and include prohibitions on aggression, genocide, slavery, racial discrimination, and the denial of self-determination.[56]

52. *See* Memorial of United States, Elettronica Sicula S.p.A. (ELSI) (U.S. v. Italy), 1987 I.C.J. Pleadings 114–15 (filed May 15, 1987); Compañía des Desarrollo de Santa Elena S.A. v. Costa Rica, ICSID (W. Bank) Case No. ARB/96/1, paras. 103–105 (Feb. 17, 2000); F.A. Mann, *Compound Interest as an Item of Damage in International Law*, in FURTHER STUDIES IN INTERNATIONAL LAW 377, 383 (1990).

53. *See* ILC Articles, *supra* note 2, arts. 42–43.

54. *Id.*, arts. 46–47.

55. *Id.*, art. 48.

56. *See* Barcelona Traction, Light & Power Co., Ltd. (Belg. v. Spain), Second Phase, 1970 I.C.J. 3, 32, para. 34 (Feb. 5); East Timor (Port. v. Austl.), 1995 I.C.J. 90, 102, para. 29 (June 30); Application of the Convention on the Prevention and Punishment of the Crime of Genocide (Bosnia & Herz. v. Yugo.), Judgment on Preliminary Objections to Jurisdiction, 1996 I.C.J. 595, para. 31 (July 11).

Espousal of Claims of a National. In some situations, the injury to the state may not be direct, but instead the consequence of an injury to one of its nationals. Thus, if John Doe from State A travels to State B where he is taken prisoner and executed without due process of law, State A is in a position to bring a claim against State B based on State B's failure to accord John Doe the minimum standard of protection due to aliens.[57] If State A presents to State B, through diplomatic channels, a claim for injury to John Doe, State A is engaging in "diplomatic protection" of John Doe by "espousing" his claim.[58]

Such espousal may be very helpful to an injured person (or his heirs); instead of standing alone, the person has the weight of her government in support of the claim against the breaching state. At the same time, however, the private claim becomes an international claim over which the claimant state enjoys exclusive control. The private claimant, therefore, can no longer pursue or dispose of the claim on her own.[59] As the D.C. Circuit Court of Appeals held in *Asociacion de Reclamantes*, the claims of private parties espoused by the Mexican government were the Mexican government's to pursue: "the fact that a claim has been espoused provides a complete defense for the defendant sovereign in any action by the private individual. . . . "[60] To the extent that government control of the claim works to the disadvantage of the injured national, U.S. courts have long recognized that recourse for the national is against her government, not pursuit of the claim against the foreign government on her own.[61]

While a state might espouse a single claim relating to an isolated incident, it is often the case that a state will espouse an entire class of claims relating to losses or injuries suffered by its nationals from a revolution or war in another state. In the course of such an espousal, the claimant government can dispose of the

---

57. *See* Chapter 10(B).

58. In 2006, the International Law Commission adopted a series of articles codifying the law on diplomatic protection of natural and legal persons. *See* U.N. Doc. A161/10, at 24 (2006).

59. *See* Note, *The French Spoliation Cases—An Unanswered Question*, 12 Va. J. Int'l L. 120 (1971) (describing the U.S. waiver of private claims of U.S. nationals against France for spoliation of their vessels in exchange for France dropping certain claims against the United States); *see also* 2 Restatement (Third) on the Foreign Relations Law of the United States § 713 cmt. a (1987) ("The claim derives from injury to an

individual, but once espoused it is the state's claim, and can be waived by the state.").

60. Asociacion de Reclamantes v. United Mexican States 735 F.2d 1517, 1523 (D.C. Cir. 1984); *see* Meade v. United States, 76 U.S. (9 Wall.) 691, 724 (1869) (finding that regardless of the attitude of the private claimant to the U.S. government's espousal of the claim, the claimant lacked the power to deprive the government of settlement authority by resorting to a private remedy).

61. *See* Gray v. United States, 21 Ct.Cl. 340, 392–93 (1886); Shanghai Power Co. v. United States, 4 Cl. Ct. 237, 240–45 (1983).

claims either by (1) receiving a lump sum payment from the breaching state which is then distributed by the claimant state to its nationals;[62] or (2) placing the espoused claims before an international claims commission for arbitration. The U.S. Supreme Court recognized in the *Dames & Moore* case that such dispositions have occurred repeatedly throughout U.S. history.[63]

The public purpose served in allowing a state to establish mechanisms for resolving claims is readily apparent if doing so allows two states to eliminate sources of transnational friction. In *American Insurance Association v. Garamendi*, the U.S. Supreme Court found that the U.S. government could displace private actions under state law by concluding a U.S.-German agreement on compensation to persons for Nazi-era injuries committed by companies and banks:

> Since claims remaining in the aftermath of hostilities may be "sources of friction" acting as an "impediment to resumption of friendly relations" between the countries involved, [*United States v. Pink*, 315 U.S. 203, 225 (1942)], there is a "longstanding practice" of the national Executive to settle them in discharging its responsibility to maintain the Nation's relationships with other countries, [*Dames & Moore v. Regan,* 453 U.S. 654, 679 (1981)]. The issue of restitution for Nazi crimes has in fact been addressed in Executive Branch diplomacy and formalized in treaties and executive agreements over the last half century, and although resolution of private claims was postponed by the Cold War, securing private interests is an express object of diplomacy today, just as it was addressed in agreements soon after the Second World War. Vindicating victims injured by acts and omissions of enemy corporations in wartime is thus within the traditional subject matter of foreign policy in which national, not state, interests are overriding, and which the National Government has addressed.[64]

Limitations on Espousal. There are certain situations, however, where an injured state may *not* espouse a person's claim. First, if the claim is brought on behalf of a person who is not a national of the injured state, the injured state cannot maintain the claim.[65]

---

62. In the United States, such distribution is normally done by the U.S. Department of Justice Foreign Claims Settlement Commission.

63. *See* Dames & Moore v. Regan, 453 U.S. 654, 679 (1981); *see also* Chapter 7(A).

64. American Ins. Ass'n v. Garamendi, 539 U.S. 396, 420–21 (2003); *accord* Deutsch v. Turner Corp., 317 F.3d 1005, 1023–24 (9th Cir. 2003) (finding that the United States "has already exercised its own exclusive authority to resolve the war, including claims arising out of it. It did not choose, however, to incorporate into that resolution a private right of action against our wartime enemies or their nationals.").

65. *See* ILC Articles, *supra* note 2, art. 44(a).

States are only entitled to pursue claims of their own nationals, not the nationals of other states. Further, even if the person is a national of the espousing state at the time the claim is filed, the state may not espouse her claim against another state if she was not a national of the espousing state when the alleged injury occurred or at any other point prior to resolution of the claim. In other words, under the "continuous nationality" rule, the nationality of the person with the espousing state must be continuous from the occurrence of the injury until the resolution of the claim. Of course, as stated at the beginning of this chapter, two or more states may always choose to craft alternative rules. For example, under the European human rights convention,[66] one member state has standing to make a claim against another for human rights violations, even if the injury is not to the nationals of the first state.[67]

An example of the continuous nationality rule may be seen in the *Loewen* case, an arbitration brought under Chapter 11 of the North American Free Trade Agreement (NAFTA). Chapter 11 allows a foreign investor from one of the three NAFTA states (Canada, Mexico, and the United States) to pursue arbitration directly against the government of a member state when that state harms the investor. In *Loewen*, a Canadian company (Loewen) sued the U.S. Government for alleged discrimination, expropriation, and denial of a minimum standard of protection stemming from Loewen's treatment before a Mississippi trial court. After filing its claim, however, Loewen's business operations were reorganized as a U.S. corporation, and the NAFTA claim was assigned to a Canadian corporation owned and controlled by that U.S. corporation. Since the real beneficiary of the NAFTA claim was now a U.S. national, the arbitral tribunal found that the "continuous nationality" rule of customary international law was not met, because the rule requires that foreign nationality be maintained from the occurrence of the injury until the issuance of an award (not just until the filing of the claim).[68]

Second, where the claim is brought on behalf of persons, those persons must first exhaust all reasonably available remedies in the national system of the breaching state.[69] Thus, under this "local remedies" rule, the injured national of State B must first pursue any judicial or administrative recourse in State A to its highest

66. Convention for the Protection of Human Rights and Fundamental Freedoms art. 33, Nov. 4, 1950, 213 U.N.T.S. 221, *as amended by* Protocol No. 11, May 11, 1994, 33 I.L.M. 960.

67. *See, e.g.,* Denmark v. Turkey, App. No. 34382/97, Eur. Ct. H.R. (Apr. 5, 2000).

68. *See* Loewen Group v. United States, Award, paras. 225–33 (NAFTA Ch. 11 Arb. Trib. June 26, 2003).

69. *See* ILC Articles, *supra* note 2, art. 44(b).

level before State B may pursue a claim against State A. As the International Court stated in the *Interhandel* case,

> "[t]he rule that local remedies must be exhausted before international proceedings may be instituted is a well-established rule of customary international law; the rule has been generally observed in cases in which a State has adopted the cause of its national whose rights are claimed to have been disregarded in another State in violation of international law. Before resort may be had to an international court in such a situation, it has been considered necessary that the State where the violation occurred should have an opportunity to redress it by its own means, within the framework of its own domestic legal system."[70]

For example, in 1998 the Republic of Guinea filed a state responsibility case against the Democratic Republic of Congo (D.R.C.) at the International Court. Guinea alleged that Ahmadou Sadio Diallo, a national of Guinea who had resided in the D.R.C. for thirty-two years, was unlawfully imprisoned without a trial by the authorities of that state. It was also claimed that Diallo's investments, businesses, and property were unlawfully expropriated. After Diallo attempted unsuccessfully in local proceedings to recover sums owed to him by companies owned by the government of the D.R.C. and companies in which it was a shareholder, Guinea claimed that, without judicial process, Diallo was expelled from the D.R.C., which Guinea maintained was unlawful. After the filing of the case, the D.R.C. objected to the admissibility of the claims, in part based on a failure to exhaust local remedies. The Court found that the D.R.C.'s objection focused solely on the issue of expulsion; it failed to challenge a lack of exhaustion with respect to the other claims. With respect to the expulsion, the Court found Diallo's expulsion was classified by the D.R.C. as a "refusal of entry," which is not appealable under D.R.C. law.[71] Further, while the D.R.C. indicated that there was a possibility to request reconsideration by an administrative authority, the Court found that

> administrative remedies can only be taken into consideration for purposes of the local remedies rule if they are aimed at vindicating a right and not at obtaining a favour, unless they constitute an essential prerequisite for the admissibility of subsequent contentious proceedings. Thus, the possibility open to Mr. Diallo of submitting a request for reconsideration of the expulsion decision to the administrative authority having taken

---

70. Interhandel (Switz. v. U.S.), 1959 I.C.J. 6, 27 (Mar. 21); *see* Elettronica Sicula S.p.A. (ELSI) (U.S. v. Italy), 1989 I.C.J. 15, 43–44, para. 53 (July 20).

71. Ahmadou Sadio Diallo (Guinea v. D.R.C.), 2007 I.C.J. para. 46 (May 24), *at* <http://www.icj-cij.org>.

it—that is to say the Prime Minister—in the hope that he would retract his decision as a matter of grace cannot be deemed a local remedy to be exhausted.[72]

At the later merits phase, the Court found that Diallo's arrest, detention, and expulsion violated his rights under the International Covenant on Civil and Political Rights and the African Charter on Human and People's Rights.[73]

Third, an injured state may not pursue a claim if it has waived that claim or acquiesced in the wrongful conduct.[74] For example, if State B insists for years that State A pay a specific sum in compensation for a capital loss, and State A eventually pays that sum, State B might be regarded as having waived any claim for a further payment of interest.[75] Acquiescence may arise if, over a period of years after the wrongful conduct occurred, State B fails to notify State A of its claim. International law does not specify a time period after which acquiescence will be deemed to have occurred.[76] Much depends on whether the injured state should have known of the wrongful conduct and whether the failure to bring a claim prejudiced the breaching state, such as through the loss of contemporaneous evidence.

Discretion to Espouse. A state is not obligated to espouse a claim of one of its nationals, regardless of whether there is merit to the claim. For example, Renatus J. Chytil and Bohumir J. Marik were nationals of Czechoslovakia when their properties were confiscated in 1939 and 1972, respectively. Both men subsequently became naturalized U.S. citizens, at which point their Czech citizenship was revoked. When Chytil and Marik sought assistance from the U.S. government in regaining their property, the Department of State declined to espouse their claims on grounds that they were not U.S. nationals at the time the claims arose.

In 1999, the two men separately sued the U.S. government in federal court, charging that the failure to espouse the claims constituted a violation of their civil rights[77] and seeking a declaratory judgment that the secretary of state, in deciding whether to espouse, may not discriminate against them on the basis of national origin. The Ninth Circuit Court of Appeals affirmed the district court's dismissal of the cases.

---

72. *Id.*, para. 47.

73. Ahmadou Sadio Diallo (Guinea v. D.R.C.), 2010 I.C.J. (Nov. 30), *at* <http://www.icj-cij.org>.

74. *Id.*, art. 45.

75. *See* Russian Indemnity Case (Russ. v. Turk.), 11 R.I.A.A. 421, 446 (1912).

76. *See* Certain Phosphate Lands in Nauru (Nauru v. Austl.), 1992 I.C.J. 240, 247, para. 13 (June 26).

77. *See* 42 U.S.C. §§ 1971, 1982, 1983 (2006).

Espousal seems particularly unsusceptible to resolution in the judicial branch. In making espousal decisions, the Secretary of State undoubtedly takes into account many factors relating to foreign relations, including the relations between the United States and the foreign country against which a person has a claim. The judiciary has no experience in espousal and has no way of considering the many other factors that espousal decisions would affect, and there is no basis upon which the judiciary can conclude that national origin is a factor that the Secretary may not consider. We therefore hold that Chytil's case presents a nonjusticiable political question.[78]

Countermeasures

In addition to invoking the breaching state's responsibility, the injured state may pursue countermeasures against the breaching state. A "countermeasure" is defined as a non-forcible act[79] that would normally be contrary to the international obligations of a state, but that is deemed permissible when taken in response to the wrongful act of another state and in order to induce cessation of, and reparation for, that act.

Chapter 5 discussed the importance of reciprocity in promoting *ab initio* compliance by states with international obligations, and the significance of "self-help" by states through the imposition of unilateral sanctions to coerce compliance with international law, since there is no centralized "international policeman." At the same time, it should be clear that the free-wheeling use of unilateral sanctions would be detrimental to the stability of the international legal system. With that in mind, state responsibility rules on countermeasures seek to identify the conditions and limitations upon a state when undertaking non-forcible actions in response to the wrongful conduct of another state.

The ILC Articles on countermeasures, which have been challenged by some states and scholars, maintain that the following conditions and limitations exist:

- An injured state may not impose countermeasures unless it has first called upon the breaching state to desist from its internationally wrongful conduct and to make reparation; further, the injured state must notify the breaching state of

78. Chytil v. Powell, 15 Fed. Appx. 515 (9th Cir. 2001); *see* Marik v. Powell, 15 Fed. Appx. 517 (9th Cir. 2001).

79. In international law, the term "reprisal" is used to describe a forcible action by one state taken in time of international armed conflict in response to a wrongful act by another state. The term "retorsion" is used to describe a responsive action taken by a state that is unfriendly, but that is not contrary to the international obligations of that state.

its intent to undertake countermeasures and offer to negotiate the matter;[80]

- An injured state may not impose countermeasures (and must suspend the countermeasures if they have already been imposed) if the breaching state ceases its wrongful conduct and the matter is placed before an international court or tribunal;[81]

- An injured state may only take countermeasures against the state responsible for the wrongful act;[82]

- An injured state may only take countermeasures in order to induce the breaching state into complying with its obligations, conforming its conduct, and making reparation;[83]

- An injured state must limit its countermeasures, at least initially, to the non-performance of its obligations to the breaching state;[84]

- An injured state must limit its countermeasures in such a way as to permit the resumption of performance of the obligations in question at some future time;[85]

- An injured state may not engage in countermeasures inconsistent with its obligations arising under: (a) the U.N. Charter's prohibition on the threat or use of force;[86] (b) fundamental human rights law; (c) prohibitions on belligerent reprisal; (d) peremptory norms of international law (*jus cogens*); or (e) diplomatic or consular law;[87]

- An injured state must adhere to any dispute settlement procedure existing with the breaching state, and cannot suspend that procedure as part of its countermeasures;[88]

- An injured state must only pursue countermeasures that are proportionate to the injury suffered;[89] and

- An injured state must cease its countermeasures when the breaching state ceases its wrongful conduct and makes reparation.[90]

An often-cited example of countermeasures is a 1970's dispute between the United States and France over air services. A U.S.

---

80. *See* ILC Articles, *supra* note 2, art. 52(1). Notification is not required for countermeasures that must be taken urgently, such as freezing foreign assets before they can be repatriated. *Id.*, art. 52(2).

81. *Id.*, art. 52(3).

82. *Id.*, art. 49(1).

83. *Id.*

84. *Id.*, art. 49(2).

85. *Id.*, art. 49(3).

86. *See* Chapter 14(A).

87. ILC Articles, *supra* note 2, art. 50.

88. *Id.*, art. 50(2)(a).

89. *Id.*, art. 51 (using the term "commensurate" rather than "proportionate").

90. *Id.*, art. 53.

carrier, Pan Am, had certain rights under a bilateral U.S.-France air services agreement for flights from the United States to Paris. Rather than fly direct to Paris, Pan Am sought to fly first to London where there would be a "change of gauge" (switching to a smaller aircraft) before completing the flight to Paris. France refused to receive such flights, even though they appeared permissible under the air services agreement. The U.S. government demanded that France honor the agreement and, when France did not, the United States responded by refusing to allow Air France to fly a route from Paris to Los Angeles. The matter was placed before an international arbitral tribunal, which concluded that the U.S. countermeasure was justified and proportionate.[91]

91. *See* Air Service Agreement of 27 March 1946 (U.S. v. Fr.), 18 R.I.A.A. 417, 444, para. 83 (1978).

Further Reading

Tal Becker, *Terrorism and the State: Rethinking the Rules of State Responsibility* (2006).

Daniel Bodansky & John R. Crook, eds., "Symposium: The ILC's State Responsibility Articles," 96 *Am. J. Int'l L.* 773 (2002).

Chittharanjan F. Amerasinghe, *Local Remedies in International Law* (2d ed. 2003).

Chittharanjan F. Amerasinghe, *Diplomatic Protection* (2008).

Ian Brownlie, *System of the Law of Nations: State Responsibility (Part I)* (1983).

James Crawford et al., eds., *The Law of International Responsibility* (2010).

James Crawford, *The International Law Commission's Articles on State Responsibility: Introduction, Text, and Commentaries* (2002).

Christine Gray, *Judicial Remedies in International Law* (1987).

Pablo de Greiff ed., *The Handbook of Reparations* (2006).

Clyde Eagleton, *The Responsibility of States in International Law* (1928).

O.Y. Elagab, *The Legality of Non-forcible Counter-measures in International Law* (1988).

Göran Lysén, *State Responsibility and International Liability of States for Lawful Acts: A Discussion of Principles* (1997).

André Nollkaemper & Harmen van der Wilt, *System Criminality in International Law* (2009).

Maurizio Ragazzi, *The Concept of International Obligations* Erga Omnes (1997).

Albrecht Randelzhofer & Christian Tomuschat, eds., *State Responsibility and the Individual: Reparation in Instances of Grave Violations of Human Rights* (1999).

Shabtai Rosenne, ed., *The International Law Commission's Draft Articles on State Responsibility: Part 1, Articles 1–35* (1991).

Dinah Shelton, *Remedies in International Human Rights Law* (2d ed. 2005).

Kimberly Trapp, *State Responsibility for International Terrorism* (2011).

Marjorie M. Whiteman, *Damages in International Law* (1937–43) (3 vols.).

PART II

Inter-Relationship of International Law and National Law

Chapter 7

FOREIGN RELATIONS LAW
OF THE UNITED STATES

The inter-relationship of international law and national law is important for the functioning of international law. The ways that states operate internally have enormous consequences for how international law is created, interpreted, and enforced. To understand any given state's relationship to international law, it is important first to analyze the constitutional structure of the state, to see how powers relating to foreign affairs are distributed within the state, both laterally (*i.e.*, among different branches) and horizontally (*i.e.*, between the central government and lower levels of government). Further, the state's constitution, statutes, and case law will reveal much about whether the state readily incorporates international law as a part of its law or whether there are impediments to such incorporation. Such law is referred to as foreign relations law.

Foreign relations law in the United States falls principally into three areas. One area concerns the division of power among the three branches of the federal government in matters touching upon foreign affairs. Another area concerns the effect of the federal government's foreign affairs power upon the conduct of the several states. The third area deals with the manner in which international law is regarded as a part of U.S. law, such as whether an individual can invoke a treaty provision before a U.S. court. This chapter provides an overview of these three areas of U.S. foreign relations law.

A. Separation of Powers

Congressional Power

Under the U.S. Constitution, Congress has several powers touching upon foreign affairs, such as the powers to lay and collect duties, provide for the common defense, regulate commerce with foreign nations, regulate naturalization, make rules regarding the law of prize, define and punish piracies and felonies committed on the high seas (as well as offenses against the law of nations), create and regulate an army and a navy, and declare war.[1] Moreover, two-thirds of the U.S. Senate must provide advice and consent before the president may ratify a treaty.[2] Congress also, of course, has the power to appropriate funds for the U.S. government and enact all laws "necessary and proper" to execute any federal power.[3] As in other areas of law, U.S. courts have interpreted these Congressional powers broadly in the field of foreign affairs when Congress chooses to act, unless there is a specific constitutional limitation on governmental power, such as in the Bill of Rights.[4]

U.S. Government Constitutional Allocation of Foreign Affairs Power

Congressional Powers (Art. I)	Executive Powers (Art. II)	Judicial Power (Art. III)
Power to appropriate funds relating to foreign affairs (*e.g.*, foreign aid, military assistance)	Vested with the executive power	Power to hear cases arising under U.S. laws and treaties, affecting ambassadors, and concerning admiralty
Power to lay and collect duties, imposts, and excises	Power to receive/appoint ambassadors	
Power to provide for common defense and to raise/support/regulate the army and navy	Commander-in-chief power	
Foreign commerce power	Power to make treaties with consent of Senate	Power to hear cases between a state or its citizens and a foreign state or its citizens
Power to establish laws on naturalization	Power to take care that the laws are faithfully executed	
Power to define and punish piracies and felonies on high seas, and offenses against law of nations		
Power to declare war and make rules concerning captures on land and water (*i.e.*, prize)		
Power to call forth militia to repel invasion		
Power to approve state-level foreign "compacts"		
Senate power to consent to treaty ratification and appointment of ambassadors		

Among these powers is Congress' power to "Define and Punish ... Offenses against the Law of Nations," the only place in the U.S. Constitution where reference is made to the "law of nations" (it is generally believed that the term "international law" was only later coined by Jeremy Bentham). The "offenses" clause allows Congress to specify the elements of offenses that exist under international law and to impose both criminal and civil sanctions for their

---

1. *See* U.S. CONST. art. I, § 8.

2. *Id.*, art. II, § 2, cl. 2.

3. *Id.*, art. I, §§ 7, 8.

4. *See* LOUIS HENKIN, FOREIGN AFFAIRS AND THE UNITED STATES CONSTITUTION 64, 80 (2d ed. 1996).

violation.[5] The first Congress invoked the law of nations when criminalizing piracy, attacks on ambassadors, and violations of safe conduct,[6] and within a few years arguably used the clause to enact statutes concerning neutrality and the slave trade. A notable challenge to Congress' use of the clause arose in the context of criminalizing the counterfeiting of foreign currency and corporate securities. In *United States v. Arjona*,[7] the Supreme Court in 1887 broadly construed the scope of the power as including punishment for conduct that harms U.S. relations with other countries. According to the Court:

> The national government ... is made responsible to foreign nations for all violations by the United States of their international obligations, and because of this congress is expressly authorized to "define and punish offenses against the law of nations." The law of nations requires every national government to use "due diligence" to prevent a wrong being done within its own dominion to another nation with which it is at peace, or to the people thereof; and because of this, the obligation of one nation to punish those who, within its own jurisdiction, counterfeit the money of another nation has long been recognized.[8]

Contentious issues continue today concerning the "offenses" clause, such as whether through it Congress has limited presidential power to conduct military commissions,[9] has criminalized not just piracy but "attempted" piracy,[10] and can properly criminalize "material support for terrorism" under the laws of war[11] or even "terrorism" itself.[12]

Many statutes enacted by Congress under this and other foreign relations powers remain effective for years, even centuries. For example, the Alien Tort Statute, discussed in section C below, was enacted in 1789 and remains in effect to this day. Other statutes are more temporary in nature, such as the annual foreign relations appropriation legislation, which contains provisions that expire at the end of the fiscal year.

5. *See* J. Andrew Kent, *Congress' Under–Appreciated Power to Define and Punish Offenses Against the Law of Nations*, 85 Tex. L. Rev. 843 (2007).

6. Crimes Act of 1790, ch. 9, §§ 25–27.

7. 120 U.S. 479 (1887); *see also* Frend v. United States, 100 F.2d 691 (1938); Ex Parte Quirin, 317 U.S. 1 (1942); Boos v. Barry, 485 U.S. 312 (1988).

8. *Arjona*, 120 U.S. at 483–84.

9. *See* Hamdan v. Rumsfeld, 548 U.S. 557 (2006).

10. *See* United States v. Hasan, 747 F.Supp.2d 599 (E.D. Va. 2010); United States v. Said, 757 F.Supp.2d 554 (E.D. Va. 2010).

11. *See* Almog v. Arab Bank, PLC, 471 F.Supp.2d 257 (E.D.N.Y. 2007).

12. *See* United States v. Yousef, 327 F.3d 56 (2d Cir. 2003).

A centerpiece of U.S. foreign relations statutes is the 1961 Foreign Assistance Act (FAA).[13] Among other things, the FAA reorganized U.S. foreign assistance programs so as to separate military and non-military aid. Military aid was expected to help U.S. allies defend themselves from attack and participate in collective security arrangements. Non-military aid was expected to foster economic growth and democracy in the developing world, combat the perceived spread of ideological threats such as communism, and address the threat of instability arising from poverty. As originally enacted in 1961, the FAA contained few restrictions on how assistance was to be provided and only general factors to be taken into account prior to the provision of assistance. Over time, however, the FAA has been amended repeatedly to contain restrictions on the conduct of the executive branch and to adjust the purposes for which military and non-military aid may be dispensed. Further, the FAA must now be read in conjunction with other statutes, such as the 1976 Arms Export Control Act (AECA),[14] which contains important restrictions on the retransfer of arms sold to U.S. allies.

One example of a restriction on executive branch conduct is FAA section 660, which precludes the executive from providing FAA funds to a foreign state's police or law enforcement personnel unless that state has a "longstanding democratic tradition, does not have standing armed forces, and does not engage in" human rights abuses.[15] Such a restriction reflects Congressional concern that U.S. aid not be used to support abuses by a foreign government against its own people. Statutes such as the FAA also often impose reporting requirements on the executive branch, so Congress can obtain information needed for fulfilling its legislative mandate, and can monitor executive actions. Thus, the FAA requires the Department of State to submit annually to Congress a "full and complete report regarding the status of internationally recognized human rights" for all U.N. member states and all states receiving U.S. foreign assistance.[16]

Annual and biennial authorization and appropriations statutes are also an important means for Congressional regulation and oversight of executive branch action in the field of foreign affairs. The Foreign Relations Authorization Act—covering one or two fiscal years—falls under the authority of the Senate Foreign Relations and House Foreign Affairs committees. The principal annual appropriations legislation—the Foreign Operations, Export Financing, and Related Appropriations Act, and the State, Commerce, and

---

13. Pub. L. No. 87–195, 75 Stat. 424 (1961) (codified as amended in scattered sections of 22 U.S.C.).

14. Pub. L. No. 94–329, 90 Stat. 729 (1976).

15. 22 U.S.C. § 2420(c) (2006).

16. FAA §§ 116(d), 502B, 22 U.S.C. §§ 2304(b), 2151n(d) (2006); *see* Trade Act of 1974, Pub. L. No. 93–618, § 504, 88 Stat. 1978, 2070–71 (1975).

Justice departments' appropriations legislation—fall under the authority of the Senate and House appropriations committees. Other authorization and appropriations statutes, such as those relating to the Department of Defense, often include important provisions on the conduct of U.S. foreign relations. The annual or biennial adoption of these statutes entails a process of negotiation among Congressional representatives, and between Congress and the executive branch, by which important initiatives in U.S. foreign relations are discussed and addressed.

For example, the Foreign Relations Authorization Act for fiscal years 1994 and 1995 contained a provision stating that the United States shall not make any voluntary or assessed contribution to "any affiliated organization of the United Nations which grants full membership as a state to any organization or group that does not have the internationally recognized attributes of statehood.... "[17] Further, the Foreign Relations Authorization Act for fiscal years 1990 and 1991 provided that "[n]o funds authorized to be appropriated by this Act or any other Act shall be available for the United Nations or any specialized agency thereof which accords the Palestine Liberation Organization the same standing as member states."[18] The language of both provisions was such that the requirements were regarded as continuing in force even after the fiscal years covered by the statutes. In October 2011, the U.N. Educational, Scientific and Cultural Organization (UNESCO) voted to admit Palestine to membership. In light of the statutory restrictions, the United States announced that it would terminate its funding of UNESCO, which comprised about 22 percent of the organization's budget.[19]

Failure to comply with such statutes entails risks for executive branch personnel; the Anti–Deficiency Act makes it a crime to spend funds in a manner not authorized by Congress, while the Miscellaneous Receipts Statute prohibits U.S. government personnel from lending or using public money without authorization.[20] At the same time, when Congress enacts a statute that imposes restrictions or requirements on executive branch conduct, the president must decide whether he believes the statute intrudes upon the president's constitutional powers. If it does, the president may issue a statement to that effect, and treat the Congressional restriction or requirement as simply advisory in nature. For example, in 2009

17. Pub. L. No. 103–236, Title IV, § 410, 108 Stat. 454 (1994).

18. Pub. L. No. 101–246, Title IV, § 414, 104 Stat. 70 (1990).

19. *See* Colum Lynch, *UNESCO Votes to Admit Palestine; U.S. Pulls Funding*, WASH. POST, Nov. 1, 2011, at A7.

20. *See* Anti–Deficiency Act, 31 U.S.C. §§ 1341–42, 1350 (2006); Miscellaneous Receipts Statute, 31 U.S.C. 3302 (2006); *see generally* Kate Stith, *Congress' Power of the Purse*, 97 YALE L.J. 1343 (1988).

Congress passed legislation that, among other things, provided that the "Secretary of the Treasury shall instruct the United States Executive Director of the International Monetary Fund to use the voice and vote of the United States to oppose any loan, project, agreement, memorandum, instrument, plan, or other program of the Fund to a Heavily Indebted Poor Country that imposes budget caps or restraints that do not allow the maintenance of or an increase in governmental spending on health care or education. . . ."[21] Although President Obama signed the legislation into law, he issued a statement that such provisions "would interfere with my constitutional authority to conduct foreign relations by directing the Executive to take certain positions in negotiations or discussions with international organizations and foreign governments. . . . I will not treat these provisions as limiting my ability to engage in foreign diplomacy or negotiations."[22]

While many statutes impose restrictions and requirements upon executive action, Congress has also statutorily delegated vast power to the executive branch for the conduct of U.S. foreign relations. Congress often allows the president to waive restrictions when necessary for U.S. national security interests, and has adopted statutes that provide the president with extensive power to address national emergencies that may arise suddenly, such as the International Emergency Economic Powers Act (IEEPA),[23] the National Emergencies Act (NEA)[24], and the Trading with the Enemy Act.[25] U.S. presidents have invoked such emergency statutes in numerous situations. These statutes can be invoked against an entire country with respect to all commerce and financial transactions or with respect to just certain sectors, such as exports from the United States of military or "dual" (commercial/military) use items. Thus, as of 2011, IEEPA sanctions imposed by the executive branch exist with respect to Belarus (since 2006), Iran (since 1979), Myanmar (since 1997), North Korea (since 2008), Russia (since 2000, to prevent the export of weapons-grade uranium), Syria (since 2004), Sudan (since 1997), and Zimbabwe (since 2003). Alternatively, these statutes can be invoked against just certain entities or persons. For example, in October 1995, President Clinton invoked IEEPA and NEA to issue an executive order that provided for economic sanctions against four international narcotics traffickers operating from Colombia (the Cali Cartel).[26] This invoca-

---

21. Supplemental Appropriations Act, 2009, Title XIV, Pub. L. No. 111–32, 123 Stat. 1919 (2009).

22. President Barack Obama Statement on Signing the Supplemental Appropriations Act, 2009, 45 DAILY COMP. PRES. DOC. (June 24, 2009); *see* Curtis A. Bradley & Eric A. Posner, *Presidential Signing Statements and Executive Power*, 23 CONST. COMMENT. 307 (2006).

23. 50 U.S.C. §§ 1701–07 (2006).

24. 50 U.S.C. §§ 1601–51 (2006).

25. 12 U.S.C. § 95a (2006).

26. *See* Exec. Order No. 12,978, 60 Fed. Reg. 54,579 (1995).

tion of the emergency statutes led Congress to adopt more targeted legislation on that topic, the Foreign Narcotics Kingpin Designation Act.[27]

For U.S. action relating to a given foreign relations issue, there may be multiple statutes and multiple executive branch agencies involved. Thus, when a humanitarian catastrophe occurs—such as from the 2011 earthquake and subsequent tsunami that devastated Japan—responsibility for the U.S. humanitarian response falls upon different agencies operating under different statutes. Civilian humanitarian programs rest primarily with the U.S. Department of State and the U.S. Agency for International Development (USAID). The former's authority relates to funds for refugee assistance[28] and admission of refugees to the United States;[29] the latter's relates to funds for foreign disaster assistance[30] and to provision of agricultural commodities and their transportation to meet emergency needs.[31] The U.S. Department of Defense has responsibility for military humanitarian programs, including humanitarian and civic assistance provided in conjunction with military activities,[32] transportation of humanitarian-relief supplies on a space-available basis,[33] foreign disaster and other humanitarian assistance,[34] and provision of excess, nonlethal supplies for humanitarian relief.[35]

Congress also has the power to enact statutes regulating certain conduct of the judicial branch concerning U.S. foreign relations. For example, the Foreign Sovereign Immunities Act[36] sets forth the exclusive basis for U.S. federal courts to consider actions brought against foreign states.

Executive Power

General Executive Power. In contrast to Congress, the president is expressly allocated few foreign affairs powers by the Constitution. The president serves as commander-in-chief of the armed forces, has the power to receive ambassadors, and has the power to appoint ambassadors and make treaties (with the consent of two

27. 21 U.S.C. §§ 1901–08 (2006); 8 U.S.C. § 1182 (2006); *see* 31 C.F.R. §§ 598.101–598.803 (2010).

28. *See* Migration and Refugee Assistance Act of 1962, 22 U.S.C. §§ 2601–06 (2006).

29. *See* 8 U.S.C. §§ 1101–60 (2006).

30. *See* FAA, 22 U.S.C. §§ 2292–92(b) (2006).

31. *See* Agricultural Trade Development and Assistance Act of 1954, Pub. L. No. 83–480, §§ 201–305, 68 Stat. 454, 457–59 (1954); *see also* FAA, 22 U.S.C. § 2318(2)(A) (2006) (authorizing the drawdown of articles and services from any U.S. agency, up to a specified aggregate value per year, for purposes of either the refugee-or disaster-assistance program).

32. *See* 10 U.S.C. § 401 (2006).

33. *See* 10 U.S.C. § 402 (2006).

34. *See* 10 U.S.C. §§ 404, 2551 (2006).

35. *See* 10 U.S.C. § 2547 (2006).

36. 28 U.S.C. §§ 1330, 1332, 1391(f), 1441(d), 1602–1611 (2006); *see* Chapter 9(C).

thirds of the Senate).[37] Nevertheless, as a practical matter, an extraordinary amount of U.S. government authority in the field of foreign affairs is exercised by the executive branch, which alone represents the United States in diplomatic relations and before U.S., foreign, and international courts. Such power not only is derived from the few express powers noted above, but also from vesting of the "executive power" in the president,[38] and from the president's duty to take care that U.S. laws (including treaties and customary international law) are faithfully executed.[39]

Much of this general executive power is derived from customary practice, often as the result of struggles between the executive and legislative branches for the right to exercise a given element of foreign affairs authority. The president has certain inherent institutional advantages in the field of foreign affairs. As a single voice (rather than the group of voices found in Congress), the president is in a much better position to articulate a single U.S. foreign policy and make credible commitments to foreign governments. Through extensive executive branch personnel based in Washington, D.C. and U.S. embassies and consulates worldwide, the president is able to obtain information about foreign affairs and implement U.S. policies in response. Pursuit of certain policies must be done expeditiously and sometimes in secret, which also favors executive branch action.

In the *Curtiss-Wright* case,[40] the Supreme Court commented upon the executive's institutional advantages. In that case, Congress had adopted a statute authorizing the president to prohibit certain arms sales if the president believed doing so would help resolve an armed conflict in South America. The president then issued a proclamation prohibiting such sales. When the defendant was thereafter indicted for violating the prohibition, the defendant challenged the ability of Congress to delegate such power to the president. Noting that the statute related to matters "external to the United States," the Court stated:

> It is important to bear in mind that we are here dealing not alone with an authority vested in the President by an exertion of legislative power, but with such an authority plus the very delicate, plenary and exclusive power of the President as the sole organ of the federal government in the field of international relations—a power which does not require as a basis for its exercise an act of Congress, but which, of course, like every other governmental power, must be exercised in subordination to the applicable provisions of the Constitution.

37. *See* U.S. Const. art. II, §§ 2 & 3.

38. *Id.*, § 1, cl. 1.

39. *Id.*, § 3.

40. United States v. Curtiss–Wright Export Corp., 299 U.S. 304 (1936).

It is quite apparent that if, in the maintenance of our international relations, embarrassment—perhaps serious embarrassment—is to be avoided and success for our aims achieved, congressional legislation which is to be made effective through negotiation and inquiry within the international field must often accord to the President a degree of discretion and freedom from statutory restriction which would not be admissible were domestic affairs alone involved.[41]

The *Curtiss-Wright* case is often cited in support of extensive presidential powers in the field of foreign affairs. Yet the president is clearly constrained by the division of powers with Congress under the Constitution, and there is a constant struggle between the two branches over the conduct of U.S. foreign relations. One analytical framework for thinking about this executive-legislative struggle is found in *Youngstown Sheet & Tube Co. v. Sawyer* (the "Steel Seizure" case).[42] During the Korean War—which entailed the deployment of U.S. forces abroad without a formal declaration of war by Congress—the U.S. steel industry was on the verge of a strike. President Truman issued an executive order, without express statutory authority, directing the secretary of commerce to seize and operate the steel mills. The president explicitly tied this action to the need for steel in the war effort, and grounded the seizure in the president's power as commander-in-chief and more generally in the vesting of the executive power in the president. The Supreme Court found the president's order unconstitutional because it was not authorized by Congress and, perhaps, was implicitly prohibited by the Taft–Hartley Act. In considering under what circumstances the exercise of executive power will be regarded as constitutional, Justice Jackson, concurring, wrote:

1. When the President acts pursuant to an express or implied authorization of Congress, his authority is at its maximum, for it includes all that he possesses in his own right plus all that Congress can delegate. . . . If his act is held unconstitutional under these circumstances, it usually means that the Federal Government as an undivided whole lacks power. . . .

2. When the President acts in absence of either a congressional grant or denial of authority, he can only rely upon his own independent powers, but there is a zone of twilight in which he and Congress may have concurrent authority, or in which its distribution is uncertain. . . . In this area, any actual test of power is likely to depend on the imperatives

41. *Id*. at 319–20.   **42.** 343 U.S. 579 (1952).

of events and contemporary imponderables rather than on abstract theories of law.

3. When the President takes measures incompatible with the expressed or implied will of Congress, his power is at its lowest ebb, for then he can rely only upon his own constitutional powers minus any constitutional powers of Congress over the matter. Courts can sustain exclusive Presidential control in such a case only by disabling the Congress from acting upon the subject.[43]

Justice Jackson stated that Truman's seizure of the steel mills was not authorized by Congress, and therefore could not fall within category one. Further, Justice Jackson stated that there were three statutory policies enacted by Congress that were inconsistent with such a seizure, and thus category two was not available. The seizure, therefore, could only fall within category three. Yet for Justice Jackson, the foreign affairs powers afforded the president under the Constitution did not support the seizure of private property in the United States. He noted that "no doctrine that the Court could promulgate would seem to me more sinister and alarming than that a president whose conduct of foreign affairs is so largely uncontrolled, and often even is unknown, can vastly enlarge his mastery over the internal affairs of the country by his own commitment of the Nation's armed forces to some foreign venture."[44]

The three categories advanced by Justice Jackson in *Youngstown* leave many questions unanswered, yet his analytical framework has been relied upon by many U.S. courts, perhaps because it allows for a pragmatic and flexible review of presidential conduct. For example, the 1981 Algiers Accords concluded by President Carter solely as executive agreements (without any Congressional approval) terminated claims that had been filed by U.S. nationals in U.S. courts against the government of Iran, in exchange for the release by Iran of U.S. nationals being held hostage. The Algiers Accords also provided for the establishment of a claims tribunal in The Hague to resolve, among other things, claims by U.S. nationals against the government of Iran. In *Dames & Moore v. Regan,*[45] claimants against the Iranian government sought a declaration that the executive action, which nullified their claims in U.S. courts, was unconstitutional. Relying heavily on *Youngstown,* the Court found the president's action valid. While there was no statutory authority expressly supporting such termination of claims, the Court found significant certain statutes that provided the president with broad authority in times of national emergency, such as IEEPA. Further,

---

43. *Id.* at 635–38.

44. *Id.* at 642.

45. 453 U.S. 654 (1981).

the Court noted Congress' longstanding acquiescence to presidential settlement of international claims by executive agreement.

From cases such as *Dames & Moore*, it is clear that guides to the scope of executive power in foreign affairs are not found in judicial definitions or even in the synthesis of decided cases. Rather, that authority is defined in an inter-branch process of action-reaction-accommodation that characterizes much of U.S. constitutional law on the separation of powers.

Treaty Power. Chapter 3(A) of this book described how treaties are made. For the United States, the president authorizes a negotiator or negotiating team to conduct treaty negotiations. If the negotiations are successful, the president authorizes someone to sign the treaty on behalf of the United States. Once signed, the treaty must be transmitted to the U.S. Senate. The transmittal documents typically include not just the treaty but also information from the U.S. Department of State describing the treaty, its significance for the United States, and the effect, if any, on U.S. law. Once the treaty has been transmitted, the Senate Foreign Relations Committee decides whether to hold a hearing, at which representatives of the executive branch and others interested in the treaty may testify. The Committee then votes on whether to send the treaty to the floor of the Senate for advice and consent. To receive consent, two-thirds of the Senate must vote in favor of the treaty, after which the president is so notified. The president may only deposit the instrument of ratification with the depositary of the treaty after receiving the Senate's consent.

If the Committee fails to report the treaty to the full Senate, or the treaty is not scheduled for a vote before the full Senate, or the treaty fails to secure the necessary two-thirds vote, the treaty can remain on the Senate's treaty calendar for further action at a later time. As of 2011, there remain on the calendar treaties extending as far back as 1949 (the oldest is a treaty concerning freedom of association and the right to organize adopted by the International Labor Organization). More recent treaties of some significance awaiting Senate consent are the U.N. Convention on the Law of the Sea,[46] the U.N. Convention on Discrimination Against Women,[47] and the Vienna Convention on the Law of Treaties.[48] To the extent that, by signing a treaty, the president generates a U.S. obligation under international law not to defeat the treaty's object and purpose (as discussed in Chapter 3(A)), then a tension arises within U.S. law whenever the Senate exercises its prerogative not to consent to the new treaty obligations. That tension might be

46. Dec. 10, 1982, S. Treaty Doc. No. 103–39 (1994), 1833 U.N.T.S. 3.

47. Dec. 18, 1979, 1249 U.N.T.S. 13.

48. May 23, 1969, 1155 U.N.T.S. 331.

decreased if the obligation not to defeat a treaty's object and purpose is construed narrowly.[49]

Chapter 3(A) also discussed how a state may attach reservations or issue "understandings" or "declarations" (RUDs) when filing its instrument of ratification. The U.S. executive branch transmittal documents will include suggested RUDs, and the Senate can condition its consent upon the inclusion of such RUDs, or upon any other RUD the Senate wishes to include. For example, when the United States ratified the International Covenant on Civil and Political Rights (ICCPR), the Senate conditioned its consent on a reservation that ICCPR Article 20 (which prohibits advocacy of national, racial or religious hatred) does not require any U.S. legislation that would restrict the right of free speech. Moreover, the Senate called for a declaration that the rights set forth in the treaty are not self-executing in U.S. law (see section C below on the doctrine of self-execution).

Of course, ratification of certain treaties may require the United States to alter its national law to conform with the treaty, since reservations may not be permitted or desirable. In such instances, the Senate's consent will usually be conditioned upon the passage of necessary implementing legislation. Thus, the failure of the United States to ratify some treaties may be due not to a failure to secure a two-thirds majority vote in the Senate but, rather, to the difficulty in obtaining simple majorities in both houses of Congress as needed to adopt the implementing legislation.

Executive Agreements. All "treaties" entered into by the United States must be submitted to the Senate for advice and consent. However, by some estimates, only about five percent of all the international agreements concluded by the United States have gone through the process set forth in the U.S. Constitution for approval of treaties. Indeed, the vast majority of international agreements entered into by the United States are never submitted to the Senate for advice and consent. While all of these agreements are viewed by other states as "treaties" within the meaning of international law, as a matter of U.S. law these other agreements are called "executive agreements" and are based on one of three other forms of legal authority.

First, if there exists a prior treaty that contemplates explicitly or implicitly follow-on international agreements, the president may conclude those agreements without obtaining further Senate approval (sometimes referred to as a "treaty-based executive agreement"). For instance, after the Senate provided advice and consent

---

49. Curtis A. Bradley, *Unratified Treaties, Domestic Politics, and the U.S.* *Constitution,* 48 Harv. Int'l L.J. 307 (2007).

to the NATO Status of Forces Agreement,[50] the president concluded, without further congressional approval, a series of bilateral
agreements with individual states in order to implement the treaty.[51]

Second, the president may conclude an executive agreement
when it is based on one of his constitutional powers (sometimes
referred to as a "sole-executive agreement"). Thus, relying solely
on his constitutional power to receive ambassadors, the president
might conclude an executive agreement with another state to
establish diplomatic relations; that agreement might even involve
the settlement of outstanding claims between the two nations. For
example, when President Roosevelt recognized the Soviet government in 1933, he also concluded an agreement by which there was
an assignment (the "Litvinov Assignment") from the Soviet government of all its rights in properties located in the United States,
rights which the Soviets had previously claimed pursuant to expropriation decrees issued after the Russian Revolution. The Assignment was part of a larger process for settling claims between the
two governments. When the U.S. Government appeared in state
courts to exercise its newly acquired rights in the properties, some
courts refused to accept that the Soviets had ever acquired rights in
the properties (and thus could not assign rights in them) because
state law denied extraterritorial effect to the Soviet expropriation
decrees. The U.S. Supreme Court, however, held that accepting the
Assignment was an essential component of the normalization of
relations between the United States and the Soviet Union, and that
the agreement was properly concluded based solely on the president's constitutional powers. Therefore, U.S. government property
rights under the Assignment could not be questioned under state
law.[52]

Third, the president may conclude an executive agreement if
he has obtained *majority* approval (not two-thirds approval) from
both houses of Congress. This third form of executive agreement
(sometimes referred to as a "congressional-executive agreement")
may be based on prior congressional approval as embodied in an
existing statute. Thus, by statute Congress has authorized the
president to conclude stratospheric ozone protection agreements
with other states,[53] project agreements with NATO states,[54] and

---

50. June 19, 1951, 4 U.S.T. 1792,
199 U.N.T.S. 67. The NATO SOFA addresses the rights and duties of U.S.
troops in NATO states, and NATO
forces in the United States.

51. *See, e.g.*, Agreement Relative to
Implementation of the Agreement be-
tween the Parties to the North Atlantic
Treaty Regarding the Status of their

Forces, U.S.-Turkey, June 23, 1954, 5
U.S.T. 1465, 233 U.N.T.S. 189.

52. *See* United States v. Belmont,
301 U.S. 324, 330 (1937); United States
v. Pink, 315 U.S. 203, 230 (1942).

53. *See* 42 U.S.C. § 7671p (2006).

54. *See* 22 U.S.C. § 2767 (2006).

numerous other kinds of agreements, typically subject to certain conditions. Whenever the president wishes to conclude such an agreement, he may do so without further legislative approval. A congressional-executive agreement may also be based on approval of the agreement by both houses of Congress *after* its negotiation. For instance, after the president completed negotiations on the North American Free Trade Agreement,[55] he submitted the agreement to both houses of Congress. After majority approval in both houses (the vote in the Senate was less than a two-thirds majority), the president proceeded to ratify the NAFTA.

It may seem startling that U.S. practice in concluding international agreements deviates so starkly from the means contemplated in Article II of the U.S. Constitution for the making of treaties. However, there is an indirect recognition in the Constitution of types of international agreements other than treaties, such as agreements by "alliance," "confederation," and "compact."[56] Further, this U.S. practice is long-standing and reflects a practical accommodation of the president's need to conclude numerous agreements, many of marginal significance, without adhering to the formal treaty process. Nevertheless, as discussed below, on occasion this practice has been challenged in U.S. courts.

Congressional concern over the extensive use of executive agreements led to the 1972 enactment of the Case Act,[57] which requires the secretary of state to transmit to Congress the text of any international agreement, other than a treaty, concluded by the president. Further, an amendment enacted in 2004 requires the secretary of state to submit annually to Congress a report that contains an index of all international agreements that the United States has signed or otherwise executed in the prior year and that are not being published in the Department's annual compilation of *United States Treaties and International Agreements*.[58] In this manner, Congress can monitor the president's practice of concluding executive agreements.

Further, so as to regularize its own practice in pursuing international agreements, the Department of State has adopted "Circular 175," an administrative instruction laying out the procedures to be followed (including consultative procedures with Congress) when considering whether an intended agreement should be concluded as a treaty or an executive agreement. In making that decision, Circular 175 calls upon the Department of State to consider the extent to which the agreement involves commitments affect-

---

55. Dec. 12, 1992, U.S.-Can.-Mex., 32 I.L.M. 289 (1993).

56. U.S. CONST. art. I, § 10; *see* LAURENCE TRIBE, AMERICAN CONSTITUTIONAL LAW § 4–5 (3d ed. 2000).

57. 1 U.S.C. § 112b (2006).

58. *Id.*, § 112b(d)(1).

ing the nation as a whole, whether the agreement will affect state laws, whether the agreement will be "self-executing" (discussed below), relevant past practice concerning similar agreements, preferences of Congress, the agreement's degree of formality, the agreement's expected duration, and general international practice in connection with the type of agreement in question.

Scope of the Treaty Power. The authority of the United States to enter into international agreements is coextensive with the foreign affairs interests of the United States.

> The treaty power, as expressed in the Constitution, is in terms unlimited except by those restraints which are found in that instrument against the action of the government or of its departments, and those arising from the nature of the government itself and of that of the States. It would not be contended that it extends so far as to authorize what the Constitution forbids, or a change in the character of the government or in that of one of the States, or a cession of any portion of the territory of the latter without its consent.... But with these exceptions, it is not perceived that there is any limit to the questions which can be adjusted touching any matter which is properly the subject of negotiation with a foreign country.[59]

Indeed, there is support for the proposition that the federal government may do by treaty what it cannot do by statute. In *Missouri v. Holland*,[60] the Supreme Court found that the federal government could regulate migratory birds pursuant to a treaty, even though a similar statute had been struck down previously by lower courts as unconstitutional. The state of Missouri asserted that, since Article I, Section 8, did not allocate to Congress power over the matter, the regulation of birds was a matter "reserved" to the states under the Tenth Amendment of the U.S. Constitution. Justice Oliver Wendell Holmes, in upholding the treaty, found that the scope of legislative powers granted to Congress did not govern the scope of the treaty power.[61]

At the same time, treaties are subject to constitutional limitations on governmental power and may not contravene specific constitutional prohibitions. In *Reid v. Covert*,[62] the defendants were civilian dependents of armed servicemen posted in the United Kingdom and Japan, and had murdered their husbands. Interna-

---

59. De Geofroy v. Riggs, 133 U.S. 258, 267 (1890); *see* Santovincenzo v. Egan, 284 U.S. 30, 40 (1931).

60. 252 U.S. 416, 433–35 (1920).

61. *See* Michael D. Ramsey, *Missouri v. Holland and Historical Textualism*, 73 Mo. L. Rev. 969 (2008); David Golove, *Treaty-Making and the Nation: The His-*

torical Foundations of the Nationalist Conception of the Treaty Power, 98 Mich. L. Rev. 1075 (2000); *but see* Nicholas Quinn Rosenkranz, *Executing the Treaty Power*, 118 Harv. L. Rev. 1867 (2005) (arguing that *Missouri* was decided incorrectly).

62. 354 U.S. 1 (1957).

tional agreements between the United States and those countries provided the United States with exclusive criminal jurisdiction over the crimes. Yet, there existed no federal or state statute in the United States granting jurisdiction to a regular court over murder committed abroad. The only recourse was to try the civilian dependents before a court-martial under the Uniform Code of Military Justice (UCMJ), a military system of justice that (at the time) provided no grand jury, no jury trial, and lacked certain other constitutional rights normally accorded civilians. After being convicted and sentenced to death, the defendants appealed to the U.S. Supreme Court. The U.S. government argued that conclusion of the U.S.-U.K. and U.S.-Japan agreements was within the power of the federal government and that the UCMJ constituted legislation necessary and proper to fulfill those international agreements. The Supreme Court noted that Article VI of the Constitution made treaties part of the supreme law of the land. Yet the Court stated:

> It would be manifestly contrary to the objectives of those who created the Constitution, as well as those who were responsible for the Bill of Rights—let alone alien to our entire constitutional history and tradition—to construe Article VI as permitting the United States to exercise power under an international agreement without observing constitutional prohibitions. In effect, such construction would permit amendment of that document in a manner not sanctioned by Article V.[63]

Although *Reid* was a plurality decision, a majority of justices in that case appeared to accept the proposition that treaties may not contravene the Constitution, a proposition that has been confirmed in later decisions.[64]

Termination of Treaties. The process for U.S. adherence to an international agreement clearly contemplates a role for both the president and Congress. The Constitution is silent, however, on the process for withdrawal from or termination of U.S. adherence to a treaty. In *Goldwater v. Carter*,[65] the D.C. Circuit Court of Appeals held that the president had the power to terminate a treaty with Taiwan without first obtaining the consent of the Senate. The court noted that "the constitutional commitment of powers to the President is notably comprehensive" and "bespeaks no limitation" in the area of foreign relations.[66] Further, the court stated that the "constitutional institution of advice and consent of the Senate ... is a special and extraordinary condition of the exercise by the President of certain specified powers under Article II [and] is not lightly to be extended," and that it "would take an unprecedented

---

63. *Id.* at 17.

64. *See, e.g.,* Breard v. Greene, 523 U.S. 371, 373 (1998).

65. 617 F.2d 697 (D.C. Cir. 1979), *vacated*, 444 U.S. 996 (1979).

66. *Id.* at 703–04.

feat of judicial construction to read into the Constitution an absolute condition precedent of congressional or Senate approval for termination of all treaties ... [that] would unalterably affect the balance of power between the two Branches.... "[67]

The Supreme Court vacated the decision in *Goldwater* without addressing the question (four justices viewed the matter as a political question, while a fifth justice saw the case as not ripe for decision). Yet in a different context, the Supreme Court has recognized that the grant to the Senate of an "advice and consent" role with regard to *approval* of a course of action does not entail the same grant with regard to *terminating* the course of action. Specifically, the Supreme Court has held that the Senate does not retain any authority to terminate "Officers of the United States" even though such officers are appointed with the "Advice and Consent of the Senate," pursuant to Article II, Section 2, of the Constitution.[68]

An example of this issue is President Bush's December 2001 announcement[69] that the United States would withdraw from the 1972 Anti–Ballistic Missile Treaty (ABM Treaty).[70] Pursuant to the terms of the treaty, the U.S. withdrawal became effective six months later, on June 13, 2002. On June 12, thirty-two members of the House of Representatives filed a lawsuit in U.S. district court against President Bush asserting that any U.S. withdrawal constitutionally required the consent of Congress. The district court held in *Kucinich v. Bush*[71] that the plaintiffs lacked standing to bring the action without Congress' approval and that the action raised a nonjusticiable political question.

War Power. As noted above, Congress has the power to declare war, raise and support an army and navy, and control the federal "purse," while the president serves as commander-in-chief of the armed forces and chief executive. These concurrent war powers sometimes are in great tension, such as when the president continued to prosecute the Vietnam War despite significant congressional opposition (Congress was unable to muster a majority to cut off funds for the war).

Concerned that the president might commit troops without congressional approval in situations short of war (which could then evolve into full-scale armed conflicts), Congress passed the 1973

---

67. *Id.* at 704–05.

68. *See* Morrison v. Olson, 487 U.S. 654, 686–90 (1988).

69. *See* Remarks Announcing the United States Withdrawal from the Anti–Ballistic Missile Treaty, 37 WEEKLY COMP. PRES. DOC. 1783 (Dec. 13, 2001).

70. Treaty on the Limitation of Anti–Ballistic Missile Systems, U.S.-U.S.S.R., May 26, 1972, 23 U.S.T. 3435; *see* Protocol to the Treaty on the Limitation of Anti–Ballistic Missile Systems, U.S.-U.S.S.R., July 3, 1974, 27 U.S.T. 1645.

71. 236 F. Supp. 2d 1 (D.D.C. 2002).

War Powers Resolution.[72] The Resolution requires consultation between the president and Congress "in every possible instance" before introducing U.S. forces into hostilities or imminent danger of hostilities. After troops are introduced into such hostilities or into a foreign territory "equipped for combat," the president is required to report the circumstances to Congress. If the president reports that troops have been introduced into hostilities or imminent danger of hostilities, the troops must be withdrawn within sixty days (extendable to ninety days), unless Congress authorizes a continuation of the action.

The War Powers Resolution represented the first overt recognition by Congress of the president's inherent power to send troops abroad for a period of time without prior Congressional approval. The Resolution, however, has not proven particularly effective. Politically, it is difficult for Congress not to support the president once U.S. troops are placed in harm's way. Further, the sixty-day withdrawal provision is not triggered when the president simply reports that he has introduced troops into a foreign state "equipped for combat"; by not mentioning "hostilities," the president avoids the withdrawal provision while maintaining an appearance of cooperation with Congress. Finally, the executive branch has consistently maintained that the withdrawal provision of the War Powers Resolution represents an unconstitutional attempt to interfere with the powers of the president as chief executive and commander-in-chief. The courts are likely to treat such disputes as a political question unless a majority of both houses of Congress forbids executive action (discussed below). Lacking judicial intervention, the effect of the Resolution on executive power is determined principally by whether U.S. public opinion supports or opposes the use of U.S. troops abroad in specific circumstances.

For the most recent large-scale deployments of U.S. military troops, Congress has passed joint resolutions authorizing the president to act. For example, Congress expressly authorized the use of military force in response to the terrorist attacks of September 2001 on the World Trade Center and the Pentagon,[73] which led to the U.S. intervention in Afghanistan in October 2001. In October 2002, Congress authorized the president to use the armed forces "as he determines to be necessary and appropriate" to "defend the national security of the United States against the continuing threat posed by Iraq" and "enforce all relevant United Nations Security Council resolutions regarding Iraq,"[74] which led to the U.S. intervention in Iraq in March 2003.

---

72. *See* 50 U.S.C. §§ 1541–48 (2006).

73. *See* Pub. L. No. 107–40, 115 Stat. 224 (2001) [hereinafter 2001 Authorization for Use of Military Force].

74. Pub. L. No. 107–243, 116 Stat. 1498 (2002).

Not all U.S. deployments, however, are on a large scale. In reaction to the outbreak of civil war in Libya in early 2011, the U.N. Security Council passed a resolution imposing an arms embargo on Libya, freezing the assets of Gaddafi and ten members of his inner circle, and restricting their travel.[75] When the violence continued, the Council adopted a second resolution demanding an immediate ceasefire and characterizing the violence as possibly "crimes against humanity." Further, the resolution established a ban on all flights within Libya (a "no-fly zone"), other than flights transporting humanitarian aid, evacuating foreign nationals, enforcing the no-fly zone, or those "deemed necessary for the benefit of the Libyan people." Importantly, the resolution authorized member states "acting nationally or through regional organizations or arrangements, and acting in cooperation with the Secretary–General, to take all necessary measures . . . to protect civilians and civilian populated areas under threat of attack in [Libya], while excluding a foreign occupation force of any form on any part of Libyan territory. . . ."[76] Consequently, a multi-state coalition commenced military operations against Libya to implement the resolution, with the North Atlantic Treaty Organization (NATO) assuming control of some aspects.

While other NATO member states conducted most of the airstrikes in Libya against Gaddafi's forces, U.S. forces flew most of the missions related to reconnaissance, surveillance, and refueling (comprising approximately one-fourth of the missions flown each day by NATO), as well as occasional airstrikes using drone (unmanned) aircraft. No U.S. ground troops or trainers were deployed into Libya. In March 2011, President Barack Obama transmitted to Congress a report "as part of my efforts to keep Congress fully informed, consistent with the War Powers Resolution." In it, he stressed that the "United States has not deployed ground forces into Libya. United States forces are conducting a limited and well-defined mission in support of international efforts to protect civilians and prevent a humanitarian disaster."[77] Thereafter, the Justice Department's Office of Legal Counsel issued an opinion defending the lawfulness of the action, stating that prior congressional approval was not required given that the limited military operations contemplated did not constitute "war" in the constitutional sense.[78]

75. *See* S.C. Res. 1970 (Feb. 26, 2011).

76. *See* S.C. Res. 1973, U.N. Doc. S/Res/1973 (Mar. 17, 2011).

77. *See* Letter from the President Regarding the Commencement of Opera-

tions in Libya, Daily Comp. Pres. Docs., 2011 DCPD No. 00193 (Mar. 21, 2011).

78. Authority to Use Military Force in Libya, 2011 WL 1459998 (O.L.C.) (Apr. 1, 2011).

Detention of Unlawful Combatants. The scope of the president's war power has been especially controversial since 2001, when the United States began pursuing extensive measures in the "war on terrorism," including the indefinite detention of persons captured on the battlefield in Afghanistan or elsewhere who were classified as "unlawful combatants." About 780 non-U.S. nationals were detained outside the United States at the Guantánamo Bay Naval Base in Cuba, while a few U.S. nationals were detained in the United States. The president initially detained these individuals without charge or trial, without access to counsel, and without any judicial review of their classification as unlawful combatants, based on various grounds, including the president's role as commander-in-chief in a time of war.

With respect to U.S. detainees, the Supreme Court found in 2004 in *Hamdi v. Rumsfeld* that U.S. nationals captured in zones of combat can be classified and detained as enemy combatants without criminal trial.[79] To the extent that explicit congressional authorization is required for their detention, it existed in the 2001 statute empowering the president to use military force against those responsible for the terrorist attacks of September 11.[80] The Court, however, concluded that "a citizen-detainee seeking to challenge his classification as an enemy combatant must receive notice of the factual basis for his classification, and a fair opportunity to rebut the Government's factual assertions before a neutral decisionmaker."[81]

With respect to non-U.S. nationals detained at Guantánamo, President George W. Bush issued a "military order" providing for prosecution for war crimes of some of the detainees before newly established military commissions, rather than in U.S. civilian courts or regular U.S. military courts.[82] The military order and its implementing regulations called for a military judge to preside over a trial of the detainee on charges of war crimes, with special rules on evidence and hearsay, before a panel of U.S. service members who would decide whether to convict and, if so, the appropriate sentence, including the death penalty. Because the detainees were held outside the territory of the United States, the executive branch argued that they were not entitled to the right of habeas corpus. Nevertheless, several detainees sought judicial review by U.S. courts of their detention. In *Rasul v. Bush*,[83] the Supreme Court held that U.S. district courts had jurisdiction under the federal

---

79. Hamdi v. Rumsfeld, 542 U.S. 507 (2004).

80. *See* 2001 Authorization for Use of Military Force, *supra* note 73.

81. Hamdi v. Rumsfeld, 542 U.S. at 532.

82. Military Order of November 13, 2001, 66 Fed. Reg. 57,833 (Nov. 16, 2001).

83. 542 U.S. 466 (2004).

habeas statute to hear the claims of detainees. Statutory habeas rights, the Court held, applied in any territory over which the United States had "exclusive jurisdiction and control" as was the case in Guantánamo Bay.

In the wake of the decision in *Rasul*, the executive branch instituted a process for reviewing whether each detainee was properly regarded as a "combatant" against the United States. These Combatant Status Review Tribunals (CSRTs) provided for an individualized assessment of each detainee, but were criticized for lax evidentiary standards, the inability of detainees to retain their own counsel, and their inability to call as witnesses persons who could testify as to their innocence. Separately, the executive branch also commenced an administrative process for "continuing threat" assessments, in which the government would determine whether a combatant was no longer a threat to the United States, and thus could be released.[84]

At the same time, Congress enacted the Detainee Treatment Act of 2005,[85] which revoked federal court jurisdiction over habeas claims by the detainees (at least with respect to claims not already pending). Instead, the DTA created jurisdiction in the D.C. Circuit Court of Appeals only to hear appeals of final decisions of the military commissions. In *Hamdan v. Rumsfeld*,[86] the Supreme Court decided that the military commission convened to try Hamdan lacked the power to proceed because its structure and procedures violated an existing statute, the Uniform Code of Military Justice (UCMJ). According to the Court, the President had a constitutional power to convene military commissions, but that power is shared with Congress, and Congress may impose limitations on the exercise of the power. Although the UCMJ largely regulates the conduct of regular military courts (courts martial), it also imposes two important limitations on the President's power to convene military commissions. First, the military commissions should not deviate unnecessarily from the procedures by which courts martial operate; military commission procedures must be uniform with those of courts martial insofar as practical.[87] In this case, the Court found that the procedures governing Hamdan's military commission did deviate in significant ways without justification, such as by allowing the accused to be excluded from the proceedings even in the absence of any disruptive conduct. Second, the military commissions must operate in accordance with the "laws of war," including the 1949 Geneva Conventions and custom-

---

84. *See* Sean D. Murphy, *Evolving Geneva Convention Paradigms in the "War on Terrorism": Applying the Core Rules to the Release of Persons Deemed "Unprivileged Combatants,"* 75 Geo. Wash. L. Rev. 1105 (2007).

85. Pub. L. No. 109–148, § 1001, 119 Stat. 2680 (2005).

86. 548 U.S. 557 (2006).

87. 10 U.S.C. § 836 (2006).

ary international law.[88] The Court found that the conflict between the United States and Al Qaeda is an "armed conflict not of an international character" that falls within the scope of Common Article 3 to the 1949 Geneva Conventions, which prohibits "the passing of sentences and the carrying out of executions without previous judgment pronounced by a regularly constituted court affording all the judicial guarantees which are recognized as indispensable by civilized peoples."[89] According to the Court, the *Hamdan* military commission was not such a court since it had not been established by congressional statute.[90] Moreover, a plurality of the Court also based its decision on the trial guarantees contained in Article 75 of Protocol I of the Geneva Conventions, a treaty which the U.S. has *not* ratified, but whose provisions reflect customary international law.[91]

In response to the Court's decision in *Hamdan*, Congress and the President collaborated to ground the President's military commissions in a new statute, the Military Commissions Act of 2006 (MCA).[92] The MCA largely maintained the structure and process for the commissions that had been developed by the executive branch. While some modifications were made to the prior scheme, modeled after rules contained in the UCMJ, the MCA still exempted the military commissions from certain key UCMJ rules, including the defendant's right to a speedy trial and the right to be warned about the possibility of self-incrimination. Importantly, the MCA clarified that persons exposed to the jurisdiction of the commissions were not just those who engaged in hostilities against the United States or its allies, but also those who purposefully and materially supported such hostilities. Further, the MCA created an executive branch Court of Military Commission Review, to which a final decision of a military commission on an issue of law could be appealed. If that appeal failed, the accused could appeal the decision to the D.C. Circuit Court of Appeals, which in turn could be reviewed by the Supreme Court.

Guantánamo detainees then challenged the constitutionality of the DTA and MCA in revoking federal court jurisdiction over their habeas claims. In *Boumediene v. Bush*,[93] the Supreme Court agreed that the habeas clause of the U.S. Constitution applies to U.S. conduct in Guantánamo[94] and that the DTA/MCA unconstitutional-

---

88. 10 U.S.C. § 821 (2006).

89. *See* Geneva Convention (III) Relative to the Treatment of Prisoners of War, Aug. 12, 1949, art. 3(1)(d), 6 U.S.T. 3316, 75 U.N.T.S. 135.

90. 548 U.S. at 628, 631, 634–35.

91. *Id*. at 633.

92. Pub. L. No. 109–366, 120 Stat. 2600 (Oct. 17, 2006).

93. 553 U.S. 723 (2008).

94. U.S. Const. art. I, § 9, cl. 2. Whether constitutional habeas rights are available with respect to U.S. conduct abroad is decided contextually, based on various factors. *See* Al Maqaleh

ly suspended the writ; the statutes did not purport to formally suspend the writ as permitted under the Constitution "in cases of rebellion or invasion the public safety" nor did they provide procedures that adequately and effectively substitute for the writ. Arguably *Boumediene* is the first time that the Court, during a time of armed conflict, has invalidated a major national security policy backed by both Congress and the President. Thereafter, Boumediene and most of his co-plaintiffs convinced a U.S. federal court judge to order their release, due to a lack of evidence that they were in fact enemy combatants.

In January, 2009, President Obama issued an executive order suspending the military commission proceedings.[95] Later that year, he signed into law the Military Commissions Act of 2009,[96] which amended the Military Commissions Act of 2006 in various respects, but still retained the basic structure of the military commissions. After the adoption of new implementing rules and procedures, President Obama in March 2011 lifted his suspension of the military commission proceedings.[97] As of late 2011, some 600 detainees had been transferred to their home or third countries (mostly to Afghanistan, Pakistan, or Saudi Arabia), 8 detainees had died in custody, and some 170 detainees remained at Guantánamo. Of those remaining custody, about a dozen had been charged with crimes, but only a few were either convicted or pled guilty.

Judicial Power

The U.S. Constitution provides that the federal judicial power extends to all cases concerning treaties, ambassadors, and admiralty and maritime jurisdiction, and cases between a state (or its nationals) and foreign states (or their nationals).[98] Since federal courts are vested with jurisdiction over matters arising under federal law, disputes concerning the interpretation of constitutional provisions and statutes relating to foreign affairs are also within

v. Gates, 605 F.3d 84 (D.C. Cir. 2010) (constitutional habeas not available to persons held at Bagram air base in Afghanistan); Johnson v. Eisentrager, 339 U.S. 763 (1950) (constitutional habeas not available to German nationals detained by U.S. military commission in China).

95. Exec. Order No. 13492, 74 Fed. Reg. 4897 (Jan. 27, 2009).

96. Pub. L. 111–84, 123 Stat. 2190 (2009).

97. *See* White House Office of the Press Secretary, Fact Sheet: New Actions on Guantanamo and Detainee Policy, at 3 (Mar. 7, 2011); *see also* Periodic Review of Individuals Detained at Guantanamo Bay Naval Station Pursuant to the Authorization for Use of Military Force, Exec. Order No. 13567, 76 Fed. Reg. 13,277 (Mar. 7, 2011); *see generally* MICHAEL JOHN GARCIA, ET AL., CONG. RESEARCH SERV., R40139, CLOSING THE GUANTÁNAMO DETENTION CENTER: LEGAL ISSUES (2011); Dept. of Defense, Military Commissions (n.d.), *at* <http://www.mc.mil>.

98. *See* U.S. CONST., art. III, § 2, cl. 1.

the scope of the judicial power. In fact, U.S. courts regularly are called upon to decide matters touching on foreign affairs, as seen in the numerous U.S. cases cited throughout this volume. When construing an ambiguous treaty, courts will often defer to the view of the executive branch as to the meaning of the treaty, given that the executive branch negotiated the treaty and can provide information as to post-ratification practice under the treaty. Yet courts do not always defer to the view of the executive branch; indeed, on the very same day, the U.S. Supreme Court decided one case that was highly deferential to the executive[99] and a second case that was not.[100] At least one survey of U.S. cases from 1984 to 2005 confirms that the executive branch's views are not always dispositive.[101]

At the same time, U.S. courts often invoke doctrines of abstention to avoid cases relating to foreign affairs. Under the "act of state" doctrine, U.S. courts have declined to pass upon the acts of foreign governments taken within their territory.[102] Under the allied doctrine of "comity," U.S. courts will sometimes defer to the judgment of a foreign forum, just as foreign fora often defer to U.S. courts.[103] Under the doctrine of "foreign non conveniens," a federal court has discretion to dismiss a case when a foreign forum has jurisdiction to hear the case, and "trial in the chosen forum would establish . . . oppressiveness and vexation to a defendant . . . out of all proportion to plaintiff's convenience, or . . . the chosen forum [is] inappropriate because of considerations affecting the court's own administrative and legal problems."[104] U.S. courts invoke the "political question" doctrine to avoid second-guessing actions of Congress or the president in the field of foreign affairs, leaving resolution of disputes between those branches to the political process. Indeed, the Supreme Court has stated that "the conduct of foreign relations is committed by the Constitution to the political departments of the Federal Government; that the propriety of the exercise of that power is not open to judicial inquiry. . . . "[105]

The modern statement of the political question doctrine is found in *Baker v. Carr*.[106] In that case (which involved the apportionment of state legislative districts), the Supreme Court identified

---

99. Sanchez-Llamas v. Oregon, 548 U.S. 331 (2006).

100. Hamdan v. Rumsfeld, 548 U.S. 557 (2006).

101. Robert M. Chesney, *Disaggregating Deference: The Judicial Power and Executive Treaty Interpretations*, 92 Iowa L. Rev. 1723 (2007).

102. *See* Chapter 9(D).

103. *See* Hilton v. Guyot, 159 U.S. 113 (1895).

104. Sinochem Int'l Co. v. Malaysia Int'l Shipping Corp., 549 U.S. 422, 429 (2007) (citing American Dredging Co. v. Miller, 510 U.S. 443, 447–448 (1993)).

105. United States v. Pink, 315 U.S. 203, 222–23 (1942); *see* Haig v. Agee, 453 U.S. 280, 292 (1981).

106. 369 U.S. 186 (1962).

six factors that weigh against judicial review, including in cases touching on foreign relations. Those factors were:

> a textually demonstrable constitutional commitment of the issue to a coordinate political department; or a lack of judicially discoverable and manageable standards for resolving it; or the impossibility of deciding without an initial policy determination of a kind clearly for nonjudicial discretion; or the impossibility of a court's undertaking independent resolution without expressing lack of the respect due coordinate branches of the government; or an unusual need for unquestioning adherence to a political decision already made; or the potentiality of embarrassment from multifarious pronouncements by various departments on one question.[107]

Courts regularly consider these principles when passing upon cases in the field of foreign affairs. For example, in *Ramirez de Arellano v. Weinberger*,[108] a U.S. national challenged the authority of the executive branch to confiscate his plantation in Honduras for military training exercises. The court concluded that the claims were not "exclusively committed for resolution to the political branches" for three reasons: federal courts historically have resolved disputes over land; adjudication of this claim was not beyond judicial expertise; and none of the circumstances of the case gave rise to prudential concerns.[109]

By contrast, in *Made in the USA Foundation v. United States*,[110] the plaintiffs were not successful in obtaining judicial review. In that case, the plaintiffs sought a judicial declaration that NAFTA was unconstitutional, because it did not receive a two-thirds majority approval in the Senate (instead, as discussed above, it was treated as a congressional-executive agreement, receiving a simple majority approval in both houses of Congress). According to the plaintiffs, NAFTA was so intrusive into matters of concern to the several states that it had to be concluded as a treaty with the consent of the Senate, the institution where the rights of the several states were uniquely protected. The Eleventh Circuit found that with respect to international commercial agreements such as NAFTA, the question of what constitutes a "treaty" requiring Senate ratification presents a nonjusticiable political question. Relying on *Goldwater v. Carter*,[111] the court in *Made in the USA*

107. *Id.* at 217.

108. 745 F.2d 1500 (D.C. Cir. 1984), *remanded for reconsideration on other grounds*, 471 U.S. 1113 (1985).

109. 745 F.2d at 1512–13; *see Lamont v. Woods*, 948 F.2d 825 (2d Cir. 1991) (declining to invoke the political question doctrine in a case challenging U.S. foreign aid to religious institutions).

110. 242 F.3d 1300 (11th Cir. 2001).

111. *Supra* note 65.

Foundation stated that "just as the Treaty Clause fails to outline the Senate's role in the abrogation of treaties, we find that the Treaty Clause also fails to outline the circumstances, if any, under which its procedures must be adhered to when approving international commercial agreements."[112]

Likewise, when a pharmaceutical company in Sudan filed a defamation suit against the United States challenging President Clinton's statement upon launching a 1998 missile strike against the company's plant (linking the company to Al Qaeda), the circuit court affirmed dismissal of the case as presenting a political question. Among other things, the court noted that the president's public justifications for "discrete military action are always offered, in part at least, with strategic military, national security, or foreign policy objectives in mind."[113]

Resort to the courts to challenge the president's power to deploy armed forces in the absence of a congressional declaration of war has also fallen victim to abstention doctrines. For example, in April 1999, seventeen members of the House of Representatives filed a lawsuit in federal court challenging President Clinton's ability to maintain a bombing campaign against the Federal Republic of Yugoslavia (in response to its treatment of Kosovar Albanians) without authorization from Congress. The complaint requested the court to issue declaratory relief that the president "is unconstitutionally conducting an offensive military attack," and that "no later than May 25, 1999, the president must terminate" such action. The court, however, dismissed the case on standing and political question grounds, noting that Congress had not expressly opposed the president's actions and that courts traditionally have been reluctant to intervene in political disputes concerning matters of war.[114] A similar outcome occurs when a Congressional authorization to the president to use force is challenged as too broad or premature. Thus, when a dozen House Democrats, three anonymous U.S. soldiers, and fifteen parents of U.S. soldiers filed suit challenging Congress' 2002 authorization allowing the president to use military force against Iraq, the district court dismissed the action on ripeness grounds saying relevant events had not yet unfolded.[115]

---

112. 242 F.3d at 1315; *see* Weinberger v. Rossi, 456 U.S. 25 (1982).

113. El-Shifa Pharm. Indus. Co. v. United States, 559 F.3d 578, 585 (D.C. Cir. 2009).

114. *See* Campbell v. Clinton, 52 F. Supp. 2d 34 (D.D.C. 1999), *aff'd*, 203 F.3d 19 (D.C. Cir. 2000); *see also* Dellums v. Bush, 752 F. Supp. 1141 (D.D.C.

1990) (dismissing a challenge by members of Congress to President George Bush's deployment of forces to assist Kuwait against Iraq's invasion).

115. Doe v. Bush, 240 F. Supp. 2d 95, 96 (D. Mass. 2003), *aff'd*, 322 F.3d 109 (1st Cir. 2003).

B. Federal–State Relations

Reasons for Federal Dominance

There are several reasons why the foreign affairs power resides in the federal government, rather than in the governments of the several states or with sub-state entities. First, there is some authority for the proposition that the foreign affairs power is a necessary attribute of sovereignty itself and therefore is inescapably embedded in the national government.[116]

Second, U.S. constitutional history makes clear that matters touching upon foreign affairs were intended to be dealt with under federal law. The men who met in Philadelphia in 1787 were dissatisfied with the lack of centralized control over foreign affairs under the Articles of Confederation, such as the inability of the central government to regulate foreign commerce. Further, the founders were concerned with the resistance of state courts to the enforcement of the 1783 treaty of peace with Great Britain, which protected persons who had remained loyal to Britain and called for repayment of U.S. debts to them. Ultimately, the Philadelphia convention sought to design a new federal government as a means of correcting these and other deficiencies.[117]

Third, all the important foreign affairs powers are explicitly denied to the states by the U.S. Constitution. The states are absolutely prohibited from entering into treaties or alliances with other nations,[118] and may not, without the consent of Congress, enter into "compacts" with foreign nations, impose duties on imports or exports, or keep military forces in times of peace.[119] Concomitantly, the Constitution explicitly assigns considerable lawmaking power to the national government in the field of foreign affairs, such as the power to regulate foreign commerce. Moreover, the Constitution's Supremacy Clause[120] expressly makes federal legislation passed pursuant to these federal constitutional powers (as well as all treaties) binding upon the several states as "the supreme Law of the Land."

Nevertheless, states and sub-state entities regularly pursue initiatives that relate to foreign affairs. Sometimes those initiatives are simply criticism or condemnation of a federal foreign affairs policy, such as the numerous resolutions adopted by cities (*e.g.,* Berkeley, California; Madison, Wisconsin; Seattle, Washington) crit-

---

116. *See Curtiss–Wright Export Corp., supra* note 40, at 318; Chinese Exclusion Case, 130 U.S. 581 (1889).

117. *See, e.g.,* THE FEDERALIST, Nos. 1, 6, 8–9, 11, 21 (Alexander Hamilton), Nos. 2–5 (John Jay), No. 49 (James Madison).

118. *See* U.S. CONST. art. I, § 10, cl. 1.

119. *Id.,* § 10, cl. 2 & 3.

120. *Id.,* art. VI, cl. 2.

icizing the U.S. intervention in Iraq in 2003. Other initiatives attempt to adopt legislation that implements an international norm, such as regional, state, and municipal controls on carbon-based emissions as required under the Kyoto Protocol (to which the United States is not a party).[121]

For example, in 1998 San Francisco adopted an ordinance requiring a review of all city policies to ensure conformance with the Convention on the Elimination of All Forms of Discrimination Against Women (CEDAW).[122] Although the United States is not a party to CEDAW, San Francisco decided that applying CEDAW would help ensure that women were receiving adequate social services and job-training, as well as promotions within city government.[123] Such initiatives may not conflict with the federal foreign affairs power, but courts are sometimes confronted with determining whether a conflict exists and, if so, whether the local law should be struck down.

States also regularly enter into "compacts" with foreign states and sub-state entities, such as for the construction or maintenance of a bridge across a boundary. What distinguishes a "compact" from a "treaty" is not clear from Constitution, but "compact" appears to be a term denoting an agreement of lesser and more local interest. While the Constitution calls for all compacts "with a foreign power" to be approved by Congress, and while there is some judicial precedent that they must be,[124] foreign compacts often are not approved by Congress and are not challenged by the federal government. Since the Supreme Court has stated that certain compacts may be concluded *among* the several states ("inter-state compacts") without the approval of Congress so long as they do not encroach upon the political power of the federal government,[125] the same approach appears to apply to foreign compacts.[126]

Bases for Striking Down State Laws

U.S. courts have readily recognized federal authority over the several states on matters concerning foreign affairs. In doing so, different bases have emerged for striking down state laws. If the federal government has enacted a treaty or statute that directly conflicts with a state law or policy, then—under the Supremacy Clause—the state law or policy will be struck down because it has

---

121. *See* Kyoto Protocol to the U.N. Framework Convention on Climate Change, Dec. 10, 1997, 37 I.L.M. 22.

122. Dec. 18, 1979, 1249 U.N.T.S. 13; *see* Chapter 10(C).

123. *See* Shanna Singh, *Brandeis's Happy Incident Revisited: U.S. Cities as the New Laboratories of International Law*, 37 G.W. Int'l L. Rev. 537 (2005).

124. Holmes v. Jennison, 39 U.S. (Pet.) 649 (1840).

125. Virginia v. Tennessee, 148 U.S. 503 (1893).

126. *See* Duncan B. Hollis, *Unpacking the Commerce Clause*, 88 Tex. L. Rev. 741 (2010).

been preempted by federal law. For example, to protest human rights violations, Massachusetts enacted in 1996 a law prohibiting its government from purchasing goods or services from individuals or companies that engaged in business with or in Myanmar (Burma), except in certain situations. In *Crosby v. National Foreign Trade Council*,[127] the Supreme Court found the law unconstitutional under the Supremacy Clause because there already existed a federal sanctions program against Myanmar.

Even if Congress has not acted, a state law may be struck down as contrary to the "foreign commerce" power reserved to Congress if the law facially discriminates against foreign commerce without a legitimate local justification and attempts to regulate conduct beyond the state's borders. The First Circuit Court of Appeals in the *Crosby* case found the Massachusetts statute unconstitutional, in part, based on this ground.[128]

Further, a state law may be struck down if it infringes on the *general* foreign affairs power of the federal government, and has more than an incidental or indirect effect on U.S. foreign policy. For example, in *Zschernig v. Miller*,[129] an Oregon resident died without a will. Heirs residing in communist East Germany sought to claim their inheritance, but encountered difficulties under Oregon's inheritance statute. That statute required proof that foreign heirs would receive their property without confiscation, in whole or in part, by their government. In striking down this requirement, the Supreme Court found that similar statutes in probate courts of various states had led to numerous inquiries into the quality and nature of foreign governments.

> It seems inescapable that the type of probate law that Oregon enforces affects international relations in a persistent and subtle way. The practice of state courts in withholding remittances to legatees residing in Communist countries or in preventing them from assigning them is notorious.... As we stated in *Hines v. Davidowitz*, [312 U.S. 52, 64 (1941)]: "Experience has shown that international controversies of the gravest moment, sometimes even leading to war, may arise from real or imagined wrongs to another's subjects inflicted, or permitted, by a government." [130]

Similar reasoning was used by the Supreme Court in the *Garamendi* case, which concerned the California Holocaust Victim Insurance Relief Act (HVIRA). HVIRA mandated broad disclosure of information by insurance companies doing business in California

---

127. 530 U.S. 363 (2000).

128. *See* National Foreign Trade Council v. Natsios, 181 F.3d 38, 66–71 (1st Cir. 1999).

129. 389 U.S. 429 (1968).

130. *Id.* at 440–41.

regarding all policies issued in Europe between 1920 and 1945, including the names of policyholders and beneficiaries, as well as a certification as to whether and how policy proceeds had been paid. When suit was brought by insurance companies for injunctive relief, the Supreme Court struck down the statute.[131] The Court affirmed the long-standing premise that "at some point an exercise of state power that touches on foreign relations must yield to the National Government's policy" so as to maintain uniformity in U.S. dealings with other nations.[132] In this instance, the executive branch had embarked on various executive agreements designed to resolve holocaust-era claims and, while those agreements did not directly preempt HVIRA, "[v]indicating victims injured by acts and omissions of enemy corporations in wartime is ... within the traditional subject matter of foreign policy in which national, not state, interests are overriding, and which the National Government has addressed."[133] By contrast, in *Medellin v. Texas*, the Supreme Court found that *Garamendi* did not support the constitutionality of a presidential directive that state courts must reopen final criminal judgments in death penalty cases involving aliens, even if doing so would help implement an obligation of the United States arising from a judgment rendered by the International Court of Justice. According to the Court, the president's limited authority to settle international claims disputes pursuant to an executive agreement could not be stretched to cover such unilateral action by the president.[134]

In the aftermath of *Garamendi*, circuit courts have grappled with whether to strike down state law provisions for reasons of interference with the federal government's general foreign affairs power, and have not always reached consistent results. Thus, in *Von Saher v. Norton Simon Museum of Art at Pasadena*, the Ninth Circuit found that, although a California statute on recovery of Nazi-looted art did not conflict with any current federal law or specific foreign policy espoused by the Executive Branch, nevertheless it was preempted because it infringed on a general foreign affairs power reserved by the Constitution exclusively to the national government. According to the court, the California statute "intrudes on the power to make and resolve war," a conclusion "buttressed by the documented history of federal action addressing the subject of Nazi-looted art" which was "so comprehensive and pervasive as to leave no room for state legislation."[135] Yet in

---

131. *See* American Ins. Ass'n v. Garamendi, 539 U.S. 396 (2003).

132. *Id.* at 413.

133. *Id.* at 420–21.

134. 128 S. Ct. 1346, 1371–72 (2008).

135. Von Saher v. Norton Simon Museum of Art at Pasadena, 592 F.3d 954, 965–66 (9th Cir. 2010); *but see* Movsesian v. Victoria Versicherung AG, 629 F.3d 901 (9th Cir. 2010) (finding that a California statute allowing claims

Museum of Fine Arts Boston v. Seger–Thomschitz, the First Circuit declined to strike down a Massachusetts statute relating to a claim for Nazi-era art, stating that (unlike in *Garamendi*) there was "no comparably express federal policy bearing on the issues."[136]

Thus, state interference with federal policies may be prohibited even when those policies are not reduced to treaty or legislation.[137] States may not act to exacerbate relations with foreign nations,[138] nor may they contravene policies advanced in a U.S. international agreement even if no direct conflict with the agreement exists.[139]

C. International Law as a Part of U.S. Law

International law has been a part of U.S. law since the founding of the nation.[140] Although there are important issues about how international law operates within the U.S. legal system—and the relative hierarchy between it and other sources of U.S. law—U.S. courts at both the state and federal level have drawn upon international law since 1776, just as the courts of England did prior to U.S. independence. In the first great treatise on U.S. law, Chancellor James Kent stated that the "faithful observance" of the law of nations "is essential to national character, and to the happiness of mankind."[141] This section considers the manner in which international law is regarded as a part of U.S. law.

Treaties in U.S. Law

The Supremacy Clause of the U.S. Constitution provides:

> This Constitution, and the Laws of the United States which shall be made in Pursuance thereof; *and all Treaties made*, or which shall be made under the Authority of the United States, *shall be the supreme Law of the Land*; and the Judges in every State shall be bound thereby, any Thing in the Constitution or Laws of any State to the Contrary notwithstanding.[142]

From the text, it appears that treaties should be regarded like statutes passed by Congress and signed by the president. Certainly, in terms of their supremacy over state law, treaties are like

arising out of life insurance policies issued to "Armenian Genocide victim[s]" does not conflict with a federal government policy forbidding the use of that term).

136. 623 F.3d 1, 12–13 (1st Cir. 2010).

137. *See* United States v. Belmont, 301 U.S. 324 (1937).

138. *See* Banco Nacional de Cuba v. Sabbatino, 376 U.S. 398 (1964).

139. *See* Kolovrat v. Oregon, 366 U.S. 187 (1961).

140. *See* Louis Henkin, *International Law as Law in the United States*, 82 MICH. L. REV. 1555 (1984).

141. JAMES KENT, COMMENTARIES ON AMERICAN LAW, pt. 1, lect. 1, at 1 (1826).

142. U.S. CONST., art. VI, cl. 2 (emphasis added).

statutes.[143] Moreover, to the extent there is a conflict between a treaty and a statute, the later-in-time rule prevails, just as it would between two statutes, unless Congress evinces a contrary intent.[144] Congress has evinced an intent in some situations that a later-in-time treaty not prevail.[145] Whenever possible, courts seek to interpret a later-in-time statute as consistent with an earlier treaty (unless Congress evinces a contrary intent) on an assumption that Congress normally does not seek to violate U.S. obligations under international law.[146]

However, there is an important way in which treaties are not like U.S. statutes. Beginning with Chief Justice Marshall's decision in *Foster v. Neilson*,[147] U.S. courts have developed a doctrine that treaties may be either "self-executing" or "non-self-executing."[148] A self-executing treaty is capable of being directly applied as part of the internal law in the United States immediately upon entry into force of the agreement; courts will look to it for the rule of decision in cases affected by its terms. Non-self-executing treaties, however, require legislation or some other source of U.S. law to implement them in the United States. For such agreements, it is the implementing legislation, not the agreement itself, that becomes the rule of decision in U.S. courts.

When will a court determine that a treaty is self-executing? Courts in the United States answer that question by focusing on different factors. Many courts determine whether an agreement is self-executing by examining the intent of the parties. For example, in *Cheung v. United States*,[149] the Second Circuit found an agreement between the United States and Hong Kong to be self-executing by reference to statements made by the executive when transmitting the agreement to Congress, to the effect that "this Agreement will not require implementing legislation." Conversely, the executive or Congress may assert at the time of its conclusion that an agreement is not a part of U.S. law in whole or in part. For example, when adhering to the Uruguay Round Agreements

---

143. *See, e.g.,* Asakura v. Seattle, 265 U.S. 332 (1924) (striking down a Seattle ordinance that discriminated against Japanese as inconsistent with a U.S.-Japan commercial treaty).

144. *See* Whitney v. Robertson, 124 U.S. 190 (1888); *see also* United States v. Palestine Liberation Org., 695 F. Supp. 1456 (S.D.N.Y. 1988) (considering the normative hierarchy between a U.S. treaty commitment to the United Nations as against a later-in-time statute affecting the PLO mission in New York).

145. *See, e.g.,* 19 U.S.C. § 3312(a)(1) (2006) (providing that U.S. statutes al-

ways prevail over the North American Free Trade Agreement).

146. *See* Murray v. Schooner Charming Betsy, 6 U.S. (2 Cranch) 64, 118 (1804); 1 RESTATEMENT (THIRD) OF THE FOREIGN RELATIONS LAW OF THE UNITED STATES §§ 114–15 (1987) [hereinafter RESTATEMENT (THIRD)].

147. 27 U.S. (2 Pet.) 253, 314 (1829).

148. *See* Thomas Buergenthal, *Self-Executing and Non Self–Executing Treaties in National and International Law,* 235 R.C.A.D.I. 303, 370 (1992).

149. 213 F.3d 82, 95 (2000).

of the World Trade Organization, Congress enacted a statute stating:

> No person other than the United States (A) shall have any cause of action or defense under any of the Uruguay Round Agreements or by virtue of congressional approval of such an agreement, or (B) may challenge ... any action or inaction by any department, agency, or any other instrumentality of the United States, any State, or any political subdivision of a State on the ground that such action or inaction is inconsistent with any such agreement.[150]

Where there is no express statement by the executive or congressional branches, some courts focus on whether the language of the treaty is susceptible to enforcement. Thus, a treaty containing hortatory or indeterminate language may be non-self-executing. Still other courts consider whether the treaty seeks to regulate a matter over which Congress as a whole has the sole competence to legislate (*e.g.*, the appropriation of funds). If so, it is not self-executing. Finally, some courts are interested in whether the treaty purports to create a private right of action; if not, the treaty might not be self-executing. Whether these are sensible distinctions to draw is subject to debate.[151]

In *Medellin v. Texas*,[152] the U.S. Supreme Court considered whether a judgment of the International Court of Justice (I.C.J.) against the United States in *Avena and Other Mexican Nationals*[153] —although admittedly creating an international law obligation binding upon the United States—could also be directly enforced by a Mexican national as domestic law in Texas state court. In deciding that the judgment was *not* directly enforceable, the Court parsed the language of three treaties. First, an optional protocol to the Vienna Convention on Consular Relations provided jurisdiction to the I.C.J. to decide cases arising under the Vienna Convention, but it did not address enforcement of the Court's decisions in national courts. Second, the United Nations Charter provided that

---

150. 19 U.S.C. § 3512(c)(1) (2006); see Bronco Wine Co. v. Bureau of Alcohol, Tobacco & Firearms, 168 F.3d 498 (9th Cir. 1999) (finding that section 3512(c) bars private actions relating to the implementation of the Uruguay Round Agreements on the theory that ensuring proper implementation of those agreements—because they are agreements between governments—should be the sole responsibility of the United States government and not of private persons through judicial processes); Corus Staal BV v. Dept. of Commerce, 395 F.3d 1343 (Fed. Cir. 2005) (finding that the Commerce Department is not obli-

gated to incorporate WTO procedures into its interpretation of U.S. law).

151. *See, e.g.,* Carlos Manuel Vázquez, *The Four Doctrines of Self–Executing Treaties*, 89 AM. J. INT'L L. 695 (1995); Jordan Paust, *Self-Executing Treaties*, 82 AM. J. INT'L L. 760 (1988). For a spirited discussion of whether *any* treaties should be self-executing, see 99 COLUM. L. REV. 1955–2258 (1999).

152. Medellin v. Texas, 128 S. Ct. 1346 (2008).

153. 2004 I.C.J. 12 (Mar. 31).

members would "undertake to comply" with I.C.J. judgments, but in Article 94 contemplated a process of enforcement through resort to the U.N. Security Council, not through national courts. Third, the Statute of the I.C.J. addressed the resolution of cases between states, but made no reference to private parties, and further provided that an I.C.J. judgment is binding only upon the states that appear before the Court in the case. As such, because "none of these treaty sources creates binding federal law in the absence of implementing legislation, and because it is uncontested that no such legislation exists, we conclude that the *Avena* judgment is not automatically binding domestic law."[154] Further, the Court stated that the responsibility for transforming an international obligation arising from a non-self-executing treaty into U.S. law falls to Congress; the president may not do so acting solely on his own authority.[155]

Since *Medellin* is the principal contemporary case in which the Supreme Court has considered the issue of self-executing treaties, considerable attention has been paid to its exact meaning. A joint task force of the ABA Section of International Law and the American Society of International Law posited three possible meanings of *Medellin*: (1) the case speaks only narrowly to the domestic enforceability of I.C.J. decisions and has no broader implications; (2) the case stands only for the proposition that treaty provisions that contemplate future action by states parties, and that are not specifically addressed to the judiciary, are not self-executing; or (3) the case broadly holds that all treaties that do not affirmatively and expressly provide for judicial enforceability are not self-executing.[156] For its part, the Senate Foreign Relations Committee in the aftermath of *Medellin* appears to have rejected the broad interpretation, asserting that "a strong presumption should exist against the conclusion in any particular case that the United States lacks the necessary authority in U.S. law to implement obligations it has assumed under treaties that have received the advice and consent of the Senate."[157] In any event, possibilities for clarifying whether treaties are judicially-enforceable in U.S. courts include (1) adoption of a broad federal statute indicating which treaties or types of treaties should be regarded as judicially-enforceable; and (2) for all new treaties, issuance of a clear statement by the executive branch

154. 128 S. Ct. at 1357.

155. *Id.* at 1368.

156. *See* ABA Section of International Law/American Society of International Law Joint Task Force on Treaties in U.S. Law, *Report* (Mar. 16, 2009), *available at* http://www.asil.org/files/Treaties TaskForceReport.pdf; *see also* David H. Moore, *Law (Makers) of the Land: The Doctrine of Treaty Non–Self–Execution,* 122 Harv. L. Rev. 32 (2009); Carlos Vázquez, *Treaties as the Law of the Land: The Supremacy Clause and the Judicial Enforcement of Treaties,* 122 Harv. L. Rev. 599 (2008).

157. Senate Foreign Relations Committee Report on Extradition Treaties with the European Union, S. Exec. Rep. No. 110–12, at 9–10 (2008).

as to whether the treaty is judicially-enforceable.[158] Further, to the extent that the problem is uncertainty as to whether the treaty supplies a private cause of action, perhaps greater reliance might be placed on existing statutes, such as 42 U.S.C. § 1983 (2006) or the federal habeas statute (29 U.S.C. § 2241(c)(3) (2006)), to supply a private cause of action to vindicate a treaty right, rather than rely on the treaty itself.[159]

Although it is clear today that both treaties and executive agreements are constitutionally acceptable instruments for conducting U.S. foreign policy, there are some differences between the two in terms of their internal legal effect. Executive agreements authorized by a federal statute or treaty have the same normative rank as the statute or treaty on which they are based, with the later-in-time having precedence. Sole-executive agreements (agreements made by the president based solely on his own constitutional power) supersede inconsistent state laws, but may not prevail against a conflicting prior federal statute.[160]

Statutes and Regulations Implementing Treaties

While considerable scholarly attention has been paid to whether treaties may be directly invoked as a part U.S. law, the influence of treaties is far more evident in the variety of U.S. statutes and regulations implementing U.S. treaty obligations. Such statutes and regulations exist in an array of fields, such as environment, human rights, aviation, health, maritime transport, and telecommunications. The treaty obligation is sometimes directly incorporated into the U.S. statute or regulation, while in other instances the international rule is repeated in near-verbatim language or is used as a key bench-mark in establishing the U.S. norm.

For example, Chapter 5(A) discussed in some detail how states worldwide have adapted their national legal systems so as to implement their obligations as members of the International Civil Aviation Organization (ICAO). The United States incorporates ICAO standards and recommended practices (SARPs) into its national law through statute and administrative regulations, using direct reference, repetition or paraphrasing of the ICAO SARPs. The same process of implementation of international treaty obligations may be seen in numerous other fields of U.S. law.[161]

---

158. Oona Hathaway et al., *International Law at Home: Enforcing Treaties in U.S. Courts*, 37 YALE J. INT'L L. 51, 91–101 (2012).

159. *Id.* at 78–83.

160. *See* 1 RESTATEMENT (THIRD), *supra* note 146, § 115 rptrs. note 5.

161. *See, e.g.,* United States v. Locke, 529 U.S. 89 (2000) (reading the Ports and Waterways Safety Act of 1972, and other U.S. statutes and regulations, as having as one aim the conformity of U.S. law with standards set forth in several treaties).

Customary International Law in U.S. Law

From early in U.S. history, the U.S. Supreme Court has construed international law (or the "law of nations") as being a part of U.S. law. Thus, in 1796, Justice Wilson stated that "[w]hen the United States declared their independence, they were bound to receive the law of nations, in its modern state of purity and refinement."[162] Likewise, in 1815 Chief Justice Marshall declared that "the Court is bound by the law of nations which is a part of the law of the land."[163]

The role of international law in U.S. law, however, was most famously addressed in *The Paquete Habana.*[164] In that case, the president of the United States ordered a naval blockade of the Cuban coast "in pursuance of the laws of the United States, and the law of nations applicable to such cases."[165] The president's proclamations, however, did not address whether civilian fishing vessels could be seized as prizes of war. After the blockade commander captured two small fishing vessels flying the Spanish flag (the *Paquete Habana* and *Lola*), the U.S. secretary of the navy instructed that Spanish fishing vessels attempting to violate the blockade were subject to capture and detention. The two vessels were then condemned before a U.S. federal court and sold in the United States as prize vessels.

In a suit by the original owners to recover the proceeds, the U.S. Supreme Court, sitting as a prize court, held that international law prohibited seizing coastal fishing vessels during time of war, and therefore affirmed an award of compensatory damages. The Court wrote:

> International law is part of our law, and must be ascertained and administered by the courts of justice of appropriate jurisdiction, as often as questions of right depending upon it are duly presented for their determination. For this purpose, where there is no treaty, and no controlling executive or legislative act or judicial decision, resort must be had to the customs and usages of civilized nations.... [166]

Since its decision in *The Paquete Habana*, the Supreme Court repeatedly has reaffirmed its position. In *Banco Nacional de Cuba v. Sabbatino,*[167] the Court stated that "it is, of course, true that United States courts apply international law as a part of our own in appropriate circumstances.... " In *Texas Industries, Inc. v. Rad-*

---

162. Ware v. Hylton, 3 U.S. (3 Dall.) 199, 281 (1796).

163. The Nereide, 13 U.S. (9 Cranch) 388, 423 (1815); *see* Anthony J. Bellia & Bradford R. Clark, *The Federal Common Law of Nations*, 109 Colum. L. Rev. 1 (2009).

164. 175 U.S. 677 (1900).

165. *Id.* at 712.

166. *Id.* at 700.

167. 376 U.S. 398, 423 (1964).

cliff Materials, Inc.,[168] the Court recognized that "international disputes implicating ... our relations with foreign nations" are one of the "narrow areas" in which "federal common law" continues to exist. Most recently, in *Sosa v. Alvarez–Machain*,[169] the Court stated that "[f]or two centuries we have affirmed that the domestic law of the United States recognizes the law of nations."

Yet the meaning of the broad language quoted above from *The Paquete Habana* has been the subject of considerable controversy. Some scholars emphasize the first sentence in the quotation, arguing that international law is automatically and directly applicable in U.S. courts whenever relevant issues are up for decision. Under this analysis, international law is one of the "Laws of the United States" that are the "supreme Law of the Land" under the Supremacy Clause (preempting state law), which the president must faithfully execute under Article II, section 3 of the Constitution.[170]

Other scholars, however, see a narrower precedent. First, they note that in *Paquete Habana* the president himself incorporated the limitations of international law into his orders. Acts in violation of those rules were therefore *ultra vires* under the president's own orders and, consequently, void. (A response to this point, however, is that the Supreme Court in *Paquete Habana* did not maintain that international law was a part of U.S. law only because of the president's proclamations.) Second, they emphasize the second sentence of the language quoted above, which says that international law only applies "where there is no treaty, and no controlling executive or legislative act or judicial decision." As such, a "controlling executive act" prevails over international law. For example, in *Garcia-Mir v. Meese*,[171] a large number of Cubans came to the United States, but the United States did not want to admit them and could not deport them elsewhere. Consequently, the U.S. attorney general ordered that they be held in detention for several months. The Cubans filed suit charging that their prolonged detention was arbitrary and thus a violation of international law. The Eleventh Circuit Court of Appeals agreed that the detention violated international law, but viewed the attorney general's decision as a "controlling executive act" that trumped international law. Other circuits have followed this approach. In *Guzman v. Tippy*,[172] the Second Circuit also found that international law norms on indefinite detention are displaced, *inter alia*, by the "controlling act" of the attorney–general's decision to detain the Mariel Cubans. Yet presumably not every action by an executive branch official consti-

---

168.   451 U.S. 630, 641 (1981).

169.   542 U.S. 692, 729 (2004).

170.   *See, e.g.*, Henkin, *supra* note 140, at 1566.

171.   788 F.2d 1446, 1453–55 (11th Cir. 1986).

172.   130 F.3d 64, 66 (2d Cir. 1997); *see* Gisbert v. U.S. Attorney General, 988 F.2d 1437 (5th Cir. 1993).

tutes a "controlling executive act," since the decisions by U.S. Navy officials to seize the two fishing vessels in *Paquete Habana* were not of sufficient weight to overcome international law.

Whatever its scope, customary international law appears to be part of the enclave of U.S. federal common law that has survived the Supreme Court's decision in *Erie Railroad Company v. Tompkins*.[173] While the Supreme Court in *Erie* directed federal courts to apply state law in the absence of federal legislative guidance, the Supreme Court in *Sosa v. Alvarez–Machain* noted that federal common law exists in various "havens of speciality," such as international law.[174]

Yet customary international law holds a rarefied position in U.S. law. Practitioners unfamiliar with customary international law tend not to invoke it. When it is invoked, judges find such law difficult to ascertain and are sometimes hostile to it.[175] A few scholars have questioned whether locating law-making authority outside U.S. institutions (*i.e.*, in the practice of states globally) fits within the U.S. political tradition.[176] Whether customary international law supersedes a pre-existing treaty or a pre-existing statute under U.S. law is unclear.[177] What is clear is that when the existence of a specific norm of customary international law is disputed by the U.S. government, U.S. courts normally will not give effect to the norm. Further, U.S. courts give special weight to views of the executive branch in interpreting customary international law.[178]

Example: Alien Tort Statute

A modern and important development in the role of international law in U.S. courts is found in recent cases decided under the Alien Tort Statute (ATS). The ATS confers original jurisdiction on

173. 304 U.S. 64 (1938).

174. 542 U.S. 692, 726–30 (2004). For a pre-*Sosa* debate on this issue, compare Curtis Bradley & Jack Goldsmith, *Customary International Law as Federal Common Law: A Critique of the Modern Position*, 110 HARV. L. REV. 815 (1997), with Harold Koh, *Is International Law Really State Law?*, 111 HARV. L. REV. 1824 (1998); Phillip C. Jessup, *The Doctrine of* Erie Railroad v. Tompkins *Applied to International Law*, 33 AM. J. INT'L L. 740 (1939).

175. *See* United States v. Yunis, 924 F.2d 1086, 1091 (D.C. Cir. 1991) ("Our duty is to enforce the Constitution, laws and treaties of the United States, not to conform the law of the land to norms of customary international law.")

176. *See* Phillip Trimble, *A Revisionist View of Customary International Law*, 33 UCLA L. REV. 665 (1986).

177. *Compare* Louis Henkin, *The Constitution and United States Sovereignty: A Century of Chinese Exclusion and Its Progeny*, 100 HARV. L. REV. 853, 867–78 (1987) (asserting that customary international law is not inferior to treaties or statutes), *with* Jack Goldklang, *Back on Board the Paquete Habana: Resolving the Conflict Between Statutes and Customary International Law*, 25 VA. J. INT'L L. 143 (1984) (finding customary international law inferior).

178. *See* 1 RESTATEMENT (THIRD), *supra* note 146, § 112 cmt. c.

federal district courts over "any civil action by an alien for a tort only, committed in violation of the law of nations or a treaty of the United States."[179] The original purpose of the statute may have been to avoid international conflict by opening U.S. federal courts (which were viewed as less political than state courts) to foreign diplomats for redress of injuries suffered at the hands of U.S. nationals, either in the United States or abroad. However, the intent of Congress when enacting the statute is not entirely clear and, because the statute lay dormant for almost 200 years, for a long time its scope was not clarified by U.S. courts.[180]

In 1980, the ATS was dramatically resurrected in *Filartiga v. Pena–Irala.*[181] In that case, a federal court used the statute to establish jurisdiction over a claim by Paraguayan plaintiffs against an official of their own government for the torture and slaying of a family member in Paraguay. The Court found that torture conducted under "color of law" was a violation of the law of nations, even when conducted by a government against its own nationals. Such a case—involving a tort that occurred abroad by an alien against another alien—highlights the extraordinary nature of the ATS. However, not all courts have been receptive to such a robust use of the statute.[182]

In 2004, the Supreme Court clarified in the *Sosa* case that the ATS is solely a jurisdictional statute; it does not itself provide a cause of action.[183] Yet such causes of action need not be found in U.S. statutes; they may be found in treaties or customary international law.

> [T]he First Congress understood that the district courts would recognize private causes of action for certain torts in violation of the law of nations, though we have found no basis to suspect Congress had any examples in mind beyond those torts corresponding to Blackstone's three primary offenses: violation of safe conducts, infringement of the rights of ambassadors, and piracy.... [T]here are good reasons for a restrained conception of the discretion a federal court should exercise in considering

---

179. 28 U.S.C. § 1350 (2006) (also referred to as the Alien Tort Claims Act or ATCA).

180. *See* Anthony J. Bellia & Bradford R. Clark, *The Alien Tort Statute and the Law of Nations*, 78 CHICAGO L. REV. 445 (2011); Anne–Marie Burley, *The Alien Tort Statute and the Judiciary Act of 1789: A Badge of Honor*, 83 AM. J. INT'L L. 461 (1989).

181. 630 F.2d 876 (2d Cir. 1980).

182. *See, e.g.*, Tel–Oren v. Libya, 726 F.2d 774, 798 (D.C. Cir. 1984) (Bork, J.,

concurring) (seeking to limit the ATS to eighteenth century torts, specifically violation of safe-conducts or passports, infringement of the rights of ambassadors, and piracy); Beanal v. Freeport–McMoran, Inc., 197 F.3d 161 (5th Cir. 1999) (finding that the environmental agreements upon which the claim was pled did not provide discernable standards for identifying international environmental torts).

183. *Sosa*, supra note 169, at 713–14.

a new cause of action of this kind. Accordingly, we think courts should require any claim based on the present-day law of nations to rest on a norm of international character accepted by the civilized world and defined with a specificity comparable to the features of the 18th-century paradigms we have recognized.[184]

Thus, to succeed on an ATS claim, three key elements must exist: (1) the claim must be filed by an alien (*i.e.*, not a national of the United States); (2) the claim must be for a tort; and (3) the action in controversy must have violated either a U.S. treaty or a "specific, universal, and obligatory" norm of international law.[185] In *Sosa*, the Supreme Court found that the third element had not been met; the plaintiff had failed to establish that there existed in either a treaty binding on the United States or customary international law a prohibition on arbitrary arrest, as contrasted with a prohibition on prolonged arbitrary detention.[186] Many ATS claims have been dismissed by lower courts for failure to show a violation of the law of nations, including claims arguing that environmental torts, fraud, or defamation violate international law.[187] Yet many other ATS claims have been viewed as cognizable, including state-sponsored torture, crimes against humanity, war crimes, and genocide.[188] For example, in *Sarei v. Rio Tinto*, the Ninth Circuit found:

> Claims for violations of the international norm proscribing war crimes are cognizable under the ATS. By ratifying the [1949] Geneva Conventions, Congress has adopted a precise, universally accepted definition of war crimes. Moreover, through enactment of a separate federal statute, Congress has incorporated this precise definition into the federal criminal law. 18 U.S.C. § 2441. Thus, Congress has clearly defined the law of nations to include a binding prohibition on the commission of war crimes. Given this, and given *Sosa*'s teachings, it follows that an allegation of a war crime states a cause of action under the ATS.[189]

---

184. *Id.* at 724–25; *see* Ernest A. Young, Sosa *and the Retail Incorporation of International Law*, 120 HARV. L. REV. F. 28, 31, 33 (2007) ("*Sosa* is best read as recognizing a federal common law implied right of action for the violation of certain [customary international law] rules of decision.... [O]nce *Sosa* recognized a federal right of action, that recognition was sufficient to bring such claims within current understandings of Article III's 'arising under' jurisdiction.").

185. *Sosa, supra* note 169, at 732–33.

186. *Id.* at 734–38.

187. *See* Flores v. Southern Peru Copper Corp., 343 F.3d 140, 172 (2d Cir. 2003); Hamid v. Price Waterhouse, 51 F.3d 1411, 1418 (9th Cir. 1995); Maugein v. Newmont Mining Corp., 298 F. Supp. 2d 1124, 1130 (D. Colo. 2004).

188. *See, e.g.*, Chavez v. Carranza, 559 F.3d 486 (6th Cir. 2009); Cabello v. Fernandez–Larios, 402 F.3d 1148 (11th Cir. 2005); Abebe–Jira v. Negewo, 72 F.3d 844 (11th Cir. 1996).

189. Sarei v. Rio Tinto, 2011 WL 5041927 (9th Cir. Oct. 25, 2011).

One difficult area has been sorting out which aspects of an ATS claim are governed by international law, including customary international law, and which aspects are governed by U.S. law. It appears generally accepted that the cause of action arises within international law, while the technical aspects of the filing of a claim remains governed by the federal rules of civil procedure. Yet there are a host of other issues, such as whether the ATS contemplates liability for aiding and abetting a violation of the law of nations, where it is less clear whether international or U.S. is the relevant source.[190]

ATS claims generally have been limited to suits against persons (natural or legal), since suits against governments must be brought under the Foreign Sovereign Immunities Act.[191] Further, the person sued must be acting in a governmental capacity (or under "color of law"), since it is generally accepted that only states can violate international law. However, U.S. case law also permits claims against non-governmental persons that are based on a handful of egregious offenses (such as piracy, slave trading, and certain war crimes), since those offenses can lead to individual liability under international law.[192]

A notable use of the ATS has been against U.S. corporations which enter into business relationships with foreign governments that engage in human rights violations.[193] For example, in 1996, villagers from Myanmar (Burma) filed a class action lawsuit in U.S. federal court against, *inter alia*, a U.S. corporation (Unocal) that was involved in a joint venture with the Myanmar government to extract natural gas. The plaintiffs alleged that the defendant was responsible under the ATS for international human rights violations, including forced labor perpetrated by the Burmese military in furtherance of the pipeline portion of the project. The district court found that corporations are within the ambit of the ATS when they engage in cooperative behavior with governments engaged in human rights violations.[194] After discovery, however, the court granted Unocal's motion for summary judgment because—as a factual matter—the corporation was not sufficiently connected to the construction and operation of the gas pipeline to sustain a claim that it

190. For an argument that federal common law peculiar to the ATS, which blends U.S. and international law into a continuum, answers all such questions, see Ingrid Weurth, *The Alien Tort Statute and Federal Common Law: A New Approach*, 85 NOTRE DAME L. REV. 1931 (2010).

191. *See* Argentine Republic v. Amerada Hess Shipping Corp., 488 U.S. 428 (1989) (finding that the ATS does not grant jurisdiction for a suit against a foreign government); *see also* Chapter 9(C).

192. *See, e.g.*, Kadic v. Karadzic, 70 F.3d 232 (2d Cir. 1995).

193. *See, e.g.*, Aguinda v. Texaco, 303 F.3d 470 (2d Cir. 2002).

194. *See* Doe v. Unocal Corp., 963 F. Supp. 880 (C.D. Cal. 1997).

engaged in a tort "in violation of the law of nations or a treaty of the United States."[195]

A three-judge panel of the Ninth Circuit Court of Appeals held that the district court erred in determining that the plaintiffs must show that Unocal controlled the Burmese military's actions in order to establish Unocal's liability. Rather, the plaintiffs needed to show only that Unocal "knowingly assisted" the military in perpetrating the abuses. Further, the court of appeals stated that the plaintiffs had produced sufficient evidence under this standard for the case to proceed to trial, although the evidence was insufficient to support claims of torture.[196] Soon thereafter, the Ninth Circuit decided to rehear the appeal before the full eleven-judge court and vacated the decision of the three-judge panel.[197] Before the Ninth Circuit could reach a final decision, however, the parties announced a settlement. Although the terms of the settlement were not released publicly, Unocal stated that it would pay the plaintiffs an unspecified amount of money and fund programs to improve the living conditions for people from the Burmese region surrounding the pipeline and "who may have suffered hardships."[198]

Other settlements, however, have been made public. In June 2009, the parties in three cases that had been consolidated—*Wiwa v. Royal Dutch Petroleum Company*, *Wiwa v. Shell Petroleum Company*, and *Wiwa v. Anderson*—reached a settlement in an amount of $15.5 million.[199] These cases involved allegations that a multinational company (Shell), its Nigerian subsidiary, and the head of the subsidiary had conspired with the Nigerian government to commit grave human rights abuses, including conduct that lead to the death of Ken Saro–Wiwa, a prominent Nigerian activist. Among other things, the settlement provided for the creation of a trust fund for the benefit of persons living in the area of the defendants' operations.

In the aftermath of the *Sosa* decision, it was unclear whether customary international law included corporate liability for human rights violations, given that there is no treaty or international tribunal decision clearly and unambiguously imposing such liability. In a case involving current and former residents of southern Sudan (allegedly victims of genocide, crimes against humanity and other violations of international law as a result of acts by the government

---

195. Doe v. Unocal Corp., 110 F. Supp. 2d 1294 (C.D. Cal. 2000); *see* Bigio v. Coca–Cola Co., 239 F.3d 440 (2d Cir. 2000).

196. *See* Doe v. Unocal Corp., 395 F.3d 932 (9th Cir. 2002).

197. *See* Doe v. Unocal Corp., 395 F.3d 978 (9th Cir. 2003).

198. Unocal Press Release on Settlement Reached in Human Rights Lawsuit (Dec. 13, 2004), *at* <http:// www.unocal. com/uclnews /2004news/121304.htm>.

199. Settlement Agreement in *Wiwa v. Royal Dutch Petroleum Co.* (S.D.N.Y. 2009), 48 I.L.M. 969 (2009).

of Sudan and a Canadian energy company, Talisman Energy, Inc.), the Second Circuit reviewed the standard set in *Sosa* and found that a corporation may be liable for aiding and abetting a government's violation of human rights, but the corporate conduct must be done *with the intention of* violating the law of nations.[200] The D.C. and Eleventh Circuits have also recognized that aiding and abetting conduct may give rise to an ATS claim.[201]

Separately, a panel of the Second Circuit in *Kiobel v. Royal Dutch Petroleum* concluded that there can be *no* cases under the ATS against corporations because corporations are not subject to liability under customary international law.[202] By contrast, the Ninth Circuit in *Sarei v. Rio Tinto* found that no rule of either customary international or U.S. law supported the proposition that the ATS only applies to natural persons and not to corporations.[203] Some judges have asserted that focusing on customary international law for this issue is misguided; that the question of whether corporations are liable for ATS purposes is a matter left to U.S. law, not customary international law.[204] Given the split in the circuits, the U.S. Supreme Court accepted certiorari in the *Kiobel* case and will likely address the matter in 2013.

Finally, the ATS is also now being used in cases relating to the U.S. "war on terrorism." In these lawsuits, the alien claimants are charging that U.S. government personnel mistreated them in violation of international law during their detention in Iraq or at Guantánamo Bay Naval Base in Cuba, or wrongfully rendered them to the custody of another state where they were mistreated.[205]

Judicial Use of International/Foreign Law

Even in the absence of a controlling treaty or statute, U.S. courts have made reference to international law and foreign law in the course of interpreting U.S. law. Such situations arise in a variety of circumstances. The U.S. court might look to the decisions of foreign courts who have interpreted a treaty of concern to the

---

200. Presbyterian Church of Sudan v. Talisman Energy, 582 F.3d 244 (2d Cir. 2009); *see also* Abdullahi v. Pfizer, 562 F.3d 163 (2d Cir. 2009); Khulumani v. Barclay Nat'l Bank Ltd., 504 F.3d 254, 260 (2d Cir. 2007).

201. *See* Romero v. Drummond Co., 552 F.3d 1303, 1315 (11th Cir. 2008); Doe v. Exxon Mobil Corp., No. 09–7125, 2011 WL 2652384, at *29 (D.C. Cir. July 8, 2011).

202. Kiobel v. Royal Dutch Petroleum, 621 F.3d 111, 125 (2d Cir. 2010) (holding that customary international law as a whole "has not to date recog-

nized liability for corporations that violate its norms").

203. Sarei v. Rio Tinto, 2011 WL 5041927 (9th Cir. Oct. 25, 2011).

204. *See Kiobel*, at 149, 174–76 (Leval, J., concurring in the judgment); *see generally* Harold Hongju Koh, *Separating Myth from Reality About Corporate Responsibility Litigation*, 7 J. INT'L ECON. L. 263, 266–67 (2004).

205. *See* Julian Ku, *The Third Wave: The Alien Tort Statute and the War on Terrorism*, 19 EMORY INT'L L.REV. 205 (2005).

U.S. court.[206] While those decisions are in no sense binding on the United States, they are viewed as relevant in parsing the intent of the parties to the treaty and maintaining harmony in treaty relations. Foreign law may also be relevant when U.S. courts are interpreting a contract that calls for the application of foreign law or are faced with a term in a U.S. statute—such as "right to custody" in a case of child abduction from a foreign country—that inescapably requires reference to foreign law.[207]

More controversially, U.S. courts have referred to international and foreign law when interpreting provisions of the U.S. Constitution. In *Roper v. Simmons*,[208] the Court referred to the U.N. Convention on the Rights of the Child[209] (to which the United States is not a party) in the course of finding Missouri's juvenile death penalty in violation of the Eighth Amendment's prohibition on "cruel and unusual punishment."[210] Justice Kennedy, writing for a 5–4 majority, stated that the Eighth Amendment's expansive language

> must be interpreted according to its text, by considering history, tradition, and precedent, and with due regard for its purpose and function in the constitutional design. To implement this framework we have established the propriety and affirmed the necessity of referring to "the evolving standards of decency that mark the progress of a maturing society" to determine which punishments are so disproportionate as to be cruel and unusual.[211]

In considering such "evolving standards of decency," the Court engaged in an extensive analysis of the rejection of the juvenile death penalty in the majority (thirty) of U.S. states, the infrequency of its use even in states where it was available, and the trend toward abolition of such punishment. For the Court, this evidence demonstrated that contemporary U.S. society views juveniles as categorically less culpable than the average criminal. The Court then stated that the "opinion of the world community, while not controlling our outcome, does provide respected and significant confirmation for our own conclusions."[212] The Court reasoned:

---

206. *See* Chapter 4(G).

207. *See, e.g.,* Furnes v. Reeves, 362 F.3d 702 (11th Cir. 2004) (determining whether a father had a "right to custody" within the meaning of 42 U.S.C. §§ 11601–11610 (2006) by analyzing relevant Norwegian law).

208. 543 U.S. 551 (2005).

209. Nov. 20, 1989, 1577 U.N.T.S. 3; *see* Chapter 10(C).

210. U.S. CONST. amend. VIII (the Court was applying the Eighth Amendment to Missouri through the amendment's incorporation by the Fourteenth Amendment).

211. *Roper*, 125 S. Ct. at 1190 (citing Trop v. Dulles, 356 U.S. 86, 100–101 (1958)).

212. *Id.* at 1200.

Our determination that the death penalty is disproportionate punishment for offenders under 18 finds confirmation in the stark reality that the United States is the only country in the world that continues to give official sanction to the juvenile death penalty. This reality does not become controlling, for the task of interpreting the Eighth Amendment remains our responsibility. Yet at least from the time of the Court's decision in *Trop [v. Dulles]*, the Court has referred to the laws of other countries and to international authorities as instructive for its interpretation of the Eighth Amendment's prohibition of "cruel and unusual punishments." 356 U.S. [86], at 102–103 [(1958)] (plurality opinion) ("The civilized nations of the world are in virtual unanimity that statelessness is not to be imposed as punishment for crime"); *see also Atkins [v. Virginia*, 536 U.S. 304], at 317, n. 21 [(2002)] (recognizing that "within the world community, the imposition of the death penalty for crimes committed by mentally retarded offenders is overwhelmingly disapproved"); *Thompson [v. Oklahoma*, 487 U.S. 815,] at 830–831, and n. 31, [(1988)] (plurality opinion) (noting the abolition of the juvenile death penalty "by other nations that share our Anglo–American heritage, and by the leading members of the Western European community," and observing that "[w]e have previously recognized the relevance of the views of the international community in determining whether a punishment is cruel and unusual"); *Enmund [v. Florida*, 458 U.S. 782,] at 796–797, n. 22 [(1982)] (observing that "the doctrine of felony murder has been abolished in England and India, severely restricted in Canada and a number of other Commonwealth countries, and is unknown in continental Europe"); *Coker [v. Georgia*, 433 U.S. 584,] at 596, n. 10 [(1977)](plurality opinion) ("It is ... not irrelevant here that out of 60 major nations in the world surveyed in 1965, only 3 retained the death penalty for rape where death did not ensue").

... Article 37 of the United Nations Convention on the Rights of the Child, which every country in the world has ratified save for the United States and Somalia, contains an express prohibition on capital punishment for crimes committed by juveniles under 18.... No ratifying country has entered a reservation to the provision prohibiting the execution of juvenile offenders. Parallel prohibitions are contained in other significant international covenants....

... [O]nly seven countries other than the United States have executed juvenile offenders since 1990: Iran, Pakistan, Saudi Arabia, Yemen, Nigeria, the Democratic Republic of Congo, and China. Since then each of these countries has either abolished capital punishment for juveniles or made public disavowal of the practice.... In sum, it is fair to say that the United States now stands alone in a world that has turned its face against the juvenile death penalty.[213]

Similarly, in *Graham v. Florida*,[214] the Court (again Justice Kennedy writing for a 5–4 majority) found that life without parole for juvenile non-homicide offenders would violate the Eighth Amendment. The Court noted that the United States was the only country with such a sentence and that such a sentence is inconsistent with that U.N. Convention on the Rights of the Child. Justice Kennedy reiterated: "The question before us is not whether international law prohibits the United States from imposing the sentence at issue in this case. The question is whether that punishment is cruel and unusual."[215]

In some cases, reference may be made to foreign or international law less to confirm one interpretation of a U.S. norm than to dispel an alternative interpretation. For instance, in 1986 Chief Justice Warren Burger concurred in upholding Georgia's antisodomy statute by claiming that sodomy was contrary to the history of Western civilization and to Judeo–Christian moral and ethical standards.[216] Similarly, in *Lawrence v. Texas*, the Texas Court of Appeals upheld Texas's antisodomy statute in part by stating that "Western civilization has a long history of repressing homosexual behavior by state action."[217] When *Lawrence* was appealed in 2003, the Supreme Court cited foreign and international laws and judicial decisions[218] protecting the right of homosexual adults to engage in intimate, consensual conduct as a means of refuting the idea that antisodomy laws were accepted worldwide.[219] Thus, foreign and international law in *Lawrence* was used by the Supreme Court not as direct authority, but to demonstrate that an opposing argument about Western civilized norms of behavior was unsustainable.

Not everyone is happy with U.S. judges looking to foreign and international law when deciding cases, especially when interpreting a constitution drafted by Americans to govern Americans. On the state level, in approximately twenty states as of 2011 some form of state constitutional amendment or state law has been proposed or enacted that would restrict or prohibit state courts from using laws

---

213. *Id.* at 1198–99; *but see* Stanford v. Kentucky, 492 U.S. 361, 369 n.1 (1989) (emphasizing "that it is *American* conceptions of decency that are dispositive" in interpreting the Eighth Amendment, not the sentencing practices of foreign states).

214. 130 S.Ct. 2011 (2010).

215. *Id.* at 2034.

216. *See* Bowers v. Hardwick, 478 U.S. 186, 210–12 (1986).

217. *See* Lawrence v. Texas, 41 S.W.3d 349, 361 (Tex. App. 2001).

218. *E.g.*, Modinos v. Cyprus, 16 Eur. Ct. H.R. 485 (1993); Norris v. Ireland, 13 Eur. Ct. H.R. 186 (1988).

219. Lawrence v. Texas, 539 U.S. 558, 576–77 (2003).

or legal doctrines from international or foreign law, or from religious doctrines, including Sharia law. For example, a "Save our State Amendment" was adopted in Oklahoma forbidding courts from considering either "international law" or "Sharia law" when deciding cases,[220] while in Tennessee the "American and Tennessee Laws for Tennessee Courts" statute focuses on preventing reference to "foreign law."[221] On the federal level, bills were introduced (but not adopted) in Congress in 2004 and 2005 that would have forbidden U.S. federal courts from using foreign and international law in their opinions, except for English law and other sources relied upon by the framers of the Constitution.[222] Separately, Supreme Court Justice Antonin Scalia dissented in the *Simmons* case, saying: "Acknowledgment of foreign approval has no place in the legal opinion of this court. . . . "[223]

Critics argue that if the purpose in using such law is solely to confirm a legal analysis already reached based on U.S. law, then using foreign or international law is wholly unnecessary. The only reason to use such law, therefore, must be to reach an outcome *not* supported by U.S. law. To critics, such an approach is undemocratic; judges are supposed to apply the laws adopted by U.S. citizens, not impose laws adopted abroad. Further, critics point to methodological problems in assessing international law. There are some 193 other states in the world; how exactly are U.S. judges supposed to survey the laws of each? What if there is a split among those laws? What if those laws reveal a widespread practice that detracts from U.S. liberties? While the modern use of foreign and international law in constitutional interpretation is sparse, critics worry that it might increase in the future.[224]

220. Okl. Enr. H.J.r. 1056 (2010). The amendment was not yet certified as of the end of 2011 due to a challenge in federal court.

221. 2010 Tenn. Pub. Acts 983.

222. *See* H.R. 4118, 108th Cong. (2004); H.R. 1658, 109th Cong. (2005).

223. *Roper*, 125 S. Ct. at 1229.

224. For a debate on this subject, see *Agora: The United States Constitution and International Law*, 98 Am. J. Int'l L. 42 (2004); *see also* Sarah Cleveland, *Our International Constitution*, 31 Yale J. Int'l L. 1 (2006).

Further Reading:

Joseph D. Becker, *The American Law of Nations: Public International Law in American Courts* (2001).

John Hart Ely, *War and Responsibility: Constitutional Limitations of Vietnam and Its Aftermath* (1993).

Louis Fisher, *Presidential Spending Power* (2d ed. 1975).

Louis Fisher, *Presidential War Power* (2d ed. 2004).

Thomas M. Franck, *Political Questions/Judicial Answers: Does the Rule of Law Apply to Foreign Affairs?* (1992).

Sofie Geeroms, *Foreign Law in Civil Litigation: A Comparative and Functional Analysis* (2004).

Michael Glennon, *Constitutional Diplomacy* (1990).

Louis Henkin, *Foreign Affairs and the United States Constitution* (2d ed. 1996).

Vicki C. Jackson, *Constitutional Engagement in a Transnational Era* (2009).

Harold Koh, *The National Security Constitution: Sharing Power After the Iran–Contra Affair* (1990).

James M. Lindsay, *Congress and the Politics of U.S. Foreign Policy* (1994).

Jordan Paust, *International Law as Law of the United States* (2d ed. 2003).

Jefferson Powell, *The President's Authority Over Foreign Affairs: An Essay in Constitutional Interpretation* (2002).

Michael D. Ramsey, *The Constitution's Text in Foreign Affairs* (2007).

John M. Rogers, *International Law and United States Law* (1999).

Abraham D. Sofaer, *War, Foreign Affairs, and Constitutional Power* (1984).

Ralph Steinhardt & Anthony D'Amato, eds., *The Alien Tort Claims Act: An Analytical Anthology* (1999).

Restatement (Third) of the Foreign Relations Law of the United States (1987) (2 vols.).

Chapter 8

NATIONAL JURISDICTION TO PRESCRIBE, ADJUDICATE, AND ENFORCE

This chapter deals with the right of a state under international law to exercise jurisdiction over persons or things outside its territory. Its principal focus is the relevant practice of the United States, but similar approaches to jurisdiction may be found in other states. Section A considers presumptions existing under U.S. law regarding whether U.S. statutes apply extraterritorially. If a U.S. statute does apply extraterritorially, Section B examines whether such application of U.S. law is viewed as permissible under international law. Finally, Section C discusses how jurisdiction can be applied extraterritorially through legislation, adjudication, and enforcement.

A. Presumptions Under U.S. Law

Congress enacts many statutes. When U.S. courts interpret those statutes, the normal presumption is that they apply only to acts performed within U.S. territory.[1] For instance, U.S. law criminalizes the possession of cocaine.[2] Yet, if a U.S. national traveled to Canada, bought and consumed a small amount of cocaine, and then returned to the United States, U.S. prosecutors and courts would not apply the U.S. law to such an act. Reasons for this presumption against extraterritoriality include the belief that Congress legislates with national (not international) concerns in mind and the idea that we should avoid unintended clashes between U.S. laws and those of other nations.[3]

At the same time, U.S. courts may not apply the presumption in places that are outside U.S. territory, but that are within U.S. control, such as U.S. military bases in Guantánamo Bay, Cuba,[4] or

---

1. *See, e.g.,* Sale v. Haitian Ctrs. Council, Inc., 509 U.S. 155, 188 (1993) (holding that a U.S. immigration statute does not apply extraterritorially); Smith v. United States, 507 U.S. 197, 204–05 (1993) (holding that the Federal Tort Claims Act does not apply extraterritorially).

2. *See* 21 U.S.C. § 959 (2006).

3. *See* EEOC v. Arabian Am. Oil Co., 499 U.S. 244, 248 (1991); *Smith,* 507 U.S. at 204; *see also* John H. Knox, *A Presumption Against Extrajurisdictionality,* 104 Am. J. Int'l L. 351 (2010).

4. *See* Rasul v. Bush, 542 U.S. 466 (2004).

elsewhere,[5] and may not apply it with respect to conduct abroad that has effects in the United States.[6] Arguably the presumption should not be applied in any situation where extraterritorial application of U.S. law helps implement international law, since doing so harmonizes U.S. laws with the laws of other nations rather than clashes with them.[7] Finally, the presumption will fall whenever Congress exercises its power to regulate conduct performed outside U.S. territory. The Supreme Court has stated that "Congress has the authority to enforce its laws beyond the territorial boundaries of the United States."[8] U.S. courts, however, are to presume that Congress has not exercised this power, unless Congress manifests a "clear intent" to reach acts performed outside U.S. territory.[9]

Congressional intent that a statute regulate conduct outside the United States can be discerned first by looking to "see whether 'language in the [relevant Act] gives any indication of a congressional purpose to extend its coverage beyond places over which the United States has sovereignty or has some measure of legislative control.' "[10] Thus, in criminalizing the possession, manufacture, or distribution of controlled substances within the United States, Congress has expressly included "acts of manufacture or distribution committed outside the territorial jurisdiction of the United States" since those acts can have effects within the United States.[11]

A recent example of this dynamic concerns the extraterritorial application of antifraud provisions of U.S. securities law. Section 10(b) of the Securities and Exchange Act of 1934 prohibits, when buying or selling securities, any manipulative or deceptive practice in contravention of rules adopted by the Securities Exchange Commission.[12] The SEC's Rule 10b–5 prohibits, among other things, the making of untrue statements when selling securities.[13] Neither the statute nor the rule indicates whether they apply to foreign commerce, such as the issuance of an untrue statement abroad by a foreign issuer of a security which is relied upon by a U.S. buyer. U.S. courts initially interpreted the statute as having an extraterritorial effect,[14] but in 2010 the U.S. Supreme Court, in *Morrison v.*

---

5. *See* Vermilya–Brown Co. v. Connell, 335 U.S. 377 (1948) (not applying the presumption to military base in Bermuda); *but see* United States v. Spelar, 338 U.S. 217 (1949) (applying the presumption to military base in Newfoundland).

6. *See, e.g.,* Hartford Fire Ins. Co. v. California, 509 U.S. 764 (1993).

7. *See* Anthony J. Colangelo, *A Unified Approach to Extraterritoriality*, 97 Va. L. Rev. 1019 (2011).

8. *EEOC*, 499 U.S. at 248.

9. *See* Foley Bros. v. Filardo, 336 U.S. 281, 285 (1949).

10. 499 U.S. at 248 (quoting *Foley Bros.*, 336 U.S. at 285).

11. 21 U.S.C. § 959(c) (2006).

12. 15 U.S.C. § 78j (2006).

13. 17 C.F.R. § 240.10b–5 (2009).

14. *See, e.g.,* Schoenbaum v. Firstbrook, 405 F.2d 200 (2d Cir. 1968).

National Australia Bank,[15] found otherwise. Writing for the majority, Justice Scalia asserted that Congress must clearly indicate in the statute whenever it wishes to apply U.S. law to conduct abroad. As such, the statute does apply to transactions involving securities traded on U.S. exchanges, or transactions involving an exchange of ownership in the United States, but does not apply to a foreign company that issues securities abroad. After the Court issued its opinion, however, Congress reacted by partially applying the U.S. law to conduct abroad. Specifically, Congress amended the law so as to authorize the executive branch (not private parties) to sue in U.S. court on fraudulent foreign transactions if there exists "conduct within the United States that constitutes significant steps in furtherance of the violation," or if conduct occurring outside the United States "has a foreseeable substantial effect within the United States."[16]

Some areas of Congressional legislation are obviously focused on acts occurring outside U.S. territory; thus, the U.S. Constitution contains a clause empowering Congress to "define and punish Piracies and Felonies committed on the high Seas, and Offences against the Law of Nations."[17] From the earliest days of the American republic, Congress has criminalized felonious conduct by U.S. and foreign citizens on the high seas. As the Supreme Court declared in 1818, "[t]he constitution having conferred on congress the power of defining and punishing piracy, there can be no doubt of the right of the legislature to enact laws punishing pirates, although they may be foreigners, and may have committed no particular offence against the United States."[18] Cases continue to arise today from U.S. statutes prohibiting unlawful acts on the high seas.[19]

The "piracies and felonies" clause is the only specific Constitutional grant of power for punishing offenses committed outside U.S. territory. Yet Congress has also expressly prohibited conduct abroad unrelated to the high seas. Illustrative statutes prohibit:

- murder of a U.S. national in a foreign country (18 U.S.C. § 1119 (2006));

- extraterritorial use of biological weapons (18 U.S.C. § 175 (2006));

---

15. 130 S.Ct. 2869 (2010).

16. Dodd–Frank Wall Street Reform and Consumer Protection Act, Pub. L. No. 111–203, § 929P(b)(1), 124 Stat. 1376, 1864 (2010) (amending 15 U.S.C. 77v(a)).

17. U.S. Const. art. I, § 8, cl. 10.

18. United States v. Palmer, 16 U.S. (3 Wheat.) 610, 630 (1818).

19. *See* United States v. Suerte, 291 F.3d 366 (5th Cir. 2002) (applying the Maritime Drug Law Enforcement Act, 46 U.S.C. App. § 1903 (2006)).

- extraterritorial crimes committed against high government officials (18 U.S.C. §§ 351, 1751 (2006));

- extraterritorial money laundering (18 U.S.C. § 1956 (2006));

- attacks on diplomats abroad (18 U.S.C. § 1116(c) (2006));

- kidnaping of a protected U.S. government employee abroad (18 U.S.C. §§ 1201(a)(4), 1201(e) (2006));

- hostage taking abroad (18 U.S.C. § 1203 (2006));

- providing assistance to foreign terrorist organizations abroad (18 U.S.C. § 2339B(d) (2006)); and

- foreign terrorist activity (18 U.S.C. § 2332b(e) (2006)).

The "clear intent" referred to in *Morrison v. National Australia Bank*, however, may not require that the statute itself expressly provide for extraterritorial application. Rather, courts consider "all available evidence about the meaning" of the statute.[20] For example, in 1998 two U.S. embassies in East Africa were bombed by terrorists. Soon thereafter, the United States took into custody several persons who had allegedly conspired in the bombings. In pre-trial proceedings in *United States v. Bin Laden*,[21] some of the defendants challenged the extraterritorial application of some of the U.S. statutes under which they were charged. Those statutes prohibited the malicious destruction of property owned or possessed by the United States, but were silent about whether the actions must occur within U.S. territory. The court acknowledged the general presumption that U.S. laws are not applied extraterritorially, but stated that, in this instance, the presumption could be overcome. Quoting from *United States v. Bowman*,[22] the court noted that the presumption did not apply to those "criminal statutes which are, as a class, not logically dependent on their locality for the Government's jurisdiction, but are enacted because of the right of the Government to defend itself against obstruction, or fraud wherever perpetrated, especially if committed by its own citizens, officers or agents."[23] Similarly, in a case involving a conspiracy to bomb U.S. commercial airliners in southeast Asia, the Second Circuit found that the relevant criminal statute covered any U.S. "flag aircraft while in flight, wherever in the world it may be."[24] Courts, therefore, may infer the intent of Congress that such

20. *Sale, supra* note 1, at 177; *see Smith, supra* note 1, at 201–03 (examining the text, structure, and legislative history of the statute).

21. 92 F. Supp. 2d 189 (S.D.N.Y. 2000).

22. 260 U.S. 94, 98 (1922).

23. 92 F. Supp. 2d at 193.

24. United States v. Yousef, 327 F.3d 56, 87 (2d Cir. 2003) (construing 18 U.S.C. § 32(a) (2006)); *see* United States v. Larsen, 952 F.2d 1099 (9th Cir. 1991) (construing 21 U.S.C. § 841(a)(1) (2006)).

statutes are to be applied extraterritorially; otherwise, it would greatly curtail the scope and usefulness of the statute.[25]

There is also a presumption in U.S. law (known as the *Charming Betsy* canon) that an act of Congress ought never be construed to violate the "law of nations" as well as foreign law if any other possible construction remains.[26] The U.S. Supreme Court

> ordinarily construes ambiguous statutes to avoid unreasonable interference with the sovereign authority of other nations. This rule of construction reflects principles of customary international law—law that (we must assume) Congress ordinarily seeks to follow.
>
> This rule of statutory construction cautions courts to assume that legislators take account of the legitimate sovereign interests of other nations when they write American laws. It thereby helps the potentially conflicting laws of different nations work together in harmony—a harmony particularly needed in today's highly interdependent commercial world.[27]

Consequently, when considering whether Congress intended a statute to be applied extraterritorially, U.S. courts typically are interested in whether the statute is compatible with the extraterritorial jurisdiction of states recognized as permissible under international law (see next section). Indeed, the U.S. statute itself may require courts to take into account what is permissible under international law. For example, Congress has defined the "special maritime and territorial jurisdiction of the United States" as including *"[t]o the extent permitted by international law*, any foreign vessel during a voyage having a scheduled departure from or arrival in the United States with respect to an offense committed by or against a national of the United States."[28] Thus, in cases involving a U.S. statute prohibiting conduct in the U.S. "special maritime and territorial jurisdiction" and being applied to a foreign vessel calling at a U.S. port, U.S. courts are required by statute to consider whether the exercise of jurisdiction is permissible under international law.

---

25. *Cf.* United States v. Mitchell, 553 F.2d 996 (5th Cir. 1977) (finding that the Marine Mammal Protection Act, 16 U.S.C. § 1361 (2006), does not criminalize a U.S. national's capture, without a U.S. permit, of a dolphin in Bahamian waters for transport to the United Kingdom).

26. *See* McCulloch v. Sociedad Nacional de Marineros de Honduras, 372 U.S. 10, 21 (1963); Murray v. Schooner Charming Betsy, 6 U.S. (2 Cranch) 64, 118 (1804); *see also* Ralph Steinhardt, *The Role of International Law as a Canon of Domestic Statutory Construction*, 43 Vand. L. Rev. 1103 (1990).

27. F. Hoffman–La Roche Ltd. v. Empagran, 542 U.S. 155, 164–65 (2004) (citations omitted).

28. 18 U.S.C. § 7(8) (2006) (emphasis added).

B. Permissible Bases of Jurisdiction Under International Law

General Approach

Over the centuries, states have developed through their practice (and in some instances, through treaties) rules on what kinds of national jurisdiction are acceptable as a matter of international law. Generally, these rules view the permissible scope of a state's jurisdiction over persons or conduct as a function of the state's linkages with those persons or conduct. The stronger the link, the more likely the exercise of jurisdiction will be regarded as permissible.

A decision often referred to in this regard is that of the Permanent Court of International Justice (PCIJ) in the *S.S. "Lotus" Case*.[29] In that case, France objected to Turkey's prosecution of a French naval lieutenant for criminal negligence stemming from a collision between his ship and a Turkish vessel on the high seas which killed several Turkish nationals. Turkey's law allowed for such prosecution, even though the act and injury occurred outside its territory. The PCIJ concluded that Turkey was free to act unless a customary international law prohibition *against* the exercise of jurisdiction could be found. After stating that territorial jurisdiction was a fundamental element of the sovereignty principle in the international legal system, the Court wrote:

> Far from laying down a general prohibition to the effect that States may not extend the application of their laws and the jurisdiction of their courts to persons, property and acts outside their territory, it leaves them in this respect a wide measure of discretion which is only limited in certain cases by prohibitive rules; as regards other cases, every State remains free to adopt the principles which it regards as best and most suitable.[30]

The Court concluded that "all that can be required of a State is that it should not overstep the limits which international law places upon its jurisdiction; within these limits, its title to exercise jurisdiction rests in its sovereignty."[31]

When considering the "limits which international law places" on a state's exercise of jurisdiction, reference typically is made to "principles" of jurisdiction that international law has come to accept in one form or another. The five principles are known as: (1) the territoriality principle; (2) the nationality principle; (3) the passive personality principle; (4) the protective principle; and (5) the universality principle. Each is discussed in turn.

---

29. 1927 P.C.I.J. (ser. A) No. 10 (Sept. 7).

30. *Id.* at 19.

31. *Id.*

Territoriality Principle

A state has absolute (but not exclusive) power to regulate conduct that occurs within its own territory. It may also act to affect interests in a *res* or the status of persons located within its territory.[32] This "territoriality principle" reflects the global community's recognition that without the power to control acts or things located in its territory, a state could not exist. Further, other states must be able to rely on that power so as to protect their rights and interests abroad. Thus, the territoriality principle in part serves to distribute competence among members of the international community.[33]

The territoriality principle acknowledges a state's ability to regulate persons or things from abroad that come within the state's territory. In *Spector v. Norwegian Cruise Line, Ltd.*,[34] the U.S. Supreme Court found that Title III of the American with Disabilities Act could be applied to foreign-flag cruise ships that enter U.S. territorial or internal waters. At the same time, in construing a provision of the statute requiring the removal of certain barriers to the disabled where "readily achievable," the Court concluded that such removal was not readily achievable if it placed the vessel in non-compliance with the International Convention for the Safety of Life at Sea,[35] which requires certain structural features on vessels. Thus, in considering the exercise of U.S. territorial jurisdiction, the Court balanced competing interests; the interests of the United States in regulating matters within its territory, with the interests in establishing a global system for the safety of vessels worldwide.

In addition, a state has jurisdiction to regulate conduct that occurs outside its territory that has, or is intended to have, substantial effects *within* its territory. This "objective territoriality" principle recognizes that, without the authority to regulate foreign acts that have national effects, a state could not fully protect its nationals and residents. Justice Oliver Wendell Holmes, Jr., stated:

> Acts done outside a jurisdiction, but intended to produce and producing effects within it, justify a State in punishing the cause of the harm as if he had been present at the effect, if the State should succeed in getting him within its power.[36]

The most controversial application of the "objective territoriality" principle is its use to regulate foreign activities that have, or threaten to have, adverse economic effects within the regulating

---

32. *See* 1 RESTATEMENT (THIRD) OF THE FOREIGN RELATIONS LAW OF THE UNITED STATES § 402(1) (1987) [hereinafter RESTATEMENT (THIRD)].

33. *See* Island of Palmas (Neth. v. U.S.), 2 R.I.A.A. 829, 839 (1928).

34. 545 U.S. 119 (2005).

35. Nov. 1, 1974, 1184 U.N.T.S. 276, 32 U.S.T. 47.

36. Strassheim v. Daily, 221 U.S. 280, 285 (1911).

state. For instance, in *United States v. Aluminum Co. of America*,[37] the Second Circuit ruled that the Sherman Antitrust Act applied to a foreign agreement intended to affect the U.S. market, even though the agreement was solely between foreign companies and performed entirely on foreign soil. In the 1982 Foreign Trade Antitrust Improvements Act, Congress confirmed that the Sherman Antitrust Act should not apply to conduct involving trade or commerce with foreign nations unless that conduct significantly harms U.S. imports or exports, or U.S. domestic commerce.[38] As such, price-fixing conduct abroad that significantly affects consumers inside the United States may be prosecuted in U.S. courts, yet similar conduct that solely affects consumers outside the United States may not.[39]

Nationality Principle

A state may exercise jurisdiction over its nationals and over their conduct even when they are physically outside the state's territory. Thus, the Foreign Corrupt Practices Act[40] expressly criminalizes certain actions by U.S. nationals and corporations even if the acts occur and only have effects abroad. The justifications for this principle are that: (1) the national owes allegiance to his or her state no matter where he or she is located; (2) states have certain responsibilities to one another for the conduct of their nationals; and (3) each state has an interest in the well-being of its nationals while they are abroad.[41]

As noted in Chapter 2(D), each state has the right to determine how a person may acquire its nationality. That nationality, however, must be based on a genuine link between the state asserting jurisdiction and the person or entity over whom jurisdiction is asserted.

A corporation is deemed to have the nationality of the state where it is incorporated.[42] Under the nationality principle, the connection provided by the act of creation is sufficient to permit a state to exercise jurisdiction over a corporation. For a state to treat a corporation *not* incorporated under its laws as its national, there must be some other genuine link between the state and the corporation. Among such links are the nationality of owners of a

---

37. 148 F.2d 416 (2d Cir. 1945).

38. *See* 15 U.S.C. § 6a (2006).

39. *See F. Hoffman–La Roche Ltd.*, *supra* note 27; *see generally* Austen L. Parrish, *The Effects Test: Extraterritoriality's Fifth Business*, 61 VAND. L. REV. 1455 (2008).

40. 15 U.S.C. §§ 78a, 78dd–1–78dd–3, 78ff (2006).

41. *See generally* Geoffrey Watson, *Offenders Abroad: The Case for Nationality–Based Criminal Jurisdiction*, 17 YALE J. INT'L L. 41 (1992).

42. *See* Barcelona Traction, Light & Power Co. (Belg. v. Spain), 1970 I.C.J. 3, 168 (Feb. 5).

substantial number of the corporation's shares, the location of the corporate management office (called the *siège social* or corporate seat in some continental corporate codes), or the location of a principal place of business. In certain circumstances (*e.g.* where the corporation is in fact only a corporate shell), a corporation may be treated as having the nationality of its shareholders for limited purposes. In other instances, a state may exercise jurisdiction over foreign branches of nationally organized corporations by virtue of its jurisdiction over the parent or home office, as long as doing so is reasonable. In general, the state may lift the corporate veil only in limited circumstances.[43]

Vessels have the nationality of the state in which they are registered and whose flag they fly regardless of the owner's nationality. Some states, such as Liberia and Panama, permit vessel registry with few requirements, except the payment of a fee. These "flags of convenience" have been challenged on the grounds that a "genuine link" must exist between the ship and the state whose flag it flies.[44] U.S. courts have held that U.S. maritime regulatory legislation applies to ships registered in foreign states when those ships have significant contacts with the United States.[45] The same general rules that determine the nationality of ocean vessels apply to aircraft under the Convention on International Civil Aviation.[46]

Passive Personality Principle

In limited circumstances, a state may assert the authority to exercise jurisdiction over acts committed abroad when they injure a national of the state (the "passive personality" principle). For example, Congress has enacted a statute making it a criminal offense for a foreigner to take a U.S. national hostage outside the United States[47] and a statute criminalizing terrorist killings of U.S. nationals abroad.[48] Further, Congress created a civil cause of action for U.S. nationals to recover treble damages for injuries from such acts.[49] Under the Torture Victim Protection Act (TVPA), Congress criminalized the extrajudicial killing and torture by foreign government officials of any individual, including U.S. nationals.[50]

This "passive personality" principle, however, has not been extended to ordinary crimes and torts that occur abroad. The Ninth Circuit Court of Appeals has stated:

43. *See* 1 RESTATEMENT (THIRD), *supra* note 32, §§ 211, 213, 403(2), 414(1) (and associated comments).

44. *See* U.N. Convention on the Law of the Sea art. 91, Dec. 10, 1982, S. TREATY DOC. NO. 103–39 (1994), 1833 U.N.T.S. 3.

45. *See* Hellenic Lines, Ltd. v. Rhoditis, 398 U.S. 306 (1970).

46. Dec. 7, 1944, 61 Stat. 1180, 15 U.N.T.S. 295.

47. *See* 18 U.S.C. § 1203 (2006).

48. *See* 18 U.S.C. § 2332 (2006).

49. *See* 18 U.S.C. § 2333 (2006).

50. *See* 28 U.S.C. § 1350 note (2006).

In general, this principle has not been accepted as a sufficient basis for extraterritorial jurisdiction for ordinary torts and crimes.... [T]he passive personality principle has become increasingly accepted as an appropriate basis for extraterritoriality when applied to terrorist activities and organized attacks on a state's nationals because of the victim's nationality.[51]

Thus, in *United States v. Columba–Colella*, a car was stolen in the United States and taken to Mexico. The thief arranged to sell the car through the defendant, who had no connection with the United States of any kind. Before the sale could be completed, the defendant was arrested and taken to the United States for trial. The Fifth Circuit Court of Appeals dismissed the charge, stating:

There is no question, of course that [the defendant's] conduct somehow affected a United States citizen. Had he been successful in his enterprise, he would have prevented the stolen car from finding its way back to its owner. But that an act affects the citizen of a state [in this way] is not a sufficient basis for that state to assert jurisdiction over the act. It is difficult to distinguish the present case from one in which the defendant had attempted not to fence a stolen car but instead to pick the pockets of American tourists in Acapulco.[52]

For the United States, one interesting application of the passive personality principle concerns crimes against U.S. nationals aboard foreign vessels on the high seas. Federal criminal statutes typically apply not only within U.S. territory but also within the "special maritime and territorial jurisdiction" of the United States (referred to *infra*). The Violent Crime Control and Law Enforcement Act of 1994[53] extended this "special maritime jurisdiction" to include, "[t]o the extent permitted by international law, any foreign vessel during a voyage having a scheduled departure from or arrival in the United States with respect to an offense committed by or against a national of the United States."[54] In *United States v. Roberts*,[55] a foreign national allegedly accosted a U.S. national on a Liberian-flagged cruise ship on the high seas. The ship began and ended its cruise in the United States. The district court found that it had jurisdiction over the case because various factors—the incident occurred on the high seas, the vessel had departed on its cruise from the United States, the stock of the company owning the vessel was traded in the United States, and the company's corpo-

---

51. United States v. Vasquez–Velasco, 15 F.3d 833, 841 n.7 (9th Cir. 1994); *see generally* Geoffrey Watson, *The Passive Personality Principle*, 28 TEX. INT'L L.J. 1 (1993).

52. United States v. Columba–Colella, 604 F.2d 356, 360 (5th Cir. 1979).

53. Pub. L. No. 103–322, § 120002, 108 Stat. 1796, 2021 (1994).

54. 18 U.S.C. § 7(8) (2006).

55. 1 F. Supp. 2d 601 (E.D. La. 1998).

rate officers were located in the United States—all indicated that it would not infringe upon the sovereignty of another nation for the United States to assert passive personality jurisdiction.[56]

Protective Principle

A state may exercise jurisdiction over conduct outside its territory that threatens its security (such as counterfeiting the state's money or fabricating its visa documents), so long as that conduct is generally recognized as criminal by states in the international community.[57]

The protective principle has had limited use in the United States, perhaps because of a common law preference for tying jurisdiction to territorial relationships. Nevertheless, U.S. courts have invoked the protective principle, for example, to punish perjury abroad before a U.S. consular officer,[58] to punish falsification of official U.S. documents abroad,[59] and to punish foreign conspiracies to smuggle drugs into the United States.[60] In the example discussed at the beginning of this chapter regarding the terrorist acts against two U.S. embassies, the court viewed the application of U.S. criminal law to those acts as mostly related to the protective principle.[61]

Universality Principle

The Basic Principle. A state may exercise jurisdiction over conduct outside its territory if that conduct is universally dangerous to states and their nationals. The justification for this principle is that states must be permitted to punish such acts wherever they may occur as a means of protecting the global community as a whole, even absent a link between the state and the parties or acts in question. "Universal jurisdiction" traditionally was asserted over the crime of piracy on the high seas and over persons engaging in the slave trade. Hence, the U.S. piracy statute provides that "[w]hoever, on the high seas, commits the crime of piracy as defined by the law of nations, and is afterwards brought into or found in the United States, shall be imprisoned for life."[62]

There is growing support for the proposition that perpetrators of the crimes of piracy, slavery, torture, genocide, war crimes, and

56. For a similar case, see United States v. Neil, 312 F.3d 419 (9th Cir. 2002).

57. *See generally* IAIN CAMERON, THE PROTECTIVE PRINCIPLE OF INTERNATIONAL CRIMINAL JURISDICTION (1994).

58. *See, e.g.,* United States v. Pizzarusso, 388 F.2d 8 (2d Cir. 1968).

59. *See, e.g.,* United States v. Birch, 470 F.2d 808 (4th Cir. 1972).

60. *See, e.g.,* United States v. Cardales, 168 F.3d 548 (1st Cir. 1999); United States v. Romero–Galue, 757 F.2d 1147 (11th Cir. 1985); United States v. Gonzalez, 776 F.2d 931 (11th Cir. 1985); Rivard v. United States, 375 F.2d 882 (5th Cir. 1967).

61. *See Bin Laden, supra* note 21, at 193–97.

62. 18 U.S.C. § 1651 (2006).

crimes against humanity are exposed to the possibility of the exercise of jurisdiction by any state based on the universality principle.[63] In addition, various terrorist acts may be subject to such jurisdiction pursuant to international treaties and perhaps even customary international law.[64] These agreements provide that parties are obligated either to extradite offenders or submit them to prosecution, even though such offenses are not committed within the party's territory and do not involve its nationals. U.S. statutes such as the Alien Tort Statute[65] and the TVPA[66] provide for civil actions in U.S. courts for egregious acts abroad by a non-U.S. national against a non-U.S. national.

A close analysis of the national laws of states worldwide, however, indicates that very few actually have national laws that assert jurisdiction solely on the basis of the universality principle.[67] For instance, in 1987 the United States enacted a statute criminalizing genocide, yet the statute was limited to offenses that occur in the United States (territoriality jurisdiction) or that are committed by U.S. nationals (nationality jurisdiction).[68] Only in 2007 did the United States amend the statute so as to cover acts committed outside the United States by a non-U.S. national, provided the person is a U.S. resident or at least present in the United States at the time of the prosecution.[69] Likewise, the United States has adopted a statute that criminalizes war crimes, but that statute is limited to offenses committed by or against U.S. military personnel or nationals (nationality or passive personality jurisdiction).[70] States appear reluctant to invoke universal jurisdiction, perhaps for fear that their courts will become a magnet for actions seeking redress for atrocities committed worldwide.

63. *See* THE PRINCETON PRINCIPLES ON UNIVERSAL JURISDICTION, princpl. 2 (2001); *see also* KATHRYN SIKKINK, THE JUSTICE CASCADE: HOW HUMAN RIGHTS PROSECUTIONS ARE CHANGING WORLD POLITICS (2011); Máximo Langer, *The Diplomacy of Universal Jurisdiction: The Political Branches and the Transnational Prosecution of International Crimes*, 105 AM. J. INT'L L. 1 (2011); UNIVERSAL JURISDICTION NATIONAL COURTS AND THE PROSECUTION OF SERIOUS CRIMES UNDER INTERNATIONAL LAW (Stephen Macedo ed., 2006); Arrest Warrant of 11 April 2000 (D.R.C. v. Belg.), 2002 I.C.J. 3, 63 (Feb. 14) (joint separate opinion of Judges Higgins, Kooijmans and Buergenthal); *id.*, 2002 I.C.J. 3, 137 (dissenting opinion of Judge *ad hoc* Van den Wyngaert).

64. *See, e.g.,* Convention for the Suppression of Unlawful Seizure of Aircraft, Dec. 16, 1970, 22 U.S.T. 1641, 860 U.N.T.S. 105; Convention for the Suppression of Unlawful Acts Against the Safety of Civil Aviation, Sept. 23, 1971, 24 U.S.T. 565, 974 U.N.T.S. 177; Convention on the Prevention and Punishment of Crimes Against Internationally Protected Persons, Including Diplomatic Agents, Dec. 14, 1973, 28 U.S.T. 1975, 1035 U.N.T.S. 167.

65. 28 U.S.C. § 1350 (2006).

66. *Supra* note 50.

67. *See* M. Cherif Bassiouni, *Universal Jurisdiction for International Crimes: Historical Perspectives and Contemporary Practice*, 42 VA. J. INT'L L. 81, 136–51 (2001).

68. *See* 18 U.S.C. § 1091(d) (2006).

69. Genocide Accountability Act of 2007, Pub. L. No. 110–151, 121 Stat. 1821.

70. *See* 18 U.S.C. § 2441(b) (2006).

Example: 1993 Belgian Statute. A recent example of the difficulty in adopting national laws that provide for universal jurisdiction may be seen with respect to Belgium. On June 16, 1993, Belgium passed the "Law Relative to the Repression of Serious Violations of the International Conventions of Geneva of August 12, 1949, and of the Protocols I and II of June 8, 1977."[71] The law allowed an individual (whether Belgian or not) to file a criminal complaint in a Belgian court against any person for international crimes in violation of the four 1949 Geneva Conventions and their additional protocols, even if the acts were committed by non-Belgians, against non-Belgians, and outside of Belgium. After a complaint had been filed, a magistrate investigated it and could issue a warrant for the arrest of the accused. In 1999, the law was amended to cover genocide and crimes against humanity.[72] The 1999 amendment provided that no immunity based on "official capacity" would preclude application of the law.

The Belgian law was widely recognized as the most far-reaching example of a state exercising "universal jurisdiction." During the first decade of its existence, some thirty legal complaints were filed against a variety of government officials worldwide, including against Rwandans for genocide, General Augusto Pinochet of Chile, Cuban President Fidel Castro, Iraqi President Saddam Hussein, Palestinian leader Yasser Arafat, and Israeli Prime Minister Ariel Sharon. In the case against Sharon—for his alleged role as Israeli defense minister in the 1982 massacre of refugees by Christian militiamen in camps outside Beirut—the Belgian Supreme Court held that official immunity protects a prime minister from prosecution while serving in office, but does not protect him after he leaves office. Moreover, the Supreme Court (reversing an earlier intermediate court ruling to the contrary) found that a prosecution may proceed against, and international arrest warrants may be issued for, a defendant located outside of Belgium.[73]

Several criminal complaints were filed against U.S. officials under the Belgian law. Among these complaints was one filed in March 2003 against former President George H. W. Bush and several of his senior advisers for their alleged roles in a U.S. attack on a Baghdad bunker in February 1991. After the United States

---

71. *See* Loi du 16 juin 1993 relative à la répression des infractions graves aux Conventions internationales de Genève du 12 août 1949 et aux Protocoles I et II du 8 juin 1977, Moniteur Belge 17751 (Aug. 5, 1993), *reprinted in* Eric David, *La Loi Belge sur Les Crime de Guerre*, 28 Rev. Belge de Droit Int'l 668, 680 (1995).

72. Loi relative à la répression des violations graves de droit international humanitaire, Moniteur Belge 9286 (Mar. 23, 1999). The amended law was reproduced in translation at 38 I.L.M. 918 (1999).

73. *See* H.S.A. v. S.A., Cour de Cassation, No. P. 02.1139.F/1 (Feb. 12, 2003), *translated and reprinted in* 42 I.L.M. 596 (2003).

complained, Belgium amended the law to provide exclusive discretion to a Belgian federal prosecutor as to whether to prosecute a criminal complaint in certain situations: (1) when the act at issue was not committed on Belgian territory; (2) when the alleged offender was not Belgian or was not located in Belgium; and (3) when the victim was not Belgian or had not resided in Belgium for at least three years.[74] The new amendment also provided that the federal prosecutor should refrain from prosecuting a complaint when, out of respect for Belgium's international obligations, the matter is better suited for either an international tribunal or another national tribunal (on the assumption that such tribunal is competent, independent, impartial, and fair). Thus, if a complaint involved no direct link to Belgium and concerned officials of a democratic state (such as the United States), it was expected that the complaint would be referred to that state.

Nevertheless, in May 2003, several Iraqi and Jordanian nationals filed a criminal complaint under the Belgian statute against a U.S. general (Tommy Franks) for alleged war crimes in commanding U.S. forces during the invasion of Iraq in March 2003. Although the complaint was immediately referred by Belgian authorities to the United States for disposition, U.S. officials expressed outrage at the commencement of such an action. Moreover, U.S. officials threatened that the existence of the Belgian law could have severe repercussions on Belgium's status as the host country of the North Atlantic Treaty Organization (NATO).

After another criminal complaint was filed in June against President George W. Bush and U.K. Prime Minister Tony Blair for the use of force against Iraq and Afghanistan, Belgium replaced the 1993 law with one of much narrower jurisdictional scope.[75] The new law limited the filing of criminal complaints to situations in which the suspect is either a Belgian national or residing in Belgium, or in which the victim is either a Belgian national or has resided in Belgium for at least three years. Once a criminal complaint is filed, a Belgian federal prosecutor retains sole and unreviewable discretion to initiate a prosecution, and may decline to do so (based on "respect for Belgium's international obligations") when there is an alternative international or national tribunal available. Further, the law precludes the filing of complaints against sitting heads of state and foreign ministers, as well as against other individuals enjoying immunity in Belgium based on treaties. Finally, the law prohibits enforcement of a prosecution against any person staying

---

74. *See* Loi modifiant la loi du 16 juin 1993 relative à la répression des violations graves du droit international humanitaire et l'article 144ter du Code judiciaire, Moniteur Belge 24846 (May 7, 2003).

75. *See* Loi relative aux violations graves du droit international humanitaire, Moniteur Belge 40506 (Aug. 7, 2003).

in Belgium either at the official invitation of Belgian authorities or in connection with an international organization based in Belgium and with which Belgium has entered into a headquarters agreement (such as NATO). In September 2003, because of the new changes in the law, the Belgian Supreme Court dismissed all pending cases against U.S. officials.

Combinations of Jurisdictional Principles

More than one jurisdictional "principle" may apply in certain cases. For instance, in *United States v. King*,[76] the defendants were prosecuted in the United States under a U.S. law that prohibited the distribution of heroin, even though the distribution occurred in Japan. The Ninth Circuit found that the application of the law to conduct that occurred in Japan was acceptable under international law based both on the territorial principle (the heroin was intended for importation into the United States and thus would have effects in the United States) and on the nationality principle (the defendants were U.S. nationals). In *Chua Han Mow v. United States*,[77] the Ninth Circuit found on similar facts (for conduct occurring in Malaysia by a Malaysian national) that both the territoriality principle and the protective principle applied.

Discretion to Exercise Permissible Jurisdiction

Even if international law permits the exercise of jurisdiction, it is wholly within the discretion of the state whether to do so. For instance, international law permits a state to enact legislation prohibiting its nationals from committing crimes abroad (based on the nationality principle), and many states have enacted such laws. However, U.S. criminal law is principally regulated by the laws of the several states (not federal law), which in most instances are not interpreted by state courts as applying outside the territory of the state, let alone outside the United States. Consequently, when a U.S. national commits a serious crime abroad, such as murder, normally there are no means for prosecuting that person in the United States, even though international law permits the United States to do so. In short, do not confuse the existence of the five principles as *in fact* establishing jurisdiction by a particular state over particular persons or conduct abroad; national laws determine whether the state has actually exercised the discretion permitted to it under international law.

Reasonableness of Exercising Jurisdiction

Even if a state has enacted a statute exercising jurisdiction under one of the principles discussed above, the exercise of jurisdic-

---

76. 552 F.2d 833 (9th Cir. 1976).   **77.** 730 F.2d 1308 (9th Cir. 1984).

tion is still unlawful under international law if it is *unreasonable*. According to the *Restatement (Third)*, various factors must be balanced in determining whether the regulation by a state over a person or activity is unreasonable, such as "the existence of justified expectations that might be protected or hurt by the regulation," "the extent to which another state may have an interest in regulating the activity," or "the likelihood of conflict with regulation by another state."[78]

This "balancing" test was called into question by the U.S. Supreme Court in *Hartford Fire Insurance Co. v. California*.[79] In that case, the Court upheld the application of the Sherman Antitrust Act to conduct by insurers located in the United Kingdom. In doing so, the Court did not engage in the type of analysis envisaged in the *Restatement (Third)*. Rather, the Court simply asked whether there was any direct conflict between U.S. and U.K. law.[80] Finding that U.K. law did not expressly prohibit companies in the U.K. from abiding by U.S. standards of antitrust law, the Court concluded that the application of U.S. law was permissible. In his dissent, Justice Scalia criticized the majority for not considering the factors outlined in the *Restatement (Third)*.[81]

Yet more recently, in *F. Hoffman LaRoche Limited*, the Supreme Court cited approvingly to the *Restatement (Third)* balancing factors in striking down the application of U.S. antitrust laws to certain defendants. In that case, the Court found unreasonable the application of U.S. antitrust laws to foreign conduct that causes foreign harm, where the plaintiff's claim arises solely from that harm. The Court found that the "application of those laws creates a serious risk of interference with a foreign nation's ability independently to regulate its own commercial affairs" and "the justification for that interference seems insubstantial."[82]

The concept of reasonableness is closely allied to the notion of comity among states. Comity is "the recognition which one nation allows within its territory to the legislative, executive or judicial acts of another nation, having due regard both to international duty and convenience, and to the rights of its own citizens or of other persons who are under the protection of its laws."[83] The practical necessity of arriving at a principled method for such accommodation was stated by Justice Jackson in *Lauritzen v.*

---

78. 1 Restatement (Third), *supra* note 32, § 403(2)(d), (g) & (h); *see* Timberlane Lumber Co. v. Bank of Am., 549 F.2d 597 (9th Cir. 1976).

79. 509 U.S. 764 (1993).

80. *Id.* at 798–799.

81. *Id.* at 814–815.

82. *F. Hoffman–LaRoche Ltd.*, *supra* note 27, at 2367.

83. Hilton v. Guyot, 159 U.S. 113, 164 (1895) (refusing to enforce a French judgment on grounds that France did not enforce U.S. judgments).

Larsen, where he distinguished between the existence of national power and the wisdom of its exercise.

> [International law] aims at stability and order through usages which considerations of comity, reciprocity and long-range interest have developed to define the domain which each nation will claim as its own. . . . [I]n dealing with international commerce we cannot be unmindful of the necessity for mutual forbearance if retaliations are to be avoided; nor should we forget that any contact which we hold sufficient to warrant application of our law to a foreign transaction will logically be as strong a warrant for a foreign country to apply its law to an American transaction.[84]

Comity is most accurately characterized as a golden rule among nations—each state should respect the laws, policies, and interests of others as it would have others respect their own in similar circumstances. In the United States, courts have resorted to the comity principle as a rationale for refusing to apply U.S. law to foreign persons or events in situations where concurrent jurisdiction exists and for refusing to give effect to a foreign state's law, if that state breached its duty of comity to the United States.

A recent example of the reasonableness standard in U.S. courts concerns the "Prosecutorial Remedies and Other Tools to End the Exploitation of Children Today Act of 2003" (also referred to as the "PROTECT Act").[85] Among other things, the PROTECT Act provides that any person who enters the United States, as well as any U.S. national or permanent resident who travels abroad, for the purpose of engaging in sexual acts with children (persons under the age of eighteen) can be prosecuted in the United States for such acts, and fined or imprisoned for up to thirty years.

In a speech to the U.N. General Assembly in September 2003, President Bush declared that "governments that tolerate this trade are tolerating a form of slavery."[86] The following day, the U.S. government announced that it had initiated the first prosecution under the PROTECT Act. A U.S. national, Michael Clark Lewis, was indicted in Seattle on charges of engaging in illicit sexual conduct in Cambodia with two boys, ages ten and thirteen. Clark reportedly admitted upon arrest that he had been engaging in such acts in Cambodia for several years and that he normally paid the children two dollars for each act.

In March 2004, Clark pled guilty to the charges, but reserved the right to challenge the legality of the statute. Clark then

84. 345 U.S. 571, 582 (1953).

85. Pub. L. No. 108–21, 117 Stat. 650 (2003) (to be codified in scattered sections of 18 U.S.C.).

86. Address to the U.N. General Assembly, 39 WEEKLY COMP. PRES. DOC. 1256, 1260 (Sept. 23, 2003).

challenged the statute on the grounds that it was not a proper exercise of extraterritorial jurisdiction and that the statute was unreasonable under international law. In rejecting the first of these grounds, the district court found that application of the statute extraterritorially could be based on the "nationality principle" or, alternatively, on the "universality principle" since "the sexual abuse of children criminalized by this statute is universally condemned."[87] In rejecting the second ground, the court accepted that "[e]ven if principles of international law serve as bases for extraterritorial application of a law, international law also requires that such application of the law be reasonable."[88] However, in this instance, the district court found application of the statute to be reasonable.

> Although there is only a minimal link between the activity sought to be regulated by this statute and the territory of the United States, several ... factors favor a finding of reasonableness here. There is a strong connection between the United States and its citizens (and resident aliens) who commit the illicit activity. The prohibition against sexual activity with young children is considered desirable and is widely accepted. There is very little likelihood of conflict with regulation by other states.[89]

The Ninth Circuit Court of Appeals agreed, noting further that "Clark himself stated to a U.S. official in Cambodia that he 'wanted to return to the United States' because he saw people dying in the Cambodian prison... Having been saved from immediate prosecution in Cambodia, it is somewhat ironic that he now challenges the law [as unreasonable] in a United States court."[90]

Concurrent Jurisdiction

International law recognizes that more than one state may have jurisdiction over a particular person or event. Concurrent jurisdiction may exist where multiple states have legitimate interests in regulating the same events or persons. Thus, if a Mexican terrorist murders a U.S. national in Canada, at least three states might have national laws extending jurisdiction over the murder. Canada no doubt would have a statute criminalizing murder within its territory (territoriality principle); the United States might criminalize it as an act of terrorism against its nationals abroad (passive personality principle); and Mexico could have a statute criminalizing murder by its nationals abroad (nationality principle). Most

87. United States v. Clark, 315 F.Supp.2d 1127, 1131 (W.D. Wash. 2004).

88. *Id.* at 1132.

89. *Id.*

90. United States v. Clark, 435 F.3d 1100, 1107 (9th Cir. 2006).

U.S. courts resort to comity in determining how to balance the exercise of concurrent authority in such circumstances.

C. Jurisdiction to Prescribe, Adjudicate, and Enforce

Thus far, this chapter has focused on the exercise of a state's jurisdiction by means of a statute. Yet states can exercise jurisdiction in different ways and, depending on what aspect of jurisdiction is being exercised, the limitations under international law may differ. The *Restatement (Third)* adopts a tri-partite characterization—jurisdiction to prescribe, jurisdiction to adjudicate, and jurisdiction to enforce.

Jurisdiction to Prescribe

Section 401(a) of the *Restatement (Third)* asserts that, under international law, a state is subject to limitations on its "jurisdiction to prescribe, *i.e.*, to make its law applicable to the activities, relations, or status of persons, or the interests of persons in things, whether by legislation, by executive act or order, by administrative rule or regulation, or by determination of a court." U.S. lawyers commonly refer to this type of jurisdiction as *subject matter jurisdiction*. As the *Restatement (Third)* notes, a state might seek to regulate conduct extraterritorially through enactment of a statute, rule, or regulation, or even extension of the law through judicial decision. Regardless of the form, the exercise of jurisdiction must fit within one of the five "principles" and must be reasonable, as discussed in Section B above.

Jurisdiction to Adjudicate

Section 401(b) of the *Restatement (Third)* asserts that, under international law, a state is subject to limitations on its "jurisdiction to adjudicate, *i.e.*, to subject persons or things to the process of its court or administrative tribunals, whether in civil or in criminal proceedings, whether or not the state is a party to the proceedings." U.S. lawyers commonly refer to this type of jurisdiction as *personal jurisdiction*. International law requires that a state exercise jurisdiction to adjudicate only in situations where it is reasonable to do so. The standard of reasonableness is not the same as the standard applied for jurisdiction to prescribe. It is entirely possible that international law would regard as reasonable the exercise by a state of subject matter jurisdiction over a person, yet not regard as reasonable the exercise of personal jurisdiction over that person (and vice versa).

For this type of jurisdiction, international law examines whether there is a particular link between the state and the person or thing when jurisdiction is asserted. Relevant links include: (1) whether the person or thing is present in the territory of the state;

(2) whether the person is a national of, or domiciled or resident in, the state; and (3) whether the person, natural or juridical, has consented to the exercise of jurisdiction or has regularly carried on business in the state.[91]

U.S. lawyers are familiar with these concepts from studying the "minimum contacts" necessary when according due process to defendants under the U.S. Constitution.[92] Typically, U.S. courts will (1) consider whether the plaintiff's claim arises out of or is related to the defendant's conduct within the forum state; (2) assess the defendant's contacts with the forum state to determine whether they constitute purposeful activity, such that being haled into court would be foreseeable; and (3) look at the "forum state's interest in adjudicating the dispute; the plaintiff's interest in obtaining convenient and effective relief, at least when that interest is not adequately protected by the plaintiff's power to choose the forum; the interstate judicial system's interest in obtaining the most efficient resolution of controversies; and the shared interest of the several States in furthering fundamental substantive social policies."[93]

Jurisdiction to Enforce

Section 401(c) of the *Restatement (Third)* asserts that, under international law, a state is subject to limitations on its "jurisdiction to enforce, *i.e.*, to induce or compel compliance or to punish noncompliance with its laws or regulations, whether through courts or by use of executive, administrative, police or other non-judicial action." Enforcement measures include ordering the production of documents, criminal sanctions (fines or imprisonment), or sanctions for the failure to comply with a judicial or administrative order.

Generally, limitations set by international law provide that a state must first have jurisdiction to prescribe before the state seeks to enforce its law, whether done through its courts or otherwise (*e.g.*, through administrative or police action). Further, international law requires that a state only exercise jurisdiction to enforce in situations where it is reasonable to do so, measured in proportion to the violation. Finally, a state may only employ enforcement measures against a person located outside its territory if the person is given reasonable notice of the claims or charges against him, the person is given an opportunity to be heard, and enforcement is through a state's courts that have jurisdiction to adjudicate.[94] A

---

91. *See* 1 Restatement (Third), *supra* note 32, § 421.

92. *See, e.g.*, Int'l Shoe Co. v. Washington, 326 U.S. 310 (1945); Asahi Metal Indus. Co. v. Superior Court, 480 U.S. 102 (1987).

93. World–Wide Volkswagen Corp. v. Woodson, 444 U.S. 286, 292 (1980) (internal citations omitted).

94. *See* 1 Restatement (Third), *supra* note 32, § 431.

state's law enforcement officers may only exercise their functions in the territory of another state with that state's consent.[95]

When the United States seeks custody of an individual located abroad, normally it pursues the matter through bilateral channels with the foreign government in whose territory the individual is located. At present, the United States has a network of bilateral extradition treaties with foreign states which obligate those states to extradite individuals to the United States under certain circumstances (and vice versa).[96] On rare occasions, however, the United States has unilaterally seized a foreign national abroad and brought him to the United States. Generally, U.S. courts have not allowed a unilateral abduction to stand in the way of an otherwise lawful exercise of U.S. jurisdiction over the defendant, absent some express treaty prohibition to the contrary. For example, in *Ker v. Illinois*, the defendant was forcibly abducted from Peru by a private individual and brought to the United States, where he was tried and convicted for larceny. While there existed a U.S.-Peru extradition treaty, the U.S. Supreme Court found that there was no U.S. governmental involvement in the abduction and that Peru had not objected to the abduction. Consequently, the Court held that "such forcible abduction is no sufficient reason why the party should not answer when brought within the jurisdiction of the court which has the right to try him for an offence, and presents no valid objection to his trial in such court."[97]

In *United States v. Alvarez–Machain*, there also existed a U.S.-Mexico extradition treaty, yet this time the abduction from Mexico was conducted with U.S. government involvement (it was sponsored by the U.S. Drug Enforcement Administration) and was objected to by Mexico.[98] Even so, the Supreme Court found that the extradition treaty did not expressly prohibit such abduction and relevant norms of international law did not support inferring such a prohibition. Therefore, the Court found that the *Ker v. Illinois* rule applied: "The fact of respondent's forcible abduction does not therefore prohibit his trial in a court in the United States for violations of the criminal laws of the United States."[99]

The Court left open whether the abduction might constitute a violation of "general international law principles" and, if so, whether such violation should result in the executive branch returning the individual to Mexico as a matter separate from the treaty. The person abducted, Dr. Humberto Alvarez–Machain, was then tried in the United States for alleged participation in the torture and

95. *Id.*, § 432.

96. *See* Chapter 13(B).

97. Ker v. Illinois, 119 U.S. 436, 444 (1886).

98. *See* 31 I.L.M. 934 (1992).

99. United States v. Alvarez–Machain, 504 U.S. 655, 670 (1992).

murder of a U.S. drug enforcement agent, but the district court directed a verdict of acquittal based on a lack of evidence. Alvarez–Machain then sued one of his kidnappers (a former Mexican police officer named Francisco Sosa) under the Alien Tort Statute, but the Supreme Court found that a norm against temporary arbitrary arrest did not exist as a matter of either treaty or customary international law.[100]

100. *See* Chapter 7(C).

Further Reading

Paul Arnell, *Law Across Borders: The Extraterritorial Application of United Kingdom Law* (2011).

Iain Cameron, *The Protective Principle of International Criminal Jurisdiction* (1994).

Lawrence Collins, *Essays in International Litigation and the Conflict of Laws* (1993).

Benedetto Conforti, *International Law and the Role of Domestic Legal Systems* (1993).

Benedetto Conforti & Francesco Francioni, eds., *Enforcing International Human Rights in Domestic Courts* (1997).

James J. Fawcett, *Declining Jurisdiction in Private International Law: Reports to the XIVth Congress of the International Academy of Comparative Law* (1995).

Geoff Gilbert, *Transnational Fugitive Offenders in International Law: Extradition and Other Mechanisms* (1998).

Michael Hirst, *Jurisdiction and the Ambit of the Criminal Law* (2003).

Andreas F. Lowenfeld, *International Litigation and the Quest for Reasonableness: Essays in Private International Law* (1996).

Stephen Macedo, ed., *Universal Jurisdiction: National Courts and the Prosecution of Serious Crimes Under International Law* (2004).

Campbell McLachlan & Peter Nygh, eds., *Transnational Tort Litigation: Jurisdictional Principles* (1996).

Karl M. Meessen, ed., *Extraterritorial Jurisdiction in Theory and Practice* (1996).

Jannet A. Pontier & Edwige Burg, *EU Principles on Jurisdiction and Recognition and Enforcement of Judgments in Civil and Commercial Matters, According to the Case Law of the European Court of Justice* (2004).

Kal Raustiala, *Does the Constitution Follow the Flag? The Evolution of Territoriality in American Law* (2009).

W. Michael Reisman, ed., *Jurisdiction in International Law* (1999).

Luc Reydams, *Universal Jurisdiction: International and Municipal Legal Perspectives* (2003).

Cedric Ryngaert, *Jurisdiction in International Law* (2008).

Chapter 9

IMMUNITY FROM
NATIONAL JURISDICTION

The prior chapter discussed limitations imposed by international law on the right of a state to extend its jurisdiction over persons or events outside the state's territory. This chapter considers further limitations on the right of a state to exercise its jurisdiction over foreign governments and officials because of the immunities they enjoy. Parts A and B of this chapter consider the immunities accorded to *persons*, whether they be diplomatic or consular personnel of a state, employed by an international organization, or heads of state. Section C deals with the immunities enjoyed by *states* (or governments). Finally, Section D explains the "act of state doctrine," under which courts generally refrain from passing upon the validity of a foreign government's official acts taken within its territory.

A. Diplomatic and Consular Immunity

Purpose of the Immunity

A longstanding feature of the international legal system is the immunity of foreign diplomatic personnel and property from proceedings before national courts or other authorities. Diplomatic immunity contributes to friendly relations among states by allowing state representatives to perform their functions without the risk of being exposed to national proceedings, which in some instances might be a form of harassment or retaliation. In general, once a government (the "sending state") accredits a person as a diplomat to another government (the "receiving state"), that person is immune with respect to acts or omissions in the exercise of his or her official functions and in other circumstances in which lack of immunity would be inconsistent with diplomatic status. The diplomat is also immune from criminal process and most civil process in the receiving state.[1]

---

1. *See* 1 Restatement (Third) of the Foreign Relations Law of the United States § 464 (1987) [hereinafter Restatement (Third)].

Diplomatic Immunity

Customary international law governing the treatment of diplomats and diplomatic property is codified in the Vienna Convention on Diplomatic Relations (VCDR).[2] The VCDR has been ratified by 187 states as of 2011, including the United States. Under the VCDR, the "person" of the diplomat is inviolable and the receiving state has an affirmative duty to protect each diplomat from an attack "on his person, freedom or dignity."[3] The receiving state may neither arrest nor detain the diplomat, and the diplomat is immune from criminal laws as well as from most civil and administrative jurisdiction.[4] Diplomats may not be compelled to give evidence[5] and they are immune from personal service, most taxes, social security provisions, and customs duties and inspections.[6] Diplomatic immunity also extends to the diplomat's family members.[7]

Diplomats are not exempt from the jurisdiction of the sending state.[8] Moreover, the sending state may expressly waive the immunity of its diplomatic personnel. An example of such a waiver is the case of Gueorgui Makharadze, a diplomat posted at the Embassy of Georgia in Washington, D.C. In January 1997, Makharadze was speeding in his car when it crashed, killing a sixteen-year-old woman and injuring four others. After reviewing the facts, the U.S. attorney's office for the District of Columbia informed the U.S. Department of State that Makharadze could be charged with negligent homicide, involuntary manslaughter, or second-degree murder. Yet because of his diplomatic status, Makharadze was immune from U.S. criminal jurisdiction. Consequently, the U.S. Department of State requested the Georgian Embassy to waive Makharadze's immunity from criminal prosecution. The Georgian government did so under VCDR Article 32. In February 1997, Makharadze was charged with one count of involuntary manslaughter and four counts of aggravated assault. In October, he pled guilty and eventually was sentenced to a term of seven to twenty-one years in prison. After more than a year of discussions among the U.S. Department of Justice, the U.S. Department of State, and the government of Georgia, an agreement was reached for Makharadze to be sent back to Georgia to serve the remainder of his term.[9]

The VCDR also provides for the protection of diplomatic property. Under the VCDR, the physical premises of a diplomatic

---

2. Apr. 18, 1961, 23 U.S.T. 3227, 500 U.N.T.S. 95 [hereinafter VCDR].

3. *Id.*, art. 29.

4. *Id.*, art. 31(1).

5. *Id.*, art. 31(2).

6. *Id.*, arts. 33–36.

7. *Id.*, art. 37.

8. *Id.*, art. 31(4).

9. *See* SEAN D. MURPHY, UNITED STATES PRACTICE IN INTERNATIONAL LAW 1999–2001 86–88 (2002).

"mission" (meaning the embassy and other diplomatic buildings) are inviolable.[10] The receiving state has an affirmative duty to assist the sending state in obtaining all necessary facilities for the functioning of the mission, such as telephone service, and to protect those facilities once established.[11] Additionally, the receiving state has an affirmative obligation to allow the embassy freedom of movement and communication.[12] The archives of an embassy are also inviolable.[13] Yet, contrary to popular belief, the land upon which the mission sits is not the "sovereign territory" of the sending state; indeed, the sending state might not even own the land or buildings that comprise the mission. Unlike its sovereign territory, the sending state may only use the premises for diplomatic functions (it cannot place an army or a nuclear missile silo on the site) and must seek permission, for instance, to install and use wireless transmitters.[14]

An example of the protection accorded diplomatic premises is a case in which a landlord sued a diplomatic mission that had fallen into arrears on its rent. The Second Circuit Court of Appeals denied the landlord the right to evict the diplomatic mission from the premises because doing so would transgress the mission's inviolability. The court stated:

> Enforcement of an owner's common law right to obtain possession of its premises upon the tenant's non-payment of rent may not override an established rule of international law. Nor under the guise of local concepts of fairness may a court upset international treaty provisions to which the United States is a party. The reason for this is not a blind adherence to a rule of law in an international treaty, uncaring of justice at home, but that by upsetting existing treaty relationships American diplomats abroad may well be denied lawful protection of their lives and property to which they would otherwise be entitled.[15]

An authoritative statement of the international law on diplomatic immunity can be found in the *United States Diplomatic and Consular Staff in Tehran* case before the International Court of Justice.[16] The United States had accused the Iranian government of seizing its embassy and consulates in Iran and of unlawfully detaining U.S. diplomats and consular officers as hostages. In its opinion, the Court stressed repeatedly that Iran had clearly breached its obligations to the United States, under both international treaties

---

10. *See* VCDR, *supra* note 2, art. 22.

11. *Id.*, arts. 22 & 25.

12. *Id.*, arts. 26–27.

13. *Id.*, art. 24.

14. *Id.*, art. 27(1).

15. 767 Third Ave. Assoc. v. Zaire, 988 F.2d 295, 296 (2d Cir. 1993).

16. United States Diplomatic and Consular Staff in Tehran (U.S. v. Iran), 1980 I.C.J. 3 (May 24).

and general international law.[17] Further, the Court emphasized the fundamental importance of the rules on diplomatic immunity, which could not be altered by alleged extenuating circumstances, such as Iran's claims of past U.S. wrongdoing.[18]

Consular Immunity

Customary international law governing the treatment of consular officers and consulates is codified in the Vienna Convention on Consular Relations (VCCR).[19] The VCCR has been ratified by 173 states as of 2011, including the United States. It prohibits the arrest or detention of consular officers except for grave crimes and under court order.[20] Consular officers are not subject to judicial jurisdiction "in respect of acts performed in the exercise of consular functions," although they may be required to give evidence and their privileges may be waived by the sending state.[21] The VCCR also obligates states, when they arrest a foreign national, to notify the national of a right to have his or her consulate informed. The failure to notify foreigners of this right has been used to challenge their convictions and sentences in U.S. court, in the Inter–American Commission on Human Rights, and in cases before the International Court of Justice.[22]

International Civil Servant Immunity

Civil servants employed by international organizations typically enjoy a variety of immunities. They are usually exempted from alien registration acts and generally have personal immunities similar to those accorded diplomats and consuls. For the United Nations, the relevant multilateral treaty is the General Convention on the Privileges and Immunities of the United Nations.[23] The General Convention provides for immunity from personal arrest and protects papers, documents and courier bags. Further, since the U.N. headquarters is in the United States, certain privileges and immunities are accorded U.N. personnel pursuant to a bilateral U.S.-U.N. agreement.[24]

Such immunities are important for international civil servants to engage in their work free from threats and interference. For example, in March 1994 the Chairman of the U.N. Commission on Human Rights appointed a Malaysian national, Dato' Param Cumaraswamy, as Special Rapporteur on the Independence of Judges

---

17. *Id.* at 30–31, 37–41.

18. *Id.* at 41–42.

19. Apr. 24, 1963, 21 U.S.T. 77, 596 U.N.T.S. 261.

20. *Id.*, art. 41.

21. *Id.*, arts. 43–45; *see* 1 RESTATEMENT (THIRD), *supra* note 1, § 465.

22. *See* Chapter 4(E).

23. Feb. 13, 1946, 21 U.S.T. 1418, 1 U.N.T.S. 15.

24. Privileges and immunities of the United Nations are discussed in greater detail in Chapter 2(B).

and Lawyers. The commission charged the special rapporteur with investigating, reporting, and making recommendations concerning allegations of attacks on the independence of judges, lawyers, and court officials worldwide. As part of this mandate, Cumaraswamy initiated an investigation into alleged judicial dependence in numerous states, including Malaysia. In November 1995, Cumaraswamy's views regarding the independence of Malaysian judges were quoted in a British magazine. Thereafter, several law suits were filed by Malaysian nationals against Cumaraswamy in Malaysian courts alleging defamation and seeking compensation.

The U.N. secretary-general informed the government of Malaysia that Cumaraswamy's statements were made in the course of his mission, which ensured his immunity from legal process in Malaysian courts. Nevertheless, Cumaraswamy's claim of immunity was rejected by those courts. In August 1998, the U.N. Economic and Social Council requested an advisory opinion on the matter from the International Court of Justice. The Court determined that the secretary-general had correctly found that Cumaraswamy, when providing the interview, was acting in the performance of his mission as special rapporteur, and was therefore immune from legal process under the General Convention. Further, the Court held that Malaysia had failed in its obligation under both the U.N. Charter and the General Convention to inform its courts of the position taken by the secretary-general.[25]

U.S. Statutory Law

The United States has enacted the VCDR into federal statutory law,[26] which extends the privileges and immunities of the convention to *all* diplomats regardless of whether the sending state is a convention party. Under the statute, the president may, on the basis of reciprocity, specify privileges and immunities for diplomats which are either more or less favorable than those specified in the VCDR. In addition, the United States may also require diplomatic missions to insure themselves against liability for the benefit of parties injured by diplomats. Purchasing liability insurance does not constitute a waiver of immunity under the VCDR.[27] (In addition to immunities, attacking a diplomat is a federal criminal offense in the United States, pursuant to a statute[28] that implements the Convention on the Prevention and Punishment of Crimes Against Internationally Protected Persons, Including Diplomatic Agents.[29])

---

25. *See* Advisory Opinion on Difference Relating to Immunity from Legal Process of a Special Rapporteur of the Commission on Human Rights, 1999 I.C.J. 62 (Apr. 29).

26. *See* 22 U.S.C. § 254a–e (2006).

27. *Id.*, §§ 254b, 254c & 254e.

28. 18 U.S.C. § 112 (2006). Both of the above-mentioned statutes protect consular officials as well.

29. Dec. 14, 1973, 1035 U.N.T.S. 167, 13 I.L.M. 41.

Separately, the International Organizations Immunities Act[30] provides immunities for international civil servants and certain other persons in the United States.

B. Head-of-State Immunity

Separate from the immunities accorded to diplomats, consular officials, and international civil servants, international law has developed the concept of "head-of-state" immunity. In the United States, head-of-state immunity is a part of federal common law. When foreign officials are sued or prosecuted in U.S. courts, they will often raise head-of-state immunity as a defense.[31] U.S. courts typically defer to the executive branch in determining whether head-of-state immunity should be accorded.[32] Further, such immunity may be waived by an individual's government.[33]

For example, in 2000 several Zimbabwe nationals filed a civil action in federal court under the Torture Victim Protection Act[34] seeking compensatory and punitive damages. The defendants included Zimbabwean President Robert Mugabe and Foreign Minister Stan Mudenge. The plaintiffs alleged that they or their deceased relatives had been subject to murder, torture, or other acts of violence under orders from President Mugabe as part of a widespread campaign to intimidate his political opponents. The U.S. Department of State argued that Mugabe, as head of a foreign state, was immune from the court's jurisdiction.[35] The department also asserted that Mudenge was immune from the court's jurisdiction, citing *The Schooner Exchange v. M'Faddon*.[36] The district

30. 22 U.S.C. §§ 288–288k (2006).

31. *See, e.g.*, United States v. Noriega, 117 F.3d 1206, 1212 (11th Cir. 1997) (rejecting head-of-state immunity for Panamanian military leader being prosecuted on drug charges); Kadic v. Karadzic, 70 F.3d 232, 248 (2d Cir. 1995) (rejecting head-of-state immunity for civilian leader of Serbs in Bosnia).

32. *See Noriega*, 117 F.3d at 1212; *see also* Mexico v. Hoffman, 324 U.S. 30 (1945); *Ex Parte* Peru, 318 U.S. 578 (1943) (indicating that U.S. courts are bound by suggestions of immunity from the executive branch); *but see* Ingrid Wuerth, *Foreign Official Immunity Determinations in U.S. Courts: The Case Against the State Department*, 51 VA. J. INT'L L. 915 (2011) (reviewing constitutional, historical, functional, and other arguments for not supporting an executive power to make binding immunity determinations).

33. *See, e.g.*, Doe v. United States, 860 F.2d 40, 44–46 (2d Cir. 1988) (finding no head-of-state immunity for former Philippine leader and his wife due to waiver by the Philippine government).

34. 28 U.S.C. § 1350 note (2006).

35. As precedent, the department cited to First Am. Corp. v. Sheikh Zayed Bin Sultan Al–Nahyan, 948 F. Supp. 1107, 1119 (D.D.C. 1996); Alicog v. Saudi Arabia, 860 F. Supp. 379, 382 (S.D. Tex. 1994), *aff'd*, 79 F.3d 1145 (5th Cir. 1996); Lafontant v. Aristide, 844 F. Supp. 128, 132 (E.D.N.Y. 1994).

36. 11 U.S. (7 Cranch) 116, 138 (1812) (Marshall, C.J.) (recognizing that, under customary international law, "the immunity which all civilized nations allow to foreign ministers" is coextensive with the immunity of the sovereign).

court accepted the Department of State's suggestion of immunity and dismissed the action as against the defendants.[37]

There is some dictum in U.S. courts in support of the proposition that head-of-state immunity for acts committed during a leader's tenure disappears when he or she steps down.[38] However, such immunity may disappear only with respect to private acts taken during a leader's tenure.[39] In 2002, several plaintiffs filed a class action lawsuit in U.S. court against Jiang Zemin, president of China, alleging torture, genocide, and other violations against practitioners of Falun Gong (a spiritual movement of Chinese origin). After the U.S. government filed a statement asserting that Jiang should be accorded head-of-state immunity, Jiang stepped down as president of China. The Seventh Circuit Court of Appeals accepted that Jiang remained immune from suit, finding that the rationale for head-of-state immunity was no less implicated after a leader has left power. Further, the Seventh Circuit found this remained the case even if the underlying claims related to violations of *jus cogens* norms.[40]

By contrast, General Augusto Pinochet, former president of Chile, was arrested in London by U.K. authorities in October 1998 after a Spanish magistrate issued an international warrant seeking his detention. Spain requested extradition on the grounds that Pinochet directed a widespread conspiracy from 1973 to 1990 to take over the government of Chile by coup and to reduce the state to submission through genocide, murder, torture, and the taking of hostages, primarily in Chile but elsewhere as well. A lower U.K. court ruled that Pinochet was immune from arrest because he was a head of state at the time the alleged crimes were committed (Pinochet was in power from 1973 to 1990).[41] On November 25, however, the House of Lords ruled that Pinochet was not immune on such grounds, given the nature of the crimes he allegedly committed.[42] Thereafter, the U.K. home secretary certified that most of the crimes set forth in the Spanish request were extraditable crimes under the U.K. Extradition Act of 1989 (except the charges of genocide), paving the way for the extradition to proceed.[43] Yet in 1999, the House of Lords found that acts of torture

37. *See* Tachiona v. Mugabe, 169 F. Supp. 2d 259 (S.D.N.Y. 2001). The Second Circuit found it unnecessary to reach this issue. *See* Tachiona v. United States, 386 F.3d 205, 220–21 (2d Cir. 2004).

38. *See In re* Doe, 860 F.2d 40, 45 (2d Cir. 1988).

39. *See, e.g.*, Philippines v. Marcos, 806 F.2d 344, 360 (2d Cir. 1986) (stating that head-of-state immunity may not reach a former head-of-state's private acts).

40. *See* Ye v. Zemin, 383 F.3d 620 (7th Cir. 2004).

41. *See* 38 I.L.M. 68 (1999); *see also* In re *Pinochet*, 93 Am. J. Int'l L. 690 (1999).

42. *See* 37 I.L.M. 1302 (1998).

43. *See* 38 I.L.M. 489 (1999).

(as well as conspiracy to commit torture) were "extraditable offenses" under the U.K. Extradition Act of 1989 only if they occurred after September 29, 1988, when the U.K. Criminal Justice Act entered into force (the Act established torture as a crime in the United Kingdom).[44] Although the judges issued seven different decisions, essentially the House of Lords found that Pinochet could not be extradited for conduct that was not criminal under U.K. law at the time it occurred. This decision significantly reduced the scope of the charges for which Pinochet could be extradited. In 2000, Pinochet was permitted to fly home to Chile because his health had deteriorated. After his return to Chile, Pinochet was stripped of his parliamentary immunity, arrested, and placed on trial for various charges, which remained ongoing at the time of his death in 2006.[45]

In October 2000, the Democratic Republic of Congo sued Belgium at the International Court of Justice, seeking the annulment of a Belgian judge's "international arrest warrant" issued for "serious violations of international humanitarian law" against Mr. Abdulaye Yerodia Ndombasi, Congo's minister for foreign affairs. Congo asserted that a sitting foreign minister was immune from such process. In a decision issued in February 2002, the Court decided that, while in office, a minister for foreign affairs traveling abroad enjoys personal immunity from the criminal jurisdiction of a foreign state. Such immunity protects the minister against any act of authority of another state which would hinder the minister in the performance of his or her duties. Notwithstanding the *Pinochet* case, the Court found that this rule applied even if the minister is suspected of having committed international crimes, such as war crimes or crimes against humanity. Consequently, the Court held that the issuance of the arrest warrant and its international circulation constituted violations of Belgium's legal obligation towards the Congo.[46] At the same time, blanket immunity ends after the minister departs from office; although he still retains functional immunity for his official acts while in office, such immunity does not extend to the commission of private acts while in office. Thereafter, Belgium withdrew the warrant.

C. State Immunity

Customary International Law on State Immunity

As with diplomatic immunity, state (or sovereign) immunity reflects the proposition that in situations where one sovereign could

44. *See* 38 I.L.M. 581 (1999).

45. *See generally* Naomi Roht-Arriaza, The Pinochet Effect: Transnational Justice in the Age of Human Rights (2005); The Pinochet Papers: The Case of Augusto Pinochet in Spain and Britain (Reed Brody & Michael Ratner eds., 2003).

46. *See* Arrest Warrant of 11 April 2000 (D.R.C. v. Belg.), 2002 I.C.J. 3 (Feb. 14).

exercise jurisdiction over the acts of another, the interests of international harmony dictate restraint by national courts and other authorities. In *Jurisdictional Immunities of the State*, the International Court of Justice stated:

> The Court considers that the rule of State immunity occupies an important place in international law and international relations. It derives from the principle of sovereign equality of States, which, as Article 2, paragraph 1, of the Charter of the United Nations makes clear, is one of the fundamental principles of the international legal order. This principle has to be viewed together with the principle that each State possesses sovereignty over its own territory and that there flows from that sovereignty the jurisdiction of the State over events and persons within that territory. Exceptions to the immunity of the State represent a departure from the principle of sovereign equality. Immunity may represent a departure from the principle of territorial sovereignty and the jurisdiction which flows from it.[47]

As such, customary international law accords immunities to a government from suits in another government's courts. To ascertain the nature of such immunities, it is necessary to review state practice in the form of "judgments of national courts faced with the question whether a foreign State is immune, the legislation of those States which have enacted statutes dealing with immunity, the claims to immunity advanced by States before foreign courts and the statements made by States.... "[48] In *Jurisdictional Immunities of the State*, the Court found that Italy violated international law by allowing civil claims to be brought in its courts against Germany for war crimes committed during World War II by German forces against Italian nationals in Italy and elsewhere. Among other things, the Court found that customary international law had not developed to the point where a state is loses its immunity before foreign courts in respect of action by its armed forces taken in the course of an armed conflict, even if that action that causes death, personal injury or damage to property on the territory of the forum state.[49] Further, the Court concluded "that, under customary international law as it presently stands, a State is not deprived of immunity by reason of the fact that it is accused of serious violations of international human rights law or the international law of armed conflict."[50] Even if those acts allegedly violate *jus*

---

47. Jurisdictional Immunities of the State (Ger. v. Italy), 2012 I.C.J. para. 57 (Feb. 3), *at* <http://www.icj-cij.org/docket/files/143/16883.pdf>.

48. *Id.*, para. 55.

49. *Id.*, para. 78.

50. *Id.*, para. 91.

cogens norms, the Court found that the existence of a *jus cogens* norm does not alter the scope and extent of national court jurisdiction, including otherwise applicable rules on state immunity, nor does the fact that there may be no other means of securing redress.[51]

The doctrine of sovereign immunity emerged as one of the earliest concepts of international law, yet until 2004 there was no global treaty seeking to codify customary international law in this area. In 2004, the U.N. General Assembly adopted the U.N. Convention on Jurisdictional Immunities of States and Their Property.[52] The convention recognizes a general immunity for states, including their various organs, constituent units or political subdivisions, their representatives (when acting in that capacity), and their agencies or instrumentalities. At the same time, the convention recognizes certain exceptions, such as when a state engages in commercial transactions[53] or when a state is involved in proceedings related to the determination of intellectual property rights.[54] Unlike the analogous U.S. statute (discussed below), the convention provides no exception to immunity for a state's expropriation of property, nor for acts of state-sponsored terrorism. In addition, the convention identifies types of state-owned property immune from suit, such as military property, property (including bank accounts) used for diplomatic missions or missions to international organizations, property of the central bank or other monetary authority of the state, and property forming part of the cultural heritage or scientific interest of the state. Although the convention has been open for adherence since January 2005, only thirteen states had joined the convention as of 2011, which has not yet entered into force.

Historical Development in the United States

In the absence of a widely adhered to global treaty on state immunity, one must examine the national laws of each state to ascertain how the principle of sovereign immunity has been implemented. In the United States, the Supreme Court in *Schooner Exchange v. M'Faddon*[55] found that a French warship in a U.S. port was immune from the jurisdiction of U.S. courts, even though the plaintiffs charged that the vessel had been illegally seized from them by France. Chief Justice John Marshall concluded that no foreign sovereign would subject itself to the absolute and exclusive power of another without an implied understanding that entry into

---

51. *Id.*, paras. 95 & 101.

52. G.A. Res. 59/38, annex (Dec. 2, 2004). For a regional treaty, see European Convention on State Immunity, May 16, 1972, ETS No. 74, 1495 U.N.T.S. 182.

53. *Id.*, G.A. Res. 59/38, annex, *supra* note 52, art. 10.

54. *Id.*, art. 14.

55. *Supra* note 36.

foreign territory included a grant of immunity from the territorial sovereign's power. This doctrine of "absolute immunity," which had its basis in principles of state sovereignty, was for centuries deemed to reflect customary international law,[56] and remains the approach taken in many countries, such as Brazil, China, and Russia.

By the 1940's, however, U.S. and European courts began considering situations in which foreign sovereign immunity should be restricted. To ascertain the boundaries of foreign sovereign immunity, U.S. courts typically sought a recommendation from the U.S. Department of State or, when no such recommendation was forthcoming, decided the matter based on past Department of State practice.[57] Yet the department's views were often unclear or contradictory. In an effort to regularize these views, the department's legal adviser in 1952 informed the Department of Justice—in a communication thereafter known as the "Tate letter"—that henceforth the Department of State would favor the theory of "restrictive" sovereign immunity (such a theory had already gained currency in various foreign states).[58] Under this theory, the Department of State would recommend immunity only when a case involved the public acts of a foreign government (*jure imperii*); it would not recommend immunity when a case involved the commercial acts of a foreign government, acts which could have been carried on by private parties (*jure gestionis*). If the Department of State made no recommendation, the characterization of an act as "governmental" or "commercial" was to be determined by the courts.[59]

For example, in *Victory Transport, Inc. v. Comisaria General*,[60] the Second Circuit held that the Spanish government's chartering of a ship to move surplus grain from the United States to Spain for distribution to the Spanish people was just like a private commercial act. Consequently, the defendant was not immune from suit to compel arbitration, although it was an arm of the Spanish government. In reaching its conclusion, the court identified five categories of acts generally treated as governmental in nature: (1) internal administrative acts, such as expulsion of an alien; (2) legislative acts, such as nationalization; (3) acts concerning the armed forces; (4) acts concerning diplomatic activity; and (5) public loans.[61]

Given the diplomatic pressures on the Department of State to recommend immunity in cases involving foreign sovereigns, and the

56. *See* Berizzi Bros. v. Steamship Pesaro, 271 U.S. 562 (1926).

57. *See, e.g., Hoffman, supra* note 32.

58. *See Changed Policy Concerning the Granting of Sovereign Immunity to Foreign Governments (Tate Letter)*, 26 STATE DEPT. BULL. 984 (1952).

59. *See, e.g.,* Nat'l City Bank of N.Y. v. China, 348 U.S. 356 (1955).

60. 336 F.2d 354 (2d Cir. 1964).

61. *Id.* at 360.

political difficulties that arose when such recommendations were not made, it was virtually impossible for the department to follow the restrictive theory consistently in determining whether to recommend immunity in specific cases.[62] Efforts to hold administrative-style hearings to determine immunity did not alleviate the problem. Consequently, the Foreign Sovereign Immunities Act of 1976 (FSIA)[63] was enacted to eliminate the Department of State's extensive role in sovereign immunity cases in favor of the judiciary determining immunity on the basis of codified rules of law.

Foreign Sovereign Immunities Act (FSIA) Generally

The FSIA provides the sole basis for obtaining jurisdiction over a foreign state in U.S. courts.[64] Considerations related to subject-matter jurisdiction and personal jurisdiction are merged under the FSIA. The FSIA grants subject matter jurisdiction for "any nonjury civil action against a foreign state" in which the foreign state is not entitled to immunity.[65] It also grants personal jurisdiction if the court has jurisdiction under § 1330(a) and service of process has been made in accordance with the FSIA.[66] Actions may be brought initially in either state or federal court, but a foreign state is guaranteed the right to remove a civil action from state to federal court.[67]

In certain circumstances, the FSIA strips away the immunity of a foreign government in U.S. courts (discussed below). The FSIA does not, however, provide a cause of action against a foreign government, except in the very limited context of certain actions against terrorist-listed states. In all other situations, for a claim to be brought successfully against a foreign government, the claimant must first establish that the government does not have immunity under the FSIA and then identify a cause of action against the government from some other source of federal or state law. Thus, if a claimant brings an action in tort against a foreign government, the claimant must first establish that the FSIA tort exception to sovereign immunity applies, and then identify a relevant tort law (probably the law of one of the several states of the United States) which supports the action. Simply establishing that the FSIA tort exception applies is not good enough for sustaining the case.

After the FSIA was enacted in 1976, an open question was whether it applied to conduct that occurred prior to that year, or

---

62. *See, e.g.*, Rich v. Naviera Vacuba, S.A., 295 F.2d 24 (4th Cir. 1961).

63. 28 U.S.C. §§ 1330, 1332, 1391(f), 1441(d), 1602–1611 (2006).

64. *See* Argentine Republic v. Amerada Hess Shipping Corp., 488 U.S. 428 (1989).

65. 28 U.S.C. § 1330(a) (2006).

66. *See* 28 U.S.C. §§ 1330(b), 1608 (2006).

67. *See* 28 U.S.C. § 1441 (2006); Delgado v. Shell Oil Co., 231 F.3d 165, 176–77 (5th Cir. 2000); Davis v. McCourt, 226 F.3d 506 (6th Cir. 2000).

even prior to the point when the U.S. government shifted away from the rule of absolute immunity. In *Austria v. Altmann*,[68] the U.S. Supreme Court found that the FSIA applies to such conduct. In that case, a U.S. national named Maria Altmann was the heir to owners of certain paintings by Gustav Klimt, which were seized by the Nazis in Austria. In 1948, the living heirs agreed to "donate" the paintings to the Austrian Gallery of the Austrian government, in exchange for export permits for other works of art. In 2000, Altmann sued the Austrian government in U.S. court, claiming that the "donation" was really a coerced seizure of the Klimt paintings. Altmann therefore based her suit on the expropriation exception of the FSIA (discussed below). Austria replied that when the allegedly wrongful conduct occurred (in 1948), the Austrian government enjoyed absolute immunity from suit in U.S. courts. The U.S. Supreme Court rejected this argument, holding that the language and structure of the FSIA revealed that Congress intended all suits filed after 1976 to fall within the scope of the FSIA, regardless of when the conduct underlying the suit occurred.

Another open question after the FSIA was enacted concerned whether the statute only covered cases against foreign governments or also covered cases against foreign government *officials* when acting in their official capacity. In *Samantar v. Yousuf*, the U.S. Supreme Court was confronted with whether Muhammad Ali Samatar, a former prime minister of Somalia, could be sued in U.S. court for allegedly overseeing government atrocities in Somalia in the 1980's. While the cause of action against Samatar arose pursuant to the Torture Victim Protection Act,[69] the threshold question was whether Samantar was immune from suit in U.S. courts. The district court held that Samantar was entitled to immunity under the FSIA (which, as discussed below, only denies immunity with respect to torts arising in the United States), but the U.S. Supreme Court unanimously disagreed, finding that the text, history, and purpose of the FSIA make clear that it only speaks to the immunity of governments, not persons.[70] As such, the Court remanded the case to the district court to determine whether Samantar was entitled to immunity under common law.

FSIA Agencies and Instrumentalities

The definition of a "foreign state" under the FSIA includes any of its political subdivisions, agencies, or instrumentalities.[71] Agencies and instrumentalities are defined as any separate legal entity which is not a U.S. national and which satisfies one of two prongs set forth in 28 U.S.C. section 1603(b)(2): the entity must either (1)

68. 541 U.S. 677 (2004).

69. 28 U.S.C. § 1350 note (2006).

70. Samantar v. Yousef, 130 S.Ct. 2278 (2010).

71. *See* 28 U.S.C. § 1603(a) (2006).

be an "organ" of a foreign state or (2) have a majority of its shares owned by a foreign state.[72] The following are examples of each prong.

"Organ" of a Foreign State. In *USX Corp. v. Adriatic Insurance Co.,*[73] a railroad sued certain insurers in state court in connection with antitrust actions against the railroad. The insurers filed contribution claims against an Ireland insurer, which removed the action to federal court on the ground that the Ireland insurer was owned by the government of Ireland and thus an "agency or instrumentality" of that government within the meaning of the FSIA. After removal, the district court allowed the Ireland insurer to amend its notice of removal to assert that it was instead an "organ" of the government of Ireland.

The Third Circuit Court of Appeals found that the district court did not abuse its discretion in allowing the amendment.[74] Further, it affirmed that the Irish insurer was in fact an "organ" of the Irish government and, in so doing, discussed the meaning of that term under the FSIA. The court noted that both the Ninth Circuit[75] and Fifth Circuit[76] had developed flexible approaches when determining whether an entity qualifies as an "organ" of a state.[77] The Third Circuit then found that such flexibility was appropriate, given Congress' desire to promote uniformity of decision (through removal to federal courts) and to avoid impairing U.S. foreign relations.[78] According to the court, the starting point in determining whether an entity is an "organ" is to assess whether the entity engages in a public activity on behalf of the foreign government.

> In making this assessment, factors employed by both the Courts of Appeals for the Ninth and Fifth Circuits are relevant, although no one is determinative: (1) the circumstances surrounding the entity's creation; (2) the purpose of its activities; (3) the degree of supervision by the government; (4) the level of government financial support; (5) the entity's employment policies, particularly regarding whether the foreign state requires the hiring of public employees and pays their salaries; and (6) the entity's obligations and privileges under the foreign state's laws. To this list, we should add an additional factor: (7) the ownership structure of the entity. Under the organ prong, as opposed to the majority ownership prong of section

---

72. *See* First Nat'l City Bank v. Banco Para El Comercio Exterior de Cuba, 462 U.S. 611, 619 (1983).

73. 345 F.3d 190 (3d Cir. 2003).

74. *Id.* at 203–06.

75. *See* EOTT Energy Operating Ltd. v. Winterthur Swiss Ins. Co., 257 F.3d 992 (9th Cir. 2001); Gates v. Victor Fine Foods, 54 F.3d 1457 (9th Cir. 1995).

76. *See* Kelly v. Syria Shell Petroleum Dev. B.V., 213 F.3d 841 (5th Cir. 2000).

77. *See USX Corp.*, 345 F.3d at 206–07.

78. *Id.* at 207–09.

1603(b)(2), a foreign state might own only 10% of an entity; it might own directly 50% of the entity; or it might own even 100% of a holding company that owns 100% of the entity. On the other hand it is possible that a foreign state might not own any portion of any entity that nevertheless is its organ as section 1603(b)(2) does not require a foreign state to have any ownership interest in an entity for it to be its organ. Courts should consider how these different ownership structures might influence the degree to which an entity is performing a function "on behalf of the foreign government."[79]

In applying these factors, the Third Circuit found that the Ireland insurer was an "organ" of the government of Ireland given the government's indirect ownership, control over the insurer's shares, and decision-making role.[80]

Ownership of Shares by a Foreign State. In *Dole Food Co. v. Patrickson*,[81] Latin American banana workers brought a class action in state court against multinational fruit and chemical companies. The companies then impleaded certain chemical companies (collectively referred to as the Dead Sea Companies) indirectly owned by the Israeli government. The district court and the Ninth Circuit Court of Appeals found that the Dead Sea Companies were not "instrumentalities" of a foreign state under the FSIA because they were indirectly owned. Further, the district court declared that the status of an FSIA entity is to be assessed at the time suit is filed. While the government of Israel indirectly owned the Dead Sea Companies at the time of the alleged wrongdoing, its ownership ended prior to the filing of the lawsuit, thus precluding the Dead Sea Companies from falling within the FSIA.

The U.S. Supreme Court affirmed, addressing both the issue of whether foreign government ownership must be direct and whether ownership must exist at the time the complaint is filed. With respect to direct ownership, the Court found that a foreign government must directly own a majority of the corporation's shares for the corporation to fall within the scope of the second prong of FSIA section 1603(b)(2). In this case, Israel never had any direct ownership of shares in the Dead Sea Companies. While at certain times there existed "intermediate corporate tiers" such that Israel indirectly owned the Dead Sea Companies, such "indirect subsidiaries" do not fall within the language of section 1603(b)(2). The Court noted that section 1603(b)(2)'s reference to ownership of "shares" demonstrated that Congress intended coverage to turn on formal corporate ownership. The Court also acknowledged that the "veil" separating corporations and their shareholders may be pierced in

79. *Id.* at 209 (footnotes omitted).   **81.** 538 U.S. 468 (2003).
80. *Id.* at 209–16.

exceptional circumstances, but found no such circumstances in this case.[82]

As for when ownership must exist, the Court found that "instrumentality" status is determined at the time of the filing of the complaint. The Court noted that section 1603(b)(2) uses the present tense in speaking of "a majority of whose shares ... is owned by a foreign state," and cited approvingly the principle that jurisdiction depends upon the state of things at the time the action is brought. In this case, the Court rejected the Dead Sea Companies' efforts to compare foreign sovereign immunity with other immunities based on status at the time of the conduct giving rise to the suit. The ownership relationship between Israel and the Dead Sea Companies ended before the suit was commenced; thus, the companies could not claim "instrumentality" status even if indirect ownership fell within the FSIA.[83]

Presumption of Separateness. While an agency or instrumentality may be regarded as governmental for purposes of the FSIA, U.S. courts nevertheless maintain a presumption of separateness, such that the acts of the former cannot automatically be imputed to the latter. Thus, if sustaining a claim requires showing government conduct (*e.g.*, an act of expropriation), then simply showing that an instrumentality engaged in the conduct is insufficient. Further, if a judgment is obtained against an instrumentality, the judgment normally can only be satisfied against the assets of that instrumentality, not against the assets of the government as a whole.

An example of this phenomenon arose in *Zappia Middle East Construction Co. v. Abu Dhabi.*[84] From 1979 to 1982, Zappia Middle East Construction Company (ZMEC) entered into eight public works construction contracts with an instrumentality of the emirate of Abu Dhabi (of the United Arab Emirates) that required periodic emirate payments. Ultimately, ZMEC filed suit in U.S. court alleging that the instrumentality forced it to "perform work outside the contracts ... and delayed making payments," requiring ZMEC to borrow funds from the Emirates Commercial Bank on unfavorable terms. Moreover, ZMEC alleged that the instrumentality would not allow ZMEC employees to leave the emirate and threatened ZMEC's owner with imprisonment. The company asserted that the U.S. court had jurisdiction under the expropriation exception to sovereign immunity contained in the FSIA.

The Second Circuit Court of Appeals rejected ZMEC's argument. Although the acts alleged were taken by the emirate's instrumentality, the court found that there is a presumption of separateness between the instrumentality and the emirate such

---

82. *Id.* at 475–77.

83. *Id.* at 478–80.

84. 215 F.3d 247 (2d Cir. 2000).

that the acts of the former cannot automatically be imputed to the latter. Since expropriation requires an act by the government itself, and since the plaintiff had failed to impute the instrumentality's conduct to the government, there could be no expropriation by the emirate's instrumentality. The emirate's refusal to pay ZMEC under the construction contracts did not constitute expropriation because "breach of a commercial contract alone does not constitute a taking pursuant to international law."[85] With respect to whether the emirate itself engaged in expropriation, the court noted that the government at no point seized control of ZMEC.

FSIA General Grant of Immunity

As a general matter, the FSIA recognizes immunity from U.S. jurisdiction for all foreign sovereigns.[86] However, the FSIA sets forth a series of exceptions to that immunity, which are discussed below. Once a defendant presents a *prima facie* case that it is a foreign sovereign, the plaintiff has the burden of showing that (under the exceptions to the FSIA) immunity should not be granted.[87] Further, the FSIA operates "[s]ubject to existing international agreements to which the United States is a party."[88] This means that the diplomatic and consular immunities of foreign states recognized under treaties such as the VCDR and VCCR remain unaltered by the FSIA.

Waiver Exception

A foreign state is subject to U.S. jurisdiction if it has either impliedly or expressly waived its immunity.[89] Once a waiver is made, it cannot be withdrawn except in a manner consistent with the terms of the waiver. An explicit waiver of immunity occurs when a foreign state waives immunity by treaty, by contract with a private party, or by a statement from an authorized official after a dispute arises.[90] An implicit waiver may occur when a foreign state agrees to arbitration in another state knowing that U.S. courts can compel or enforce the arbitration, or agrees that the law of another state will govern a contract.[91] Immunity may also be waived by a failure to raise it as a defense in the first responsive pleading.

85. *Id.* at 252.

86. *See* 28 U.S.C. § 1604 (2006).

87. *See, e.g.*, Cabiri v. Ghana, 165 F.3d 193 (2d Cir. 1999).

88. 28 U.S.C. § 1609 (2006).

89. *See* 28 U.S.C. § 1605(a)(1) (2006).

90. *See, e.g.*, Aquamar S.A. v. Del Monte Fresh Produce N.A., Inc., 179 F.3d 1279 (11th Cir. 1999) (giving effect to an express waiver by Ecuador's ambassador to the United States).

91. *But see* S & Davis Int'l v. Yemen, 218 F.3d 1292 (11th Cir. 2000) (finding that Yemen's agreement to arbitrate did not demonstrate the requisite intent to waive its sovereign immunity to suit in U.S. court).

U.S. courts are not quick to find an implied waiver of immunity, as doing so might negate the overall purpose of the FSIA to preserve the immunity of foreign states for traditional public functions. For example, in *Blaxland v. Commonwealth Director of Public Prosecutions*, a U.S. resident, Christopher Blaxland, served as director of a publicly listed Australian company and some affiliated companies from 1986 to 1989. After resigning from the companies, Blaxland was charged by Australian authorities with fraud and other improper use of his position—charges Blaxland asserted to be politically motivated. When he failed to appear for trial in Australia, an Australian court issued a warrant for his arrest, and the Australian government filed an extradition request with the U.S. government. Blaxland was extradited by the United States in October 1997, but he was ultimately acquitted in Australia.[92]

Upon returning to the United States, Blaxland filed suit against the Australian government and two of its employees for malicious prosecution, abuse of process, intentional infliction of emotional distress, and false imprisonment. The defendants claimed immunity under the FSIA. Blaxland responded that the Australian government and its employees implicitly waived their immunity from suit in U.S. courts by seeking extradition. The Ninth Circuit noted that in *Siderman de Blake v. Argentina*,[93] Argentina was found to have implicitly waived its immunity by filing a letter rogatory with a California court to obtain assistance in a bogus fraud action in an Argentinean court. In *Blaxland*, however, the court found no such waiver because "the Australian government did not itself apply to our courts for assistance but instead invoked its rights under the Extradition Treaty by applying to the executive branch of our government."[94] The court expressed a concern that interpreting extradition requests as implied waivers of immunity could "interfere with foreign policy and threaten the ethos of the extradition system,"[95] and noted that the same position had recently been taken by the Supreme Court of Canada.[96]

Commercial Activity Exception

A foreign state is not immune from the jurisdiction of U.S. courts where its "action is based upon a commercial activity," so long as it is carried out in, or has a "direct effect" in, the United States.[97] A "commercial" activity may be regular conduct or an individual transaction, so long as its nature, rather than its pur-

---

92. Blaxland v. Commonwealth Dir. of Pub. Prosecutions, 323 F.3d 1198, 1201–03 (9th Cir. 2003).

93. 965 F.2d 699 (9th Cir. 1992).

94. *Blaxland*, 323 F.3d at 1206.

95. *Id*. at 1208.

96. *See* Schreiber v. Canada (Attorney General), 2002 S.C.R. 62.

97. 28 U.S.C. § 1605(a)(2) (2006).

pose, is the determining factor.[98] Courts look to whether the foreign government was acting as a regulator of the market, in which case the action is not commercial, or whether it was acting like a private player within the market, in which case the action is commercial.[99] The claim must be based on the commercial activity, rather than merely related to it.[100]

Congress explicitly left the "direct effect" requirement to judicial discretion on a case-by-base basis, yet a committee report offered examples of such effects: commercial transactions performed, in whole or in part, in the United States; import-export transactions involving sales to, or purchases from, the United States; business torts occurring in the United States; and an indebtedness incurred by a foreign state which negotiates or executes a loan agreement in the United States.[101]

For example, in *Lyon v. Agusta S.P.A.*,[102] two U.S. nationals were killed in 1993 when an airplane designed, manufactured, and owned by certain Italian companies—which were instrumentalities of the government of Italy—crashed in Santa Monica, California. When the survivors brought suit, the Italian companies moved to dismiss the action on the basis of immunity under the FSIA. The Ninth Circuit Court of Appeals found that the companies' acts of designing, manufacturing and owning the airplanes was in connection with a commercial activity. Although that activity was outside the territory of the United States, it caused a direct effect in the United States by resulting in an accident. As such, the requirements of the FSIA exception were met, and the case was not dismissed.

By contrast, in *Virtual Countries v. South Africa*, a Seattle-based corporation named Virtual Countries owned various Internet domain names, including <www.southafrica.com>, which it used to provide access to news, weather, travel, and other information relating to countries worldwide. In October 2000, the Republic of South Africa issued a press release stating that it intended to seek the rights to the Internet domain name <www.southafrica.com> by taking appropriate steps before the World Intellectual Property Organization and the Internet Corporation for Assigned Names and Numbers.[103] One week later, Virtual Countries sued the Republic of

---

98. *See* 28 U.S.C. § 1603(d).

99. *See* Argentina v. Weltover, Inc., 504 U.S. 607, 614 (1992).

100. *See, e.g.*, Saudi Arabia v. Nelson, 507 U.S. 349 (1993) (finding that a government's imprisonment and alleged torture of a U.S. national is not a "commercial activity," even though the national's presence in Saudi Arabia was

pursuant to an employment contract with the government).

101. *See* H.R. Rep. No. 94–1487, at 15 (1976).

102. 252 F.3d 1078 (9th Cir. 2001).

103. The Internet Corporation for Assigned Names and Numbers was established in 1998 as a nonprofit, private-sector corporation that coordinates some

South Africa and the South African Tourism Board in U.S. court seeking declaratory relief (that South Africa lacked rights to the domain name) and injunctive relief (to prevent any arbitration or judicial proceeding challenging Virtual Countries' rights). The district court granted the defendants' motion to dismiss the action for lack of subject matter jurisdiction under the FSIA.

In affirming the dismissal, the Second Circuit agreed that the FSIA's commercial activity exception did not apply since there was no "direct effect in the United States" from the issuance of the press release in South Africa. The court explained that

> even accepting the plaintiff's account for purposes of the motion to dismiss, the press release's effect falls at the end of a long chain of causation and is mediated by numerous actions by third parties. First, the Republic issued the press release. Then wire services and newspapers in South Africa and elsewhere obtained the release and wrote articles about it. Current or potential investors—perhaps in the United States, perhaps in other countries, and perhaps in both—and a potential strategic business partner in South Africa allegedly then learned of the release's contents. Drawing on news reports, they then formed their own independent assessments of the Republic's intentions and the possible effect of those intentions on Virtual Countries and people who would do business with it.... Only then could investors and the prospective business partner have decided to give effect to their doubts as to the validity of the plaintiff's current registration of southafrica.com and their fears of reprisal by the Republic, by declining to invest in or do business with Virtual Countries.

> . . . .

> ... Defining "direct effect" to permit jurisdiction when a foreign state's actions precipitate reactions by third parties, which reactions then have an impact on a plaintiff, would foster uncertainty in both foreign states and private counterparties. Neither could predict when an action would create jurisdiction, which would hinge on third parties' independent reactions and conduct, even if in individual cases, such as the one at bar, a particular effect might be foreseeable. To permit jurisdiction in such cases would thus be contrary to the predictability interest fostered by the statute.[104]

of the Internet's technical management functions. *See ICANN Fact Sheet* (n.d.), *at* <http://www.icann.org/general/factsheet.html>.

104. Virtual Countries v. South Africa, 300 F.3d 230, 237–38 (2d Cir. 2002).

Expropriation Exception

A foreign state is not immune from the jurisdiction of U.S. courts in an action "in which rights in property taken in violation of international law are in issue and that property or any property exchanged for that property" is either (1) "present in the United States in connection with a commercial activity carried on in the United States by the foreign state" or (2) "owned and operated by an agency or instrumentality of the foreign state ... engaged in a commercial activity in the United States."[105] This exception, therefore, contemplates suits involving property that was nationalized or expropriated by a foreign government without compensation, so long as there is an appropriate nexus with a commercial activity in the United States.

For example, in *Anderman v. Austria*,[106] the plaintiffs were Jews in Austria (and their heirs) at the time of the German Anschluss (the 1938 German annexation of Austria). In 2001, the plaintiffs sued the government of Austria, alleging that it deprived them in 1938 and thereafter of property through theft, intimidation, coercion and discriminatory taxes. The government of Austria asserted that it was immune from suit. The plaintiffs sought to invoke several FSIA exceptions concerning waiver, commercial activity, and expropriation. In finding that the expropriation exception to immunity did not apply, the district court noted that the plaintiffs had not alleged that the property at issue (or any property exchanged for the property) was present in the United States in connection with an Austrian government commercial activity.[107] Moreover, the court found that only one of the plaintiffs had alleged that the government of Austria owned or operated any such property.[108] As such, most of the plaintiffs could not invoke the FSIA expropriation exception.

In *Nemariam v. Republic of Ethiopia*,[109] Eritreans brought an action against the Government of Ethiopia and the Central Bank of Ethiopia alleging an unlawful taking of bank and non-bank accounts in Ethiopia. The D.C. Circuit Court of Appeals found that FSIA Section 1605(a)(3) applies only to *tangible* property, a position that has been taken by other courts.[110] Therefore, the plaintiffs had not brought an action concerning "rights in property." Moreover,

---

105. 28 U.S.C. § 1605(a)(3) (2006).

106. 256 F. Supp. 2d 1098 (C.D. Cal. 2003); *see* Rodriguez v. Costa Rica, 297 F.3d 1 (1st Cir. 2002) (finding that claims for breach of contract, personal injury, and damage to or loss of property did not fall within the FSIA "expropriation" exception).

107. *See Anderman*, 256 F. Supp. 2d at 1110.

108. *Id.* at 1110–11.

109. 491 F.3d 470 (D.C. Cir. 2007).

110. *See, e.g.*, Citizens Bank of Md. v. Strumpf, 516 U.S. 16, 21 (1995) (bank account "consists of nothing more or less than a promise to pay, from the bank to the depositor").

since the Ethiopian Government had only "frozen" the bank accounts, the plaintiffs had not brought an action concerning property that is "owned or operated" by a foreign state.

Inheritance/Immovable Property Exception

A foreign state is not immune from actions involving rights in property in the United States acquired by succession or gift, or rights in immovable property situated in the United States.[111] As such, a foreign state that own's real property in the United States, or that is a party to litigation involving a will or estate, cannot invoke sovereignty immunity. Difficult issues can arise, however, as to what constitutes an action involving "rights in immovable property."

For example, in *Permanent Mission of India*,[112] India had failed over the course of several years to pay taxes on a building it owned for the portion being used as residential units for employees below the rank of ambassador. The unpaid taxes eventually converted into tax liens and New York City sought a declaratory judgment in court as to the validity of the lien. Justice Thomas, writing for the Supreme Court, held that since the effect of a tax lien was to inhibit the right to convey land, a lawsuit to establish the validity of a lien implicated rights in immovable property. As such, India was not immune from suit.[113] By contrast, in *City of New York v. Permanent Mission of India*,[114] the Second Circuit found that apartments owned by India and Mongolia to house personnel of their consulates or missions to the United Nations were exempt from city tax. In that instance, however, the exemption derived not from the FSIA, but from an exercise of authority by the U.S. Secretary of State under the Foreign Missions Act,[115] which provides the Secretary discretion to determine that certain benefits should be accorded to a particular foreign government's missions, as a means of promoting reciprocal treatment for U.S. missions.

Tort Exception

A foreign state is not immune from tort actions involving money damages where the damage occurred in the United States, including actions for personal injury, death, and loss or damage to property caused by a tortious act or omission of the foreign state or its agents.[116] Thus, if an embassy driver negligently hits another car

---

111. *See* 28 U.S.C. § 1605(a)(4) (2006).

112. 551 U.S. 193 (2007).

113. *See* Nicholas P. Shapiro, *The Immovable Property Exception to a State's Sovereign Immunity—Permanent Mission of India to the United Nations v.* *City of New York*, 31 Suffolk Transnat'l L. Rev. 719 (2008).

114. City of N.Y. v. Permanent Mission of India, 618 F.3d 172 (2d Cir. 2010).

115. 22 U.S.C. §§ 4301–16 (2006).

116. *See* 28 U.S.C. § 1605(a)(5) (2006).

in Washington, D.C., the victim can sue the foreign government in federal court, using District of Columbia tort law for the cause of action.

One important limitation on this "tort exception" is that the damage or loss must occur in the United States.[117] The "United States" includes "all territories and waters, continental or insular, subject to the jurisdiction of the United States."[118] U.S. embassies do not fall within this exception because the ground on which an embassy stands remains the territory of the host state.[119] Consequently, a person in a U.S. embassy abroad who is physically attacked by an agent of the local government cannot file a suit in U.S. court against the foreign government using the FSIA tort exception. Further, while the exception does not state that the tortious act or omission must occur in the United States (as opposed to the damage or loss), several courts have so held.[120]

States remain immune, however, if the tort claim is based upon the discharge of a discretionary function, or if it arises from "malicious prosecution, abuse of process, libel, slander, misrepresentation, deceit or interference with contract rights."[121] For example, in *Blaxland v. Commonwealth Director of Public Prosecutions* (discussed above), a U.S. resident, Christopher Blaxland, filed suit against the Australian government and two of its employees for malicious prosecution, abuse of process, intentional infliction of emotional distress, and false imprisonment. The Ninth Circuit Court of Appeals held that the claims involved torts and that some of the alleged harm occurred in the United States; thus, the claims *prima facie* fell within the scope of the FSIA tort exception to immunity. The court further noted, however, that the tort exception expressly states that it does not apply to claims "arising out of" malicious prosecution or abuse of process. As such, the court found that only Blaxland's claim for false imprisonment fell within the scope of the FSIA tort exception. Yet the false imprisonment claim was also defective since Blaxland's imprisonment was in the United States by the U.S. government acting under a valid legal process.[122]

Arbitration Exception

A foreign state is not immune from the jurisdiction of U.S. courts in any case where the action is brought to enforce an agreement made by the foreign state with a private party to submit

117. *See Amereda Hess, supra* note 64, at 439.

118. 28 U.S.C. § 1603(c) (2006).

119. *See* McKeel v. Iran, 722 F.2d 582, 588 (9th Cir. 1983).

120. *See, e.g.,* Persinger v. Iran, 729 F.2d 835 (D.C. Cir. 1984).

121. 28 U.S.C. §§ 1605(a)(5)(A) & (B) (2006).

122. *Blaxland, supra* note 92, at 1202–06.

to arbitration differences which may arise with respect to a defined legal relationship, whether contractual or not, concerning a subject matter capable of settlement by arbitration under U.S. law, or to confirm an award made pursuant to such an arbitration.[123]

For example, in *International Insurance Co. v. Caja Nacional de Ahorro y Seguro*,[124] a U.S. insurance company (International Insurance) purchased reinsurance from an Argentinian insurance company (Caja) pursuant to two contracts that contained an arbitration clause in the event that a dispute arose. Caja subsequently failed to pay more than U.S. $2 million in indemnity obligations. In 2000, International Insurance initiated an arbitration in the United States and won a default award after Caja failed to appear. International Insurance then filed a petition in a U.S. court for confirmation of the arbitral award. Caja appeared and claimed immunity as an instrumentality of a foreign government.[125]

The Seventh Circuit Court of Appeals rejected the claim of immunity.

> Section 1605(a)(6)(A) of the FSIA provides that a foreign state or instrumentality is not immune from the jurisdiction of American courts in any proceeding to confirm an arbitral award where that foreign state or instrumentality agreed to submit to arbitration and the arbitration takes place in the United States. Article XX of each of the parties' reinsurance contracts provides that Caja would "submit to the jurisdiction of any court of competent jurisdiction within the United States and will comply with all requirements necessary to give such court jurisdiction.... " Article XXI of each contract contained a provision that arbitration would occur in Chicago, Illinois, unless some other location was mutually agreed upon by the parties. By agreeing to a contract designating Chicago, Illinois as the site of arbitration, even if it is a foreign instrumentality, Caja waived its immunity in a proceeding to confirm the arbitral award.[126]

Terrorist State Exception

This exception to immunity permits civil suits for monetary damages against foreign states that cause personal injury or death "by an act of torture, extrajudicial killing, aircraft sabotage, hostage taking, or the provision of material support or resources ...

---

123. *See* 28 U.S.C. § 1605(a)(6) (2006); *see, e.g.,* Creighton Ltd. v. Qatar, 181 F.3d 118 (D.C. Cir. 1999).

124. 293 F.3d 392 (7th Cir. 2002); *but see* Monegasque de Reassurances S.A.M. v. Nak Naftogaz, 311 F.3d 488 (2d Cir. 2002) (dismissing proceeding to confirm arbitral award under doctrine of *forum non conveniens*).

125. *Int'l Ins. Co.*, 293 F.3d at 393–94.

126. *Id.* at 397.

for such an act. . . . "[127] Under this exception, the claimant or victim must have been a U.S. national when the terrorist act occurred and the foreign state must have been designated by the secretary of state as a state sponsor of terrorism. As of 2011, Cuba, Iran, Sudan and Syria were designated as terrorist states. After creating this exception, Congress also passed a civil liability provision that establishes a cause of action against an agent of a foreign state that acts under the conditions specified in the exception.[128] The civil liability statute provided that the agent shall be liable for "money damages which may include economic damages, solatium, pain and suffering, and punitive damages."

Since enactment of this exception in 1996, numerous cases have been filed by U.S. nationals against terrorist states. For example, in April 1995 a suicide bomber drove a van loaded with explosives into a bus passing through the Gaza Strip, killing seven Israeli soldiers and one U.S. national, a twenty-year-old college student spending a semester abroad in Israel. The Shaqaqi faction of Palestine Islamic Jihad (a terrorist group funded by the government of Iran) claimed responsibility for the explosion. The deceased's father, Stephen M. Flatow, sued Iran, invoking the FSIA terrorist state exception. In March 1998, a U.S. district court found that Iran was not immune from suit and was responsible for the death of Michelle Flatow. The court held Iran and its officials jointly and severally liable for compensatory and punitive damages in an amount of U.S. $247 million.[129]

Claimants under this exception, however, have experienced some difficulties. First, the civil liability statute (known as the "Flatow Amendment") as originally enacted was more narrow than the exception itself. The Flatow Amendment conferred a right of action only against an "official, employee, or agent of a foreign state," not against the foreign state itself. In *Cicippio-Puleo v. Iran*, the D.C. Circuit Court of Appeals affirmed that the Flatow Amendment did not create a private right of action against a foreign government and found that the cause of action is limited to claims against officials in their individual, as opposed to official, capacities.[130] As such, the portion of the claim against the government of Iran was dismissed. Only in 2007 was the provision rewritten so as to create a private right of action against the state itself.

---

127. 28 U.S.C.A. § 1605A (West. Supp. 2010).

128. *See* 28 U.S.C. § 1605 note (2006).

129. *See* Flatow v. Iran, 999 F. Supp. 1 (D.D.C. 1998); *see also* Alejandre v. Cuba, 996 F. Supp. 1239, 1253 (S.D.Fla. 1997); Daliberti v. Iraq, 97 F. Supp. 2d 38 (D.D.C. 2000).

130. *See* Cicippio–Puleo v. Iran, 353 F.3d 1024, 1033–36 (D.C. Cir. 2004). In light of this decision, earlier district court cases holding governments liable under the Flatow Amendment (such as the *Flatow* case, *supra* note 129) appear to have been incorrectly decided.

Second, plaintiffs bringing such cases must comply with the jurisdictional requirement within the terrorist state exception. Specifically, claimants must afford foreign states "a reasonable opportunity to arbitrate the claim in accordance with accepted rules of arbitration" if "the act occurred in the foreign state against which the claim has been brought.... "[131] In *Simpson v. Libya*, the plaintiff sued Libya for hostage-taking and torture when her cruise ship made an emergency stop at a Libyan port. Shortly thereafter, she mailed the Libyan government an offer to arbitrate, subject to certain conditions. Among the conditions was that the plaintiff would not be required to leave the United States. The D.C. Circuit Court of Appeals found that the offer was timely and that the conditions were reasonable.[132]

Third, even in situations where the foreign state fails to appear, plaintiffs must establish to the satisfaction of the court that the foreign state was liable for the conduct in question. For example, in 1996 Yaron and Efrat Ungar were killed by members of Hamas in Beit Shemesh, Israel. In 2000, the family of Yaron Ungar filed a claim against Iran and its intelligence service based on the terrorist state exception. Iran failed to appear and the district court issued a default. Nevertheless, after hearing the evidence presented by the plaintiffs at the evidentiary hearing, the court in *Ungar v. Iran* held that they had failed to establish a causal link between Iran and this specific attack. In particular, the court pointed to confessions by the killers indicating that they received no training from Iran, obtained funding and weapons from sources other than Hamas, and were only loosely connected to Hamas. The district court concluded that the plaintiffs had not "established a legally sufficient evidentiary base for a reasonable jury to find that the acts of the defendants were a necessary condition or a 'but for' cause of the Ungars' deaths."[133]

Fourth, the relationship of the United States with those states that are designated as "terrorist states" changes over time; in recent years Libya, Iraq, North Korea, and Serbia have all been removed from the list of "terrorist states."[134] When this happens, plaintiffs may experience difficulties, even for suits brought (or based upon acts that occurred) prior to the de-listing of the state. For example, Iraq was designated as a state sponsor of terrorism in 1990. In 2003, various plaintiffs filed suit in U.S. court against Iraq

131. 28 U.S.C.A. § 1605A(a)(2)(A)(iii).

132. *See* Simpson v. Libya, 326 F.3d 230, 233–34 (D.C. Cir. 2003).

133. Ungar v. Iran, 211 F. Supp. 2d 91, 98 (D.D.C. 2002).

134. The State Department lists state sponsors of terrorism pursuant to § 6(j) of the Export Administration Act of 1979, 50 App. U.S.C. § 2405(j) (2006), § 620A of the Foreign Assistance Act, 22 U.S.C. § 2371 (2006), and § 40(d) of the Arms Export Control Act, 22 U.S.C. § 2780(d) (2006).

alleging mistreatment by Iraqi officials during and after the 1991 Gulf War, at a time when Saddam Hussein ruled Iraq. After the U.S. intervention in Iraq in 2003, Hussein was toppled from power, and replaced by a new, democratic government. Congress then enacted a statute that authorized the president to "make inapplicable with respect to Iraq" laws that apply "to countries that have supported terrorism."[135] On the basis of that authority, the president issued a determination that purported to restore Iraq's immunity in U.S. courts, including with respect to pending suits.[136] Although the D.C. Circuit held in 2004 that Congress had not authorized the restoration of such immunity,[137] the Supreme Court found in 2009 that by virtue of the 2003 statute and the president's determination, Iraq's immunity had been restored, thus blocking suits against Iraq for acts committed by Iraq during Hussein's regime.[138]

Finally, claimants who obtain judgments have had considerable difficulty enforcing those judgments, due to the lack of assets from terrorist states located within U.S. jurisdiction. Various claimants have sought to attach and execute against the properties and bank accounts of terrorist states, but the U.S. government often has intervened, noting that the properties are protected under diplomatic or consular conventions, or are owned by the U.S. government in trust. Congress has adopted new statutes in an effort to assist claimants, going so far as allowing certain claimants to obtain compensatory (but not punitive) damages directly from the U.S. government.[139]

Counterclaims Exception

If a foreign state brings an action in U.S. court, it is not immune from the jurisdiction of U.S. courts for any counterclaim arising out of the same transaction or occurrence, so long as the counterclaim does not seek relief exceeding the amount sought by the foreign state.[140] For example, in *Cabiri v. Ghana*,[141] the government of Ghana sued in U.S. court to evict the family of Bawol Cabiri (a former Ghana government employee) from their New York home, which they had obtained as part of his employment contract. Cabiri counterclaimed for, among other things, breach of

---

135. Emergency Wartime Supplemental Appropriations Act (EWSAA), § 1503, Pub. L. No. 108–11, 117 Stat. 559, 579 (2003).

136. Presidential Determination No. 2003–23, 68 Fed. Reg. 26,459 (May 16, 2003).

137. Acree v. Republic of Iraq, 370 F.3d 41 (D.C. Cir. 2004). The plaintiffs

judgment, however, was vacated on other grounds.

138. Iraq v. Beaty, 556 U.S. 848 (2009).

139. For a discussion, see Sean D. Murphy, United States Practice in International Law, 2002–2004, 67–72 (2005).

140. *See* 28 U.S.C. § 1607 (2006).

141. 165 F.3d 193 (2d Cir. 1999).

his employment contract. The government of Ghana asserted that it was immune from suit under the FSIA. The Second Circuit Court of Appeals, however, held that Cabiri's breach of contract claim was permissible since it arose "out of the same transactions as the eviction proceeding: Cabiri's employment contract and his termination."[142]

Extent of Liability

If a foreign state is not entitled to immunity from U.S. jurisdiction, it is generally liable as if it were a private party.[143] However, a foreign state will only be subject to punitive damages in two circumstances. First, punitive damages may be awarded for cases falling under the terrorist state exception. Second, punitive damages may be awarded in a wrongful death action if the law of the place where the act occurred provides only for punitive damages.[144]

Attachment and Execution

Even if a foreign state is not immune from suit in U.S. courts, its assets are generally presumed to be immune from attachment or execution.[145] After a judgment is issued against a foreign government, the FSIA provides that a reasonable time must pass before the judgment holder is allowed to execute the judgment.[146] If a reasonable time has elapsed, a foreign government's property is still immune from attachment or execution unless, under FSIA section 1610, three conditions are met. First, the property must be "used for a commercial activity in the United States" (thus, diplomatic and consular properties are generally immune from attachment and execution).[147] Second, the property must fit within one of several secondary requirements contained in FSIA section 1610. These secondary requirements largely parallel the exceptions to immunity contained in FSIA section 1605 (a government is not immune from attachment or execution if it has waived the immunity, or if the attachment or execution is based upon an order confirming an arbitral award, and so on). Third, even if the property is used for commercial purposes and one of the secondary requirements is met, the property still remains immune if it is used for the purposes of a foreign government's central bank or military.[148]

---

142. *Id.* at 198.

143. *See* 28 U.S.C. § 1606 (2006); *see also* State Bank of India v. NLRB, 808 F.2d 526 (7th Cir. 1986).

144. *See, e.g.,* Harris v. Polskie Linie Lotnicze, 820 F.2d 1000 (9th Cir. 1987).

145. *See* 28 U.S.C. § 1609 (2006).

146. *Id.,* § 1610(c).

147. *See, e.g.,* City of Englewood v. Libya, 773 F.2d 31, 36–37 (3d Cir. 1985) (finding that although the purchase of certain property was a commercial transaction, its use as a diplomatic residence "as a matter of law ... is not commercial activity").

148. *See* 28 U.S.C. § 1611 (2006); *see, e.g.,* Olympic Chartering v. Ministry

For example, in *Venus Lines Agency v. CVG Industria Venezolana de Aluminio*, a U.S. shipping company (Venus Lines) contracted with a Venezuelan government instrumentality (Venalum) for the delivery of aluminum products. After a contract dispute arose, Venus Lines commenced arbitration against Venalum and sought to attach certain aluminum products in its custody that were owned by Venalum. Venalum replied that the assets were immune from prejudgment attachment. Venus Lines claimed Venalum had waived its right to immunity by declaring in the contract that Venus Lines "shall have the right to attach the cargo for the payment of the freight. . . . " The Eleventh Circuit Court of Appeals agreed that this language was sufficiently explicit to cover a waiver of immunity from prejudgment attachment.[149]

D. Act of State Doctrine

Act of State Doctrine Generally

The act of state doctrine is essentially a rule of judicial self-restraint that has developed in the United States and many other states in one form or another.[150] Under this rule, U.S. courts decline to "sit in judgment" on the acts of a foreign government when those acts are taken within the foreign government's territory. The principal motivation for this self-restraint appears to be a desire that disputes involving the acts of foreign governments in their own territories be resolved through diplomatic means, not through litigation in national courts.[151]

An early application of this doctrine in the United States is illustrated in *Underhill v. Hernandez*.[152] In 1892, revolution broke out in Venezuela, led by General Hernandez, who assumed control of the city of Bolivar. Underhill, a U.S. national, wished to leave the city, but was prevented by Hernandez because Underhill had constructed the city's waterworks and was needed to help operate the system. Eventually the revolutionaries succeeded in seizing control of the entire country and Underhill was able to leave Venezuela. Upon his return to the United States, he sued Hernandez for violations of Venezuelan tort law. The U.S. Supreme Court viewed Hernandez's action as that of a sovereign and so affirmed the dismissal of the case based on the act of state doctrine.

---

of Indus. & Trade of Jordan, 134 F. Supp. 2d 528 (S.D.N.Y. 2001).

149. Venus Lines Agency v. CVG Industria Venezolana de Aluminio, 210 F.3d 1309, 1311–12 (11th Cir. 2000).

150. *See* 1 RESTATEMENT (THIRD), *supra* note 1, § 443 rptrs. n. 12.

151. *See generally* OPPENHEIM'S INTERNATIONAL LAW 365–71 (9th ed., Robert Jennings & Arthur Watts eds., 1992).

152. 168 U.S. 250 (1897).

Every sovereign State is bound to respect the independence of every other sovereign State, and the courts of one
country will not sit in judgment on the acts of the government
of another done within its own territory. Redress of grievances
by reason of such acts must be obtained through the means
open to be availed of by sovereign powers as between themselves.[153]

Later cases have suggested that the doctrine either was required by
principles of comity[154] or was a special choice of law rule.[155]

Since the act of state doctrine is frequently invoked in cases in
U.S. courts involving foreign governments, discussion of the doctrine is often grouped with discussion of sovereign immunity. It
must be emphasized, however, that the act of state doctrine is
relevant in *any case* where the validity of a foreign government's
act, taken in its own territory, is at issue. Such cases may arise
when the foreign government itself is not a party. For instance, if a
foreign government issues a decree ordering that certain property
be transferred within its territory from John to Jane, and John
sues Jane in a U.S. court to recover the property, Jane may raise as
a defense that the court cannot pass upon the validity of the foreign
government's conduct given the act of state doctrine. By contrast,
sovereign immunity issues arise only in cases in which one of the
parties is alleged to be a foreign government (or one of its organs,
agencies, or instrumentalities).

Sabbatino Case

A landmark decision in the U.S. Supreme Court on the act of
state doctrine is *Banco Nacional de Cuba v. Sabbatino.*[156] In that
case, the Cuban government had nationalized a company in which
U.S. investors had an interest. Subsequently a U.S. commodities
broker, who had contracted to purchase a shipload of sugar from
the company, entered into a new agreement to buy the sugar from
the Cuban government. After gaining possession of the shipping
documents (and hence of the sugar), the broker made payment to
the U.S. investors rather than the Cuban government. Banco
Nacional de Cuba then sued in U.S. court to obtain possession of
the funds from the investors, represented at that point by a
temporary receiver (Sabbatino). Sabbatino defended on the grounds
that title to the sugar never passed to Cuba because the expropriation violated international law.

---

153. *Id.* at 252.

154. *See, e.g.*, Oetjen v. Cent. Leath-
er Co., 246 U.S. 297 (1918); Ricaud v.
Am. Metal Co., 246 U.S. 304 (1918).

155. *See, e.g.*, Am. Banana Co. v.
United Fruit Co., 213 U.S. 347 (1909).

156. 376 U.S. 398 (1964).

Although lower courts held that the act of state doctrine did not apply because the taking violated international law, the Supreme Court stated that the adjudication of this claim risked serious embarrassment to the executive branch because the international law concerning compensation for expropriation was unclear. Justice Harlan summarized the holding as follows:

> [W]e decide only that the Judicial Branch will not examine the validity of a taking of property within its own territory by a foreign sovereign government, extant and recognized by this country at the time of suit, in the absence of a treaty or other unambiguous agreement regarding controlling legal principles, even if the complaint alleges that the taking violates customary international law.[157]

Exceptions to the Doctrine

Since the act of state doctrine has evolved in the United States principally through judicial decisions, the exact contours of the doctrine are somewhat vague. In several cases, courts have declared that there are certain situations where the act of state doctrine should not be applied. It must be noted, however, that U.S. decisions are inconsistent in interpreting and applying these exceptions.[158]

Exception when Congress So Directs. U.S. courts will not apply the act of state doctrine when they are directed by statute not to do so. Shortly after the Supreme Court's decision in *Sabbatino*, Congress passed the "Second Hickenlooper Amendment" to the Foreign Assistance Act of 1964, which provides:

> [N]o court in the United States shall decline on the ground of the federal act of state doctrine to make a determination on the merits giving effect to the principles of international law in a case in which a claim of title or other right to property is asserted by any party including a foreign state ... based upon ... a confiscation or other taking after January 1, 1959, by an act of that state in violation of the principles of international law....[159]

This statute essentially reversed the Supreme Court's decision in *Sabbatino*, with the result that on remand the lower court found the Cuban taking invalid.[160] Subsequent cases have construed the *Sabbatino* Amendment narrowly to limit its effect to situations in

---

157. *Id.* at 428; *see* 1 Restatement (Third), *supra* note 1, § 443.

158. *See generally* Michael Ramsey, *Acts of State and Foreign Sovereign Obligations*, 39 Harv. Int'l L.J. 1 (1998); Michael Bazyler, *Abolishing the Act of State Doctrine*, 134 U. Pa. L. Rev. 325 (1986).

159. 22 U.S.C. § 2370(e)(2) (2006).

160. *See* Banco Nacional de Cuba v. Farr, Whitlock & Co., 383 F.2d 166 (2d Cir. 1967).

which the property whose title is in dispute is physically present in the United States (*e.g.*, funds from the sale of sugar).

Exception When Department of State So Advises. In *Bernstein v. Van Heyghen Freres*,[161] Judge Learned Hand applied the act of state doctrine to avoid passing upon the validity of the coercive taking of property from a Jewish plaintiff by Nazi officials (even though World War II was over and the Nazis were no longer in power). In a nearly identical case seven years later, the Department of State informed the Second Circuit by letter that U.S. foreign relations did not require judicial abstention in cases involving Nazi confiscations. Consequently, the court did not apply the act of state doctrine.[162] Under this so-called "*Bernstein* exception," the act of state doctrine is not applied when the Department of State explicitly indicates to the court that such an application is not required for the conduct of U.S. foreign relations.

Whether the *Bernstein* exception has been fully accepted by the U.S. Supreme Court, however, remains unclear. In *First National City Bank v. Banco Nacional de Cuba*,[163] the Court considered whether to adjudicate the validity of a Cuban taking of Citibank's property. The Department of State wrote to the Court that the act of state doctrine need not apply. While a majority of justices found the doctrine inapplicable, only a minority was willing to recognize the *Bernstein* exception and regard the executive's statement as conclusive on the matter.[164]

Treaty Exception. In *Kalamazoo Spice Extraction Co. v. Ethiopia*,[165] the district court was asked to decide a counterclaim by a U.S. defendant for the expropriation of his property by the revolutionary government of Ethiopia. Although the U.S.-Ethiopia Treaty of Amity and Economic Relations[166] included a standard of "prompt payment of just and effective compensation" in the event that one party expropriated property belonging to nationals of the other, the district court applied the act of state doctrine and dismissed the case. Before the appeal was heard, the Department of State transmitted a letter to the Sixth Circuit stating: "When, as in this case, there is a controlling legal standard for compensation, we believe that adjudication would not be inconsistent with foreign policy interests under the Act of State Doctrine." On appeal, the Sixth Circuit accepted the position expressed in the letter. It is not clear whether courts will apply this "treaty exception" without first receiving the government's position. This exception appears to

161. 163 F.2d 246 (2d Cir. 1947).

162. *See* Bernstein v. N.V. Nederlandsche–Amerikaansche Stoomvaart–Maatschappij, 210 F.2d 375 (2d Cir. 1954).

163. 406 U.S. 759 (1972).

164. *See* Alfred Dunhill of London, Inc. v. Cuba, 425 U.S. 682 (1976).

165. 729 F.2d 422 (6th Cir. 1984).

166. U.S.-Eth., Sept. 7, 1951, 4 U.S.T. 2134, 206 U.N.T.S. 41.

reflect the proposition advanced in *Sabbatino* that applying the act of state doctrine is appropriate when there is insufficient consensus on the applicable international law rule, yet inappropriate when such consensus exists (*e.g.*, in a treaty).

Exception for Extraterritorial Government Action. The act of state doctrine does not apply where the foreign government seeks to affect property located outside its territory.[167] Situs questions become particularly important in cases involving actions against intangibles, such as credits, debts or securities.

Exception for Commercial Activities. In *Alfred Dunhill of London, Inc. v. Cuba*,[168] three justices argued that the act of state doctrine did not apply to a foreign sovereign's commercial acts, even though those acts were done within its own territory. According to those justices, such acts are incapable of examination in U.S. courts only if U.S. jurisdiction over the conduct is limited under international jurisdictional principles.

Exception where Validity of Act is Not in Question. In *W.S. Kirkpatrick & Co. v. Environmental Tectonics Corp.*,[169] the plaintiff was an unsuccessful bidder on a contract with the government of Nigeria. The successful bidder (the defendant) had allegedly bribed a Nigerian government official in order to get the contract, in violation of U.S. law. The Supreme Court declined to apply the act of state doctrine, stating that the question before it was not whether to "declare invalid the official act of a foreign sovereign performed within its own territory." Rather, the issue before the court was whether an unlawful motivation could be imputed to a foreign official in the performance of his duties so as to satisfy U.S. requirements for a civil recovery by the plaintiff.[170]

Exception for Counterclaims. In *First National City Bank v. Banco Nacional de Cuba*,[171] a foreign government filed a claim and a U.S. national responded with a counterclaim. The foreign government raised the act of state doctrine as a defense to the counterclaim. The Supreme Court declined to apply the doctrine. Justice Douglas took the position that the act of state doctrine should not be applied to counterclaims.[172] None of the other justices, however, found that issue dispositive.

Exception for Human Rights Cases. U.S. courts usually do not apply the act of state doctrine to dismiss cases alleging human rights violations by a foreign government in its territory.[173] Indeed,

167. *See* Iraq v. First Nat'l City Bank, 353 F.2d 47 (2d Cir. 1965).

168. *Supra* note 164.

169. 493 U.S. 400 (1990).

170. *Id.* at 405.

171. *Supra* note 163.

172. *Id.* at 770–73 (citing to Nat'l City Bank v. China, 348 U.S. 356 (1955).

173. *See, e.g.*, Forti v. Suarez–Mason, 672 F. Supp. 1531, 1544–47 (N.D. Cal. 1987) (finding that the act of state doctrine does not bar an action for tor-

when enacting the Torture Victim Protection Act[174]—which provides a civil remedy to persons who suffer torture or extrajudicial killing by, or under the authority of, a foreign government—a Congressional committee indicated that it did not intend the act of state doctrine to apply to such claims.[175]

---

ture abroad brought under the Alien Tort Statute, 28 U.S.C. § 1350 (2006)).

174.   28 U.S.C. § 1350 note (2006).

175.   *See* S. Rep. No. 102–249, at 8 (1991).

Further Reading

Reed Brody & Michael Ratner, eds., *The Pinochet Papers: The Case of Augusto Pinochet in Spain and Britain* (2000).

James Cooper–Hill, *The Law of Sovereign Immunity and Terrorism* (2006).

Joseph W. Dellapenna, *Suing Foreign Governments and Their Corporations* (2d ed. 2003).

Eileen Denza, *Diplomatic Law: Commentary on the Vienna Convention on Diplomatic Relations* (3d ed. 2008).

Andrew Dickinson et al., *State Immunity: Selected Materials and Commentary* (2004).

Hazel Fox, *The Law of State Immunity* (2d ed. 2008).

Michael Wallace Gordon, *Foreign State Immunity in Commercial Transactions* (1991) (looseleaf).

Charles J. Lewis, *State and Diplomatic Immunity* (3d ed. 1990).

Luke T. Lee, *Consular Law and Practice* (3d ed. 2008).

Ellen L. Lutz & Caitlin Reiger, eds., *Prosecuting Heads of State* (2009).

William H. Manz, ed., *Foreign Sovereign Immunities Act of 1976, with Amendments: A Legislative History of Pub. L. No. 94–583* (2000) (2 vols.).

Grant V. McClanahan, *Diplomatic Immunity: Principles, Practices, Problems* (1989).

Ivor Roberts, *Satow's Diplomatic Practice* (6th ed. 2009).

Beth Stephens & Michael Ratner, *International Human Rights Litigation in U.S. Courts* (1996).

Rosanne van Alebeek, *The Immunities of States and their Officials in International Criminal Law and International Human Rights Law* (2008).

PART III

SPECIALIZED AREAS OF INTERNATIONAL LAW

Chapter 10

HUMAN RIGHTS

A. Introduction

Although it is common to note that traditional international law was concerned only with relations among states, in fact it has always been concerned with protecting persons. From its earliest origins, an important component of international law has been the protection of diplomats and envoys sent from one state to another, and the protection of combatants and non-combatants from the excesses of warfare. Further, international law has always addressed the treatment by one state of another's nationals, an area known as "state responsibility for injury to aliens."[1] These protections, however, were cast as obligations that a state owed to the *state* of the foreigner's nationality, not obligations owed directly to the foreigner. Hence, the person had no standing to complain of wrongful conduct under international law.

Traditional international law also spoke to the protection of persons against the acts of their *own* governments. Thus, the idea of a state intervening to protect the other state's nationals (a doctrine now referred to as "humanitarian intervention") was advanced by early scholars of international law, such as Grotius and Vattel.[2] Grotius maintained that resort to war was lawful— both under natural law and the law of nations—if a ruler was inflicting "upon his subjects such treatment as no one is warranted in inflicting."[3] By the 1800's, European powers embarked on interventions to protect from persecution Christians located within the Ottoman Empire, such as France's intervention in Syria in 1860–61. This, in turn, led the Ottoman Empire to grant various concessions to the European powers regarding the treatment of minorities within its empire, concessions that appeared in treaties such as the General Treaty of Paris of 1856 and the Treaty of Berlin of 1878.[4]

---

1. *See infra* sec. B.

2. *See* SEAN D. MURPHY, HUMANITARIAN INTERVENTION: THE UNITED NATIONS IN AN EVOLVING WORLD ORDER 43–46 (1996).

3. 2 HUGO GROTIUS, DE JURE BELLI AC PACIS LIBRI TRES (ON THE LAW OF WAR AND PEACE), bk. 2, ch. 25, para. 8 (Francis Kelsey trans., 1925) (1646).

4. General Treaty for the Re-establishment of Peace, Mar. 30, 1856, 46 BRIT. & FOREIGN STATE PAPERS 8, 12 (1855–56); Treaty for the Settlement of Affairs in the East, July 13, 1878, 69 BRIT. & FOREIGN STATE PAPERS 749, 753 (1877–78).

Among other things, those treaties obligated Turkey to treat its subjects on the basis of religious and racial non-discrimination.

Indeed, the 1800's saw sporadic efforts to codify rules of international law for the protection of persons, such as treaties to abolish slavery and the slave trade, some of which set up international anti-slavery courts.[5] These treaties were partly an altruistic effort to protect individuals from rulers who held their subjects in (or sold them into) slavery, yet were also an attempt by states that had abolished slavery to avoid a competitive disadvantage with those states that had not. Instruments codifying rules protecting combatants and non-combatants emerged at this time, such as the 1864 Geneva Convention on the wounded and sick, and the 1868 St. Petersburg Declaration on explosive projectiles.[6] The latter expressed, with respect to a particular weapon, the broader customary principle prohibiting the infliction of unnecessary suffering upon combatants in time of war.

By the 1900's, codification of norms protecting individuals began to broaden. The 1899 and 1907 Hague conferences led to the adoption of important treaties regulating the conduct of warfare.[7] After World War I, the Covenant of the League of Nations established a "mandate" system whereby certain states became responsible for administering the defeated powers' colonies. The administering states agreed to promote the well-being of the peoples of those colonies, an obligation supervised by the League's Mandates Commission. Further, a series of post-war treaties concluded between the victorious powers and newly-emerged states or newly-independent states in Europe (such as Czechoslovakia, Hungary, and Poland) required the new states to protect ethnic, linguistic, or religious minorities located within their territory.[8] Minorities could file grievance petitions with the League, which on several occasions sought advice from the Permanent Court of International Justice about the treatment of minorities.[9] After the formation of the International Labor Organization (ILO) in 1919, dozens of treaties

5. *See* General Act of the Conference of Berlin Concerning the Congo, Feb. 26, 1885, 3 AM. J. INT'L L. SUPP. 7 (1909); General Act for the Repression of the African Slave Trade, July 2, 1890, 27 Stat. 886; *see* Jenny S. Martinez, *Anti-Slavery Courts and the Dawn of International Human Rights Law*, 117 YALE L.J. 550 (2008).

6. Geneva Convention for the Amelioration of the Condition of the Wounded in Armies in the Field, Aug. 22, 1864, 22 Stat. 940; St. Petersburg Declaration Renouncing the Use, in Time of War, of Explosive Projectiles Under 400 Gram-

mes Weight, Dec. 11, 1868, 2 AM. J. INT'L L. SUPP. at 95–96 (1907).

7. *See* Chapter 14(B).

8. *See, e.g.,* Treaty of Peace between the Principal Allied and Associated Powers and Hungary, June 4, 1920, 15 AM. J. INT'L L. SUPP. 1, 1–4 (1921).

9. *See, e.g.,* Advisory Opinion on Minority Schools in Albania, 1935 P.C.I.J. (ser. A/B) No. 64 (Apr. 6); *see generally* JULIUS STONE, INTERNATIONAL GUARANTEES OF MINORITY RIGHTS: PROCEDURE OF THE COUNCIL OF THE LEAGUE OF NATIONS IN THEORY AND PRACTICE (1932).

were concluded concerning basic standards on labor and social welfare, such as the Convention Concerning Forced or Compulsory Labour.[10] Moreover, the ILO's law-making process entailed a unique ability for government, labor, and management representatives to appear and vote before the ILO Conference. The 1926 Slavery Convention (and its 1956 supplementary convention) helped define and protect persons from a wide range of institutionalized practices, such as debt bondage, serfdom, and illegal transfers of children.[11]

In the aftermath of World War II, the movement to codify international human rights dramatically accelerated due to a global interest in transferring to the international arena the essential civil, political, and economic rights secured at great cost in many national arenas. If a single event may be regarded as the key turning point, that event would be the 1945 establishment by France, the Soviet Union, the United Kingdom, and the United States of an International Military Tribunal (IMT) at Nuremberg to try Germans for atrocities committed during World War II. While the Allied states were interested in punishing German leaders for their aggression, they were also horrified by the widespread and systematic atrocities committed by the Axis powers against their own nationals, particularly Germany's extermination of some six million Jews in Germany and German-occupied territories. The IMT was charged not just with the prosecution of Germans for war crimes against the Allied Powers and their nationals (*e.g.*, aggression and other war crimes), but also with "crimes against humanity" committed by German leaders against their own people in times of war *or* peace. The IMT, therefore, became the starting point for rapidly developing laws that would protect persons against genocide, violence, and other harmful acts inflicted by their own governments, and for recognizing on a broad scale that persons in power had responsibilities under international law that, if transgressed, could lead to personal and criminal accountability.

From Nuremberg to the present, human rights law has evolved in both its substance and process. Whereas prior to Nuremberg there were merely a handful of treaties that addressed narrow protections for persons, since Nuremberg an array of global and regional treaties covering political, civil, cultural, economic, and other rights have entered into force. Whereas the prior focus had been on granting protections for persons from wrongful treatment by foreign governments, the focus is now on protecting persons

10. June 28, 1930, 39 U.N.T.S. 55 (ILO Convention No. 29).

11. *See* Slavery Convention, Sept. 25, 1926, 60 L.N.T.S. 253, as amended by protocol of Oct. 23, 1953, 182 U.N.T.S. 51; Supplementary Convention on the Abolition of Slavery, the Slave Trade, and Institutions and Practices Similar to Slavery, Sept. 7, 1956, 226 U.N.T.S. 3.

from any governmental action, including that of their own government. Whereas before the emphasis had been on recognizing the rights of governments to protect their nationals against other governments, the emphasis has switched to recognizing the rights held by persons themselves. Before Nuremberg, only governments brought claims to vindicate these rights, yet after Nuremberg mechanisms developed for persons to bring their own claims, sometimes against a foreign government and sometimes against their own government. Whereas before Nuremberg culpable behavior by leaders of a state might presage a claim against the state, such behavior now serves as the basis of criminal liability of the leader himself.

B. State Responsibility for Injury to Aliens

Before the emergence of modern human rights law, international law had established rules on the responsibility of a state to protect aliens within its jurisdiction. While a state was not obligated to allow an alien to enter its territory, once it did, the state was obligated to treat the alien in accordance with a reasonable standard of decency. At the same time, the alien was required to accept the substantive and procedural law of the state to whom the alien had voluntarily traveled (which need not accord aliens all the rights held by the local population, such as the right to vote); so long as the alien was treated decently, the alien could not complain that the local law was less desirable than that of his home state. Hence, the law in this area sought to balance the right of the host state to maintain its substantive and procedural law with its obligation to treat the alien decently.

States and international tribunals have struggled with what is meant by treating an alien "decently" or "reasonably." Some states have taken the position that so long as the same protection is accorded to aliens as is accorded to local nationals, then there is no violation of international law. In other words, so long as an alien receives "national treatment" in the protection of his or her person and property, the state has no further obligation to the alien. For example, in the *Rosa Gelbtrunk* case before the U.S.-Salvador Claims Commission in 1902, the U.S. claimants' property in El Salvador was unlawfully looted by soldiers. The El Salvador government, however, declined to pay compensation. The commission held for El Salvador, finding that the claimants "were not in any way discriminated against" since they were treated the same as El Salvador nationals whose property was looted.[12]

---

12. United States (Rosa Gelbtrunk claim) v. Salvador, 15 R.I.A.A. 463, 466 (1902).

Yet the position that an alien is never entitled to treatment more favorable than that accorded to local nationals is not accepted by international law and practice. Rather, there has emerged a standard referred to as the "minimum standard of treatment" which sets a threshold below which treatment of an alien may not fall regardless of how local nationals are treated. Under this standard, a host state is expected to provide a minimum level of police protection for aliens and their property within its territory, and to accord them at least minimal substantive and procedural rights.

The U.S.-Mexican Claims Commission grappled with this standard in its 1926 *Neer* case. In that case, Paul Neer was a U.S. national employed as superintendent of a mine in Mexico. In November 1924, Neer was traveling by horseback when he was stopped by a gang of armed men, leading to a shoot-out in which Neer was killed. Thereafter, Mexican police authorities conducted what Neer's wife considered a lackluster investigation. When a claim was brought against Mexico, the claims commission stated:

> [T]he propriety of governmental acts should be put to the test of international standards, and ... the treatment of an alien, in order to constitute an international delinquency, should amount to an outrage, to bad faith, to wilful neglect of duty, or to an insufficiency of governmental action so far short of international standards that every reasonable and impartial man would readily recognize its insufficiency. Whether the insufficiency proceeds from deficient execution of an intelligent law or from the fact that the laws of the country do not empower the authorities to measure up to international standards is immaterial.[13]

The commission noted that Mexico's investigation could have been better, but there was a "full record" of the police having conducted an investigation, including visiting the location where the killing occurred, examining the corpse, and questioning witnesses. Further, certain suspects were arrested, although later released due to lack of evidence. The commission concluded that it was "not prepared to hold that the Mexican authorities have shown such lack of diligence or such lack of intelligent investigation in apprehending and punishing the culprits as would render Mexico liable before this Commission."[14]

Modern tribunals continue to express the minimum standard of treatment in terms of outrageous behavior by the host government. In *Waste Management, Inc. v. Mexico* case, an arbitral panel

---

13. United States (L.F.H. Neer Claim) v. Mexico, 4 R.I.A.A. 60, 61–62 (1926).

14. *Id.* at 62.

convened under the North American Free Trade Agreement (NAF-TA)[15] stated:

> [T]he minimum standard of treatment of fair and equitable treatment is infringed by conduct attributable to the State and harmful to the claimant if the conduct is arbitrary, grossly unfair, unjust or idiosyncratic, is discriminatory and exposes the claimant to sectional or racial prejudice, or involves a lack of due process leading to an outcome which offends judicial propriety—as might be the case with a manifest failure of natural justice in judicial proceedings or a complete lack of transparency and candour in an administrative process.[16]

Likewise, in *Glamis Gold*, a different NAFTA panel asserted that the minimum standard of treatment is violated only by conduct that is "sufficiently egregious and shocking—a gross denial of justice, manifest arbitrariness, blatant unfairness, a complete lack of due process, evident discrimination, or a manifest lack of reasons."[17] One way the standard might be breached is if the host state makes specific assurances or commitments to the alien investor so as to induce certain expectations, but then arbitrarily reneges on those assurances or commitments.

As indicated in the above quotes, the "minimum standard of treatment" includes the idea that an alien should not be denied the benefits of due process of law before a state's courts or administrative tribunals. Such treatment is regarded as a "denial of justice." A denial of justice might arise from an unwarranted delay or obstruction in an alien's access to local courts, a gross deficiency in the administration of the judicial process with respect to an alien's claim, or a manifestly unjust judgment by a local court regarding an alien's claim. At the same time, as the Turkish–American Claims Commission in the *Pirocaco* case concluded: "As a general rule, a denial of justice resulting from improper action of judicial authorities can be predicated only on a decision of a court of last resort."[18] In essence, international law accepts that errors are inevitable in any system of justice. Consequently, when evaluating whether a state has met its obligation to provide an adequate system of justice, international law takes into account that system's ability to correct its errors through appellate mechanisms made available in the state's system.

15. U.S.-Can.-Mex., Dec. 17, 1992, 32 I.L.M. 289 & 605.

16. Waste Mgmt., Inc. v. Mexico, Award, para. 98 (NAFTA Ch. 11 Arb. Trib. Apr. 30, 2004), *reprinted in* 43 I.L.M. 967 (2004).

17. Glamis Gold Ltd. v. United States, Award, para. 616 (NAFTA Ch. 11 Arb. Trib. June 8, 2009), *reprinted in* 48 I.L.M. 1035 (2009).

18. Christo G. Pirocaco v. Turkey (1923), *reprinted in* FRED K. NIELSEN, AMERICAN-TURKISH CLAIMS SETTLEMENT UNDER THE AGREEMENT OF DECEMBER 24, 1923, 587, 599 (1937).

A NAFTA tribunal considered the denial of justice standard in the *Mondev* case. In December 1978, the City of Boston and the Boston Redevelopment Authority (BRA) concluded a commercial real estate development contract with a partnership owned by a Canadian company, Mondev International (Mondev). A dispute arose under the contract and Mondev sued BRA in Massachusetts court. A jury found in favor of Mondev, but on appeal the Massachusetts Supreme Judicial Court found against Mondev, based in part on BRA's immunity under a Massachusetts statute. Mondev's petitions for a rehearing by the Massachusetts Supreme Judicial Court and for certiorari to the U.S. Supreme Court were denied. In 1999, Mondev filed a NAFTA claim asserting, among other things, that various actions of the Massachusetts Supreme Court constituted "flagrant procedural deficiencies" or "gross defects in the substance of the judgment itself," and thus constituted a denial of justice under customary international law. The NAFTA tribunal considered this allegation in light of the International Court of Justice's decision in the *ELSI* case.[19]

> In the *ELSI* case, a Chamber of the [International] Court [of Justice] described as arbitrary conduct that which displays "a wilful disregard of due process of law, ... which shocks, or at least surprises, a sense of judicial propriety".... The test is not whether a particular result is surprising, but whether the shock or surprise occasioned to an impartial tribunal leads, on reflection, to justified concerns as to the judicial propriety of the outcome.... In the end the question is whether, at an international level and having regard to generally accepted standards of the administration of justice, a tribunal can conclude in the light of all the available facts that the impugned decision was clearly improper and discreditable, with the result that the investment has been subjected to unfair and inequitable treatment. This is admittedly a somewhat open-ended standard, but it may be that in practice no more precise formula can be offered to cover the range of possibilities.[20]

Applying this standard to Mondev's claim, the tribunal found that the Massachusetts Supreme Judicial Court's decisions were either applying settled Massachusetts contract or procedural law or, if applying new law, "fell well within the interstitial scope of lawmaking exercised by courts such as those of the United States.... "[21]

---

19. *See* Elettronica Sicula S.p.A. (ELSI) (U.S. v. Italy), 1989 I.C.J. 15, para. 128 (July 20).

20. Mondev Int'l v. United States, Award, para. 127 (NAFTA Ch. 11 Arb. Trib. Oct. 11, 2002), *reprinted in* 42 I.L.M. 85 (2003) (footnotes omitted).

21. *Id.*, paras. 133, 136–37.

Traditionally, only the state of the person's nationality was entitled to bring a claim against the offending state. As the Permanent Court of International Justice explained: "[I]n taking up the case of one of its nationals, by resorting to diplomatic action or international judicial proceedings on his behalf, a State is in reality asserting its own right, the right to ensure in the person of its nationals respect for the rules of international law."[22] Thus, a state would "espouse" the claim of its national and then proceed diplomatically to resolve the claim, either by a settlement agreement or arbitration.[23] In modern situations, however, persons may be empowered to bring claims directly against foreign governments, such as by investors against host states under the NAFTA.

When modern human rights law first developed, the area of state responsibility for injury to aliens provided a useful starting point. Protections of "decency" accorded to aliens were considered relevant in developing protections to be accorded to nationals as against their own government. As time has passed, and human rights law has become more refined, the tables have turned. Increasingly, norms associated with modern human rights law are being read back into the law on state responsibility for injury to aliens, to clarify concepts such as "minimum standard of treatment" and "denial of justice." Indeed, it is now commonly accepted that states may invoke human rights standards on behalf of their nationals with respect to conduct by other states.

C. Global Human Rights Instruments

Modern human rights law centers around important treaties (and institutions) adopted since World War II. Human rights treaties, in turn, have had a significant (albeit not thorough) influence on the constitutions, laws, judicial decisions, and policies of states worldwide.[24] The following are some of the most important of these treaties.

U.N. Charter and Human Rights

When the four powers (China, Soviet Union, United Kingdom, and United States) met at Dumbarton Oaks in 1944 to complete the

22. Panevezys–Saldutiskis Railway (Est. v. Lith.), 1939 P.C.I.J. (ser. A/B) No. 76, at 16 (Feb. 28).

23. See Chapter 6(E).

24. See BETH A. SIMMONS, MOBILIZING FOR HUMAN RIGHTS: INTERNATIONAL LAW IN DOMESTIC POLITICS (2009); CHRISTOF HEYNS & FRANS VILJOEN, THE IMPACT OF THE UNITED NATIONS HUMAN RIGHTS TREATIES ON THE DOMESTIC LEVEL (2002); Ryan Goodman & Derek Jinks, *Measuring the Effects of Human Rights Treaties*, 14 EUR. J. INT'L L. 171 (2003); *but see* Oona A. Hathaway, *Do Human Rights Treaties Make a Difference?*, 111 YALE L.J. 1935 (2002) (arguing that such treaties are relatively ineffective); Oona A. Hathaway, *Testing Conventional Wisdom*, 14 EUR. J. INT'L L. 185 (2003) (same); Michael J. Gilligan & Nathaniel H. Nesbitt, *Do Norms Reduce Torture?*, 38 J. LEGAL STUD. 445 (2009).

first draft of a United Nations Charter, their principal focus was on the creation of an organization that could maintain international peace and security, not on the promotion and protection of human rights. Indeed, those states had reasons to avoid the question of human rights, whether due to Soviet gulags used to suppress political opposition, the U.K. maintenance of colonial possessions, or the U.S. toleration of racial discrimination and segregation.

At the general conference at San Francisco in 1945, however, other states and non-governmental organizations pressed for references to the protection of human rights in the Charter. Rather strikingly, the preamble to the U.N. Charter begins with "We the Peoples of the United Nations" rather than "We states" or "We governments," a clear recognition that the new organization was the product of the will of persons, not just governments.[25] Further, the preamble states that, among other things, the "Peoples" are determined "to reaffirm faith in fundamental human rights.... "[26] Article 1 then states that one of the purposes of the United Nations is to "develop friendly relations among nations based on respect for the principle of equal rights and self-determination of peoples, and to take other appropriate measures to strengthen universal peace," while another is to "achieve international co-operation in ... promoting and encouraging respect for human rights and for fundamental freedoms for all without distinction as to race, sex, language, or religion."

Despite these initial provisions, the U.N. Charter provides just a basic framework for developing the law or process of human rights. None of the extraordinary powers accorded to the Security Council explicitly refers to human rights; instead, the emphasis is on maintaining international peace and security. Chapter IX on "International Economic and Social Cooperation" contains two brief articles of direct relevance. Article 55 provides that:

> With a view to the creation of conditions of stability and well-being which are necessary for peaceful and friendly relations among nations based on respect for the principle of equal rights and self-determination of peoples, the United Nations shall promote:
>
> a. higher standards of living, full employment, and conditions of economic and social progress and development;
>
> b. solutions of international economic, social, health, and related problems; and international cultural and educational cooperation; and

25. U.N. Charter pmbl.   **26.** *Id.*

    c. universal respect for, and observance of, human rights and fundamental freedoms for all without distinction as to race, sex, language, or religion.

Article 55 is important for four reasons. First, whereas many states are not a party to the various human rights treaties discussed below, 193 states are party to the U.N. Charter and are thereby obligated to abide by Article 55. Second, Article 55 made clear that human rights and fundamental freedoms were no longer a matter solely of internal concern for states; all states agreed that the United Nations could properly promote such rights and freedoms. Third, Article 55 made an important link between the maintenance of international peace and the promotion of human rights; it asserts that the stability necessary for peaceful relations is dependant, in part, upon a universal respect for human rights. Thus, while the U.N. Charter is skewed toward peace and security, embedded in Article 55 is a recognition that achieving peace can only be accomplished with an eye to human rights. Fourth, while the exact substance of those human rights is not described (proposals by various delegations at San Francisco in this regard failed), Article 55 clearly prohibits distinctions based on race, sex, language, or religion. Article 56 then provides: "All Members pledge themselves to take joint and separate action in co-operation with the Organization for the achievement of the purposes set forth in Article 55."

Powers accorded to organs other than the Security Council laid the groundwork for subsequent development of the meaning of these human rights. Under Chapter IV, the General Assembly "shall initiate studies and make recommendations for the purpose of . . . assisting in the realization of human rights and fundamental freedoms for all without distinction as to race, sex, language, or religion."[27] Under Chapter X, the Economic and Social Council (ECOSOC) is also empowered to make recommendations on this topic and is called upon to establish a commission for the promotion of human rights[28] (now known as the U.N. Human Rights Council). Under Chapter XII, the (now-dormant) U.N. trusteeship system is instructed to encourage such rights and freedoms.[29]

Both skeptics and supporters of human rights law can find support in the U.N. Charter. For skeptics, the operative gerunds contained in these provisions ("promoting," "taking appropriate measures," "encouraging," and "assisting in the realization of") are, at best, tepid, and provide little concrete direction to states. To the extent that mandates are assigned to particular organs, it is to organs that have only the power of recommendation (*e.g.*, the

---

27. *Id.*, art. 13(1)(b).   **29.** *Id.*, art. 76.

28. *Id.*, arts. 62 & 68.

General Assembly; ECOSOC), not the power to bind states (*i.e.*, the Security Council). For supporters, however, these provisions laid the legal groundwork for the United Nations' efforts to create new instruments that codified and developed the field of human rights. Some scholars have even gone so far as to say that when a global human rights treaty has garnered widespread support among states, the norms reflected in the treaty bind non-parties, because the norms either reflect customary international law or illuminate the obligations under Articles 55–56 to which all states are bound.

Shortly after adoption of the U.N. Charter, efforts were made in U.S. courts to use the Charter to strike down discriminatory state laws. Although concurring opinions before the U.S. Supreme Court suggested that Articles 55 and 56 were now a part of U.S. federal law that prohibited racial discrimination,[30] the California Supreme Court found in 1952 that the U.N. Charter's human rights provisions were not self-executing and thus did not preempt state law.[31] In *Sei Fujii v. California*, the plaintiffs challenged a California statute that prevented aliens ineligible for citizenship from acquiring real property, arguing that the statute conflicted with Articles 55–56. According to the California Supreme Court:

> The provisions in the charter pledging cooperation in promoting observance of fundamental freedoms lack the mandatory quality and definiteness which would indicate an intent to create justiciable rights in private persons immediately upon ratification. Instead, they are framed as a promise of future action by the member nations.[32]

Since that decision, U.S. courts have consistently declined to allow the U.N. Charter's human rights articles to be used as a means of striking down federal or state laws.[33]

Universal Declaration of Human Rights

At the time the U.N. Charter was adopted in 1945, it was accepted that an "international Bill of Rights" would be one of the first actions taken by the fledgling organization. The newly-formed U.N. Commission on Human Rights took up the task and quickly realized that the creation of a binding instrument would take a considerable amount of time. Consequently, the commission decided first to create a non-binding instrument that states would more readily accept, which it transmitted through ECOSOC to the Gen-

---

30. *See* Oyama v. California, 332 U.S. 633, 649–50, 673 (1948) (concurring opinions of Justices Black and Murphy).

31. *See* Sei Fujii v. California, 38 Cal. 2d 718, 722–25 (1952). On the doctrine of non-self-executing treaties, see Chapter 7(C).

32. 38 Cal. 2d at 724.

33. *See, e.g.*, United States v. Noriega, 746 F. Supp. 1506, 1533–34 (S.D. Fla. 1990).

eral Assembly. In December 1948, the General Assembly adopted unanimously the Universal Declaration on Human Rights,[34] albeit with eight abstentions (including states from the Soviet bloc).

Over the course of thirty articles, the Universal Declaration contains an impressive listing of key human rights, including the following:

- all persons are born free and equal in dignity and rights (art. 1);

- all persons have the right to life, liberty, and security (art. 3);

- no one shall be held in slavery or tortured (arts. 4–5);

- all persons are entitled to equal protection under the law (arts. 6–7);

- there shall be no arbitrary arrest, detention, or exile (art. 9);

- all persons have the right to a fair trial (arts. 10–11);

- all persons have a right of privacy (art. 12);

- each person has a right to a nationality, to freedom of movement and residence in his or her state, to leave and return to his or her state, and to seek asylum elsewhere (arts. 13–15);

- all persons have a right to marry and to have a family (art. 16);

- all persons have a right to own property (art. 17);

- all persons have a right to freedom of thought, conscience, religion, and assembly (arts. 18–20);

- each person has a right to participate in the government of his country (art. 21);

- each person has a right to social security, employment, rest and leisure, education, and a standard of living adequate for his or her health and well-being (arts. 22–26);

- these rights are to be held without discrimination of any kind (art. 2); and

- each person has a right to sue to a remedy in national tribunals for acts violating fundamental rights granted under national law (art. 8).

At the same time, the Universal Declaration recognizes that each person has duties to his community so as to ensure respect for the rights and freedoms of others, and to meet "the just require-

---

34. G.A. Res. 217 (Dec. 10, 1948) [hereinafter Universal Declaration]. For the important role of non-governmental organizations (NGOs) in the drafting, see WILLIAM KOREY, NGOS AND THE UNIVERSAL DECLARATION OF HUMAN RIGHTS: "A CURIOUS GRAPEVINE" (1998).

ments of morality, public order and the general welfare in a democratic society."[35]

As noted above, the Universal Declaration was not adopted as a binding instrument, nor was it ever reduced to treaty form or ratified by states through the typical treaty process. Over time, many scholars have declared that the Universal Declaration is partly or entirely legally binding upon states. One argument for the legal force of the Universal Declaration is that it serves as an authoritative statement of the rights to which states have committed themselves under Articles 55–56 of the U.N. Charter. Another argument is that the Universal Declaration has passed into customary international law. For instance, when the Second Circuit Court of Appeals in the *Filartiga* case sought to determine whether state-sponsored torture violated customary international law, the court found it relevant that the Universal Declaration prohibited torture. The court stated:

> For although there is no universal agreement as to the precise extent of the "human rights and fundamental freedoms" guaranteed to all by the Charter, there is at present no dissent from the view that the guaranties include, at a bare minimum, the right to be free from torture. This prohibition has become part of customary international law, as evidenced and defined by the Universal Declaration of Human Rights ... which states, in the plainest of terms, "no one shall be subjected to torture."[36]

In the *Sosa* case, however, the U.S. Supreme Court asserted that because the Universal Declaration was non-binding at its inception, it could not "establish the relevant and applicable rule of international law"[37]—in that instance, whether temporary arbitrary arrest violated the law of nations. In any event, it is clear that the Universal Declaration has served as a template for numerous subsequent treaties on human rights, as discussed below.

Human Rights Covenants (ICCPR and ICESCR)

After completing work on the Universal Declaration of Human Rights, the U.N. Commission on Human Rights set about the task of concluding a legally-binding instrument. As predicted, that task resulted in protracted negotiations among states, which ultimately culminated in 1966 with the adoption of two treaties: the International Covenant on Civil and Political Rights (ICCPR);[38] and the International Covenant on Economic, Social and Cultural Rights

---

35. *Id.*, art. 29.

36. Filartiga v. Pena–Irala, 630 F.2d 876, 882 (2d Cir. 1980).

37. Sosa v. Alvarez–Machain, 542 U.S. 692, 734–35 (2004).

38. Dec. 16, 1966, 999 U.N.T.S. 171 [hereinafter ICCPR].

(ICESCR).[39] As suggested by their titles, the first covenant focuses on clarifying and detailing the civil and political rights envisaged in the Universal Declaration, while the latter focuses on the same with respect to economic and social rights. For example, while the Universal Declaration contains a fairly simple statement that "[e]veryone has the right to life,"[40] the ICCPR contains a more detailed article addressing, among other things, the status of the death penalty. Collectively, the human rights provisions of the U.N. Charter, the Universal Declaration, and the two covenants have been referred to as the "International Bill of Human Rights."

ICCPR. As of 2011, the ICCPR has 167 parties, including the United States. It details the civil and political rights held by persons, including rights to self-determination, life, freedom from torture, freedom of opinion and expression, and equality under the law. While many of these rights are recognized in the Universal Declaration, some rights, such as the right not to be imprisoned for debt or the right of a child to be accorded "such measures of protection as are required by his status as a minor,"[41] do not appear in the Universal Declaration.

ICCPR Article 2(1) provides: "Each State Party to the present Covenant undertakes to respect and to ensure to all individuals within its territory and subject to its jurisdiction the rights recognized in the present Convention, without distinction of any kind . . . " While this language imposes a straight-forward obligation upon states to ensure the rights set forth in the ICCPR, the language has led to debate. Some observers maintain that areas outside a state's "territory," even if under its "jurisdiction," are not covered since the obligation is with respect to individuals *both* within its territory and under its jurisdiction.[42] In support of that position, the preparatory work to the ICCPR indicates that the words "within its territory and" were proposed by the United States in 1950 so as not to assume an obligation with respect to territories occupied or leased by the United States, such as occurred after World War II in Germany and Japan.[43] Thus, the U.S. government has maintained that the ICCPR does not apply to al Qaeda and Taliban individuals being held at Guantánamo Bay Naval Base in Cuba because that location is outside U.S. territory. Other observers, however, maintain that the language of Article 2 was

39. Dec. 16, 1966, 993 U.N.T.S. 3 [hereinafter ICESCR].

40. Universal Declaration, *supra* note 34, art. 3.

41. ICCPR, *supra* note 38, arts. 11 & 24(1).

42. *See* Michael J. Dennis, *Application of Human Rights Treaties Extraterritorially in Times of Armed Conflict and Military Occupation*, 99 AM. J. INT'L L. 119 (2005); MANFRED NOWAK, UN COVENANT ON CIVIL AND POLITICAL RIGHTS 41 (1993).

43. *See* Dennis, *supra* note 42, at 123–24.

meant to be expansive, covering areas *either* within a state's territory or under its jurisdiction. Indeed, the Human Rights Committee established by the ICCPR has asserted that "the enjoyment of Covenant rights is not limited to citizens of States Parties but must also be available to all individuals ... who may find themselves in the territory or subject to the jurisdiction of the State Party."[44] Further, in *Legal Consequences of the Construction of a Wall*, the International Court advised that

> while the jurisdiction of States is primarily territorial, it may sometimes be exercised outside the national territory. Considering the object and purpose of the International Covenant on Civil and Political Rights, it would seem natural that, even when such is the case, States parties to the Covenant should be bound to comply with its provisions.[45]

Separate from the issue of coverage, the ICCPR contains important qualifications within several provisions. The ICCPR does not prohibit all government taking of life; rather, it provides that "[n]o one shall be *arbitrarily* deprived of his life."[46] The ICCPR does not prohibit all government interference with the privacy of a person; rather, it states that "[n]o one shall be subjected to *arbitrary* or *unlawful* interference with his privacy.... "[47] Thus, it is insufficient to show that government action is being taken against one's life or privacy; one must prove that such action was arbitrary or unlawful. Similarly, the ICCPR protects freedom of religion, but allows states to impose limitations as "prescribed by law" and as "necessary to protect public safety, order, health, or morals or the fundamental rights and freedoms of others."[48] Thus, a professed religion requiring the smoking of hallucinogenic drugs or the killing of dogs might be restricted by a state on the grounds of public health or morals.

Moreover, the ICCPR contains a clause that allows states to derogate from their obligations "[i]n time of public emergency which threatens the life of the nation and the existence of which is officially proclaimed," so long as it does so only "to the extent strictly required by the exigencies of the situation."[49] In such instances, the state is permitted to suspend its obligations, except for seven of the most fundamental rights contained in the ICCPR.

---

44. Human Rights Committee, General Comment No. 31, U.N. Doc. CCPR/C/21/Rev.1/Add.13, para. 10 (2004).

45. Legal Consequences of the Construction of a Wall in the Occupied Palestinian Territory, 2004 I.C.J. 136, para. 109 (July 9); *see generally* MARKO MILANOVIC, EXTRATERRITORIAL APPLICATION OF HUMAN RIGHTS TREATIES: LAW, PRINCIPLES, AND POLICY (2011).

46. ICCPR, *supra* note 38, art. 6(1) (emphasis added).

47. *Id.*, art. 17(1) (emphasis added).

48. *Id.*, art. 18.

49. *Id.*, art 4(1). A state that undertakes such a derogation must inform all other state parties. *Id.*, art. 4(3).

These fundamental rights concern: (1) the right to life; (2) the right not to be tortured; (3) the right not to be held in slavery; (4) the right not to be imprisoned for debt; (5) the right not to be found guilty of an offense made criminal *ex post facto*; (6) the right to recognition as a person before the law; and (7) the right to freedom of thought, conscience, and religion. In the *Lawless Case*,[50] the European Court of Human Rights construed a similar provision, finding that the Irish government was justified in declaring a public emergency in response to terrorist activities and in detaining persons without trial, since the detentions were subject to various safeguards to prevent abuses (e.g. Parliamentary scrutiny).

There are two protocols to the ICCPR which states may join if they wish. The First Optional Protocol[51] creates a procedure for individuals to send a communication to the ICCPR Human Rights Committee, and is discussed in Section D below. The Second Optional Protocol expressly abolishes the death penalty, although it allows states to use the death penalty for serious military crimes committed in time of war.[52] At present, 114 states are party to the first protocol and 73 states are party to the second protocol. The United States is a party to neither protocol.

In June 1992, the United States ratified the ICCPR, yet filed several reservations, understandings, and declarations (RUDs).[53] For instance, although ICCPR Article 20(2) provides that "advocacy of national, racial or religious hatred that constitutes incitement to discrimination, hostility or violence shall be prohibited by law," the United States filed a reservation stating that the ICCPR did not authorize or require any law that would restrict free speech under the U.S. Constitution. Further, the United States filed an understanding that distinctions based upon race, color, sex, and other characteristics are permitted "when such distinctions are, at minimum, rationally related to a legitimate governmental objective."[54] By declaration, the United States asserted that the substantive rights recounted in ICCPR Articles 1 though 27 are not self-executing as a matter of U.S. law, a declaration that has been given effect by U.S. courts.[55]

ICESCR. As of 2011, the ICESCR has 160 parties, not including the United States. This covenant, as its title suggests, focuses on economic, social and cultural rights, many of which were identified in the Universal Declaration. It spells out in greater detail

---

50. 1 Eur. Ct. H.R. (ser. A) (1960).

51. First Optional Protocol to the ICCPR, Dec. 16, 1966, 999 U.N.T.S. 302, 6 I.L.M. 383.

52. Second Optional Protocol to the ICCPR, Dec. 15, 1989, 29 I.L.M. 1464.

53. *See* 138 Cong. Rec. 8068 (1992) [hereinafter ICCPR RUDs].

54. *Id.* at 8070.

55. *See, e.g., Sosa*, 542 U.S. at 735; Igartua De La Rosa v. United States, 32 F.3d 8, 10 n.1 (1st Cir. 1994).

what is meant by the right to work, the right to form trade unions, the right to social security, and the right to food, clothing, and housing.

Article 2(1) of the ICESCR provides that states undertake to implement these rights, but notes several caveats:

Each State Party to the present Covenant undertakes to take steps, individually and through international assistance and co-operation, especially economic and technical, to the maximum extent of its available resources, with a view to achieving progressively the full realization of the rights recognized in the present Covenant by all appropriate means, including particularly the adoption of legislative measures.

Unlike ICCPR Article 2(1), the several caveats in ICESCR Article 2(1) are a ready indication that states are not prepared to accept wholesale obligations to provide social security, employment, food and shelter to their nationals. Whereas a state's agreement not to infringe upon freedom of religion can be a cost-free undertaking, a state's agreement to provide social security is clearly not cost-free, and many states (especially in the developing world) are simply not in a position to adhere to such an obligation. Thus, Article 2 recognizes that there can be a "progressive" realization of these rights over a period of time. At the same time, some of the ICESCR's obligations apply immediately, such as the undertaking that the rights "enunciated in the present Covenant will be exercised without discrimination of any kind. . . ."[56]

Under Part IV of the Covenant, certain monitoring functions are assigned to the U.N. Economic and Social Council (ECOSOC), but in 1985, ECOSOC delegated those functions to a body of independent experts known as the Committee on Economic, Social and Cultural Rights (CESCR).[57] As discussed in Section D below, States parties submit reports to the Committee on their implementation of the Covenant; the Committee examines each report, indicates areas of concern, and provides recommendations to the states parties. In 2008, the General Assembly adopted an Optional Protocol to the Covenant which provides the Committee competence to receive and consider petitions by individuals, with respect to states that have ratified the Optional Protocol.[58]

The United States has not ratified the ICESCR or the Optional Protocol. Although signed by President Carter in 1977 (along with the ICCPR) and transmitted to the Senate in 1978, the Senate declined to consent to ratification of the ICESCR. While senators' concerns varied, much of the resistance appears related to the

---

56. ICESCR, *supra* note 39, art. 2(2).

57. ECOSOC Res. 1985/17 (May 28, 1985).

58. G.A. Res. 63/117 (Dec. 10, 2008).

political culture of the United States. At its inception, the United States embedded political and civil rights in the fabric of its constitution (*i.e.*, the Bill of Rights), which sought to constrain government action. Yet early U.S. political culture did not embrace economic and social rights whereby U.S. nationals could claim economic entitlements from their government. Although certain economic entitlements now exist with the passage of statutes protecting vulnerable groups (*e.g.*, the poor and the elderly), U.S. political philosophy remains largely oriented toward a belief in the free market and the promotion of capitalism free of government control. As such, U.S. leaders remain skeptical of and uncertain about what it means to guarantee various ICESCR rights, such as a "right to work," as provided in ICESCR Article 6. To the extent that it means that the U.S. government must find an unemployed worker a new job and perhaps pay him a salary if one cannot be found, the United States is unwilling at this time to accept such an obligation.

Other Key Human Rights Treaties

Convention Against Genocide. The extermination of millions of individuals in the Holocaust aroused the U.N. General Assembly in December 1948 to adopt the Convention Against Genocide,[59] which entered into force in 1951. The convention provides that genocide, whether committed in times of peace or war, is a crime under international law which states undertake to prevent and punish, including by enactment of necessary legislation.[60] The convention defines genocide as certain acts, such as killing, injuring, or forcibly transferring persons, "with intent to destroy, in whole or in part, a national, ethnical, racial or religious group ... ,"[61] and applies to persons whether they are rulers or private individuals.

For example, in September 1998, the International Criminal Tribunal for Rwanda (ICTR) convicted a former Rwandan mayor, Jean Paul Akayesu, of genocide (as well as crimes against humanity and war crimes).[62] The ICTR found that during the genocide in Rwanda, more than 2,000 Tutsis were killed in Akayesu's commune, while many others were exposed to violence (including rape) and other forms of hatred. Akayesu personally supervised the murder of various Tutsis and failed to take any steps to stop the killings. As the first conviction by the ICTR, the decision was of significance; in fact, it was the first genocide conviction by any

---

59. Convention on the Prevention and Punishment of the Crime of Genocide, Dec. 9, 1948, 78 U.N.T.S. 277; *see* THE UN GENOCIDE CONVENTION: A COMMENTARY (Paola Gaeta, ed. 2009); JOHN QUIGLEY, THE GENOCIDE CONVENTION: AN INTERNATIONAL LAW ANALYSIS (2006).

60. *Id.*, arts. I & V.

61. *Id.*, art. II.

62. *See* Prosecutor v. Akayesu, Judgment, Case No. ICTR–96–4–T (Int'l Crim. Trib. Rwanda Sept. 2, 1998), *reprinted in* 37 I.L.M. 1399 (1998).

international court. In October 1998, Akayesu was sentenced to life imprisonment (the ICTR does not issue the death penalty).

As of 2011, there are 142 parties to the Convention Against Genocide. The United States ratified the convention in November 1988, subject to various RUDs.[63] One reservation provides that "nothing in the Convention requires or authorizes legislation or other action by the United States of America prohibited by the Constitution of the United States as interpreted by the United States."[64] The United States implements the convention through the Genocide Convention Implementation Act of 1987, as amended.[65]

Unfortunately, when an apparent genocide arises, states may resist labeling it "genocide" because doing so triggers an obligation to prevent it. This appears to have been the case for the United States in April 1994 with respect to the genocide that unfolded in Rwanda. By contrast, in July 2004, the U.S. Congress adopted a concurrent resolution declaring that genocide was occurring in Darfur, Sudan. The resolution referred to the definition of "genocide" in the Convention Against Genocide and stated that "in Darfur, Sudan, an estimated 30,000 innocent civilians have been brutally murdered, more than 130,000 people have been forced from their homes and have fled to neighboring Chad, and more than 1,000,000 people have been internally displaced.... "[66] Thereafter, U.S. Secretary of State Colin Powell declared that the atrocities in Darfur constituted genocide.[67] At the initiative of the United States, the U.N. Security Council adopted a resolution providing, among other things, for the creation of a commission to investigate the atrocities in Darfur and to determine whether they constituted genocide.[68] The secretary-general established an International Commission of Inquiry,[69] which in February 2005 concluded that the government of Sudan had not pursued a policy of genocide, because it found no evidence of genocidal intent on the part of central government authorities.[70]

63. *See* 28 I.L.M. 754 (1989) [hereinafter Genocide RUDs].

64. *Id*. at 782.

65. 18 U.S.C. § 1091 (2006).

66. S. Con. Res. 133, pmbl, 108th Cong. (2004). The resolution garnered unanimous support in the House and passed by a voice vote in the Senate.

67. *See* Secretary of State Colin L. Powell, The Crisis in Darfur, Written Remarks before the Senate Foreign Relations Committee (Sept. 9, 2004), *at* <http://www.state.gov>; *see also* Statement on the Situation in Sudan, 40 Weekly Comp. Pres. Doc. 1909 (Sept. 9, 2004) (statement by President Bush that "we have concluded that genocide has taken place in Darfur").

68. *See* S.C. Res. 1564 (Sept. 18, 2004).

69. *See* U.N. Doc. S/2004/812 (Oct. 4, 2004).

70. U.N. Doc. S/2005/60 at 4 (Jan. 25, 2005).

Yet in 2010, the International Criminal Court issued a warrant for the arrest of Sudan's President, Omar al Bashir, for three counts of genocide. Among other things, the warrant stated that there were reasonable grounds to believe that President al Bashir played a role in coordinating a Sudanese government military campaign in which the targeted villages and towns "were selected on the basis of their ethnic composition and that towns and villages inhabited by other tribes, as well as rebel locations, were bypassed in order to attack towns and villages known to be inhabited by civilians belonging to the Fur, Masalit and Zaghawa ethnic groups."[71]

Convention on Elimination of Racial Discrimination. In 1966, the U.N. General Assembly adopted a convention on the elimination of racial discrimination (CERD),[72] which entered into force in 1969. Under CERD, parties undertake to eliminate racial discrimination, including by rescinding laws and regulations that create or perpetuate such discrimination.[73] "Racial discrimination" is defined as

> any distinction, exclusion, restriction or preference based on race, colour, descent, or national or ethnic origin which has the purpose or effect of nullifying or impairing the recognition, enjoyment or exercise, on an equal footing, of human rights and fundamental freedoms in the political, economic, social, cultural or any other field of public life.[74]

As of 2011, there are 175 parties to CERD. In 1992, the United States signed CERD and, after receiving the Senate's consent, ratified it in 1994 subject to various RUDs.[75] Since the United States took the position that its laws, policies and government institutions are fully consistent with the provisions of the convention that it accepted, it did not enact implementing legislation. In its first report to the CERD committee, the United States asserted:

> Racial discrimination by public authorities is prohibited throughout the United States, and the principle of non-discrimination is central to governmental policy throughout the country. The legal system provides strong protections against and remedies for discrimination on the basis of race, colour, ethnicity or national origin by both public and private actors. These laws and policies have the genuine support of the overwhelm-

71. Second Warrant of Arrest for Omar Hassan Ahmad Al Bashir, ICC Doc. ICC–02/05–01/09–95 at 5 (July 12, 2010); *see also* Chapter 13(E).

72. International Convention on the Elimination of All Forms of Racial Discrimination, Dec. 21, 1965, 660 U.N.T.S. 195, 5 I.L.M. 350 [hereinafter CERD].

73. *Id.*, art. 2(d).

74. *Id.*, art. 1(1); *see* Advisory Opinion on Legal Consequences for States of the Continued Presence of South Africa in Namibia, 1971 I.C.J. 16, 57 (June 21).

75. *See* 140 Cong. Rec. 14,326 (1994) [hereinafter CERD RUDs].

ing majority of the people of the United States, who share a common commitment to the values of justice, equality, and respect for the individual.[76]

At the same time, the report conceded that "even though U.S. law is in conformity with the obligations assumed by the United States under the treaty, American society has not yet fully achieved the Convention's goals. Additional steps must be taken to promote the important principles embodied in its text."[77]

While CERD prohibits racial discrimination, it accepts that special measures "for the sole purpose of securing adequate advancement of certain racial or ethic groups" are permissible, provided they are not "continued after the objectives for which they were taken have been achieved."[78] Such a limitation on affirmative action was quoted approvingly by Justice Ginsberg in her concurring opinion to the U.S. Supreme Court's 2003 decision in *Grutter v. Bollinger*.[79] In that case, the Court found that a University of Michigan law school admissions policy designed to promote the racial diversity of the student body did not violate the Equal Protection Clause of the Fourteenth Amendment.[80] Noting, however, that race-conscious admissions policies must have a "logical end point," the Court expressed its expectation that "25 years from now, the use of racial preferences will no longer be necessary to further the interest approved today."[81] In her concurring opinion, Justice Ginsburg (joined by Justice Stephen Breyer) stated:

> The Court's observation that race-conscious programs "must have a logical end point," . . . accords with the international understanding of the office of affirmative action. The International Convention on the Elimination of All Forms of Racial Discrimination, ratified by the United States in 1994, . . . endorses "special and concrete measures to ensure the adequate development and protection of certain racial groups or individuals belonging to them, for the purpose of guaranteeing them the full and equal enjoyment of human rights and fundamental freedoms." . . . But such measures, the Convention instructs, "shall in no case entail as a consequence the maintenance of unequal or separate rights for different racial groups after the objectives for which they were taken have been achieved." [S]ee also . . . Convention on the Elimination of All Forms of Discrimination against Women, Annex to G.A. Res.

---

76. U.S. Dep't of State, Initial Report of the United States of America to the UN Committee on the Elimination of Racial Discrimination 2, para. 6 (2000).

77. *Id.*, para. 8.

78. CERD, *supra* note 72, art. 1(4).

79. 539 U.S. 306 (2003).

80. *See* U.S. Const. amend. XIV, § 1 ("nor [shall any State] deny to any person within its jurisdiction the equal protection of the laws").

81. *Grutter*, 539 U.S. at 343.

34/180, 34 U.N. GAOR Res. Supp. (No. 46) 194, U.N. Doc. A/34/46, Art. 4(1) (1979) (authorizing "temporary special measures aimed at accelerating *de facto* equality" that "shall be discontinued when the objectives of equality of opportunity and treatment have been achieved").[82]

Convention on Discrimination Against Women. In the post-World War II period, treaties began to emerge protective of women's rights. In 1948, the Organization of American States adopted the Inter–American Convention on the Granting of Political Rights to Women.[83] Twenty-four states of the Western Hemisphere have joined the convention as of 2011, including the United States. In 1952, the U.N. General Assembly adopted the U.N. Convention on the Political Rights of Women,[84] which as of 2011 has 122 states parties, including the United States. The latter convention provides that women shall be entitled to vote, women shall be eligible for election in all publicly elected bodies, and women shall be entitled to hold public office and to exercise all public functions, all on equal terms with men.[85]

In December 1979, the U.N. General Assembly adopted the Convention on the Elimination of All Forms of Discrimination Against Women (CEDAW),[86] which entered into force in 1981. Like CERD, the convention calls upon parties to eliminate discrimination, including by rescinding laws and regulations that create or perpetuate such discrimination.[87] "Discrimination against women" is defined as

> any distinction, exclusion, or restriction made on the basis of sex which has the effect or purpose of impairing or nullifying the recognition, enjoyment or exercise by women, irrespective of their marital status, on a basis of equality of men and women, of human rights and fundamental freedoms in the political, economic, social, cultural, civil or any other field.[88]

As of 2011, there are 187 parties to CEDAW. Many states who have adhered to the convention have filed reservations to protect national or religious practices that discriminate against women. The United States signed CEDAW in July 1980, and President Carter submitted the treaty to the U.S. Senate for advice and consent later that year. Although the Senate Foreign Relations Committee (SFRC) held hearings on CEDAW in 1988 and 1990, the committee did not act on the treaty. In 1994, the SFRC recommended that the full Senate grant advice and consent, subject to

---

82. *Id.* at 344.

83. May 2, 1948, O.A.S. T.S. No. 3.

84. Dec. 20, 1952, 193 U.N.T.S. 135.

85. *Id.*, arts. 1–3.

86. Dec. 18, 1979, 1249 U.N.T.S. 13 [hereinafter CEDAW].

87. *Id.*, art. 2(f).

88. *Id.*, art. 1.

certain RUDs,[89] but the Senate took no action. In 2002, the SFRC again held hearings on a proposed Senate resolution to grant advice and consent to CEDAW. However, the U.S. Department of State expressed concerns that the CEDAW Committee had issued objectionable reports on certain countries.[90] In particular, the department noted that the CEDAW Committee (1) had criticized Belarus for reinstating Mother's Day, which the CEDAW Committee regarded as continuing a sex-role stereotype; (2) had criticized China for criminalizing prostitution, since the CEDAW Committee viewed prostitution as resulting from poverty and economic deprivation; and (3) had criticized Croatia for limiting access to abortions.[91] As of 2011, the United States has not joined CEDAW.

Convention Against Torture. In December 1984, the U.N. General Assembly adopted the Convention Against Torture,[92] which entered into force in 1987. The convention defines torture in part as

> any act by which severe pain or suffering, whether physical or mental, is intentionally inflicted on a person for such purposes as obtaining from him or a third person information or a confession, punishing him for an act he or a third person has committed ... , or intimidating or coercing him or a third person, ... when such pain or suffering is inflicted by or at the instigation of ... a public official.... [93]

The convention requires all parties to prevent acts of torture in territory under its jurisdiction, and precludes parties from extraditing a person to another state where there are substantial grounds for believing the person would be tortured.[94] The convention also requires parties to exercise jurisdiction over such offenses on board its flag vessels or when committed abroad by one of its nationals.[95] If an offender turns up in a party's territory, the party must either submit the matter to prosecution or extradite the individual to another party for prosecution.[96] In 2002, the U.N. General Assembly adopted an Optional Protocol to the Convention,[97] which establishes a system for regular visits by independent international and

89. *See* Marian Nash, *Contemporary Practice of the United States*, 89 Am. J. Int'l L. 96, 102 (1995).

90. *See* Letter from Secretary of State Colin L. Powell to Senator Joseph R. Biden, Jr. (July 8, 2002) (on file with author).

91. *See* U.N. Doc. A/55/38, para. 361 (Jan. 31, 2000) (regarding Belarus); U.N. Doc. A/54/38/Rev.1, paras. 288–89 (Feb. 3, 1999) (regarding China); U.N. Doc. A/53/38, paras. 109, 117 (May 14, 1998) (regarding Croatia).

92. Convention Against Torture and Other Cruel, Inhuman or Degrading Treatment or Punishment, Dec. 10, 1984, S. Treaty Doc. No. 100–20 (1988), 1465 U.N.T.S. 85 [hereinafter Convention Against Torture].

93. *Id.*, art. 1.

94. *Id.*, arts. 2–3.

95. *Id.*, art. 5(1).

96. *Id.*, arts. 7–8.

97. G.A. Res. 57/199, annex (Dec. 18, 2002).

national bodies to places where people are deprived of their liberty, in order to prevent torture and other cruel, inhuman or degrading treatment or punishment.

As of 2011, there are 149 parties to the Convention Against Torture. On November 20, 1994, the United States became a party to the convention, subject to various RUDs.[98] As discussed in Chapter 5(C), the United States enacted a statute that authorizes federal criminal prosecution of U.S. nationals who commit torture abroad, as well as of any perpetrator (regardless of nationality) present in the United States.[99] Otherwise, the United States implements the convention through existing federal and state statutes and regulations, since torture was already prohibited as a tool of state authority prior to U.S. adherence to the convention.

Convention on the Rights of the Child. In November 1989, the U.N. General Assembly adopted the U.N. Convention on the Rights of the Child,[100] which entered into force in September 1990. The convention calls for parties to accord a variety of protections for human beings under the age of eighteen (unless they obtain adult status at an earlier age under national law).[101] These protections include the rights to life, to a name from birth, to acquire a nationality, to not be separated from parents against one's will, to express one's views freely, to freedom of association, to privacy, and to access to information.[102]

As of 2011, every state except the United States and Somalia has ratified the Convention on the Rights of the Child. The United States signed the convention in 1995, but U.S. resistance to ratification has centered on the fact that the convention largely covers matters left to the several states in the United States, which the United States prefers not to federalize. Nevertheless, as discussed in Chapter 7(C), the U.S. Supreme Court in *Roper v. Simmons*[103] referred to this convention in finding Missouri's juvenile death penalty violative of the Eighth Amendment's prohibition on cruel and unusual punishment.

In May 2000, the U.N. General Assembly adopted two optional protocols to the convention, entitled Optional Protocol on the Involvement of Children in Armed Conflict and Optional Protocol on the Sale of Children, Child Prostitution and Child Pornography.[104] Among other things, the first protocol bars compulsory

---

98. *See* 136 Cong. Rec. 17,486 (1990) [hereinafter Torture RUDs].

99. *See* 18 U.S.C. §§ 2340, 2340A & 2340B (2006).

100. Nov. 20, 1989, 1577 U.N.T.S. 3 [hereinafter Convention on the Rights of the Child].

101. *Id.*, art. 1.

102. *Id.*, arts. 6–7, 9, 12–17.

103. 543 U.S. 551 (2005).

104. G.A. Res. 54/263 (May 25, 2000) (annexes I & II).

recruitment of children under the age of eighteen for military service, requires that states which voluntarily recruit children under the age eighteen describe the steps they will take to ensure the protection of such enlistees (*e.g.*, showing parental consent and reliable proof of age), and requires that states cooperate in prevention and rehabilitation efforts for children victimized by war. The second protocol defines as criminal acts the "sale of children," "child prostitution," and "child pornography;" establishes grounds for jurisdiction over, and extradition of, criminal offenders; and provides for international cooperation in pursuing offenders. A state may become a party to either protocol without being a party to the underlying convention.

In 2000, the United States joined other members of the Security Council in passing a resolution urging all members to sign and ratify the protocol on the involvement of children in armed conflict.[105] Moreover, President Clinton signed both protocols, which were then transmitted to the U.S. Senate for advice and consent.[106] In June 2002, the Senate unanimously provided advice and consent to ratification. With respect to the Children in Armed Conflict Protocol, the Senate added two additional understandings, including one that provides "that nothing in the Protocol establishes a basis for jurisdiction by any international tribunal, including the international criminal court."[107] With respect to the Sale of Children Protocol, the Senate added a declaration that the protocol is non-self-executing and fulfilled by current U.S. law, and added a further understanding concerning the implementation of the protocol in the U.S. federal system.[108] In December 2002, the United States deposited with the United Nations the instruments of ratification for both protocols.

Convention on the Rights of Persons with Disabilities. In December 2006, the U.N. General Assembly adopted the Convention on the Rights of Persons with Disabilities (CRPD)[109] which, as of 2011, has been adhered to by 105 states. The United States signed the convention, but has not ratified it as of 2011. The convention generally obligates states to "undertake to ensure and promote the full realization of all human rights and fundamental freedoms for all persons with disabilities without discrimination of any kind on

---

105. *See* S.C. Res. 1314, para. 4 (Aug. 11, 2000).

106. *See* 146 Cong. Rec. 7573 (2000); White House Press Release on Message from the President to the Senate on Children's Rights (July 25, 2000), *reprinted in* 2000 WL 1120135.

107. 148 Cong. Rec. S5717 (daily ed. June 18, 2002).

108. *Id.* at S5718–19.

109. G.A. Res. 61/106, annex I (Dec. 13, 2006), 46 I.L.M. 441 (2007); *see generally* Frédéric Mégret, *The Disabilities Convention: Human Rights of Persons with Disabilities or Disability Rights?*, 30 Hum. Rts. Q. 494 (2008).

the basis of disability."[110] Among other things, states are obligated to ensure the equal rights and advancement of women and girls with disabilities (Article 6), to protect children with disabilities (Article 7), and to guarantee that persons with disabilities enjoy their inherent right to life on an equal basis with others (Article 10).

Convention on Enforced Disappearance. The U.N. General Assembly also in December 2006 adopted the International Convention for the Protection of All Persons from Enforced Disappearance (CPED).[111] Under the CPED, no state may subject a person to "enforced disappearance," which is defined as:

> the arrest, detention, abduction or any other form of deprivation of liberty by agents of the State or by persons or groups of persons acting with the authorization, support or acquiescence of the State, followed by a refusal to acknowledge the deprivation of liberty or by concealment of the fate or whereabouts of the disappeared person, which place such a person outside the protection of the law.[112]

The CPED entered into force in December 2010 and, as of 2011, has thirty states parties, not including the United States.

Labor Conventions. As noted *supra* in Section A of this chapter, the International Labor Organization (ILO) played a key role in advancing human rights at a relatively early period of the human rights era. From the early twentieth century up to 2011, the ILO has adopted 189 conventions protective of worker's rights. The ILO has identified eight of those conventions as "fundamental" since they cover subjects that are considered as fundamental principles and rights at work: freedom of association and the effective recognition of the right to collective bargaining; the elimination of all forms of forced or compulsory labor; the effective abolition of child labor; and the elimination of discrimination in respect of employment and occupation.[113]

For example, on June 17, 1999, the ILO unanimously adopted a convention to eliminate the "worst forms of child labour."[114] The

---

110. G.A. Res. 61/106, annex II, art. 4.

111. G.A. Res. 61/488, annex (Dec. 20, 2006).

112. *Id.*, arts. 1–2.

113. These fundamental principles were identified by the International Labor Conference in its 1998 Declaration on Fundamental Principles and Rights at Work, June 1998, 37 I.L.M. 1237 (1998); *see also* Philip Alston, *Core Lab-*

our Standards and the Transformation of the International Labour Rights Regime, 15 Eur. J. Int'l L. 457 (2004). As of 2011, 135 states having ratified all of the fundamental conventions, while the United States has ratified two.

114. Convention Concerning the Prohibition and Immediate Action for the Elimination of the Worst Forms of Child Labour, June 17, 1999, ILO No. C182, 38 I.L.M. 1207.

convention provides that each party "shall take immediate and effective measures to secure the prohibition and elimination of the worst forms of child labour," including penal and other sanctions.[115] The convention defines a "child" as any person under the age of 18, and states that "the worst forms of child labour" comprise: (1) all forms of slavery or practices similar to slavery, such as the sale and trafficking of children, debt bondage and serfdom, and forced or compulsory labor, including forced or compulsory recruitment of children for use in armed conflict; (2) using, procuring or offering a child for prostitution, the production of pornography, or pornographic performances; (3) using, procuring, or offering a child for illicit activities, in particular for the production and trafficking of drugs as defined in relevant international treaties; and (4) work which, by its nature or the circumstances in which it is carried out, is likely to harm the health, safety, or morals of children.[116] The convention also obligates parties to provide for the rehabilitation and social integration of children removed from the worst forms of child labor, access to free basic education, and (wherever possible and appropriate) vocational training.[117] At the insistence of the United Kingdom and the United States, the convention permits the voluntary enlistment of children under age eighteen to serve in a state's armed services.

In August 1999, President Clinton transmitted the convention to the Senate for advice and consent,[118] which was granted in November subject to various RUDs.[119] The president then deposited the U.S. instrument of ratification and the United States became a party when the convention entered into force in December 2000. Separately, President Clinton in June 1999 ordered U.S. executive branch agencies to take appropriate actions to enforce U.S. laws prohibiting the manufacture or importation of goods produced by forced child labor.[120]

Not all labor-related conventions were crafted within the ILO. For example, forty-five states have joined the International Convention on the Protection of the Rights of All Migrant Workers and Members of their Families (ICRMW), which was adopted by the U.N. General Assembly in 1990.[121] The ICRMW obligates states parties to accord various rights to migrant workers, including the freedom to leave any state without restriction.[122]

115. *Id.*, art. 1.

116. *Id.*, arts. 2–3.

117. *Id.*, art. 7.

118. *See* S. Exec. Rep. 106–12 (1999).

119. *See* 145 Cong. Rec. 14,226 (1999).

120. *See* Exec. Order No. 13,126, 64 Fed. Reg. 32,383 (June 12, 1999).

121. G.A. Res. 45/158, annex (Dec. 18, 1990).

122. *Id.*, art. 8.

U.S. Adherence to Human Rights Treaties

As noted above, the United States has adhered to various major human rights agreements adopted since World War II (*e.g.*, ICCPR, CERD, and the conventions against genocide, torture, and child labor), yet has declined to join others (*e.g.*, ICESCR, CEDAW, and the Convention on the Rights of the Child). Debate over whether the United States should join such treaties has existed since the 1950's. Proponents view the treaties as largely reflecting U.S. values and existing law, and regard adherence as a means of projecting and securing U.S. values worldwide. Opponents, however, express concern about how the treaties affect U.S. law, both through the substantive norms expressed in the treaties and the structural aspect of federalizing matters traditionally left to the several states. For many years, southern legislators feared that adherence to such treaties would provide Congress with the power to enact civil rights laws that otherwise could not be supported under Congress' Article I powers. Some even saw the Convention Against Genocide as potentially supporting claims against the U.S. government for the treatment of African–Americans and Native–Americans. Moreover, the economic and social rights within the ICESCR were viewed askance during the Cold War, for they appeared to some as communism in disguise.[123]

Reflecting these concerns, Senator John Bricker in the 1950's advocated adoption of various amendments to the U.S. Constitution that would preclude treaties from being self-executing. The Bricker amendments were defeated, but only after a commitment from the Eisenhower administration that the United States would not ratify new human rights treaties. Hence, for decades the United States declined to submit major human rights treaties to the Senate, such as the ICCPR and the ICESCR. With the election of President Jimmy Carter in 1976, however, the executive branch began favoring an aggressive promotion of human rights worldwide. Among other things, it signed and sent to the Senate major human rights treaties.

To the extent that the United States has adhered to such conventions, it has (as noted above) invariably filed important RUDs. While these RUDS vary considerably, they tend to fall into one of four categories. First, some RUDs simply reject provisions contained within the treaty, such as a reservation to CERD rejecting any limitation on hate speech inconsistent with the First Amendment's protection of free speech,[124] or rejecting the jurisdic-

---

123. *See generally* NATALIE KAUFMAN, HUMAN RIGHTS TREATIES AND THE SENATE: A HISTORY OF OPPOSITION (1990); DUANE TANANBAUM, THE BRICKER AMENDMENT CONTROVERSY: A TEST OF EISENHOWER'S POLITICAL LEADERSHIP (1988).

124. *See* CERD RUDs, *supra* note 75, para. I(1).

tion of the International Court of Justice over disputes arising under the treaty.[125] Second, some RUDs attempt to interpret vague treaty provisions, such as a reservation clarifying that the Convention Against Torture's prohibition on "cruel, inhuman, or degrading treatment" means such treatment as is prohibited by the U.S. Constitution (which speaks only of "cruel and unusual" punishment).[126] Third, some RUDs assert that the treaty's core provisions are not self-executing as a matter of U.S. law, meaning that they cannot be enforced in U.S. courts,[127] while others state that the president may not ratify the treaty until implementing legislation has been enacted.[128] Fourth, some RUDs seek to acknowledge the federal structure of the United States by asserting that the federal government will only adhere to the treaty with respect to matters within its jurisdiction, while other matters will be left to state and local governments.[129]

Views differ as to the propriety of RUDs when joining human rights treaties. Some critics characterize the U.S. approach as bad policy: one of fear and arrogance that "weakens America's voice as a principled defender of human rights around the world and diminishes America's moral influence and stature."[130] Further, some argue that U.S. RUDs violate the object and purpose of the treaties and, as such, are void.[131]

Others, however, note the widespread practice of states in filing reservations to human rights treaties; one-third of the parties to the ICCPR have reserved to its substantive provisions.[132] As such, it seems doubtful that all RUDs violate the treaty's object and purpose. Certainly, U.S. courts have upheld U.S. reservations to human rights treaties.[133] To the extent a RUD is violative of the treaty's object and purpose, several states and scholars maintain that the reserving state has not become a party to the treaty, for a state cannot be bound to a treaty provision to which it has not consented. As for whether the U.S. approach is good policy, some argue that RUDs "reflect a sensible accommodation of competing domestic and international considerations," bridging "the political divide between isolationists who want to preserve the United

---

125. *Id.*, para. I(3).

126. *See* Torture RUDs, *supra* note 98, para. I(1); *see also* ICCPR RUDs, *supra* note 53, para. I(2).

127. *See, e.g.,* ICCPR RUDs, *supra* note 53, para. III(1).

128. *See, e.g.,* Genocide RUDs, *supra* note 63, para. III.

129. *See, e.g.,* ICCPR RUDs, *supra* note 53, para. II(5).

130. Kenneth Roth, *The Charade of US Ratification of International Human* *Rights Treaties*, 1 Chi. J. Int'l L. 347, 347 (2000).

131. *See* Chapter 3(A).

132. *See* Catherine J. Redgwell, *Reservations to Treaties and Human Rights Committee General Comment No. 24(52)*, 46 Int'l & Comp. L.Q. 390, 393 (1997).

133. *See, e.g.,* Beazley v. Johnson, 242 F.3d 248, 266–68 (5th Cir. 2001); *Ex Parte* Pressley, 770 So. 2d 143, 148 (Ala. 2000); Domingues v. Nevada, 961 P.2d 1279, 1280 (Nev. 1998).

States's sovereign prerogatives, and internationalists who want the United States to increase its involvement in international institutions...."[134]

D. Global Human Rights Institutions

Global human rights treaties operate within a system of institutions that promote, monitor, and implement compliance with the

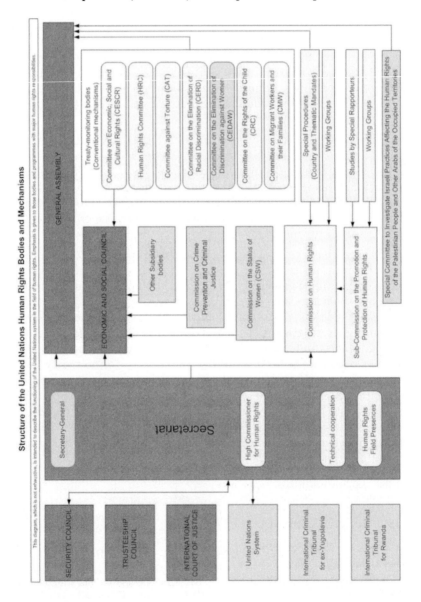

134. Curtis A. Bradley & Jack L. Goldsmith, *Treaties, Human Rights, and* *Conditional Consent*, 149 U. Pa. L. Rev. 399, 402 (2000).

treaties. Four particular institutions of significance are: (1) the committees established by several of the global human rights treaties; (2) the U.N. Human Rights Council; (3) the U.N. High Commissioner for Human Rights; and (4) the U.N. High Commissioner for Refugees. Each is discussed in turn.

Human Rights Committees

In addition to creating substantive obligations for parties, several human rights treaties also establish a committee of experts that serves important functions. Although the Convention Against Genocide created no such committee (and thus has no permanent institution to monitor compliance), there now exist the following committees:

- Human Rights Committee (established by the ICCPR);[135]

- Committee on Economic, Social and Cultural Rights;[136]

- Committee on the Elimination of Racial Discrimination;[137]

- Committee on the Elimination of Discrimination Against Women;[138]

- Committee on Torture;[139]

- Subcommittee on Prevention of Torture;[140]

- Committee on the Rights of the Child;

- Committee on Migrant Workers;

- Committee on the Rights of Persons with Disabilities;[141]

- Committee on Enforced Disappearance;

- ILO Committee of Experts on the Application of Conventions and Recommendations; and

- ILO Committee on Freedom of Association.

---

135. *See* Thomas Buergenthal, *The U.N. Human Rights Committee*, 5 MAX PLANCK U.N. YRBK. 341 (2001); DOMINIC MCGOLDRICK, THE HUMAN RIGHTS COMMITTEE: ITS ROLE IN THE DEVELOPMENT OF THE INTERNATIONAL COVENANT ON CIVIL AND POLITICAL RIGHTS (1991).

136. This committee was not created by the ICESCR itself, but developed from resolutions adopted by ECOSOC. *See* ECOSOC Res. 1985/17 (May 22, 1985).

137. *See* Rüdiger Wolfrum, *The Committee on the Elimination of Racial Discrimination*, 3 MAX PLANCK U.N. YRBK. 489 (1999).

138. *See* HUMAN RIGHTS OF WOMEN: NATIONAL AND INTERNATIONAL PERSPECTIVES 228–56 (Rebecca J. Cook ed., 1994).

139. *See* Chris Ingelse, *The Committee Against Torture: One Step Forward, One Step Back*, 18 NETH. Q. HUM. RTS. 307 (2000).

140. This subcommittee implements the 2002 Optional Protocol to the Convention against Torture.

141. G.A. Res. 61/106, annex II (Dec. 13, 2006).

Each committee is composed of a certain number of experts nominated and elected by the parties to the relevant treaty. The number of experts for these committees vary: for example, the first three committees listed above have eighteen experts, while the fourth consists of twenty-three experts. All experts serve in their individual capacities, not as representatives of governments. These committees have assumed important institutional functions: receiving reports from parties; commenting on compliance and other issues; dealing with inter-state complaints; and, when authorized, receiving and addressing petitions filed by individuals.

Reporting System. Except for the Subcommittee on Prevention of Torture (which focuses on visiting places of detention), all such committees are charged with periodically receiving reports on each party's implementation of the treaty. After reviewing a report, the committee may address questions to the reporting state to clarify or supplement the report. Often, a state will orally present its report to the committee in a public session, at which committee members may ask questions and make comments. The committee then privately considers the report and issues its reaction in writing, addressed to the relevant state and to the meeting of the parties of the treaty. This reaction, referred to as "Concluding Observations" by the Committee on Human Rights, not only critiques the state in question, but also (over time and in conjunction with other reactions) clarifies the meaning of treaty provisions and the manner in which they should be implemented. Having said that, committees have no adjudicatory power to declare a state in violation of the treaty. For a brief discussion of the first U.S. report to the Committee on Torture and its reaction, see Chapter 5(A).

In addition to commenting on the reports of parties, committees issue "general comments" addressed to the parties generally. Such comments provide interpretive guidance to the parties and guide the committee when reviewing the reports of states. For example, the Human Rights Committee's General Comment 24[142] asserts that a state may not file a reservation that is incompatible with the object and purpose of the human rights treaty, that it is for the committee to decide whether a reservation is incompatible, and that, if incompatible, the state is still bound to the treaty minus the reservation. The United States objected strenuously to General Comment 24, arguing that the Human Rights Committee had not been accorded such a power of interpretation, that the committee was setting aside established treaty law and the primacy of state consent, and that there was no basis in international law for severing a reservation from the ratification instrument.[143] Most

---

142. *See* Chapter 3(A).

143. *See* Observations by the United States on General Comment No. 24(52),

of the Human Rights Committee's general comments have not been so controversial. Indeed, some U.S. courts have found the committee's commentary helpful and persuasive.[144]

Inter-State Complaint System. Several of these committees have a role in overseeing an inter-state complaint system. The ICCPR, ICRMW, and Convention Against Torture provide their respective committees with jurisdiction to decide complaints filed by one party against another only if the parties have by written declaration accepted such jurisdiction (simply adhering to the treaty does not establish jurisdiction). By contrast, any state that ratifies the CERD accepts automatically the jurisdiction of the Committee on the Elimination of Racial Discrimination over inter-state complaints.

Under the ICRMW and Convention Against Torture, the system is similar to a mediation process; the committee's role is to try to find a friendly solution to the matter and, if it cannot, simply to report on the facts of the dispute without issuing a decision. By contrast, under ICCPR Article 41, it is then possible for the parties to consent to the creation of an *ad hoc* conciliation commission that would make findings of fact and issue a non-binding decision as to how the matter should be resolved. Under the CERD, the committee's role is limited to determining whether the complaint is admissible; if it is admissible, it is placed before an *ad hoc* conciliation commission.

As of 2011, these inter-state complaint systems have not been invoked.

Individual Petition System. In addition to these monitoring systems, parties to the ICCPR, ICESCR, CERD, CEDAW, CRPD, and Convention Against Torture may accept an individual petition system. Parties to the ICCPR, ICESCR, CRPD, and CEDAW accept this system by ratifying an optional protocol, whereas parties to the CERD and Convention Against Torture do so by declaration. The ICRMW provides for individual communications to be considered by its committee, but these provisions will become operative only once ten states parties make the necessary declaration under Article 77 of the ICRMW. The ILO Committee on Freedom of Association can review complaints against states which allege a violation of the right of freedom of association.

For example, by adhering to the ICCPR's First Optional Protocol, a state recognizes the competence of the Human Rights Committee to receive and consider communications from individuals

reprinted in 3 INT'L HUM. RTS. REP. 265 (1996).

144. *See, e.g.*, United States v. Duarte–Acero, 208 F.3d 1282, 1287 (11th Cir. 2000); United States v. Benitez, 28 F. Supp. 2d 1361, 1364 (S.D. Fla. 1998).

claiming to be victims of an ICCPR violation by that state. After exhausting local remedies, individuals may file a petition with the Human Rights Committee, which then transmits the petition to the state whose conduct is in question. Upon receiving the state's views and possibly further views of the petitioner, the petition is examined by the Human Rights Committee. The Committee might determine that the petition is inadmissible (*e.g.*, for failure to exhaust local remedies), or it can address the petition on the merits. Once the Committee reaches a finding on the petition (referred to as "Views"), it is transmitted to the petitioner and the state in question, and reported to the U.N. General Assembly through ECOSOC.

As of 2011, 114 of the 167 parties to the ICCPR have ratified the First Optional Protocol. The United States is among those states that have not done so. A lower number of states (53 out of 175 states and 56 out of 149 states respectively) have accepted the CERD's and the Convention Against Torture's individual petition system, not including the United States, while 79 out of 187 states party to CEDAW have accepted its individual petition system.

Investigation of Torture. In addition to the above systems, the Convention Against Torture authorizes its committee to undertake an investigation on its own initiative when it receives "reliable information" that torture is being "systematically practised" in a state.[145] The committee does not need the state's consent to conduct an investigation, yet does need its consent to enter the state's territory for purposes of the investigation. When joining the Convention Against Torture, a state may declare that it does not accept the committee's competence to conduct such investigations, although most parties have not exercised this option. Such investigations have occurred with respect to Peru and Turkey.

U.N. Human Rights Commission and Council

In 1946, the United Nations created a Human Rights Commission consisting of 53 states elected by the U.N. Economic and Social Council for three year terms.[146] Over the course of its life, the commission was an important global institution capable of helping develop key human rights instruments and investigating systematic abuses of human rights worldwide.[147] As noted above, the commission was instrumental in drafting the Universal Declaration of

---

145. Convention Against Torture, *supra* note 92, art. 20.

146. A similar Commission on the Status of Women was created in 1946, consisting of forty-five states elected by ECOSOC based on equitable geographic distribution. This commission was in-

strumental in the creation of the optional protocol to CEDAW allowing for an individual petition system.

147. *See generally* Howard Tolley, Jr., The U.N. Commission on Human Rights (1987).

Human Rights and the two covenants (ICCPR and ICESCR). By the late 1990's, however, there was considerable dissatisfaction with the commission; some observers criticized it as an ineffective "talk shop" for "hypocrites." For instance, in 2001, the United States was not elected to the commission, whereas Sudan—a state that independent human rights groups accused of permitting slavery and committing gross abuses against political and religious freedom—was elected.

In September 2005, a meeting of heads of states and governments at the U.N. General Assembly resolved to create a new U.N. Human Rights Council, which would be responsible for the functions previously performed by the Human Rights Commission.[148] The council was created in March 2006, this time consisting of 47 states elected by and reporting to the General Assembly.[149] Like its predecessor (and unlike the human rights committees associated with specific treaty regimes), the Human Rights Council consists of representatives of *governments*, not experts independent of governments. The council's work consists of various elements.

One element is the "Universal Periodic Review" (UPR), a process for reviewing the human rights records of all 193 U.N. member states once every four years. For each UPR, the state under review is expected to report to the council on the actions they have taken to improve human rights and fulfill their human rights obligations. The United States underwent its UPR in 2010–2011 and submitted a comprehensive report, one that reflected a series of consultations undertaken by the U.S. government with various sectors of the U.S. public. Among other things, the United States acknowledged the need for improvement in several areas, such as racial justice, women's rights, gay and lesbian rights, disability rights, and discrimination against Muslims and U.S. nationals of South Asian and Arab descent.[150]

Another element of the council's work is an advisory committee, consisting of eighteen independent experts, which provides expertise to the council on thematic human rights issues (the committee replaces an earlier sub-commission on the promotion and protection of human rights). In performing its functions, the advisory committee is expected to interact with states, national human rights institutions, non-governmental organizations, and civil society groups.

148. 2005 World Summit Outcome, U.N. Doc. A/60/L.1, paras. 157–60 (Sept. 15, 2005).

149. G.A. Res. 60/251 (2006).

150. Report of the United States Submitted to the UN High Commission-er for Human Rights in Conjunction with the Universal Periodic Review (Aug. 2010), *at* <http://www.state.gov/documents/organization/146379.pdf>.

A third element is a complaints procedure, which allows individuals and organizations to bring alleged human rights violations to the attention of the council. The purpose of the complaint procedure is to identify consistent patterns of gross violations of human rights and fundamental freedoms occurring anywhere worldwide. The procedure operates through two working groups: a Working Group on Communications (formed from members of the advisory committee, who are charged with determining whether a complaint deserves investigation) and a Working Group on Situations (formed from members of the council itself, which investigate the matter and report to the council).

Finally, the council creates and monitors certain mechanisms or "mandates" that investigate specific countries or thematic human rights issues (these mandates are also referred to as "special procedures"). As of 2011, there are 33 thematic mandates and 8 country-specific mandates, being performed in some instances by one expert (as special rapporteur, independent expert, or special representative of the Secretary–General) and in others by a working group of experts (usually composed of five members, one from each region of the world), working in their personal capacity and without salary. The exact mandate in each instance is spelled out in the resolution by the council creating the mechanism, which can last no longer than six years. Examples of recently-established thematic mandates include: contemporary forms of slavery (2007); access to safe drinking water and sanitation (2008); cultural rights (2009); freedom of peaceful assembly and of association (2010); and discrimination against women in law and in practice (2010).

The Office of the High Commissioner for Human Rights (discussed below) provides the council with support for the discharge of these tasks, including personnel, policy, research and logistical support.

U.N. High Commissioner for Human Rights

In 1994, the U.N. General Assembly created the position of U.N. High Commissioner for Human Rights to serve as the "United Nations official with principal responsibility for United Nations human rights activities under the direction and authority of the Secretary–General.... "[151] By creating this position, the United Nations placed a "human face" on U.N. human rights activities; a single individual can now call attention to human rights abuses and implore states to do better. The high commissioner is appointed by the secretary-general with the approval of the U.N. General Assembly (with due regard to geographical rotation) for a four-year, renewable term, and heads the Office of the High Commissioner of Human Rights (OHCHR).

151. *See* G.A. Res. 48/141 (Dec. 20, 1993).

Though based in Geneva, the OHCHR has offices and field operations worldwide, and coordinates U.N. programs in the human rights field, monitors human rights crises in various countries, trains government officials to prevent human rights abuses, and engages in dialogue with relevant governments about improving their human rights records. To date, the high commissioners have been: José Ayala Lasso (Ecuador); Mary Robinson (Ireland); Sergio Vieira de Mello (Brazil); Louise Arbour (Canada); and Navanethem Pillay (South Africa).

U.N. High Commissioner for Refugees

In 1950, the U.N. General Assembly created the position of U.N. High Commissioner for Refugees. While initially focused on the resettlement of more than one million refugees displaced during World War II, the high commissioner is now concerned with displaced persons worldwide. The high commissioner is appointed by the secretary-general with the approval of the U.N. General Assembly (with due regard being paid to geographical rotation) for a four-year, renewable term, and heads the U.N. Office of the High Commissioner for Refugees (UNHCR). Though based in Geneva, the OHCHR has offices and field operations worldwide, and helps coordinate U.N. programs in the field of refugees affairs. As of 2011, there have been ten high commissioners; António Guterres (Portugal) currently holds the position.

In performing its functions, the UNHCR monitors whether states are abiding by the U.N. Convention Relating to the Status of Refugees[152] and its associated protocol.[153] While the United States is not a party to the convention, it is derivatively bound to the convention's core provisions through its adherence to the protocol. In the case of *INS v. Aguirre–Aguirre*,[154] the Ninth Circuit Court of Appeals found a UNHCR handbook useful when interpreting U.S. obligations under the protocol, but the U.S. Supreme Court reversed, stating that the lower court did not give appropriate deference to the interpretation adopted by the U.S. Board of Immigration Appeals.

E.   Regional Human Rights Instruments/Institutions

Europe

In 1949, ten West European states banded together to form an international organization known as the Council of Europe, whose governing body is a Committee of Ministers and whose Parliamen-

---

152. July 28, 1951, 19 U.S.T. 6259, 189 U.N.T.S. 150 [hereinafter Refugee Convention].

153. Protocol Relating to the Status of Refugees, Jan. 31, 1967, 19 U.S.T. 6223, 606 U.N.T.S. 267.

154.   526 U.S. 415 (1999).

tary Assembly consists of parliamentarians from member states.[155] Among other things, members of the Council of Europe pledged to protect human rights and fundamental freedoms. Since it was apparent that it would take many years to develop the global human rights instruments that became the ICCPR and ICESCR, the Council of Europe member states in 1950 adopted the European Convention for the Protection of Human Rights and Fundamental Freedoms (European Convention),[156] which set forth a variety of civil and political rights (*e.g.*, the right to life, the right to be free from torture, and so on) and created institutions to monitor adherence.[157] Since 1950, the European Convention has been amended by thirteen protocols that considerably expand upon and clarify these rights. For example, Protocol No. 6, adopted in 1983, abolished the death penalty in peacetime.[158] As of 2011, 47 states were party to the European Convention.

The European Convention clearly governs the conduct of European governments within their own territory, in relation to their own nationals and non-nationals. As such, the Convention is primarily focused on European public order and the provision of rights in the legal space (espace juridique) of Europe.[159] However, the Convention will be applied to the conduct of a European state outside its territory in situations when the state is exercising control and authority over an individual or an area, such as the control exercised by the United Kingdom through its soldiers in Iraq during 2003–2004.[160]

In addition, other human rights have been declared by the Council of Europe through the European Social Charter,[161] which focuses on economic and social rights, and through conventions on topics such as torture, minorities, cloning, trafficking in persons, abuse of children, and violence against women. Separately, the European Union in 2000 crafted a non-legally binding Charter of Fundamental Rights, which over the course of fifty-four articles spells out protections for the integrity of the person, laborers, access to justice, and other matters.[162]

155. *See* Statute of the Council of Europe, May 5, 1949, 87 U.N.T.S. 103, Europ. T.S. No. 1.

156. Nov. 4, 1950, 213 U.N.T.S. 221, Europ. T.S. No. 5 [hereinafter European Convention].

157. *See generally* ROBIN C.A. WHITE & CLARE OVEY: JACOBS, WHITE AND OVEY: THE EUROPEAN CONVENTION ON HUMAN RIGHTS (5th ed. 2010).

158. *See* Protocol No. 6 to the European Convention, Apr. 28, 1983, Europ. T.S. No. 114.

159. Banković v. Belgium, 11 B.H.R.C. 435 (2001).

160. Al-Skeini v. United Kingdom, 50 I.L.M. 995 (2011).

161. European Social Charter, Oct. 18, 1961, 529 U.N.T.S. 89, Europ. T.S. No. 35, *amended by* protocols of May 5, 1988, Oct. 21, 1991, and Nov. 9, 1995. A revised, integrated European Social Charter was completed March 5, 1996, and entered into force in 1999. *See* Europ. T.S. No. 163.

162. *See* Charter of Fundamental Rights of the European Union, Dec. 7, 2000, 2000 O.J. (C 364) 1.

Initially, there were two principal institutions of the European human rights system: the European Commission of Human Rights (commission) and the European Court of Human Rights (ECHR). The commission, however, was abolished by Protocol No. 11,[163] and the ECHR was transformed from a part-time body into a full-time court.

The ECHR consists of a number of judges equal to the number of states party to the European Convention (at present 47 judges). As noted in Chapter 3(F), judges are elected by the Parliamentary Assembly of the Council of Europe for a non-renewable term of nine years. Any contracting state,[164] or any natural or legal person claiming to be a victim of a violation of the European Convention,[165] may lodge an application with the ECHR alleging a breach by a contracting state of one of the European Convention's rights. Admissibility requirements (*e.g.*, whether a petition is well-founded or whether local remedies have been exhausted) apply principally to individual, not inter-state petitions.[166] Consequently, individual petitions are normally first assigned to a judge or a committee of three judges to decide whether the petition is admissible.

If admissible, a petition is transmitted to a seven-judge chamber which is empowered to reach its own decision on admissibility and to address issues of merits and remedies. In doing so, the chamber may invite the parties to submit evidence and written observations, including any claims for "just satisfaction" by the petitioner. A hearing is then held, after which the chamber decides the matter by majority vote. The chamber's decision can be referred to a grand chamber of seventeen judges for review.[167] Once final, the decision is binding on the state to which it is directed.[168] Each year the ECHR issues hundreds of judgments, thereby establishing a formidable corpus of human rights jurisprudence.

As of 1970, the ECHR may issue advisory opinions on legal questions concerning the interpretation of the convention and its protocols, when requested by the Committee of Ministers of the Council of Europe.[169] Advisory opinions are given by the grand chamber and adopted by majority vote.

In addition to the work of the Council of Europe, European human rights have been advanced by the Organization for Security

---

163. Protocol No. 11 to the European Convention, May 11, 1994, Europ. T.S. No. 155.

164. European Convention, *supra* note 156, art. 33; *see also* Søren C. Prebensen, *Inter-State Complaints under Treaty Provisions—The Experience under the European Convention on Human Rights*, 20 Hum. Rts. L.J. 446 (1999).

165. *See* European Convention, *supra* note 156, art. 34.

166. *Id.*, art. 35.

167. *Id.*, art. 43.

168. *Id.*, art. 46.

169. *See* Protocol No. 2 to the European Convention, June 5, 1963, Europ. T.S. No. 44.

and Cooperation in Europe (OSCE). As discussed in Chapter 3(F), the 1975 Helsinki Final Act played an extremely important role in fostering human rights in Europe during the Cold War and thereafter. Among other things, the OSCE has focused on protecting the rights of national minority groups to prevent ethnic conflict in Europe. Indeed, the OSCE has created a High Commissioner on National Minorities charged with providing early warnings of situations where national minorities might be threatened, as a means of forestalling the outbreak of armed conflict.[170]

Americas

The inter-American human rights system is based on two separate instruments: the 1948 Charter of the Organization of American States (OAS Charter)[171] and the 1969 American Convention on Human Rights (American Convention).[172] Other instruments on torture, forced disappearances, and violence against women have also been concluded.

Human Rights under the OAS Charter. Under the OAS Charter, parties proclaim the fundamental rights of the individual and the need for states to respect those rights. While those rights are not spelled out in detail, a non-legally binding declaration adopted by American states in 1948, called the American Declaration of the Rights and Duties of Man (Declaration),[173] arguably provides greater content to them. In 1960, OAS member states created, as an autonomous entity, the Inter–American Commission on Human Rights with the task of promoting the human rights set forth in the Declaration. Seven years later, these states adopted a protocol to the OAS Charter (which entered into force in 1970), formally establishing the commission as an organ of the OAS.[174]

The commission consists of seven members elected by the OAS General Assembly from a list of candidates proposed by OAS governments. Members act in their personal capacity; they do not represent their government. A member from the United States virtually always serves on the commission, yet election is not guaranteed. In 2003, the United States nominated a lawyer known for expertise in medical malpractice and health law. The OAS

---

170. *See* Wolfgang Zellner, On the Effectiveness of the OSCE Minority Regime (1999).

171. Apr. 30, 1948, 2 U.S.T. 2394, 119 U.N.T.S. 3, as amended by protocols of 1967, 1985, 1992, and 1993 [hereinafter OAS Charter]. For a brief discussion of the OAS, see Chapter 2(B).

172. Nov. 22, 1969, 1144 U.N.T.S. 123, 9 I.L.M. 673, as amended by protocols of Nov. 14, 1988, 28 I.L.M. 156, and

June 8, 1990, 29 I.L.M. 1447 [hereinafter American Convention].

173. OAS Res. XXX (May 2, 1948), *reprinted in* Basic Documents Pertaining to Human Rights in the Inter-American System, OAS/Ser.L/V/1.4 Rev. 9 at 17 (2003).

174. *See* Thomas Buergenthal, *The Revised OAS Charter and the Protection of Human Rights*, 69 Am. J. Int'l L. 828 (1975).

General Assembly then elected four new members to the commission but did not elect the U.S. national. The following year, however, a U.S. national known for expertise in human rights law was elected.

Based in Washington, D.C., the commission has assisted in the drafting of OAS human rights instruments, provided advice on human rights to OAS organs, and educated states in their human rights obligations by sponsoring conferences and publications. It conducts investigations into human rights conditions in a particular state if it receives credible evidence of large-scale violations, which sometimes entails on-site investigations and hearing from witnesses. Further, the commission receives communications from states and individuals alleging violations of human rights, and issues final reports regarding those allegations. The commission has competence under Article 42 of the American Convention to supervise a reporting process, but as of 2011 has not exercised that function.

Numerous communications to the commission have concerned whether the United States is adhering to human rights standards. In some instances, these petitions were dismissed by the commission as inadmissible for failure to exhaust local remedies or failure to state facts tending to establish a violation of rights under the American Declaration or other relevant instruments.[175] In other cases, the commission has found the petition admissible, and held the United States in violation of its obligations under international law. For example, in February 2002, a petition was filed before the commission on behalf of Napoleon Beazley, a U.S. national on death row for an offense committed when he was seventeen years old. The commission issued precautionary measures requesting the United States not to execute Beazley pending the outcome of the commission's proceedings, yet Beazley was subsequently executed by the state of Texas. In December 2003, the commission determined that, in executing a juvenile offender, the United States had violated an international norm of *jus cogens* (the right to life), as set forth in Article 1 of the American Declaration. Consequently, the commission recommended that the United States provide a remedy (including compensation) to Beazley's next of kin. The commission also found that the United States violated its obligations as an OAS member by failing to abide by the commission's request that Beazley not be executed.[176] The commission's conclu-

---

175. *See, e.g.,* Lares–Reyes, Case 12.379, Inter–Am. C.H.R., Report No. 19/02 (2002); Walker, Case 12.049, Inter–Am. C.H.R., Report No. 62/03 (2003).

176. *See* Beazley, Case 12.412, Inter–Am. C.H.R., Report No. 101/03 (2003).

sion in this and similar cases[177] may have influenced the Supreme Court's 2005 decision in *Roper v. Simmons*, finding the death penalty for juveniles unconstitutional.[178]

Not all petitions filed with the commission against the United States have involved the death penalty. In the *Statehood Solidarity Committee* case, the commission concluded that the United States violated Article II (right to equality before the law) and XX (right to vote and to participate in government) of the American Declaration by denying residents of the District of Columbia the opportunity to vote for members of the U.S. Congress.[179] In the *Mary and Carrie Dann* case, the commission considered a petition by members of a U.S. Indian tribe, who asserted that the U.S. government interfered with their use and occupation of ancestral lands in violation of the American Declaration. The U.S. government argued that the issue was not one of human rights, but of land title and land use, which had been fully and fairly litigated in U.S. courts. The commission, however, concluded that the United States had violated the American Declaration by failing to ensure the petitioners' right to property under conditions of equality.[180] In 2002, the commission issued precautionary measures in favor of the detainees at Guantánamo Bay Naval Base, requesting the United States to clarify their status under international law, and subsequently requesting the United States to address various human rights concerns, including methods used for their interrogation and their transfer to third countries for interrogation.[181] In 2006, the commission decided that the United States had failed to give effect to the precautionary measures, resulting in irreparable harm to the fundamental rights of the detainees.[182]

The United States engages in the work of the Inter–American Commission, including the submission of "observations" to the commission with respect to petitions filed regarding conduct of the U.S. government. Yet the United States regards the Inter–American Commission as simply a consultative organ of the OAS, which is authorized to examine communications from individuals and groups, but is not authorized to issue binding decisions as against OAS states that are not parties to the American Convention, including the United States. Moreover, the United States does not

---

177. *See, e.g.,* Domingues, Case 12.285, Inter–Am. C.H.R., Report No. 62/02 (2002).

178. *See* Chapter 7(C).

179. *See* Statehood Solidarity Comm., Case 11.204, Inter–Am. C.H.R., Report No. 98/03 (2003).

180. *See* Dann, Case 11.140, Inter–Am. C.H.R., Report No. 75/02 (2002).

181. *See* Inter.-Am. C.H.R., Precautionary Measure 259/02–Detainees being Held by the United States at Guantánamo Bay (Mar. 12, 2002), 41 I.L.M. 532 (2002); for subsequent requests, see 45 I.L.M. 667–681 (2006).

182. *See* Inter.-Am. C.H.R. Resolution 2/06 (July 28, 2006); *see also* Inter.-Am. C.H.R. Resolution 2/11 (Aug. 2, 2011).

accept that the American Declaration, a non-legally-binding instrument, can create obligations binding upon the United States, and therefore does not accept views of the commission that the United States can violate that instrument (as a non-party to the American Convention, the United States also cannot violate that treaty).

Human Rights under the American Convention. Separate from the OAS Charter, the American Convention serves as an important component of the inter-American human rights system. Twenty-five of thirty-five Western Hemisphere states have ratified the American Convention, not including the United States. The American Convention sets forth various human rights, similar to those found in the European Convention on Human Rights and Fundamental Freedoms.

The American Convention authorizes the Inter–American Commission to receive petitions from individuals charging American Convention contracting states with violations of human rights[183] (thus, the commission plays an important role under the OAS Charter and, separately, under the American Convention). The commission first determines whether the petition is admissible, based on whether local remedies have been exhausted and other factors. If admissible, it then investigates the matter and attempts to achieve a friendly settlement. If no such settlement can be reached, the commission prepares a report on its findings and recommendations. The American Convention also authorizes the commission to consider inter-state petitions so long as the states in question consented when they ratified the convention. No such petition has yet been filed.

The American Convention also created an Inter–American Court of Human Rights.[184] Based in San José, Costa Rica, the court consists of seven judges who are nationals of OAS member states and who are elected by the contracting states to the American Convention. The judges serve for seven-year terms and may be re-elected no more than once. If a contracting state to the American Convention declines to accept recommendations issued by the commission concerning an individual petition, the commission or another contracting state can take the case to the court.

The court may also hear contentious cases between states so long as the states in question have consented to the court's jurisdiction. A state does not accept the court's contentious jurisdiction merely by ratifying the American Convention. Rather, a state either must consent *ad hoc* to any case brought against it or, when it joins

183. *See* American Convention, *supra* note 172, arts. 34–51.

184. *Id.*, arts. 52–69; *see* Laurence Burgorgue-Larsen & Ubeda de Torres, The Inter-American Court of Human Rights: Case Law and Commentary (2011).

the convention, must declare that it recognizes as binding the jurisdiction of the court on matters relating to interpretation or application of the convention. As of 2011, such declarations had been filed by twenty-one states. Further, the commission participates in all contentious proceedings before the court. Individuals are not permitted to bring cases before the court, but they may participate in proceedings once initiated.

Decisions of the court are final and binding on states that have accepted the court's jurisdiction. Important and well-publicized cases have arisen on various issues, including charges that the Honduran government engaged in a policy of forced disappearances in the early 1980's,[185] or that Guatemalan police engaged in abduction, torture, and murder of street children.[186] As of 2011, the Court has issued approximately 150 judgments.

At the request of any OAS member state or the commission, the court may issue advisory opinions that interpret the American Convention or "other treaties concerning the protection of human rights in the American states."[187] The court has opined that the "other treaties" it may interpret are not only OAS or inter-American treaties, but any treaty relevant to the enjoyment or enforcement of human rights in an American state.[188] Separately, the Court has weighed in on whether an OAS member state (*e.g.*, the United States) that has not ratified the American Convention is legally bound by the provisions of the American Declaration, which was adopted as a non-binding instrument. The court declared that "for the member states of the [OAS], the [American] Declaration is the text that defines the human rights referred to in the Charter.... [T]he Declaration is for these States a source of international obligations related to the Charter of the Organization."[189]

Since the United States has not ratified the American Convention, it is not exposed to the Court's jurisdiction. U.S. courts have not regarded as binding, nor generally followed, decisions or opinions of the Court.[190]

---

185. *See* Fairén Garbi & Solis Corrales v. Honduras, Inter.-Am. Ct. H.R. (ser. C) No. 6 (1989).

186. *See* Villagran Morales ("Street Children"), Inter.-Am. Ct. H.R. (ser. C) No. 63 (2000).

187. American Convention, *supra* note 172, art. 64(1).

188. *See* Advisory Opinion on "Other Treaties" Subject to the Advisory Jurisdiction of the Court, Inter.-Am. Ct. H.R. (ser. A) No. 10, para. 48 (1982).

189. Advisory Opinion on Interpretation of the American Declaration of the Rights and Duties of Man Within the Framework of Article 64 of the American Convention on Human Rights, Inter.-Am. Ct. H.R. (ser. A) No. 10, para. 45 (1989).

190. *See, e.g.*, United States v. Li, 206 F.3d 56 (1st Cir. 2000); United States v. Lombera–Camorlinga, 206 F.3d 882 (9th Cir. 2000).

Africa

In 1981, the Organization of African Unity (OAU) adopted the African Charter on Human and Peoples' Rights (African Charter),[191] which entered into force in 1986. When the African Union succeeded the OAU in 2002, its constituent instrument did not indicate the African Union's relationship to the African Charter.[192]

The African Charter sets forth a variety of civil, political, economic, and social rights for individuals and "peoples." For instance, peoples have the right to self-determination and to freely dispose of their natural resources.[193] Moreover, the African Charter sets forth *duties* that individuals have as well. For example, the charter imposes a duty on every individual "to respect his parents at all times" and "to maintain them in case of need."[194] Provisions unique to Africa also appear within the charter, such as the duty "to preserve and strengthen positive African cultural values in . . . relation with other members of the society. . . . "[195] Member states to the African Charter are obligated to recognize these rights and duties as a part of their national laws.

As is the case with global human rights treaties, member states are obligated to report biennially on their implementation of the charter.[196] Reports are submitted to an African Commission on Human and Peoples' Rights created by the charter, which consists of eleven persons nominated by member states and elected for six year terms by the Assembly of Heads of State and Government.[197] The commission reviews these reports and pursues its own studies in fulfilling its mandate to give views and recommendations to member states.[198] Like the U.N. Human Rights Council, the African Commission has appointed rapporteurs and working groups to investigate particular topics or member states.

The commission may also entertain inter-state petitions[199] (so long as local remedies have been exhausted) and issue a report which is transmitted to the Assembly of Heads of State and Government. The only inter-state petition to date was filed in 1999 when the Democratic Republic of the Congo (DRC) submitted an inter-state complaint against Burundi, Uganda, and Rwanda alleging serious human rights abuses inflicted within the DRC's territo-

---

191. June 27, 1981, 21 I.L.M. 58 [hereinafter African Charter].

192. *See generally* RACHEL MURRAY, HUMAN RIGHTS IN AFRICA: FROM THE OAU TO THE AFRICAN UNION (2004); VINCENT NMEHIELLE, THE AFRICAN HUMAN RIGHTS SYSTEM: ITS LAWS, PRACTICE, AND INSTITUTIONS (2001).

193. *See* African Charter, *supra* note 191, arts. 20–21.

194. *Id.*, art. 29(1).

195. *Id.*, art. 29(7).

196. *Id.*, art. 62.

197. *Id.*, arts. 30–42.

198. *Id.*, art. 45(1)(a).

199. *Id.*, arts. 47–49.

ry. (In tandem, the DRC filed cases against these three states at the International Court of Justice).

An individual petition system also exists, yet is limited to petitions that concern "serious or massive violations of human and peoples' rights. . . . "[200] Further, the commission must first receive permission from the Assembly of Heads of State and Government before investigating the matter. As of 2011, the commission has issued decisions based on several hundred petitions. For example, in 1997 the commission condemned the trial in Nigeria of persons by special military courts without appeal.[201]

Finally, the commission is empowered to "[i]nterpret all the provisions of the present Charter at the request of a State party, an institution of the OAU or an African Organization recognized by the OAU."[202]

In 1998, OAU states adopted an additional protocol[203] to the African Charter to create an African Court on Human and Peoples' Rights. After the formation of the African Union in 2002 to replace the OAU, a different protocol was adopted creating a Court of Justice for the African Union. Then, in July 2008, the African Union decided to merge the African Court on Human and Peoples' Rights and the Court of Justice of the African Union so as to form a single court, known as the African Court of Justice and Human Rights, based in Arusha, Tanzania.[204]

The Court consists of sixteen judges representing the different geographic regions of Africa, who have jurisdiction to decide matters relating to both the constituent instruments of the African Union and the African Charter on Human and Peoples' Rights. The African Commission is empowered to bring human rights cases before the African Court against an AU state, which it did in March 2011, charging that the Libyan government of Muammar Gaddafi had engaged in massive human rights violations. After reviewing the matter, the African Court issued a provisional measures order that Libya "must immediately refrain from any action that would result in loss of life or violation of physical integrity of persons, which could be a breach of the provisions of the [African] Charter or of other international human rights instruments to which it is a party."[205]

---

200. *Id.*, art. 58(1).

201. *See* Constitutional Courts Project v. Nigeria, Comm. 60/91 (Oct. 1995), *reprinted in* 18 Hum. Rts. L.J. 28 (1997).

202. African Charter, *supra* note 191, art. 45(3).

203. *See* Protocol to the African Charter on the Establishment of the African Court on Human and Peoples'

Rights, June 10, 1998, 12 Afr. J. Int'l & Comp. L. 187 (2000).

204. Protocol on the Statute of the African Court of Justice and Human Rights, 48 I.L.M. 334 (2009). The Court's Statute is annexed to the protocol.

205. African Commission v. Libya, App. No. 004/2011, Order for Provisional Measures, para. 25 (Mar. 25, 2011).

F. Immigration and Refugees

Under both international and national law, states have extensive authority regarding whether aliens may enter and remain within their territory. As such, questions concerning acquisition of nationality, immigration, asylum, and refugees are largely handled by each state's national laws. Nevertheless, with the rise of human rights law and (to a certain extent) trade and investment law, international treaties and customary norms have helped shape national laws and policies, and are often invoked by persons in national courts.[206]

As a general matter, the ICCPR provides that an alien lawfully present in a state "may be expelled therefrom only in pursuance of a decision reached in accordance with law," and should be allowed to argue his or her case before a competent authority.[207] Further, the Refugee Convention and its associated protocol[208] call upon states to accord certain protections to persons who have a "well-founded fear of being persecuted [in their country of origin] for reasons of race, religion, nationality, membership of a particular social group or political opinion.... "[209] While it is within the discretion of a state to grant such refuge, states are barred from expelling the refugee (save on grounds of national security or public order) and cannot expel or return ("refouler") a refugee to a state "where his life or freedom would be threatened on account of his race, religion, nationality, membership of a particular social group or political opinion."[210] In *Sale v. Haitian Centers Council*,[211] however, the U.S. Supreme Court held that the U.S. obligation on expulsion or return under the Refugee Convention is not intended to have an extraterritorial effect, and therefore does not apply when the alien is interdicted outside U.S. territory (*e.g.*, on the high seas).

Similarly, Article 3(1) of the Convention Against Torture provides that "[n]o State Party shall expel, return or extradite a person to another State where there are substantial grounds for believing that he would be in danger of being subjected to torture." Other instruments are also relevant, although they speak less directly to the issue of immigration. For example, the Universal Declaration of Human Rights and the ICCPR both provide that the family is entitled to protection as a "fundamental group unit of

---

206. *See generally* GUY GOODWIN-GILL & JANE MCADAM, THE REFUGEE IN INTERNATIONAL LAW (3d ed. 2007); AGNÈS HURWITZ, THE COLLECTIVE RESPONSIBILITY OF STATES TO PROTECT REFUGEES (2009); REFUGEES, ASYLUM SEEKERS AND THE RULES OF LAW (Susan Kneebone ed., 2009).

207. ICCPR, *supra* note 38, art. 13.

208. *See supra* notes 152–53.

209. Refugee Convention, *supra* note 152, art. 1(A)(2).

210. *Id.*, arts. 32(1) & 33(1).

211. 509 U.S. 155 (1993).

society.''[212] Such instruments have been invoked by aliens seeking to be reunited with their families or to avoid being separated by deportation. Regional restrictions also may exist. Thus, under Article 3 of the European Convention on Human Rights, the parties may not deport a person if there are substantial grounds to believe that the person would face a real risk of torture or inhuman or degrading treatment in the receiving country.[213]

The principal U.S. statute on immigration and nationality is the Immigration and Nationality Act (INA).[214] To immigrate to the United States, an alien must show that he fits within a qualifying category (*e.g.*, to join a spouse or parent already resident in the United States or to work at employment designated for preferential treatment) and is not ineligible (*e.g.*, for having a serious criminal record or being a danger to national security). While there is no limitation on the immigration of immediate family relatives, limits exist for other family relationships and employment-related immigration. Separately, there is a pool of persons admitted each year (about 50,000) through a lottery system designed to admit a highly diverse group. Alternatively, an alien outside the United States might seek permission to immigrate as a refugee.

U.S. law also provides for sending aliens back to their home country. If an alien has been admitted into the United States through normal immigration procedures, then the process for sending the alien home is *deportation*. If the alien did not properly enter (*e.g.*, the alien snuck across the border or the alien's ability to enter was challenged at the border by the Immigration and Naturalization Service), then the process is to *exclude* the alien from the United States. Whether someone is subject to exclusion can be confusing in that a person challenged at the border can be paroled into the United States until their case is resolved, but they are still regarded as being constructively at the border. Deportation and exclusion proceedings are collectively referred to as *removal* of the alien. If the Department of Homeland Security initiates a removal, the alien can challenge the removal through extensive administrative proceedings, involving immigration judges sitting in 54 immigration courts throughout the United States (which are part of the Department of Justice's Executive Office for Immigration Review), a 15–member Board of Immigration Appeals (created by the U.S. Attorney–General), and rarely the U.S. Attorney–General herself. Once administrative appeals are exhausted, the matter usually can

212. Universal Declaration, *supra* note 34, art. 16(3); ICCPR, *supra* note 38, art. 23(1).

213. *See, e.g.,* Chahal v. United Kingdom, 1996 Eur. Ct. H.R. 54; Saadi v. Italy, 2008 Eur. Ct. H.R. 179.

214. Pub. L. No. 82–414, 66 Stat. 163 (1952) (codified as amended 8 U.S.C. §§ 1101–1524 (2006)).

be taken to the federal court of appeals for the circuit where the process is occurring.[215]

Any person who is physically present in the United States may apply for asylum, in which case the matter is referred to an asylum officer in the Department of Homeland Security. As is the case for persons from outside the United States seeking refugee status, a person seeking asylum must have been persecuted or have a well-founded fear of persecution in his home country on account of race, religion, nationality, membership in a particular social group, or political opinion. Further the person cannot fall within certain statutory disqualifications, such as having previously committed a particularly serious crime. If the asylum officer does not grant asylum, the case is referred to an immigration court.[216]

The United States implements its obligations under the treaties noted above through relevant provisions in U.S. immigration laws. For example, U.S. law has been amended to implement the U.S. obligation not to expel or return a refugee to a state where his life or freedom would be threatened "because of the alien's race, religion, nationality, membership of a particular social group or political opinion."[217]

---

215. *See* John R.B. Palmer, Stephen W. Yale–Loehr & Elizabeth Cronin, *Why Are So Many People Challenging Board of Immigration Appeals Decisions in Federal Court?*, 20 GEO. IMMIGR. L.J. 1 (2005).

216. *See generally* DEBORAH E. ANKER, LAW OF ASYLUM IN THE UNITED STATES (2011).

217. 8 U.S.C. § 1231(b)(3) (2006).

Further Reading

Philip Alston & James Crawford, eds., *The Future of UN Human Rights Treaty Monitoring* (2000).

Anne F. Bayefsky, ed., *The UN Human Rights Treaty System in the 21st Century* (2000).

Anne F. Bayefsky, *The UN Human Rights Treaty System: Universality at the Crossroads* (2001).

Andrew Clapham, *Human Rights Obligations of Non–State Actors* (2006).

Robert C. Divine & R. Blake Chisam, *Immigration Practice* (2010–2011 ed.)

David Forsythe, ed., *Encyclopedia of Human Rights* (2009) (5 vols.).

Anne T. Gallagher, *The International Law of Human Trafficking* (2010).

Hurst Hannum, ed., *Guide to International Human Rights Practice* (4th ed. 2004).

Christof Heyns & Frans Viljoen, eds., *The Impact of the United Nations Human Rights Treaties on the Domestic Level* (2002).

Sarah Joseph et al., *The International Covenant on Civil and Political Rights: Cases, Materials, and Commentary* (2d ed. 2004).

Menno T. Kamminga & Martin Scheinin, eds., *The Impact of Human Rights Law on General International Law* (2009).

Susan Marks & Andrew Clapham, *International Human Rights Lexicon* (2005).

Theodor Meron, *International Law in the Age of Human Rights* (2004).

Jo M. Pasqualucci, *The Practice and Procedure of the Inter–American Court of Human Rights* (2003).

Dinah Shelton, *Regional Protection of Human Rights* (2008).

Guglielmo Verdirame, *The UN and Human Rights: Who Guards the Guardians?* (2011).

Frans Viljoen, *International Human Rights Law in Africa* (2007).

Kirsten A. Young, *The Law and Process of the U.N. Human Rights Committee* (2002).

David Weissbrodt & Connie de la Vega, *International Human Rights Law: An Introduction* (2010).

Robin C.A. White et al., *Jacobs, White, and Ovey: The European Convention on Human Rights* (2010).

Chapter 11

LAW OF THE SEA

A. Introduction

Until the 1950's, the basic principles of the law of the sea had their source in customary international law. In 1958, the United Nations convened the first U.N. Conference on the Law of the Sea (UNCLOS I), which succeeded in adopting four conventions on: (1) the territorial sea and contiguous zone; (2) the high seas; (3) the continental shelf; and (4) the fishing and conservation of living resources of the high seas. While the first three conventions were ratified by numerous states (including the United States) and are regarded as reflecting customary international law, the fourth convention (as well as an optional protocol on dispute settlement) obtained less adherence.

UNCLOS I was a considerable success, yet it failed to resolve important issues concerning the law of the sea, such as the breadth of the territorial sea. Consequently, the United Nations convened a second conference (UNCLOS II) in 1960, but insufficient time had passed to allow states to resolve their differences, and the conference failed.

In 1973, the third U.N. Conference on the Law of the Sea (UNCLOS III) was convened. Nine years later, the conference adopted the U.N. Convention on the Law of the Sea (LOSC), which sought to establish a comprehensive legal framework governing the uses of the oceans through a single treaty.[1] The LOSC addressed the topics covered by the 1958 conventions, filled in various gaps in those conventions, and went further by tackling topics such as the management of the sea-bed's mineral resources located beyond national jurisdiction (the deep sea-bed).

During the two-year period that the LOSC was open for signature, 159 states signed the LOSC. Although they voted in favor of adopting the LOSC, the United States and several other industrialized states (including Germany and the United Kingdom) did not sign it, due to concerns regarding Part XI (and related annexes) on the deep sea-bed. In the hope of overcoming the impasse, the U.N. secretary-general informally pursued, over a four-year period, a

---

1. *See* U.N. Convention on the Law of the Sea, Dec. 10, 1982, S. TREATY DOC. No. 103–39 (1994), 1833 U.N.T.S. 3 [hereinafter LOSC].

further "implementing" agreement designed to reform Part XI. After the implementing agreement was adopted by the General Assembly in 1994,[2] most industrialized states ratified the LOSC, which entered into force on November 16, 1994.

In 1994, President Clinton submitted the LOSC and the 1994 implementing agreement to the U.S. Senate (see section E below). As of 2011, however, the Senate had not granted consent to ratification. Nevertheless, the United States remains bound to all four 1958 conventions and has accepted many of the LOSC's provisions as reflecting customary international law.[3]

Under the LOSC and associated customary rules, the law of the sea is organized based on major maritime zones (see Section B below), as well as on functional uses of the sea (Section C). The LOSC also has created a flexible yet binding process for resolution of disputes arising under the convention (Section D).

B. Major Maritime Zones

The seas cover about seventy percent of the Earth's surface. Much of the contemporary law of the sea can be understood through reference to rules that apply within maritime zones that are layered outward from coastal states. As a general matter, zones closer to the state's coast envisage higher levels of coastal state sovereignty or control over activities within the zone, whereas zones further from the coast envisage lesser coastal state control and greater freedom for other states.

Baselines and Internal Waters

The starting point for establishing maritime zones are the "baselines." The baselines of a state serve dual functions. They demarcate the state's internal waters from external waters and provide the lines from which the outer limits of maritime zones will be measured. Thus, all waters of a state that are landward of its baselines are internal waters and are treated as if they were part of the state's land territory. Waters seaward of a state's baselines are the principal focus of the law of the sea.

LOSC Article 5 provides that "the normal baseline for measuring the breadth of the territorial sea is the low-water line along the coast as marked on large-scale charts officially recognized by the coastal State." This general rule works well for coasts that are relatively smooth. However, it is less useful for states that have

---

2. *See* Agreement Relating to the Implementation of Part XI of the United Nations Convention on the Law of the Sea of 10 December 1982, July 28, 1994, S. Treaty Doc. No. 103–39, at 263 (1994), 1836 U.N.T.S. 41; *see also* Bernard H. Oxman, *Law of the Sea Forum: The*

1994 Agreement on Implementation of the Seabed Provisions of the Convention on the Law of the Sea, 88 Am. J. Int'l L. 687 (1994).

3. *See generally* S. Treaty Doc. No. 103–39 (1994).

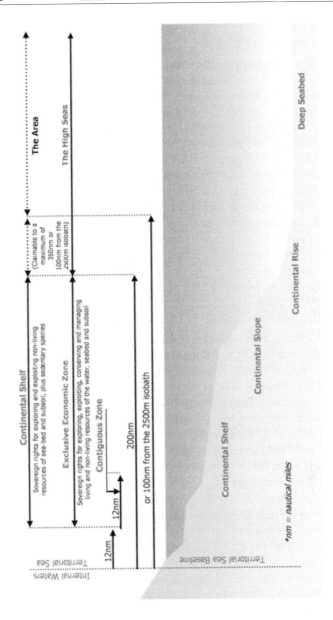

extensive indentations in their coasts or that are fringed with islands, because it is very cumbersome and confusing to ascertain the location of the maritime zones measured from such highly irregular features. Moreover, the general rule is unhelpful in dealing with natural features commonly found along coasts, such as bays, river mouths, low-tide elevations, or reefs. The LOSC has developed special rules for drawing baselines with respect to those natural features, as well as artificial harbors.

For instance, to handle coasts that are deeply indented, the LOSC allows a state to draw a series of straight lines using the outermost points along the coast. Yet there are limits to how a state may draw such "straight baselines." LOSC Article 7(3) provides that these straight baselines "must not depart to any appreciable extent from the general direction of the coast, and the sea areas lying within the lines must be sufficiently closely linked to the land domain to be subject to the régime of internal waters." Further, under Article 7(4), straight baselines "shall not be drawn to and from low-tide elevations, unless lighthouses or similar installations which are permanently above sea level have been built upon them" or where doing so has received "general international recognition." Article 7(5) instructs that "account may be taken . . . of economic interests peculiar to the region concerned, the reality and the importance of which are clearly evidenced by long usage." Such rules, however, are inherently flexible, allowing states considerable latitude when drawing straight baselines.

While these rules are codified in the LOSC, they emerged in large part from the International Court of Justice's decision in the Anglo–Norwegian *Fisheries* case.[4] In that case, Norway sought to exclude U.K. vessels from fishing off the coast of Norway north of the Arctic circle. The dispute turned on whether Norway was properly drawing baselines using not only its mainland, but also islands, islets, rocks and reefs (known as the "skjærgaard" or "rock rampart") off its coast. The Court concluded that Norway's method of drawing straight baselines through use of the skjærgaard was consistent with the practice of states and not opposed by other states. Consequently, the U.K. vessels had no right to fish in the waters from which they were being excluded. The Court outlined various considerations that were subsequently adopted in the 1958 U.N. Convention on the Territorial Sea and Contiguous Zone, and later incorporated in the 1982 LOSC. Thus, the Anglo–Norwegian *Fisheries* case is a good example of the interplay of customary international law and treaty law, and the importance of judicial decisions in crystalizing beliefs as to the content of customary international law.

As noted above, once baselines are established, waters landward of the baselines are internal waters. The coastal state enjoys full territorial sovereignty over its internal waters, with the exception that there is a right of innocent passage (see below) through waters enclosed by a straight baseline that previously had not been

---

4. Fisheries Case (U.K. v. Nor.), 1951 I.C.J. 116 (Dec. 18); *see* C. Wal- dock, *The Anglo–Norwegian Fisheries Case*, 28 Brit. Y.B. Int'l L. 114 (1951).

considered internal waters.[5] There is no general right under international law for foreign vessels to enter a state's internal waters.[6] At the same time, a state's international ports are presumed to be open to international non-military vessels, subject to any technical conditions for entry set by the state (*e.g.*, being escorted by a harbor pilot). Further, customary international law and various treaties (such as treaties of friendship, commerce, and navigation) contemplate a right of entry to a port when a vessel is in distress.

Once a foreign vessel is in a state's internal waters, it is exposed to that state's criminal and civil jurisdiction. Thus, a merchant vessel visiting a port may be seized for customs violations and exposed to actions *in rem* against the ship. In practice, coastal states do not exercise jurisdiction over matters concerning a foreign vessel's internal activities (such as theft by one crew member from another); rather, they leave such matters to authorities on the vessel or to the state which granted the vessel the right to sail under its flag (the "flag state"). Coastal states will exercise their jurisdiction, however, when requested by the captain or flag state, or when an issue affects the peace or good order of the port.[7]

Territorial Sea

When the law of the sea first emerged, there were disagreements about whether the high seas should be subject to state sovereignty or should be free to navigation and use by all. Yet, even then, there was a general consensus that coastal states enjoyed some rights to regulate activities in seas immediately adjacent to their coasts. Differences of view concerning this "territorial sea" zone focused on its breadth, the nature of coastal states' rights in the zone, and the right of other states' vessels to pass through the zone. Considerable consensus has formed on these three points with the adoption of the LOSC.

With respect to the breadth of the territorial sea, many states initially advocated for a distance at which the sea could be controlled by shore-based cannons, which was a distance of approximately three nautical miles. This "cannon-shot" rule garnered widespread but never uniform acceptance. Scandinavian states, for example, consistently maintained that their territorial sea extended four nautical miles. By the final stages of LOSC negotiations, states were able to reach consensus on a wider breadth for the territorial

5. *See* LOSC, *supra* note 1, art. 8(2).

6. *See* Military and Paramilitary Activities in and against Nicaragua (Nicar. v. U.S.), 1986 I.C.J. 14, para. 213 (June 27); *but see* Saudi Arabia v. ARAMCO, 27 I.L.M. 117, 212 (1963) ("[a]ccording to a great principle of international law, ports of every state must be open to foreign merchant vessels").

7. *See* Wildenhus' Case, 120 U.S. 1 (1887). On the subject generally, see V.D. Degan, *Internal Waters*, 17 Neth. Y.B. Int'l L. 3 (1986).

sea, driven in large part by a desire of all states to have full sovereign control over fishing and pollution occurring near their coasts. LOSC Article 3 provides that a coastal state may claim a territorial sea extending no more than twelve nautical miles from its baselines. President Ronald Reagan proclaimed such a zone for the United States in 1988.[8]

With respect to the coastal state's rights in the territorial sea, the LOSC provides that the coastal state's sovereignty extends beyond its land territory and internal waters to the territorial sea, subject to the provisions of the LOSC and other rules of international law, such as rules on sovereign and diplomatic immunities.[9] The coastal state's sovereignty extends not just to the waters, but also to the airspace above the waters and to the sea-bed and subsoil below the waters.[10] This extension of sovereignty means that the coastal state can control activities in the territorial sea largely in the same manner as it controls activities in its internal waters or on its land territory.

Yet, while the coastal state has extensive control over the territorial sea, the LOSC places some key limitations on the exercise of that sovereignty. The coastal state may not (1) legislate so as to hamper or levy charges on vessels engaged in "innocent passage;"[11] (2) enforce its laws over crimes committed on a vessel engaged in such passage except in limited circumstances;[12] or (3) arrest a vessel in connection with liabilities not incurred on its voyage through the territorial sea.[13] Further, the coastal state has duties to foreign vessels which enter the territorial sea, such as to buoy and mark channels, keep navigable waters clear, and provide rescue services.[14]

With respect to the entry by foreign vessels into the territorial sea, a right of "innocent passage" was generally accepted early in the development of the law of the sea. As codified in the LOSC, "passage" means passing through the territorial sea in a continuous and expeditious manner. Such passage includes stopping and anchoring when doing so is incidental to ordinary navigation or is compelled by distress.[15] "Innocent" passage means passage that "is not prejudicial to the peace, good order or security of the coastal State."[16] The LOSC enumerates a series of activities that are not considered innocent, such as engaging in weapons practice, spying,

---

8. *See* Proclamation 5928 of December 27, 1988, 54 Fed. Reg. 777 (Jan. 9, 1989).

9. *See* LOSC, *supra* note 1, arts. 2(1) & 2(3).

10. *Id.*, art. 2(2).

11. *Id.*, art. 24(1).

12. *Id.*, art. 27.

13. *Id.*, art. 28.

14. *Id.*, arts. 22(1) & 24(2); *see* Fisheries Jurisdiction (U.K. v. Ice.), 1973 I.C.J. 3, 28 at n. 8 (separate opinion of Judge Fitzmaurice).

15. *See* LOSC, *supra* note 1, art. 18.

16. *Id.*, art. 19(1).

propaganda, wilful and serious pollution, fishing, and "any other activity not having a direct bearing on passage."[17] This list suggests an objective standard, whereby the specific activity (not the coastal state's interpretation of that activity) serves as the touchstone for innocence. At the same time, the final item in the list appears to encompass a wide range of activities (activities not having a "direct bearing on passage") even if they are not prejudicial to the coastal state, thus potentially diminishing the right of innocent passage. In an effort to avoid such an implication, the United States and Soviet Union in 1989 issued a "uniform interpretation" of international law governing innocent passage in which they stated that the LOSC sets out "an exhaustive list of activities that would render passage not innocent."[18]

Vessels not engaged in innocent passage may be excluded from a state's territorial sea. Further, "[t]he coastal State may, without discrimination ... among foreign ships, suspend temporarily in specified areas of its territorial sea the innocent passage of foreign ships if such suspension is essential for the protection of its security, including weapons exercises."[19]

The LOSC does not expressly address the issue of innocent passage by warships through the territorial sea. The convention grants a right of innocent passage to the "ships of all States" without distinction between military and non-military vessels,[20] and it contemplates specific rules relating to innocent passage by submarines (which at present are all warships).[21] As such, it appears that the LOSC assumes that warships are entitled to innocent passage. Nevertheless, some forty states argue that they are permitted to require that foreign warships obtain authorization before entering their territorial sea. Major maritime powers reject and challenge such requirements. In the U.S.-Soviet "uniform interpretation" referred to above, both states agreed that all ships, including warships, enjoy the right of innocent passage.[22]

Contiguous Zone

Prior to the modern codification of the law of the sea, some states claimed a jurisdictional zone outside their territorial sea, usually for customs and security purposes. For example, during the alcohol prohibition era in the United States (1920–33), the United States enforced its prohibition laws against foreign vessels hovering just outside the U.S. territorial sea as a means of preventing them from "running whiskey" into the United States at night or when

17. *Id.*, art. 19(2).
18. 28 I.L.M. 1444, para. 3 (1989).
19. LOSC, *supra* note 1, art. 25(3).
20. *Id.*, art. 17.

21. *Id.*, art. 20.
22. *See* 28 I.L.M. 1444, para. 2 (1989).

the "coast was clear."[23] Other states, such as the United Kingdom, asserted that international law provided for no such contiguous zone.

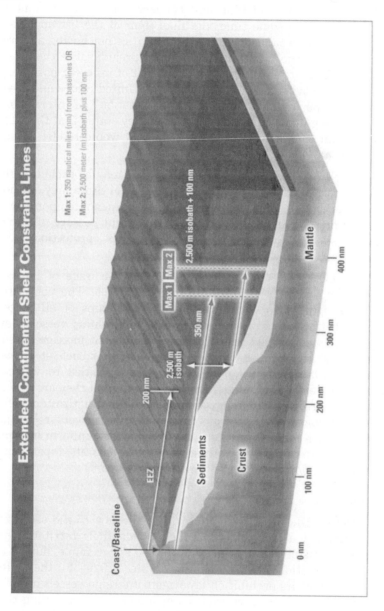

23. *See* Schroeder v. Bissell (Over the Top Case), 5 F.2d 838 (D. Conn. 1925).

As codified in LOSC Article 33, a coastal state may exercise control over a contiguous zone extending no more than twenty-four nautical miles from the baselines, as necessary: (1) to "prevent infringement of its customs, fiscal, immigration or sanitary laws and regulations within its territory or territorial sea;" or (2) to "punish infringement of [those] laws and regulations committed within its territory or territorial sea." Thus, the zone exists only for certain limited purposes (it is not a general security zone) and a coastal state may undertake enforcement action against vessels in the zone only for covered offenses that have or likely will be committed within its territory or territorial sea, but not for actions occurring in the contiguous zone itself. The enforcement action may include stopping and boarding the vessel, and seizing the vessel and bringing it into port if evidence of an offense or likely offense is uncovered.[24]

States are not obligated to declare a contiguous zone. Indeed, only about one-third of all coastal states have declared such zones, including the United States.[25]

Continental Shelf

See *Continental Shelf* photo on previous page.

Geologically, the sea-bed that slopes away from the coast typically consists of a gradual slope (the continental shelf proper), followed by a steep slope (the continental slope), and then a more gradual slope leading to the deep sea-bed floor. These three areas— collectively known as the "continental margin"—are rich in natural resources, including oil, natural gas, and certain minerals.

In 1945, President Harry Truman issued a proclamation declaring that the United States "regards the natural resources of the subsoil and sea-bed of the continental shelf beneath the high seas but contiguous to the coasts of the United States as appertaining to the United States, subject to its jurisdiction and control."[26] Thereafter, several other states advanced similar claims and, in 1969, the International Court of Justice recognized that

> the rights of the coastal State in respect of the area of continental shelf that constitutes a natural prolongation of its land territory into and under the sea exist *ipso facto* and *ab initio*, by virtue of its sovereignty over the land, and as an extension of it in an exercise of sovereign rights for the purpose of exploring the seabed and exploiting its natural resources.[27]

In the LOSC, the "continental shelf" is legally defined as comprising the sea-bed and subsoil of the submarine areas that

---

24. *See generally* A.V. Lowe, *The Development of the Concept of the Contiguous Zone*, 52 BRIT. Y.B. INT'L L. 109 (1981).

25. *See* Proclamation No. 7219 of August 2, 1999, 64 Fed. Reg. 48,701 (Sept. 8, 1999).

26. Proclamation No. 2667 of October 1, 1945, 10 Fed. Reg. 12,303 (Oct. 2, 1945).

27. North Sea Continental Shelf (FRG v. Den.; FRG v. Neth.), 1969 I.C.J. 3, 23, at para. 19 (Feb. 20).

extend beyond the territorial sea throughout the natural prolongation of the land territory to the continental margin's outer edge.[28] Moreover, if that natural prolongation falls short of 200 nautical miles from the baselines, the legal continental shelf includes the sea-bed out to a distance of 200 nautical miles from the baselines. (In other words, a state may always claim as its "continental shelf" the area extending out to 200 nautical miles from its baselines regardless of the geology). If the natural prolongation extends *beyond* 200 nautical miles from the baselines, the coastal state's legal continental shelf continues until the natural prolongation ends, but under no circumstances may it exceed either: (1) 350 nautical miles from the baselines; or (2) 100 nautical miles beyond the 2,500 meter isobath (a line connecting the depth of 2,500 meters).[29] In determining where the natural prolongation ends, the coastal state may either develop a line based on the thickness of the sedimentary cover at the outer limit of the continental shelf or, alternatively, based on a distance of 60 nautical miles from the foot of the continental slope.[30]

Where the continental shelf extends beyond 200 nautical miles, it is left to the coastal state, in the first instance, to delineate the outer limits of the continental shelf.[31] The LOSC provides, however, that by no later than ten years after a coastal state becomes a LOSC party,[32] it shall submit oceanographic information relevant to the limits of its continental shelf to a twenty-one person "Commission on the Limits of the Continental Shelf" established under the convention. The commission reviews the information and then makes recommendations to the coastal state regarding the delimitation of the continental shelf. If the coastal state establishes its continental shelf on the basis of those recommendations, the recommendations are considered "final and binding."[33]

28. *See* LOSC, *supra* note 1, art. 76(1).

29. *Id.*, art. 76(5).

30. *Id.*, art. 76(4).

31. *Id.*, art. 76(7); *see* INTERNATIONAL LAW ASSOCIATION, LEGAL ISSUES OF THE OUTER CONTINENTAL SHELF, 72 I.L.A. REP. CONF. 215 (2006); David A. Colson, *The Delimitation of the Outer Continental Shelf between Neighboring States*, 97 AM. J. INT'L L. 91 (2003); CONTINENTAL SHELF LIMITS: THE SCIENTIFIC AND LEGAL INTERFACE (Peter J. Cook & Chris M. Carleton, eds. 2000).

32. This time limit was altered by a decision of the convention parties in May 2001, so that no state was required to submit information prior to 2009.

33. LOSC, *supra* note 1, art. 76(8) & Annex II. The convention does not expressly indicate whether delimitations *not* based on the commission's recommendations are to be regarded as invalid. *See* Michael Sheng-ti Gau, *The Commission on the Limits of the Continental Shelf as a Mechanism to Prevent Encroachment upon the Area*, 10 CHINESE J. INT'L L. 3 (2011); Ted L. McDorman, *The Role of the Commission on the Limits of the Continental Shelf: A Technical Body in a Political World*, 17 INT'L J. MARINE & COASTAL L. 301 (2002).

The coastal state has sovereign rights over the natural resources of its continental shelf, and can exclude all other states from exploiting those resources. Those resources consist of

> the mineral and other non-living resources of the sea-bed and subsoil together with living organisms belonging to sedentary species, that is to say, organisms which, at the harvestable stage, either are immobile on or under the sea-bed or are unable to move except in constant physical contact with the sea-bed or the subsoil.[34]

While the LOSC permits a state to claim a continental shelf extending beyond 200 nautical miles from its baselines (subject to the above-stated limits), it also sets forth a formula by which the "coastal State shall make payments or contributions in kind in respect of the exploitation of the non-living resources" in those areas.[35] Those payments are made to the convention's "Authority" (discussed below) for distribution "on the basis of equitable sharing criteria, taking into account the interests and needs of developing States, particularly the least developed and the land-locked among them."[36]

Exclusive Economic Zone

Even before the LOSC was adopted, many states, including the United States, declared fishery conservation zones extending outside their territorial seas.[37] Thus, it was no surprise that states agreed in the LOSC to permit coastal states to claim an "exclusive economic zone" (EEZ) of up to 200 nautical miles from their baselines within which they may exercise extensive rights in relation to natural resources. Shortly after the LOSC's adoption, President Reagan proclaimed an EEZ for the United States within 200 nautical miles of its coast even though the United States had not signed the LOSC.[38] The rapid acceptance of this concept may be seen in the International Court of Justice's 1985 observation (before the LOSC entered into force) that it was "incontestable that ... the exclusive economic zone ... is shown by the practice of States to have become a part of customary law...."[39]

Under LOSC Article 56(1)(a), the coastal state in the EEZ has "sovereign rights for the purpose of exploring and exploiting, conserving and managing" both the living and non-living natural resources of the sea-bed, its subsoil, and superadjacent waters (these rights in part duplicate the coastal state's rights in the

34. LOSC, *supra* note 1, art. 77(4).

35. *Id.*, art. 82(1).

36. *Id.*, art. 82(4)

37. For the United States, see Proclamation No. 2668 of October 1, 1945, 10 Fed. Reg. 12,304 (Oct. 2, 1945).

38. *See* Proclamation No. 5030 of March 10, 1983, 48 Fed. Reg. 10,605 (Mar. 14, 1983).

39. Continental Shelf (Libya/Malta), 1985 I.C.J. 13, para. 34 (June 3).

continental shelf). As such, the coastal state has extensive control over fishing activities in the EEZ (see Section C below). Moreover, Article 56(1)(a) accords the coastal state sovereign rights with regard to other activities for economic exploitation and exploration of the zone, such as "the production of energy from the water, current and winds." The coastal state also has jurisdiction in the EEZ over artificial islands, installations and structures, marine scientific research, and the protection and preservation of the marine environment.[40]

Other states, however, also have rights in the EEZ, which must be respected by the coastal state.[41] Vessels of other states generally enjoy the same navigational freedoms that they have on the high seas,[42] but they are subject to the coastal state's regulations regarding pollution control throughout the EEZ. Similarly, other states' aircraft generally enjoy overflight freedom in the EEZ, yet they are subject to the coastal state's powers on matters such as the dumping of wastes. Other states also enjoy the freedom to lay submarine cables and pipelines in the EEZ, subject to certain provisions relating to those cables or pipelines being broken or damaged,[43] and a provision on obtaining coastal state consent to the route of the pipelines.[44] Finally, in exercising their rights in the EEZ, other states must have due regard to the rights and duties of the coastal state.[45]

All land territory, including islands, can generate both a continental shelf and an EEZ. Thus, even a small island can provide the basis for claims to a continental shelf and EEZ covering hundreds of square kilometers, which in part explains why states sometimes argue intensely over sovereignty concerning even the smallest of islands. However, "[r]ocks which cannot sustain human habitation or economic life of their own shall have no exclusive economic zone or continental shelf."[46] If all coastal states were to establish 200 nautical mile EEZs, they would cover just over one-third of the total area of the sea. Yet within those EEZs would be found more than ninety percent of all fish stocks that are presently commercially exploitable.

High Seas

With the gradual expansion of state control over waters adjacent to their coasts, the area of the high seas has been significantly diminished. Under the contemporary law of the sea, the high seas are defined as "all parts of the sea that are not included in the

---

40. *See* LOSC, *supra* note 1, art. 56(1)(b); *see also id.*, arts. 60 & 246.

41. *Id.*, art. 56(2).

42. *Id.*, arts. 58(1) & 87.

43. *Id.*, arts. 112–15.

44. *Id.*, art. 79(3).

45. *Id.*, art. 58(3).

46. *Id.*, art. 121(3).

exclusive economic zone, in the territorial sea or in the internal waters of a State, or in the archipelagic waters of an archipelagic State."[47]

In general, the high seas are open to all states. The LOSC provides a non-exhaustive list of the freedoms all states enjoy on the high seas: freedoms of navigation, overflight, fishing, laying and maintenance of submarine cables and pipelines, scientific research, and artificial installation construction.[48] A state is obligated to have "due regard for the interests of other States" in exercising these high seas rights and rights relating to the sea-bed area.[49] Further, states have specific duties, such as to negotiate and agree upon measures necessary for the conservation of high seas fisheries. The high seas are also to "be reserved for peaceful purposes."[50]

As a general matter, the flag state has the exclusive right to exercise jurisdiction over its vessels on the high seas. Thus, penal or disciplinary proceedings against a person for causing a collision on the high seas rest either with the flag state or the state of the person's nationality.[51] There are, however, some exceptions to the exclusivity of the flag state's jurisdiction. All states may exercise jurisdiction over pirate vessels, with piracy defined as acts of violence, detention or depredation committed for private ends by the crew or passengers of a private ship (or aircraft) against another ship (or aircraft) or persons or property on board, on (or over) the high seas.[52] All states may also exercise jurisdiction over unauthorized broadcasting on the high seas.[53] Further, warships may board vessels suspected of engaging in piracy, slave trade, and certain other acts.[54]

In recent years, the menace of piracy on the high seas has provoked considerable attention by the international community. In 2010 alone, pirates launched more than 200 attacks off the Horn of Africa which, when successful, resulted in ransoms averaging $5 million per vessel.[55] In response, many states deployed naval vessels to the region to monitor major sea lanes and seize pirates when spotted on the high seas. If caught, the pirates are exposed to prosecution in the courts of the capturing state, as recognized in the LOSC and the 1958 Convention on the High Seas. In 2010,

---

47. *Id.*, art. 86.

48. *Id.*, art. 87(1).

49. *Id.*, art. 87(2).

50. *Id.*, art. 88.

51. *Id.*, art. 97. This rule reversed the Permanent Court of Justice's ruling in the S.S. "Lotus" (Fr. v. Turk.), 1927 P.C.I.J. (ser. A) No. 10 (Sept. 7), which held that the state whose vessel was harmed had concurrent jurisdiction.

52. *See* LOSC, *supra* note 1, art. 101; *see also* ALFRED P. RUBIN, THE LAW OF PIRACY (2d ed. 1998).

53. *See* LOSC, *supra* note 1, art. 109.

54. *Id.*, art. 110.

55. *See* LAUREN PLOCH ET AL., CONG. RESEARCH SERV., R40528, *Piracy Off the Horn of Africa* (2011).

Kenya established a special court within its national system to try suspected pirates operating from Somalia in the Gulf of Aden; several international organizations and states provided funding to Kenya to support the court, and concluded agreements allowing for the transfer of persons to Kenya for trial.[56] In the United States, the piracy statute allows punishment for "the crime of piracy as defined by the law of nations,"[57] which requires U.S. courts to grapple with the exact contours of what constitutes "piracy" under international law.[58]

One of the difficulties in undertaking enforcement actions on the high seas is the ability of offenders to flee from the high seas back into territorial waters once detected by an enforcement vessel. The ability of pirates to flee into Somalia's territorial waters resulted in the adoption by the Security Council of path-breaking resolutions authorizing states and regional organizations "cooperating" with the Transitional Federal Government of Somalia to enter those territorial waters and use "all necessary means" (and even to enter Somalia itself to use "all necessary measures") to repress acts of piracy, including seizing and disposing of vessels, arms and related equipment used for piracy.[59]

Various initiatives have been undertaken to secure flag state consent to the stopping and boarding of vessels on the high seas that are suspected of engaging in certain illicit activities. For example, in May 2003, the United States launched a multilateral effort to combat the transportation of weapons of mass destruction (WMD), called the "Proliferation Security Initiative" (PSI).[60] Among other things, PSI member states have committed themselves to take specific actions: to board suspicious vessels flying their own flags; to consent to the boarding of their flag vessels by other states; to stop and search suspicious vessels in their territorial or contiguous zones; to require suspicious aircraft in their airspace to land for inspection; to carry out rigorous inspections at

---

56. *See, e.g.*, EU–Kenya Exchange of Letters on the Conditions and Modalities for the Transfer of Persons Suspected of Having Committed Acts of Piracy, 48 I.L.M. 747 (2009).

57. 18 U.S.C. § 1651 (2006).

58. *Compare* United States v. Said, 757 F.Supp.2d 554 (E.D. Va. 2010) (limiting the statutory offense of piracy to sea robbery) *with* United States v. Hasan, 747 F. Supp. 2d 599 (E.D. Va. 2010) (allowing the offense to cover violent acts committed on the high seas for private ends, even in the absence of an actual robbery); *see Agora: Piracy Prosecutions*, 104 Am. J. Int'l L. 397 (2010).

59. *See* S.C. Res. 1846, para. 10 (Dec. 2, 2008); S.C. Res. 1851, para. 6 (Dec. 16, 2008); *see also* S.C. Res. 1816 (June 2, 2008); S.C. Res. 2020 (Nov. 22, 2011); *see also* Mahnoush Arsanjani & W. Michael Reisman, *East African Piracy and the Defense of World Public Order*, in Law of the Sea in Dialogue 137 (Holger Hestermeyer et al., eds. 2011); J. Ashley Roach, *Countering Piracy Off Somalia: International Law and International Institutions*, 104 Am. J. Int'l L. 397 (2010).

60. *See* Daniel H. Joyner, *The Proliferation Security Initiative: Nonproliferation, Counterproliferation, and International Law*, 30 Yale J. Int'l L. 507 (2005).

their ports and airfields; and not to transport WMD cargoes to or from states of concern. In furtherance of this initiative, the United States has concluded agreements with states that serve as flags of convenience (*e.g.*, Liberia[61] and Panama[62]) regarding the boarding of their flag vessels on the high seas. Among other things, Liberia and Panama agreed that if the United States requests permission to board and inspect their ships suspected of transporting WMD, a failure to respond to that request within two hours will be deemed as consent by the flag state.

Deep Sea–Bed Area

Under the LOSC, the deep sea-bed "Area" consists of the "seabed and ocean floor and subsoil thereof, beyond the limits of national jurisdiction."[63] Thus, it is the area outside the continental shelf areas claimed by coastal states. The LOSC's principal focus regarding the deep sea-bed area relates to equitable exploitation of its mineral-rich resources, which include baseball-size nodules lying on the sea-bed floor formed by processes of accretion, and containing cobalt, copper, iron, manganese, and nickel.

At the time LOSC negotiations began, developing states thought that deep sea-bed mining would bring immense profits and should be exploited only under the auspices of a U.N. entity as part of the "common heritage of mankind," rather than by private firms (predominantly from the developed states) acting for their own gain.[64] The provisions of Part XI of the LOSC, therefore, called for the establishment of an "International Sea–Bed Authority" (Authority) that would control access by private entities to deep sea-bed mining sites, and would limit extraction so as not to impinge excessively on land-based mining. The private entities would be taxed and the proceeds distributed to all states. Moreover, the Authority itself could engage in mining through the establishment of a new entity called the "Enterprise." A private entity seeking access to a potential mining area would have to identify two sites, one for itself and one for exploitation by the Authority either through the Enterprise or by some association with developing states. Finally, the Authority would have the ability to compel states to transfer to it, on "fair commercial terms," mining technology that was not available on the open market.

61. Agreement Concerning Cooperation to Suppress the Proliferation of Weapons of Mass Destruction, Their Delivery Systems, and Related Materials by Sea, U.S.-Liber., Feb. 11, 2004, *at* <http://www.state.gov/t/np/trty/>.

62. Agreement Concerning Cooperation to Suppress the Proliferation of Weapons of Mass Destruction, Their Delivery Systems, and Related Materials by Sea, U.S.-Pan., May 12, 2004, *at* <http://www.state.gov/t/np/trty/>.

63. LOSC, *supra* note 1, art. 1(1).

64. *See* G.A. Res. 2749 (Dec. 17, 1970).

Industrialized states viewed the Authority as irrational, expensive and inefficient, and declined to sign the LOSC after it was adopted. After the sixtieth ratification was deposited in November 1993, the LOSC was set to enter into force in November 1994. At the same time, it had become increasingly clear that extraction of deep sea-bed resources was not commercially feasible using existing technology. Consequently, in an effort to bring the major industrialized states into the regime, further negotiations were conducted leading to a 1994 agreement on the implementation of Part XI of the LOSC.[65]

The 1994 implementing agreement retained the framework for deep sea-bed mining, but with radical changes. As a result, there exists only a skeletal Authority, based in Jamaica, that will develop over time in response to changing circumstances. The Authority has three principal organs: a plenary Assembly; a thirty-six state Council; and a secretariat.[66] The 1994 implementing agreement restructures the Authority's decision-making processes, so that all important decisions are to be made by the Council (the Assembly can only refuse to confirm the Council's decisions). Further, important Council decisions now require consensus on certain issues and a super-majority vote on others. The latter process involves a four-chamber system that protects the interests of different factions, including industrialized states.

Since there is no planned commercial mining in the deep sea-bed area, the 1994 implementing agreement provides that the Enterprise not be established as yet; it begins operating only when the Council decides that it should. Moreover, once established, the Enterprise will be required to conduct its initial mining operations through joint ventures and will not operate independently.[67]

Straits and Archipelagos

Straits. A strait is a narrow stretch of water connecting two larger bodies of water. Given the importance of allowing vessels to pass through straits used for international navigation between one part of the high seas and another, the International Court of Justice—even before adoption of the LOSC—recognized a customary rule of international law that innocent passage cannot be suspended by a coastal state in such straits.[68]

When LOSC negotiators agreed to allow states to claim territorial seas as far out as twelve nautical miles from their baselines, it

---

65. *See supra* note 2.

66. *See* LOSC, *supra* note 1, art. 158.

67. *See generally* L.D.M. Nelson, *The New Deep Sea–Bed Mining Regime*, 10 INT'L J. MAR. & COASTAL L. 189 (1995).

68. *See* Corfu Channel (U.K. v. Alb.), 1949 I.C.J. 4, 28 (Apr. 9).

was understood that this would eliminate in many straits the navigational freedoms enjoyed on the high seas. While there would still be a right of innocent passage through the strait, the loss of broader freedoms was viewed by major maritime states as jeopardizing their interests. Consequently, it was agreed that the LOSC should not only recognize coastal states' interests in expanded territorial seas, but also protect the interests of major maritime states regarding passage through straits by creating special rules on "transit passage." These rules apply with respect to straits that are so narrow that they contain no EEZ and no high seas.

"Transit passage" provides vessels with the traditional freedom of navigation and overflight that exists on the high seas solely for the continuous and expeditious passage through the strait.[69] When engaging in transit passage, vessels must refrain from the threat or use of force and must comply with internationally accepted regulations and practices on safety and pollution.[70] While the coastal state may legislate on certain matters regarding the passage of vessels through the strait, it may not suspend transit passage for security or any other reasons.[71]

Archipelagos. An archipelago is a group of closely interrelated islands that form an intrinsic geographical, economic, and political entity.[72] Where an archipelagos forms a single state, the LOSC allows the archipelagic state to draw "archipelagic baselines" around the state, joining the outermost points of its outermost islands or reefs,[73] rather than create separate maritime zones for each island. The LOSC also sets certain limits on the state's ability to draw archipelagic baselines, such as maintaining a ratio of land-to-water (within the baselines) of no less than one-to-one and no more than one-to-nine.

Once baselines are drawn, the archipelagic state may claim maritime zones over waters seaward of these baselines (territorial sea, contiguous zone, EEZ, and so on). Waters landward of these baselines are "archipelagic waters;" they are not territorial waters, nor are they internal waters unless they fall landward of closing lines across river mouths, bays or harbors of individual islands drawn in accordance with LOSC rules on normal baselines.[74] An archipelagic state must recognize other states' rights in its archipelagic waters as may exist in other agreements, and must recognize traditional fishing rights of neighboring states.[75] Further, the LOSC provides that vessels enjoy the same right of innocent passage through these archipelagic waters as they enjoy through territorial

---

69. *See* LOSC, *supra* note 1, art. 38(2).

70. *Id.*, arts. 39(1) & 39(2).

71. *Id.*, arts. 42(1) & 44.

72. *Id.*, art. 46.

73. *Id.*, art. 47(1).

74. *Id.*, art. 50.

75. *Id.*, art. 51(1).

seas; rights which may only be suspended in limited circumstances.[76] Several states—such as the Bahamas, Indonesia, and the Philippines—have elected to draw archipelagic baselines.

Delimitation of Maritime Boundaries

As the law of the sea maritime zones pushed sovereign control further out from the baselines, states encountered overlapping claims to areas of the sea and continental shelf. Thus, states adjacent to each other along the same coastal stretch, or states bordering opposite sides of a strait or small sea, encountered conflicting claims to their territorial seas, exclusive economic zones, or continental shelves. To resolve such claims, states typically have entered into bilateral agreements (or multilateral agreements if more than two states are involved). For instance, the United States has concluded several bilateral agreements with Mexico regarding maritime boundaries.[77] When such claims cannot be resolved by agreement, they have sometimes been submitted to international dispute resolution, such as before the International Court of Justice.[78]

To resolve these claims, states look to general rules embodied in the LOSC and customary international law. For the delimitation of the territorial seas of states *opposite* each other, the normal practice is to use a median line (a line equidistant from the closest points of the two states' coasts). For territorial sea delimitation of states *adjacent* to each other, a median line is sometimes drawn outwards from the coast, while other times a simple perpendicular line is used. In either type of delimitation, special circumstances may be taken into account. LOSC Article 15 provides:

> Where the coasts of two States are opposite or adjacent to each other, neither of the two States is entitled, failing agreement between them to the contrary, to extend its territorial sea beyond the median line every point of which is equidistant from the nearest points on the baselines from which the breadth of the territorial seas of each of the two States is measured. The above provision does not apply, however, where it is necessary by reason of historic title or other special circumstances to delimit the territorial seas of the two States in a way which is at variance therewith.

76. *Id.*, art. 52.

77. *See, e.g.*, Treaty with Mexico on Delimitation of Continental Shelf, U.S.-Mex., June 9, 2000, S. TREATY DOC. No. 106–39 (2000).

78. *See, e.g.*, Delimitation of the Maritime Boundary in the Gulf of Maine Area (Can./U.S.), 1984 I.C.J. 246 (Oct. 12); Maritime Delimitation & Territorial Questions between Qatar & Bahrain (Qatar v. Bahr.), 2001 I.C.J. 39 (Mar. 16).

LOSC Article 83(1) provides somewhat less guidance for the delimitation of the continental shelf. It states:

> The delimitation of the continental shelf between States with opposite or adjacent coasts shall be effected by agreement on the basis of international law, as referred to in Article 38 of the Statute of the International Court of Justice, in order to achieve an equitable solution.

In practice, states and international tribunals have been unwilling to apply automatically an equidistance principle for delimiting the continental shelf. In the *North Sea Continental Shelf* cases, application of the equidistance principle would have resulted in a very small continental shelf for Germany (compared with Denmark and the Netherlands) due to the concave coastline of the three states along the North Sea. Instead, the Court stated that

> delimitation is to be effected by agreement in accordance with equitable principles, and taking account of all the relevant circumstances, in such a way as to leave as much as possible to each Party all those parts of the continental shelf that constitute a natural prolongation of its land territory into and under the sea, without encroachment on the natural prolongation of the land territory of the other.... [79]

"Relevant circumstances" that have been taken into account by dispute fora include the overall coastal configuration, the length of the parties' coasts, the presence of islands, and the parties' prior conduct (such as an agreement on a provisional boundary line). After negotiation among the three states, Germany was accorded a larger portion of the continental shelf.

Hot Pursuit Across Maritime Zones

One difficulty with enforcing the law of the sea is that maritime vessels are inherently mobile—they may quickly flee from an area under a state's jurisdiction to another area of the seas not under the state's jurisdiction. Consequently, for centuries states have recognized a customary right for a state's military vessel to engage in "hot pursuit" of a foreign vessel which has violated the state's laws within its internal waters or territorial sea, even if the arrest is ultimately made on the high seas.

The LOSC maintains this concept for pursuits that begin not just in internal waters or the territorial sea, but also in the contiguous zone, the EEZ, archipelagic waters, or waters above the continental shelf. The pursuit that commences in a particular zone must be for enforcement of an offense that occurred in that zone.

---

79. North Sea Continental Shelf I.C.J. 3, at para. 101 (Feb. 20).
(F.R.G. v. Den.; F.R.G. v. Neth.), 1969

The pursuit may use necessary and reasonable force to effect an arrest, but the pursuit must be continuous and must end as soon as the vessel enters another state's territorial sea.[80]

C. Regulation of Certain Uses of the Sea

Maritime Pollution

Vessels that transport goods across the seas are among the principal sources of pollution of the marine environment. Such pollution may derive from the vessel's propulsion emissions, the vessel's discharge of garbage or sewage, or the accidental or deliberate spillage of cargo. For instance, oil tankers once used sea water to clean their oil tanks (or to serve as ballast water in the oil tanks), and then discharged the oily sea water back into the sea, causing significant harm to the marine environment.

Various types of global, regional, and bilateral treaties have sought to mitigate marine pollution. On the global level, the International Maritime Organization (IMO) in 1973 developed the Convention for the Prevention of Pollution from Ships (MARPOL Convention)[81] to deal with all forms of intentional pollution of the sea from vessels (other than dumping). The MARPOL Convention originally included a general framework agreement and two obligatory annexes containing technical regulations: Annex I (on prevention of pollution by oil) and Annex II (on control of pollution by noxious liquid substances in bulk). Other annexes have been added in subsequent years, which the parties may join at their discretion: Annex III (on prevention of pollution by harmful substances carried by sea in packaged form); Annex IV (on prevention of pollution by sewage from ships); Annex V (on prevention of pollution by garbage from ships); and Annex VI (on prevention of air pollution from ships).

By way of example, Annex VI prohibits the deliberate emission of ozone-depleting substances by vessels (regulation 12), limits the emission of nitrogen oxides from marine diesel engines (regulation 13), creates stringent sulfur oxide emission controls in the Baltic Sea and other designated areas (regulation 14), regulates the emission of volatile organic compounds during transfer of cargoes between tankers and terminals (regulation 15), and sets international standards for shipboard incinerators and fuel-oil quality (regulations 16 and 18). Annex VI also applies to fixed and floating platforms and drilling rigs, with some exceptions (regulation 19).

---

80. *See* LOSC, *supra* note 1, art. 111. For an example, see William C. Gilmore, *Hot Pursuit: The Case of R. v. Mills and Others*, 44 Int'l & Comp. L.Q. 949 (1995).

81. Nov. 2, 1973, 1340 U.N.T.S. 184, 12 I.L.M. 1319.

To address the dumping of wastes at sea by vessels and aircraft (other than disposal of wastes incidental to the normal operation of such vessels and aircraft), states adopted the Convention on the Prevention of Marine Pollution by Dumping of Wastes and Other Matter (originally known as the London Dumping Convention and now simply the London Convention).[82] The London Convention (1) lists certain substances, such as mercury, that may not be dumped at sea (the "black list"); (2) lists other substances, such as pesticides, that may be dumped only if authorized by a special permit issued by a party to the convention (the "grey list"); and (3) allows the dumping of all other substances and wastes only if authorized by a general permit issued by a party to the convention, which may be conditioned on factors such as the method of disposal and the disposal site. A 1996 protocol to the London Convention that has entered into force for 41 states severely restricts the types of substances that may be dumped.[83]

The most important source of marine pollution is from land-based activities. While several regional treaties address this issue,[84] there is as yet no global convention. This absence no doubt reflects the difficulty of regulating on a global level activities falling squarely within the territorial sovereignty of states and encompassing an enormous range of polluters (ranging from industrial wastes to agricultural pesticides to grass fertilizers used by homeowners).

The LOSC reinforces these treaty-based standards on marine pollution by placing an obligation on all states to adopt laws and regulations that give effect to generally accepted international rules and standards.[85] Flag states are obligated to enforce such laws and regulations against their vessels.[86] When a vessel enters a port, the port state may also pursue enforcement actions.[87] Finally, a coastal state is permitted to enforce laws and regulations on maritime pollution within maritime zones under its authority subject to certain constraints, such as being non-discriminatory and not hampering innocent passage.[88]

Fishing

Historically, fish outside territorial waters have been open to exploitation by fishing vessels from any state. Yet with modern technological advances in locating, harvesting, and storing fish (such as the use of drift nets that are thirty feet in depth and up to

---

82. Dec. 29, 1972, 26 U.S.T. 2403, 1046 U.N.T.S. 120, as amended.

83. *See* 36 I.L.M. 1, 7 (1997).

84. *See, e.g.,* MALGOSIA FITZMAURICE, INTERNATIONAL LEGAL PROBLEMS OF THE ENVIRONMENTAL PROTECTION OF THE BALTIC SEA (1992).

85. *See* LOSC, *supra* note 1, arts. 207–12.

86. *Id.*, art. 217.

87. *Id.*, art. 218.

88. *Id.*, art. 220.

thirty miles in length), fish stocks worldwide have suffered from biologically unsustainable exploitation. The modern law of the sea, therefore, has sought to regulate access to fishery resources, both in the EEZ and on the high seas.

As noted above, in the EEZ the coastal state has "sovereign rights for the purpose of exploring and exploiting, conserving and managing" the living and non-living natural resources of the sea-bed, its subsoil, and superadjacent waters.[89] At the same time, the coastal state must ensure that the living resources in the EEZ are maintained at or restored to "levels which can produce the maximum sustainable yield, as qualified by relevant environmental and economic factors ... and taking into account fishing patterns, the interdependence of stocks and any generally recommended international minimum standards.... "[90] Further, in fulfilling its obligation to promote the optimum utilization of EEZ living resources, the coastal state must establish the total allowable catch and either itself harvest that catch or allow the fishing vessels of other states to do so.[91] Where a coastal state has permitted access to its EEZ for foreign fishing vessels, it may enforce its regulations against those vessels by "boarding, inspection, arrest and judicial proceedings.... "[92]

Of course, fish do not confine themselves to the EEZ of a particular coastal state. They may migrate among EEZs (shared fish stocks) and between EEZs and the high seas (straddling fish stocks). Some fish spend their entire life cycle on the high seas. LOSC Article 63(1) calls upon states with shared fish stocks "to agree upon the measures necessary to co-ordinate and ensure the conservation and development of such stocks.... " To that end, many states have agreed upon cooperative arrangements for managing shared stocks.[93]

With respect to straddling fish stocks and fish stocks that spend their entire life cycle on the high seas, LOSC Articles 117–20 impose a duty on interested states to cooperate in the management and conservation of high seas living resources, making use where appropriate of international fishery commissions. In furtherance of that cooperation, many states have concluded the U.N. Convention on the Conservation and Management of Straddling Fish Stocks and Highly Migratory Fish Stocks,[94] which entered into force in

89. *Id.*, art. 56(1)(a).

90. *Id.*, art. 61(3).

91. *Id.*, arts. 61–62, 69–70.

92. *Id.*, art. 73(1).

93. *See, e.g.*, Treaty Concerning Pacific Salmon, U.S.-Can., Jan. 28, 1985,

T.I.A.S. 11,091, 1469 U.N.T.S. 357 (further amended in June 1999).

94. Agreement for the Implementation of the Provisions of the United Nations Convention on the Law of the Sea of 10 December 1982 Relating to the Conservation and Management of Straddling Fish Stocks and Highly Migratory

2001. The convention sets out detailed principles to be followed by a coastal state within its EEZ and by all states on the high seas. Where a regional organization or arrangement exists to implement these principles, the convention obligates states to use that organization or arrangement or to refrain from fishing in that region. Where a regional organization or arrangement does not exist, the convention calls upon states to establish one.

Several such regional organizations or arrangements now exist. For example, the United States is a party to the Northwest Atlantic Fisheries Organization (NAFO). Each year, NAFO establishes a total allowable catch for the high seas area of the Northwest Atlantic, which is then divided into quotas allocated to NAFO member states. The most recently established regional arrangement covers the last major area of the world's oceans that lacked a regional management regime—the Western and Central Pacific Ocean.[95] Two-thirds of the world's tuna catch comes from this region.

Despite these cooperative efforts among states to manage fish on the high seas, fish stocks worldwide are under enormous stress. Consequently, some coastal states have been aggressive in extending the reach of their national laws. In the *Fisheries Jurisdiction* case (Spain v. Canada),[96] Spain charged that Canada violated international law by: (1) passing a law/regulations allowing Canadian enforcement actions on the high seas to prevent excessive fishing of stocks that migrated between the high seas and Canada's exclusive economic zone; and (2) seizing a Spanish fishing vessel on the high seas allegedly engaged in such fishing. The Court dismissed the case on jurisdictional grounds, since Canada only accepted the Court's compulsory jurisdiction with reservations, one of which carved out any dispute concerning "conservation and management measures taken by Canada with respect to vessels fishing in the [North Atlantic Fisheries Organization] Regulatory Area ... and enforcement of such measures." The most significant element of the Court's decision was the finding that "conservation and management measures" in fishing treaties and national legislation can include a broad variety of activities; thus, Canada's actions were within the scope of its reservation to the Court's jurisdiction.[97] Some of the separate and dissenting opinions also address the issue of what constitutes "conservation and management measures."[98]

Fish Stocks, Aug. 4, 1995, 2167 U.N.T.S. 88, 34 I.L.M. 1542.

95. *See* Convention on the Conservation and Management of Highly Migratory Fish Stocks in the Western and Central Pacific Ocean, Sept. 5, 2000, 40 I.L.M. 278.

96. Fisheries Jurisdiction (Spain v. Can.), 1998 I.C.J. 432 (Dec. 4).

97. *Id.* at 461–62, paras. 70–71.

98. *Id.* at 474 (separate opinion of Judge Oda) (finding the Court's references to fishing treaties and national legislation "meaningless" and "mislead-

Protection of Whales

To safeguard against the loss of whale stocks, the 1946 International Convention for the Regulation of Whaling (ICRW)[99] established a schedule of regulations that lists particular species covered by the ICRW, as well as the controls on each of those species. Amendments to the schedule require a three-fourths majority vote of the International Whaling Commission (IWC) created by the ICRW. Once adopted, an amendment is binding on all parties except those that have filed objections with the IWC within ninety days. In 1982, the IWC voted to amend the schedule in order to phase out commercial whaling, leading to a complete moratorium in 1986—except for aboriginal whaling and scientific research. This moratorium has had a significant effect in restoring the populations of certain whale stocks, although states (and their scientists) differ on exactly how well whale stocks are doing.

The ICRW moratorium met with considerable opposition from some states. Japan and three other states lodged objections to the moratorium from the start, stating that the purpose of the ICRW was to promote and maintain whale fishery stocks, not to ban whaling completely. For those states, the moratorium does not apply since, as noted above, amendments to the ICRW schedule are not binding on states that file objections. Iceland did not initially file an objection. Yet after the IWC began extending the moratorium annually—even in the face of scientific evidence that certain whale stocks were recovering or had recovered—Iceland officially withdrew from the IWC in 1992. According to Iceland, the IWC had wholly disregarded the ICRW's purpose and requirements.

In light of growing resistance to the moratorium, in 1994 the IWC adopted a "revised management procedure" (RMP) for calculating allowable catches of whales based on population data and taking into account uncertainties. The IWC, however, chose not to implement the RMP, and the moratorium on commercial whaling remained in place.[100] Instead, the commission embarked on the development of a "revised management scheme" (RMS) that would

ing"); *id.* at 496 (dissenting opinion of Vice–President Weeramantry, dissenting opinions of Judges Bedjaoui and Vereshchetin) (arguing that the unilateral exercise of jurisdiction by a coastal state against non-flag state vessels on the high seas does not constitute "conservation and management measures" or even enforcement of such measures, since there is no right under international law to enact such measures unilaterally with respect to the high seas).

99. Dec. 2, 1946, 62 Stat. 1716, 161 U.N.T.S. 72. The convention is implemented in U.S. law by the Whaling Convention Act of 1949, 16 U.S.C. §§ 916–916*l* (2006).

100. *See* David D. Caron, *The International Whaling Commission and the North Atlantic Marine Mammal Commission: The Institutional Risks of Coercion in Consensual Structures*, 89 Am. J. Int'l L. 154, 160–61 (1995).

contain appropriate measures for ensuring that states adhered to the RMP.

In October 2002, Iceland filed an instrument of adherence to the ICRW with the United States (the depositary for the ICRW), which was conditioned on a reservation to the commercial whaling moratorium. The reservation sought to induce the IWC into implementing the RMP and RMS by stating that Iceland would not authorize whaling by its vessels if progress is made in the negotiation of the RMS and, upon completion of that negotiation, the moratorium is lifted within a reasonable time. As of 2011, however, the ICRW moratorium on commercial whaling remained in place.

Recovery of Underwater Artifacts

Recovery of artifacts located on the floor of the sea is increasingly feasible due to technological advances in underwater survey and recovery techniques. Since such artifacts are often valuable, states have enacted a variety of laws determining whether, and subject to what conditions, the recovery of artifacts is to be permitted. Under the LOSC, coastal states have jurisdiction to regulate activity that affects "underwater cultural heritage" in areas over which they have sovereignty, including territorial seas.[101] Further, coastal states have authority over the removal of "objects of an archaeological and historical nature" in the contiguous zone.[102] Beyond the contiguous zone, the LOSC establishes no special role for the coastal state. All states, however, "have the duty to protect objects of an archaeological and historical nature found at sea and shall co-operate for this purpose."[103] With respect to the deep seabed or the "Area," the LOSC provides that underwater cultural heritage "shall be preserved or disposed of for the benefit of mankind as a whole, particular regard being paid to the preferential rights of the State" of origin.[104]

In 2001, the U.N. Educational, Scientific and Cultural Organization (UNESCO) adopted a convention to protect underwater cultural heritage.[105] The convention defines "underwater cultural heritage" as artifacts that have been underwater for at least one hundred years.[106] It also provides that, within the territorial sea, the coastal state must require that any activities directed at underwater cultural heritage be in accordance with the convention's annex, which contains rules and standards for underwater archeology.[107] With respect to underwater cultural heritage located outside

101. LOSC, *supra* note 1, arts. 2, 7.

102. *Id.*, arts. 33(1), 303.

103. *Id.*, art. 303(1).

104. *Id.*, art. 149.

105. *See* Convention on the Protection of the Underwater Cultural Heritage, Nov. 6, 2001, 41 I.L.M. 40.

106. *Id.*, art. 1(1)(a).

107. *Id.*, art. 7, annex.

the territorial sea but within a state's continental shelf or EEZ, the convention provides that all states must require their nationals to notify the coastal state of any discoveries or planned activities regarding the artifacts.[108] Other states may inform the coastal state that they are interested in such artifacts based "on a verifiable link," but it is the coastal state, acting as a "Coordinating State," that has extensive rights regarding any activities directed at those artifacts.[109] With respect to underwater cultural heritage located on the deep sea-bed ("the Area"), the flag state of the vessel that locates an artifact, or is planning an activity, must notify other states and the International Sea–Bed Authority of any discoveries or proposed activities. A "Coordinating State" is then appointed by all interested states, and charged with implementing protective measures, including authorization for recovery, as agreed upon by the interested states.[110]

As of 2011, 40 states have ratified the convention. The United States does not support the convention because it believes the convention accords too much control to the coastal state over artifacts outside its territorial waters. Instead, the United States has pursued bilateral agreements with states regarding specific sunken vessels, such as agreements with the United Kingdom relating to the RMS *Titanic*,[111] which sank in 1912, and with France relating to the *LaBelle*,[112] which sank in 1686.

D. Dispute Settlement

The LOSC promotes the peaceful settlement of LOSC disputes. In section 1 of part XV, the LOSC calls for an expeditious exchange of views between two parties whenever a dispute may arise, and for resolution of the dispute by whatever means agreed upon by the parties. If this is not possible, either party may request that the other party agree to use the LOSC conciliation procedure.[113] Under this procedure, each party chooses two conciliators (of which one may be its national) from a list established by LOSC parties. The four conciliators then select a fifth to serve as chairperson. After considering the views of both parties, the panel issues a report in which it makes non-binding recommendations.

If the dispute is incapable of settlement under section 1 of part XV, either party may resort to the compulsory dispute settlement

---

108. *Id.*, art. 9(1)(a).

109. *Id.*, arts. 9(5), 10(3)(b).

110. *Id.*, arts. 11–12.

111. *See* Agreement Concerning the Shipwrecked Vessel RMS Titanic, U.S.-U.K., art. 3, June 18, 2004, *at* <http://www.state.gov/g/oes/rls /or/2004/33709. htm>.

112. *See* Agreement Regarding the Wreck of *La Belle*, U.S.-Fr., art. 1(2), Mar. 31, 2003, 2003 WL 21312330 (Treaty).

113. *See* LOSC, *supra* note 1, art. 284 & annex V.

provisions contained in section 2, so long as none of its exceptions apply. For example, most disputes concerning the exercise by a coastal state of its sovereign rights or jurisdiction within the EEZ are not subject to LOSC compulsory dispute settlement.[114] Otherwise, disputes arising under the LOSC or its implementing agreements shall be resolved before one of four dispute resolution fora: (1) the International Tribunal for the Law of the Sea (ITLOS), established under LOSC Annex VI;[115] (2) the International Court of Justice;[116] (3) a general arbitral tribunal, established pursuant to LOSC Annex VII; or (4) an arbitral tribunal composed of specialists in certain areas (fisheries, environmental protection, marine scientific research, or navigation), established pursuant to LOSC Annex VIII.

When a state signs the LOSC, or at any point thereafter, it may indicate which of the four fora it selects for compulsory dispute settlement (if it fails to select a forum, it is deemed to have selected Annex VII arbitration). If two parties to a dispute have both selected the same forum, then that forum is used to resolve the dispute, unless the parties agree otherwise.[117] If two states have selected different fora, and cannot agree on a forum, the dispute is submitted to Annex VII arbitration.[118] All these fora apply LOSC and other rules of international law, and their decisions are final and binding on the parties.[119] In practice, many LOSC parties have not selected a forum, while others have accepted ITLOS (*e.g.*, Argentina), the International Court of Justice (*e.g.*, Germany), or Annex VII arbitration (*e.g.*, the United States, although not yet an LOSC party, has indicated it will select this forum).

An example of the LOSC dispute resolution process is the *Southern Bluefin Tuna* case. In that case, Australia and New Zealand charged that Japan was violating its LOSC obligations by not limiting its catch of southern bluefin tuna on the high seas. In July 1999, the two states notified Japan that they intended to institute LOSC Annex VII arbitration and to seek provisional measures of protection from ITLOS pending constitution of the arbitral tribunal, as permitted under LOSC Article 290(5). In a decision rendered in August 1999, ITLOS found that the arbitral tribunal would likely have jurisdiction over the dispute. Consequently, ITLOS imposed certain limitations on Japanese fishing pending the arbitral tribunal's decision.[120]

---

114. *Id.*, arts. 297–298.

115. *See* Chapter 4(F).

116. *See* Chapter 4(D).

117. *See* LOSC, *supra* note 1, art. 287(4).

118. *Id.*, art. 287(5).

119. *Id.*, arts. 293 & 296.

120. *See* Southern Bluefin Tuna (N.Z. v. Japan; Austl. v. Japan), Provisional Measures (ITLOS Aug. 27, 1999), *reprinted in* 38 I.L.M. 1624 (1999).

Thereafter, a tribunal of five arbitrators was formed, presided over by former International Court of Justice Judge (and President) Stephen Schwebel. The tribunal found that it lacked jurisdiction over the dispute.[121] It noted that in Article 16 of the Convention for the Conservation of Southern Bluefin Tuna,[122] all three states had agreed that disputes arising under the convention would be resolved by binding third-party settlement only with the consent, in each case, of all the parties to the dispute. According to the tribunal, the effect of the agreement was to exclude compulsory dispute settlement under that convention and under the LOSC, since the LOSC was an "umbrella" or "framework" agreement designed to allow states to choose the means for resolving disputes. Since it lacked jurisdiction over the merits of the dispute, the tribunal revoked the provisional measures imposed by ITLOS.[123]

Part XI of the LOSC, relating to the deep sea-bed, creates a "Sea-bed Disputes Chamber" of ITLOS, which has jurisdiction over certain disputes concerning the deep sea-bed (*e.g.*, between the Authority and a state party to the LOSC).[124] Further, the Sea-bed Disputes Chamber has authority to "give advisory opinions at the request of the Assembly or the Council on legal questions arising within the scope of their activities."[125] In response to certain questions posed by the Council, the Chamber issued its first advisory opinion in 2011 entitled *Responsibilities and Obligations of States Sponsoring Persons and Entities with Respect to Activities in the Area*.[126] Among other things, the Chamber clarified that a state that sponsors contractors who engage in exploratory activities on the deep sea-bed is responsible for supervising them, including any drilling, dredging or excavation. Further, states must engage in a precautionary approach with respect to such activities, must use best environmental practices, and must conduct environmental impact assessments.

E. Should the United States Ratify the LOSC?

As noted in section A above, President Clinton in 1994 submitted the LOSC and the 1994 implementing agreement to the U.S. Senate for advice and consent.[127] The Senate Foreign Relations

---

121. *See* Southern Bluefin Tuna (Austl. & N.Z. v. Japan), Jurisdiction and Admissibility (Int'l Arb. Trib. Aug. 4, 2000), *reprinted in* 39 I.L.M. 1359 (2000).

122. May 10, 1993, 1819 U.N.T.S. 360.

123. For a critique of this decision, taking the view that some form of *compulsory* dispute settlement is integral to the LOSC, see Bernard H. Oxman, *Com-*

plementary Agreements and Compulsory Jurisdiction, 95 Am. J. Int'l L. 277 (2001).

124. *See* LOSC, *supra* note 1, arts. 186–90.

125. *Id.*, art. 191.

126. Case No. 17, Advisory Opinion (Feb. 1, 2010), 50 I.L.M. 458 (2011).

127. *See* S. Treaty Doc. No. 103–39 (1994).

Committee (SFRC) did not schedule hearings on the LOSC, however, until October 2003, by which time 143 states had become parties to the convention, including virtually all North Atlantic Treaty Organization (NATO) states, China, and Russia. Although the SFRC unanimously reported favorably on the LOSC in 2004,[128] a vote before the full Senate had not been held as of the end of 2011. Among other things, critics of the LOSC charged that "this accord would constitute the most egregious transfer of American sovereignty, wealth, and power to the U.N. since the founding of that 'world body.' "[129]

In urging the Senate to provide its consent, the executive branch argued that (1) maintaining the status quo was untenable; (2) the advantages of joining the LOSC outweighed the disadvantages; and (3) U.S. adherence to binding dispute settlement could be crafted to protect U.S. interests. With respect to maintaining the status quo, the U.S. Department of State legal adviser argued:

> U.S. [maritime] mobility and access have been preserved and enjoyed over the past twenty years largely due to the Convention's stable, widely accepted legal framework. It would be risky to assume that it is possible to preserve *ad infinitum* the stable situation that the United States currently enjoys. Customary international law may be changed by the practice of States over time and therefore does not offer the future stability that comes with being a party to the Convention.[130]

As to the advantages of joining the LOSC, the legal adviser asserted that:

- U.S. accession would enhance the authoritative force of the Convention, likely inspire other States to join, and promote its provisions as *the* governing rules of international law relating to the oceans.

- The United States would be in a stronger position invoking a treaty's provisions to which it is party, for instance in a bilateral disagreement where the other country does not understand or accept them.

---

128. *See* S. Exec. Rpt. 108–10 (2004); *see also* Michael J. Mattler, *The Law of the Sea Convention: A View from the U.S. Senate*, in International Energy Policy, the Arctic and the Law of the Sea 33 (Myron H. Nordquist et al. eds., 2005).

129. Frank Gaffney, Jr., *Don't Get LOST*, Nat'l Rev. Online, Mar. 18, 2004, *at* <http://www.nationalreview.com/gaffney/gaffney200403181156.asp>; *see* Charles Babington, *Criticism Deep–Sixes*

Senate Vote on Sea Treaty, Wash. Post, Apr. 25, 2004, at A4.

130. *Accession to the 1982 Law of the Sea Convention and Ratification of the 1994 Agreement Amending Part XI of the Law of the Sea Convention: Hearing Before the S. Comm. on Foreign Relations*, 108th Cong. 12 (2003) (statement of William H. Taft, IV, U.S. Department of State Legal Adviser) [hereinafter Taft testimony].

- While we have been able to rely on diplomatic and operational challenges to excessive maritime claims, it is desirable to establish additional methods of resolving conflict.

- The Convention continues to be implemented in various fora, both within the Convention and outside the Convention (such as at the International Maritime Organization or IMO). The United States would be in a stronger position defending its military and other interests in these fora if it were a party to the Convention.

- Becoming a party to the Convention would permit the United States to nominate members for both the Law of the Sea Tribunal and the Continental Shelf Commission. Having U.S. members on those bodies would help ensure that the Convention is being interpreted and applied in a manner consistent with U.S. interests.

- Becoming a party to the Convention would strengthen our ability to deflect potential proposals that would be inconsistent with U.S. interests, including freedom of navigation.[131]

By contrast, the legal adviser argued that the disadvantages of joining the LOSC were minimal. Payments to the convention's institutions would be modest. There would be a new bureaucracy for deep sea-bed mining, yet that bureaucracy had been restructured in ways that met the objections raised by the United States. The United States also would have to pay for the exploitation of the continental shelf beyond 200 miles from shore based on a percentage of oil/gas production, but

> the revenue-sharing provisions of the Convention are reasonable. The United States has one of the broadest shelves in the world. . . . The revenue-sharing provision was instrumental in achieving guaranteed U.S. rights to these large areas. It is important to note that this revenue-sharing obligation does not apply to areas within 200 nautical miles and thus does not affect current revenues produced from the U.S. Outer Continental Shelf. Most important, this provision was developed by the United States in close cooperation with representatives of the U.S. oil and gas industry. The industry supports this provision. Finally, with a guaranteed seat on the Finance Committee of the International Seabed Authority, we would have an absolute veto over the distribution of all revenues generated from this revenue-sharing provision.[132]

As for the dispute resolution process, the legal adviser noted that the LOSC allows states, when joining the convention, to

---

131. *Id.* at 11–12.   **132.** *Id.* at 10–11.

submit a declaration opting out of such procedures for disputes: (1) regarding maritime boundaries between neighboring states; (2) regarding military activities and certain law enforcement activities; and (3) in respect of which the U.N. Security Council is exercising the functions assigned to it under the U.N. Charter.[133] The executive branch recommended that the United States opt out of the dispute settlement procedures with regard to all three categories. It also recommended that the United States declare that its adherence to the convention was conditioned on the understanding that "each Party has the exclusive right to determine which of its activities are 'military activities' and that such determination is not subject to review."[134]

133. *See* LOSC, *supra* note 1, art. 298(1).

134. Taft Testimony, *supra* note 130, at 6–7.

Further Reading:

David Joseph Attard, *The Exclusive Economic Zone in International Law* (1987).

Peter B. Beazley, *Maritime Limits and Baselines* (3d ed. 1987).

E.D. Brown, *The International Law of the Sea* (1994) (2 vols.).

William T. Burke, *The New International Law of Fisheries: UNCLOS 1982 and Beyond* (1994).

Hugo Caminos, ed., *Law of the Sea* (2000).

Jonathan Charney et al., *International Maritime Boundaries* (1993–2002) (4 vols.).

R.R. Churchill & A.V. Lowe, *The Law of the Sea* (3d ed. 1999).

R.B. Clark, *Marine Pollution* (5th ed. 2001).

Gudmundur Eiriksson, *The International Tribunal for the Law of the Sea* (2000).

David Freestone, et al., eds., *The Law of the Sea: Progress and Prospects* (2006).

Natalie Klein, *Maritime Security and the Law of the Sea* (2011).

Marion Markowski, *The International Law of EEZ Fisheries: Principles and Implementation* (2010).

Francis Ngantcha, *The Right of Innocent Passage and the Evolution of the International Law of the Sea: The Current Regime of "Free" Navigation in Coastal Waters of Third States* (1990).

Myron H. Nordquist, *United Nations Convention on the Law of the Sea: A Commentary* (1985–2002) (6 vols.).

D.P. O'Connell, *The International Law of the Sea* (1982) (2 vols.).

J. Ashley Roach & Robert W. Smith, *United States Responses to Excessive Maritime Claims* (2d. ed. 1996).

U.S. Commission on Ocean Policy, *An Ocean Blueprint for the 21st Century: Final Report of the U.S. Commission on Ocean Policy* (2004).

Francisco O. Vicuña, *The Exclusive Economic Zone: Regime and Legal Nature Under International Law* (1989).

James C.F. Wang, *Handbook on Ocean Politics and Law* (1991).

José A. Yturriaga, *The International Regime of Fisheries: From UNCLOS 1982 to the Presential Sea* (1997).

Chapter 12

INTERNATIONAL
ENVIRONMENTAL LAW

International environmental law is a relatively recent branch of international law concerned with the preservation and enhancement of the global environment. To address transnational environmental problems, such as ozone depletion, climate change, and loss of biological diversity, states have developed a network of agreements and institutions, as well as certain legal principles and techniques, that are unique to this field of international law.

A. Structural Overview

Historical Background

Early Days. In the nineteenth and early twentieth centuries, states began concluding agreements regulating international fishing and protecting certain fauna (such as birds and seals) and various plant species. For example, the bilateral treaty at issue in *Missouri v. Holland*[1] concerned the protection of birds migrating between the United States and Canada. Some regional conventions also emerged, such as the 1940 Convention on Nature Protection and Wildlife Preservation in the Western Hemisphere.[2] That convention promoted conservation through the establishment of national parks and wilderness reserves.[3] The decision on whether to establish parks and reserves was left to the wide discretion of the parties. The parties also agreed on the importance of protecting migratory birds and certain species listed in an annex.[4] The annex, however, is not a comprehensive list of species but, rather, a compilation of national lists.

In this early period, states also concluded agreements to regulate the use of water along boundaries, such as the Treaty Relating to the Boundary Waters and Questions Arising Along the Boundary[5] between Canada and the United States, which remains in force today. As discussed in Chapter 4(A), the treaty provides a frame-

---

1. 252 U.S. 416 (1920); *see* Chapter 7(C).

2. Oct. 12, 1940, 56 Stat. 1354, 161 U.N.T.S. 193.

3. *Id.*, art. II(1).

4. *Id.*, art. VIII.

5. U.S.-U.K., Jan. 11, 1909, 36 Stat. 2448, 12 Bevans 319.

work for resolving disputes between the two states over activities affecting shared water resources.

Stockholm Conference. Contemporary international environmental law arose after developments at the national level in the 1960's, when governments and the public at large became aware of the significant environmental threats posed by the rapid growth in population, industrial pollution, and human consumption of natural resources. In 1968, the U.N. General Assembly proposed the convening of a global conference on the human environment, to be held in Stockholm, Sweden.[6] The 1972 Stockholm Conference brought together, for the first time, representatives from 113 states, as well as from hundreds of international and non-government organizations, to discuss the global environment. Two key achievements occurred at Stockholm.

First, the conference adopted at its closing plenary session a Declaration on the Human Environment.[7] The Stockholm Declaration contained important preambular language and a series of politically-binding principles to be followed by governments and their peoples in preserving and improving the human environment for the benefit and posterity of all people. In general, the Stockholm Declaration advanced certain ethical and moral values in favor of preserving the human environment, while at the same time recognizing that economic and scientific realities would limit the steps that could be taken.[8] For instance, Principle 2 of the Stockholm Declaration declared:

> The natural resources of the earth including the air, water, land, flora and fauna and especially representative samples of natural ecosystems must be safeguarded for the benefit of present and future generations through careful planning or management, as appropriate.

While many of these principles were vague and conditional, they reflected a commitment of states to the global environment that thereafter shaped the development of more specific international environmental agreements, national laws, and institutional initiatives.

Second, the Stockholm Conference adopted a politically-binding Action Plan containing 109 recommendations for future action in addressing international environmental problems. Special attention was paid to identifying and responding to environmental threats and to supporting such responses financially and institutionally (through education and training). As a result of the Action Plan,

---

6. *See* G.A. Res. 2398 (Dec. 3, 1968).

7. 11 I.L.M. 1416 (1972) [hereinafter Stockholm Declaration].

8. *See* Louis Sohn, *The Stockholm Declaration on the Human Environment,* 14 Harv. Int'l L.J. 423 (1973).

the U.N. General Assembly in 1972 created the U.N. Environment Programme (UNEP), based in Nairobi, Kenya.

From Stockholm to Rio. In the twenty years after the Stockholm Conference, states moved rapidly to develop international environmental law across a range of sectors. Some global agreements continued to focus on wildlife protection. Thus, the 1971 Ramsar Convention[9] calls upon parties to engage in the "wise use" of wetlands by undertaking environmental impact assessments, making wetland inventories, establishing nature reserves, training wetland managers, consulting other parties, and assisting in operations of the convention. Article 2(4) requires each party to designate one wetland of international importance for the Ramsar Convention List. A party that lists a wetland is required to promote its conservation and "wise use," yet the convention provides no specific guidance (*e.g.*, whether the wetland must be kept in its natural condition or whether it should remain in private ownership) and subsequent guidelines developed by the parties are nonbinding. Further, any wetland placed on the convention list may be removed by a party.[10]

With respect to the protection of endangered species, the 1973 Convention on International Trade in Endangered Species of Wild Fauna and Flora (CITES)[11] established a global system for strictly regulating trade in species threatened with extinction and limiting trade in species that may become extinct or that are of concern to member states. Although not adopted in treaty form, the U.N. General Assembly's 1982 World Charter for Nature contained twenty-four articles calling for the integration of nature conservation into the laws and practices of states.[12]

Such conservation agreements, however, were not limited to wildlife. Through the 1972 UNESCO World Heritage Convention[13] states voluntarily commit themselves to protect cultural monuments and natural sites within their territory that are recognized to be of such universal value that safeguarding them concerns humanity as a whole. Parties recognize that they have a duty to identify and protect the cultural and natural heritage that lies within their territory, but they are not obligated to place any sites

9. Convention on Wetlands of International Importance Especially as Waterfowl Habitat, Feb. 2, 1971, 996 U.N.T.S. 243, 11 I.L.M. 963, 969, as amended by the Paris Protocol, Dec. 3, 1983, 22 I.L.M. 698.

10. If a state removes a wetland from the list, the state "should as far as possible compensate for any loss of wetland resources" by finding ways to protect the affected waterfowl. *Id.*, art. 4(2).

11. Mar. 3, 1973, 27 U.S.T. 1087, 993 U.N.T.S. 243 [hereinafter CITES].

12. *See* G.A. Res. 37/7 (Oct. 28, 1982).

13. Convention Concerning the Protection of the World Cultural and Natural Heritage, Nov. 23, 1972, 27 U.S.T. 37, 1037 U.N.T.S. 151 [hereinafter World Heritage Convention].

on the World Heritage Site List and the convention is "without prejudice to property rights provided by national legislation.... "[14] Since such sites are often located in poorer states, placing sites on the World Heritage Site List is often viewed as a means of obtaining assistance, whether technical or financial, for conservation projects.

States also turned their attention to pollution of the atmosphere, land, and areas outside national jurisdiction. With respect to atmospheric pollution, the industrialized states of Europe and North America joined together in 1979 to conclude the Convention on Long–Range Transboundary Air Pollution (LRTAP).[15] The LRTAP Convention regulates emissions of sulfur dioxide, nitrous oxide, and other long-range pollutants through a series of protocols. With respect to land-based pollutants, the 1989 Basel Convention on the Control of Transboundary Movements of Hazardous Wastes and Their Disposal[16] provides for environmentally sound management and disposal of hazardous wastes transported across borders, principally through use of a notice-and-consent regime. With respect to areas outside the sovereignty of states, the Protocol on Environmental Protection to the Antarctic Treaty[17] provides an integrated approach to environmental protection of that fragile ecosystem. As for the oceans, the U.N. Convention on the Law of the Sea (LOSC) was adopted in 1982 and entered into force in 1994, containing extensive and innovative provisions on the protection and preservation of the marine environment.[18]

In addition to these global instruments, dozens of regional and bilateral international environmental agreements were adopted, such as the 1968 African Convention on the Conservation of Nature and Natural Resources.[19] The European Community also adopted several environmental regulations and directives that are binding on its member states.[20]

Rio Conference. On the twentieth anniversary of the Stockholm Conference, the U.N. General Assembly convened another conference, this time in Rio de Janeiro, Brazil. The 1992 U.N. Conference on Environment and Development (UNCED) involved representatives from 172 states, as well as thousands of representatives from international and non-governmental organizations. From the outset, however, there was a tension between the developed states and

14. *Id.*, art. 6(1).

15. Nov. 13, 1979, T.I.A.S. No. 10,-541, 1302 U.N.T.S. 217 [hereinafter LRTAP].

16. Mar. 22, 1989, S. Treaty Doc. No. 102–5 (1991), 1673 U.N.T.S. 57 [hereinafter Basel Convention].

17. Oct. 4, 1991, 30 I.L.M. 1455.

18. *See* U.N. Convention on the Law of the Sea, Dec. 10, 1982, S. Treaty Doc. No. 103–39 (1994), 1833 U.N.T.S. 3, 397 (1982) [hereinafter LOSC]; *see also* Chapter 11.

19. Sept. 15, 1968, 1001 U.N.T.S. 3.

20. *See* Ludwig Krämer, EC Environmental Law (2003).

developing states. The developed states desired stronger global environmental regulation, while the developing states were unwilling to assume the burdens of such regulation if doing so impeded their economies. As a result, efforts to blend environmental and developmental objectives pervaded the work of the conference. Ultimately, UNCED led to three key achievements.

First, important global conventions on climate change and biological diversity were opened for signature at the conference. The conference also adopted a politically-binding statement of principles on conservation and management of forests.[21]

Second, UNCED adopted the Rio Declaration on Environment and Development containing twenty-seven politically-binding principles that built upon the Stockholm Declaration, with particular emphasis on integrating environmental protection and economic development ("sustainable development").[22] Thus, Rio Declaration Principle 4 provides: "In order to achieve sustainable development, environmental protection shall constitute an integral part of the development process and cannot be considered in isolation from it." Like the Stockholm Declaration, the Rio Declaration is not legally-binding, but is often referred to in negotiations or litigation as an authoritative statement of states' political commitments.

Third, UNCED adopted a politically-binding action program for the twenty-first century, called "Agenda 21."[23] Over the course of forty chapters, Agenda 21 provides extensive recommendations for addressing more than 100 international environmental topics, such as changing consumption patterns (chapter four), freshwater resources (chapter eighteen), and the role of indigenous peoples (chapter twenty-six). Of particular relevance, Agenda 21 contains chapters on international institutional arrangements (chapter thirty-eight) and international legal instruments and mechanisms (chapter thirty-nine). Throughout Agenda 21, there is an emphasis on the development of national legislation and programs to implement its recommendations. UNCED called for the establishment of a high-level U.N. commission to monitor the implementation of Agenda 21, which led to the creation of the U.N. Sustainable Development Commission (CSD), based in New York.

Recent Developments

In the two decades following the UNCED conference, states have taken steps to implement Agenda 21 through the passage of

---

21. *See* 31 I.L.M. 881 (1992).

22. *See* 31 I.L.M. 874 (1992) [hereinafter Rio Declaration]; *see also* Nico Schrijver, *The Evolution of Sustainable Development in International Law: Inception, Meaning and Status*, 329 R.C.A.D.I. 217 (2007).

23. *See* AGENDA 21: PROGRAM OF ACTION FOR SUSTAINABLE DEVELOPMENT, RIO DE JANEIRO, U.N. Doc. A/CONF. 151/26 (vols. I, II, & III) (1992).

national legislation and programs. Further, the global community has continued to develop international environmental law through adoption of new agreements or protocols to existing agreements. Thus, in 1994 states adopted the U.N. Convention to Combat Desertification in Those Countries Experiencing Serious Drought and/or Desertification, Particularly in Africa.[24] In 2000, states adopted the Cartegena Protocol on Biosafety to the Convention on Biological Diversity,[25] which established a notice-and-consent regime for the export of living, genetically-modified organisms that are to be introduced into the environment of the importing state (*e.g.*, genetically-modified seeds for planting). In 2010, states adopted a supplementary protocol to the Cartegena Protocol that establishes rules on liability for damage to biodiversity resulting from living modified organisms.[26]

Some of these treaties are quite detailed. For example, in 2001 states adopted the Stockholm Convention on Persistent Organic Pollutants,[27] which addresses hazardous chemicals that resist degradation and can travel long distances through air and water (persistent organic pollutants or POPs). The Stockholm Convention requires parties to establish control measures covering the production, import, export, disposal and use of twelve POPs that fall into three general categories: pesticides (aldrin, chlordane, dichlorodiphenyltrichloroethane (DDT), dieldrin, endrin, heptachlor, mirex and toxaphene); industrial chemicals (hexachlorobenzene (HCB) and polychlorinated biphenyls (PCBs)); and unintentional by-products of industrial and combustion processes (dioxins, furans, HCB, and PCBs). The control provisions call for reducing and eliminating the production and use of intentionally produced POPs, eliminating unintentionally produced POPs where feasible, and managing and disposing POP waste in an environmentally sound manner.[28] The convention allows parties to register exemptions from the control measures by notifying the convention's secretariat in writing, but those exemptions expired in 2009, five years after entry into force of the Stockholm Convention.[29] The listing of POPs in the annexes may be amended and new annexes added pursuant to procedures set forth in the convention.[30] Amendments in 2009 added nine more POPs for those parties who accept the amendments. The Stockholm Convention also calls on parties to exchange information on reduction and elimination techniques, promote public education and

24. June 17, 1994, 1954 U.N.T.S. 3, 33 I.L.M. 1328.

25. Jan. 29, 2000, 39 I.L.M. 1027.

26. Nagoya-Kuala Lumpur Supplementary Protocol on Liability and Redress to the Cartegena Protocol on Biosafety, UNEP Doc. UNEP/ CBD/BS/COP–MOP/5/17 (2010), *reprinted in* 50 I.L.M. 105 (2011).

27. May 22, 2001, 40 I.L.M. 532.

28. *Id.*, arts. 3 & 5–6.

29. *Id.*, art. 4(4).

30. *Id.*, arts. 21–22.

awareness of POPs, develop and promote research and monitoring techniques regarding POPs and elimination strategies, provide technical assistance and financial support to developing states and states with transitional economies in implementing the convention, and report periodically to the conference on implementation measures and effectiveness.[31] The Stockholm Convention as of 2011 has 176 parties, not including the United States.

Another detailed treaty is the 2003 Framework Convention on Tobacco Control (FCTC).[32] The FCTC addresses a wide range of issues relating to tobacco and smoking, such as tax and non-price-related measures to reduce tobacco demand, protections for non-smokers from exposure to smoke ("passive smoking"), regulation of tobacco contents and packaging, public awareness of the consequences of smoking, restrictions on tobacco advertising and sponsorship, addiction and cessation programs, illicit trade in tobacco products, sales to minors, and tobacco-related research and information sharing among parties. Structurally, the FCTC establishes a conference of the parties, appoints the WHO as secretariat, and calls for financial assistance to developing parties and parties with transitional economies. As of 2011, 174 states are parties to the FCTC, not including the United States.

There is concern, however, that too much attention is being placed on crafting new treaties, and not enough on finding ways to promote state adherence to and compliance with treaties already in force. Scholars have begun to seriously study national implementation of and compliance with environmental agreements. Two scholars have noted that

> [o]ne cannot simply read domestic legislation to determine whether countries are complying. While some claim that most states comply with most international treaties most of the time, there are reasons to believe that national implementation of and compliance with international accords is not only imperfect but often inadequate, and that such implementation as takes place varies significantly among countries.[33]

Since the Rio Conference, other fields of international law—such as trade, human rights, and armed conflict—have become increasingly responsive to international environmental concerns. In an advisory opinion by the International Court of Justice on the legality of the threat or use of nuclear weapons, the Court declined

31. *Id.*, arts. 9–15.

32. May 21, 2003, 42 I.L.M. 518 [hereinafter FCTC].

33. ENGAGING COUNTRIES: STRENGTHENING COMPLIANCE WITH INTERNATIONAL ENVIRONMENTAL ACCORDS 2 (Edith Brown Weiss & Harold K. Jacobson eds., 1998); *see* Tseming Yang, *International Treaty Enforcement as a Public Good: Institutional Deterrent Sanctions in International Environmental Agreements*, 27 MICH. J. INT'L L. 1131 (2006).

to answer the question solely by reference to environmental agreements. The Court, however, declared that it

> recognizes that the environment is not an abstraction but represents the living space, the quality of life and the very health of human beings, including generations unborn. The existence of the general obligation of States to ensure that activities within their jurisdiction and control respect the environment of other States or of areas beyond national control is now part of the corpus of international law relating to the environment.[34]

The following year, the International Court confronted the difficulties of balancing environmental protection with economic development in *Gabčíkovo-Nagymaros Project*.[35] That case involved a 1977 treaty between Hungary and Czechoslovakia (to which Slovakia succeeded) for constructing a system of locks and dams on the Danube River. As evidence emerged regarding the environmental consequences of the project, Hungary suspended its involvement. The Court found that Hungary breached the treaty and that the breach was not justified by "ecological necessity." At the same time, the Court found that Slovakia violated its obligations by proceeding on its own with a variant of the project. The Court concluded that the treaty remained in force and that the parties should negotiate a resolution of their dispute in good faith. In doing so, the Court noted:

> Throughout the ages, mankind has, for economic and other reasons, constantly interfered with nature. In the past, this was often done without consideration of the effects upon the environment. Owing to new scientific insights and to a growing awareness of the risks for mankind—for present and future generations—of pursuit of such interventions at an unconsidered and unabated pace, new norms and standards have been developed, set forth in a great number of instruments during the last two decades.... This need to reconcile economic development with protection of the environment is aptly expressed in the concept of sustainable development.[36]

International and Non-governmental Organizations

The Stockholm Declaration called upon states to "ensure that international organizations play a co-ordinated, efficient and dynamic role for the protection and improvement of the environment."[37] International organizations are quite important to all

---

34. Advisory Opinion on Legality of the Threat or Use of Nuclear Weapons, 1996 I.C.J. 226, 241, at para. 29 (July 8).

35. Gabčíkovo-Nagymaros Project (Hung./Slovk.), 1997 I.C.J. 7 (Sept. 25).

36. *Id.*, para. 140.

37. Stockholm Declaration, *supra* note 7, princ. 25.

fields of international law,[38] but they are especially significant in this field for several reasons: (1) they allow states to pool their scientific knowledge about threats to the global environment; (2) they allow states to develop international rules and standards as a means of addressing those threats; (3) they provide a forum for resolving ambiguities in the rules and standards, and for adapting the rules to rapidly-changing conditions; (4) they provide a means for monitoring state adherence to rules and standards; and (5) they allow states to coordinate the provision of financial and other resources to states experiencing difficulty in complying with norms and standards.[39] The two most important international environmental institutions focused solely on international environmental problems are the U.N. Environment Program (UNEP) and the U.N. Sustainable Development Commission (CSD), both created by the U.N. General Assembly.[40]

UNEP, a special intergovernmental body within the United Nations, was the first U.N. agency to be assigned an environmental agenda. The UNEP Governing Council consists of representatives from fifty-eight states elected by the U.N. General Assembly, who meet every two years to adopt decisions on UNEP initiatives and programs. The UNEP High–Level Committee of Ministers and Officials, composed of representatives from thirty-six states, meets on a regular basis to prepare draft decisions for the Governing Council and review the work of the secretariat. The UNEP Executive Director, appointed by the U.N. secretary-general, oversees the day-to-day operations of UNEP's secretariat, which is based at UNEP's headquarters in Nairobi, Kenya (there are also regional offices worldwide). Finally, a Committee of Permanent Representatives, consisting of representatives from all U.N. member states, meets four times per year and serves as a communications link between UNEP and its member governments.[41]

A key function of UNEP is to coordinate environmental initiatives and programs within the U.N. system and with institutions outside the United Nations. For example, UNEP created a Global Environmental Monitoring System (GEMS), which pools information obtained from the monitoring of ecosystems by scientists worldwide. Another key function of UNEP is its development of rules and standards in the global environment field. Since its inception, UNEP has sponsored more than forty multilateral envi-

---

38. *See* Chapter 2(B).

39. *See* ABRAM CHAYES & ANTONIA CHAYES, THE NEW SOVEREIGNTY: COMPLIANCE WITH INTERNATIONAL REGULATORY AGREEMENTS 1–17 (1995).

40. *See generally* Marvin S. Soroos, *Global Institutions and the Environment: An Evolutionary Perspective, in*

THE GLOBAL ENVIRONMENT: INSTITUTIONS, LAW, AND POLICY 27 (Norman J. Vig & Regina S. Axelrod eds., 1999).

41. *See* Maria Inova, *UNEP in Environmental Governance: Design, Leadership, Location,* 10:1 GLOBAL ENV. POL. 30 (2010).

ronmental agreements at the global and regional levels, as well as numerous statements of principles that are not legally binding but provide important guidance for states.[42]

The CSD is a commission of the U.N. Economic and Social Council (ECOSOC) and consists of representatives from fifty-three states elected by ECOSOC. The principal function of the CSD is to monitor and make recommendations concerning the implementation of Agenda 21 (discussed above) at the international, regional, and national levels. Reflecting the emphasis of the 1992 UNCED, the CSD is concerned with integrating environmental and developmental objectives, and to that end receives reports from other international institutions and states. The CSD meets annually, yet also establishes *ad hoc* expert groups to engage in work between its sessions.[43]

Many other U.N. agencies, regional organizations, and supranational organizations also play a role in the development of international environmental law, such as the Food and Agriculture Organization (FAO), the World Health Organization (WHO), the U.N. Development Programme (UNDP), and the World Bank group. In 1991, UNEP, UNDP, and the World Bank jointly established a "Global Environment Facility" (GEF) to serve as a source of grant funds for incremental costs incurred by developing states in achieving global environmental benefits in four areas: ozone depletion, climate change, conservation of biological diversity, and protection of international waters. The GEF is the largest multilateral source of grant funds for environmental protection and operates as the financial mechanism for the Climate Change and Biological Diversity conventions. To scrutinize whether the World Bank complies with its environmental (and other) policies and procedures when issuing its loans, an Inspection Panel was created in 1994 with the authority to receive claims of affected parties from the borrower's territory, carry out independent investigations, and make recommendations to the Bank's Board of Executive Directors.[44]

Most contemporary global agreements relating to international environmental law establish a conference of the parties and a secretariat (and sometimes a scientific commission). The conference of the parties typically meets annually or biennially to interpret and monitor compliance with the treaty, and to adapt the treaty through adoption of adjustments, amendments, or protocols. The secretariat is an important standing institution typically charged

42. For further information, see <http://www.unep.org>.

43. For further information, see <http://www.un.org/esa/sustdev/csd. htm>.

44. *See* IBRAHIM SHIHATA, THE WORLD BANK INSPECTION PANEL: IN PRACTICE (2000).

with assisting the conference of the parties, coordinating the flow of information among the parties, and assisting states in complying with the treaty through the transfers of financial or other support, training and education programs, and the development of model national legislation. Rather than create a new secretariat, some agreements call for an existing institution, such as UNEP, to serve as the secretariat.

There are numerous international non-governmental organizations that play an important role in the development of international environmental law. These organizations help galvanize public support for environmental initiatives and channel that support to governments and to negotiations of international instruments. Indeed, such organizations often participate in multilateral negotiating conferences as observers, which allows them to speak on issues under negotiation. The World Wildlife Fund (WWF) is an excellent example of such an organization.[45]

Key Principles

Agreements are the primary means by which states commit themselves to specific obligations to protect and enhance the global environment. In developing, interpreting, and implementing agreements, states often refer to certain principles, which some states regard as having legal force while others view them as simply shaping legal obligations developed in agreements. The following are some of these principles.

Principles of Common Heritage and Common Concern of Humankind. The principle of the common *heritage* of humankind (or "mankind") maintains that all humans have a stake in resources located outside the territory of states, such as the high seas, the deep sea-bed, Antarctica, and outer space. As such, no state should exhaust the resources of these global commons and all are obliged to cooperate peacefully in managing them.[46] The principle of the common *concern* of humankind, which is less widely adopted in agreements, speaks to a similar concept with respect to resources located *within* states. Thus, even though most biological diversity is located within states, the preamble of the Biological Diversity Convention asserts that "the conservation of biological diversity is a common concern of humankind. . . . "[47]

---

45. *See* <http://www.worldwildlife. org>; *see generally* THE INTERNATIONAL POLITICS OF THE ENVIRONMENT: ACTORS, INTERESTS, AND INSTITUTIONS (Andrew Hurrell & Benedict Kingsbury eds., 1992).

46. *See, e.g.*, Treaty on Principles Governing the Activities of States in the Exploration and Use of Outer Space,

Including the Moon and Other Celestial Bodies, Jan. 27, 1967, 18 U.S.T. 2410, 610 U.N.T.S. 205.

47. Convention on Biological Diversity pmbl., June 5, 1992, 1760 U.N.T.S. 79, 31 I.L.M. 818 [hereinafter Biological Diversity Convention].

Prevention of Environmental Harm Principle. Stockholm Principle 21 provides:

> States have, in accordance with the Charter of the United Nations and the principles of international law, the sovereign right to exploit their own resources pursuant to their own environmental policies, and the responsibility to ensure that activities within their jurisdiction or control do not cause damage to the environment of other States or of areas beyond the limits of national jurisdiction.

Rio Declaration Principle 2 (adopted twenty years after the Stockholm Declaration) reiterated this language, but added the words "and developmental" before "policies." This principle contains two contrasting notions: one stressing the inherent sovereignty of states; the other stressing that states must ensure that their activities (including activities by their nationals) do not harm the environment beyond their territory. In practice, this principle is not viewed as prohibiting *all* transboundary environmental harm; indeed, pollution drifts across borders regularly without claims that the polluting state is violating international law. Rather, the principle is usually interpreted as prohibiting significant (or substantial) damage or, alternatively, as requiring a state to exercise due diligence in seeking to prevent such damage (thus imposing an obligation of conduct rather than an obligation of result). Cases often cited in support of this principle are the *Trail Smelter* arbitration (1941)[48] and the *Lake Lanoux* arbitration (1957).[49]

Precautionary Principle. The precautionary principle generally provides that where there are threats of serious or irreversible damage, a lack of scientific certainty that such threats will materialize should not be used as a reason for postponing cost effective measures to prevent potential environmental degradation.[50] Some version of this principle appears in virtually all international environmental agreements adopted since 1990. Like the principle on prevention of environmental harm, the precautionary principle seeks to avoid environmental damage. Yet this principle is more concerned with the difficulties in predicting future environmental harm with scientific certainty, and calls upon states to tip the balance in favor of acting now. The United States and some other countries prefer to refer to a "precautionary approach," due to a belief that this concept is not a legal principle but, rather, an

---

48. 3 R.I.A.A. 1938, 1962 (1941) (asserting a duty on the part of Canada to protect the United States from injurious transboundary air pollution generated by a Canadian smelter).

49. 12 R.I.A.A. 281 (1957) (holding that if France had adversely affected waters that flowed into Spain, France would have violated Spanish rights); *see* Chapter 4(A).

50. *See* Rio Declaration, *supra* note 22, princ. 15.

approach that may lead to different results depending on social and economic costs.

"Polluter Pays" Principle. The polluter pays principle provides that the polluter who creates an environmental harm should be forced to pay the costs of remedying that harm. The essential idea in this principle is to force polluters to internalize costs that would otherwise be imposed on others, so that polluters will consider environmental factors when making economically efficient decisions.[51]

Principle of Non–Discrimination. This principle provides that each state should ensure that its environmental protection regime, when addressing pollution originating within the state, does not discriminate between pollution affecting the state and pollution affecting other states. An important example of this may be seen in multinational agreements on environmental impact assessments, which require states to assess the extraterritorial environmental effects of projects within their jurisdiction in the same manner as they do the national effects.[52]

Principle of Common but Differentiated Responsibilities. This principle recognizes that because developed states have contributed disproportionately to global environmental degradation, and because they command greater financial and technological resources, those states have a special responsibility in shouldering the burden of pursuing global sustainable development.[53] Some version of this principle appears in virtually all global environmental agreements adopted since 1990.

Principle of Intergenerational Equity. This principle stresses that in meeting the needs of present generations, the needs of future generations should not be sacrificed.[54]

Techniques of Legal Regulation

While all international environmental agreements seek in some way to protect or preserve the global environment, they employ a variety of techniques to regulate the behavior of states. In order to obtain reliable information on threats to the global environment, an agreement may contain provisions requiring a state to monitor and report on activities that may affect the quality of the environment.[55] With respect to specific development projects, an agreement

---

51. *Id.,* princ. 16.

52. *See, e.g.,* Convention on Environmental Impact Assessment in a Transboundary Context, Feb. 25, 1991, 30 I.L.M. 800 [hereinafter Espoo Convention].

53. *See* Rio Declaration, *supra* note 22, princ. 7.

54. *Id.,* princ. 3; *see* EDITH BROWN WEISS, IN FAIRNESS TO FUTURE GENERATIONS: INTERNATIONAL LAW, COMMON PATRIMONY, AND INTERGENERATIONAL EQUITY (1989).

55. *See, e.g.,* LOSC, *supra* note 18, art. 204; Biological Diversity Convention, *supra* note 47, art. 7.

may require the state to engage in an environmental impact assessment (EIA) so that the environmental consequences of the project are considered, as well as possible alternatives that are more environment-friendly. An entire agreement may be devoted to an EIA[56] or discrete provisions within agreements.[57]

Rather than simply monitor and assess adverse environmental effects, an agreement may require a state to apply the best available technology (BAT) or use the best practical means for avoiding such effects.[58] Whether a particular technology is BAT depends on various factors, such as its economic feasibility. An agreement may set standards regarding the manner in which products are produced (*e.g.*, a ban on fishing with driftnets that sweep large quantities of non-targeted species into the net) or regarding the product itself (*e.g.*, a regulation controlling the sulfur content of fuels). Many agreements establish limits on environmentally harmful emissions or discharges from a particular source, such as factories or oil tankers.[59] If the risk of environmental harm is particularly high, an agreement may severely restrict or outright ban certain products or processes, such as a ban on the production of specified persistent organic pollutants. When establishing these regulations, the agreements may call for the state to impose a licensing or permitting system, a labeling system, or import/export restrictions as the means of regulation.

Rather than have the state impose specific restrictions, a few recent agreements call for or allow market-based measures that encourage efficiency in activities that pollute the environment. Such measures might involve taxing the polluter for emissions—a technique that does not bar pollution but creates an economic disincentive to pollute—or might involve a system of limited but negotiable permits to pollute, so that the most economically productive entity can purchase rights to pollute from less economically productive entities, which would be "bought out" of their ability to pollute.[60]

Techniques for Imposing Liability

In certain discrete areas in which states can agree that compensation for harm to human health or the environment is appropriate, states have negotiated detailed liability regimes imposing liability directly on the responsible state itself or (more often) on

---

56. *See, e.g.*, Espoo Convention, *supra* note 52.

57. *See, e.g.*, Biological Diversity Convention, *supra* note 47, art. 14(1)(a).

58. *See* LRTAP Convention, *supra* note 15, art. 6.

59. *See, e.g.*, International Convention for the Prevention of Pollution from Ships, Nov. 2, 1973, 1340 U.N.T.S. 184, as amended Feb. 17, 1978, 1340 U.N.T.S. 61.

60. *See* Kyoto Protocol, discussed below.

the private entities associated with the harm. Compensation may be allowed for loss of life or personal injury, yet the total amount of compensation to be paid by a defendant is typically limited or "capped" at a certain level, for which the defendant obtains insurance. Three standards of care may be discerned in these regimes: absolute liability (where the defendant is liable for any harm that was caused by his activity); strict liability (where the defendant is liable for any harm that was caused by his activity, but various defenses are available); and liability based on fault (where it must be shown that the defendant acted negligently, recklessly, or with an intent to commit the harm). As is the case in most national law systems, absolute or strict liability has been employed where the underlying activity is ultra-hazardous or dangerous.

International State Liability Regime. It is possible to assign liability to a state even if the state itself is not at fault. Thus, under the 1972 Convention on International Liability for Damage Caused by Space Objects,[61] the state that launches a space object, procures the launch, or from whose territory the object is launched is absolutely liable to pay compensation to another state for damage caused by the space object on the surface of the earth or to aircraft in flight. The fact that a private individual or entity launched the space object is irrelevant. If two or more states are associated with the launch, they are jointly and severally liable.[62] It should be noted, however, that exoneration from liability is permitted to the extent that the claimant state (or its nationals) contributed to the damage by gross negligence or an intentional act or omission.[63] Claims are resolved through a process of negotiation between states; thus, harmed nationals must convince their government to pursue a claim against the state responsible for the harm, which the government may not wish to do for political reasons. If a claim is presented, a claims commission may be used whose decision is final and binding "if the Parties have so agreed."[64] Only one claim has been presented under this treaty, for damage from a satellite that fell to earth, resulting in the payment of three million dollars by the U.S.S.R. to Canada.[65] Limited provisions imposing state liability may also be found in treaties on damage caused in outer space,[66] in the Antarctic,[67] on the high

---

61. Mar. 29. 1972, 24 U.S.T. 2389, 961 U.N.T.S. 187.

62. *Id.*, art. 5.

63. *Id.*, art. 6.

64. *Id.*, arts. 14 & 19.

65. *See* Claim Against the USSR for Damage Caused by Soviet Cosmos 954, Jan. 23, 1979, *reprinted in* 18 I.L.M. 899 (1979); Protocol, Can.-U.S.S.R., Apr. 2, 1981, 20 I.L.M. 689.

66. *See* Treaty on Principles Governing the Activities of States in the Exploration and Use of Outer Space, Including the Moon and Other Celestial Bodies *supra* note 46, art. 7.

67. *See* Convention on the Regulation of Antarctic Mineral Resource Activities art. 8, June 2, 1988, 27 I.L.M. 868 [hereinafter CRAMRA] (providing for state liability for failure to oversee

seas,[68] from military cooperation,[69] and in some situations where nationals have failed to provide compensation under an international civil liability regime.[70]

The success to date in creating effective conventions imposing liability on states for harm caused by their nationals has been minimal. Indeed, some international law theorists doubt that imposition of liability upon states is an effective means of regulating transnational behavior.[71] Among other things, the adversarial nature of inter-state claims may impede inter-state cooperation and planning that are desirable for regulating other aspects of the problem.

International Civil Liability Regimes. A civil liability regime exposes persons or corporate entities to liability for damage they cause to the nationals of another state. One advantage of this regime is that it allows victims a direct remedy without resort to inter-state claims. Moreover, it channels liability directly to the entity causing the harm, thus forcing it to internalize the costs of its behavior. To accomplish this, states that join such regimes must alter rules that would otherwise apply in their national legal systems, so as to affect directly the legal rights and remedies available to private entities.

Most states, however, have been very reluctant to conclude and implement international civil liability regimes. For states that only benefit from such regimes, joining presents little difficulty. Yet for states whose nationals are likely to lose more than to gain from the exposure to liability, there is little incentive to join. Successes to date in creating such regimes have occurred principally in areas where there is a lucrative and beneficial good or service that occasionally has sudden, adverse consequences. In these instances, states have found common ground in constructing regimes that allow compensation for the occasional adverse consequence, but

the activities of its nationals). CRAMRA likely will never enter into force due to lack of support from a sufficient number of Antarctic Treaty consultative parties and to the adoption of the Protocol on Environmental Protection to the Antarctic Treaty and its Annex VI. *See* Annex VI on Liability Arising from Environmental Emergencies, June 17, 2005, to the Protocol on Environmental Protection to the Antarctic Treaty, Oct. 4, 1991, 30 I.L.M. 1455. Annex VI provides that persons, whether governmental or not, who organize activities in the Antarctic Treaty area and who fail to take prompt and effective response action to environmental emergencies arising from such activities, shall be liable to pay the costs of response action taken by governments.

68. *See* LOSC, *supra* note 18, arts. 139 & 235; International Convention Relating to Intervention on the High Seas in Cases of Oil Pollution Casualties, Nov. 29, 1969, 26 U.S.T. 765, 970 U.N.T.S. 211.

69. *See, e.g.,* NATO Status of Forces Agreement art. 8, June 19, 1951, 4 U.S.T. 1792, 199 U.N.T.S. 67.

70. *See* Vienna Convention on Civil Liability for Nuclear Damage art. 7, May 21, 1963, 1063 U.N.T.S. 265, 2 I.L.M. 727, as amended.

71. *See, e.g.,* CHAYES & CHAYES, *supra* note 39, 1–28.

also set limits on recovery to protect the industry providing the good or service.

There are generally two sub-types of international civil liability regimes: regimes that focus simply on enhancing the ability of nationals to sue in national courts using existing substantive law (process-oriented regimes); and regimes that focus on enhancing the ability to sue *and* establish substantive law to be applied by national courts (process-and-substance-oriented regimes).

A process-oriented international civil liability regime generally obligates the parties to open their courts to jurisdiction over claims for conduct occurring in one state that causes injury in another state. This approach is well developed in Europe with the Brussels and Lugano conventions.[72] Thus, under Article 5(3) of the Brussels Convention, a foreign defendant can be sued in tort before the courts of the state where the "harmful event occurred."[73] Further, it is possible to provide access to a state's courts for governments acting on behalf of their nationals, such as exists in the Convention on the Protection of the Environment between Denmark, Finland, Norway, and Sweden (the 1974 Nordic Convention).[74] This process-oriented approach, however, is not found in other regions of the world, nor yet in a global convention.

There are several inherent difficulties to this approach. First, by avoiding a uniform substantive law, this approach may only provide foreign claimants with the same unlikelihood of recovery that already exists for local claimants. Second, the Brussels/Lugano and Nordic conventions work because they are among states with similar legal systems. Yet if some states are more generous in allowing recovery than other states (as is likely for a regime created on a global level), then this process-oriented approach invites significantly different substantive outcomes in similar cases brought in different states.

72. *See* Brussels Convention on Jurisdiction and Enforcement of Judgments in Civil and Commercial Matters, Sept. 27, 1968, 1262 U.N.T.S. 153, 8 I.L.M. 229, as amended (harmonizing rules of jurisdiction and procedures for recognition and enforcement of judgments among EU States); Lugano Convention on Jurisdiction and Enforcement of Judgments in Civil and Commercial Matters, Sept. 16, 1988, 1988 O.J. (L 319) 9, 28 I.L.M. 620 (harmonizing such rules and procedures among EU States and European Free Trade Area States). In December 2000, the European Commission adopted a regulation that amends the terms of the Brussels and Lugano conventions and transforms them into a European Union legal instrument which is binding and directly applicable to member States. *See* Council Regulation (EC) 44/2001, Jurisdiction and the Recognition and Enforcement of Judgments in Civil and Commercial Matters, Dec. 22, 2000, 2001 O.J. (L 12) 1.

73. *See, e.g.,* G.J. Bier v. Mines de Potasse, Judgment No. 21/76, 1976 Common Mkt. Rep. (CCH) 7814, 7816.

74. Feb. 19, 1974, 1092 U.N.T.S. 279, 13 I.L.M. 591.

Rather than solely provide access to national courts, an international civil liability regime can also establish the central features of substantive law to be applied uniformly by national courts. A process-and-substance-oriented international civil liability regime instructs national courts to accept jurisdiction over claims and accord standing to foreign plaintiffs, yet also dictates substantive rules regarding the standard of liability, burden of proof, bases for exoneration from liability, types of damages available, and limits on recovery (if any). The regime identifies the appropriate type of defendant, normally channeling liability to the entity owning or operating a dangerous facility or a carrier of hazardous materials, provided there is a connection between that entity and the harm suffered by the claimant. The regime might also address compulsory insurance or other financial guarantees to be held by potential defendants. This approach avoids some of the process-oriented regime difficulties by creating a uniform law.

Most process-and-substance-oriented international civil liability regimes address ultra-hazardous or dangerous activities, where a single event causes unique, enormous or widespread harm. The best developed global regime of this type exists in the field of maritime discharge of oil. There are about ninety-five states party to the 1969 International Convention on Civil Liability for Oil Pollution Damage (1969 CLC),[75] which covers damage caused within a party's territory, territorial sea or exclusive economic zone by discharges from ships carrying oil as cargo. Owners of such ships are liable, even without fault, for discharges that cause harm, although certain defenses are available (*e.g.*, negligent acts of governments with respect to aids to navigation) and the contributory liability of the claimant may be established in certain circumstances. The shipowner's sole liability is under the convention; no action may be brought against a shipowner outside the convention, nor may any action be brought against other entities, such as the shipowner's employees or agents. Liability is limited on the basis of the ship's tonnage and an absolute ceiling exists so long as the owner agrees to establish a fund to pay damages. Shipowners carrying more than a certain tonnage of bulk oil must maintain insurance to meet their liability. Further, actions for damages may be brought only in the courts of states where the damage occurred or preventive measures have been taken. Judgments issued by these courts must be recognized, with very limited exceptions, by every party.

Another example of a process-and-substance-oriented international civil liability regime exists in the area of nuclear power. The Paris Convention on Third Party Liability in the Field of Nuclear

---

75. Nov. 29, 1969, 973 U.N.T.S. 3, 9 I.L.M. 45, as amended.

Energy[76] was developed by the Organisation for Economic Co-operation and Development (OECD) and has fourteen parties, several of which have no nuclear installations. A separate convention established by the International Atomic Energy Agency (IAEA), the Vienna Convention on Civil Liability for Nuclear Damage,[77] has thirty-two parties. The two regimes, which have been linked in a joint protocol,[78] channel liability (up to certain limits) to the operator of a nuclear installation (whether private or a state) for injury or loss of life proven to be causally connected to a nuclear incident at the installation. Similar conventions have been developed to address damage from ships carrying nuclear material.[79]

Examples of process-and-substance-oriented regimes also exist for damage from carriage of dangerous goods by sea[80] and (among European states) by land,[81] from sea-bed exploitation,[82] and at transport terminals engaged in international trade.[83] Perhaps the most ambitious European effort is the 1993 Lugano Convention on Civil Liability,[84] which addresses harm to human health and the environment from a range of "dangerous activities." Although the Lugano Convention has proven unpalatable to some European states, it channels liability to all persons and companies (and state and other agencies) exercising control over dangerous activities that cause damage, with no limitations on liability. The scope of damage extends to all deaths or bodily harm. Liability is not imposed if the activity was taken for the benefit of the person damaged. Since 1993, no European states have ratified the convention. Resistance to the convention apparently turns on a belief that its scope is too wide and too vague in both its definitions and legal rules.[85]

76. July 29, 1960, 956 U.N.T.S. 251, *reprinted in* 55 AM. J. INT'L L. 1082 (1960), as amended.

77. *Supra* note 70.

78. *See* Joint Protocol Relating to the Application of the Vienna Convention and the Paris Convention, Sept. 21, 1988, *reprinted in* 42 NUCLEAR L. BULL. 56 (1988).

79. *See* Brussels Convention on the Liability of Operators of Nuclear Ships, May 25, 1962, *reprinted in* 57 AM. J. INT'L L. 268 (1963); Brussels Convention Relating to Civil Liability in the Field of Maritime Carriage of Nuclear Material, Dec. 17, 1971, 974 U.N.T.S. 255, 11 I.L.M. 277.

80. *See* International Convention on Liability and Compensation for Damage in Connection with the Carriage of Hazardous and Noxious Substances by Sea, May 3,1996, 35 I.L.M. 1415.

81. *See* Convention on Civil Liability for Damage Caused During the Carriage of Dangerous Goods by Road, Rail and Inland Navigation Vessels, Oct. 10, 1989, U.N. Doc. ECE/TRANS/79 (1989).

82. *See* Convention on Civil Liability for Oil Pollution Damage Resulting From Offshore Operations, Dec. 17, 1976, 16 I.L.M. 1450.

83. *See* U.N. Convention on the Liability of Operators of Transport Terminals in International Trade, Apr. 19, 1991, 30 I.L.M. 1503.

84. Convention on Civil Liability for Damage Resulting from Activities Dangerous to the Environment, June 21, 1993, 32 I.L.M. 1228 [hereinafter Lugano Convention].

85. *See* Commission of the European Communities, *White Paper on Environmental Liability*, at 25, COM (2000) 66 final (Feb. 9, 2000).

There are also process-and-substance-oriented regimes directed at *trade* in certain types of products considered potentially dangerous to human health or the environment. The 1999 Basel Protocol on Liability and Compensation for Damage Resulting from Transboundary Movements of Hazardous Wastes and their Disposal[86] seeks to establish a comprehensive regime for liability, and for adequate and prompt compensation, for damage resulting from transboundary movements of hazardous wastes, including illegal traffic in such wastes. Under the Basel Protocol, the person who notifies the importing state of the shipment shall be liable for damage until the disposer has taken possession of the hazardous wastes; thereafter, the disposer shall be liable for damage. Further, any person shall be liable for damage caused or contributed by their lack of compliance with the Basel Convention or by their wrongful intentional, reckless or negligent acts or omissions.[87] However, compensation may be reduced or disallowed "if the person who suffered the damage ... has caused or contributed to the damage having regard to all circumstances."[88] Claims must be filed within certain time periods and recovery is limited based on the tonnage of the shipment. Claims may be filed in the courts of the state where the damage was suffered, the state where the damage occurred, or the state where the defendant has his or her habitual residence or principal place of business. Potentially liable persons are obligated to establish insurance, bonds, or other financial guarantees during their period of potential liability. Final judgments issued by a competent court are enforceable in the courts of other states who are party to the Basel Protocol, with certain limited exceptions.[89]

Process-and-substance-oriented international civil liability regimes also have their limits. States typically preclude liability when the injured person contributed to the harm or undertook responsibility for handling the harmful material. For instance, with respect to the 1999 Basel Protocol, the strict liability of the exporter of hazardous wastes ends once the disposer in the importing state takes possession of the wastes. Even if harm subsequently occurs from the release of hazardous wastes into the environment, there is no liability under the Basel Protocol against the original exporter. This outcome is a recognition that by consenting to the import of hazardous wastes, the importing state and importer bear responsibility for any harm that ultimately occurs. Indeed, shifting responsibility to the importing state and importer is regarded as desirable since otherwise the incentive on them to manage the wastes in an environmentally sound manner is dramatically decreased.

86. Dec. 10, 1999, U.N. Doc. UNEP/ CHW.1/WG/1/9/2 (1999).

87. *Id.*, arts. 4–5.

88. *Id.*, art. 9.

89. *Id.*, arts. 12–14, 17, 21 & annex B.

Even the most far-reaching international civil liability regime, the Lugano Civil Liability Convention, found it necessary to recognize that defendants should not be liable for damage incurred in the normal exercise or operation under national regulatory measures of the "dangerous activity" in question. Moreover, the convention provides that operators will not be liable for damage arising from the dangerous activity if the damage is caused by pollution generally accepted in the locality.[90] Thus, there is a reluctance to impose international civil liability in situations where local public authorities have sanctioned an activity and where the transnational damage is no different than other types of damage tolerated locally.

While international civil liability regimes are perhaps growing in number, they remain a relatively undeveloped area of international law and to date have met with minimal success in terms of ratification. For example, the United States has traditionally avoided liability conventions due to a desire not to preempt the tort law of its several states, including placing limits on the amount of permissible recovery. As such, it belongs to none of the oil pollution, nuclear, or hazardous wastes/substances liability conventions. The failure to attract key states to these liability regimes should not be underestimated, for it defeats their entire purpose. For instance, although considerable effort has been placed on developing international civil liability regimes in the field of nuclear energy, when one of the reactors of the Chernobyl nuclear power plant exploded in April 1986—emitting a radioactive cloud that contaminated a number of European states—the Vienna and Paris conventions on civil liability for nuclear damage did not apply since the Soviet Union was not a party. Thus, no claim could be brought against the Soviet Union under the conventions.

International Fund Regime. It is also possible to create an "international fund" regime, such as the 1971 International Convention on the Establishment of an International Fund for Compensation for Oil Pollution Damage.[91] Linked to the 1969 CLC (discussed above), this fund pays compensation, within certain limits, when a shipowner is incapable of meeting its obligations or the damages exceed the shipowner's liability limit. The fund is supported by pro rata contributions from persons (including governments) operating installations that receive seaborne crude and heavy fuel oil in annual quantities exceeding 150,000 tons. The source of the contributions into the fund (the "shippers" or cargo owners) is therefore not the same as those initially liable under the

---

90. *See* Lugano Convention, *supra* note 84, art. 8(d) (exempting an operator who has complied with operating conditions authorized under national regulatory measures).

91. Dec. 18, 1971, 1110 U.N.T.S. 57, 11 I.L.M. 284, as amended.

1969 CLC (shipowners), which spreads the risk of liability. The fund is governed by an "Assembly" of parties to the convention, which meets annually; administrative functions are performed by a secretariat. The fund is an entity capable of suing and being sued in the parties' national courts. Thus, claimants can bring suit against the shipowner and, should they believe recourse to the fund is available, against the fund as well. The fund has been involved in dozens of cases since its inception.

Other efforts to develop international funds have met with less success. While the parties to the Basel Convention initially considered the establishment of both a compensation fund and a fund to be used in cases of emergency,[92] ultimately neither fund was established.

B. Regulation in Important Sectors

Ozone Depletion

General Overview. The agreements designed to prevent the depletion of the stratospheric ozone layer are an excellent example of a sophisticated and successful international environmental regime. Beginning in the 1980's, scientists became convinced that certain widely used chemicals were migrating up to the stratosphere where they caused a chemical reaction that destroyed ozone molecules, allowing increased ultraviolet rays from the sun to pass through the ozone layer and harm human health and the environment on the earth. To address this problem, states adopted the Vienna Convention for the Protection of the Ozone Layer in 1985.[93] Under that convention, the parties agreed to cooperate in the monitoring and scientific assessment of stratospheric ozone depletion, and to take appropriate measures to prevent it from occurring.[94] The convention was a "framework convention" in the sense that it envisaged subsequent agreements on specific emissions obligations as scientific knowledge developed.

In 1987, the parties adopted the Montreal Protocol on Substances that Deplete the Ozone Layer (Montreal Protocol).[95] The Montreal Protocol provided for the progressive reduction by specified dates of the production and consumption of certain types of ozone-depleting chemicals—chlorofluorocarbons and halons—listed in annexes to the Protocol. Further amendments to the Montreal Protocol have allowed additional chemicals to be added to the control list (the list appears in Annex E to the Protocol); such

---

92. *See* U.N. Doc. UNEP/CHW.1/6 (1992); U.N. Doc. UNEP/CHW.1/11 (1992).

93. Mar. 22, 1985, T.I.A.S. 11,097, 1513 U.N.T.S. 293.

94. *Id.*, arts. 2–3.

95. Sept. 16, 1987, S. TREATY DOC. NO. 100–10 (1987), 1522 U.N.T.S. 3 [hereinafter Montreal Protocol]; *see* RICHARD BENEDICK, OZONE DIPLOMACY (1998).

amendments require ratification by states through normal process-es. In addition, the Montreal Protocol permits the conference of parties to make "adjustments" to the control measures on listed chemicals without further state ratification, provided that the ad-justments are supported by two-thirds of the parties, where that two-thirds represents at least half of global consumption of the chemical in question.[96] Various exceptions exist to the limits im-posed by the protocol, mostly for developing states, but also for states that can demonstrate a need to deviate from their limits for important reasons.

Example: Methyl Bromide. An example of the method for listing and adjusting ozone-depleting chemicals is that of methyl bromide, a widely used agricultural fumigant that depletes the stratospheric ozone layer when released into the atmosphere. The Montreal Protocol originally did not list methyl bromide, yet at the fourth meeting of the Conference of the Parties in Copenhagen in 1992, the protocol was amended to include methyl bromide as a covered chemical.[97] (As of 2011, 194 states, including the United States, have ratified the Copenhagen Amendment.[98]) While the Copenhagen Amendment simply provided that states shall not exceed annually their 1991 levels of consumption and production of methyl bromide, subsequent meetings of the parties decided to phase out methyl bromide completely. In particular, the 1997 Montreal adjustment required states to reduce their consumption and production levels of methyl bromide to zero beginning January 2005.[99]

There are, however, some exceptions to this phase-out. Devel-oping states are allowed an additional ten years beyond 2005 before they must phaseout their consumption and production. Further, the Montreal adjustment provided that the parties can "decide to permit the level of production or consumption that is necessary to satisfy uses agreed by them to be critical uses."[100] The parties issued a decision stating that the use of methyl bromide should qualify as "critical" only if the state seeking the exemption deter-mines both that "the lack of availability of methyl bromide for that use would result in a significant market disruption" and that there were "no technically and economically feasible alternatives."[101] Un-der the parties' decision, an expert panel would review the request

---

96. *Id.*, art. 2(9).

97. *See* Adjustments and Amend-ment to the Montreal Protocol on Sub-stances that Deplete the Ozone Layer annex III, art. 1(I), Nov. 23, 1992, 32 I.L.M. 874, 880–81.

98. The United States ratified the amendment in 1994.

99. *See* Report of the Ninth Meeting of the Parties to the Montreal Protocol on Substances that Deplete the Ozone Layer, annex III, U.N. Doc. UNEP/OzL.Pro.9/12 (1997).

100. *Id.*

101. *Id.*, Decision IX/6.

for an exemption and make recommendations to the meeting of the parties.

In 2003, eleven states (including the United States) requested a critical-use exemption to allow them to continue producing and consuming methyl bromide. All eleven states claimed that since technically and economically feasible alternatives to methyl bromide had not yet been developed, the chemical's continued use was required as an essential pesticide for important crops, such as peppers, strawberries, and tomatoes. An extraordinary meeting of the parties (the first ever) held in Montreal in March 2004 granted an exemption to the eleven states for 2005. In subsequent years, further exemptions have also been granted, but for decreasing numbers of states and decreasing levels.[102]

Noncompliance Procedure. As noted in Chapter 5(A), one important feature of the Montreal Protocol is the noncompliance procedure called for in Article 8 and developed thereafter by decisions of the Conference of the Parties. Under this procedure, a party having difficulties in meeting its obligations, or a party with concerns about another party's fulfillment of its obligations, may report the issue to an implementation committee. The implementation committee gathers information, including on-site monitoring, and reports on the matter to the Conference of the Parties, which decides upon the steps necessary to bring the state into full compliance. Such steps initially might include providing assistance to the non-compliant state in the form of technology transfer, training, or financing. If a state remains non-compliant, a warning may be issued and ultimately a suspension of rights and privileges under the protocol.

Global Climate Change

When coal, oil, wood, and natural gas are burned, they create gases (such as carbon dioxide) that rise into the atmosphere and form a screen comparable to the tinted glass of a greenhouse. By trapping solar heat in the earth's atmosphere, these "greenhouse gas" (GHG) emissions are causing global warming, which over time may have dramatic effects on the global climate, causing polar ice to melt, ocean levels to rise, and worldwide temperatures and precipitation levels to change significantly. Contemporary understanding of existence of global climate change has benefitted from the work of an Intergovernmental Panel on Climate Change (IPCC), which was established in 1988 by the United Nations Environment Program and the World Meteorological Organiza-

---

102. *See* Meeting of the Parties to the Montreal Protocol, *Decision XXII/6: Critical–Use Exemptions for Methyl Bro-* *mide for 2011 and 2012,* U.N. Doc. UNEP/OzL.Pro.22/9, at 31–32 (2010).

Intergovernmental Panel on Climate Change

Assessment of Climate Changes 1961-1990

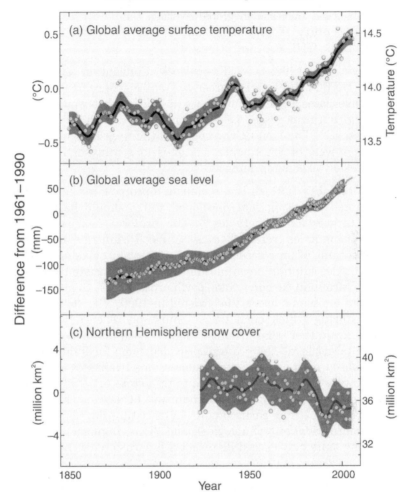

tion.[103] The IPCC is an intergovernmental body that reviews and assesses scientific, technical and socio-economic information produced worldwide, with the help of thousands of scientists. Since its inception the IPCC has periodically issued reports analyzing climate change, its likely causes, and its potential effects (the fourth report was issued in 2007). The graphic on the following page indicates some of the data confirmed by the IPCC regarding global average increases in surface temperature and sea levels from 1961 to 1990, as well as the decrease in snow cover in the northern

103. *See* G.A. Res. 43/53 (Dec. 6, 1988); *see also* <http://www.ipcc.ch/index.htm>.

hemisphere. While there are some "climate sceptics" that view global warming as simply part of the natural cycle of the earth's climatic changes, the IPCC's fourth report concluded that "[m]ost of the observed increase in global average temperatures since the mid–20th century is very likely due to the observed increase in anthropogenic GHG concentrations."[104]

Under the 1992 U.N. Framework Convention on Climate Change (UNFCCC),[105] states agreed to stabilize concentrations of all greenhouse gases in the atmosphere at a level that would prevent dangerous anthropogenic (*i.e.*, human) interference with the climate system.[106] The UNFCCC recognized the necessity of returning to earlier levels of greenhouse gas emissions, but set no specific timetables or targets for doing so.[107]

In December 1997, in Kyoto, Japan, a protocol to the UNFCCC was adopted accepting that developed states should be bound to specific targets and timetables.[108] The protocol obliges some 38 developed countries (referred to as "Annex I countries") to reduce their emissions of four greenhouse gases (carbon dioxide, methane, nitrous oxide, sulphur hexafluoride) and two associated groups of gases (hydrofluorocarbons and perfluorocarbons) by collectively 5.2% from emissions levels that existed in 1990. The "commitment period" during which such targets must be reached was set at 2008–2012. Rather than rigidly require each state to meet an absolute target level, the protocol provided some flexibility through market-based mechanisms, such as emissions trading (a state emitting below its target can trade credits to a state emitting above its target), a "clean development mechanism" (a developed state may exceed its target if it earns credits by assisting developing states with climate-friendly technologies), and "joint implementation" (a developing state may exceed its target if it earns credits by assisting another developed state).

Ratification of the Kyoto Protocol, however, was slowed by its failure to resolve a substantial number of issues concerning its operation. Difficulties included: (1) rules for how the various flexibility mechanisms would actually operate; (2) the means for counting carbon "sinks" (which remove greenhouse gases from the atmosphere), such as farmland, rangeland, and forests toward parties' reduction commitments; and (3) the means for determining and addressing a party's noncompliance. At a session of the conference of the parties in July 2001 in Bonn, Germany, key compro-

104. IPCC, *Climate Change 2007: Synthesis Report* 39 (2007).

105. May 9, 1992, S. Treaty Doc. No. 102–38 (1992), 1771 U.N.T.S. 107.

106. *Id.*, art. 2.

107. *Id*, art. 4.

108. *See* Kyoto Protocol to the U.N. Framework Convention on Climate Change, Dec. 10, 1997, 37 I.L.M. 22.

mises were reached by developed states on implementing the Kyoto Protocol, including the use of carbon sinks as a means of earning emission credits. Meeting in Morocco four months later, the conference of the parties reached final agreement on details for implementing the Kyoto Protocol.

The Kyoto Protocol entered into force in 2005 and as of 2011 has 193 parties, including many developing countries that have no obligations with respect to its targets and timetable. The United States announced that it would not ratify the protocol on various grounds, including its view that the emissions targets were not scientifically based or environmentally effective, and that developing states should also be bound to the targets. The administration of George W. Bush pursued voluntary measures for addressing climate change,[109] such as a non-binding partnership among fourteen countries to reduce methane gases from gas pipelines and to encourage the capture and use of methane from coal mines, solid waste landfills, and oil wells.[110] (Methane is a greenhouse gas twenty-three times more potent than carbon dioxide in trapping global heat in the atmosphere.) Among other things, the partners committed to identify and promote multilateral, bilateral, and private sector cooperation for methane recovery, through use of a formal steering group and other administrative structures. Similarly, in July 2005, the United States joined Australia, China, India, Japan, and South Korea in a non-binding Asia–Pacific Partnership on Clean Development and the Climate. Under this pact, the six states (which represent about half of global greenhouse gas emissions) pledged to cooperate in the development, deployment, and transfer of more efficient technologies to meet climate change concerns, consistent with the UNFCCC. Further, various initiatives unfolded at the state and local level in the United States to promotion reductions in greenhouse gas emissions.

Many observers view the Kyoto Protocol as failing to achieve the objective of controlling meaningfully greenhouse gas emissions, though it may be the first step in doing so. A key problem has been that developing countries such as China and India are not covered by the protocol, while the United States—which could be covered— has not joined the protocol, thus leaving outside of the regime major greenhouse gas emitters. Further, the use of 1990 as a base period created a certain illusion as to reductions, for that year was the last in which the Soviet Union and eastern bloc countries operated extraordinarily inefficient factories that emitted extensive greenhouse gases. Those emissions immediately began to drop after the collapse of communism and well in advance of the adoption of

---

109. *See* 38 WEEKLY COMP. PRES. DOCS. 232, 234–35 (Feb. 14, 2002).

110. *See* Terms of Reference for the Methane to Markets Partnership (Nov. 16, 2004).

the Kyoto Protocol, yet countries can claim "reductions" since 1990 even if their emissions have increased during the life of the protocol.[111] Moreover, since the commitment period of the protocol ends in 2012, the political will must exist to adopt and adhere to further commitment periods.

With that in mind, the parties to the UNFCCC adopted a "Copenhagen Accord" in 2009 which created a non-binding system of "pledge and review" for both developed and developing states;[112] those commitments were formally brought into the UNFCCC process by agreements reached at Cancun in 2010. Then, in December 2011, the Kyoto Protocol parties met in Durban, South Africa, where they decided they would adopt in 2012 an amendment to the protocol establishing a second commitment period covering the years 2013–2017 or 2013–2020. The parties are expected to submit their proposed emissions/reductions targets in the lead up to the adoption of the 2012 amendment.

Moreover, the UNFCCC Conference of the Parties (also meeting in Durban) decided to "to launch a process to develop *a protocol, another legal instrument or an agreed outcome with legal force* under the [UNFCCC] *applicable to all Parties*, through a subsidiary body under the Convention hereby established and to be known as the Ad Hoc Working Group on the Durban Platform for Enhanced Action."[113] Thus, the exact legal form of the new instrument was not agreed upon; some countries, such as India, did not support a legally-binding instrument. Whatever form it takes, however, the instrument will apply to all states, including developing countries. With respect to the timetable, the Durban Platform stated that the working group "shall complete its work as early as possible but no later than 2015 in order to adopt this protocol, legal instrument or agreed outcome with legal force at the twenty-first session of the Conference of the Parties and for it to come into effect and be implemented from 2020."[114]

Biological Diversity

Contemporary concern with an integrated approach to the protection and preservation of global biological diversity is perhaps the logical outgrowth of numerous early international instruments on nature conservation and protection of flora and fauna. The 1992 Biological Diversity Convention defines biological diversity as:

111. *See generally* MATTHEW J. HOFF-MAN, CLIMATE GOVERNANCE AT THE CROSS-ROADS (2011).

112. Copenhagen Accord (Dec. 18, 2009), *in* U.N. Doc. CC/CP/2009/11/Add.1 (2009).

113. Establishment of an Ad Hoc Working Group on the Durban Platform for Enhanced Action, U.N. Doc. FCCC/CP/2011/L.X, para. 2 (Dec. 11, 2011) ("Durban Platform for Enhanced Action") (emphasis added).

114. *Id.*, para. 4.

the variability among living organisms from all sources including, *inter alia*, terrestrial, marine and other aquatic ecosystems and the ecological complexes of which they are a part; this includes diversity within species, between species and of ecosystems.[115]

Since the industrial revolution, pollution, urbanization, population growth, and the exploitation of natural resources have profoundly threatened biological diversity, leading to the extinction of many species worldwide at a rate far faster than would occur naturally.

The Biological Diversity Convention is a comprehensive umbrella instrument for protecting and preserving biological diversity. Recognizing that other agreements address the protection of particular species, the convention is directed principally at the rights and responsibilities of states at the national level with respect to biological diversity generally. Thus, the convention requires states to identify important components of biological diversity within their jurisdiction, and to monitor activities that may have adverse impacts on that diversity.[116] Further, it requires states to use this information to develop national strategies and plans for protecting and preserving biological diversity, thereby integrating concerns for biological diversity into national decision making.[117] The convention expresses a preference for *in-situ* conservation (in a natural habitat), but recognizes the complementary role of *ex situ* conservation (in a controlled environment, such as a "gene bank").[118]

In the course of negotiating the convention, the economic value of genetic resources could not be ignored. The convention states that decisions on access to genetic resources rest with the national government where the resource is located.[119] At the same time, it provides that states should facilitate access to such resources for environmentally sound uses and on mutually agreed upon terms.[120] Since genetic resources can be used to develop new biotechnology applications (such as new pharmaceuticals), the convention provides that states should take measures to share in a fair and equitable way the results of biotechnology applications with the state providing the resource.[121]

In the wake of the Biological Diversity Convention, states have continued to conclude agreements for the protection of specific species, whether on land or at sea. For example, after eight years of negotiations, Russia and the United States signed a bilateral Agree-

115. Biological Diversity Convention, *supra* note 47, art. 2.

116. *Id.*, art. 7.

117. *Id.*, arts. 6 & 10.

118. *Id.*, arts 8–9.

119. *Id.*, art. 15(1).

120. *Id.*, art. 15(2) & (3).

121. *Id.*, art. 19(2).

ment on the Conservation and Management of the Alaska–Chukot-ka Polar Bear Population in October 2000.[122] The agreement builds on conservation measures established in a 1973 multilateral agreement on polar bears.[123] The earlier agreement allowed the taking of polar bears for subsistence purposes by native people so long as it was done at a sustainable harvest level. The new agreement specifically addresses the polar bear population in the waters and adjacent coastal areas of the Chukchi, East Siberian, and Bering Seas. Among other things, the new agreement states that native peoples may take such polar bears for subsistence purposes only if: (1) the take is consistent with the earlier agreement; (2) the take does not include females with cubs, cubs less than one year of age, or bears in dens, including bears preparing to enter dens or who have just left dens; (3) no use is made during the take of aircraft, large motorized vessels, or large motorized vehicles; and (4) no use is made of poisons, traps, and snares for the purpose of taking polar bears. Polar bears also may be taken for the conduct of scientific research, for the purpose of rescuing or rehabilitating orphaned, sick, or injured animals, or when human life is threatened.[124] The new agreement also defines "sustainable harvest level" as

> a harvest level which does not exceed net annual recruitment to the population and maintains the population at or near its current level, taking into account all forms of removal, and considers the status and trend of the population, based on reliable scientific information.[125]

In addition, the new agreement establishes a U.S.-Russia Polar Bear Commission, which will make scientific determinations as necessary to establish harvest limits and carry out other responsibilities under the terms of the agreement.[126]

C. Cross–Sectoral Issues

Trade and Environment

International environmental agreements affect trade in various ways. They may impose trade sanctions as a means of encouraging non-parties to join the agreement or as a means of promoting compliance after a state has joined. They may also directly restrict or prohibit trade in certain types of products as a means of fulfilling the purpose of the agreement. For example, the 1989 Basel Conven-

---

122. U.S.-Russ., Oct. 16, 2000, S. Treaty Doc. No. 107–10, at 5 (2002) [hereinafter Polar Bear Agreement].

123. *See* Agreement on the Conservation of Polar Bears, Nov. 15, 1973, 27 U.S.T. 3918, 13 I.L.M. 13. Russia and the United States, as well as Canada,

Denmark, and Norway, are parties to the 1973 agreement.

124. *See* Polar Bear Agreement, *supra* note 122, art. 6.

125. *Id.*, art. 1

126. *Id.*, art. 8.

tion on transboundary movements of hazardous wastes provides that a party may not export to, nor import from, a non-party any hazardous wastes, unless the party has a separate agreement with the non-party which is as environmentally sound as the Basel Convention.[127] Further, even between parties, there may be no hazardous waste trade, except pursuant to the notice-and-consent regime set forth in the Basel Convention (a state wishing to prohibit such imports may do so).[128]

Whenever international environmental agreements (or national environmental laws) interfere with free trade, the values underlying both fields come into conflict. In fact, there are often concerns that international trade obligations may be used to strike down laws designed to protect the environment. The principal forum for adjudicating such conflicts has been the dispute settlement process before the World Trade Organization (WTO), which looks to trade agreements such as the General Agreement on Tariffs and Trade (GATT).

Under the GATT, trade restrictions are generally impermissible if they: (1) treat imports from one state less favorably than like products from another state (thus violating the most-favored-nation principle in GATT Article I); (2) treat imports less favorably than like local products (thus violating the national treatment principle in GATT Article III); or (3) constitute quantitative restrictions, such as quotas or bans (thus violating GATT Article XI). At the same time, GATT Article XX provides that impermissible trade restrictions may be justified if: (1) they are not applied in a manner which constitutes arbitrary or unjustifiable discrimination or a disguised restriction on trade; and (2) they constitute measures necessary to protect human, animal, or plant life or health, or constitute measures relating to the conservation of exhaustible natural resources (so long as those measures are made in conjunction with restrictions on national production or consumption).

An example of these provisions before the WTO is the "shrimp-turtle case." Various states sued the United States over a U.S. law that protected endangered sea turtles by restricting imports of shrimp and shrimp products caught without using "turtle excluder devices" (TEDs) or equally effective means of protecting turtles.[129] In 1998, the WTO appellate body found that the U.S. import restrictions violated the GATT and that the Article XX exception could not be invoked because—while the law was designed to conserve sea turtles and those turtles were an "exhaustible natural resource"—the *manner* in which the United States implemented its

---

127. *See* Basel Convention, *supra* note 16, arts. 4(5) & 11.

128. *Id.*, arts. 4 & 6.

129. *See* 16 U.S.C. § 1537 note (2006).

law constituted arbitrary and unjustifiable discrimination. Part of this discrimination derived from the overall prohibition on imports of shrimp harvested by certain states, even though their vessels used turtle-excluder devices comparable to those considered acceptable for U.S. vessels.[130] Thereafter, rather than change or repeal the law, the United States pursued various steps to bring its implementation of the law into compliance with its GATT obligations, such as being more flexible in certifying foreign programs. When Malaysia subsequently challenged the U.S. implementation of the appellate body report, the appellate body found the U.S. implementation GATT-compliant.[131]

The North American Free Trade Agreement (NAFTA)[132] also contains provisions on environmental protection. For instance, Article 1114(2) states that "it is inappropriate to encourage investment by relaxing domestic health, safety or environmental measures." Article 104 provides that where there is a conflict between NAFTA and trade sanctions called for in certain international environmental agreements (such as the Montreal Protocol on ozone-depleting substances), the latter shall prevail. Further, the NAFTA parties concluded a side agreement on environmental cooperation[133] addressing government transparency and enforcement actions regarding environmental protection, and creating private rights of action for violations of environmental laws and regulations. Many of these provisions are now included in bilateral trade agreements concluded by the United States with its trading partners.

States might also use environmental or conservation norms as a means of justifying the expropriation of foreign investment. For example, in *Southern Pacific Properties*[134] a company entered into an agreement in 1974 with the government of Egypt to develop tourist complexes at the pyramid area near Cairo and elsewhere, but thereafter political opposition to the project developed. Consequently, the government issued a decree in May 1978 declaring the relevant land to be public property, purportedly due to the presence

---

130. *See* Appellate Body Report, *United States—Import Prohibition of Certain Shrimp and Shrimp Products*, WT/DS58/AB/R (Oct. 12, 1998).

131. *See* Appellate Body Report, *United States—Import Prohibition of Certain Shrimp and Shrimp Products*, WT/DS58/AB/RW (Oct. 22, 2001), reprinted in 41 I.L.M. 149 (2002); *see also* Panel Report, *EC Measures Affecting Asbestos and Asbestos–Containing Products*, WT/DS135/R (Sept. 18, 2000) (upholding under Article XX a 1996 French

ban on imports of chrysotile asbestos from Canada).

132. U.S.-Can.-Mex., Dec. 17, 1992, 32 I.L.M. 289, 605.

133. *See* North American Agreement on Environmental Cooperation, U.S.-Can.-Mex., Sept. 14, 1993, 32 I.L.M. 1480.

134. Southern Pacific Properties (Middle East) Ltd. v. Egypt (Jiménez de Aréchaga, Amin El Mahdi & Pietrowski, arbs. May 20, 1992), *reprinted in* 106 I.L.R. 501, 589 (1993).

of "antiquities" which had to be protected due to Egypt's adherence to the World Heritage Convention.[135] Shortly thereafter, Egypt nominated the pyramid fields for inclusion on the World Heritage Convention list of sites. The company argued, among other things, that Egypt did not rely on the convention when it canceled the project, and that Egypt only invoked the convention as a *post hoc* rationalization for its expropriation. While accepting Egypt's contention that antiquities were present on the land, the ICSID Tribunal rejected the argument that Egypt was obligated under the World Heritage Convention to expropriate the property. The Tribunal stated that under the convention "the choice of sites to be protected is not imposed externally, but results instead from the State's own voluntary nomination" and that "the UNESCO Convention by itself does not justify the measures taken by the Respondent.... "[136] Similar cases have arisen under NAFTA's investor-state dispute resolution process. For example, in *Metalclad Corp. v. Mexico*,[137] a NAFTA arbitration panel found that Mexico expropriated the property interest of a U.S. investor when it issued a permit allowing the U.S. investor to construct a hazardous waste disposal facility, yet failed to prevent Mexican local authorities from interfering with its operation, purportedly on environmental grounds.

Extraterritorial Application of Environmental Law

Where national environmental laws are applied to conduct that occurs extraterritorially, an issue arises regarding the propriety (under international law) of a state unilaterally using its law to control or influence activities occurring outside its borders. International law recognizes the ability of a state to prescribe legislation on the basis of certain principles, such as the territorial principle.[138] National laws used to protect or preserve the foreign environment, however, do not fall neatly within such principles. Even if they did, the national laws must be reasonable, taking into account such factors as the extent to which another state has an interest in regulating the affected activity.

Since U.S. environmental laws are adopted principally to address environmental concerns within the United States, U.S. courts have resisted applying those laws to conduct (or effects) in foreign countries. For example, in *Amlon Metals, Inc. v. FMC Corp.*,[139] a district court found that the Resource Conservation and Recovery Act did not provide a cause of action for damage in the United Kingdom from hazardous wastes shipped from the United States.

135. *Supra* note 13.

136. *Southern Pacific Properties*, 106 I.L.R. at 625, para. 154.

137. 119 I.L.R. 615 (ICSID W. Bank 2001), *reprinted in* 40 I.L.M. 36 (2001).

138. *See* Chapter 8(B).

139. 775 F. Supp. 668 (S.D.N.Y. 1991).

For such a cause of action, the plaintiffs would have to look to U.K. law before U.K. courts. Similarly, in *Born Free USA v. Norton*,[140] the plaintiffs sought an injunction to stop the import of eleven elephants from Swaziland, charging that, in granting import permits, the U.S. Fish and Wildlife Service had failed to conduct an environmental impact review as required by the National Environmental Policy Act (NEPA).[141] The district court accepted that Swaziland was obligated to issue export permits for African elephants since they are listed as an endangered species under CITES.[142] Further, under CITES and the Endangered Species Act,[143] the United States is obligated to issue import permits. The district court, however, declined to enjoin the import, stating:

> In the present case, the Court is not dealing with environmental effects in a no-man's land such as Antarctica, where the United States has some real measure of control; rather, it is dealing with environmental affects [sic] in a foreign sovereign nation. That nation has made an independent determination to proceed with the export of the elephants under CITES, has concluded that the export will not be detrimental to the species, and has determined that if the export is not possible, it will be necessary to cull the elephants. Absent some further indication from Congress, this Court is not inclined to take the step of requiring [the Fish and Wildlife Service] to conduct an environmental analysis aimed at second-guessing the validity of Swaziland's determination.[144]

As indicated by the district court's decision, in situations where the conduct (or effects) at issue occur outside the national jurisdiction of any country, U.S. courts are more inclined to apply U.S. environmental laws. For example, in *Environmental Defense Fund, Inc. v. Massey*,[145] the D.C. Circuit Court of Appeals found that NEPA required an environmental impact statement for major federal actions affecting the quality of the human environment in Antarctica. Similarly, the Ninth Circuit Court of Appeals in *Natural Resources Defense Council v. Winter*[146] found that NEPA applied to navy sonar tests being conducted on the high seas or within the U.S. exclusive economic zone and affirmed a preliminary injunction limiting the tests. However, the U.S. Supreme Court vacated the injunction on national security grounds, finding that the environ-

---

140. 278 F. Supp. 2d 5 (D.D.C. 2003).

141. 42 U.S.C. §§ 4321–4370f (2006). Under NEPA, an agency must prepare an environmental impact statement for any proposed "major Federal actions significantly affecting the quality of the human environment." 42 U.S.C. § 4332(C).

142. *Supra* note 11.

143. 16 U.S.C. §§ 1531–1544 (2006).

144. 278 F. Supp. 2d at 20.

145. 986 F.2d 528 (D.C. Cir. 1993).

146. 518 F.3d 658 (9th Cir. 2008).

mental concerns were "plainly outweighed" by the Navy's interest in effective, realistic training of its sailors.[147] NEPA has also been applied to testing done in the exclusive economic zone of a foreign state (as opposed to its territorial waters).[148]

Finally, in situations where the conduct at issue occurred abroad, yet the effects occurred in the United States, U.S. courts have exercised jurisdiction. For example, in *Pakootas v. Teck Cominco Metals*,[149] the U.S. Environmental Protection Agency (EPA) issued an administrative order under the Comprehensive Environmental Response, Compensation, and Liability Act (CERCLA)[150] to a Canadian corporation, Teck Cominco Metals, Ltd. (Teck), directing it to conduct a "remedial investigation/feasibility study." Teck owned and operated a smelter in Trail, British Columbia, approximately ten miles north along the Columbia River from the U.S.-Canada border.[151] The purpose of the administrative order was to have Teck investigate and determine the full nature of contamination at the Trail smelter site and whether contaminants were migrating into the Columbia River and then into the United States. Teck refused to comply with the order, contending that CERCLA could not be applied extraterritorially to actions by a Canadian corporation taken within Canada.

In 2004, U.S. members of the Confederated Tribes of the Colville Reservation sued Teck in U.S. court under the "citizen suit" provision of CERCLA to enforce the administrative order. Teck moved to dismiss the case. The district court found that it had personal jurisdiction over Teck under Washington state's "long-arm" statute, since the plaintiffs alleged that Teck had engaged in intentional acts expressly aimed at, and causing effects in, Washington. The parties then contested whether the court had subject matter jurisdiction, with the defendant arguing that the case involved an impermissible extraterritorial application of CERCLA to conduct occurring outside U.S. borders. The circuit court concluded that the case did not involve extraterritorial application of the statute, even though Teck's facility was located in Canada:

> The location where a party arranged for disposal or disposed of hazardous substances is not controlling for purposes of assessing whether CERCLA is being applied extraterritorially, because CERCLA imposes liability for releases or threatened releases of hazardous substances, and not merely for disposal

---

147. Winter v. Natural Resources Defense Council, 555 U.S. 7 (2008).

148. *See* Center for Biological Diversity v. Nat'l Sci. Found., C 02–5065JL, 2002 WL 31548073 (N.D. Cal. Oct. 30, 2002).

149. 452 F.3d 1066 (9th Cir. 2006).

150. 42 U.S.C. §§ 9601–9675 (2006).

151. For the famous case regarding transboundary air pollution from the same smelter, see *Trail Smelter* arbitration, *supra* note 48.

or arranging for disposal of such substances. Because the actual or threatened release of hazardous substances triggers CERCLA liability, and because the actual or threatened release here, the leaching of hazardous substances from slag that settled at the Site, took place in the United States, this case involves a domestic application of CERCLA.[152]

As such, the court declined to dismiss the complaint.

152.   452 F.3d at 1078.

Further Reading:

Regina S. Axelrod et al., eds., *The Global Environment: Institutions, Law, and Policy* (2d ed. 2005).

Scott Barrett, *Environment and Statecraft: The Strategy of Environmental Treaty-making* (2003).

Patricia Birnie, Alan Boyle, & Catherine Redgwell, *International Law and the Environment* (3d ed. 2009).

Daniel Bodansky, *The Art and Craft of International Environmental Law* (2010).

Daniel Bodansky et al., eds., *The Oxford Handbook of International Environmental Law* (2007).

Alex G. Oude Elferink & Erik J. Molenaar, *The International Legal Regime of Areas Beyond National Jurisdiction* (2010).

Francesco Francioni, ed., *Environment, Human Rights and International Trade* (2001).

Xue Hanqin, *Transboundary Damage in International Law* (2003).

Stephen Humphreys, ed., *Human Rights and Climate Change* (2010).

Alexandre Kiss & Dinah Shelton, *International Environmental Law* (3d ed. 2004).

Marie–Louise Larsson, *The Law of Environmental Damage: Liability and Reparation* (1999).

Fiona Macmillan, *WTO and the Environment* (2001).

Linda Malone & Scott Pasternack, *Defending the Environment: Civil Society Strategies to Enforce International Environmental Law* (2004).

Stephen C. McCaffrey, *The Law of International Watercourses* (2d ed. 2007).

Fiona McConnell, *The Biodiversity Convention: A Negotiating History* (1996).

Elisa Morgera, *Corporate Accountability in International Environmental Law* (2009).

Fred L. Morrison & Rüdiger Wolfrum, eds., *International, Regional, and National Environmental Law* (2000).

Sebastian Oberthür & Herman Ott, *The Kyoto Protocol: International Climate Policy for the 21st Century* (1999).

Daniel D. Perlmutter & Robert L. Rothstein, *The Challenge of Climate Change: Which Way Now?* (2011).

Philippe Sands, *Principles of International Environmental Law* (2d ed. 2003).

Edella C. Schlager, et al., eds., *Navigating Climate Change Policy: The Opportunities of Federalism* (2011).

Erich Vranes, *Trade and the Environment* (2009).

Yearbook of International Environmental Law (published annually by Oxford University Press).

Chapter 13

INTERNATIONAL CRIMINAL LAW

A. Introduction

All states have national criminal justice systems that create and enforce laws in the hope of deterring and punishing criminal behavior. In most instances, such behavior is not transnational in nature, yet it sometimes spans borders or the suspected offender might have left one state's jurisdiction and entered another's. In these instances, states value reciprocal cooperation in order to investigate criminal behavior, gather evidence for use in prosecutions, and apprehend fugitives. Cooperation may occur as a matter of comity or friendly cooperation, or it may be based on legally binding treaties or customary norms.

Chapter 8 discussed the bases of national jurisdiction (including criminal jurisdiction) viewed as permissible under international law, while Chapter 9 noted certain immunities that diplomats and heads of state have from national jurisdiction. This chapter explores other important aspects of contemporary international criminal law. First, in pursuing enforcement of national criminal law, states have found it useful to conclude treaties providing for cooperation on information-sharing, evidence-gathering, and extradition. Second, special treaties have developed that augment national law enforcement efforts in important subject matter areas that have an inescapable transnational dimension, such as terrorism, narcotics, corruption, and cyber-crime. Third, states have developed treaties that impose criminal liability on individuals for large-scale atrocities committed in times of war and peace, such as genocide or crimes against humanity. Finally, as a means of prosecuting individuals for atrocities, states have created standing and *ad hoc* international criminal tribunals to supplement national tribunals. Each of these aspects is discussed in turn.

B. General Transnational Cooperation

Mutual Legal Assistance (Evidence Gathering)

The first step in pursuing transnational criminal behavior is the investigation of the crime, including gathering documentary and witness evidence. A prosecutor might seek evidence from abroad simply by a unilateral order, such as a grand jury subpoena directed at U.S. nationals or U.S. residents located abroad, for which they can be held in contempt if they fail to comply.[1] Yet when law enforcement authorities are interested in obtaining evidence abroad, often they will rely on assistance from their foreign counterparts. Historically, such cooperation has occurred on an informal basis, as a matter of international comity, although (as discussed below) there are now treaties that address this issue.[2] For the United States, much of this work is coordinated through the U.S. Department of State Office of the Legal Adviser and the U.S. Department of Justice Office of International Affairs.

To the extent a foreign court needs to be enlisted in obtaining evidence for an investigation or trial, a local court can communicate formally with its foreign counterpart by means of "letters rogatory" (or letter of request). U.S. courts have regularly sought assistance from foreign courts by means of letters rogatory. When this is done, the letter must be issued under the seal of the U.S. court and the signature of the U.S. judge. Further, some foreign states require that the U.S. letter be authenticated by the local U.S. embassy or consulate. Conversely, U.S. federal courts are authorized to assist foreign and international tribunals in the taking of statements or the production of documents upon receipt of a letter rogatory from abroad (or a request from an interested party in the foreign case).[3] The U.S. Department of State is authorized to act as the intermediary for transmission of letters rogatory from foreign courts to U.S. courts, but it is also common for these courts to directly communicate with one another. In general, however, the process for letters rogatory can be extremely slow and cumbersome, and therefore is disfavored unless absolutely necessary.

In the past fifty years, states have also concluded a network of bilateral treaties to regularize and improve the effectiveness of cooperation between governments on criminal matters. Typically referred to as "mutual legal assistance in criminal matters treaties" (MLATs), these treaties generally provide for a "requested state" to assist a "requesting state's" law enforcement efforts by: (1) sharing with the requesting state useful information in the requested state's possession; (2) searching for and seizing evidence located in the requested state; (3) serving summons on and tracing suspects or witnesses located in the requested state; and (4) taking written testimony from such persons. Sometimes an MLAT will allow a representative of the requesting state to be present during

---

1. *See* 28 U.S.C. §§ 1783–84 (2006); *see also* Marc Rich & Co. v. United States, 707 F.2d 663 (2d Cir. 1983) (affirming power of U.S. court to subpoena bank records controlled by a Swiss bank whose U.S. subsidiary was charged with tax evasion).

2. With respect to obtaining evidence in non-criminal matters, see Convention on the Taking of Evidence Abroad in Civil or Commercial Matters, Mar. 18, 1970, 23 U.S.T. 2555, 847 U.N.T.S. 231.

3. *See* 28 U.S.C. §§ 1781–82 (2006).

certain tasks, such as the taking of statements. While most proceedings are criminal in nature, MLATs often obligate parties to assist with respect to any proceedings that might arise—criminal, civil, or administrative. Unlike letters rogatory, courts are not necessarily involved in the MLAT process.

The treaty instrument allows states to commit to cooperation generally, yet subject to exceptions deemed important. Thus, a requested state might reserve the right to decline to conduct a search and seizure unless certain conditions are satisfied (*e.g.*, a court order from the requesting state). A treaty might also allow states to refuse a request relating to the investigation of an offense that is political in nature or that arises out of discrimination on the basis of race, sex, religion, or nationality. Some MLATs require that the offense satisfy the "principle of double criminality," meaning that the offense be criminal under the laws of both the requesting and requested states (discussed further below).

In any event, the requested state follows its own national laws and practices for gathering the requested evidence. Some MLATs, however, try to encourage the requested state to comply also with the laws and practices of the requesting state, in order to avoid problems of admissibility of evidence in the courts of the requesting state.

When concluding such an agreement, each country designates a central authority responsible for direct communication between states on matters within the scope of the treaty. For the United States, the central authority is the Department of Justice. All told, the United States has concluded more than sixty MLATs with states of greatest interest to U.S. law enforcement. U.S. MLATs exist with neighbors (Canada, Mexico), major allies (*e.g.*, Germany, Japan, Netherlands, United Kingdom), and states in Africa (*e.g.*, Egypt, Morocco), Asia (*e.g.*, Australia, Philippines), the Carribean (*e.g.*, Barbados, Jamaica), Eastern Europe (*e.g.*, Czech Republic, Hungary), and South America (*e.g.*, Brazil, Panama). Similar diversity may be found in U.S. extradition treaties, which are discussed in the next section.

In 1959, the Council of Europe adopted a Convention on Mutual Legal Assistance in Criminal Matters,[4] which has had a significant influence on the development of MLATs by European states. Moreover, since many countries (particularly in the developing world) do not have MLATs with one another, the United Nations in 1990 adopted a model MLAT.[5]

---

4. Apr. 20, 1959, Europ. T.S. No. 30, as amended by protocol.

5. *See* G.A. Res. 45/117, annex (Dec. 14, 1990), *reprinted in* 30 I.L.M. 1419 (1991).

More recently, in June 2003, the European Union and United States signed an MLAT[6] which provides for cooperation between the United States and all twenty-seven E.U. member states (previously the United States had MLATs with just eighteen E.U. states). This MLAT contains a number of innovative provisions. Article 4 establishes a detailed mechanism for receiving information on bank accounts, allowing the United States to request information from an existing network of European national registries. Article 5 calls for the establishment of joint investigative teams between the United States and E.U. member states to facilitate criminal investigations or prosecutions. Article 6 calls for cooperation in the use of video-conferencing technology to take testimony, including the punishment in the requested state of persons who make intentionally false statements during such testimony. Article 9 sets out certain parameters for the vexing issue of disclosure to, and use by, a requesting state of personal data.

Extradition

Extradition Generally. Once a state has investigated and charged an offender, the issue of extradition arises if the offender is located in another state. "Extradition" refers to the formal process by which an individual is delivered from the state where he is located to a requesting state to face prosecution, or if already convicted, to serve a sentence. Since there is no general requirement under international law for a state to extradite an offender, treaties have emerged as the principal means for ensuring that extraditions occur in a dependable fashion. In 1990, the United Nations adopted a model extradition treaty to assist states in developing such treaties.[7]

Extradition treaties vary considerably, but they usually grapple with three particular issues. First, the offense at issue must be a crime in both the requesting and the requested states. This "principle of dual criminality" serves the purpose of ensuring that the offense is serious and that a requested state will not be embarrassed by assisting in the punishment of an act that the requested state tolerates under its own law. Some treaties address this principle by incorporating a list of offenses regarded by both parties as crimes (these lists must then be regularly updated). Modern treaties contain broad, catch-all clauses that simply acknowledge the principle, leaving it to the requested state to determine whether the principle is satisfied with regards to a particular request. Second, extradition treaties typically contain the "rule of speciali-

---

6. *See* Agreement on Mutual Legal Assistance in Criminal Matters, U.S.-E.U., June 25, 2003, 2003 O.J. (L 181) 34, 43 I.L.M. 758.

7. *See* G.A. Res. 45/116, annex (Dec. 14, 1990), *reprinted in* 30 I.L.M. 1407 (1991).

ty," which requires that an offender only be tried for the crime for which he or she was extradited. Thus, a state may not request extradition based on offense X and then prosecute the person for offenses X, Y, and Z. Whether the offender may raise the rule of specialty as a defense or whether it may only be raised by the state from which the offender was extradited is a matter of some dispute.[8] Third, most extradition treaties do not allow extradition for "political offenses," meaning an offense arising from political activism, such as treason, sedition, or espionage.[9] Determining whether an offense is a "political offense," however, is not always easy, especially when the crime committed is merely incidental to political activism.

Extradition to and from the United States. When a U.S. prosecutor seeks extradition of an offender located abroad, he or she must obtain approval from the U.S. Department of Justice under a statute that allows extradition when there "is a treaty or convention for extradition between the United States and any foreign government. . . . "[10] Conversely, extradition from the United States normally may proceed only when there is a treaty[11] or statute authorizing extradition, such as a statute relating to terrorist acts[12] or to an international criminal tribunal.[13] If the United States receives a request for extradition that is supported by a treaty or statute, a U.S. court will issue an arrest warrant. A hearing is then conducted to determine if the extradition may proceed, at which point the offender may raise objections. Assuming there are no valid objections, the court then certifies to the U.S. secretary of state that the extradition may occur; the final decision to extradite lies with the secretary.

As of 2011, the United States has in force extradition treaties with more than one hundred foreign states. As was the case with MLATs, the European Union and United States signed an extradition treaty in June 2003.[14] The treaty does not eliminate bilateral extradition agreements between the United States and E.U. member states; rather, it supplements and selectively amends them. For example, the U.S./E.U. treaty sets forth a detailed list of criteria that a requested state must take into account when faced with competing extradition requests from several states. Further, the

---

8. *Compare* United States v. Puentes, 50 F.3d 1567 (11th Cir. 1995) (finding the offender has standing to invoke the rule), *with* United States v. Van Cauwenberghe, 827 F.2d 424 (9th Cir. 1987) (finding standing only for the state who extradited the offender).

9. *See* Quinn v. Robinson, 783 F.2d 776 (9th Cir. 1986).

10. 18 U.S.C. § 3184 (2006).

11. *See* 18 U.S.C. §§ 3181(a), 3184 (2006).

12. *See* 18 U.S.C. §§ 3181(b).

13. *See* Ntakirutimana v. Reno, 184 F.3d 419 (5th Cir. 1999).

14. *See* Agreement on Extradition, U.S.-E.U., June 25, 2003, 2003 O.J. (L 181) 27, 43 I.L.M. 749.

treaty broadens the range of extraditable offenses, requiring extradition for every offense punishable in both the requesting and requested state by more than one year in prison.[15]

Example of Extradition Treaty. In 2003, the United States and United Kingdom negotiated a new extradition treaty designed, in part, to bring their bilateral relationship in line with the U.S./E.U. extradition treaty noted above. Under the 1972 U.S./U.K. extradition treaty, each state was only obligated to extradite persons accused or convicted of offenses listed on a schedule annexed to the treaty, as well as other offenses listed in relevant U.K. extradition law and considered felonies under U.S. law.[16] In contrast, under the 2003 treaty, the parties agree to extradite for any "extraditable offense," defined as an offense "punishable under the laws in both States by deprivation of liberty for a period of one year or more or by a more severe penalty."[17] When transmitting the treaty to the Senate in April 2004, the U.S. government asserted that the use of such a "pure" dual criminality clause "obviates the need to renegotiate or supplement the Treaty as additional offenses become punishable under the laws in both States."[18]

Article 4 of the treaty establishes bases for denial of extradition, including extradition sought for a political offense. Article 4(2) sets forth seven categories of offenses that shall not be considered political offenses, including "an offense for which both Parties have the obligation pursuant to a multilateral international agreement to extradite the person sought or to submit the case to their competent authorities for decision as to prosecution."[19] Article 7 provides that a state that does not allow capital punishment may refuse to extradite to a state that allows capital punishment, unless the latter "provides an assurance that the death penalty will not be imposed or, if imposed, will not be carried out."[20] Article 18(2) of the treaty states that an extradited person "may not be the subject of onward extradition *or surrender* for any offense committed prior to extradition to the Requesting State unless the Requested State consents."[21] The use of the term "surrender" was intended to make

---

15. *Id.*, arts. 4(1), 10.

16. *See* Extradition Treaty arts. I & III, U.S.-U.K., June 8, 1972, 28 U.S.T. 227, 30 U.N.T.S. 167. This treaty was supplemented in 1985. *See* Supplementary Treaty, U.S.-U.K., June 25, 1985, T.I.A.S. 12,050, 1556 U.N.T.S. 369.

17. Extradition Treaty arts. 1 & 2(1), U.S.-U.K., Mar. 31, 2003, S. TREATY DOC. NO. 108–23, at 1, 4 (2003) [hereinafter 2003 Extradition Treaty].

18. S. TREATY DOC. NO. 108–23 at V (2003).

19. 2003 Extradition Treaty, *supra* note 17, art. 4(2)(a). As discussed in the next section, there are numerous multilateral conventions containing a "prosecute or surrender" obligation.

20. Similar formulations may be seen in recent U.S. extradition treaties with Argentina, France, India, Republic of Korea, Peru, and Poland.

21. 2003 Extradition Treaty, *supra* note 17, art. 18(2) (emphasis added).

clear that the United Kingdom will not surrender to the International Criminal Court any person extradited by the United States.[22]

C. Transnational Cooperation Concerning Important Sectors

In addition to the general cooperation that occurs through MLATs and extradition treaties, states have adopted innovative law enforcement instruments in discrete areas by which they define, and commit themselves to punish, certain serious crimes (or extradite offenders to jurisdictions where they can be punished). This section discusses some of these areas.

Terrorism

The General Assembly has characterized "terrorism" as "criminal acts intended or calculated to provoke a state of terror in the general public, a group of persons or particular persons for political purposes."[23] Further, the Special Tribunal for Lebanon recently asserted that terrorism under customary international law consists of

> the following three key elements: (i) the perpetration of a criminal act (such as murder, kidnapping, hostage-taking, arson, and so on), or threatening such an act; (ii) the intent to spread fear among the population (which would generally entail the creation of public danger) or directly or indirectly coerce a national or international authority to take some action, or to refrain from taking it; (iii) when the act involves a transnational element.[24]

Many observers, however, regard there as not yet existing a universally-accepted definition of "terrorism" for purposes of international law. Part of the difficulty has been differences of opinion over whether certain groups are "terrorists" engaged in unlawful violence or "freedom fighters" pursuing national liberation, self-determination, or other worthy causes.[25]

Instead of a single, all-encompassing treaty on the subject, the global community has concluded several antiterrorist conventions

---

22. Article 98(2) of the Rome Statute of the International Criminal Court, July 17, 1998, 2187 U.N.T.S. 3 [hereinafter Rome Statute], provides that the ICC may not proceed with a request for surrender that "would require the requested State to act inconsistently with its obligations under international agreements pursuant to which the consent of a sending State is required to surrender a person of that State to the Court.... "

23. Declaration on Measures to Eliminate International Terrorism, G.A. Res. 60/49, annex, para. 3 (Dec. 9, 1994).

24. Interlocutory Decision on the Applicable Law: Terrorism, Conspiracy, Homicide, Perpetration, Cumulative Charging, Case No. STL–11–01/1, para. 85 (Feb. 16, 2011).

25. *See generally* BEN SAUL, DEFINING TERRORISM IN INTERNATIONAL LAW (2006).

that require parties to make it an offense under their national criminal law to engage in: offenses on, or hijacking or sabotage of, aircraft;[26] the taking of hostages;[27] crimes against certain protected persons;[28] maritime terrorism;[29] the manufacture or transport of unmarked plastic explosives;[30] terrorist bombings;[31] the financing of terrorism;[32] and nuclear terrorism.[33] These conventions also require parties either to extradite alleged offenders or submit the matter to prosecution in their own courts, a principle referred to as *aut dedere aut judicare*.[34] Thus, when an act of terrorism occurs that falls within the scope of one of these treaties and the perpetrator turns up in a party's territory, that party is supposed to have a national law allowing for prosecution of the offense (even if the offense occurred abroad), and is supposed to either submit the matter to prosecution or extradite the perpetrator to a state willing to prosecute. In this fashion, these treaties strive to preclude safe havens for terrorists.

While these treaties are not universally adhered to, the U.N. Security Council and General Assembly have called upon states to become parties to such instruments "as soon as possible" and as a "matter of priority."[35] The United States is a party to these

26. *See* Convention on Offences and Certain Other Acts Committed on Board Aircraft, Sept. 14, 1963, 20 U.S.T. 2941, 704 U.N.T.S. 219; Convention for the Suppression of Unlawful Seizure of Aircraft, Dec. 16, 1970, 22 U.S.T. 1641, 860 U.N.T.S. 105 (and its optional Protocol of Sept. 10, 2010); Convention for the Suppression of Unlawful Acts Against the Safety of Civil Aviation, Sept. 23, 1971, 24 U.S.T. 565, 974 U.N.T.S. 177 (supplemented by protocol of February 24, 1988 on violence at airports); Convention on the Suppression of Unlawful Acts Relating to International Civil Aviation, Sept. 10, 2010, 50 I.L.M. 141 (2011).

27. *See* International Convention Against the Taking of Hostages, Dec. 17, 1979, T.I.A.S. 11,081, 1316 U.N.T.S. 205.

28. *See* U.N. Convention on the Prevention and Punishment of Crimes Against Internationally Protected Persons, Including Diplomatic Agents, Dec. 14, 1973, 28 U.S.T. 1975, 1035 U.N.T.S. 167.

29. Convention for the Suppression of Unlawful Acts against the Safety of Maritime Navigation, Mar. 10, 1988, IMO Doc. SUA/CONF/15/Rev.1 (1988); Protocol for the Suppression of Unlaw-

ful Acts against the Safety of Fixed Platforms Located on the Continental Shelf, Mar. 10, 1988, IMO Doc. SUA/CONF/16/Rev.2 (1988).

30. *See* Convention on the Marking of Plastic Explosives for the Purpose of Detection, Mar. 1, 1991, U.N. Doc. S/22393 (1991), 30 I.L.M. 726.

31. *See* International Convention for the Suppression of Terrorist Bombings, G.A. Res. 52/164, annex (Dec. 15, 1997).

32. *See* International Convention for the Suppression of the Financing of Terrorism, Dec. 9, 1999, S. Treaty Doc. No. 106–49 (2000), G.A. Res. 54/109, annex (Dec. 9, 1999).

33. *See* Convention on the Physical Protection of Nuclear Material, Mar. 3, 1980, T.I.A.S. 11080, IAEA Doc. IN-FCIRC/274/Rev.1 (1980); International Convention for the Suppression of Acts of Nuclear Terrorism, G.A. Res. 59/290, annex (Apr. 13, 2005).

34. *See generally* M. Cherif Bassiouni & Edward M. Wise, Aut Dedere Aut Judicare: The Duty to Extradite or Prosecute in International Law (1995).

35. S.C. Res. 1373, para. 3(d) (Sept. 28, 2001); G.A. Res. 49/60, annex, para. 8 (Feb. 17, 1995).

conventions and adopts implementing legislation as necessary.[36] Other treaties have been concluded on a regional level, such as conventions against terrorism adopted by the Council of Europe[37] and by the Organization of American States.[38]

Narcotics

Various multilateral, regional, and bilateral agreements have been concluded to promote cooperation among states in combating illegal trafficking in narcotics. The 1961 Single Convention on Narcotic Drugs[39] seeks to limit the use of narcotics with cannabis, coca, and opium-like effects solely to scientific and medical purposes. To that end, it obligates parties to restrict to licensed persons the cultivation, manufacture, and distribution of such narcotics. Further, the convention created an International Narcotics Control Board, to which the parties must report the amount of narcotics produced, consumed, or seized in their territory. The 1971 Convention on Psychotropic Substances[40] was developed in response to the diversification and expansion of the spectrum of drugs beyond those addressed in the 1961 Single Convention. It introduced controls over mind-altering and synthetic drugs, including import and export restrictions, based on the risk of abuse and therapeutic value of the drug. The 1988 U.N. Convention Against the Illicit Traffic in Narcotic Drugs and Psychotropic Substances[41] regulates the precursor chemicals to drugs controlled by the Single Convention and the Convention on Psychotropic Substances. It also contains important provisions related to money laundering and other drug-related crimes.

On the regional level, various instruments have been concluded. For example, the Declaration of Cartagena Concerning the Production of, Trafficking in and Demand for Illicit Drugs[42] sets forth a series of understandings and general commitments to ad-

36. *See, e.g.,* Terrorist Bombings Convention Implementation Act of 2002, Pub. L. No. 107–197, Title I, 116 Stat. 721 (2002); Suppression of the Financing of Terrorism Convention Implementation Act of 2002, Pub. L. No. 107–197, Title II, 116 Stat. 724 (2002).

37. Convention on the Prevention of Terrorism, May 16, 2005, COE Doc. CM(2005)34 addendum 1 final (May 3, 2005); Convention on Laundering, Search, Seizure and Confiscation of the Proceeds from Crime and on the Financing of Terrorism, May 16, 2005, COE Doc. CM(2005)35 final (May 3, 2005); European Convention on the Suppression of Terrorism, Jan. 27, 1977, Europ. T.S. No. 90.

38. *See* Inter–American Convention Against Terrorism, June 3, 2002, S. TREATY DOC. NO. 107–18 (2002), O.A.S. T.S. No. A–66, 42 I.L.M. 19; Inter–American Convention to Prevent and Punish the Acts of Terrorism Taking the Form of Crimes Against Persons and Related Extortion That Are of International Significance, Feb. 2, 1971, 27 U.S.T. 3949, 1438 U.N.T.S. 194.

39. Mar. 30, 1961, 18 U.S.T. 1407, 520 U.N.T.S. 204.

40. Feb. 21, 1971, 32 U.S.T. 543, 1019 U.N.T.S. 175.

41. Dec. 20, 1988, S. TREATY DOC. NO. 101–4, 1582 U.N.T.S. 95.

42. Feb. 15, 1990, T.I.A.S. No. 12,-411.

dress drug trafficking and consumption in Bolivia, Colombia, Peru, and the United States. Such instruments provide a framework for bilateral agreements. Thus, the United States has concluded with Colombia an Agreement to Suppress Illicit Traffic by Sea,[43] which authorizes each party to board and search private or commercial vessels of the other's nationality, except within the other party's territorial waters (the United States has concluded more than twenty such bilateral agreements with South American and Caribbean states). Likewise, the United States and Colombia have concluded a Memorandum of Understanding Concerning Cooperation in the Seizure and Forfeiture of Property and Proceeds of Illicit Trafficking in Narcotic Drugs,[44] which establishes an information-sharing regime to combat narcotics-related money laundering.

Corruption

Transnational criminal behavior involves a wide range of corrupt practices, including bribery, embezzlement, and money laundering. Efforts to combat such corruption occur both through cooperative arrangements, such as the Financial Action Task Force (FATF) established by the Organisation for Economic Co-operation and Development (OECD), and through treaties. Several regional conventions on corruption have been developed by the OECD,[45] the OAS,[46] the Council of Europe,[47] and the African Union.[48]

On the global level, the U.N. General Assembly in October 2003 adopted the U.N. Convention Against Corruption.[49] Over the course of eight chapters and seventy-one articles, the convention lists a variety of measures states are obligated to take to strengthen international efforts to fight the corruption of public officials. The convention sets forth preventive measures that states must undertake, including the adoption of anticorruption policies and practices, and the use of a body (or bodies) to ensure implementation of such policies and practices.[50] Further, the convention specifically requires parties to criminalize embezzlement, money laundering, and the bribing of government officials (local or foreign) in relation

43. U.S.-Colom., Feb. 20, 1997, Temp. State Dep't No. 97–57, 1997 WL 193931.

44. U.S.-Colom., July 24, 1990, T.I.A.S. No. 12,417.

45. *See* OECD Convention on Combating Bribery of Foreign Public Officials in International Business Transactions, Dec. 18, 1997, OECD Doc. DAFFE/IME/BR(97)20, 37 I.L.M. 1; *see also* THE OECD CONVENTION ON BRIBERY: A COMMENTARY (Mark Pieth et al. eds., 2007).

46. *See* Inter–American Convention Against Corruption, Mar. 29, 1996, OAS Doc. B–58, 35 I.L.M. 724.

47. *See* Council of Europe Criminal Law Convention on Corruption, Jan. 27, 1999, Europ. T.S. No. 173, 38 I.L.M. 505.

48. *See* Convention on Preventing and Combating Corruption, July 11, 2003, *at* <http://www.africa-union.org>.

49. Oct. 31, 2003, G.A. Res. 58/4, annex (Oct. 31, 2003).

50. *Id.*, ch. II.

to the conduct of international business. The convention also calls upon parties to "consider adopting" laws to establish other criminal offenses, including trading in influence, abuse of functions, and illicit enrichment. The convention contains a series of articles on measures for promoting adherence to these criminal laws (*e.g.*, measures for freezing and confiscating the proceeds of a crime, overcoming bank secrecy laws, and cooperation among law enforcement authorities). Part of the convention is devoted to international cooperation, and addresses issues such as extradition and procedures for mutual legal assistance.[51] A section on asset recovery establishes a system whereby assets recovered in one jurisdiction can be returned to the beneficial owners located in another.[52] As of 2011, 154 states are parties to the Convention, including the United States.

Organized Crime

During the second half of the 1990's, states became concerned about the rapid spread of organized crime across borders, a phenomenon related to the end of the Cold War. In November 2000, the U.N. General Assembly adopted the U.N. Convention against Transnational Organized Crime (TOC Convention),[53] the first global agreement designed specifically to combat criminal groups operating internationally. The convention contains two optional protocols that focus on especially difficult issues of organized crime: trafficking in persons and the smuggling of migrants.

The TOC Convention requires parties to ensure that their national criminal laws meet certain criteria with respect to the four offenses characteristic of transnational organized crime: (1) participation in an organized criminal group; (2) laundering the proceeds of serious crime; (3) corruption of national public officials; and (4) obstructing justice by intimidating witnesses and law enforcement officials. Further, the TOC Convention sets out detailed mechanisms for extraditing fugitives and assisting foreign criminal investigations and prosecutions. As of 2011, 164 states are parties to the TOC Convention, including the United States.

Important provisions are contained in the protocols as well. For example, the alien smuggling protocol obligates parties to accept the return of smuggled migrants who are their nationals or permanent residents at the time of return. While such an obligation has been regarded as part of customary international law, the protocol codifies it in treaty form for the first time. Parties who intercept

51. *Id.*, ch. IV

52. *Id.*, ch. V.

53. Nov. 15, 2000, S. TREATY DOC. NO. 108–16 (2003), G.A. Res. 55/25, annexes I (main convention), II (protocol on trafficking in persons), & III (protocol on smuggling migrants) (Nov. 15, 2000).

smuggled migrants also must take appropriate measures to preserve and protect their rights. Since migrant smuggling by sea is
common, the protocol sets forth procedures for interdicting vessels
engaged in such smuggling.[54]

Cybercrime

With the advent of the personal computer and the Internet, the
potential for transnational computer crime has grown dramatically:
computer "viruses" can be unleashed that cause enormous damage
worldwide; personal and financial information of an individual in
one state can be stolen from across the globe; and pornography can
be posted on and widely distributed by the Internet.[55]

Investigation of and enforcement against computer crimes requires "real-time" coordination by law enforcement authorities
operating across borders in tracing electronic communications. The
principal convention to date is the Council of Europe's Convention
on Cybercrime,[56] which entered into force in July 2004. The convention requires parties to criminalize certain conduct related to computer systems, such as gaining illegal access into a computer system
(known as "hacking").[57] Further, it requires parties to ensure that
certain investigative procedures are available to enable national law
enforcement authorities to investigate cybercrime offenses effectively and obtain electronic evidence (such as computer data) of
crime. Among other things, the convention is designed to make it
possible to trace immediately the source of a computer attack, no
matter when or where it might occur. Finally, the convention
requires parties to cooperate in investigations and assist in the
extradition of fugitives sought for crimes identified under the
convention. As of 2011, 32 states have ratified the convention,
including the United States. Indeed, the Bush administration declared in its 2003 National Strategy to Secure Cyberspace that
joining the convention was a key U.S. objective.[58]

Due largely to U.S. resistance, the convention did not include
provisions designed to eliminate racist Internet sites by defining
and criminalizing "hate speech" on computer networks. A key
objective of such provisions would have been to prevent "unlawful
hosting," whereby persons interested in posting racist comments
aimed at one state do so by locating their Internet servers in
another state with less strict hate-speech regulations. The United

54. David McClean, Transnational
Organized Crime: A Commentary on the
United Nations Convention and Its Proto-
cols (2007).

55. *See* Duncan B. Hollis, *An e–SOS
for Cyberspace*, 52 Harv. Int'l L.J. 373
(2011).

56. Nov. 23, 2001, S. Treaty Doc. No.
108–11 (2003), Europ. T.S. No. 185.

57. *Id.*, art. 2.

58. White House, National Security
Strategy to Secure Cyberspace, at 52
(Feb. 2003).

States opposed such provisions out of a concern that they might infringe upon constitutionally-protected free speech and expression in the United States. While the convention ultimately contained no hate-speech provisions, the Council of Europe in January 2003 adopted a hate-speech optional protocol to the convention.[59] The protocol requires, among other things, that parties criminalize "distributing, or otherwise making available, racist and xenophobic material to the public through a computer system."[60] By 2011, twenty states have ratified the protocol, but the United States has neither signed nor ratified the protocol, and is not expected to do so.

D. International Crimes

The subject matter areas discussed in the prior section principally involve cooperation among states with respect to the prosecution of national crimes. To the extent that such crimes are regarded as a part of international law (*e.g.*, the crime of terrorism), it might be said that the crime originated in a national context and transitioned into international law. There are, however, certain crimes that arise as a matter of international law through conventions and customary rules, which then (at least in some instances) become crimes prosecuted under national law. Such crimes (crime of aggression, war crimes, crimes against humanity, and genocide) are being actively pursued before international criminal tribunals and hybrid courts operating within national legal systems. This section discusses the general and specific elements of these crimes.

General Elements of International Crimes

A detailed discussion of the elements of international crimes is beyond the scope of this volume, but various core concepts should be noted. First, international criminal law operates on the basis of *individual* criminal responsibility, meaning that a person cannot be held accountable for an act that he or she did not participate in or perform. Yet direct performance is not necessary; international criminal law encompasses incitement, planning, attempt, and conspiracy to commit a crime. Particular attention is paid to the concept of "command responsibility," whereby superiors in a line of command may be held accountable for the acts of their subordinates. Command responsibility generally is found where a superior knows that an offense is about to happen or is happening and fails to prevent the offense, or where a superior intentionally or

---

59. Additional Protocol to the Convention on Cybercrime, Concerning the Criminalisation of Acts of a Racist and Xenophobic Nature Committed through Computer Systems, Jan. 28, 2003, Europ. T.S. No. 189.

60. *Id.*, art. 3(1).

negligently fails to supervise a subordinate where an imminent offense is discernible and could be prevented.[61]

Second, for any given offense, there usually are "objective" and "subjective" elements. The objective element refers to specific facts that must occur to satisfy a particular criminal offense (*e.g.*, for the offense of murder, someone must be killed). The subjective element refers to the *mens rea* or mental state of the alleged offender. While the requisite *mens rea* differs according to the crime and is not well-settled under international custom, the offender must have an intent to bring about a particular result (*e.g.*, an intent to kill someone) or an awareness that a course of conduct entails an unjustifiable risk that a harmful consequence will follow (sometimes referred to as recklessness). In some cases, gross negligence may be adequate for establishing an international crime.[62] As discussed below, the major atrocity crimes address both objective and subjective elements.

Third, international criminal law recognizes circumstances that preclude wrongfulness. For example, if an offender establishes that he was acting in self-defense, the act will be regarded as justified. The act may also be excused in other situations, such as if the offender was a minor incapable of criminal intent, was mentally unsound, or was so intoxicated that his *mens rea* was negated. The defense that an offender was following superior orders (from either military or civilian authorities) is not an accepted excuse, but it may be taken into account in mitigating an offender's sentence. Offenders, however, can plea as an excuse that they acted out of necessity or under duress (*e.g.*, the offender feared for his life and had no alternative). Offenders may also be excused if they acted mistakenly regarding the facts of a situation, such as a reasonable belief that one is shooting an armed combatant rather than a defenseless civilian. By contrast, a mistake or ignorance in understanding the law normally is no excuse, a principle referred to as *ignorantia legis non excusat*.

Crime of Aggression

After World War II, both the International Military Tribunal (IMT) at Nuremberg and the International Military Tribunal for the Far East (IMTFE) at Tokyo tried individuals for crimes against peace or crimes of aggression. The IMT Charter provided that crimes against peace involved "planning, preparation, initiation or waging of a war of aggression, or a war in violation of international treaties, agreements or assurances, or participation in a Common Plan or Conspiracy for the accomplishment of any of the forego-

---

61. *See* GUENAEL METTRAUX, THE LAW OF COMMAND RESPONSIBILITY (2009).

62. *See* ANTONIO CASSESE, INTERNATIONAL CRIMINAL LAW 171–75 (2003).

ing."[63] An important issue at the time was whether resort to war had been banned under international law as of the 1930's and, if so, whether resort to war by government leaders constituted a crime for which they, in their personal capacity, could be punished. In the judgment rendered against the twenty-two Nuremberg defendants in 1946, the IMT reviewed evidence of the progressive banning of the resort to war under international law, including the 1928 General Treaty for the Renunciation of War (Pact of Paris or Kellogg–Briand Pact).[64] It then found: "All these expressions of opinion, and others that could be cited, so solemnly made, reinforce the construction which the Tribunal placed upon the Pact of Paris, that resort to a war of aggression is not merely illegal, but is criminal."[65] The IMT then determined that Hermann Göring, Rudoph Hess, Wilhelm Keitel, and other German leaders were guilty of the crime of aggression.

In 1946, the U.N. General Assembly affirmed the principles of law set forth in the IMT Charter.[66] Yet further efforts to define "aggression" proved problematic. Any definition was invariably linked to the right of states to use force in international relations under Article 2(4) of the U.N. Charter[67] and, while blatant examples of aggression could be readily agreed upon, more nuanced forms of aggression were politically controversial. The major powers generally sought wide latitude in their ability to conduct foreign relations and expressed concern that the Security Council also have latitude to preserve international peace and security. In 1974, the General Assembly adopted a resolution defining aggression,[68] which has served as a reference point for cases addressing the use of force in international law.[69] However, the resolution has been challenged as not reflecting customary international criminal law and is not viewed as comprehensive in scope.

From 1946 to the present, no international or national tribunal has conducted a trial for the crime of aggression; thus, greater content and specificity of the norm has not been achieved. The

---

63. Charter of the International Military Tribunal, art. 6(a), *annexed to* Agreement for the Prosecution and Punishment of the Major War Criminals of the European Axis, Aug. 8, 1945, 59 Stat. 1544, 82 U.N.T.S. 279 [hereinafter IMT Charter].

64. Aug. 27, 1928, 46 Stat. 2343, 94 L.N.T.S. 57.

65. Göring and Others, Judgment and Sentence (Int'l Military Trib. Sept. 30, 1946), *in* 22 TRIAL OF THE MAJOR WAR CRIMINALS BEFORE THE INTERNATIONAL MILI-TARY TRIBUNAL, NUREMBERG, 14 NOVEMBER 1945–1 OCTOBER 1946, 411 at 465 (1947).

66. *See* G.A. Res. 95(I) (Dec. 11, 1946).

67. *See* Chapter 14(A).

68. *See* G.A. Res. 3314 (Dec. 14, 1974); *see also* BENJAMIN B. FERENCZ, DEFINING INTERNATIONAL AGGRESSION: THE SEARCH FOR WORLD PEACE (1975) (2 vols.).

69. *See, e.g.,* Military and Paramilitary Activities in and against Nicaragua (Nicar. v. U.S.), 1986 I.C.J. 14, para. 195 (June 27).

International Criminal Court (ICC) will only exercise jurisdiction over such a crime after amendment of the Rome Statute.[70]

Most scholars believe that there must be criminal intent on the part of the individual to commit the act of aggression. According to the former president of the International Criminal Tribunal for the former Yugoslavia, "[i]t must be shown that the perpetrator intended to participate in aggression and was aware of the scope, significance, and consequences of the action taken or, at least, knowingly took the risk of bringing about the consequences of that action (*recklessness*)."[71] For example, in 1987 Iraqi aircraft attacked the *USS Stark* in the Persian Gulf, killing and injuring several U.S. servicemen and severely damaging the ship. If the responsible Iraqi officials truly did not intend to attack a U.S. ship in international waters, and instead thought they were attacking a belligerent Iranian warship, the requisite criminal intent for the crime of aggression did not exist. As it happened, the United States accepted Iraq's assertion that it did not intend to attack a U.S. ship, and the two states negotiated a claims agreement to settle the matter.

War Crimes

As discussed in more detail in Chapter 14(B), conventional and customary international law contain certain rules regarding how states may conduct themselves during an armed conflict (known as *jus in bello*). Not all violations of such law are war crimes; only serious violations qualify. For instance, a soldier's theft of a loaf of bread does not constitute a war crime even though the 1907 Hague Regulations state that private property is to be respected in times of war.[72] Determining exactly which violations qualify as war crimes may be simple (*e.g.*, the summary execution of prisoners of war), yet may also require a study of whether international or national tribunals have prosecuted similar violations as war crimes, or whether national legislation or military manuals indicate that such violations are criminal.

In general, war crimes may arise from the use of prohibited means or methods of warfare (*e.g.*, using poisoned weapons or intentionally shelling civilians), or from acts taken against persons not involved in active hostilities (*e.g.*, abusing interned civilians). The latter, when perpetrated in the course of an international armed conflict, are referred to as "grave breaches" of international humanitarian law. For example, the 1949 Geneva Convention on protection of civilians defines grave breaches as

70. *See infra* this chapter, Section E.

71. Cassese, *supra* note 62, at 115.

72. *See* Prosecutor v. Tadić, Decision on the Defence Motion for Interlocutory Appeal on Jurisdiction, Case No. IT–94–1–AR72, para. 94 (Int'l Crim. Trib. former Yugo. Oct. 2, 1995).

wilful killing, torture or inhuman treatment, including biological experiments, wilfully causing great suffering or serious injury to body or health, unlawful deportation or transfer or unlawful confinement of a protected person, compelling a protected person to serve in the forces of a hostile Power, or wilfully depriving a protected person of the rights of a fair and regular trial . . . , taking of hostages and extensive destruction and appropriation of property, not justified by military necessity and carried out unlawfully and wantonly.[73]

Such war crimes need not be perpetrated by soldiers; they can also be committed by civilians against enemy soldiers or civilians.

Traditionally, war crimes have been associated with serious violations committed during the course of an international armed conflict. Current law, however, indicates that an individual may also be criminally liable for violations committed in the course of an internal armed conflict.[74] Regardless, the conduct must be connected to an *armed conflict* (international or internal) in order to distinguish it from an ordinary criminal offense.

As with the crime of aggression, the individual must have a criminal intent, meaning an intent to bring about the consequences of the unlawful act. Such an intent is recognized in the Geneva Convention language quoted above by repeated use of the word "wilful." Similar language requiring intent may be found in other law of war treaties, such as Additional Protocol I to the 1949 Geneva Conventions.[75]

Unlike the crime of aggression, national and international tribunals have prosecuted individuals for war crimes on numerous occasions, such that there is a rich and growing body of case law that helps identify and clarify the law in this area. The IMT and IMTFE charters included jurisdiction over war crimes,[76] as have *ad hoc* international criminal tribunals created since that time. Further, the 1998 Rome Statute of the ICC sets forth in Article 8 an extensive list of acts that constitute war crimes, and the ICC has adopted "Elements of Crimes" that must be established in order to indict persons for war crimes.[77]

---

73. Geneva Convention Relative to the Protection of Civilian Persons in Time of War art. 147, Aug. 12, 1949, 6 U.S.T. 3526, 75 U.N.T.S. 287 [hereinafter Geneva Convention IV].

74. *See, e.g., Tadić, supra* note 72, paras. 96–134.

75. Protocol Additional to the Geneva Conventions of 12 August 1949, and Relating to the Protection of Victims of International Armed Conflicts arts. 11 &

85(3), June 8, 1977, 1125 U.N.T.S. 609 [hereinafter Protocol I].

76. *See, e.g.,* IMT Charter, *supra* note 63, art. 6(b).

77. *See* Rome Statute, *supra* note 22, art. 8; Report of the First Session of the Assembly of the Parties to the Rome Statute of the International Criminal Court, ICC Doc. ICC–ASP/1/3, pt. II(B), at 125–55 (Sept. 3–10, 2002) [hereinafter ICC Elements of Crimes].

Crimes Against Humanity

The IMT at Nuremberg also had jurisdiction over "crimes against humanity," which it defined as:

> murder, extermination, enslavement, deportation, and other inhumane acts committed against any civilian population, before or during the war, or persecutions on political, racial or religious grounds in execution of or in connection with any crime within the jurisdiction of the Tribunal, whether or not in violation of the domestic law of the country where perpetrated.[78]

Whereas at the time of World War II war crimes were firmly established as a part of international law, crimes against humanity was a relatively new concept that had not yet passed into customary international law. This presented an obstacle to the IMT, since one of the core principles of international criminal law is *nullum crimen sine lege*: a person may not be held criminally liable if he performed an act that was not a criminal offense at the time it was performed. Despite this principle, the IMT convicted several individuals of crimes against humanity, without explaining why such law was settled at the time the acts in question were committed. The novelty of the crime was somewhat tempered by the IMT Charter's requirement that it be committed "in execution of or in connection with" some other crime within the Tribunal's jurisdiction (such as war crimes), and by the tribunal's invocation of this crime only for acts that occurred during (and not prior to) the war.

In the aftermath of Nuremberg, the law on crimes against humanity developed such that it no longer required a link with an armed conflict. There has also emerged a notion that the act must not only be grave (*e.g.*, murder, extermination, enslavement, rape), but must be part of a "widespread or systematic attack" directed against a civilian population.[79] Thus, to establish this crime, a prosecutor normally must demonstrate a government policy favoring the commission or omission of an act; isolated or occasional acts are insufficient. While crimes against humanity can arise under customary international law from acts against enemy combatants, the statutes of contemporary international tribunals (including the ICC) limit such crimes to acts against civilians, which includes non-combatants (*i.e.*, captured or wounded soldiers who have laid down their arms). As with the crimes discussed above, the person committing the crime must intend to bring about the result of his acts, or at least be aware of the risk that such a result will ensue.[80]

---

78. IMT Charter, *supra* note 63, art. 6(c).

79. *See* Rome Statute, *supra* note 22, art. 7; *see also* ICC Elements of Crimes, *supra* note 77, at 116–24.

80. *See, e.g.*, Prosecutor v. Blaskić, Judgment, Case No. IT–95–14–T, paras. 247 & 251 (Int'l Crim. Trib. former Yugo. Mar. 3, 2000).

Genocide

The IMT did not have jurisdiction over the crime of genocide. Only with the adoption of the 1948 Convention Against Genocide was genocide (whether committed in time of peace or war) declared a crime under international law, which states undertake to prevent and punish, including by enactment of necessary legislation.[81] As noted in Chapter 10, the convention defines genocide as acts, such as killing, injuring, or forcibly transferring persons, committed "with intent to destroy, in whole or in part, a national, ethnical, racial or religious group.... "[82] The convention criminalizes not only genocide, but also conspiracy and attempt to commit genocide, incitement to genocide, and complicity in genocide. Moreover, the convention applies to both government officials and private individuals.[83]

Genocide has rarely been charged in national proceedings, but recent *ad hoc* criminal tribunals have charged and convicted individuals of genocide. For example, in the *Akayesu* case, the International Criminal Tribunal for Rwanda (ICTR) convicted a former Rwandan mayor, Jean Paul Akayesu, of genocide (as well as war crimes and crimes against humanity) for the killing of more than 2,000 Tutsis in Akayesu's commune.[84] In the course of doing so, the ICTR defined each of the four groups identified in the convention (national, ethnical, racial, and religious). For instance, an "ethnical" group's members share a common language or culture, while a racial group is one that shares hereditary physical traits regardless of language, culture, citizenship or religion.[85] Yet the ICTR did not limit the crime to these four groups. Rather, it asserted that "any stable and permanent group" could qualify for protection. The ICTR also clarified that rape and sexual violence can constitute genocide in the same way as other acts of serious bodily or mental harm, so long as such acts were committed with an intent to destroy a particular group.[86] Moreover, the individual charged must intend to produce the act in question, though such intent may be inferred from various facts.[87] While the ICTR trial chamber asserted that incitement or instigation of genocide must be "direct and public," the appeals chamber determined that instigation has a broader ambit, at least under the relevant provision of the ICTR

---

81. *See* Convention on the Prevention and Punishment of the Crime of Genocide arts. I & V, Dec. 9, 1948, 78 U.N.T.S. 277.

82. *Id.*, art. II.

83. *Id.*, arts. III & IV.

84. Prosecutor v. Akayesu, Judgment, Case No. ICTR–96–4–T (Int'l Crim. Trib. Rwanda Sept. 2, 1998), *reprinted in* 37 I.L.M. 1399 (1998).

85. *Id.*, paras. 513–514.

86. *Id.*, paras. 596–98.

87. *Id.*, paras. 498, 523.

statute.[88] In a separate case before the ICTR, the former Prime Minister of Rwanda, Jean Kambanda, pled guilty to genocide, the first such plea before an international criminal tribunal, and the first genocide conviction of a head of government.

In addition to the jurisprudence emerging from *ad hoc* tribunals, the 1998 Rome Statute of the ICC repeats in Article 6 the definition of genocide found in the convention, while the ICC's "Elements of Crimes" indicates the elements to be established when indicting persons for such a crime.[89]

E.   International Criminal Tribunals

As a means of prosecuting war crimes, crimes against humanity, and genocide, the global community has over the past twenty years established *ad hoc* international criminal tribunals, special courts of a quasi-international character, and, perhaps most significantly, a permanent International Criminal Court (ICC). Such tribunals are important for promoting deterrence of and retribution for atrocities, but also (through case law) for clarifying and developing principles of international criminal law.

Ad Hoc *U.N. Tribunals for Yugoslavia and Rwanda*

In the early 1990's, the U.N. Security Council created two *ad hoc* international criminal tribunals, one relating to the former Yugoslavia and the other to Rwanda. These tribunals were not created by treaty. Rather, they were established pursuant to two Security Council resolutions anchored in the Council's powers to maintain international peace and security under Chapter VII of the U.N. Charter. The two resolutions adopted "statutes" for each tribunal, which serve as the principal instruments for determining the tribunals' mandate, organization, and powers.[90] The jurisdiction of both tribunals covers war crimes, crimes against humanity, and genocide (not the crime of aggression), but is limited to crimes committed during certain times and in certain places. Both tribunals share the same appeals chamber, so as to promote consistency in the decisions of the two tribunals. All U.N. members are obligated to cooperate with the tribunals on matters such as gathering of evidence and apprehension of indictees. The tribunals are funded through the United Nations and donations from states. Their 2010–11 budgets were approximately $300 million for the ICTY and $245 million for the ICTR.

---

88.   *See* Prosecutor v. Akayesu, Case No. ICTR–96–4–A, paras. 470–83 (Int'l Crim. Trib. Rwanda June 1, 2001).

89.   *See* Rome Statute, *supra* note 22, art. 6; ICC Elements of Crimes, *supra* note 77, at 113–15.

90.   *See* S.C. Res. 827 (May 25, 1993) (adopting the ICTY statute); S.C. Res. 955 (Nov. 8, 1994) (adopting the ICTR statute).

The International Criminal Tribunal for the former Yugoslavia (ICTY) has jurisdiction over war crimes, crimes against humanity, and genocide occurring since 1991 in the territory of what was once the Socialist Federal Republic of Yugoslavia (what is now Bosnia–Herzegovina, Croatia, Kosovo, Macedonia, Montenegro, Slovenia, and Serbia). The ICTY is based in The Hague, The Netherlands, and consists of a prosecutor's office, a registry, and judges (who elect one of their own to serve as president of the ICTY), all located in a building maintained under tight security. The prosecutor's office is headed by a chief prosecutor, and is responsible for investigating, indicting, and prosecuting persons who have committed crimes within the ICTY's jurisdiction. The registry handles all administrative aspects of the ICTY, including personnel, security and public relations. The judges preside over trials, determine guilt or innocence, and sentence the guilty. Judges sit in one of three trial chambers (with no jury) or on the appeals chamber. There are sixteen permanent judges elected by the U.N. General Assembly for a term of four years (all sixteen may be re-elected). Further, a maximum of nine *ad litem* judges, drawn from a pool of twenty-seven judges elected by the General Assembly, may serve upon appointment of the Secretary–General for one or more specific trials for a period of up to three years. An ICTY prison is maintained within a local Dutch prison, where persons indicted by the ICTY are kept while their trials are pending. If an indictee is convicted, he or she is transferred to a cooperating state where the person serves out the sentence in that state's prison system. The ICTY is not empowered to issue the death penalty, but can issue life sentences.

As of mid–2011, the ICTY had indicted 161 persons and concluded proceedings against 126 of them (2 indictees were in pre-trial proceedings, 17 indictees were on trial, and 16 indictees were in appeal proceedings). Of the 126 proceedings that had been concluded: 20 indictments were withdrawn by the prosecutor; 10 indictees died prior to transfer to the ICTY; 6 indictees died in ICTY custody; 9 were acquitted by the trial chamber; 4 were acquitted by the appeals chamber; 20 indictees pled guilty, while 44 indictees were convicted after trial (sentences ranged from 2 to 40 years); and 13 were transferred to national jurisdictions for prosecution.[91]

In the course of these ICTY proceedings, more than 4,000 witnesses testified in ICTY proceedings. The outcome of a recently completed trial provides a flavor for the decisions of the ICTY:

> The case of *Prosecutor v. Ante Gotovina et al.*—with three accused—involves nine counts of crimes against humanity and

91. See ICTY, *Key Figures of ICTY Cases* (Sept. 13, 2011).

violations of the laws or customs of war allegedly committed against the Serb population in 14 municipalities in the southern portion of the Krajina region in the Republic of Croatia in 1995. This is the first trial before the Tribunal involving crimes allegedly committed against the Serb population in Croatia. The judgement, which was tentatively anticipated to be rendered in March, was delivered on 15 April 2011. Ante Gotovina, who held the rank of Colonel General in the Croatian army and was the Commander of the Split Military District, and Mladen Marka, who held the position of Assistant Minister of Interior in charge of Special Police matters, were convicted of persecution, deportation, plunder, wanton destruction, two counts of murder, inhumane acts and cruel treatment. They were sentenced to 24 and 18 years of imprisonment, respectively. Ivan ermak, who was the Commander of the Knin Garrison, was acquitted of all charges.[92]

While at one time there were many ICTY indictees that were at large, over the years fugitives were brought into custody due to arrests by their own or third-party governments, or from indictee's own surrender. Even high ranking political and military officials were taken into custody, including former Serbian President Slobodan Milosević (transferred to the ICTY by Serbia in 2001), former President of "Republika Srpska" Radovan Karadzić (transferred in 2008), and former head of the Bosnian Serb Army General Ratko Mladić (transferred in 2011). The last fugitive (the former president of the "Republic of Serbian Krajina," Goran Hadzić) was arrested by Serbia in July 2011.

The International Criminal Tribunal for Rwanda (ICTR) has jurisdiction over war crimes, crimes against humanity, and genocide occurring in Rwanda and its neighboring states in 1994. Having been created just one year later, the ICTR was closely modeled after the ICTY. The ICTR prosecutor's office, registry, and judges are based in Arusha, Tanzania. As of mid–2011, the ICTR had issued about 90 indictments: 2 indictments were withdrawn by the prosecutor; 2 indictees had died in ICTR custody, 1 indictee was awaiting trial, 6 indictees were at trial, 17 indictees were in appeal proceedings, 10 indictees were acquitted, 42 indictees pled guilty or were convicted after trial; 3 were transferred to national jurisdictions for prosecution; and 9 indictees remained at large.[93]

In December 2010, the U.N. Security Council decided to establish an "International Residual Mechanism for Criminal Tribunals" charged with finishing the remaining tasks of the ICTY and ICTR,

92. Letter from the ICTY President to the President of the Security Council, U.N. Doc. S/2011/316, para. 25 (May 18, 2011).

93. *See* ICTR, Status of Cases, *at* <http://www.unictr.org/Cases/Statusof Cases/tabid/204/Default.aspx>.

and to maintain their respective legacies.[94] The Residual Mechanism operates in accordance with its own Statute (annexed to the Security Council's resolution) which, for example, precludes it from issuing new indictments, except against those who interfere with the administration of justice or give false testimony. At the same time, the Residual Mechanism will continue to exercise the jurisdiction, rights, obligations and essential functions of the ICTY and ICTR so as to complete their work. The Residual Mechanism's branch for the ICTR is scheduled to commence operations in July 2012, while its branch for the ICTY will commence operations in July 2013.

Permanent International Criminal Court

Creation of the ICC. After the creation of the ICTY and ICTR in the early 1990's, a movement rapidly developed for the creation of a permanent International Criminal Court (ICC). Most states, however, were not interested in creating such an institution through Security Council fiat; indeed, concerns had already been expressed about the propriety of a political organ consisting of just a few states (the Security Council) creating *ad hoc* judicial bodies (the ICTY and ICTR) capable of binding all states. Rather, states coalesced around the idea of creating a treaty-based ICC, such that states could affirmatively choose whether to join. For many states, only an institution built upon widespread consent could engender the political and moral authority necessary for an ICC to succeed. Consequently, negotiations commenced on the drafting of such a treaty, which culminated with the adoption of the Rome Statute in July 1998[95] and its entry into force on July 1, 2002. As of 2011, 115 states were parties to the Rome Statute, not including the United States.

The ICC is based in the Hague and its structure is similar to that of the tripartite *ad hoc* tribunals: a prosecutor's office charged with investigating, indicting, and prosecuting persons suspected of crimes; a registry responsible for administrative aspects; and a group of judges sitting at trial and appellate levels. The Rome Statute parties elect eighteen judges for staggered terms, so that one-third of the terms expire every three years. In 2003, the contracting states unanimously elected Luis Moreno–Ocampo of Argentina as the first ICC Chief Prosecutor. In 2012, he will be succeeded by Fatou Bensouda of Gambia.

Jurisdiction. Although the ICC has a wider range of jurisdiction than the *ad hoc* tribunals, its jurisdiction is nevertheless

---

94. S.C. Res. 1966 (Dec. 22, 2010).

95. *See* Rome Statute, *supra* note 22; *see also* Otto Trifferer, Commentary on the Rome Statute of the International Criminal Court (2d ed. 2008).

limited. First, the ICC only has jurisdiction over crimes committed after the Rome Statute entered into force;[96] crimes committed prior to July 1, 2002 do not fall within its ambit. States who ratify or accede to the Rome Statute after July 1, 2002, are only exposed to the ICC's jurisdiction after that point, unless they grant the ICC jurisdiction retroactively to July 1, 2002.[97]

Second, the ICC only has jurisdiction over "the most serious crimes of concern to the international community as a whole"— specifically war crimes, crimes against humanity, and genocide.[98] Other crimes, such as terrorism or drug trafficking, were consciously excluded from the Rome Statute, since some states believed the ICC should remain narrowly focused in order to succeed.

Third, the 1998 Rome Statute contemplated the activation of jurisdiction over the crime of aggression at a future point when the crime would be defined and the conditions for its operation would be elaborated.[99] In 2010, at the first ICC "review conference" held in Kampala, Uganda, the ICC states parties adopted four important amendments to the Rome Statute to that effect, amendments which must now be ratified by each state party.[100] The amendments essentially equate an "act of aggression" with a violation of Article 2(4) of the U.N. Charter, though illuminated by reference to language from the General Assembly's 1974 Definition of Aggression.[101] Further, the amendments provide that the "crime of aggression" is the "planning, preparation, initiation or execution" of an act of aggression by a senior leader, but only in situations where the act "by its character, gravity and scale" constitutes a "manifest violation" of the U.N. Charter.[102] While a situation involving aggression can be referred to the ICC by the U.N. Security Council, in the face of inaction by the Security Council the ICC prosecutor can initiate his or her own investigation and indictments.[103] These amendments provide greater clarity to the ICC's jurisdiction over the crime of aggression, but the states parties at Kampala decided that such jurisdiction still would not be activated until they reach a further decision sometime after 2016 and until at least thirty states parties have ratified the amendments.[104] Even then, the jurisdiction will not extend to states that are not parties to the Rome Statute (such as the United States), nor to state parties who file a declaration indicating that they do not accept such jurisdiction.[105]

---

96. *Id.*, art. 11(1).

97. *Id.*, arts. 11(2) & 12(3).

98. *Id.*, arts. 5–8.

99. *Id.*, art. 5(2).

100. *See* First ICC Review Conference: Resolution and Declarations, 49 I.L.M. 1325 (2010).

101. *Id.*, ICC Doc. RC/Res. 6, annex I, art. 8*bis*, para. 2.

102. *Id.*, art. 8*bis*, para. 1.

103. Id., art. 15*bis*, paras. 6–8.

104. *Id.*, art. 15*bis*, paras. 2–3; art. 15*ter*, paras. 2–3.

105. *Id.*, art. 15*bis*, paras. 4–5; *see* Stefan Barriga & Leena Grover, *A His-*

Finally, under Articles 12 and 13 of the Rome Statute, the ICC may only investigate and prosecute acts in the following situations:

- the state where the alleged crime was committed is a party to the Rome Statute (including where the crime was committed on an aircraft or vessel of the state);

- the person suspected of committing the crime is a national of a party to the Rome Statute;

- the state where the alleged crime was committed, or whose national is suspected of committing the crime, consents *ad hoc* to the jurisdiction of the ICC (*e.g.*, although not a party to the Rome Statute, Côte d'Ivoire (or Ivory Coast) filed a declaration in April 2003 with the ICC stating that it "accepts the jurisdiction of the Court for the purposes of identifying, investigating and trying the perpetrators and accomplices of acts committed on Ivorian territory since the events of 19 September 2002"); or

- the crime is referred to the ICC by the Security Council under Chapter VII of the U.N. Charter (*e.g.*, in March 2005 the Security Council referred to the ICC crimes allegedly occurring in the Darfur region of Sudan[106] and in February 2011 referred the Libyan government's violence against civilians in Libya[107]).

Complementarity. One important design feature of the ICC is the concept of "complementarity," which means that the ICC will only commence an investigation into a potential crime if there is no state with jurisdiction that is willing and genuinely able to carry out an investigation or prosecution.[108] The fact that a state has investigated a matter and decided against prosecution is not a basis for the ICC to exercise jurisdiction, unless there is something disingenuous about the state's conduct. In considering whether to investigate the possibility of crimes in Sudan, the ICC prosecutor conducted an assessment in 2004–05 of Sudan's laws, institutions, and procedures, and interviewed numerous Sudanese government officials. Based on this assessment, the prosecutor determined that possible atrocities in Sudan fell within the jurisdiction of the ICC notwithstanding the principle of complementarity, given the absence of criminal proceedings in Sudan relating to cases on which the prosecutor was likely to focus. The prosecutor noted that the

toric Breakthrough on the Crime of Aggression, 105 Am. J. Int'l L. 517 (2011).

106. *See* S.C. Res. 1593 (Mar. 31, 2005).

107. *See* S.C. Res. 1970 (Feb. 26, 2011).

108. *See* Rome Statute, *supra* note 22, art. 17(1); *see also* David A. Kaye, *Justice Beyond the Hague: Supporting the Prosecution of International Crimes in National Courts* (Council on Foreign Relations, June 2011); Jann Kleffner, Complementarity in the Rome Statute and National Criminal Jurisdictions (2009).

assessment was part of an ongoing process and that it was possible at a later time that the ICC would be precluded from pursuing cases if there were "genuine national investigations or prosecutions."[109]

Progress to Date. For crimes over which the ICC has jurisdiction, the prosecutor can initiate an investigation on the basis of a referral from any state party, a referral from the U.N. Security Council, or by the prosecutor himself *proprio motu* on the basis of information received from individuals or organizations. As of 2011, three states parties to the Rome Statute (Uganda, the Democratic Republic of the Congo (DRC), and the Central African Republic (CAR)) had referred to the ICC situations concerning alleged atrocities by rebel groups occurring on their territories, while the Security Council had referred the situations in Sudan (Darfur) and in Libya. Further, a pre-trial chamber had granted the prosecutor authorization to open investigation *proprio motu* concerning the violence that occurred in Kenya during its 2007 elections and in the Ivory Coast during its 2010–2011 elections.

As of the end of 2011, no trials had yet been completed, but several were in either pre-trial or trial phases. With respect to Uganda, five warrants of arrest were issued against the top five members of the Lords Resistance Army, but one of those indictees died and the four others remained at large. With respect to the DRC, four cases were being heard before ICC trial courts against alleged leaders of rebel groups, with four indictees in custody and one still at large. For the CAR, one case had been initiated against the commander of the Movement for the Liberation of Congo, who was in custody. Four cases were also filed relating to the situation in Sudan and two indictees were in custody, while three remained at large, including the Sudan's head of state, President Omar Hassan Ahmad Al Bashir. For Libya, a case was initiated against three indictees: Libyan leader Muammar Gaddafi, his son Saif Al–Islam Gaddafi, and his brother-in-law Abdullah Al–Senussi. The proceedings against Gaddafi were terminated upon his death in Libya in November 2011; the other two reportedly were in custody in Libya, but had not been transferred to the ICC.

For the Kenya situation, two cases had been filed and six indictees had appeared before the ICC. With respect to the Ivory Coast, its former president—Laurent Gbagbo—was indicted for crimes against humanity (murder, rape and other forms of sexual violence, persecution and "other inhuman acts") and was extradit-

109. Report of the Prosecutor of the International Criminal Court, Mr. Luis Moreno Ocampo, to the Security Council Pursuant to UNSCR 1593, at 4 (June 29, 2005), *at* <http://www.icc-cpi.int/>.

ed to The Hague in November 2011, making him the first former head of state to be tried by the ICC.

U.S. Attitude to the ICC. As discussed in Chapter 3(A), the United States initially signed the Rome Statute, but then informed the depositary that it did not intend to seek ratification. While that failure to ratify ensures that the ICC will not have jurisdiction based solely on atrocities having occurred in the United States or by U.S. nationals, it is possible that the ICC could have jurisdiction over atrocities committed by U.S. personnel abroad in states that have either ratified the Rome Statute or consented *ad hoc* to ICC jurisdiction. Consequently, starting in 2001, the U.S. government embarked on various initiatives to ensure that U.S. personnel abroad could not be placed before ICC jurisdiction. The principal legal device underlying these initiatives is the American Service-members' Protection Act (ASPA),[110] which contains four main elements.

First, ASPA section 2004 prohibits (1) any U.S. court and any state or local government from responding to a request for cooperation from, or otherwise providing support to, the ICC; (2) U.S. agencies from transferring a letter rogatory or any other ICC request for cooperation to the U.S. entity to whom it is addressed; (3) the federal government, and any state or local government, from extraditing a person from the United States to the ICC; and (4) ICC investigative activities on U.S. territory. Section 2006 requires the president to ensure that procedures are in place to prevent the transfer of classified national security information to the ICC. At the same time, under sections 2011–2012, the president may on a case-by-case basis decide to engage in cooperation prohibited under sections 2004 and 2006, so long as this authority is not delegated and is reported to Congress. Moreover, section 2015 essentially allows U.S. cooperation with the ICC with respect to the prosecution of foreign nationals.

Second, ASPA prohibits the deployment of U.S. forces with U.N. peacekeeping missions unless they are protected from the ICC. Section 2005 states that it is U.S. policy to seek permanent exemption from the ICC for U.S. forces participating in U.N. peacekeeping operations. The section bars U.S. participation in such operations unless the president certifies that (1) the U.N. Security Council exempted U.S. forces from ICC jurisdiction in the Council's authorizing resolution; (2) the ICC does not have jurisdiction within the states in which U.S. forces will be deployed; (3) the states where U.S. forces will be deployed have entered into bilateral agreements with the United States agreeing not to transfer U.S.

---

110. 2002 Supplemental Appropriations Act for Further Recovery from and Response to Terrorist Attacks on the United States, Pub. L. No. 107–206, §§ 2001–2015, 116 Stat. 820 (2002) [hereinafter ASPA].

personnel to the ICC; or (4) notwithstanding a lack of protection from the ICC, the U.S. national interest justifies participation in the operation.

The United States sought but failed to obtain from the Security Council a permanent exemption for military forces of states that are not a party to the Rome Statute. The United States then proposed that the Security Council take advantage of Article 16 of the Rome Statute, which provides:

> No investigation or prosecution may be commenced or proceeded with under this Statute for a period of 12 months after the Security Council, in a resolution adopted under Chapter VII of the Charter of the United Nations, has requested the Court to that effect; that request may be renewed by the Council under the same conditions.

In response, the Security Council adopted a resolution in 2002 requesting

> that the ICC, if a case arises involving current or former officials or personnel from a contributing State not a Party to the Rome Statute over acts or omissions relating to a United Nations established or authorized operation, shall for a twelve-month period starting 1 July 2002 not commence or proceed with investigation or prosecution of any such case, unless the Security Council decides otherwise.[111]

The same Security Council request to the ICC was adopted in 2003.[112] In 2004, however, the other members of the Security Council resisted renewing the request, in part as a reaction to reports of U.S. abuse of Iraqi prisoners of war. Consequently, the Security Council's request lapsed.

Third, beginning in July 2003, ASPA section 2007 barred U.S. military assistance to states that are a party to the Rome Statute. Moreover, a separate U.S. law passed in late 2004 deprived such states of U.S. economic support funds, which accounted for about U.S. $2.5 billion of U.S. foreign assistance in 2005.[113] Under these laws, such military and economic assistance was prohibited unless: (1) the president waived the prohibition in the U.S. national interest with respect to a particular state; (2) the president waived the prohibition with respect to a state that has entered into a bilateral agreement with the United States agreeing not to transfer U.S.

---

111. S.C. Res. 1422, para. 1 (July 12, 2002).

112. *See* S.C. Res. 1487, para. 1 (June 12, 2003).

113. *See* Foreign Operations, Export Financing, and Related Programs Appropriations Act of 2005, § 574, *as enacted by* Division D of the Consolidated Appropriations Act of 2005, Pub. Law No. 108–447 (2004).

force personnel to the ICC; or (3) the state was a member of NATO, was a major non-NATO ally,[114] or was Taiwan.

Because of these provisions, many states risked losing U.S. military and economic assistance if they ratified or acceded to the Rome Statute without agreeing to exempt U.S. personnel. The United States concluded bilateral agreements designed to satisfy the ASPA with 100 states.[115] In the course of doing so, the United States suspended (for differing periods of time) all military assistance to thirty-five states (*e.g.*, Colombia, Croatia, and Ecuador) that had refused to conclude such agreements.[116] The United States maintained that these agreements were permissible because Article 98(2) of the Rome Statute provides:

> The Court may not proceed with a request for surrender which would require the requested State to act inconsistently with its obligations under international agreements pursuant to which the consent of a sending State is required to surrender a person of that State to the Court, unless the Court can first obtain the cooperation of the sending State for the giving of consent for the surrender.[117]

These "Article 98" agreements, however, were unpopular and President Bush had to issue numerous waivers for countries that declined to conclude such agreements. In 2008, ASPA was amended to eliminate such funding restrictions.

Fourth, the most controversial ASPA provision (section 2008)—which has prompted some to refer to ASPA as the "Hague Invasion Act"—provides that the president "is authorized to use all means necessary and appropriate to bring about the release of any person described in subsection (b) who is being detained or imprisoned by, on behalf of, or at the request of the International Criminal Court."[118] Such persons include U.S. government employees and employees of the governments of U.S. allies.[119]

F. Hybrid Courts

In addition to the ICTY, ICTR, and ICC, various smaller tribunals or courts have been established to address serious viola-

---

114. Major non-NATO allies are designated in accordance with section 517 of the Foreign Assistance Act of 1961, 22 U.S.C. § 2321k (2000). Such allies include Australia, Bahrain, Egypt, Israel, Japan, Jordan, New Zealand, and South Korea.

115. *See* U.S. Dep't of State Press Release, U.S. Signs 100th Article 98 Agreement (May 3, 2005).

116. *See* Elizabeth Becker, *U.S. Suspends Aid to 35 Countries over New In-*

ternational Court, N.Y. Times, July 2, 2003, at A12 (reporting that U.S. $47.6 million in aid and U.S. $613,000 in military education programs were affected); Presidential Determination No. 2003–27 (July 1, 2003).

117. Rome Statute, *supra* note 22, art. 98(2).

118. ASPA, *supra* note 110, § 2008(a).

119. *Id.* § 2008(b).

tions of international humanitarian law. Such tribunals or courts are often not international in the sense of being independent of a national legal system, yet they have certain design features that allow international participation as a means of promoting meaningful accountability.[120]

Cambodia Extraordinary Chambers

The Khmer Rouge, a communist organization that governed Cambodia from 1975 to 1979, murdered, starved, and exposed Cambodians to forced labor resulting in the death of an estimated 1.7 million people. (When these deaths are taken as a proportion of the total population, the Khmer Rouge was the most lethal regime of the twentieth century). In December 1978, Vietnamese troops invaded Cambodia and deposed the Khmer Rouge. The Vietnamese, however, were assisted by defections from the Khmer Rouge, while other Khmer Rouge members retreated to the west where they continued to control a portion of Cambodia. Consequently, no members of the Khmer Rouge regime were brought to justice. Vietnam ultimately left Cambodia after installing a government, but civil strife continued for more than a decade. In 1991, the Cambodian political factions signed an agreement calling for elections and disarmament. The remaining Khmer Rouge members fought against the elections and the result, yet most members had surrendered or been captured by 1999.

In 2001, Cambodia enacted a law creating "extraordinary chambers" in its courts to try former leaders of the Khmer Rouge, which the U.N. General Assembly welcomed.[121] Further, the United Nations and Cambodia in 2003 signed an agreement on U.N. involvement with these extraordinary chambers.[122] The chambers have jurisdiction over serious violations of Cambodian criminal law and international humanitarian law committed from April 1975 to January 1979. The trial chamber consists of three Cambodian judges and two international judges, while the appeals chamber consists of four Cambodian judges and three international judges. The foreign judges are appointed by Cambodia's Supreme Council of the Magistracy upon nomination by the U.N. secretary-general. A decision of the trial chamber requires an affirmative vote of at least four judges, while the appeals chamber requires an affirmative vote of at least five judges. There are foreign and Cambodian "co-

---

120. *See generally* INTERNATIONALIZED CRIMINAL COURTS (Cesare Romano et al., eds. 2004); Laura Dickinson, *The Promise of Hybrid Courts*, 97 AM. J. INT'L L. 295 (2003).

121. *See* G.A. Res. 57/228B (May 13, 2003).

122. *See* Agreement Concerning the Prosecution Under Cambodian Law of Crimes Committed During the Period of Democratic Kampuchea, Cambodia–U.N., June 6, 2003, *at* <http://www.cambodia.gov.kh/krt/english/draft%20agreement.htm>.

prosecutors" who appear in the cases, and foreign and Cambodian "co-investigating judges" who investigate cases. The chamber's office of administration is headed by a Cambodian director and a foreign deputy director appointed by the U.N. secretary-general. The maximum penalty that can be issued is life imprisonment.

As of 2011, five indictees were in custody: three were in trial; one had her proceedings suspended for health reasons; and one was appealing a sentence of 35 years' imprisonment. Unfortunately, many significant Khmer Rouge leaders have died, included its leader during 1975–79, Pol Pot.

East Timor Special Panels

In August 1999, the people of East Timor opted by referendum for independence from Indonesian rule. Immediately after the vote, extensive violence broke out in which East Timorese militias who were opposed to independence attacked East Timorese civilians, unchecked (and sometimes assisted) by Indonesian military and police. Some estimates indicated that 2,000 people were murdered and 500,000 were forced to flee their homes, alongside widespread destruction and looting of property. A U.N. Transitional Administration in East Timor (UNTAET) was then established to administer East Timor until it became stable enough to function as a fully independent nation.[123]

UNTAET determined that it was important to bring the perpetrators of the atrocities to justice, but the East Timor judicial system was very weak, with few experienced judges and lawyers, and poor facilities. Consequently, UNTAET, in conjunction with a national consultative council of East Timorese, issued regulations that created a system of district courts for East Timor. The Dili District Court was granted exclusive jurisdiction over war crimes, crimes against humanity, genocide and other serious crimes (murder, sexual offenses, and torture), so long as they were committed between January 1 and October 25, 1999. The regulations also created special panels within the Dili District Court to exercise this jurisdiction, composed of both East Timorese and international judges.[124] Thus, although the panels were part of the East Timor national court system (*e.g.*, appeals from the panels were made to East Timor courts), each panel consisted of one Timorese and two foreign judges. Further, a serious crimes unit was created to conduct investigations and indict persons for prosecution before the special panels. Finally, the regulations called for foreign prosecutors and judges to assist local lawyers. When East Timor became an

123. *See* S.C. Res. 1272 (Oct. 25, 1999).

124. *See* UNTAET Regulation No. 2000/11 on the Organization of Courts in East Timor (Mar. 6, 2000), *at* <http://www.un.org/peace/etimor/untaetR/Reg 11.pdf>.

independent country in May 2002, UNTAET and the consultative council ceased to exist, but the system for the special panels was maintained.

Although hampered by shortages of resources and staff, the serious crimes unit filed 95 indictments with the special panels covering 391 persons. The special panels convicted 84 individuals for atrocities pursuant to 55 trial proceedings that many regarded as conforming to international standards. At the same time, critics noted that the special panels were unable to bring to justice persons located outside East Timor, including high-level Indonesian indictees, such as the former Indonesian Minister of Defence and Commander of the Indonesian National Military (TNI), several high-ranking TNI commanders, and the former Governor of East Timor.[125] Due to lack of funding, the special panels ceased operating in 2006.[126]

Supreme Iraqi Criminal Tribunal

After the 2003 U.S.-led intervention in Iraq, coalition authorities appointed an Iraqi Governing Council consisting of local Iraqi leaders. Shortly after its creation, the council decided to establish a special criminal tribunal to try high-level officials of former Iraqi President Saddam Hussein's Baath Party for crimes committed under his reign. In December 2003, the Governing Council issued a "Statute of the Iraqi Special Tribunal."[127] The statute established a tribunal with jurisdiction over any Iraqi national or resident who, from July 1968 to May 2003, committed genocide, crimes against humanity, or serious war crimes, or who violated specified Iraqi laws (*e.g.*, using military force against an Arab country). The tribunal consisted of one or more trial chambers (five judges each), an appeals chamber (nine judges), investigative judges, a prosecutor's department, and an administrative department.[128]

As a general matter, the personnel of the tribunal were to be Iraqi nationals. Yet the statute provided that the Iraqi Governing Council[129] may appoint non-Iraqi judges. Further, the tribunal president was required to appoint non-Iraqi nationals to act in an advisory capacity to (or as observers of) the trial and appeals chambers, and provide assistance and monitor the tribunal's due

---

125. *See* Report to the Secretary–General of the Commission of Experts to Review the Prosecution of Serious Violations of Human Rights in Timor–Leste (the then East Timor) in 1999 (May 26, 2005), U.N. Doc. S/2005/458, annex II (July 15, 2005).

126. *See* Caitlin Reiger & Marieke Wierda, The Serious Crimes Process in Timor-Leste: In Retrospect (2006).

127. Statute of the Iraqi Special Tribunal, Dec. 10, 2003, *reprinted in* 43 I.L.M. 231 (2004) [hereinafter Iraqi Special Tribunal Statute].

128. *Id.*, arts. 1, 3–4, & 10–14

129. The Iraqi Governing Council was created during the coalition occupation of Iraq. It has since been disbanded and replaced by the current Iraqi government.

process standards. The chief tribunal investigative judge was also required to appoint non-Iraqi nationals to act in an advisory capacity or as observers with respect to the investigation and prosecution of cases (for the same purposes as above).[130]

The statute provided various rights to defendants, including the presumption of innocence, access to counsel, a public trial, adequate time to prepare a defense, the opportunity to present evidence and cross-examine prosecution witnesses, and a prohibition against self-incrimination. Penalties that may be imposed on defendants were set forth in the Iraqi criminal code of 1969, which includes life imprisonment and the death penalty.[131]

Due to concerns that the tribunal had been established by an occupying force, the Iraqi Interim Government passed a new statute in 2005, built upon the earlier statute, which changed the tribunal's name to the "Supreme Iraqi Criminal Tribunal."[132] The tribunal remained an independent judicial body, but was not required under the new law to appoint non-Iraqi nationals as advisers (it continued to permit the discretionary appointment of non-Iraqi judges). Thereafter, the tribunal proceeded with the trials of former Iraqi President Saddam Hussein, former Vice President Taha Yassin Ramadan, former deputy Prime Minister Tariq Aziz, a senior official named Ali Hassan al-Majid (also known as "Chemical Ali"), and other former senior officials of Saddam Hussein's regime. Hussein himself was found guilty on November 5, 2006, of charges relating to a massacre at the town of Dujail. After an appeal was rejected, Hussein was executed by hanging on December 30. Other defendants were also convicted and sentenced either to death or to life imprisonment; one defendant, the former governor of Mosul (Taher Tawfiq Al-ani) was released due to insufficient evidence.

Kosovar Special Panels

In March/April 1999, NATO states conducted an extensive bombing campaign against the Federal Republic of Yugoslavia (Serbia & Montenegro) to prevent its government from engaging in ethnic cleansing and atrocities in the autonomous province of Kosovo. The intervention led to the deployment of a U.N. Interim Administration in Kosovo (UNMIK) to administer the province until the situation could be stabilized. Years of civil conflict, however, had left the local judicial system in disarray; resources were scarce and trained judges or lawyers were inexperienced. At the

---

130. Iraqi Special Tribunal Statute, *supra* note 127, arts. 4(d), 6(b), 6(c), 7(n), 7(o), & 28.

131. *Id.*, arts. 20 & 24.

132. *See* Law of the Supreme Iraqi Criminal Tribunal, Law No. 10, Official Gazette of the Republic of Iraq (Oct. 18, 2005). The law and other information on the tribunal is available at <http://www.loc.gov/law/help/hussein/index.php>.

same time, numerous persons were being held in custody on suspicion of having committed atrocities.

Consequently, U.N. administrators promulgated regulations allowing foreign judges to sit with Kosovar judges on special panels within the Kosovar court system, and allowing foreign lawyers to participate in the criminal proceedings.[133] The regulations provided that the courts apply local law so long as it did not conflict with human rights standards present in international law.[134] Thereafter, Kosovar courts conducted numerous trials for war crimes. After Kosovo declared independence in 2008, a new law was passed replacing the panels with Kosovo national courts in which judges and prosecutors from a European Union Rule of Law Mission in Kosovo (EULEX) play a role.

Sierra Leone Special Court

After extensive efforts by the Economic Community of West African States, the Organization of African Unity, the United Nations, and interested states, the government of Sierra Leone and the Revolutionary United Front (RUF) signed a peace agreement in July 1999 to end the country's civil war.[135] In addition to providing for a cease-fire between the parties and for disarmament of the RUF, the agreement granted an "absolute and free pardon and reprieve to all combatants and collaborators in respect of anything done by them in pursuit of their objectives. . . . "[136] The special representative of the U.N. secretary-general, however, appended to his signature a statement that the United Nations understood the amnesty provisions of the agreement as not applying to international crimes of genocide, crimes against humanity, war crimes, and other serious violations of international humanitarian law.

In May 2000, the RUF began resisting disarmament and resumed hostilities, taking hostage some 500 members of the U.N. Mission in Sierra Leone.[137] In August 2000, the U.N. Security Council requested that the secretary-general negotiate with the Sierra Leone government for the establishment of a special court that would combine elements of Sierra Leone and international law to try Sierra Leone nationals accused of atrocities during the course

---

133. *See, e.g.,* UNMIK Regulation No. 2000/64 on Assignment of International Judges/Prosecutors and/or Change of Venue (Dec. 15, 2000).

134. *See* UNMIK Regulation No. 1999/24 on the Law Applicable in Kosovo (Dec. 2, 1999).

135. *See* Peace Agreement Between the Government of Sierra Leone and the Revolutionary United Front of Sierra Leone, July 7, 1999, *reprinted in* Letter Dated 12 July 1999 from the Chargé d'Affaires ad interim of the Permanent Mission of Togo to the United Nations Addressed to the President of the Security Council, U.N. Doc. S/1999/777, annex (1999).

136. *Id.,* art. IX(2).

137. *See* Steven Mufson, *Sierra Leone's Peace Succumbs to Its Flaws,* WASH. POST, May 8, 2000, at A1.

of the conflict.[138] Given the extensive atrocities that had occurred, the Sierra Leone government wished to provide for a system of accountability. Yet the local justice system had been severely damaged by years of civil war and associated corruption, such that it could not handle large-scale atrocity trials. Moreover, the new government did not want full responsibility for the politically-charged trial of RUF leader Foday Sankoh. Consequently, the Sierra Leone government agreed to the creation of a special court charged with hearing cases concerning war crimes, crimes against humanity, and other serious violations of international humanitarian law, as well as certain violations of local law, such as child abuse and arson (the crime of genocide was not included since it did not occur in Sierra Leone).[139]

Unlike the other courts and tribunals previously referred to in this section, the Special Court of Sierra Leone is not part of a national legal system. Rather, it is a product of an international agreement between the United Nations and the Sierra Leone government.[140] The chief prosecutor is appointed by the U.N. secretary-general and the deputy prosecutor is appointed by the Sierra Leone government. The two trial chambers each consist of two foreign judges appointed by the secretary-general and one local judge appointed by the Sierra Leone government. The appellate chamber consists of three foreign judges and two local judges, similarly appointed. A registry provides administrative support, while a defense office is responsible for ensuring that all indictees are represented by qualified attorneys, who are appointed in the event the indictee is indigent.

As of 2011, the special court has indicted 21 individuals for war crimes, crimes against humanity, and other serious violations of international humanitarian law, of whom several have been convicted and are serving terms of as much as 50 years imprisonment. Once convicted, defendants can be sentenced to as much as life imprisonment, but not to the death penalty.[141]

Special Tribunal for Lebanon

In February 2005 a car bomb exploded in Beirut killing former Lebanese Prime Minister Rafiq Hariri and more than twenty others. Hariri's vocal opposition to Syrian involvement in Lebanese affairs led to speculation that the attack was a political assassina-

---

138. *See* S.C. Res. 1315 (Aug. 14, 2000).

139. *See generally* <http://www.sc-sl. org>.

140. *See* Agreement on the Establishment of a Special Court for Sierra Leone, Sierra Leone–U.N., Jan. 16,

2002, U.N. Doc. S/2002/246, app. II, attach. (2002).

141. *See* Charles Chernor Jalloh, *Special Court for Sierra Leone: Achieving Justice?*, 32 MICH. J. INT'L L. 395 (2011).

tion directed by Syrian authorities in conjunction with Hariri's Lebanese opponents. Due to concerns about the capability and impartiality of Lebanese investigation, the U.N. Security Council, with the approval of the Lebanese government, established a U.N. International Independent Investigation Commission to provide technical assistance to the Lebanese authorities.[142] After the Commission issued its first report,[143] Lebanese authorities arrested four Lebanese generals for conspiracy in the murder of Hariri.

In December 2005, the Government of Lebanon asked the United Nations to assist in establishing a Special Tribunal for Lebanon for prosecuting those responsible for Hariri's death. The Security Council requested the Secretary–General to negotiate a treaty with the Lebanese government to that end,[144] but difficulties in securing from the Lebanese Parliament consent to the treaty led to a stalemate in the process. Consequently, in May 2007 the Security Council established the tribunal based upon its U.N. Charter Chapter VII powers[145] (invocation of Chapter VII, however, was at the request of Lebanon's Prime Minister). The absence of Lebanon's approval by treaty distinguishes this tribunal from those of Cambodia or Sierra Leone; at the same time, the Special Tribunal for Lebanon is not a subsidiary organ of the Security Council but, rather, a separate international organization created by the Security Council. A further aspect that distinguishes this tribunal is that it is charged with applying Lebanese law (specifically, the Lebanese Penal Code) rather than international law, for a "terrorist act," not for war crimes, crimes against humanity, or genocide.

The tribunal, which began functioning in March 2009, is a hybrid tribunal composed of the judges, the registry, the prosecutor, and a defense office. The judges are both Lebanese and international judges—of which the latter are in the majority—selected by the U.N. secretary–general from a list compiled by the Lebanese judiciary (for the Lebanese judges) or from nominations by U.N. member states (for the international judges).[146] A prosecutor and a registrar were also appointed by the secretary–general, while a deputy prosecutor was appointed by the government of Lebanon after consultation with the secretary–general. The tribunal is located in the Netherlands near The Hague. Half of its funding comes from the government of Lebanon and half from voluntary donations by U.N. member states.

In 2009, at the tribunal's request, Lebanese authorities deferred the case concerning Hariri's assassination to the tribunal,

142. S.C. Res. 1595 (Apr. 7, 2005).

143. *See* Report of the Int'l Independent Investigation Commission, U.N. Doc. S/2005/662 (Oct. 20, 2005).

144. S.C. Res. 1644 (Dec. 12, 2005).

145. S.C. Res. 1757 (May 30, 2007).

146. *Id.*, annex (Statute of the Special Tribunal for Lebanon).

including the results of Lebanon's investigations, judicial records, and other information. After reviewing the information, the tribunal ordered the release of the four generals due to a lack of credible evidence warranting indictment.[147] In 2011, however, the prosecutor indicted and issued arrest warrants for several members of the militant group Hezbollah. Given Hezbollah's strong political backing within the Lebanese Parliament, as of 2011 the likelihood of Lebanese cooperation with the Special Tribunal in arresting the indictees and transferring them to the Netherlands was in doubt.

147. *See* Orders Regarding Detention of Persons and Memorandum of Understanding, 48 I.L.M. 1149 (2009).

Further Reading

M. Cherif Bassiouni, *A Guide to International Criminal Law* (2008).

M. Cherif Bassiouni, *International Extradition: United States Law and Practice* (5th ed. 2007).

M. Cherif Bassiouni, ed., *International Criminal Law* (3d ed. 2008) (3 vols.).

M. Cherif Bassiouni, *The Legislative History of the International Criminal Court* (2005) (3 vols.).

Antonio Cassese, *International Criminal Law* (2d ed. 2008).

Antonio Cassese, ed., *The Oxford Companion to International Criminal Justice* (2009).

Robert Cryer et al., *An Introduction to International Criminal Law and Procedure* (2d ed. 2010).

Mark A. Drumbl, *Atrocity, Punishment and International Law* (2007).

John R.W.D. Jones & Steven Powles, *International Criminal Practice* (3d ed. 2003).

Rachel Kerr, *The International Criminal Tribunal for the Former Yugoslavia: An Exercise in Law, Politics, and Diplomacy* (2004).

Guénaï Mettraux, *International Crimes and the Ad–Hoc Tribunals* (2005).

Steven R. Ratner et al., *Accountability for Human Rights Atrocities in International Law: Beyond the Nuremberg Legacy* (3d ed. 2009).

Cesare P.R. Romano et al., eds., *Internationalized Criminal Courts and Tribunals: Sierra Leone, East Timor, Kosovo, and Cambodia* (2004).

Leila Sadat, *The International Criminal Court and the Transformation of International Law: Justice for the New Millennium* (2002).

Arvinder Sambei & John R.W.D. Jones, *Extradition Law Handbook* (2005).

William A. Schabas, *An Introduction to the International Criminal Court* (4th ed. 2011).

Benjamin N. Schiff, *Building the International Criminal Court* (2008).

Carsten Stahn & Mohamed M. El Zeidy, *The International Criminal Court and Complementarity: From Theory to Practice* (2011).

Gerhard Werle, *Principles of International Criminal Law* (2d ed. 2009).

Alexander Zahar & Göran Sluiter, *International Criminal Law: A Critical Introduction* (2008).

Chapter 14

USE OF ARMED FORCE AND ARMS CONTROL

The maintenance of international peace and security was the primary reason for creating the United Nations. Under the U.N. Charter Article 2(3), all member states are required to "settle their international disputes by peaceful means in such a manner that international peace and security, and justice, are not endangered." Article 33(1) lists several dispute settlement mechanisms as the first resort in lieu of using military force: negotiation; mediation; conciliation; arbitration; or judicial settlement.[1] Nevertheless, states often resort to the use of military force to resolve disputes, which implicates further Charter provisions and customary rules. Moreover, the resort to the use of force implicates rules on methods of warfare and on protections for vulnerable persons in times of war. This chapter addresses these rules and protections, as well as treaties developed to control the spread of weapons.

A. *Jus Ad Bellum*

International law traditionally has divided the law of warfare into two categories: laws governing whether a state may resort to war (*jus ad bellum*) and laws governing how a state must conduct itself after the war has begun (*jus in bello*). Both branches share certain principles, such as those relating to necessity and proportionality. Yet they are kept distinct to preserve the idea that no matter whether a state resorts to war lawfully or unlawfully (*jus ad bellum*), all belligerents must abide by certain norms during the conflict (*jus in bello*). This section addresses the first branch, while the following section addresses the second.

General Prohibition on the Use of Force

The principle that the use of force is generally prohibited in international relations is embodied in Article 2(4) of the U.N. Charter. It provides:

All Members shall refrain in their international relations from the threat or use of force against the territorial integrity or

1. *See* Chapter 4.

political independence of any State, or in any other manner inconsistent with the Purposes of the United Nations.

A state cannot commit a "threat or use of force" against a state that consents to the conduct at issue. Thus, if Germany consents to the presence of U.S. military forces at bases in Germany, the presence of those forces in German territory cannot be a violation of Article 2(4). Once the consent is withdrawn, however, if the forces are not removed then a violation arises. In the *D.R.C. v. Uganda* case, the International Court of Justice found that the D.R.C. initially had consented to the presence of Ugandan troops in its eastern territory, so as to help combat rebels that were operating across the border. When that consent was withdrawn in August 1998, Uganda's failure to withdraw its military forces from the D.R.C.'s territory constituted a violation of Article 2(4).[2]

Difficult issues can arise as to whether an entity that grants consent is competent to do so. U.S. interventions in Grenada in 1983 and in Panama in 1989 were justified in part on the basis of, respectively, an invitation by the "Governor–General of Grenada" (appointed by the Queen Elizabeth II, as queen of Grenada) and by the elected president of Panama who had not been allowed to assume office.[3] Presumably any group that becomes unhappy with its government cannot simply invite foreign forces to intervene militarily to oust that government. As the International Court has noted in the context of the broader and allied doctrine of non-intervention:

> [The principle of non-intervention] would certainly lose its effectiveness as a principle of law if intervention were to be justified by a mere request for assistance made by an opposition group in another State.... Indeed, it is difficult to see what would remain of the principle of non-intervention in international law if intervention, which is already allowable at the request of the government of a State, were also to be allowed at the request of the opposition.[4]

The issue of consent can also arise in the context of a government consenting in advance, such as by treaty, to a future intervention in the event that certain circumstances arise. For example, African states under Article 4(h) of the African Union Constitutive Act[5] have granted to the African Union Assembly the right to

---

2. Armed Activities on the Territory of the Congo (D.R.C. v. Uganda), 2005 I.C.J. 168, 224, para. 149 (Dec. 19).

3. *See* LAW AND FORCE IN THE NEW INTERNATIONAL ORDER 111–85 (Lori Damrosch & David Scheffer eds., 1991).

4. Military and Paramilitary Activities in and against Nicaragua (Nicar. v. U.S.), 1986 I.C.J. 14, 126 (June 27).

5. Constitutive Act of the African Union, art. 4(h), July 11, 2000, OAU Doc. CAB/LEG/23.15 (2000).

intervene in a member state "in respect of grave circumstances, namely war crimes, genocide and crimes against humanity."[6]

The language of Article 2(4) prohibits not just the *use* of force, but the *threat* to use force as well. The concept of "threat" is not defined in the Charter, but might be conceived of as "an explicit or implicit promise of a future and unlawful use of armed force against one or more states, the realization of which depends on the threatener's will."[7] For example, Guyana authorized an oil rig to engage in exploratory drilling on a part of the continental shelf in dispute between Guyana and Suriname. A Surinamese patrol boat approached the rig in the middle of the night and, by radio, ordered it to leave within twelve hours "or the consequences will be yours." In September 2007, an arbitral panel convened under the Law of the Sea Convention found that Suriname's conduct was not mere law enforcement activity; rather, it constituted a violation of U.N. Charter Article 2(4) as an unlawful *threat* to use force.[8]

The broad term "use of force" (rather than "war") reflects a desire to prohibit not only conflicts arising from a formal state of war, but the resort to armed conflict generally. As such, many scholars interpret Article 2(4) as prohibiting all uses of force deemed permissible prior to enactment of the Charter, such as armed reprisal by a state to punish the unlawful act of another state.

By contrast, some scholars have argued that the phrase "against the territorial integrity and political independence of any state" limits the prohibition to uses of force that are above a threshold at which the territorial integrity or political independence of a state is impugned. Under this interpretation, use of force directed at altering territorial or political structures (*e.g.*, an effort to annex territory) is prohibited, but uses of force not so directed (*e.g.*, to rescue nationals or to protect human rights) is permissible. Indeed, proponents of the doctrine of humanitarian intervention argue that the right of a government to protect itself by invoking Article 2(4) is contingent on that government fulfilling its duty, as a government, to protect the rights of its people. If a government fails in that responsibility to protect ("R2P") its people, other states are entitled to intervene to protect them.

Critics of this more permissive interpretation, however, contest whether state practice supports such a permissible interpretation.

---

6. *See* Ben Kioko, *The Right of Intervention under the African Union's Constitutive Act: From Non–Interference to Non–Intervention*, 85 INT'L REV. RED CROSS 807 (2003).

7. Marco Roscini, *Threats of Armed Force and Contemporary International Law*, 54 NETH. INT'L L. REV. 229, 235 (2007); *see generally* NIKOLAS STÜRCHLER, THE THREAT OF FORCE IN INTERNATIONAL LAW (2007).

8. Award of the Arbitral Tribunal (Guyana v. Suriname), para. 445 (Sept. 17, 2007), 47 I.L.M. 164 (2008).

Thus, with respect to the "responsibility to protect," a 2005 U.N. high-level panel of experts appointed by the Secretary–General (writing in the wake of the 2003 U.S. intervention in Iraq) agreed that there existed an "emerging norm that there is a collective international responsibility to protect," but concluded that armed force may be used to fulfill the responsibility only if so authorized by the Security Council.[9] The U.N. secretary–general generally endorsed the high-level panel's approach,[10] as did the General Assembly in its 2005 World Summit Outcome document,[11] though admittedly neither expressly ruled out the unilateral use of force. As such, state practice does not evince a settled doctrine that the "responsibility to protect" permits non-U.N. forcible humanitarian intervention. Many governments regard avoiding "bad" interventions as more important than authorizing "good" interventions, given the availability of the Security Council to decide which interventions should be pursued to promote international peace and security.

More generally, critics see such permissive interpretations as eroding the strength of the overall prohibition on the use of force. They note that the phrase "against the territorial integrity and political independence of any state" was inserted in Article 2(4) at the San Francisco conference in 1945 as an effort to enhance the overall prohibition, not curtail it.[12] Further, these critics find support in decisions of the International Court of Justice, which disfavors the resort to force by states. In the *Corfu Channel* case, the Court was unsympathetic to the United Kingdom's claim that it could intervene in Albanian territorial waters to vindicate U.K. rights of innocent passage. The Court took the position that, regardless of the United Kingdom's motive in clearing unlawful mines, the action was a violation of Albanian territorial integrity. Further, the Court was unmoved by arguments that unilateral action was necessary in the face of the U.N. Security Council's inability or unwillingness to act:

> The Court can only regard the alleged right of intervention as the manifestation of a policy of force, such as has, in the past, given rise to most serious abuses and such as cannot, whatever

9. *See* U.N. Secretary–General, Report of the High-level Panel on Threats, Challenges and Change, para. 203, U.N. Doc. A/59/565 (Dec. 2, 2004); *see also id.* at paras. 196, 272.

10. In Larger Freedom: Towards Development, Security and Human Rights for All, Report of the Secretary–General, U.N. Doc. A/59/2005, para. 135 (Mar. 21, 2005).

11. 2005 World Summit Outcome, U.N. Doc. A/60/L.1, paras. 138–39 (Sept. 15, 2005). For a general discussion, see Carsten Stahn, *Responsibility to Protect: Political Rhetoric or Emerging Legal Norm?*, 101 Am. J. Int'l L. 99 (2007).

12. *See* Ian Brownlie, International Law and the Use of Force by States 265–68 (1963).

be the present defects in international organization, find a place in international law.[13]

In short, the Court (and most states and scholars) believes that a strong prohibition on the use of force is necessary, since the creation of loopholes would provide states with far too much discretion in deciding when they may resort to war.

Exactly what kinds of action constitute a "use of force" is debatable, but the General Assembly's 1974 resolution defining aggression[14] sets out various scenarios that would appear to violate Article 2(4):

- invasion by one state of another, such as occurred when Iraq invaded Kuwait in August 1990;

- bombardment by one state of another, such as occurred when Japan bombed Pearl Harbor in December 1941 or NATO states bombed Serbia in March/April 1999 in relation to Serb actions in Kosovo;

- blockade by one state of another's coasts or ports, such as occurred when the United States precluded shipments of missiles to Cuba in October 1962;

- attack by one state whether on land or sea against another state's armed forces, such as when Israel attacked the *USS Liberty* in international waters (fourteen miles off the Sinai peninsula) during the 1967 Arab–Israeli war;

- use of a state's military forces, who are deployed in a host state with its consent, in a manner that contravenes such consent;

- allowing a state to use another state's territory to attack a third state; and

- sending armed bands or groups from one state into another to carry out acts of armed force of such gravity as to constitute an armed attack.

The 1974 Definition does not address many types of actions that might be regarded as unlawful uses of force. Developed and developing states have at times divided over whether extreme forms of political or economic coercion violate Article 2(4), with the former saying it does not while the latter maintains that it does.[15] As a practical matter, however, when a state unilaterally imposes economic sanctions upon another state, or severs diplomatic rela-

13. Corfu Channel (U.K. v. Alb.), 1949 I.C.J. 4, 35 (Apr. 9).

14. *See* G.A. Res. 3314 (Dec. 14, 1974); *see also* Chapter 13(D).

15. *See, e.g.*, JULIUS STONE, CONFLICT THROUGH CONSENSUS 115–36 (1977).

tions, doing so is not regarded by other states as a violation of Article 2(4).

Modern technologies have introduced a further area of uncertainty. For example, in 2010, a malicious computer virus (known as the Stuxnet worm) was detected on computers in Iran. The virus was designed to make quick changes in the rotational speed of motors, shifting them rapidly up and down. Such a change of speed severely sabotaged thousands of centrifuges spinning in Iran to enrich uranium, which can either be used to fuel nuclear reactors or to build nuclear bombs. Many speculated that the virus was deployed into Iran by a foreign government concerned that Iran was pursuing a nuclear weapons program.[16] If such a "cyberattack" could be proven, would it constitute a use of force in violation of Article 2(4) of the U.N. Charter? What about a covert flooding of Iran's economy with counterfeit currency or an infiltration of Iran's banking system so as to scramble or corrupt Iranian banking data?[17]

Despite such uncertainties, a large variety of transboundary uses of force are regarded as unlawful under U.N. Charter Article 2(4). The U.N. Charter, however, recognizes two exceptions to the prohibition set forth in Article 2(4): states may resort to force when they are acting in self-defense or under authorization by the U.N. Security Council. Each exception is discussed in turn.

Inherent Right of Self–Defense

Article 51. The use of force in self-defense has always been recognized as legitimate in international law. Article 51 of the Charter makes this explicit by stating:

> Nothing in the present Charter shall impair the inherent right of individual or collective self-defence if an armed attack occurs against a Member of the United Nations, until the Security Council has taken measures necessary to maintain international peace and security. Measures taken by Members in the exercise of this right of self-defence shall be immediately reported to the Security Council. . . .

Article 51 does not grant a right of self defense but, rather, preserves a right that predated the U.N. Charter under customary international law.[18] At the same time, Article 51 requires that there

---

16. See David E. Sanger, *Iran Fights Malware Attacking Computers*, N.Y. TIMES, Sept. 26, 2010, at 4.

17. See Michael N. Schmitt, *Computer Network Attack and the Use of Force in International Law: Thoughts on a Normative Framework*, 37 COLUM. J. TRANSNAT'L L. 885 (1999); Matthew C.

Waxman, *Cyber-Attacks and the Use of Force: Back to the Future of Article 2(4)*, 36 YALE J. INT'L L. 421 (2011); see also RICHARD A. CLARKE & ROBERT K. KNAKE, CYBER WAR (2010).

18. See Military and Paramilitary Activities *supra* note 4, para. 176.

be an "armed attack" prior to the resort to self-defense; force or intervention below the level of an "armed attack" does not trigger a right of self-defense.[19] Consequently, while there is common agreement that a state may respond in self-defense to blatant attacks on its security (*e.g.*, an invasion of its territory),[20] disagreements have arisen over the resort to self-defense in situations where the force (or threat of force) is less clear.

For example, in *Military and Paramilitary Activities in and against Nicaragua*, the United States alleged that Nicaragua was sending armed bands, groups, or irregulars across a border against El Salvador, or providing weapons or logistical support to such groups, which justified the United States acting in collective-self defense in support of El Salvador. The Court, however, found that even if such allegations were true, Nicaragua's conduct did not qualify as an "armed attack," since it did not involve acts of armed force of such gravity that they amounted to an armed attack.[21] Moreover, the Court found that there was insufficient evidence that the support was imputable to Nicaragua.

Protection of Nationals. On various occasions since 1945, when nationals of states have been threatened abroad, states have reacted by using armed force to conduct a rescue operation. Such threats do not fit easily within the language of Article 51, yet states characterize their actions as a lawful exercise of the right of self-defense, thereby implicitly viewing the threats to nationals abroad as an "armed attack."[22] This practice suggests that the nature of an initial "armed attack" need not be conventional in the sense of military forces from one state invading another to seize territory.

Temporal Issues: Anticipatory or Preemptive Self–Defense. When a state resorts to self-defense, it remains a matter of debate whether a state may: (1) only respond to an armed attack that has already occurred; (2) respond to an imminent armed attack that has not yet occurred (anticipatory self-defense); or (3) respond to an armed attack that is not imminent but may occur at some point in the future if action is not taken (preemptive self-defense). The views of states and scholars on this issue fall into three schools: strict constructionists who reject anticipatory and preemptive self-

---

19. *Id.*, para. 249; *see* Elizabeth Wilmshurst, *The Chatham House Principles of International Law on the Use of Force in Self–Defence*, 55 Int'l & Comp. L.Q. 963, princpl. 2 (2006).

20. *See*, *e.g.*, Eritrea–Ethiopia Claims Commission, Partial Award on the *Jus ad Bellum*, Ethiopia's Claims 1–8, *dispositif* at para. B(1) (Dec. 19, 2005), 45 I.L.M. 430 (2006) (finding that Eritrea violated U.N. Charter Article 2(4) by invading and occupying parts of Ethiopia or Ethiopian-administered territory in May 1998).

21. *Military and Paramilitary Activities*, *supra* note 4, paras. 230–31.

22. *See* Tom Ruys, *The Protection of Nationals Doctrine Revisited*, 13 J. Conflict & Sec. L. 233 (2008); Natalino Ronzitti, Rescuing Nationals Abroad Through Military Coercion and Intervention on Grounds of Humanity (1985).

defense; those who accept self-defense against imminent threats; and those who accept self-defense against not just imminent threats, but distant threats that are qualitatively grave.

Adherents to the strict constructionist school note that Article 51 acknowledges a right of self-defense "if an armed attack occurs" against a U.N. Member. Such language has a temporal character; an armed attack must first occur before the resort to self-defense. As such, neither anticipatory self-defense nor preemptive self-defense can be lawful, since there can be no defensive action prior to the armed attack actually occurring. Thus, Ian Brownlie asserted that "the view that Article 51 does not permit anticipatory action is correct and ... arguments to the contrary are either unconvincing or based on inconclusive pieces of evidence."[23] For Louis Henkin, allowing anticipatory action "would replace a clear standard with a vague, self-serving one, and open a loophole large enough to empty the rule."[24] When pressed, some strict constructionists accept that anticipatory or preemptive action, while illegal, in some circumstances "may be justified on moral and political grounds and the community will eventually condone or met out lenient condemnation."[25]

Adherents to the imminent threat school accept that the language of Article 51 speaks of self-defense in response to an armed attack, yet note that the language points to a right that pre-existed the Charter (the "inherent right" of self-defense). Customary international law prior to 1945 recognized the ability of a state to defend against not only an existing attack but also in anticipation of an imminent attack. The principal precedent relied upon for anticipatory self-defense is the 1836 *Caroline* incident, in which the United Kingdom asserted that its resort to force against a schooner named *Caroline*, located in U.S. territory, was permissible self-defense because the schooner had previously been used (and might be used again) to ferry supplies across the border to Canadian rebels resisting U.K. rule. U.S. Secretary of State Daniel Webster responded that self-defense is confined to "cases in which the 'necessity of that self-defence is instant, overwhelming, and leaving no choice of means, and no moment for deliberation.' "[26] Thereafter, Webster's response was widely cited with approval. For adherents to the imminent threat school, Webster's formulation embraces anticipatory self-defense and was preserved in Article 51. A second argument employed by this school expands the meaning of the term

---

23. Ian Brownlie, International Law and the Use of Force by States 278 (1963).

24. Louis Henkin, International Law: Politics and Values 121 (1995).

25. Antonio Cassese, International Law 310–11 (2d ed. 2005).

26. Letter from Daniel Webster to Lord Ashburton (Aug. 6, 1842), *quoted in* 2 John Bassett Moore, A Digest of International Law 412 (1906).

"armed attack." While a narrow interpretation of armed attack might envisage only a use of force that has been consummated, a broader interpretation would view it as including an attack that is imminent and unavoidable. Finally, this school emphasizes state practice since 1945, which arguably demonstrates an acceptance by states of self-defense when an attack is imminent and unavoidable. For example, reference is made to the 1962 "quarantine" of Cuba by the United States, the 1967 Arab–Israeli war, the 1981 Israeli attack against an Iraqi nuclear facility, and the 1986 U.S. bombing raids against Libya.

Adherents to the qualitative threat school agree that a state need not await an actual armed attack, but believe that the requirement of an imminent threat is misplaced. For this school, the world has changed significantly since 1945, particularly with the advent of weapons of mass destruction and the rise of global terrorism. Confining ourselves to the temporal strictures of the *Caroline* standard is a recipe for paralysis in the face of today's grave threats.[27] For these adherents, President John Kennedy had it right when he identified the nuclear age as one in which the actual firing of a weapon was no longer the touchstone for determining whether a nation is in peril. Rather than emphasize the temporal nature of a future attack, this school looks to other qualitative factors, such as the probability that an attack will occur at some future point, the availability of non-forcible means for addressing the situation, and the magnitude of harm an attack would inflict. Where these qualitative factors indicate a high probability of a grave future attack, a state may act as necessary and proportionate in preemptive self-defense.

A doctrine of preemptive self-defense was advanced by the Bush Administration in a September 2002 report to the U.S. Congress on national security. Among other things, the report asserted an evolving right under international law for the United States to use military force preemptively against the threat posed by "rogue states" possessing WMDs. It stated: "For centuries, international law recognized that nations need not suffer an attack before they can lawfully take action to defend themselves against forces that present an imminent danger of attack.... We must adapt the concept of imminent threat to the capabilities and objectives of today's adversaries."[28]

Defense Against Non-State Actors. Another area of debate is whether a state may only engage in self-defense against an attack

27. *See* Myres S. McDougal & Florentino P. Feliciano, Law and Minimum World Public Order: The Legal Regulation and International Coercion 217 (1961).

28. White House, The National Security Strategy of the United States of America 15 (Sept. 17, 2002).

by another state, or whether it may also do so against a non-state actor. Article 51 speaks of the right of self-defense by a "Member of the United Nations" against an armed attack without clarifying who or what must conduct the armed attack. (In contrast, Article 2(4) of the Charter speaks of a use of force by one "Member" against "any state.") If Article 51 recognizes an inherent right that preceded the enactment of the Charter, that right appears to have included self-defense against non-state actors. For instance, the *Caroline* incident concerned self-defense against attacks by non-state actors (in that case, U.K. defense against support by U.S. nationals for a rebellion in Canada).

Recent state practice suggests that the initial "armed attack" need not be made by a government. Al Qaeda, a terrorist organization based in Afghanistan, orchestrated a series of airplane hijackings in the United States on September 11, 2001, which led to the collapse of the World Trade Center, extensive damage to the Pentagon, and the death of some 3,000 people. After unsuccessfully demanding that the de facto government of Afghanistan (the Taliban) hand over the terrorists, the United States exercised its right of self-defense by pursuing a military campaign in Afghanistan against both al Qaeda and the Taliban. In its report to the U.N. Security Council explaining why it was exercising its right of self-defense, the United States did not assert that the Afghan government attacked the United States but, rather, that the Afghan government was unwilling to prevent Al Qaeda attacks.

> The attacks on 11 September 2001 and the ongoing threat to the United States and its nationals posed by the Al–Qaeda organization have been made possible by the decision of the Taliban regime to allow the parts of Afghanistan that it controls to be used by this organization as a base of operation. Despite every effort by the United States and the international community, the Taliban regime has refused to change its policy. From the territory of Afghanistan, the Al–Qaeda organization continues to train and support agents of terror who attack innocent people throughout the world and target United States nationals and interests in the United States and abroad.[29]

The global reaction to the U.S. action was largely supportive. The Security Council passed two resolutions prior to the U.S. military response declaring that the terrorist attacks threatened international peace and security, and expressly recognizing in this context the right of self-defense.[30]

29. U.N. Doc. S/2001/946 (Oct. 7, 2001).

30. *See* S.C. Res. 1368 (Sept. 12, 2001); S.C. Res. 1373 (Sept. 28, 2001).

In the Israeli *Wall* advisory opinion, however, the International Court of Justice took a contrary position. In that case, Israel argued that its construction of a lengthy barrier spanning hundreds of kilometers across certain areas of the West Bank was a non-violent measure necessary for preventing terrorism in Israeli civilian areas, and that the barrier was wholly consistent with Israel's right of self-defense under Article 51. The Court rejected this argument, stating that "Article 51 of the Charter ... recognizes the existence of an inherent right of self-defence in the case of armed attack *by one State against another State*" and that consequently Article 51 had no relevance to the case.[31]

The Court's opinion, however, generated considerable criticism, much of which noted that many regarded the attacks by Al Qaeda of 9/11 as justifying a response in self-defense.[32] The Court may have signaled a retreat from its position in 2005 in *Armed Activities on the Territory of the Congo (DRC v. Uganda)*. In that case the Court stated that, given the facts at issue, there was "no need to respond to the contentions of the Parties as to whether and under what conditions contemporary international law provides for a right of self-defense against large-scale attacks by irregular forces."[33] Both Judges Kooijmans and Simma stated in separate opinions that, if the Court still viewed Article 51 as restricted to self-defense only against an attack by another state, then the Court is out-of-step with both the Security Council and state practice.[34] According to Judge Kooijmans:

> If the activities of armed bands present on a State's territory cannot be attributed to that State, the victim State is not the object of an armed attack by it. But if the attacks by the irregulars would, because of their scale and effects, have [been] classified as an armed attack had they been carried out by regular armed forces, there is nothing in the language of Article 51 of the charter that prevents the victim State from exercising its *inherent* right of self-defence.[35]

While this area of the law may be somewhat unsettled, the trend seems to favor the view that states may act in self-defense against a non-state actor in circumstances where the host state is unable or unwilling to stop conduct that, by its gravity, constitutes an armed attack. Recent transboundary defensive actions by states,

---

31. Advisory Opinion on Legal Consequences of the Construction of a Wall in the Occupied Palestinian Territory, 2004 I.C.J. 136, 194, at para. 139 (July 9) (emphasis added).

32. *See, e.g.,* Sean D. Murphy, *Self-Defense and the Israeli Wall Advisory Opinion: An Ipse Dixit from the ICJ?*, 99 Am. J. Int'l L. 62 (2005).

33. Armed Activities on the Territory of the Congo *supra* note 2, at 223.

34. *Id.*, sep. op. Judge Kooijmans, at 313–14, para. 28; *id.*, sep. op. Judge Simma, at 337, para. 11.

35. *Id.*, sep. op. Judge Kooijmans, at 314, para. 29.

undertaken without apparent consent of the host state and eliciting no condemnation by the Security Council include: various cross-border operations by Turkey into Iraq against the Kurdish separatist guerillas; the 2008 action by Colombian military forces to bomb and attack in Ecuador guerrillas of the Revolutionary Armed Forces of Colombia (FARC); Israel's 2006 sending of military forces into, and bombing portions of, southern Lebanon in an effort to strike at the Hezbollah movement; and the U.S. air strike inside Syria in October 2008 reportedly to stem the flow of foreign fighters and weapons from that country into Iraq.[36]

The issue was on vivid display in May 2011 when the founder of Al Qaeda, Osama bin Laden, was shot and killed inside a private residential compound in Abbottabad, Pakistan, by U.S. Navy SEALs and CIA operatives. Abbottabad is a city fully under the control of the government of Pakistan; indeed, it hosts a military facility for the training of new recruits. By most accounts, the government of Pakistan was unaware of bin Laden's presence in Abbottabad. The covert operation was ordered by President Barack Obama without consulting or obtaining the consent of the government of Pakistan, apparently to avoid any possibility of Al Qaeda learning of the planned operation. The U.S. Department of State legal adviser, Harold Koh, explained the legal justification as follows:

> Given bin Laden's unquestioned leadership position within al Qaeda and his clear continuing operational role, there can be no question that he was the leader of an enemy force and a legitimate target in our armed conflict with al Qaeda. In addition, bin Laden continued to pose an imminent threat to the United States that engaged our right to use force, a threat that materials seized during the raid have only further documented. Under these circumstances, there is no question that he presented a lawful target for the use of lethal force. By enacting the [Authorization to Use Military Force statute (AUMF)], Congress expressly authorized the President to use military force "against ... *persons* [such as bin Laden, whom the President] determines planned, authorized, committed, or aided the terrorist attacks that occurred on September 11, 2001 ...in order to prevent any future acts of international terrorism against the United States by such ... persons" (emphasis added). Moreover, the manner in which the U.S. operation was conducted—taking great pains both to distinguish between legitimate military objectives and civilians and to avoid excessive incidental injury to the latter—followed the principles of

36. *See generally* NOAM LUBELL, EX-   STATE ACTORS (2010).
TRATERRITORIAL USE OF FORCE AGAINST NON-

distinction and proportionality described above, and was designed specifically to preserve those principles, even if it meant putting U.S. forces in harm's way. Finally, consistent with the laws of armed conflict and U.S. military doctrine, the U.S. forces were prepared to capture bin Laden if he had surrendered in a way that they could safely accept.[37]

Targeted Killings, Including Use of Drone Aircraft. The death of bin Laden highlighted not just the issue of self-defense against non-state actors, but also the degree to which specific persons can be targeted when using transboundary military force. This issue of targeted killings often arises in the context of the use of unmanned or "drone" aircraft, which are operated remotely. The United States has frequently used drone aircraft in recent years, especially in Afghanistan and Pakistan, but also elsewhere, such as in Libya, Iraq, Somalia and Yemen, when going after alleged terrorists. For example, in September 2011, U.S. drone aircraft fired upon a convoy in Yemen, successfully killing a U.S. national named Anwar al-Awlaki, who the U.S. government alleged was a senior recruiter and spokesman for Al Qaeda in the Arabian Peninsula.

Opponents of such targeted killings are uneasy with the idea that lethal armed force is being used outside the classic circumstances of an armed conflict between two states, and maintain that targeted attacks, at least in some circumstances, constitute a form of extrajudicial killing, in violation of human rights norms.[38] Yet proponents of such action argue that so long as the conduct is properly classified as necessary and proportionate self-defense against an enemy belligerent (such as Al Qaeda), then it matters not whether the attack targets a particular individual, nor whether the aircraft is manned or unmanned. The U.S. State Department legal adviser, Harold Koh, asserted in 2010 that "a state that is engaged in an armed conflict or in legitimate self-defense is not required to provide targets with legal process before the state may use lethal force." Further, "under domestic law, the use of lawful weapons systems—consistent with the applicable laws of war—for precision targeting of specific high-level belligerent leaders when acting in self-defense or during an armed conflict is not unlawful,

---

37. Harold Hongju Koh, *The Lawfulness of the U.S. Operation Against Osama bin Laden*, Opinio Juris (May 19, 2011), at <http://opiniojuris.org>; *see* Jordan J. Paust, *Self-Defense Targetings of Non–State Actors and Permissibility of U.S. Use of Drones in Pakistan*, 19 J. Transnat'l L. & Pol. 237 (2010).

38. *See* Philip Alston, Report of the Special Rapporteur on Extrajudicial,

Summary or Arbitrary Executions, Addendum, Study on Targeted Killings, U.N. Doc. A/HRC/ 14/24/Add.6 (May 28, 2010); *see generally* Targeted Killings: Law and Morality in an Asymmetrical World (Claire Finkelstein et al., eds., 2012); Nils Melzer, Targeted Killing in International Law (2008).

and hence does not constitute 'assassination' " in violation of U.S. restrictions.[39]

Collective Self–Defense. Article 51 recognizes an inherent right of individual *or collective* self-defense. Several regional defense agreements provide for collective self-defense, such as the North Atlantic Treaty,[40] which is the charter for the North Atlantic Treaty Organization (NATO). NATO consists of twenty-four European states, the United States, and Canada. Under Article 5 of the North Atlantic Treaty, the parties agree that an armed attack against one party shall be considered an attack against all NATO parties, such that all parties will assist the attacked party by taking actions as they deem necessary. NATO's North Atlantic Council invoked Article 5 for the first time in the aftermath of the September 2001 terrorist incidents noted above.[41]

In *Military and Paramilitary Activities in and against Nicaragua,* the International Court stated that even if Nicaragua had engaged in an "armed attack" against El Salvador, for the United States to engage in collective self-defense in support of El Salvador or any other State in the region, there must be a contemporaneous request for such assistance from the victim state, which the Court concluded did not exist on the facts of the case.[42] Further, if truly acting in collective self-defense, the Court indicated that a state is obligated under Article 51 to notify the U.N. Security Council that it is doing so, a step that had not been taken by the United States.[43]

Necessity and Proportionality. An important rule of customary international law associated with the right of self-defense is that the defensive force must be necessary and proportionate to the armed attack that gave rise to the right. Reference in support of this proposition is typically made to the *Caroline* incident (discussed above). When insurgents in Canada received private support from within the United States, the British responded by attacking and burning a vessel in a U.S. port, the *Caroline.* U.S. Secretary of State Daniel Webster asserted that the action was neither necessary nor proportionate, as required under international law,[44] a legal standard the United Kingdom fully accepted. That this standard endures under the U.N. Charter was confirmed by the International Court of Justice in its *Advisory Opinion on Legality of the Threat or Use of Nuclear Weapons,* where it stated:

---

39. Harold Hongju Koh, Legal Adviser, U.S. Dep't of State, Address at the Annual Meeting of the American Society of International Law (Mar. 25, 2010).

40. Apr. 4, 1949, 63 Stat. 2241, 34 U.N.T.S. 243.

41. *See* 40 I.L.M. 1268 (2001).

42. *Military and Paramilitary Activities, supra* note 4, at paras. 233–34.

43. *Id.,* at paras. 235–36.

44. *See* 29 Brit. & Foreign State Papers 1129, 1138 (1937).

The submission of the exercise of the right of self-defence to the conditions of necessity and proportionality is a rule of customary international law. As the Court stated in the case concerning Military and Paramilitary Activities in and against Nicaragua (Nicaragua v. United States of America), there is a "specific rule whereby self-defence would warrant only measures which are proportional to the armed attack and necessary to respond to it, a rule well established in customary international law" (I.C.J. Reports 1986, p. 94, para. 176). This dual condition applies equally to Article 51 of the Charter, whatever the means of force employed.[45]

In considering whether force is "necessary," the International Court of Justice and scholars typically first consider whether there are peaceful alternatives to self-defense, such as pursuing available diplomatic avenues.[46] This might entail determining whether the attacker has been asked to desist from further attacks and to make reparation for the injuries it has caused. Assuming that no reasonable alternative means exist, the concept of "necessity" focuses on the nature of the target pursued by the defender; where the target is the source (or one of the sources) of the threat to the defender, it is considered "necessary" defense to attack that target. "Necessity," however, does not require a defender to limit itself to actions that merely repel an initial attack; a state may use force in self-defense to remove a continuing threat to future security,[47] such as the United States pursuing action against Japan in the 1940s until its militarist regime had capitulated. An example of a lack of necessity may be seen in *Military and Paramilitary Activities in and against Nicaragua*, where the International Court said that the U.S. conduct against Nicaragua was not necessary to help El Salvador defend, since El Salvador had already successfully repulsed the rebel offensive at the time the United States acted.[48] Likewise, in the *Oil Platforms* case, the Court found that the United States did not complain to Iran about the military activities allegedly undertaken from the platforms, nor proved that the platforms were the source of the threat to the United States in the Gulf such that attacking them was necessary for eliminating that threat.[49]

"Proportionality" does not require that the force be a mirror image of the initial attack, nor that the defensive actions be

---

45. 1996 I.C.J. 226, para. 41 (July 8) [hereinafter Nuclear Weapons Advisory Opinion]. For a brief discussion of the case, see Chapter 4(D).

46. *See* YORAM DINSTEIN, WAR, AGGRESSION AND SELF-DEFENCE 237 (4th ed. 2005).

47. *See* JUDITH GARDAM, NECESSITY, PROPORTIONALITY AND THE USE OF FORCE BY STATES 4–8 (2004).

48. *Military and Paramilitary Activities, supra* note 4, at para. 237.

49. *See* Oil Platforms (Iran v. U.S.), 2003 I.C.J. 161, 196–98 (Nov. 6).

restricted to the particular geographic location in which the initial attack occurred. Rather than focus on the form, substance, or strength of the initial attack, proportionality calls for assessing the result sought for eliminating that threat and the means being used to achieve that result.[50] As suggested by Professor Roberto Ago, a rapporteur for the International Law Commission on the rules of state responsibility and later judge on the International Court of Justice, "in the case of action taken for the specific purpose of halting and repelling an armed attack, this does not mean that the action should be more or less commensurate with the attack. Its lawfulness cannot be measured except by its capacity for achieving the desired result."[51] Such reasoning is reflected in the national military manuals adopted by many states; for instance, the *U.S. Commander's Handbook on the Law of Naval Operations* indicates that proportionality imposes a "requirement that the use of force be in all circumstances limited in intensity, duration and scope to that which is reasonably required to counter the attack or threat of attack and to ensure the continued safety of U.S. forces.... "[52]

In *Military and Paramilitary Activities in and against Nicaragua*, the International Court found that the U.S. actions against Nicaragua were not proportionate, since the U.S. conduct (*e.g.*, mining of ports and attacks on oil installations) was excessive as compared to Nicaragua's aid to El Salvador rebels.[53] In the *Oil Platforms* case, the International Court signaled that, if it were proved that a shore-based missile had been launched by Iran against a U.S. flag vessel, a proportionate defensive response could include destroying an Iranian oil platform elsewhere in the Gulf, so long as the platform was shown to be engaged in assisting attacks on U.S. vessels in the Gulf. In other words, the Court found that a proportionate defensive response to a missile attack on a vessel was not limited to infliction of a missile attack in response, nor limited to the targeting of the facility from which the missile was launched. At the same time, the Court stated that, in a situation where the attack consists of the single mining of a ship (which was damaged but not sunk), a defensive response that destroys numerous vessels and aircraft of the attacker, as well as oil platforms, is disproportionate in scale to the threat.[54] The thrust of the Court's *dicta* was to consider the nature of the threat being faced by the defender and whether the defensive conduct, by its nature and scale, was de-

---

50. *See* GARDAM, *supra* note 47, at 8–19; Enzo Cannizzaro, *The Role of Proportionality in the Law of Counter–Measures*, 12 EUR. J. INT'L L. 889, 892 (2001).

51. Roberto Ago, *Addendum to Eighth Report on State Responsibility*, U.N. Doc. A/CN.4/318 & Add., at 104 (1979).

52. ANNOTATED SUPPLEMENT TO THE COMMANDER'S HANDBOOK ON THE LAW OF NAVAL OPERATIONS § 4.3.2 (A.R. Thomas & J.C. Duncan eds., 1999).

53. *Military and Paramilitary Activities, supra* note 4, para. 237.

54. *See Oil Platforms, supra* note 49, at 198–99.

signed to eliminate that threat. Similarly, in *Armed Activities on the Territory of the Congo*, the Court indicated that the armed "taking of airports and towns many hundreds of kilometers from [the defending state's] border would not seem proportionate to the series of transborder attacks it claimed had given rise to the right of self-defence, nor to be necessary to that end."[55]

Peace Enforcement by the Security Council

In addition to the exercise of self-defense, states are permitted to use force when authorized by the U.N. Security Council. Under the Charter, the Security Council has the primary responsibility for maintaining international peace and security.[56] Both the General Assembly and the secretary-general may bring to the attention of the Security Council situations which are likely to endanger international peace and security.[57] Under Chapter VII of the Charter, the Security Council has the authority to determine the existence of any "threat to the peace, breach of the peace, or act of aggression," and to decide upon either non-forcible or forcible measures to restore peace and security.[58] All member states are bound by such decisions.[59]

The Charter originally envisaged states entering into agreements with the United Nations so that armed forces could be quickly called up by the Security Council.[60] No such agreements, however, were ever concluded. As a result, any Security Council measure authorizing the use of force typically leads to the deployment on an *ad hoc* basis of national contingents under national command in support of the Security Council objective.

From 1945 to 1990, the Security Council rarely invoked its powers under Chapter VII as ideological conflicts between the East and West resulted in one or more of the permanent members of the Security Council vetoing such initiatives. During this period, the only Security Council authorization to use force against a "breach of the peace" was in response to North Korea's attack on South Korea in 1950 (at a time when the Soviet Union was boycotting the Security Council and was therefore unable to cast a veto). The Security Council recommended that states furnish "such assistance" to South Korea as necessary to repel the attack and "restore international peace and security in the area."[61] Forces from various states deployed to Korea under U.S. command with the authority to use the U.N. flag in the course of its operations.

---

55. Armed Activities on the Territory of the Congo, *supra* note 2, para. 147.

56. *See* U.N. Charter arts. 24 & 39.

57. *Id.*, arts. 11(3) & 99.

58. *Id.*, arts. 39, 41 & 42.

59. *Id.*, art. 25.

60. *Id.*, arts. 43–46.

61. S.C. Res. 83 (June 27, 1950).

When the Soviet Union returned to the Security Council and blocked further action, the General Assembly began to exercise some of the Council's power, relying to some extent on the so-called "Uniting for Peace Resolution," which provides in part:

> [The General Assembly] *Resolves* that if the Security Council, because of lack of unanimity of the permanent members, fails to exercise its primary responsibility for the maintenance of international peace and security in any case where there appears to be a threat to the peace, breach of the peace or act of aggression, the General Assembly shall consider the matter immediately with a view to making appropriate recommendations to Members for collective measures, including in the case of a breach of the peace or act of aggression the use of armed force when necessary, to maintain or restore international peace and security.[62]

The Uniting for Peace Resolution, however, never became a significant means of conflict management, as the states best equipped to engage in "peace enforcement" actions were unwilling to assign to the General Assembly authority in this area. Rather, those states ultimately preferred that such authority remain with the Security Council and, if it failed to authorize action, to proceed either unilaterally or under the authority of a regional organization.

Beginning in 1990, with the end of the Cold War and the decline of East–West tensions, the Security Council became more active in authorizing the deployment of military force. After Iraq invaded Kuwait in August 1990, the Security Council imposed trade sanctions on Iraq and authorized a forcible maritime interception operation by states acting in defense of Kuwait.[63] Ultimately, the Security Council authorized states "to use all necessary means to uphold and implement" Security Council resolutions that demanded Iraq's immediate and unconditional withdrawal.[64] Under the authority of that resolution, a U.S.-led multinational coalition commenced an air campaign against Iraq in January 1991. That operation concluded forty-two days later after coalition ground forces swept through Kuwait and into southern Iraq, setting up a buffer zone between the two states. The Security Council then adopted a cease-fire resolution that required Iraq to renounce its claims to Kuwait, accept a process for demarcation of the Iraq–Kuwait boundary, pay compensation for losses incurred during its invasion, and accept a U.N. inspection commission to oversee the elimination of Iraqi weapons of mass destruction.[65]

---

62. G.A. Res. 377 (Nov. 3, 1950).

63. *See* S.C. Res. 665 (Aug. 25, 1990).

64. *See* S.C. Res. 678 (Nov. 29, 1990).

65. *See* S.C. Res. 687 (Apr. 3, 1991).

In the 1990's, the Security Council also began authorizing the deployment of military force to address widespread human rights violations, such as: the 1992 authorization for a U.S.-led coalition of states to intervene in Somalia to reopen food supply lines;[66] the 1993 authorization for NATO to use air power to protect six enclaves of Bosnian Muslims in Bosnia–Herzegovina;[67] the 1994 authorization for France to intervene in Rwanda to protect civilians from ethnic violence between Hutus and Tutsis;[68] and the 1994 authorization for a U.S.-led coalition to oust a military junta in Haiti and restore its democratically-elected president.[69] In September 2005, a meeting of the U.N. General Assembly (consisting of heads of states and governments) declared that

> [t]he international community, through the United Nations, ... has the responsibility to use appropriate diplomatic, humanitarian and other peaceful means ... to help protect populations from genocide, war crimes, ethnic cleansing and crimes against humanity. In this context, we are prepared to take collective action, in a timely and decisive manner, through the Security Council, in accordance with the Charter, including Chapter VII, on a case-by-case basis and in cooperation with relevant regional organizations as appropriate, should peaceful means be inadequate and national authorities manifestly fail to protect their populations from genocide, war crimes, ethnic cleansing and crimes against humanity.[70]

While prior Security Council measures of this kind have had some positive effects, critics charge that the Security Council too often fails to act in a timely fashion, if at all. Further, critics charge that if the Security Council is to maintain its status as arbiter of the use of force, it must reform its membership to include more permanent members (such as Germany or Japan) and non-permanent members (perhaps increasing the total size from fifteen to twenty-one or twenty-five).

Peace Enforcement by Regional Organizations

Chapter VIII of the U.N. Charter encourages regional organizations to maintain international peace and security consistent with U.N. principles. It also envisages enforcement action by regional organizations, yet only with Security Council authorization.[71]

---

66. *See* S.C. Res. 794 (Dec. 3, 1992).

67. *See* S.C. Res. 836 (June 4, 1993).

68. *See* S.C. Res. 929 (June 22, 1994).

69. *See* S.C. Res. 940 (July 31, 1994) (forcible intervention ultimately was not necessary as the military junta agreed to step down).

70. 2005 World Summit Outcome, *supra* note 11, para. 139.

71. *See* U.N. Charter, arts. 52–53.

The most relevant regional organizations in this regard are found in the Americas, Africa, and the Middle East. In the Americas, the principal agreements are the Inter–American Treaty of Reciprocal Assistance (the Rio Treaty)[72] and the Charter of the Organization of American States (OAS Charter).[73] The OAS Charter expressly provides that "[w]ithin the United Nations, the Organization of American States is a regional agency."[74] Both the Rio Treaty and the OAS Charter recognize the territorial integrity and inviolability, sovereignty, and political independence of the parties. Moreover, they bind the parties not to use force against each other and authorize the collective use of force for the maintenance of peace and security on the continent. If an American state is attacked, that state may invoke its inherent right of self-defense under U.N. Charter Article 51; these regional agreements recognize the principle of collective self-defense to meet such an attack. The charters of the African Union and the Arab League contain similar provisions.

The OAS "quarantine" of Cuba is the primary example of the use of force by a regional organization purportedly under the authority of Chapter VIII. In 1962, U.S. spy planes determined that the Soviet Union was equipping Cuba to launch long-range missiles. After the OAS recommended that states take all measures necessary to ensure that Cuba could not receive missiles that might threaten the American continent, naval vessels from the United States and other American states turned back Soviet vessels headed to Cuba with arms. The United States argued that the action did not violate U.N. Charter Article 2(4) because it was permissible under Chapter VIII. Yet many observers doubted the validity of this legal justification given the absence of Security Council authorization.[75]

An example in Africa of peace enforcement by a sub-regional organization is the 1990 intervention in Liberia by states acting under the authority of the Economic Community of West African States (ECOWAS). When civil conflict broke out in Liberia, leading to extensive refugee flows to neighboring states, the sixteen states of ECOWAS decided to deploy military forces to Liberia to quell the fighting. Similar to the Cuban crisis, there was no advance authorization by the Security Council, and the intervention appeared outside the scope of ECOWAS's institutional authority. Nevertheless, the international community tolerated the intervention, and

72. Sept. 2, 1947, 62 Stat. 1681, 21 U.N.T.S. 77.

73. Apr. 30, 1948, 2 U.S.T. 2394, 119 U.N.T.S. 3, as amended by protocols of 1967, 1985, 1992, and 1993.

74. *Id.*, art. 1.

75. For subsequent reflections by the Department of State's legal adviser, see ABRAM CHAYES, THE CUBAN MISSILE CRISIS (1974).

the intervention was subsequently endorsed by the Security Council.[76]

In the Middle East, the 22–nation League of Arab States itself has not deployed military forces, but has played an important role in actions by the U.N. Security Council and other blocs of states. On February 22, 2011, after civil war broke out in Libya, the League suspended Libya's membership and then, on March 12, decided to call upon

> the Security Council to bear its responsibilities towards the deteriorating situation in Libya, and to take the necessary measures to impose immediately a no-fly zone on Libyan military aviation, and to establish safe areas in places exposed to shelling as a precautionary measure that allows the protection of the Libyan people and foreign nationals residing in Libya, while respecting the sovereignty and territorial integrity of neighboring States.[77]

Such action demonstrated League support for the rebel forces opposing the Libyan government of Muammar Gaddafi. (Similarly, the six-nation Gulf Cooperation Council declared the Libyan government to be illegitimate and opened up contacts with Libyan rebels.) The statement encouraged NATO and European Union states to support military intervention in Libya and discouraged China and Russia from vetoing such action at the Security Council.[78] When the Security Council on March 17 authorized the use of force to protect civilians in Libya, it noted the League's decision.[79]

Mixed Bases for the Use of Force

When states engage in the use of force, they will sometimes use multiple arguments for why force is justified, rather than solely argue that an action constitutes self-defense. For instance, in March 1999 NATO used military force (for the first time in its history) against a non-NATO state, the Federal Republic of Yugoslavia (FRY). As there was no Security Council resolution expressly authorizing the use of force, NATO states had to develop positions regarding why the action was lawful.

The U.S. position referred to various factors that, when taken together, the United States believed justified the action. These factors included: the commission by the FRY military and police of serious and widespread violations of international law in the FRY

---

76. *See* S.C. Res. 788 (Nov. 19, 1992).

77. Council of the League of Arab States, Res. 7360, para. 1 (Mar. 12, 2011).

78. *See* Richard Leiby & Muhammad Mansour, *Arab League Asks U.N. for No-fly Zone over Libya*, WASH. POST, Mar. 12, 2011, at A1.

79. S.C. Res. 1973, pmbl. (Mar. 17, 2011).

province of Kosovo against Kosovar Albanians; the threat that FRY actions in Kosovo could lead to a wider conflict in Europe; the FRY failure to comply with agreements with NATO and the Organization for Security and Cooperation in Europe regarding FRY actions in Kosovo; the FRY failure to comply with Security Council resolutions regarding FRY actions in Kosovo; the FRY failure to cooperate with the International Criminal Tribunal for the former Yugoslavia; and the FRY failure to abide by its own unilateral commitments.

For its part, the FRY viewed the NATO campaign as an unlawful use of force. Consequently, during the course of the bombing campaign, the FRY filed cases against ten NATO states before the International Court of Justice, along with a request for interim measures of protection. The Court denied that request and dismissed the two cases brought against Spain and the United States since the jurisdictional grounds pled by the FRY were plainly untenable.[80] The other eight cases were also dismissed on jurisdictional grounds in 2004.

U.N. Peacekeeping

Even during 1945–1990, when the United Nations was largely ineffective in engaging in "peace enforcement" activities, the United Nations had success in dealing with hostilities through the use of multilateral "peacekeeping." Beginning as early as 1948, the Security Council (and sometimes the General Assembly) has authorized on several occasions the deployment of military or police forces to maintain peace *based on the consent* of the states where the forces were to be deployed. In response to a request from the U.N. secretary-general, states volunteer personnel, equipment, supplies, or other support for a peacekeeping mission, and are then reimbursed from the mission budget at agreed rates. Peacekeepers remain members of their national establishment, but are under the operational control of the United Nations.

These peacekeeping missions are not specifically provided for in the U.N. Charter, yet are based either on the Security Council's overall Chapter VI power to recommend appropriate procedures or methods for resolving disputes peacefully, or its power in Chapter VII to issue binding decisions to restore international peace and security. The General Assembly's formal role in peacekeeping is small, being restricted principally to its function as a forum for

---

80. For a discussion of the legality of NATO's intervention, see Symposium, *The International Legal Fallout from* *Kosovo*, 12 Eur. J. Int'l L. 391 (2001); *Editorial Comments*, 93 Am. J. Int'l L. 824 (1999).

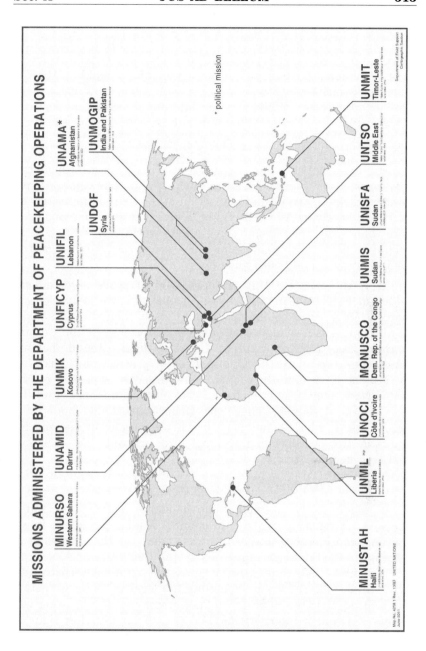

public discussion of the issues,[81] although the ICJ has suggested that the Assembly's role may be somewhat greater than the language of the Charter suggests.[82]

---

81. *See* U.N. Charter, arts. 10–12, 14.

82. *See* Advisory Opinion on Certain Expenses of the United Nations, 1962 I.C.J. 151 (July 20).

Different peacekeeping missions have served different functions, such as: assisting in a return to peace through mediation efforts; supervising a cease fire agreement; monitoring the disarmament of factions pursuant to a peace agreement; patrolling a buffer zone; and, more recently, monitoring elections and helping to rebuild failed states. While serving different functions, peacekeeping operations tend to share certain key elements. First, the presence of the peacekeepers is predicated on consent of the states in which they operate. Second, the peacekeepers strive to maintain impartiality as between states or factions. Finally, peacekeepers are lightly armed or unarmed and, as such, are neither equipped nor authorized to engage in military action other than as necessary to protect themselves. As of 2011, the United Nations has deployed more than sixty peacekeeping operations worldwide, with sixteen pending in places such as Afghanistan, Cyprus, East Timor, Kosovo, the Middle East, and South Sudan.

As is the case for U.N. authorization of peace enforcement, there can be significant difficulties in obtaining Security Council approval for a peacekeeping operation. Closely related to the political difficulties is the high cost of such operations. In the *Certain Expenses* case, the International Court of Justice found that expenses connected with the maintenance of peacekeeping forces in the Middle East and the Congo were properly expenses of the United Nations and could be assessed to all U.N. member states by the General Assembly. Thus, the General Assembly apportions these costs to all U.N. members based on a scale of assessments applicable to peacekeeping, taking into account the economic wealth of member states.

Example: 2003 Intervention in Iraq

In March 2003, a small group of states (led by the United States) intervened in Iraq. In the months leading up to the intervention, considerable attention was paid to the doctrine of "preemptive self-defense" advanced by the Bush Administration in its September 2002 report to Congress on national security (referred to above). Yet when explaining the legal basis for its action against Iraq, the United States did not assert that the invasion was permissible under international law due to an evolving right of preemptive self-defense. Rather, the United States asserted that the invasion was lawful because it was authorized by the Security Council.[83]

---

83. *See* Letter Dated 20 March 2003 from the Permanent Representative of the United States of America to the United Nations Addressed to the President of the Security Council, U.N. Doc. S/2003/351 (Mar. 20, 2003); *see also* William H. Taft, IV & Todd F. Buchwald, *Preemption, Iraq, and International Law*, 97 Am. J. Int'l L. 557, 563 (2003); Marc Weller, Iraq and the Use of Force in International Law (2010).

The United States noted that in order to address Iraq's 1990 invasion of Kuwait, the Security Council had adopted Resolution 678 in November 1990, which authorized U.N. Member States to "use all necessary means" to uphold Security Council resolutions relating to Iraq and to "restore international peace and security in the area."[84] After Iraqi forces were expelled from Kuwait, the Security Council adopted a cease-fire resolution (Resolution 687) in April 1991,[85] which imposed extensive disarmament obligations on Iraq as conditions of the ceasefire established under it. According to the United States, Resolution 687 suspended the authorization to use force against Iraq, yet did not terminate such authorization. Iraq "materially breached" its disarmament obligations by failing to disclose, discontinue, and destroy its WMD programs. The Security Council recognized that Iraq was in "material breach" of its obligations on several occasions, including in October 2002 when it unanimously adopted Resolution 1441. That resolution gave Iraq "a final opportunity to comply with its disarmament obligations" and warned Iraq of "serious consequences" if it failed to do so.[86] The United States argued that this material breach of Resolution 687 removed the basis of the ceasefire and revived the authority to use force under Resolution 678. As precedent for such a revival, the United States pointed to prior Security Council practice. For example, the United States argued that, in January 1993, the Security Council had recognized that a material breach of Resolution 687 by Iraq revived the authority to use force in the form of limited aerial bombings. In light of these factors, the United States maintained that the use of force in March 2003 was necessary given Iraq's noncompliance. The same legal theory was asserted by other members of the U.S.-led coalition.

In emphasizing the myriad Security Council resolutions enacted to deal with Iraq, the United States was able to contain the precedent set by its intervention. In principle, the U.S. legal theory serves as precedent only for future circumstances where an open-ended authorization for the use of force is issued by the Security Council and then stayed by a cease-fire resolution.[87]

B. *Jus In Bello*

The prior section dealt with whether a state may resort to the use of force. This section is concerned with the law applicable after the fighting begins. This law sometimes is referred to as the *jus in bello* (law in war) or as "international humanitarian law." Whatev-

---

84. S.C. Res. 678, *supra* note 64, para. 2.

85. *Supra* note 65.

86. S.C. Res. 1441, paras. 2 & 13 (Nov. 8, 2002).

87. For a critique of the U.S. legal theory, see Sean D. Murphy, *Assessing the Legality of Invading Iraq*, 92 GEO. L.J. 173 (2004).

er its nomenclature, such law can be divided into two general areas: *restrictions on methods* of warfare (referred to as "Hague law"); and *protections for victims* of warfare (referred to as "Geneva law"). Both bodies of law have witnessed widespread adherence by states, as reflected in the ratification of treaty instruments and the absorption of norms into national military manuals or instructions,[88] although actual warfare deviates from the norms to greater and lesser degrees.

Restrictions on Methods of Warfare

1899 and 1907 Peace Conferences. From the earliest origins of the law of nations, uncodified rules have existed regarding the methods of warfare that a state may pursue. During the American Civil War, Professor Francis Lieber of Columbia University was asked to develop written instructions for Union Army compliance with the laws of war, which were promulgated by President Lincoln in 1863 as General Order No. 100. The Lieber Code heavily influenced the development of codes of military conduct by other states, as well as efforts to develop international instruments on the subject. For example, in 1868 states agreed to prohibit the use of bullets that explode upon contact.[89] Such bullets not only disable the soldier, but also cause extraordinary suffering and make medical treatment extremely difficult.

By the end of the 1800's, advances in the technology of warfare made clear that enormous amounts of unnecessary suffering could be inflicted upon an enemy's soldiers and that certain weapons were so horrible that they should not be used even if they could assist in achieving a military objective. Consequently, at the prompting of Czar Alexander II of Russia, twenty-six states met for a peace conference at The Hague in 1899 (and returned in 1907 at the prompting of U.S. President Theodore Roosevelt, along with an additional eighteen states), in part to establish rules on how states may conduct warfare. At these two conferences, states adopted various instruments, including:

- a declaration banning the discharge of projectiles and explosives from balloons or by other similar methods;

- a declaration banning the use of projectiles whose only object is the diffusion of asphyxiating or deleterious gases;

- a declaration banning the use of bullets which expand in the human body ("dum-dum" bullets);

---

88. *See, e.g.,* U.S. DEP'T OF THE ARMY FIELD MANUAL FM 27–10, THE LAW OF LAND WARFARE (July 18, 1956); U.K. MINISTRY OF DEFENCE, THE MANUAL OF THE LAW OF ARMED CONFLICT (2004).

89. *See* St. Petersburg Declaration Renouncing the Use, in Time of War, of Explosive Projectiles Under 400 Grammes Weight, Dec. 11, 1868, 2 AM. J. INT'L L. SUPP. 95–96 (1907).

- a convention on the laws and customs of war on land, attaching the 1907 Hague Regulations Respecting the Laws and Customs of War on Land (Hague Regulations);

- conventions on the rights and duties of neutral powers in case of war on land and in case of war at sea; and

- conventions concerning the status of enemy merchant ships, the conversion of such ships into warships, the laying of mines, naval bombardment, and the right of capture in naval war.[90]

These instruments had an enduring influence, for they codified at the global level core principles that animate the *jus in bello*: the need to protect persons or property unless military necessity requires otherwise; the need to distinguish between civilian and non-civilian targets; the need to weigh the benefits gained from striking a military objective against the collateral damage to civilians and civilian property; and, generally, the need for humanity in warfare.

1907 Hague Regulations. Of the instruments adopted in 1899 and 1907, the 1907 Hague Regulations[91] are most often referred to today. The Hague Regulations state that the laws of war apply not only to armies, but also to militia and volunteer corps who: (1) are commanded by a person responsible for his subordinates; (2) have a fixed distinctive emblem recognizable at a distance; (3) carry arms openly; and (4) conduct their operations in accordance with the laws of war.[92]

The Hague Regulations then set forth a series of restrictions on how enemy soldiers may be harmed. At a general level, the Hague Regulations declare that the "right of belligerents to adopt means of injuring the enemy is not unlimited" and bar the use of "arms, projectiles, or material calculated to cause unnecessary suffering."[93] At a more specific level, the Hague Regulations forbid: using poison or poisoned weapons; killing treacherously; killing someone who has laid down his arms; declaring that no quarter will be given; improperly using a flag of truce; and forcing enemy nationals to serve in one's army.[94] Since bombardment and sieges were an important element of warfare at the time, the Hague Regulations prohibited attacks on undefended towns, required that warnings be issued prior to a bombardment, and called for the sparing of

---

90. These instruments, and other instruments referred to in this section, are reprinted in DOCUMENTS ON THE LAWS OF WAR (Adam Roberts & Richard Guelff eds., 3d ed. 2000).

91. Regulations Respecting the Laws and Customs of War on Land [hereinafter Hague Regulations], *annexed to* Convention Respecting the Laws and Cus-

toms of War on Land, Oct. 18, 1907, 36 Stat. 2277, 187 Consol. T.S. 227 [hereinafter 1907 Hague Convention].

92. Hague Regulations, *supra* note 91, art. 1.

93. *Id.*, arts. 22 & 23(e).

94. *Id.*, art. 23.

properly-marked buildings dedicated to religion, art, science, or charity, as well as historic monuments and hospitals.[95]

Once a belligerent seizes enemy territory, the Hague Regulations set forth the obligations of the occupying power. The occupying power is required to "take all the measures in his power to restore, and ensure, as far as possible, public order and safety, while respecting, unless absolutely prevented, the laws in force in the country."[96] Among other things, the pillage and confiscation of private property is forbidden, but private goods and services may be requisitioned for use of the occupying army if paid for in cash immediately or as soon as possible.[97] The occupying power may seize property of the enemy state that could be used for military operations, yet can only use in trust public buildings, real estate, forests, and agricultural estates in a manner that maintains their sustainability.[98]

Martens Clause. An enduring element of the 1899 and 1907 Hague conferences is the recognition that codes of conduct cannot address all conceivable actions that may occur, especially as new technological developments arise. Consequently, the drafters of the Hague Convention on land warfare (to which the Hague Regulations are attached) inserted a clause providing that even if a law-of-war code did not expressly apply to a specific situation, states were still bound to certain dictates of humanity.

> Until a more complete code of the laws of war has been issued, the high contracting Parties deem it expedient to declare that, in cases not included in the Regulations adopted by them, the inhabitants and the belligerents remain under the protection and the rule of the principles of the law of nations, as they result from the usages established among civilized peoples, from the laws of humanity, and the dictates of the public conscience.[99]

This clause—known as the Martens clause after the Russian diplomat who called for its insertion—is an important gap-filler in circumstances where law of war instruments fall short. Thus, in the 1996 advisory opinion of the International Court of Justice on the legality of nuclear weapons, the Court found no treaty provision or customary international law norm specifically prohibiting the use of nuclear weapons. However, the Court relied upon the enduring significance of the Martens clause to find that certain cardinal principles contained in law of war treaties (the need to distinguish combatants from non-combatants and the need to avoid unneces-

---

95. *Id.*, arts. 25–27.

96. *Id.*, art. 43.

97. *Id.*, arts. 46–47 & 52.

98. *Id.*, arts. 53 & 55.

99. 1907 Hague Convention, *supra* note 91, pmbl.

sary suffering to combatants) must be applied to new forms of military technology.[100] As such, the Court found that the use of nuclear weapons in most circumstances was prohibited.

States have continued to codify restrictions on methods of warfare in an effort to keep up with evolving technologies. In 1923, rules on aerial warfare were developed by states meeting in the Hague,[101] some of which are looked to as an expression of customary international law in this area. A 1925 Geneva protocol prohibited the use of asphyxiating, poisonous or other gases, and of bacteriological methods of warfare.[102] Further, a 1936 London protocol[103] codified an agreement among key states regarding submarine warfare against merchant ships (but did not prevent Germany's unrestricted air and submarine warfare against merchant ships during World War II). A 1954 Hague convention and protocol on the protection of cultural property sought to delineate in greater detail the duty of attacked states to mark, and the duty of attacking states to take all necessary steps to avoid harm to, such properties.[104] Modern developments in restrictions on weaponry are discussed in Section C below.

Protections for Victims of Warfare

1949 Geneva Conventions. The 1899 and 1907 Hague conferences focused principally on the means and methods of warfare. While the Hague Regulations paid some attention to protections for prisoners of war, as did a 1929 Geneva Convention, the watershed for establishing protections for the victims of warfare occurred with the adoption in 1949 of four detailed Geneva Conventions. These conventions were:

- Geneva Convention Relative to the Amelioration of the Condition of the Wounded and Sick in Armed Forces in the Field (Geneva Convention I);[105]

- Geneva Convention Relative to the Amelioration of the Condition of Wounded, Sick and Shipwrecked Members of

100. *See* Nuclear Weapons Advisory Opinion, *supra* note 45, para. 78.

101. *See* 17 Am. J. Int'l L. Supp. 245 (1923).

102. *See* Protocol for the Prohibition of the Use in War of Asphyxiating, Poisonous or Other Gases, and of Bacteriological Methods of Warfare, June 17, 1925, 26 U.S.T. 571, 94 L.N.T.S. 65.

103. *See* Procès-Verbal Relating to the Rules of Submarine Warfare Set Forth in Part IV of the Treaty of Lon-

don, Nov. 6, 1936, 31 Am. J. Int'l L. Supp. 137 (1937).

104. *See* Hague Convention for the Protection of Cultural Property in the Event of Armed Conflict, May 14, 1954, 249 U.N.T.S. 240 (the protocol of the same date appears at 249 U.N.T.S. 358) [hereinafter Hague Cultural Property Convention]; *see also* Roger O'Keefe, The Protection of Cultural Property in Armed Conflict (2011).

105. Aug. 12, 1949, 6 U.S.T. 3114, 75 U.N.T.S. 31.

Armed Forces at Sea (Geneva Convention II);[106]

● Geneva Convention Relative to the Treatment of Prisoners of War (Geneva Convention III);[107] and

● Geneva Convention Relative to the Protection of Civilian Persons in Time of War (Geneva Convention IV).[108]

Every state has ratified or acceded to the 1949 Geneva Conventions, an extraordinarily high level of adherence. While in almost all instances the conventions are binding as a matter of treaty law, they have also passed into customary international law.[109] Any study of these conventions should take account of the International Committee of the Red Cross (ICRC) commentary conducted under the general editorship of Jean Pictet.[110]

The 1949 Geneva Conventions set forth in remarkable detail protections for the victims of warfare. As a means of monitoring state compliance, the conventions call for belligerents to appoint "protecting powers" (third countries empowered to undertake various steps) at the outbreak of a conflict, to inquire after the treatment of a belligerent's nationals, to visit nationals who have been interned, to assist in communications from such persons to their families, and to help repatriate persons at the end of hostilities. This role can be (and often is) fulfilled by the ICRC.

Geneva Convention III. Of the 1949 conventions, Geneva Conventions III and IV are of the greatest practical significance. Geneva Convention III provides as a core protection that:

> Prisoners of war must at all times be humanely treated. Any unlawful act or omission by the Detaining Power causing death or seriously endangering the health of a prisoner of war in its custody is prohibited, and will be regarded as a serious breach of the present Convention....

> Likewise, prisoners of war must at all times be protected, particularly against acts of violence or intimidation and against insults and public curiosity.

> Measures of reprisal against prisoners of war are prohibited.[111]

The convention then sets forth detailed provisions as to how prisoners are to be treated when taken into captivity and during

106. Aug. 12, 1949, 6 U.S.T. 3217, 75 U.N.T.S. 85.

107. Aug. 12, 1949, 6 U.S.T. 3316, 75 U.N.T.S. 135 [hereinafter Geneva Convention III].

108. Aug. 12, 1949, 6 U.S.T. 3526, 75 U.N.T.S. 287 [hereinafter Geneva Convention IV].

109. *See* Chapter 3(B).

110. *See* INTERNATIONAL COMMITTEE OF THE RED CROSS, THE GENEVA CONVENTIONS OF 12 AUGUST 1949: COMMENTARY (Jean S. Pictet ed., 1952–60) (4 vols.).

111. Geneva Convention III, *supra* note 107, art. 13.

their internment (such as the provision of food, clothing, medical treatment, and quarters).[112] Various provisions deal with whether prisoners may be required to engage in labor, whether they may have communications with the protecting power (or ICRC), and whether they may be punished for violating camp rules.[113] A prisoner may be tried and even executed for violation of the law, including the commission of war crimes, but the convention sets forth various protections to ensure that the trial is conducted appropriately. Finally, the convention addresses the manner in which captivity should be terminated and the prisoner repatriated.[114]

Normally, Geneva Convention III is relevant to the treatment of persons who are to be detained in prisoner of war camps. Yet, in some instances, the convention is also relevant to persons held in a prison. For example, in 1988 a U.S. federal grand jury indicted on drug charges General Manual Antonio Noriega, the head of the Panamanian Defense Forces and *de facto* ruler of Panama. In 1989, U.S. military forces invaded Panama, seized Noriega, and brought him to the United States for trial. In 1992, Noriega was found guilty and sentenced to forty years in prison, after which he petitioned the court to declare that he was entitled to the rights and privileges of a prisoner of war during his prison term, such as receiving visits from the ICRC. The district court concluded that Noriega was a prisoner of war under Geneva Convention III. As such, he was "entitled to the full range of rights under the treaty, which has been incorporated into U.S. law. Nonetheless, he can serve his sentence in a civilian prison ... so long as he is afforded the full benefits of the Convention."[115] By 2007, Noriega was entitled to be released on parole, but the government of France sought his extradition for criminal charges in France. Noriega attempted to argue that, as a prisoner of war, the United States had to repatriate him to Panama, rather than extradite him to France. The Eleventh Circuit Court of Appeals affirmed Noriega's status as a prisoner of war but found that, under the Military Commissions Act of 2006, Noreiga was barred from invoking Geneva Convention III as a source of habeas rights in a U.S. court.[116] In 2010, Noriega was extradited to France, where he was tried, convicted, and sentenced to seven years' imprisonment, without any status as a prisoner of war. In 2011, France agreed to extradite Noriega to Panama to stand trial there for human rights abuses.

Geneva Convention IV. Geneva Convention IV seeks to protect civilians in times of armed conflict. The convention's core provisions draw a distinction between a state's obligation to enemy

---

112. *Id.*, pt. III, §§ I–II.

113. *Id.*, pt. III, §§ III & V–VI.

114. *Id.*, pt. IV.

115. United States v. Noriega, 808 F.Supp. 791 (S.D. Fla. 1992).

116. Noriega v. Pastrana, 564 F.3d 1290, 1292 (11th Cir. 2009).

aliens in its territory and its obligation to enemy aliens in occupied enemy territory. Some obligations apply in either territory, such as the obligations: to treat all persons humanely; to protect them from acts of violence and physical suffering; not to take them hostage; and not to pillage their property.[117] Other protections apply only with respect to enemy aliens present in the state's territory, such as the right of a person placed under internment to have the action considered as soon as possible by an appropriate court.[118] In occupied territory, numerous provisions address the role of the occupying power and its relationship to persons under occupation. For example, individual or forced mass transfers (as well as deportations) of protected persons are prohibited, although the occupying power may evacuate persons for their security or as military operations demand.[119]

Common Article 3. All four of the 1949 Geneva Conventions have in common an article 3, which addresses "armed conflict not of an international character". Common article 3 was quite unusual at the time it was enacted, for prior law of war agreements had dealt exclusively with norms operating between states, not between a state and a non-state entity (such as an insurgent or rebel force).

While the drafters of the 1949 Geneva Conventions were willing to address this issue, they were not willing to apply the conventions wholesale to such armed conflicts.[120] Instead, under common Article 3, parties to the conflict (*e.g.*, the government and rebels) are bound to treat humanely all persons taking no active part in the hostilities. To that end, common Article 3 prohibits subjecting such persons to acts of violence, hostage-taking, humiliating or degrading treatment, and the passing of sentences or carrying out of executions without judgment by a regularly constituted court in accordance with due process. Common Article 3 is, therefore, a useful minimum standard of treatment so long as there is an "armed conflict," which means something more than mere riots or civil disturbances. Unfortunately, states often are unwilling to classify an internal situation as an "armed conflict" within the meaning of common Article 3 for fear that it might provide some basis of legitimacy to the insurgent group. Further, the standards established in common Article 3 are very broad and lack the detail provided by the 1949 Geneva Conventions for conflicts between states.

The International Court of Justice has declared that the standards set by common Article 3 are relevant to *all* armed conflicts, including those that are international.

---

117. Geneva Convention IV, *supra* note 108, arts. 108 & 32–34.

118. *Id.*, art. 43.

119. *Id.*, art. 49.

120. *Cf.* Hague Cultural Property Convention, *supra* note 104, art. 19 (applying the convention to internal conflicts).

There is no doubt that, in the event of international armed conflicts, these rules also constitute a minimum yardstick, in addition to the more elaborate rules which are also to apply to international conflicts; and they are rules which, in the Court's opinion, reflect what the Court in 1949 called "elementary considerations of humanity."[121]

The United States regards its obligations under common Article 3 as applying to its military actions against Al Qaeda, thus recognizing that the state/non-state actor conflict need not be an internal one. As discussed in Chapter 7(A), the Supreme Court found that the conflict between the United States and Al Qaeda is an "armed conflict not of an international character" that falls within the scope of Common Article 3 to the 1949 Geneva Conventions, thereby imposing certain obligations upon the United States when trying Al Qaeda detainees before a military commission.[122] In 2007, President George Bush issued an executive order interpreting the restrictions of common Article 3 as permitting the U.S. detention program, provided it did not entail heinous conduct, such as torture.[123]

Protocols to the 1949 Geneva Conventions. In addition to the 1949 Geneva Conventions, states adopted two protocols to those conventions in 1977. Those protocols are:

- Protocol Additional to the Geneva Conventions of 12 August 1949, and Relating to the Protection of Victims of International Armed Conflicts (Protocol I);[124] and

- Protocol Additional to the Geneva Conventions of 12 August 1949, and Relating to the Protection of Victims of Non–International Armed Conflicts (Protocol II).[125]

Adherence to these protocols is very high; as of 2011, 171 states have adhered to Protocol I and 166 states have adhered to Protocol II. Any study of these protocols should take account of the ICRC commentary.[126]

As its name indicates, Protocol I focuses on codifying and developing the law relating to international armed conflict. It does so by clarifying and advancing the law both on protection of victims and on means/methods of war. With respect to the protection of victims, Protocol I revisits, clarifies, and expands upon the various

---

121. Military and Paramilitary Activities in and against Nicaragua, *supra* note 4, at para. 218 (citing the *Corfu Channel* case).

122. *See* Hamdan v. Rumsfeld, 548 U.S. 557 (2006).

123. *See* Exec. Order No. 13,440 (July 20, 2007).

124. June 8, 1977, 1125 U.N.T.S. 3 [hereinafter Protocol I].

125. June 8, 1977, 1125 U.N.T.S. 609 [hereinafter Protocol II].

126. *See* COMMENTARY ON THE ADDITIONAL PROTOCOLS OF 8 JUNE 1977 TO THE GENEVA CONVENTIONS OF 12 AUGUST 1949 (Yves Sandoz et al. eds., 1987).

protections addressed in the earlier Hague Regulations and 1949 Geneva Conventions. In particular, Article 75 lays down a series of fundamental protections to which all persons "in the power of a Party to the conflict" are entitled without discrimination. Those protections include a prohibition on any act of violence against persons (including murder and torture), outrages upon personal dignity, or collective punishments. In March 2011, the U.S. executive branch announced that the U.S. government will "out of a sense of legal obligation ... treat the principles set forth in Article 75 as applicable to any individual it detains in an international armed conflict, and expects all other nations to adhere to these principles as well."[127]

Among its provisions on means/methods of war, Protocol I asserts that it is "prohibited to employ methods or means of warfare which are intended, or may be expected, to cause widespread, long-term and severe damage to the natural environment" and that "[n]o person parachuting from an aircraft in distress shall be made the object of attack during his descent."[128] Protocol I also clarifies the standards to be employed when deciding whether to launch an attack, with a heavy emphasis on distinguishing between civilian and military targets. Article 52 states:

> 1. Civilian objects shall not be the object of attack or of reprisals. Civilian objects are all objects which are not military objectives as defined in paragraph 2.

> 2. Attacks shall be limited strictly to military objectives. In so far as objects are concerned, military objectives are limited to those objects which by their nature, location, purpose or use make an effective contribution to military action and whose total or partial destruction, capture or neutralization, in the circumstances ruling at the time, offers a definite military advantage.

> 3. In case of doubt whether an object which is normally dedicated to civilian purposes, such as a place of worship, a house or other dwelling or a school, is being used to make an effective contribution to military action, it shall be presumed not to be so used.

Further, Protocol I contains important language on precautions to be taken by military planners, stating that they should "do everything feasible to verify that the objectives to be attacked are neither civilians nor civilian objects," and that "an attack should be cancelled or suspended if it becomes apparent that the objective is not

---

127. White House Office of the Press Secretary, Fact Sheet: New Actions on Guantanamo and Detainee Policy, at 3 (Mar. 7, 2011).

128. Protocol I, *supra* note 124, arts. 35(3) & 42(1).

a military one" or that "the attack may be expected to cause incidental loss of civilian life ... which would be excessive in relation to the concrete and direct military advantage anticipated."[129] When engaging in an attack, Protocol I emphasizes the need to protect cultural objects, the natural environment, and objects indispensable to the survival of the civilian population, such as drinking water installations.[130] Article 56 prohibits attacks on dams, dykes, and nuclear electrical generating stations (even if they are military objectives) if doing so "may cause the release of dangerous forces."

Protocol II focuses on codifying and developing the law relating to non-international armed conflict, and thus extends the reach of common Article 3. The protocol covers conflicts between the armed forces of a state and "dissident armed forces or other organized armed groups which, under responsible command, exercise such control over a part of its territory as to enable them to carry out sustained and concerted military operations and to implement this Protocol."[131] Although shorter and less-detailed than Protocol I, Protocol II also lays down a series of fundamental protections to which all persons in internal conflicts are entitled without discrimination.[132]

The United States has not ratified either protocol. While Protocol I focuses on codifying and developing the law relating to international armed conflict, it also covers armed conflicts involving peoples "fighting against colonial domination and alien occupation and against racist regimes in the exercise of their right of self-determination.... "[133] Indeed, Protocol I provides that the 1949 Geneva Conventions apply in their entirety to these types of armed conflicts.[134] Some states, including the United States, oppose this expansive approach, claiming that it accords far too much protection and legitimacy to non-state groups, including terrorist organizations.[135] President Reagan requested that the Senate consent to ratification of Protocol II, but opposed U.S. ratification of Protocol I. In 2011, the administration of President Obama again requested that the Senate consent to ratification of Protocol II, noting that:

> An extensive interagency review concluded that United States military practice is already consistent with the Protocol's provi-

129. *Id.*, art. 57(2).

130. *Id.*, arts. 53–55.

131. Protocol II, *supra* note 125, art. 1.

132. *Id.*, art. 4.

133. Protocol I, *supra* note 124, art. 1(4).

134. *Id.*, art. 3(a).

135. For a discussion, see Agora, *The U.S. Decision Not to Ratify Protocol I to the Geneva Conventions on the Protection of War Victims*, 81 Am. J. Int'l L. 910 (1987) & 82 Am. J. Int'l L. 784 (1988); *see also* Theodor Meron, *The Time Has Come for the United States to Ratify Geneva Protocol I*, 88 Am. J. Int'l L. 678 (1994).

sions. Joining the treaty would not only assist us in continuing to exercise leadership in the international community in developing the law of armed conflict, but would also allow us to reaffirm our commitment to humane treatment in, and compliance with legal standards for, the conduct of armed conflict.[136]

Although it has not ratified either protocol, the United States appears to regard significant portions of both protocols as expressing customary international law.[137]

In December 2005, a third additional protocol (Protocol III)[138] was adopted to create an additional emblem alongside the red cross and red crescent, known as the red crystal. As of 2011, 59 states had adhered to it, including the United States.

Customary International Law. In many instances implicating international humanitarian law, there will be a treaty containing detailed provisions. Yet given the brevity of common Article 3 and Protocol II, for non-international armed conflicts reliance solely upon treaty law may be difficult. Consequently, an important issue is to what extent there exist norms in customary international law that are binding upon contending parties to a non-international armed conflict. In 2005, a study was prepared under the auspices of the International Committee of the Red Cross that analyzed state practice worldwide so as to codify customary rules of international humanitarian law for both international and non-international armed conflicts.[139] The two-volume study identified 161 rules (149 of which apply to non-international armed conflicts) falling into six general areas: the principle of distinction between combatants and civilians; specially protected persons or objects (*e.g.*, medical persons and cultural monuments); methods of warfare; restrictions on the use of weapons; treatment of civilians and persons *hors de combat* (outside the fight); and implementation of such obligations. The study has attracted considerable attention, but has been criticized by some governments[140] and scholars[141] for both its methodology and its conclusions.

---

136. White House Office of the Press Secretary, Fact Sheet: New Actions on Guantanamo and Detainee Policy, at 3 (Mar. 7, 2011).

137. *See* Michael J. Matheson, *The United States Position on the Relation of Customary International Law to the 1977 Protocols Additional to the 1949 Geneva Conventions*, 2 Am. U. J. Int'l L. & Pol'y 419 (1987).

138. Dec. 8, 2005, 45 I.L.M. 558 (2006).

139. International Committee of the Red Cross, Customary International Humanitarian Law (Jean–Marie Henckaerts & Louise Doswald–Beck eds., 2005) (2 vols.).

140. For the U.S. government position, see 46 I.L.M. 511 (2007); for the response of one of the authors of the study, see 46 I.L.M. 957 (2007).

141. *See, e.g.,* Perspectives on the ICRC Study on Customary International Humanitarian Law (Elizabeth Wilmshurst & Susan Breau eds., 2007).

Example: 2003 Intervention in Iraq

During the 2003 intervention in Iraq by the U.S.-led coalition (discussed above), various allegations were made by both sides concerning non-compliance with the laws of war. Iraqi state television broadcast pictures of U.S. prisoners of war, some of whom looked bruised and dazed, being questioned about why they had come to Iraq. Iraq also broadcast footage of dead U.S. soldiers lying in pools of blood. Among other things, the United States intercepted an Iraqi communication indicating that some U.S. personnel may have been executed by their captors. Such acts prompted charges from the United States that Iraq was violating its obligations under the laws of war by exposing prisoners to public curiosity and physical abuse. The U.S. House and Senate each passed resolutions condemning Iraq's actions, demanding that Iraq abide by Geneva Convention III, and supporting efforts to hold Iraqi officials accountable for such violations.[142]

In addition to Iraq's mistreatment of prisoners of war, the United States charged that Iraq had engaged in other violations of the laws of war, such as the deceptive use of white flags to lure enemy troops, the use of civilians as human shields at military installations, the use of protected facilities (such as hospitals or ambulances) to house military units, and attacks on the Iraqi civilian population to prevent them from fleeing to safety. Moreover, Iraqi paramilitary forces engaged in fighting while dressed in civilian clothing, making their detection very difficult. Their conduct led to the deaths of numerous coalition soldiers from ambushes and suicide bombings, and increased the risk that Iraqi civilians would be mistaken for combatants.

Although the United States made extensive use of highly precise weapons-delivery systems in targeting Iraqi installations and forces, criticism arose concerning collateral civilian casualties from U.S. attacks. For example, large explosions occurred in civilian areas of Baghdad, which the Iraqi government blamed on indiscriminate U.S. bombing. While U.S. officials conceded that the explosions might have been caused by errant U.S. missiles or bombs, they denied that the United States was engaged in indiscriminate attacks and suggested that the explosions might have been caused by faulty Iraqi missiles, Iraqi antiaircraft fire falling back to earth, or even (for propaganda purposes) the Iraqi government itself. Moreover, U.S. officials asserted that they had avoided bombing dozens of high-priority Iraqi targets due to a concern for collateral civilian casualties, making it harder for the United States

142. *See* S. Con. Res. 31, 108th   Cong. (2003).
Cong. (2003); H.R. Con. Res. 118, 108th

to achieve its air-campaign goals. Nevertheless, extensive collateral civilian casualties did occur, although the exact number of Iraqi civilians killed and wounded in the course of the conflict is unknown.

The U.S.-led coalition captured about seven thousand combatants. These persons were regarded as prisoners of war unless a military tribunal determined otherwise (persons determined to be noncombatants were released). After the Iraqi government capitulated, many Iraqi prisoners of war were released, but others viewed as continuing threats remained in detention, along with civilians regarded as threats or criminals. The largest of the U.S. detention facilities was Abu Ghraib prison, located outside Baghdad. Representatives of the ICRC were allowed access to Abu Ghraib detainees, and regularly submitted observations and recommendations to the United States regarding treatment of the detainees. After several months, the ICRC concluded that abuse of Iraqi detainees by U.S. military intelligence personnel as part of interrogation processes was widespread, harsh, and brutal, and, in some cases, "might amount to torture.... "[143] An investigation by the U.S. Central Command reached a similar conclusion, finding that

> between October and December 2003, at the Abu Ghraib Confinement Facility ... , numerous incidents of sadistic, blatant, and wanton criminal abuses were inflicted on several detainees. This systemic and illegal abuse of detainees was intentionally perpetrated by several members of the military police guard force ... of the Abu Ghraib Prison.... The allegations of abuse were substantiated by detailed witness statements ... and the discovery of extremely graphic photographic evidence.[144]

Thereafter, the U.S. Army charged several U.S. military personnel with the physical and sexual abuse of prisoners at Abu Ghraib.

As for the status of the coalition forces in Iraq as "occupying powers," in May 2003 the U.N. Security Council adopted Resolution 1483, which reaffirmed Iraq's sovereignty and territorial integrity, recognized the right of the Iraqi people to establish a representative government based on the rule of law, and empowered a special U.N. representative to coordinate humanitarian and refugee

---

143. REPORT OF THE INTERNATIONAL COMMITTEE OF THE RED CROSS (ICRC) ON THE TREATMENT BY COALITION FORCES OF PRISONERS OF WAR AND OTHER PROTECTED PERSONS BY THE GENEVA CONVENTIONS IN IRAQ DURING ARREST, INTERNMENT AND INTERROGATION, para. 24 (Feb. 2004).

144. ARTICLE 15–6 INVESTIGATION OF THE 800TH MILITARY POLICE BRIGADE, pt. 1 (findings of fact), para. 5. (n.d.) (commonly referred to as the Taguba Report, after its author, Major General Antonio Taguba); *see generally* THE TORTURE PAPERS: THE ROAD TO ABU GHRAIB (Karen Greenberg & Joshua Dratel eds., 2005).

activities.[145] At the same time, the resolution recognized the United States and United Kingdom as "occupying powers under unified command" and demanded that they comply with their obligations under international law. The resolution asserted that the occupying powers were an "authority" with the responsibility to "promote the welfare of the Iraqi people through the effective administration of the territory, including in particular working towards the restoration of conditions of security and stability and the creation of conditions in which the Iraqi people can freely determine their own political future."[146] Thereafter, U.S. and U.K. civilian administrators undertook a massive program for reforming Iraq's political, legal, economic and regulatory systems, repealing numerous Iraqi laws and creating a process for the drafting and adoption of a new Iraqi constitution.[147]

C. Arms Control

Background

The control of arms or weaponry arises in two different areas. First, as noted in the preceding section, the 1907 Hague Regulations provide that the "right of belligerents to adopt means of injuring the enemy is not unlimited."[148] This rule has animated subsequent agreements by states to prohibit the use of certain kinds of weapons in warfare, including conventional weapons, biological weapons, chemical weapons, and nuclear weapons. Second, even for weapons that have not been outright prohibited, states have found it in their interests to limit the number of such weapons possessed by states, with limitations sometimes expressed in ratios based on the sizes of the participating states. Indeed, the United States and the Soviet Union engaged in important bilateral arms agreements during the Cold War, some of which remain important in the post-Soviet era.

Conventional Weapons

In 1980, states adopted the Convention on Prohibitions or Restrictions on the Use of Certain Conventional Weapons Which May Be Deemed to Be Excessively Injurious or to Have Indiscriminate Effects (CCW)[149] as a framework convention for regulating the use of conventional arms in armed conflict. In addition to the convention itself, states may join any of its five protocols, which regulate specific kinds of conventional arms: nondetectable frag-

---

145. *See* S.C. Res. 1483 pmbl. & paras. 8–9 (May 22, 2003).

146. *Id.*, pmbl. & para. 4.

147. *See* Gregory H. Fox, *The Occupation of Iraq*, 36 Geo. J. Int'l L. 195 (2005).

148. Hague Regulations, *supra* note 91, art. 22.

149. Oct. 10, 1980, S. Treaty Doc. No. 103–25, at 7 (1994), 1342 U.N.T.S. 137.

ments;[150] mines and booby traps;[151] incendiary weapons;[152] blinding laser weapons;[153] and explosive remnants of war.[154] The United States is a party to the first two protocols.

For example, the protocol on explosive remnants of war (ERW), adopted in 2003, addresses a formidable threat to civilians in post-conflict societies. Article 3 of the protocol calls upon each party, after the cessation of hostilities and as soon as feasible, to mark, clear, remove, or destroy ERW in its territory. Article 4 provides that parties during a conflict "shall to the maximum extent possible and as far as practicable record and retain information on the use of explosive ordnance or abandonment of explosive ordnance," and that they shall, "without delay after the cessation of active hostilities and as far as practicable, subject to these parties' legitimate security interests, make available such information to the party or parties in control of the affected area ... or, upon request, to other relevant organisations." Article 5 obligates parties to undertake "all feasible precautions" to protect civilians from ERW, including "warnings, risk education, ... marking, fencing and monitoring of territory affected by explosive remnants of war," as provided in a technical annex. Article 6 obligates parties to take measures protective of humanitarian organizations that operate in ERW areas. The technical annex, to be implemented on a voluntary basis, lists best practices for achieving the protocol's objectives.

Separately, states adopted during the Cold War the Treaty on Conventional Armed Forces in Europe (CFE Treaty).[155] Under the CFE Treaty, North American and European states set specific limits on a range of conventional weapons, such as tanks, artillery, aircraft, helicopters, and armored combat vehicles. Further, the CFE Treaty provides for extensive monitoring and verification procedures.

More recently, states have been concerned with the international small arms trade, particularly its effect on conflict-prone states in Africa and parts of Asia. In December 1999, the U.N. General Assembly launched a conference to address this issue.

---

150. *See* Protocol I on Non-detectable Fragments, Oct. 10, 1980, S. Treaty Doc. No. 103–25, at 15 (1994), 1342 U.N.T.S. 168.

151. *See* Protocol II on Prohibitions or Restrictions on the Use of Mines, Booby–Traps and Other Devices, Oct. 10, 1980, *as amended* May 3, 1996, S. Treaty Doc. No. 105–1, at 45 (1997), 2048 U.N.T.S. 133.

152. *See* Protocol III on Prohibitions or Restrictions on the Use of Incendiary Weapons, Oct. 10, 1980, S. Treaty Doc.

No. 105–1, at 64 (1997), 1342 U.N.T.S. 171.

153. *See* Protocol IV on Blinding Laser Weapons, Oct. 13, 1995, S. Treaty Doc. No. 105–1, at 68 (1997), 35 I.L.M. 1218.

154. *See* Protocol V on Explosive Remnants of War, Nov. 28, 2003, U.N. Doc. CCW/MSP/2003/2 (2003), 45 I.L.M. 1348 (2006).

155. Nov. 19, 1990, S. Treaty Doc. No. 102–8 (1991), 30 I.L.M. 1.

Although some states sought a legally-binding agreement, other states (notably the United States) resisted an agreement that would constrain the legitimate weapons trade or infringe upon national rights to own small arms. On July 21, 2001, the participating states adopted a voluntary, politically-binding program of action calling upon states to pursue a variety of national, regional, and global measures against the illicit international trade in small arms.[156]

A key concern in recent years has been the use of cluster bombs, which disperse sub-munitions or "bomblets" that may not detonate upon impact, but instead can lie undisturbed for years. In some situations, the bomblets are brightly colored, and can appear to children to be toys. In May 2008, a diplomatic conference of states meeting in Dublin adopted the Convention on Cluster Munitions (CCM),[157] which prohibits all use, stockpiling, production and transfer of cluster munitions, defined as being "a conventional munition that is designed to disperse or release explosive sub-munitions each weighing less than 20 kilograms, and includes those explosive sub-munitions."[158] Various articles in the Convention concern assistance to victims, clearance of contaminated areas, and destruction of existing stockpiles. The convention entered into force in August 2010 and as of 2011 has 66 states parties. Several states that produce or stockpile cluster munitions, however, have declined to join the convention, including China, Brazil, India, Israel, Pakistan, Russia, and the United States. The United States maintains that the proper venue for discussing the issue is in the context of the CCW and that new technologies (including auto-destruct mechanisms) can address many of the concerns with such weapons.

Chemical and Biological Weapons

Chemical weapons use the toxic properties (as opposed to explosive properties) of chemicals to produce physical or physiological effects, while biological weapons disseminate infectious diseases or natural toxins. Chemical weapons include chlorine, phosgene, mustard gas, and nerve gases (*e.g.*, sarin). Biological weapons include bacteria (*e.g.*, anthrax), viruses (*e.g.*, smallpox), or toxins (*e.g.*, ricin).

Three separate multilateral agreements ban the use of chemical and biological weapons. The 1925 Geneva protocol referred to in the prior section[159] bans the use in war of "asphyxiating, poisonous

---

156. *See* Report of the United Nations Conference on the Illicit Trade in Small Arms and Light Weapons in All Its Aspects, U.N. Doc. A/CONF.192/15, at 7 (2001).

157. Convention on Cluster Munitions, May 30, 2008, 48 I.L.M. 354 (2009).

158. *Id.*, art. 2(2); *see* THE CONVENTION ON CLUSTER MUNITIONS: A COMMENTARY (Gro Nystuen et al., eds. 2010).

159. *See supra* note 102.

or other gases," as well as "bacteriological methods of warfare." The protocol does not, however, ban the production or possession of such weapons.

The 1972 Biological Weapons Convention bans the development, production, stockpiling or acquisition of biological agents or toxins "of types and in quantities that have no justification for prophylactic, protective, or other peaceful purposes."[160] Although the convention contains no inspection or verification provisions, in 1987 the parties established an annual non-binding data exchange, known as "confidence-building measures" (CBMs). Further, in 1994 the parties decided to establish a special conference of the parties to consider the creation of verification measures, including the adoption of a legally-binding protocol. Such a protocol was ultimately drafted, but in July 2001 the United States announced that it could not support the protocol since it did not believe that the mechanisms envisioned would provide useful, accurate and complete information on illicit activity, and might have adverse effects on legitimate commercial activities (*e.g.*, exposing lawful trade secrets).

The 1993 Chemical Weapons Convention (CWC)[161] forbids parties from developing, producing, stockpiling, or using chemical weapons, and requires all parties to destroy existing chemical weapons ten years after the convention's entry into force, which occurred in 1997. The CWC has two verification regimes designed to ensure compliance: one involves routine visits by teams of inspectors while the other involves challenge inspections initiated by a member state against another member state when noncompliance is suspected. The CWC created the Organization for the Prohibition of Chemical Weapons (OPCW), which is based in The Hague.

Nuclear Weapons

Nuclear weapons are devices whose explosive energy derives from nuclear fission (splitting the nucleus of an atom) or a combination of nuclear fission and fusion (joining isotopes of hydrogen). The Nuclear Nonproliferation Treaty (NPT)[162] prohibits all states from possessing nuclear weapons, except China, France, Russia, the United Kingdom, and the United States. Some states with nuclear capabilities (*e.g.*, India, Israel, Pakistan), however, have not joined

---

160. Convention on the Prohibition of the Development, Production, and Stockpiling of Bacteriological (Biological) and Toxin Weapons, and on Their Destruction, art. 1, Apr. 10, 1972, 26 U.S.T. 583, 1015 U.N.T.S. 163.

161. Convention on the Prohibition of the Development, Production, Stock-piling and Use of Chemical Weapons and on Their Destruction, Jan. 13, 1993, S. Treaty Doc. No. 103–21 (1993), 1974 U.N.T.S. 45.

162. Treaty on the Non–Proliferation of Nuclear Weapons, July 1, 1968, 21 U.S.T. 483, 729 U.N.T.S. 161 [hereinafter NPT].

the treaty. Under the NPT, nuclear-weapons states are obligated to keep nuclear weapons from non-nuclear-weapons states, while at the same time sharing nuclear technology for peaceful purposes. While nuclear weapons states may possess nuclear weapons, they are also obligated under the NPT to work toward nuclear disarmament.[163]

The NPT recognizes the right of non-nuclear-weapons states to use nuclear technology for peaceful purposes so long as they conclude a bilateral "safeguards agreement" with the International Atomic Energy Agency (IAEA) to ensure compliance.[164] Since 1968, all but about 15 non-nuclear-weapons members of the NPT have concluded safeguards agreements with the IAEA which, among other things, allow the IAEA to conduct inspections of declared nuclear facilities on short notice. Although nuclear-weapons states are not required to enter into IAEA safeguards agreements,[165] in 1977 the United States concluded a bilateral safeguards agreement with the IAEA to demonstrate its commitment to the NPT, to encourage other states to complete safeguards agreements, and to eliminate the perception that the U.S. nuclear industry had an unfair commercial advantage in not being subject to IAEA inspections.[166] Under the agreement, the United States made available for IAEA inspection on short notice more than two hundred U.S. nuclear facilities, except in cases where the United States determines that access would implicate national security concerns.[167]

The discovery of an Iraqi nuclear weapons program during the 1990–91 Gulf War revealed certain gaps in the IAEA safeguards agreements, prompting the IAEA to adopt in 1997 an "additional protocol" that would amend existing agreements. The additional protocol requires states to provide broader declarations to the IAEA about the locations and activities of their nuclear programs, and expands the access rights of the IAEA. As of 2011, 139 IAEA member states have signed an additional protocol, even though not required by the NPT. A U.S.-IAEA additional protocol was signed in 1998 and entered into force in 2009.[168] Among other things, the additional protocol requires the United States to disclose more information to the IAEA, such as data regarding research on

163. *See generally* Mohamed Ibrahim Shaker, *The Evolving Regime of Nuclear Non-Proliferation*, 321 R.C.A.D.I. 9 (2006).

164. NPT, *supra* note 162, arts. II & III.

165. *Id.*

166. *See* Agreement for the Application of Safeguards in the United States of America, U.S.-IAEA, pmbl., Nov. 18,

1977, 32 U.S.T. 3059, 1261 U.N.T.S. 371.

167. *Id.*, art. I.

168. *See* Protocol Additional to the Agreement Between the United States of America and the International Atomic Energy Agency for the Application of Safeguards in the United States of America, with Annexes, U.S.-IAEA, June 12, 1998, S. Treaty Doc. No. 107–7 (2002).

nuclear fuel cycles and development activities that do not involve nuclear material but are funded, authorized, or controlled by the United States.[169] The new protocol also shortens the advance-notice period for "complementary access" (access not specially managed to address sensitive information) to twenty-four hours and, under exceptional circumstances, to less than two hours.[170] The protocol, however, maintains the national security exclusion of the original safeguards agreement.[171]

Separately, the Limited Test Ban Treaty[172] bans all nuclear explosions except underground tests. While many nuclear-weapons states (including the United States) follow a self-imposed moratorium on underground nuclear tests, India and Pakistan both conducted such tests in 1998. In 1996, the U.N. General Assembly adopted a Comprehensive Nuclear Test Ban Treaty (CTBT) that prohibits states from conducting any nuclear tests, whether for purposes of weapons development or otherwise, and establishes a system for monitoring seismic incidents and on-site inspections.[173] Although the United States signed the convention in 1996, a Senate vote in October 1999 failed to achieve the requisite consent of two-thirds of the Senate (the vote was 51–48).

One of the most important areas of nuclear arms control over the past half century has been the effort by the United States and Russia (or the Soviet Union) to restrict their strategic nuclear warheads. In 1969, the United States and the Soviet Union commenced negotiations that led to a Strategic Arms Limitation Treaty (SALT I). Generally speaking, that agreement called for both states to maintain at existing levels their strategic ballistic missile launchers. These negotiations also led to conclusion of the Treaty on the Limitation of Anti–Ballistic Missile Systems (ABM Treaty).[174] As amended in 1973, the ABM Treaty provided that the United States and the Soviet Union each could have only one restricted ABM deployment area, thus precluding either state from developing a nationwide ABM defense. Since each side retained the ability to retaliate against the other, the ABM Treaty was thought to make it far less likely that either side would resort to a nuclear first-strike. The United States withdrew from the ABM Treaty in 2002 so that it could develop and deploy a national missile defense system capable of stopping ballistic missiles launched by "rogue" states, such as North Korea.

---

169. *Id.*, art. 2(a)(i).

170. *Id.*, art. 4(b).

171. *Id.*, art. 1.

172. Treaty Banning Nuclear Weapon Tests in the Atmosphere, in Outer Space and Under Water, Aug. 5, 1963, 14 U.S.T. 1313, 480 U.N.T.S. 43.

173. *See* G.A. Res. 50/245 (Sept. 10, 1996).

174. U.S.-U.S.S.R., May 26, 1972, 23 U.S.T. 3435.

In 1977, the two states commenced negotiations of a second Strategic Arms Limitation Treaty (SALT II), which was the first nuclear arms treaty that sought to reduce significantly strategic nuclear arms, calling for reductions to no more than 2,250 of all categories of "delivery vehicles," meaning land-based inter-continental ballistic missiles, submarine-launched ballistic missiles, or bomber aircraft. The treaty also banned new programs for improving strategic missiles. Although signed by both sides in 1979, within six months the Soviet Union had invaded Afghanistan, and the U.S. Senate declined to consent to ratification. Nevertheless, both sides honored the terms of the agreement until 1986, when the Reagan Administration charged that the Soviets were no longer abiding by it.

In 1987, the United States and the Soviet Union signed the Treaty on the Elimination of Intermediate–Range and Shorter–Range Missiles (INF Treaty), which entered into force on June 1, 1988. The INF Treaty required elimination of some 800 U.S. and 1,800 Soviet ground-launched missiles with ranges between 500 and 5,500 kilometers, along with their launchers. Implementation of the treaty was completed by 1991. The treaty, however, is of unlimited duration and still prohibits the United States and Russia (as the successor state to the Soviet Union) from possessing, producing, or flight testing intermediate-and short-range missile systems.

In 1991, the United States and Soviet Union agreed to a new Strategic Arms Reduction Treaty (START I), which required both sides to reduce their holdings of nuclear warheads to 6,000 and their delivery vehicles to no more than 1,600.[175] Since negotiation of the treaty was concluded just months before the collapse of the Soviet Union, an annex to the treaty was negotiated so as to impose its terms on the newly emerged states in which the relevant armaments existed: Russia, Belarus, Kazakhstan, and Ukraine (the latter three countries agreeing to transport the armaments to Russia for disposal). Once fully implemented, the treaty led to the disposal of nearly eighty percent of existing strategic nuclear weapons. In 1993, the two states agreed to reduce nuclear warheads below 3,500 each in a treaty known as START II.[176] START II, however, never entered into force.

In 1997, START III negotiations were launched but broke down before agreement could be reached. Instead, in May 2002, the United States and Russia signed a Treaty on Strategic Offensive Reductions (SORT or Treaty of Moscow),[177] in which they agreed to

---

175. *See* Treaty on the Reduction and Limitation of Strategic Offensive Arms, U.S.-U.S.S.R., July 31, 1991, S. TREATY DOC. No. 102–20 (1991).

176. *See* Treaty on Further Reductions and Limitations of Strategic Offen-sive Arms, U.S.-Russ., Jan. 3, 1993, S. TREATY DOC. No. 103–1 (1993).

177. Strategic Offensive Reductions Treaty, U.S.-Russ., May 24, 2002, S. TREATY DOC. No. 107–8 (2002).

reduce nuclear warheads on launchers to between 1,700 and 2,200 warheads. By its terms, SORT was set to expire in December 2012, but was superseded by a "New START" Treaty, which was concluded in April 2010.[178] Under that treaty, strategic nuclear missile launchers are to be reduced by half and a new inspection and verification regime is established.

Each year the U.S. Department of State submits a report to Congress pursuant to Section 403 of the Arms Control and Disarmament Act, as amended,[179] on adherence to and compliance with arms control, nonproliferation, and disarmament agreements and commitments by both the United States and other countries. The 2011 report concluded that "the United States and the majority of the other participating nations are adhering to their obligations and commitments and have indicated their intention to continue doing so," but that "there are compliance questions and concerns—and in some instances findings of serious treaty violations—involving a relatively small number of countries."[180]

Confidence–Building

In 1992, with the end of the Cold War, a large number of states signed a Treaty on Open Skies, which established a regime for unarmed observation flights by states parties over each other's territories. Parties are allowed to conduct on short-notice a limited number of flights, during which they can use certain sensors (such as infra-red sensors) for the purpose of detecting violations of arms treaties or movements of armed forces. The Treaty entered into force in 2002 and at present has 34 parties from Europe and North America, including Russia and the United States.

Further, under the auspices of the Organization for Security and Cooperation in Europe (OSCE), a politically-binding confidence-building regime has emerged, most recently set forth in a document adopted at Vienna in 1999 (known as Vienna Document 1999). The regime allows for participating states to engage in on-site visits, inspections, and observations regarding military activities, for exchanges of data, and for cooperative activities between military forces. In 2010, almost 100 inspections and 50 visits of units and formations were conducted by participating states.[181]

---

178. *See* Treaty on Measures for the Further Reduction and Limitation of Strategic Offensive Arms, U.S.-Russ., Apr. 8, 2010, Treaty Doc. No. 111–5 (2010), *reprinted in* 50 I.L.M. 340 (2011); *see generally* AMY F. WOOLF, CONG. RESEARCH SERV., R41219, *The New START Treaty: Central Limits and Key Provisions* (2011).

179. 22 U.S.C. § 2593a (2006).

180. U.S. Dep't of State, *Report on Adherence to and Compliance with Arms Control, Nonproliferation, and Disarmament Agreements and Commitments* 2 (Aug. 2011).

181. *Id.*, at 16.

Further Reading:

Philip Alston & Euan MacDonald, eds., *Human Rights, Intervention and the Use of Force* (2008).

Emily Crawford, *The Treatment of Combatants and Insurgents Under the Law of Armed Conflict* (2010).

Olivier Corten, *The Law Against War: The Prohibition on the Use of Force in Contemporary International Law* (2010).

Anthony Cullen, *The Concept of Non–International Armed Conflict in International Humanitarian Law* (2010).

Yoram Dinstein, *The Conduct of Hostilities under the Law of International Armed Conflict* (2004).

Yoram Dinstein, *War, Aggression and Self Defence* (5th ed. 2011).

Claude Emanuelli, *International Humanitarian Law* (2009).

Dieter Fleck, *The Handbook of Humanitarian Law in Armed Conflicts* (2d ed. 2008).

George P. Fletcher & Jens David Ohlin, *Defending Humanity: When Force is Justified and Why* (2008).

Thomas M. Franck, *Recourse to Force: State Action Against Threats and Armed Attacks* (2002).

Judith Gardam, *Necessity, Proportionality, and the Use of Force by States* (2004).

Christine Gray, *International Law and the Use of Force* (3d ed. 2008).

James A. Green, *The International Court of Justice and Self–Defence in International Law* (2009).

Leslie C. Green, *The Contemporary Law of Armed Conflict* (3d ed. 2008).

Christopher Greenwood, *Essays on War in International Law* (2006).

Daniel H. Joyner, ed., *Arms Control Law* (2012).

Fritz Kalshoven & Liesbeth Zegveld, *Constraints on the Waging of War: An Introduction to International Humanitarian Law* (3d ed. 2001).

Vaughn Lowe et al., eds., *The United Nations Security Council and War* (2008).

Larry May, *War Crimes and Just War* (2007).

Lindsay Moir, *Reappraising the Resort to Force: International Law, Jus ad Bellum, and the War on Terror* (2010).

Nigel S. Rodley, *The Treatment of Prisoners Under International Law* (3d ed. 2009).

A.P.V. Rogers, *Law on the Battlefield* (2d ed. 2004).

Tom Ruys, *"Armed Attack" and Article 51 of the UN Charter: Evolutions in Customary Law and Practice* (2010).

Gary D. Solis, *The Law of Armed Conflict: International Humanitarian Law in War* (2010).

Yearbook of International Humanitarian Law (published annually by Cambridge University Press).

Chapter 15

INTERNATIONAL LEGAL RESEARCH

Chapter 3 dealt with the methods associated with the creation of international law. This chapter introduces specific textual and online sources that international lawyers employ when they search for authority on a given point of law. The presentation assumes that the reader has an understanding of the conceptual framework and sources of international law described in the first part of this book.

A. Treatises and Other Scholarly Material

Treatises are the most useful starting point for research in international law. These books, usually written by leading scholars or practitioners in the field, provide an analytical exposition of the law and contain extensive citations to all relevant authorities. Such treatises exist in many languages and translations. The following are recent English-language treatises:

Anthony Aust, *Handbook of International Law* (2005).

Ian Brownlie, *Principles of Public International Law* (7th ed. 2008).

Antonio Cassese, *International Law* (2d ed. 2005).

Lung–Chu Chen, *An Introduction to Contemporary International Law: A Policy–Oriented Perspective* (2d ed. 2000).

Malcolm Evans, *International Law* (3d ed. 2010).

Malcolm Shaw, *International Law* (6th ed. 2008).

In addition to these recent treatises, there are older "classic" treatises on the subject that are highly respected and continue to be used:

J.L. Brierly, *The Law of Nations* (Humphrey Waldock ed., 6th ed. 1963).

Louis Henkin, How Nations Behave (2d ed. 1979).

D.P. O'Connell, *International Law* (2d ed. 1970) (two vols.).

Oppenheim's International Law (Robert Jennings & Arthur Watts eds., 9th ed. 1992).

539

Oscar Schachter, *International Law in Theory and Practice* (1991).

Various encyclopedias, dictionaries, and restatements are available for research on specific topics or terms. For example, the four-volume *Encyclopedia of Public International Law* (Rudolph Bernhardt ed., 1991–2001) contains hundreds of essays and bibliographies by leading scholars and practitioners from around the globe. This print version updates and supplements a twelve-volume series published in 1981–1990. Moreover, in 2008, an online version was launched entitled the *Max Planck Encyclopedia of Public International Law* at <http://www.mpepil.com> under the general editorship of Professor Rüdiger Wolfrum, the Director of the Max Planck Institute for Comparative Public Law and International Law. The online version updates the print version and is expected itself to be available in print in 2012.

Various dictionaries provide useful information on words or terms commonly used in international law, including: *Parry and Grant Encyclopedic Dictionary of International Law* (J. Craig Barker & John Grant eds., 3d ed. 2009); Aaron X. Fellmeth & Maurice Horwitz, *Guide to Latin in International Law* (2009); Gerard Gilbertson, *Harrap's German and English Glossary of Terms in International Law* (2d ed. 2004); James Fox, *Dictionary of International and Comparative Law* (3d ed. 2003); Edmund Osmanczyk, *Encyclopedia of the United Nations and International Agreements* (Anthony Mango ed., 3d ed. 2003) (4 vols.).

Published by the American Law Institute (ALI), the *Restatement (Third) on the Foreign Relations Law of the United States* (1987) (two volumes) (supplemented annually) is a highly valued international law research tool. U.S. courts generally view it as the most authoritative U.S. scholarly statement of contemporary international law. The *Restatement (Third)* deals with public international law and the relevant U.S. law bearing on the application of international law in and by the United States (including where U.S. law differs from international law). Each section consists of a statement of the "black letter law," followed by comments and reporters' notes. The latter are particularly useful because of their careful analysis of and citations to the relevant international law authorities. Unlike the comments, the reporters' notes state the views of the reporters only and their substance is not endorsed as such by the ALI. (The ALI adopted in 1965 the *Restatement (Second) on the Foreign Relations Law of the United States*. Although forming part of the *Restatement (Second)* series, no earlier official version was ever published.)

Casebooks are widely used in the United States for the study of law and can be useful reference tools for international law research. Besides reproducing the major international and national judicial decisions dealing with international law questions, casebooks usually also contain extensive notes, comments and valuable bibliographic information. A casebook is often accompanied by a supplementary volume of basic documents, containing the texts of major international agreements and other materials of importance. The supplements themselves are a useful source of sometimes hard to find information and documentation. The following are among the major U.S. casebooks published over the past decade:

Barry E. Carter & Allen S. Weiner, *International Law* (6th ed. 2011).

Lori F. Damrosch, Louis Henkin, Sean D. Murphy & Hans Smit, *International Law: Cases and Materials* (5th ed. 2009).

Jeffrey L. Dunoff, Steven R. Ratner & David Wippman, *International Law: Norms, Actors, Process: A Problem–Oriented Approach* (3d ed. 2010).

Mark W. Janis & John E. Noyes, *Cases and Commentary on International Law* (4th ed. 2011).

Mary Ellen O'Connell, Richard F. Scott & Naomi Roht–Arriaza, *The International Legal System: Cases and Materials* (6th ed. 2010).

Jordan J. Paust, Jon M. Van Dyke, & Linda A. Malone, *International Law and Litigation in the U.S.* (3d ed. 2009).

W. Michael Reisman, Mahnoush H. Arsanjani, Siegfried Wiessner & Gayl S. Westerman, *International Law in Contemporary Perspective* (2d ed. 2004).

In addition to international law casebooks of a general type, more and more specialized casebooks are now also being published. These deal with a variety of subjects, including international organizations, human rights, national security law, law of the sea, international civil litigation, international criminal law, international environmental law, international business transactions, trade law, and European Union law.

For research involving contemporary international law issues, it is imperative to check the periodical literature on the subject. In the United States, there are some seventy student-edited and about seventeen peer-edited journals focusing on international or comparative law.[1] Further, articles dealing with international topics appear not only in specialized international law journals published in the United States and abroad, but also in general law reviews. Articles published in U.S., U.K. and some Commonwealth law journals are

---

1. *See* Gregory Crespi, *Ranking International and Comparative Law Jour-* *nals: A Survey of Expert Opinion,* 31 Int'l Law. 869 (1997).

indexed in the *Index to Legal Periodicals* (1886–) and the *Current Law Index* (1980–). Material on international law appearing in foreign journals and in a selected number of U.S. reviews are noted in the *Index to Foreign Legal Periodicals* (1960–). An even more comprehensive bibliographic guide, published by the Max Planck Institute for Comparative Public Law and International Law, is *Public International Law: A Current Bibliography of Books and Articles* (1975–). It provides access to more than 1,000 journals and collected works from all parts of the world.

Some of the leading law journals in the field of public international law are:

American Journal of International Law (1907–) (leading U.S. law review on this subject).

European Journal of International Law (1990–).

Indian Journal of International Law (1960–).

International and Comparative Law Quarterly (1952–).

International Lawyer (1966–) (a practice-oriented journal, published by the International Law Section of the American Bar Association).

Leiden Journal of International Law (1988–).

Recueil des Cours (1924–) (reprints of the course lectures, in English and French, offered each summer at the Hague Academy of International Law by leading international lawyers, usually containing extensive bibliographies).

Revue Générale de Droit International Public (1894–) (contains articles in French).

Zeitschrift für Ausländisches Öffentliches Recht und Völkerrecht (title in English is the *Heidelberg Journal of International Law*) (1929–) (contains articles in German and English).

Many foreign-language international law journals publish a significant number of articles in English. Hence, the mere fact that a citation to an article points to a Dutch, French or German international law review, for example, does not exclude the possibility that the piece appears in English. Where this is not the case, moreover, English summaries are at times provided. Foreign international law journals as a rule also reproduce or summarize decisions of national tribunals, legislation, and governmental pronouncements of interest to international lawyers.

For a series of excellent audio-visual lectures in international law by leading scholars and practitioners, see the U.N. Audio–Visual Library of International Law, *at* <http://www.un.org/law/avl/>.

B. International Agreements

International Agreements Generally

Article 102 of the U.N. Charter provides that every international agreement entered into by a U.N. member state shall be registered with and published by the U.N. Secretariat. Consequently, the principal source for the official texts of multilateral and bilateral agreements on a worldwide basis for the years 1946 forward is the *United Nations Treaty Series* (U.N.T.S.) (1946–). U.N.T.S. presently contains more than 50,000 international agreements and related documents, and texts are provided in their official languages. Texts may also be accessed online, for a fee, from the U.N. treaty collection at <http://treaties.un.org>.

For treaty texts not yet published in U.N.T.S., reference may be made to *International Legal Materials* (I.L.M.) (1962–). Published bimonthly by the American Society of International Law, the I.L.M. is a very current source for texts of selected significant international agreements. I.L.M. is available for full text searching on the *WESTLAW* electronic database, in the *ILM* file (1980–), and on the *LEXIS/NEXIS* electronic database, in the *INTLAW* library and the *ILMTY* file (1980–).

For treaties predating the United Nations, reference should be made to the *League of Nations Treaty Series* (L.N.T.S.) (1920–44). As the predecessor treaty compilation to U.N.T.S., this set provides texts of treaties from 1920 to 1944. Index volumes are available with the set, but there is no cumulative index. The L.N.T.S. is also available at <http://treaties.un.org.>.

For treaties predating the League of Nations, reference should be made to *Consolidated Treaty Series 1648–1919* (1969–86). Edited by Clive Parry and published by Oceana Publications, this series is the major compilation of treaties on a worldwide basis from 1648 to 1919, without subject indexes, but with chronological and party indexes.

Some Internet sites seek to provide the texts of the most important international agreements, as well as links to sites containing other agreements.[2] Moreover, Oceana Publications provides access, for a fee, to more than 15,000 treaties and international agreements at <http://www.oceanalaw.com>.

For indexes allowing you to determine the existence of an international agreement on a particular subject or involving a particular state, the best place to start is the United Nations' *Multilateral Treaties Deposited with the Secretary–General* (1981–). This is an annual cumulative index to 507 major multilateral

---

2. *See, e.g.,* <http://fletcher.tufts.edu/multilaterals.html>.

treaties deposited with the United Nations. Citations are given to U.N.T.S., if available, along with information on the date of entry into force and a list of the parties. This index also provides updates on treaty status and amendments. An online version of this index is available at <http://treaties.un.org>. For a cumulative index on CD–ROM for all U.N.T.S. agreements, see William S. Hein & Company's *United Nations Master Treaty Index on CD–Rom* (1995–).

Another useful index is Christian Wiktor, *Multilateral Treaty Calendar—Repertoire des Traités Multilateraux*, 1648–1995 (1998). The *Multilateral Treaty Calendar* contains a detailed subject index and chronological list of all multilateral treaties concluded between 1648–1995. For each treaty entry, citations to relevant print treaty compilations are included, along with information concerning treaty amendments, modifications, extensions, and terminations.

International Agreements of the United States

There are various official sources that may be checked to locate an international agreement to which the United States is a party. For international agreements that the United States concluded more than approximately eight years ago, reference can be made to the Department of State's series entitled *United States Treaties and Other International Agreements* (U.S.T.) (1950–). U.S.T. is the official bound publication of U.S. international agreements arranged chronologically. This series also includes relevant presidential proclamations, diplomatic correspondence, and conference documents. Once an agreement is concluded, however, it may take up to eight years before the agreement appears in a U.S.T. volume. The *USTREATIES* library available in *WESTLAW* also provides access to treaties found in this source.

For U.S. international agreements not in U.S.T., reference may be made to the individual pamphlets issued by the Department of State in the *Treaties and Other International Acts Series* (T.I.A.S.) (1946–). The individual pamphlets issued in this series are numbered chronologically, but these too lag behind the conclusion of an agreement by about five years. Once an international agreement is published in U.S.T. (see above), the U.S.T. contains a T.I.A.S. to U.S.T. conversion table. The predecessor series to T.I.A.S. was the Department of State's *Treaty Series* (T.S.) (1908–46).

For U.S. treaties not in one of the above sources, reference may be made to *Senate Treaty Documents* (1981–), published in both pamphlet and microfiche form. These documents, which are numbered sequentially within each Congress (*e.g.*, S. Treaty Doc. No. 99–1), contain the texts of treaties as submitted to the Senate for its advice and consent, as well as useful explanatory messages from the president and the secretary of state. Once a treaty is submitted to the Senate, it retains the treaty document number through subsequent Congresses, until consent is granted or denied, or the treaty is withdrawn by the executive branch. Before 1981, such information was found in *Senate Executive Documents* (1895–1980), which were lettered sequentially within each session of Congress (*e.g.*, Exec. Doc. A). Researchers should also be aware of the *Senate Executive Reports,* issued by the Senate Foreign Relations Committee after its consideration of individual treaties, containing the committee's analysis of a treaty and its recommendation as to consent by the whole Senate. Some of these documents may also be found at <http://www.gpoaccess.gov/serialset/cdocuments>.

For U.S. international agreements not in one of the above sources, reference may be made to unofficial sources, such as *International Legal Materials* (I.L.M.) (noted above) or *Hein's United States Treaties and Other International Agreements Current Service* (1990–). The latter is a microfiche set providing full-text reproductions of current U.S. international agreements that have not yet been assigned T.I.A.S. numbers.

For pre–1950 U.S. international agreements (predating the U.S.T. series), reference should be made to *United States Statutes at Large* (1789–). This source published all ratified U.S. treaties from 1776 to 1949 and all executive agreements from 1931 to 1951. Volume 64, Part 3, at B1107, conveniently indexes by state all international agreements published in *Statutes at Large* for the period 1776–1949. Volume 8 conveniently collects together all the texts of ratified U.S. treaties from 1776–1845. After 1949, U.S. international agreements were published in T.I.A.S. and U.S.T., not in *Statutes at Large.* The *United States Statutes at Large* series can be accessed online at <http://memory.loc.gov/ammem/amlaw/lwsl.html>.

Another useful source of pre–1950 U.S. international agreements is *Treaties and Other International Agreements of the United States of America, 1776–1949* (1968–1976) (commonly known as "Bevans," since it was compiled by Charles I. Bevans of the U.S. Department of State). Volumes 1–4 are multilateral agreements arranged chronologically by date of signature, while volumes 5–12 are bilateral agreements arranged by state. Oceana Publications' *Unperfected Treaties of the United States of America, 1776–1976* (1976–1994), provides the texts of proposed U.S. treaties from 1776 to 1976 that never entered into force.

For indexes allowing you to determine the existence of a U.S. international agreement on a particular subject or with a particular state, the best place to start is the Department of State's *Treaties in Force: A List of Treaties and Other International Agreements of the United States in Force on [Year]* (1944–) (T.I.F.). Published annually, T.I.F. indexes only U.S. international agreements in force as of January 1 of each year of publication. International agreements are arranged by broad topics and by state, with citations to the U.S.T. or T.I.A.S. series as appropriate. T.I.F. can be downloaded in Adobe Acrobat from the U.S. Department of State's Internet site at <http://www.state.gov/s/l/>. To identify even more recent international agreements that the United States has concluded, or recent actions with respect to a U.S. agreement (*e.g.*, accession by a foreign government to a multilateral treaty to which the United States is a party), reference may be made to the "Treaty Actions" section of the Department of State Internet site noted above.

Further, the Case Act[3] requires the secretary of state to submit annually to Congress a report that contains an index of all international agreements that the United States has signed or otherwise executed in the prior year and that are not being published in the Department's T.I.F. This index, however, may be submitted in classified form.

Alternatively, reference may be made to William S. Hein & Company's *Guide to United States Treaties in Force* (Igor Kavass ed., 1982–). This commercial publication expands on the indexing of TIF by including agreements that have entered into force during the year after TIF's publication. It also includes non-binding and other unrecorded international agreements, as well as updates on treaty status and amendments. Further, *Hein's U.S. Treaty Index on CD–Rom* (1991–), provides citations for international agreements from 1776 to the present, as well as information concerning subsequent history, including amendments and status updates.

International Agreements on Electronic Databases

For those with access to the *WESTLAW* and *LEXIS/NEXIS* electronic databases, international agreements are available in various libraries and files of those databases. For example, *U.S. Treaties and Other International Agreements* from June, 1979 to the present may be found in *WESTLAW: USTREATIES*. Likewise, basic documents of international economic law may be found in *LEXIS: INTLAW* library, *BDIEL* file.

C. State Practice

Contemporary Practice of Governments

As discussed in Chapter 3, governmental pronouncements and official positions on questions of international law play a vital role in the creation of customary international law. Evidence of this

---

3. 1 U.S.C. § 112b (2006).

practice is, therefore, carefully collected by foreign offices and/or legal scholars in different states.[4]

Both periodical journals and yearbooks on international law are an excellent source of information regarding a state's practice in the field of international law for a given year. Often they include cases from national courts interpreting international laws, reviews of the international practice of particular states or regions, essays by scholars on topics of contemporary importance, and excerpts from national statutes that touch upon international issues. Some significant yearbooks include:

African Yearbook of International Law—Annuaire Africain de Droit International (1993–).

Annuaire de l'Institut de Droit International (1877–).

Annuaire Francais de Droit International (1955–).

Asian Yearbook of International Law (1991–).

British Yearbook of International Law (1920–).

Canadian Yearbook of International Law—Annuaire Canadien de Droit International (1963–).

Finnish Yearbook of International Law (1990–).

German Yearbook of International Law—Jahrbuch fur Internationales Recht (1948–).

Italian Yearbook of International Law (1975–).

Japanese Yearbook of International Law (1961–).

Max Planck Yearbook of United Nations Law (1997–).

Netherlands Yearbook of International Law (1970–).

South Africa Yearbook of International Law (1978–).

A useful compendium on how different states organize their treaty-making through national law and practice is Duncan B. Hollis et al., *National Treaty Law and Practice* (2005), which analyzes the law and practice of nineteen states: Austria, Canada, Chile, China, Colombia, Egypt, France, Germany, India, Israel, Japan, Mexico, the Netherlands, Russia, South Africa, Switzerland, Thailand, the United Kingdom, and the United States. Each chapter follows a common outline and contains an essay on a state's treaty law and practice along with excerpts of relevant treaty-related legislation and documentation.

4. *See* Sources of State Practice in International Law (Maria Smolka–Day & Ralph Gaebler eds., 2001).

Practice of the United States

Researchers interested in obtaining information about the practice of the United States in international law should refer to the U.S. Department of State's Internet site at <http://www.state.gov>. Further, until 1999 the Department of State issued monthly the *Department of State Dispatch* (1990–99), which provided Department of State news and policy documents. It is also available via *WESTLAW* in the *USDPTSDIS* library. The predecessor to the *Department of State Dispatch* was the *Department of State Bulletin* (1939–89). The *Bulletin,* also published monthly, is a good source of information for historical materials and policy statements of the Department of State. Each quarterly issue of the *American Journal of International Law* contains a section on *Contemporary Practice of the United States Relating to International Law,* which summarizes the U.S. position on recent developments in international law, with extracts of relevant documents and citations to further sources.

The following volumes of past U.S. practice are also useful:

Sean D. Murphy, *United States Practice in International Law, Vol. 1: 1999–2001* (2002); *id., Vol. 2: 2002–2004* (2005). These volumes provide a comprehensive overview of the United States' involvement in international law during the course of the three-year periods covered. Unlike the other volumes listed below, these volumes were not prepared under the auspices of the U.S. government.

Digest of United States Practice in International Law, 1989–90 (2003); *id., 1991–1999* (2006) (2 vols.); *id., 2000* (2001); *id., 2001* (2002); *id., 2002* (2003); *id., 2003* (2004); *id., 2004* (2006); *id., 2005* (2007); *id., 2006* (2007); *id., 2007* (2008); *id., 2008* (2010); *id., 2009* (2011). This U.S. Department of State digest, reproduces without commentary extracts of Department of State documents for the covered year, such as speeches and court pleadings.

Digest of United States Practice in International Law: Cumulative Index, 1989–2006 (2007). This volume indexes the above for the years covered.

Cumulative Digest of United States Practice in International Law: 1981–88 (1993–95). This U.S. Department of State digest covers developments during 1981–88 and was published in three volumes.

Digest of United States Practice in International Law (1973–80). This U.S. Department of State digest covers developments from 1973 to 1980 and was published in eight volumes plus a cumulative index volume.

Marjorie M. Whiteman, *Digest of International Law* (1963–73). This U.S. Department of State digest primarily covers developments from 1940 to 1960 and was published in fifteen volumes.

Green Haywood Hackworth, *Digest of International Law* (1940–44). This U.S. Department of State digest primarily covers developments from 1906 to 1939 and was published in eight volumes.

John Bassett Moore, *A Digest of International Law* (2d ed. 1906). This U.S. Department of State digest covers developments from 1776 to 1906 and was published in eight volumes.

Francis Wharton, *A Digest of the International Law of the United States* (1886). This digest is considered the first true digest of U.S. practice in international law and was published in three volumes.

Digest of the Published Opinions of the Attorneys–General, and of the Leading Decisions of the Federal Courts with Reference to International Law, Treaties, and Kindred Subjects [1877] (rev. ed. reprinted by William S. Hein & Company in 1998). The original edition, prepared by John L. Cadwalader, was the first subject compilation of official texts on U.S. practice in international law.

D. International Organization Practice

Practice of International Organizations Generally

Every international organization records its work, typically through annual reports prepared by the secretariat for the plenary organs or the member states. Such publications by lesser-known international organizations may be difficult to locate, although the Internet sites of most international organizations are very helpful. An excellent resource for ascertaining which international organizations exist, what they do, and relevant bibliographic resources is *Bowett's Law of International Institutions* (Philippe Sands & Pierre Klein, 6th ed. 2009). For a directory profiling more than 5,000 international organizations—and more than 24,000 non-governmental organizations—including the organization's purpose, history, publications, technical and regional commissions, and consultative and working relationships with other organizations, reference should be made to the *Yearbook of International Organizations* (1967–). The directory is available online for a subscription fee at <http://www.uia.org/organizations/oraccess.htm>.

Practice of the United Nations

The legally relevant practice of the United Nations is periodically recorded in the official multi-volume *Repertory of Practice of*

United Nations Organs (1958–). This publication analyzes the practice by reference to individual provisions of the U.N. Charter. Another very useful research tool on the practice of the United Nations and its specialized agencies is the *United Nations Juridical Yearbook* (1962–). It reproduces, *inter alia,* important opinions rendered by the legal officers of the United Nations and the specialized agencies, summaries of the decisions of the U.N. and I.L.O. Administrative Tribunals and of national tribunals bearing on the work of the United Nations, and selected resolutions and other legally significant information. Each volume also contains a useful systematic bibliography.

Although not designed for lawyers as such, the *Yearbook of the United Nations* (1946–), which chronicles the activities of the United Nations on an annual basis, is a useful research tool. It provides the reader with a thorough overview of the work of individual U.N. organs, together with often hard to find citations to the relevant documents bearing on the subject under consideration. The annual *Report of the Secretary–General on the Work of the Organization* performs a similar function by summarizing the activities of the different U.N. organs.

The resolutions of the U.N. General Assembly and the Security Council are issued in separate publications. The resolutions of U.N. subsidiary organs can be found in the annual reports these bodies submit to their respective parent organs.

The United Nations Internet site is very comprehensive and well organized. Many important U.N. documents, including Security Council and General Assembly resolutions, can be retrieved online at <http://www.un.org>. This site also contains a research guide to retrieve other U.N. documents. For a U.N.-oriented Internet site set up by Yale University, see <http://www.library.yale.edu/un/index.html>.

Useful recent treatises on the United Nations are:

Benedetto Conforti, *The Law and Practice of the United Nations* (3d rev. ed. 2005).

Oscar Schachter & Christopher Joyner, eds., *United Nations Legal Order* (1995) (2 vols.) (revised/abridged as Christopher Joyner, ed., *The United Nations and International Law* (1997)).

Thomas G. Weiss & Sam Daws, eds., *Oxford Handbook on the United Nations* (2007).

International Law Commission

The activities of the International Law Commission of the United Nations are described in four print sources. First, the *Yearbook of the International Law Commission* (1949–) reproduces records of meetings which took place in a given year (vol. I) and the texts of major reports produced during the year, including the annual report to the General Assembly (vol. II). Many of these studies are comprehensive legal monographs of great practical and scholarly authority, and thus are a valuable resource for international lawyers. Second, *The Work of the International Law Commission* (7th ed. 2007) gives an overview of the I.L.C.'s activities and reproduces the full text of legal instruments drafted under its aegis. Third, the *Analytical Guide to the Work of the International Law Commission, 1949–1997* (1998) describes the work of the I.L.C. on legal issues falling within its mandate with references to source materials. Fourth, a useful collection of volumes are: *The International Law Commission 1949–1998: Volume One: The Treaties, Part I* (Arthur Watts ed., 2001); *The International Law Commission 1949–1998: Volume Two: The Treaties, Part II* (Arthur Watts ed., 2004); *The International Law Commission 1949–1998: Volume Three: Final Draft Articles of the Material* (Arthur Watts ed., 2001); *The International Law Commission 1999–2009: Volume IV: Treaties, Final Draft Articles and Other Materials* (Michael M. Wood, Arnold A. Pronto eds., 2011). For information online about the I.L.C., see <http://www.un.org/law/ilc/index.htm>.

E. Judicial and Arbitral Decisions

The best general source for finding recent international judicial and arbitral decisions, as well as some national court decisions dealing with international law issues, is *International Law Reports* (1950–). Each volume includes a digest of cases, a table of treaties, and a subject index. A cumulative index exists for volumes 1–80. The predecessors to this series were *Annual Digest and Reports of International Law Cases* (1933–49) and *Annual Digest of International Law Cases* (1919–32). For online access to international law jurisprudence, the best source is *Oxford Reports on International Law, at* <http://ildc.oxfordlawreports.com>, which provides access to a wide range of cases, along with an explanatory headnote. Another useful site for searching tribunal decisions is Worldcourts, *at* <http://www.worldcourts.com/>. A useful website providing information on the courts and tribunals themselves is hosted by the Project on International Courts and Tribunals, *at* <http://www.pict-pcti.org>.

Various collections focus just on arbitral decisions. The most comprehensive collection of international arbitral decisions is the United Nations publication *Reports of International Arbitral Awards* (1948–), where selected decisions rendered since the 1890's are reproduced. Other early collections are James Scott, *Hague Court Reports* (ser. 1, 1916) (ser. 2, 1932) and John Moore, *International Arbitrations* (1898).

International Legal Materials often reprints important decisions of international judicial and arbitral decisions, as well as U.S. and foreign court decisions relating to international law. Each quarterly issue of the *American Journal of International Law* summarizes important decisions of such tribunals, as do several of the other journals listed in Section A. Other specialized law reviews follow a similar practice in their field. Thus, *Human Rights Law Journal* reproduces major decisions of the European and Inter–American human rights tribunals and of other international human rights bodies. Important national court decisions are also reported in the various national yearbooks listed in Section C.

The International Court of Justice publishes decisions in volumes entitled *Reports of Judgments, Advisory Opinions and Orders* (1947–). Other materials relating to International Court proceedings are issued in *Pleadings, Oral Arguments and Documents* (1948–). The United Nations has published *Summaries of Judgments, Advisory Opinions, and Orders of the International Court of Justice, 1948–1991* (1992); *id., 1992–1996* (1998); *id., 1997–2002* (2003); *id., 2003–2007* (2008). Thereafter, unpublished summaries may be found at <http://www.un.org/law/ICJsummaries>. The Max Planck Institute has published many of the Court's decisions in an analytical format. *See Digest of the Decisions of the International Court of Justice, 1976–1985* (1990); *Digest of the Decisions of the International Court of Justice, 1959–1975* (1978). Further information relating to the work of the International Court and its jurisdiction can be found in the annual *Yearbook of the International Court of Justice* (1947–) or online at <http://www.icj-cij.org>. The Permanent Court of International Justice followed an official publication practice similar to that of the International Court.

Decisions of the Court of Justice of the European Union are found in the official *Reports of Cases before the Court of Justice and the Court of First Instance* (1990–) and predecessor series on cases before the Court. Unofficial commercial collections published in the United Kingdom (*Common Market Law Reports*) and in the United States (*CCH Common Market Reports*) are also available. Information may also be found online at <http://www.europa.eu.int/cj/index.htm>. The European Court of Human Rights publishes *Publications of the European Court of Human Rights: Series A, Judgments and Decisions* (1960–) and *European Court of Human Rights: Series B, Pleadings, Oral Arguments and Documents* (1960–). These materials are also available online at <http://www.echr.coe.int>. Decisions of the European Court of Human Rights (and the now-dissolved European Commission of Human Rights) are also reproduced in the *Yearbook of the European Convention on Human Rights* (1960–). The *Yearbook*, however, does not always reprint material in full.

From 1982 to 1987, the Inter–American Court of Human Rights used a two-series approach similar to that of its European counterpart; namely, *Series A: Judgments and Opinions* and *Series B: Pleadings, Oral Arguments and Documents.* In 1987 it added a third series, entitled *Series C: Decisions and Judgments.* The Court recently added *Series D: Pleadings, Oral Arguments and Documents (Relative to Series C)* and *Series E: Provisional Measures.* These materials may be found online at <http://www1.umn.edu/humanrts/iachr/iachr.html>. Decisions of the Inter–American Court of Human Rights and the Inter–American Commission of Human Rights are published in their separate *Annual Reports to the OAS General Assembly* and can be accessed online at <http://www.corteidh.or.cr/public_ing/reports.html>. For an annual yearbook reporting on the Court, see *Anuario Interamericano de Derechos Humanos* (1968–).

For a multi-volume collection containing decisions of the various international criminal tribunals, see *Annotated Leading Cases of International Criminal Tribunals* (André Kip & Göran Sluiter, eds.) (32 vols.). Other useful sources are: *ICTY Judicial Reports/Recueils Judiciaires* (1997–) (published by Martinus Nijhoff); *Substantive and Procedural Aspects of International Criminal Law: The Experience of International and National Courts* (Gabrielle McDonald & Olivia Swaak–Goldman eds., 2000) (containing commentary in volume one and documents and cases in volume two); John Jones, *The Practice of the International Criminal Tribunals for the former Yugoslavia and Rwanda* (2d ed. 2000). ICTY and ICTR decisions can also be found online at <http://www.un.org/icty/index.html> and <http://www.ictr.org>. Information on the permanent International Criminal Court may be found at <http://www.icc-cpi.int>.

The International Tribunal for the Law of the Sea publishes decisions in volumes entitled *Reports of Judgments, Advisory Opinions and Orders* (1997–) and its proceedings in volumes entitled *Pleadings, Minutes of Public Sittings and Documents* (1997–). Some of these materials may be found online at <http://www.itlos.org/>.

The World Trade Organization (WTO) publishes: *The Legal Texts: Results of the Uruguay Round of Multilateral Trade Negotiations* (1999); *Basic Instruments and Selected Documents* (2003–) (BISD contains various documents pertaining to the operation and scope of the WTO); *The WTO Dispute Settlement Procedures: A Collection of the Legal Texts* (2004); and *Dispute Settlement Reports* (1996–). WTO decisions and legal texts may also be found online at <http://www.wto.org> or at <http://www.worldtradelaw.net>.

NAFTA dispute settlement decisions can also be found at <http://www.naftaclaims.com>.

F. General Internet Research

There is an extraordinary array of information on international law available on the Internet, although the researcher needs to be discriminating in seeking out sites containing accurate and current information.[5] The following Internet sites contain general information regarding international law and/or extensive links to relevant Internet sites.

<http://www.eisil.org>. The Electronic Information System for International Law (E.I.S.I.L.), created by the American Society of International Law, operates as an open database of primary and other authenticated international law materials. E.I.S.I.L. has links to international organizations, international courts, treaty collections, and other international law materials.

<http://www.un.org>. The United Nations Internet site has links to U.N. created tribunals and courts, including the International Court of Justice, the Tribunal for the Law of the Sea, the International Criminal Court, the International Criminal Tribunal for the former Yugoslavia and the International Criminal Tribunal for Rwanda (see prior section). The site also contains treaty information, committee information and extensive documents (such as maps and photographs) covering both U.N. history and current events relating to international law.

<http://www.state.gov>. The U.S. Department of State Internet site contains extensive information relating to U.S. involvement in international law and institutions, as well as many related links to Internet sites. For example, the Internet sites of the World Trade Organization, North American Free Trade Agreement, Free Trade Area of the Americas, and Asian–Pacific Economic Cooperation can all be accessed by links from the "Trade Policy and Programs" page on the Department of State Internet site.

<http://www.asil.org>. The American Society of International Law Internet site provides links to publications and activities of the American Society of International Law, as well as "Insights" papers on topics of current interest.

<http://LLRX.com/international_law.html>. LLRX is a free Internet journal focused on international law issues. This Internet site provides an international law resource center containing numerous links to international law articles and resources.

Several academic institutions worldwide have created Internet sites designed to provide extensive links to other Internet sites

---

5. *See generally ASIL Guide to Electronic Resources for International Law* (Marci Hoffman et al. eds., 3d ed. 2003), at <http://www.asil.org/resource/home.htm>.

relating to international law or institutions, such as New York University Law School's Guide to Foreign and International Legal Database's, *at* <http://www.law.nyu.edu/library/research/foreign_intl/index.htm>.

G. Further Reference Works

Most U.S. guides to legal research also contain sections on international law. For works specifically addressing international law research, see *Guide to International Legal Research* (2009) (compiled by the editors and staff of the George Washington University International Law Review); Jeanne Rehberg & Radu Popa, *Accidental Tourist on the New Frontier: An Introductory Guide to Global Legal Research* (1998); Ellen Schaffer & Randall Snyder, *Contemporary Practice of Public International Law* (1997); Claire Germain, *Germain's Transnational Law Research* (1991–) (looseleaf binder).

Cases Index

References are to Pages

T

Tachiona v. Mugabe, *301*
Tachiona v. U.S., *301*
Tadi, Prosecutor v., *468–69*
Tel–Oren v. Libya, *261*
Territorial and Maritime Dispute in the Caribbean Sea (Nicar. v. Honduras), *47*
Texaco v. Libya, *116*
Texas Indus. v. Radcliff Materials, *258–59*
Thompson v. Oklahoma, *267*
Timberlane Lumber Co. v. Bank of Am., *286*
Trail Smelter (U.S. v. Can.), *129, 426, 449*
Treatment in Hungary of U.S. Aircraft and Crew (U.S. v. Hungary), *161*
Treatment in Hungary of U.S. Aircraft and Crew (U.S. v. U.S.S.R.), *161*
Trop v. Dulles, *266–67*

U

Underhill v. Hernandez, *323–24*
Ungar v. Iran, *320*
U.S. v. _____ (see opposing party)
U.S. Diplomatic and Consular Staff in Tehran (U.S. v. Iran), *161, 203, 297–98*
USX Corp. v. Adriatic Ins. Co., *308–09*

V

Van Cauwenberghe, U.S. v., *457*
Vasquez–Velasco, U.S. v., *280*
Venus Lines Agency v. CVG Industria, *323*
Vermilya–Brown Co. v. Conell, *272*
Victory Transport, Inc. v. Comisaria General, *305*

Vienna Convention on Consular Relations (Para. v. U.S.), *157–58*
Villagran Morales (Street Children) Case, *376*
Virginia v. Tennessee, *250*
Virtual Countries v. South Africa, *313–14*
Von Saher v. Norton Simon Museum, *252*

W

Wiwa v. Royal Dutch Petroleum, *264*
W.S. Kirkpatrick & Co. v. EnvironmentalTectonics Corp., *327*
Walker Case, *373*
Ware v. Hylton, *258*
Waste Management, Inc. v. Mexico, *136, 337–38*
Weinberger v. Rossi, *248*
Westland Helicopters, *52*
Whitney v. Robertson, *254*
Wildenhus' Case, *387*
Wimbledon Case, *210*
Winter v. Natural Res. Def. Council, *448–49*
World–Wide Volkswagen Corp. v. Woodson, *290*

Y

Ye v. Zemin, *97, 301*
Yeager v. Iran, *204*
Youngstown Sheet & Tube Co. v. Sawyer, *231–32*
Yousef, U.S. v., *225, 274*
Yunis, U.S. v., *260*

Z

Zappia Middle East Construction Co. v. Abu Dhabi, *310–11*
Zschernig v. Miller, *251*

Treaties Index

563

H

Hague Convention on Protection of Cultural Property, *519*

Hague Convention on Land Warfare, *518*

Hague Convention on Land Warfare Annexed Regulations (Hague Regulations), *12, 517–18, 529*

High Seas Convention, *100, 383*

I

Illicit Traffic by Sea (U.S.–Colom.), Agreement to Suppress, *462*

Illicit Traffic in Narcotic Drugs, U.N. Convention against the, *461*

Illicit Trafficking in Narcotics Drugs (U.S.-Colom.), Memorandum on, *462*

ILO Conventions, *358–59, 363, 365*

Intermediate–Range and Shorter–Range Missiles (INF) Treaty, *535*

Intervention on the High Seas in Cases of Oil Pollution Casualties Convention, *430*

Int'l Commercial Arbitration, Inter–American Convention on, *198*

Int'l Court of Justice, Statute of the, *77, 92, 101, 103, 142–51, 256*

Int'l Covenant on Civil and Political Rights (ICCPR), *9, 345–48, 361, 363–66, 379–80*

Int'l Covenant on Civil and Political Rights First Protocol, *348*

Int'l Covenant on Civil and Political Rights, Second Protocol, *348*

Int'l Covenant on Economic, Social and Cultural Rights (ICESCR), *346, 348–50, 363–66*

Int'l Covenant on Economic, Social and Cultural Rights, Optional Protocol, *349*

Investment (U.S.–Jordan), Treaty Concerning, *130*

J

Jurisdiction and Enforcement of Judgments, Brussels Convention on, *431*

Jurisdiction and Enforcement of Judgments, Lugano Convention on, *431*

K

Kellogg–Briand Pact (General Treaty for the Renunciation of War), *17, 467*

Kyoto Protocol to the Climate Change Convention, *250, 428, 440–42*

L

La Belle Agreement (U.S.–France), *408*

Law of the Sea Convention, *129–30, 132, 166–67, 233, 279, 383–413, 418, 427, 430*

Law of the Sea Convention Agreement Implementing Part XI, *383–84*

League of Nations Covenant, *28*

Legal Recognition of Personality of Int'l NGOs Convention, *70*

Liability for Carriage of Hazardous Substances by Sea Convention, *433*

Liability of Operators of Nuclear Ships Convention, *433*

Liability of Operators of Transport Terminals Convention, *433*

London Convention on Prevention of Marine Pollution by Dumping, *403*

Long–Range Transboundary Air Pollution Convention (LRTAP), *418, 428*

M

Marking of Plastic Explosives Convention, *460*

MARPOL Convention (Prevention of Pollution from Ships), *402–03, 428*

Molotov–Ribbentrop Accords (Ger.-USSR), *36*

Montevideo Convention on the Rights and Duties of States, *34*

Montreal Protocol to the Vienna Convention for Protection of the Ozone Layer, *113, 183, 436–38*

Mutual Legal Assistance in Criminal Matters Agreement (Council of Europe), *455*

Mutual Legal Assistance in Criminal Matters Agreement (U.S.-E.U.), *456*

Mutual Legal Assistance in Criminal Matters Model U.N. Agreement, *455*

N

NATO Status of Forces Agreement, *235, 430*

NATO Status of Forces Implementing Agreement (U.S.–Turkey), *235*

Subject Index

References are to Pages

†